**PHILIP'S** | **ROAD**

CW00542062

2021 BIG ATLAS BRITAIN & IRELAND

CONTENTS

Inside back cover: **County and unitary authority boundaries**

www.philips-maps.co.uk

First published in 2009 by Philip's
a division of Octopus Publishing Group Ltd
www.octopusbooks.co.uk
Carmelite House, 50 Victoria Embankment
London EC4Y 0DZ
An Hachette UK Company
www.hachette.co.uk

Twelfth edition 2020
First impression 2020

ISBN 978-1-84907-524-4 spiral-bound
ISBN 978-1-84907-532-9 perfect-bound

Cartography by Philip's
Copyright © 2020 Philip's

Map data

This product includes mapping data licensed from Ordnance Survey®, with the permission of the Controller of Her Majesty's Stationery Office. © Crown copyright 2020. All rights reserved. Licence number 100011710

The map of Ireland on pages XII–XIII is based upon the Crown Copyright and is reproduced with the permission of Land & Property Services under delegated authority from the Controller of Her Majesty's Stationery Office, © Crown Copyright and database right 2020, PMLPA No 100503, and on Ordnance Survey Ireland by permission of the Government © Ordnance Survey Ireland / Government of Ireland Permit number 9220.

While every reasonable effort has been made to ensure that the information compiled in this atlas is accurate, complete and up-to-date at the time of publication, some of this information is subject to change and the Publisher cannot guarantee its correctness or completeness.

The information in this atlas is provided without any representation or warranty, express or implied and the Publisher cannot be held liable for any loss or damage due to any use or reliance on the information in this atlas, nor for any errors, omissions or subsequent changes in such information.

The representation in this atlas of any road, drive or track is no evidence of the existence of a right of way.

Information for National Parks, Areas of Outstanding Natural Beauty, National Trails and Country Parks in Wales supplied by the Countryside Council for Wales.

Information for National Parks, Areas of Outstanding Natural Beauty, National Trails and Country Parks in England supplied by Natural England. Data for Regional Parks, Long Distance Footpaths and Country Parks in Scotland provided by Scottish Natural Heritage.

Gaelic name forms used in the Western Isles provided by Comhairle nan Eilean.

Data for the National Nature Reserves in England provided by Natural England. Data for the National Nature Reserves in Wales provided by Countryside Council for Wales. Darparwyd data'n ymwneud â Gwarchodfeydd Natur Cenedlaethol Cymru gan Gyngor Cefn Gwlad Cymru.

Information on the location of National Nature Reserves in Scotland was provided by Scottish Natural Heritage.

Data for National Scenic Areas in Scotland provided by the Scottish Executive Office. Crown copyright material is reproduced with the permission of the Controller of HMSO and the Queen's Printer for Scotland. Licence number C02W0003960.

Printed in Malaysia

*Data from Nielsen Total Consumer Market 2016 weeks 1–52

Road map symbols

Motorway, toll motorway
Motorway junction – full, restricted access
Motorway service area – full, restricted access
Motorway under construction

Primary route – dual, single carriageway
Service area, roundabout, multi-level junction
Numbered junction – full, restricted access
Primary route under construction
Narrow primary route
Primary destination

Derby

A road – dual, single carriageway
A road under construction, narrow A road

B road – dual, single carriageway
B road under construction, narrow B road

Minor road – over 4 metres, under 4 metres wide
Minor road with restricted access

Distance in miles
Scenic route
Toll, steep gradient – arrow points downhill
Tunnel

National trail – England and Wales
Long distance footpath – Scotland

Railway with station
Level crossing, tunnel
Preserved railway with station

National boundary
County / unitary authority boundary

Car ferry, catamaran
Passenger ferry, catamaran
Hovercraft
Ferry destination
Car ferry – river crossing
Principal airport, other airport

National park
Area of Outstanding Natural Beauty – England and Wales
National Scenic Area – Scotland
forest park / regional park / national forest
Woodland

Beach
Linear antiquity
Roman road
Hillfort, battlefield – with date
Viewpoint, nature reserve, spot height – in metres
Golf course, youth hostel, sporting venue
Camp site, caravan site, camping and caravan site
Shopping village, park and ride

Adjoining page number – road maps

Relief

Feet	metres
3000	914
2600	792
2200	671
1800	549
1400	427
1000	305
0	0

Road map scale
1: 200 000 • 1 cm = 2 km • 1 inch = 3·15 miles

0 1 2 3 4 5 6 7 8 9 10 km
0 1 2 3 4 5 6 miles

Parts of Scotland
1: 250 000 • 1 cm = 2.5 km • 1 inch = 3.94 miles

0 1 2 3 4 5 6 7 8 9 10 11 12 km
0 1 2 3 4 5 6 7 8 miles

Orkney and Shetland Islands
1: 340 000 • 1 cm = 3.4 km • 1 inch = 5.37 miles

0 2 4 6 8 10 12 km
0 1 2 3 4 5 6 7 8 miles

Approach map symbols

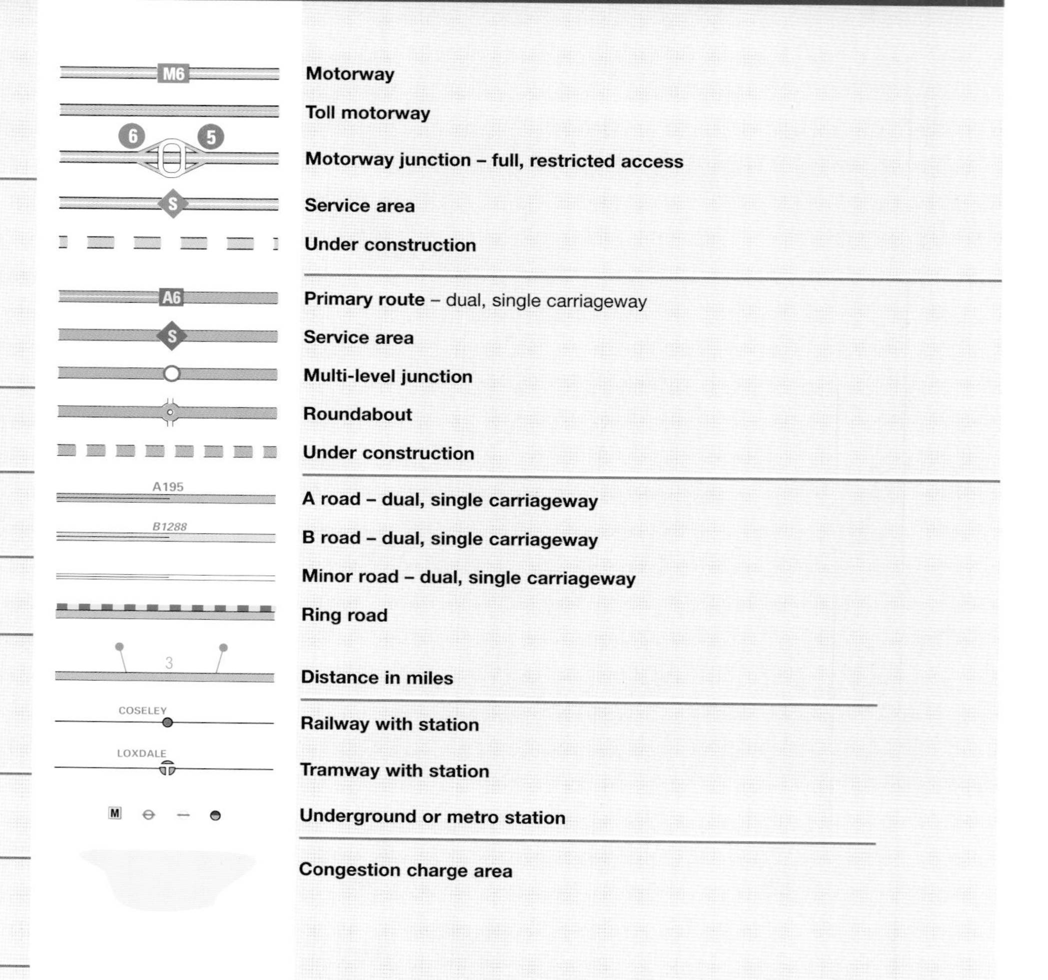

Motorway
Toll motorway
Motorway junction – full, restricted access
Service area
Under construction

Primary route – dual, single carriageway
Service area
Multi-level junction
Roundabout
Under construction

A road – dual, single carriageway
B road – dual, single carriageway
Minor road – dual, single carriageway
Ring road

Distance in miles
Railway with station
Tramway with station
Underground or metro station
Congestion charge area

Town plan symbols

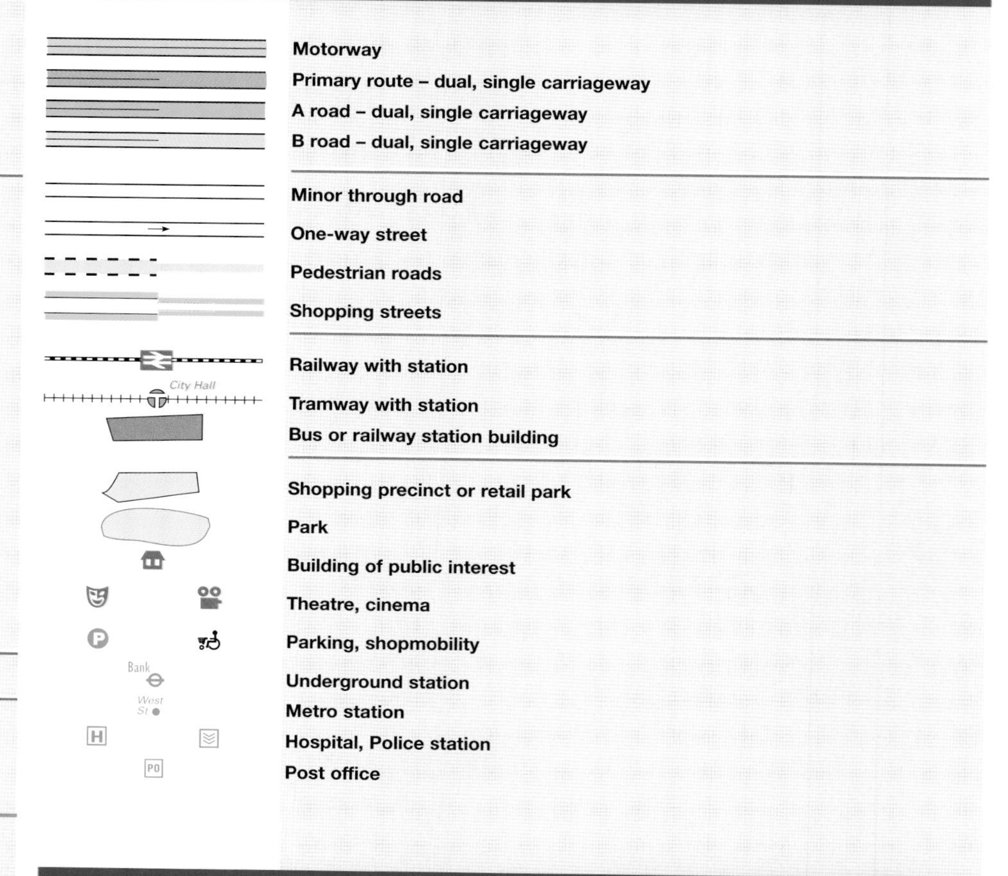

Motorway
Primary route – dual, single carriageway
A road – dual, single carriageway
B road – dual, single carriageway

Minor through road
One-way street
Pedestrian roads
Shopping streets

Railway with station
Tramway with station
Bus or railway station building

Shopping precinct or retail park
Park
Building of public interest
Theatre, cinema
Parking, shopmobility
Underground station
Metro station
Hospital, Police station
Post office

Tourist information

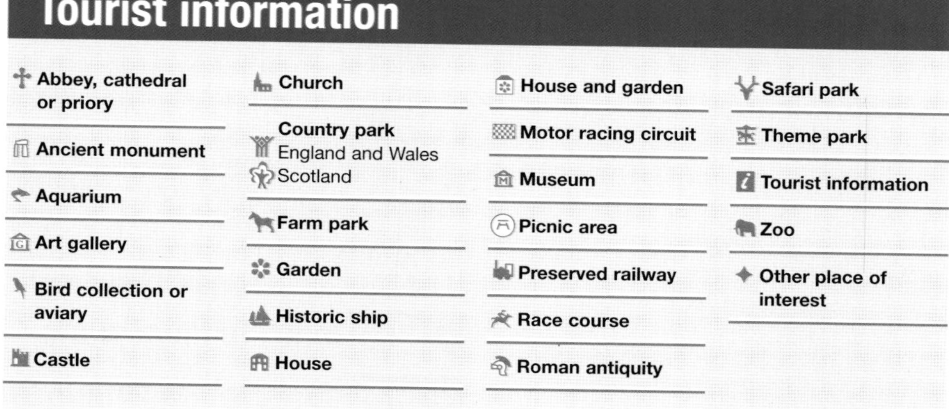

† Abbey, cathedral or priory

Church

House and garden

Safari park

Ancient monument

Country park
England and Wales
Scotland

Motor racing circuit

Theme park

Aquarium

House and garden

Museum

Tourist information

Art gallery

Farm park

Picnic area

Zoo

Garden

Preserved railway

Other place of interest

Bird collection or aviary

Historic ship

Race course

Castle

House

Roman antiquity

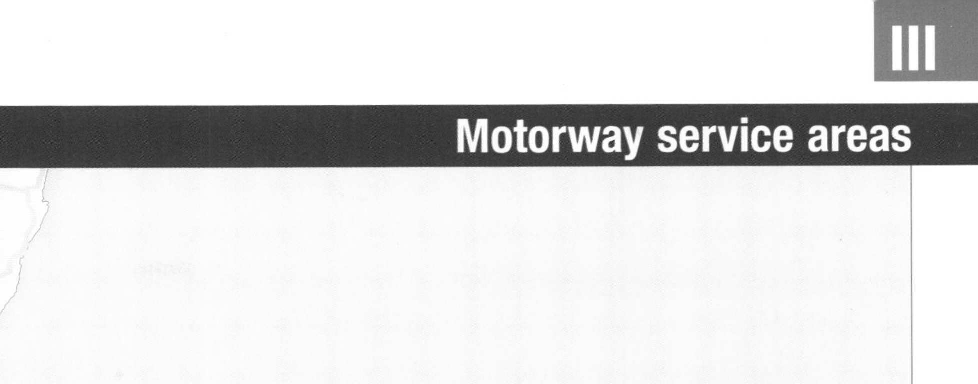

Motorway service areas

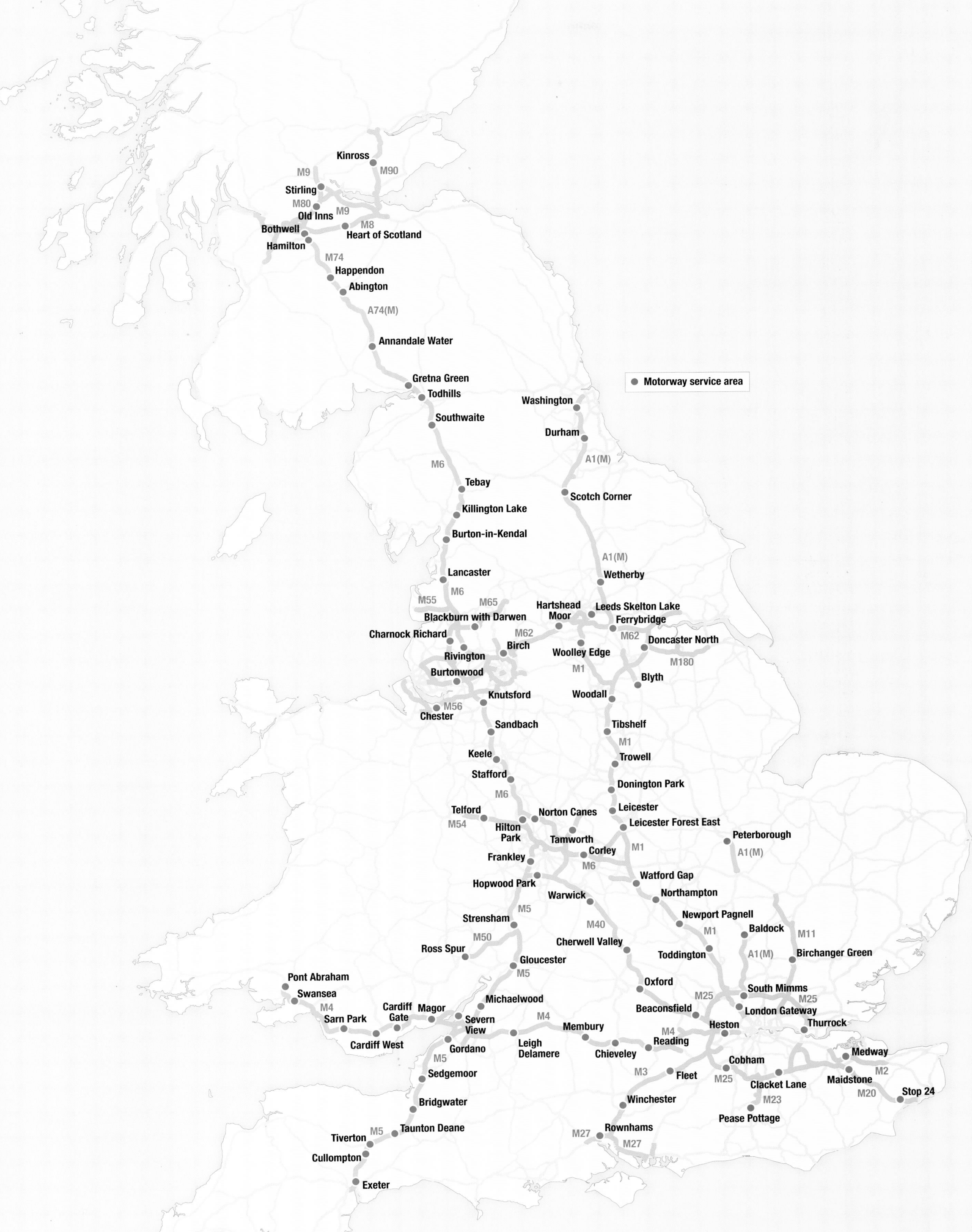
Motorway service area
Kinross
Stirling
Old Inns
Bothwell
Hamilton
Heart of Scotland
Happendon
Abington
Annandale Water
Gretna Green
Todhills
Southwaite
Washington
Durham
Tebay
Scotch Corner
Killington Lake
Burton-in-Kendal
Lancaster
Wetherby
Blackburn with Darwen
Hartshead Moor
Leeds Skelton Lake
Ferrybridge
Charnock Richard
Birch
Woolley Edge
Doncaster North
Rivington
Burtonwood
Blyth
Knutsford
Woodall
Chester
Sandbach
Tibshelf
Keele
Trowell
Stafford
Donington Park
Telford
Norton Canes
Leicester
Hilton Park
Tamworth
Leicester Forest East
Peterborough
Corley
Frankley
Watford Gap
Hopwood Park
Warwick
Northampton
Strensham
Newport Pagnell
Baldock
Cherwell Valley
Ross Spur
Toddington
Birchanger Green
Gloucester
Pont Abraham
Oxford
Swansea
South Mimms
Michaelwood
Beaconsfield
London Gateway
Cardiff Gate
Magor
Sarn Park
Severn View
Heston
Thurrock
Membury
Cardiff West
Gordano
Leigh Delamere
Reading
Chieveley
Medway
Cobham
Sedgemoor
Fleet
Clacket Lane
Maidstone
Stop 24
Bridgwater
Winchester
Pease Pottage
Taunton Deane
Tiverton
Rownhams
Cullompton
Exeter

Restricted motorway junctions

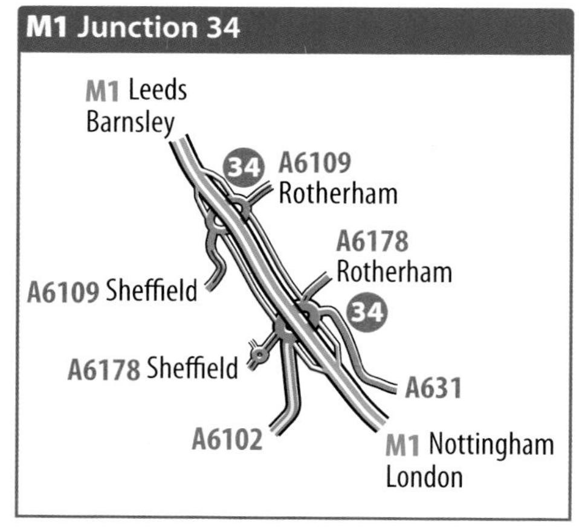

M1 Junction 34

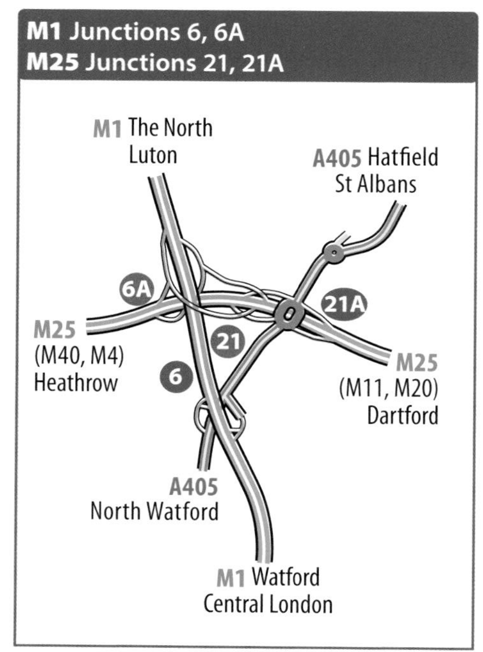

M1 Junctions 6, 6A
M25 Junctions 21, 21A

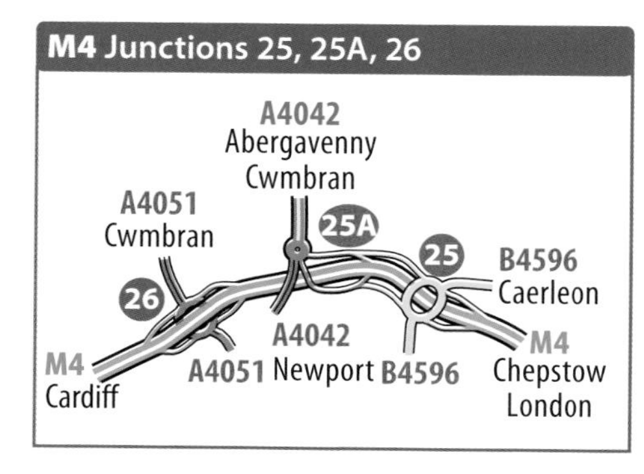

M4 Junctions 25, 25A, 26

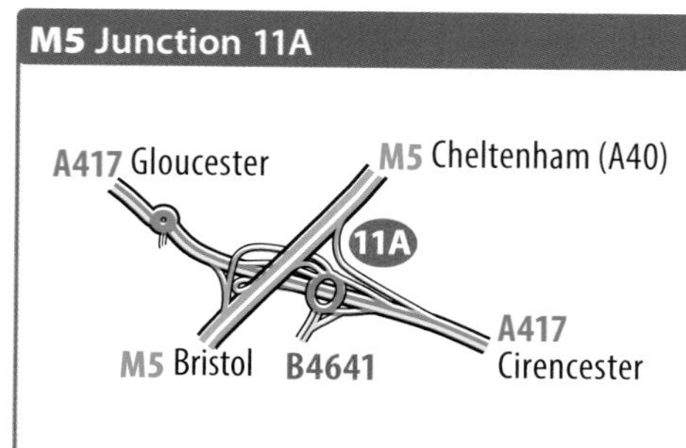

M5 Junction 11A

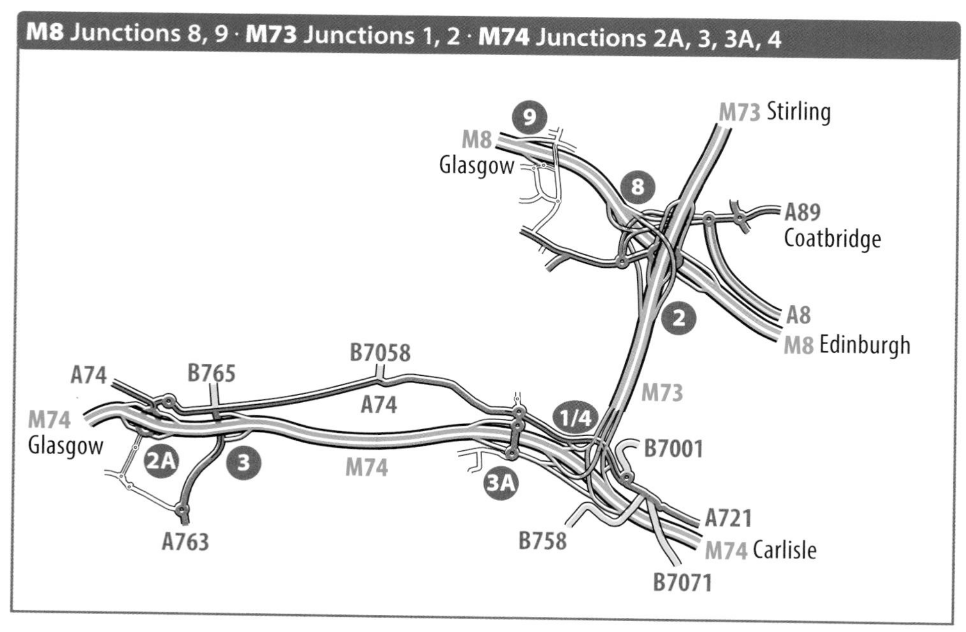

M8 Junctions 8, 9 · M73 Junctions 1, 2 · M74 Junctions 2A, 3, 3A, 4

M1	Northbound	Southbound
2	No exit	No access
4	No exit	No access
6A	No exit. Access from M25 only	No access. Exit to M25 only
7	No exit. Access from A414 only	No access. Exit to A414 only
17	No access. Exit to M45 only	No exit. Access from M45 only
19	No exit to A14	No access from A14
21A	No access	No exit
23A		Exit to A42 only
24A	No exit	No access
35A	No access	No exit
43	No access. Exit to M621 only	No exit. Access from M621 only
48	No exit to A1(M) southbound	

M3	Eastbound	Westbound
8	No exit	No access
10	No access	No exit
13	No access to M27 eastbound	
14	No exit	No access

M4	Eastbound	Westbound
1	Exit to A4 eastbound only	Access from A4 westbound only
2	Access from A4 eastbound only	Access to A4 westbound only
21	No exit	No access
23	No access	No exit
25	No exit	No access
25A	No exit	No access
29	No exit	No access
38		No access
39	No exit or access	No exit
41	No access	No exit
41A	No exit	No access
42	Access from A483 only	Exit to A483 only

M5	Northbound	Southbound
10	No exit	No access
11A	No access from A417 eastbound	No exit to A417 westbound

M6	Northbound	Southbound
3A	No access.	No exit. Access from M6 eastbound only
4A	No exit. Access from M42 southbound only	No access. Exit to M42 only
5	No access	No exit
10A	No access. Exit to M54 only	No exit. Access from M54 only
11A	No exit. Access from M6 Toll only	No access. Exit to M6 Toll only
20	No exit to M56 eastbound	No access from M56 westbound
24	No exit	No access
25	No access	No access
30	No exit. Access from M61 northbound only	No access. Exit to M61 southbound only
31A	No access	No access
45	No access	No exit

M6 Toll	Northbound	Southbound
T1		No exit
T2	No exit, no access	No access
T5	No exit	No access
T7	No access	No exit
T8	No access	No exit

M8	Eastbound	Westbound
6	No exit	No access
6A	No access	No exit
7	No Access	No exit
7A	No exit. Access from A725 northbound only	No access. Exit to A725 southbound only
8	No exit to M73 northbound	No access from M73 southbound
9	No access	No exit
13	No exit southbound	Access from M73 southbound only
14	No access	No exit
16	No exit	No access
17	No exit	
18		No exit
19	No exit to A814 eastbound	No access from A814 westbound
20	No exit	No access
21	No access from M74	No exit
22	No exit. Access from M77 only	No access. Exit to M77 only
23	No exit	No access
25	Exit to A739 northbound only. Access from A739 southbound only	
25A	No exit	No access
28	No exit	No access
28A	No exit	No access
29A	No exit	No access

M9	Eastbound	Westbound
2	No access	No exit
3	No access	No exit
6	No access	No exit
8	No exit	No access

M11	Northbound	Southbound
4	No exit	No access
5	No access	No exit
8A	No access	No exit
9	No access	
13	No access	
14	No exit to A428 westbound	No access. Access from A14 westbound only

M20	Eastbound	Westbound
2	No access	No exit
3	No exit. Access from M26 eastbound only	No access. Exit to M26 westbound only
10A	No Exit	No access
11A	No access	No exit

M23	Northbound	Southbound
7	No exit to A23 southbound	No access from A23 northbound
10A	No exit	No access

M25	Clockwise	Anticlockwise
5	No exit to M26 eastbound	No access from M26 westbound
19	No access	No exit
21	No exit to M1 southbound. Access from M1 southbound only	No exit to M1 southbound. Access from M1 southbound only
31	No exit	No access

M27	Eastbound	Westbound
10	No exit	No access
12	No access	No exit

M40	Eastbound	Westbound
3	No exit	No access
7	No exit	No access
8	No exit	No access
13	No exit	No access
14	No access	No exit
16	No access	No exit

M42	Northbound	Southbound
1	No exit	No access
7	No access. Exit to M6 northbound only	No exit. Access from M6 northbound only
7A	No access. Exit to M6 southbound only	No exit
8	No exit. Access from M6 southbound only	Exit to M6 northbound only. Access from M6 southbound only

M45	Eastbound	Westbound
M1 J17	Access to M1 southbound only	No access from M1 southbound
With A45	No access	No exit

M48	Eastbound	Westbound
M4 J21	No exit to M4 westbound	No access from M4 eastbound
M4 J23	No access from M4 westbound	No exit to M4 eastbound

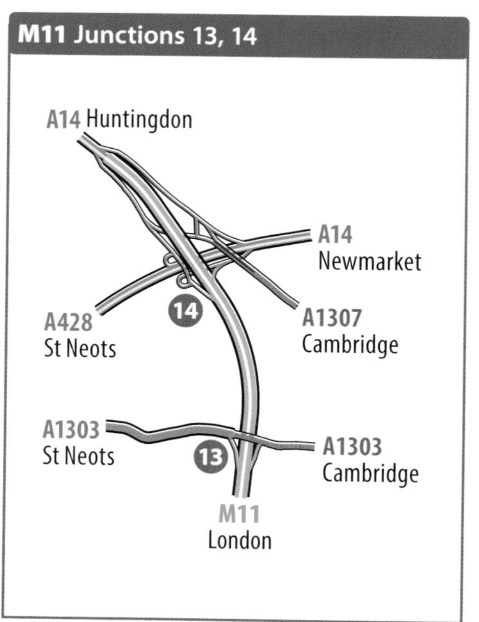

M11 Junctions 13, 14

M49	Southbound	Northbound
18A	No exit to M5 northbound	No access from M5 southbound

M53	Northbound	Southbound
11	Exit to M56 eastbound only. Access from M56 westbound only	Exit to M56 eastbnd only. Access from M56 westbound only

M56	Eastbound	Westbound
2	No exit	No access
3	No access	No exit
4	No exit	No access
7		No access
8	No exit or access	No exit
9	No access from M6 northbound	No access to M6 southbound
15	No exit to M53	No access from M53 northbound

M57	Northbound	Southbound
3	No exit	No access
5	No exit	No access

M58	Eastbound	Westbound
1	No exit	No access

M60	Clockwise	Anticlockwise
2	No exit	No access
3	No exit to A34 northbound	No exit to A34 northbound
4	No access from M56	No exit to M56
5	No exit to A5103 southbound	No exit to A5103 northbound
14	No exit	No access
16	No exit	No access
20	No access	No exit
22		No access
25	No access	
26		No exit or access
27	No exit	No access

M61	Northbound	Southbound
2	No access from A580 eastbound	No exit to A580 westbound
3	No access from A580 eastbound. No access from A666 southbound	No exit to A580 westbound
M6 J30	No exit to M6 southbound	No access from M6 northbound

M62	Eastbound	Westbound
23	No access	No exit

M65	Eastbound	Westbound
9	No access	No exit
11	No exit	No access

M66	Northbound	Southbound
1	No access	No exit

M67	Eastbound	Westbound
1A	No access	No exit
2	No exit	No access

M69	Northbound	Southbound
2	No exit	No access

M73	Northbound	Southbound
2	No access from M8 eastbound	No exit to M8 westbound

M74	Northbound	Southbound
3	No access	No exit
3A	No exit	No access
7	No exit	No access
9	No exit or access	No access
10		No exit
11	No exit	No access
12	No exit	No exit

M77	Northbound	Southbound
4	No exit	No access
6	No exit	No access
7	No exit	No access
8	No access	No access

M80	Northbound	Southbound
4A	No access	No exit
6A	No exit	No access
8	Exit to M876 northbound only. No access	Access from M876 southbound only. No exit

M90	Northbound	Southbound
1	Access from A90 northbound only	No access. Exit to A90 south-bound only
2A	No access	No exit
7	No exit	No access
8	No access	No exit
10	No access from A912	No exit to A912

M180	Eastbound	Westbound
1	No access	No exit

M621	Eastbound	Westbound
2A	No exit	No access
4		No access
5	No access	No exit
6	No exit	No access

M876	Northbound	Southbound
2	No access	No exit

A1(M)	Northbound	Southbound
2	No access	No exit
3		No access
5	No exit	No exit, no access
14	No exit	No access
40	No access	No exit
43	No exit. Access from M1 only	No access. Exit to M1 only
57	No access	No exit
65	No access	No exit

A3(M)	Northbound	Southbound
1	No exit	No access
4	No access	No exit

A38(M)	with Victoria Rd, (Park Circus) Birmingham	
Northbound	No exit	
Southbound	No access	

A48(M)	Northbound	Southbound
M4 Junc 29	Exit to M4 eastbound only	Access from M4 westbound only
29A	Access from A48 eastbound only	Exit to A48 westbound only

A57(M)	Eastbound	Westbound
With A5103	No access	No exit
With A34	No access	No exit

A58(M)		Southbound
With Park Lane and Westgate, Leeds		No access

A64(M)		Eastbound	Westbound
With A58 Clay Pit Lane, Leeds		No access from A58	No exit to A58

A74(M)	Northbound	Southbound
18	No access	No exit
22		No exit to A75

A194(M)	Northbound	Southbound
A1(M) J65 Gateshead Western Bypass	Access from A1(M) northbound only	Exit to A1(M) southbound only

M3 Junctions 13, 14 · M27 Junction 4

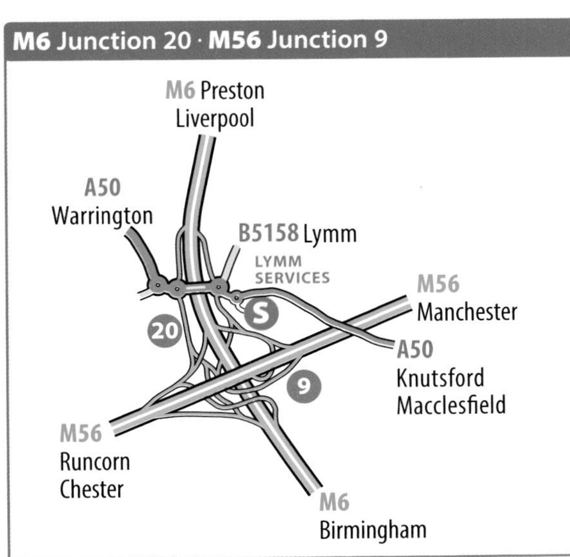

M6 Junctions 3A, 4A · M42 Junctions 7, 7A, 8, 9
M6 Toll Junctions T1, T2

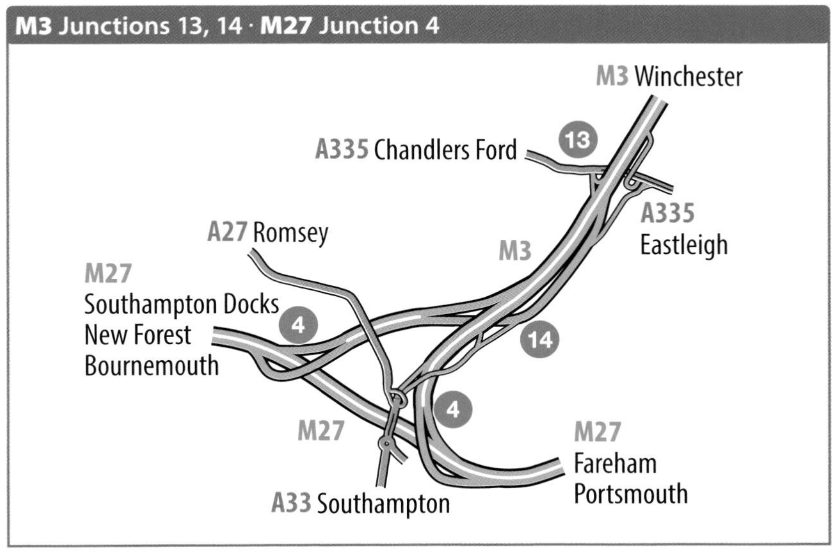

M6 Junction 20 · M56 Junction 9

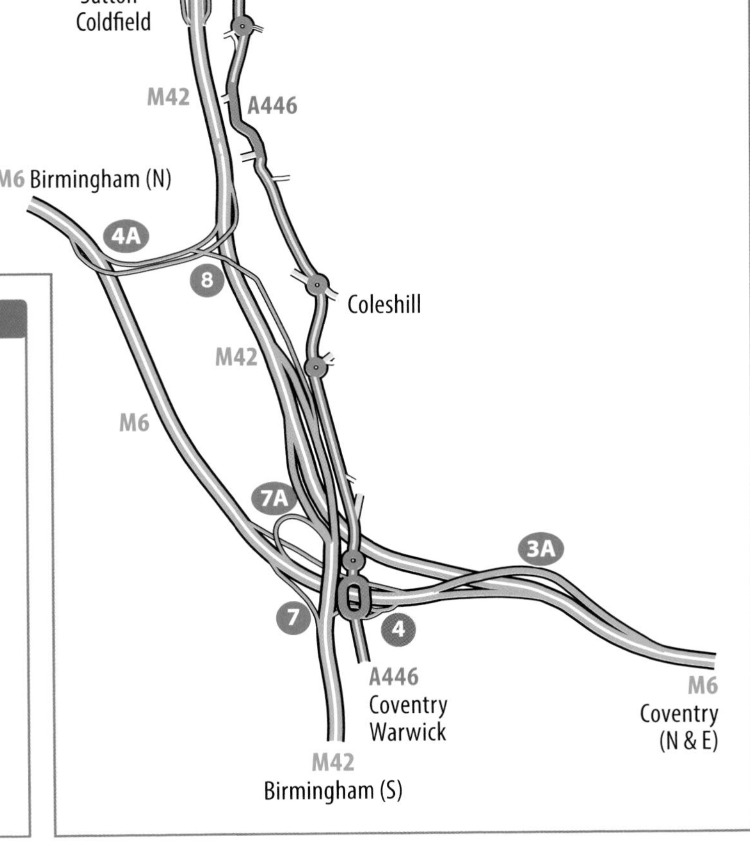

M62 Junctions 32A, 33 · A1(M) Junctions 40, 41

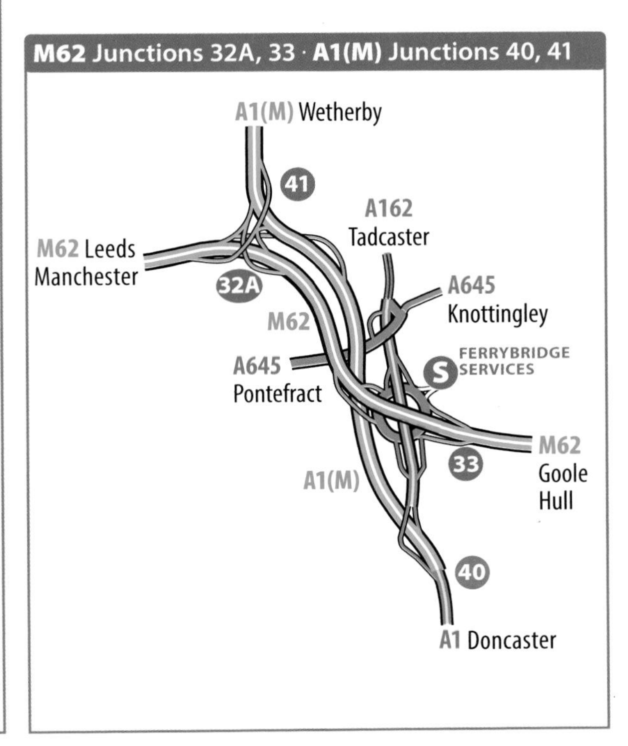

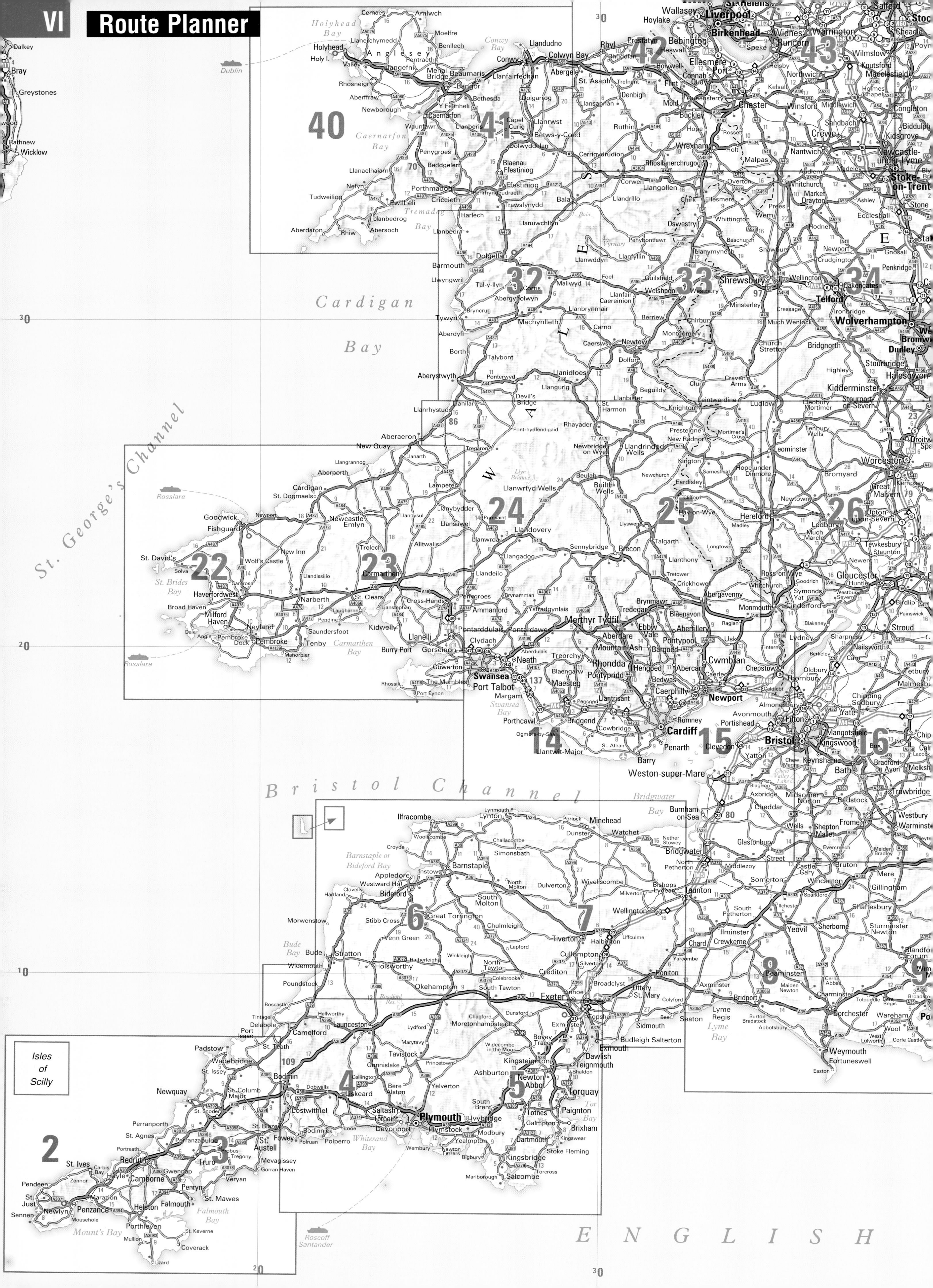
Holyhead Bay
Holyhead
Holy I.
Anglesey
Amlwch
Cemaes
Moelfre
Benllech
Llangefni
Beaumaris
Menai Bridge
Bangor
Rhosneigr
Aberffraw
Newborough
Caernarfon
Caernarfon Bay
Llanberis
Bethesda
Capel Curig
Conwy Bay
Llandudno
Conwy
Colwyn Bay
Llanfairfechan
Abergele
Rhyl
Prestatyn
Holywell
Flint
St. Asaph
Denbigh
Ruthin
Mold
Buckley
Llanrwst
Betws-y-Coed
Blaenau Ffestiniog
Ffestiniog
Cerrigydrudion
Penygroes
Beddgelert
Llanaelhaiarn
Nefyn
Tudweilog
Pwllheli
Criccieth
Porthmadog
Llanbedrog
Abersoch
Aberdaron
Rhiw
Tremadog Bay
Harlech
Bala
Trawsfynydd
Corwen
Llangollen
Wrexham
Hope
Rossett
Holt
Malpas
Wallasey
Hoylake
Liverpool
Birkenhead
Bebington
Heswall
Ellesmere Port
Chester
Widnes
Runcorn
Warrington
St. Helens
Salford
Northwich
Knutsford
Wilmslow
Macclesfield
Winsford
Middlewich
Sandbach
Congleton
Crewe
Nantwich
Kidsgrove
Newcastle-under-Lyme
Stoke-on-Trent
Whitchurch
Market Drayton
Stone
Ashley
Eccleshall
Oswestry
Ellesmere
Chirk
Wem
Shrewsbury
Welshpool
Newport
Penkridge
Wellington
Telford
Oakengates
Wolverhampton
Dudley
Stourbridge
Halesowen
Kidderminster
Stourport-on-Severn
Much Wenlock
Bridgnorth
Church Stretton
Minsterley
Montgomery
Chirbury
Newtown
Caersws
Llanidloes
Llangurig
Machynlleth
Mallwyd
Dolgellau
Barmouth
Llwyngwril
Tal-y-llyn
Abergynolwyn
Corris
Tywyn
Aberdyfi
Borth
Talybont
Aberystwyth
Ponterwyd
Devil's Bridge
Cardigan Bay
Llanrhystud
Aberaeron
New Quay
Lampeter
Tregaron
Rhayader
Knighton
Presteigne
New Radnor
Ludlow
Leominster
Tenbury Wells
Cleobury Mortimer
Craven Arms
Clun
Llandrindod Wells
Builth Wells
Llanwrtyd Wells
Newbridge on Wye
Kington
Hay-on-Wye
Hereford
Bromyard
Worcester
Great Malvern
Ledbury
Upton-upon-Severn
Tewkesbury
Much Marcle
Ross-on-Wye
Gloucester
Stroud
Cardigan
St. Dogmaels
Aberporth
Newcastle Emlyn
Llandysul
Llanybydder
Fishguard
Goodwick
St. David's
Solva
Haverfordwest
St. Brides Bay
Broad Haven
Milford Haven
Neyland
Pembroke
Pembroke Dock
Tenby
Saundersfoot
Narberth
St. Clears
Carmarthen
Carmarthen Bay
Kidwelly
Llanelli
Burry Port
Gorseinon
Llandovery
Llangadog
Llandeilo
Ammanford
Cross Hands
Brecon
Sennybridge
Talgarth
Crickhowell
Abergavenny
Monmouth
Merthyr Tydfil
Tredegar
Ebbw Vale
Brynmawr
Blaenavon
Abertillery
Pontypool
Usk
Cwmbran
Chepstow
Newport
Caerphilly
Bedwas
Pontypridd
Rhondda
Aberdare
Mountain Ash
Treorchy
Maesteg
Neath
Swansea
Port Talbot
The Mumbles
Swansea Bay
Porthcawl
Bridgend
Cowbridge
Cardiff
Penarth
Barry
Llantwit Major
Clevedon
Portishead
Bristol
Avonmouth
Filton
Yate
Thornbury
Keynsham
Bath
Bradford on Avon
Weston-super-Mare
Cheddar
Wells
Shepton Mallet
Frome
Warminster
Glastonbury
Street
Bridgwater
Bridgwater Bay
Burnham-on-Sea
Minehead
Watchet
Dunster
Porlock
Lynton
Ilfracombe
Barnstaple
Barnstaple or Bideford Bay
Bideford
Appledore
Westward Ho!
Clovelly
Hartland
Great Torrington
South Molton
Dulverton
Wiveliscombe
Taunton
Wellington
Tiverton
Cullompton
Crediton
Honiton
Exeter
Exmouth
Sidmouth
Budleigh Salterton
Okehampton
Holsworthy
Bude
Bude Bay
Stratton
Launceston
Camelford
Padstow
Wadebridge
Newquay
Bodmin
Liskeard
Lostwithiel
Fowey
St. Austell
Mevagissey
Truro
Redruth
Camborne
Hayle
St. Ives
Penzance
Newlyn
St. Just
Helston
Falmouth
Falmouth Bay
Mount's Bay
Lizard
Coverack
Tavistock
Plymouth
Saltash
Torpoint
Plymstock
Ivybridge
Kingsbridge
Salcombe
Dartmouth
Totnes
Paignton
Torquay
Brixham
Newton Abbot
Teignmouth
Dawlish
Chard
Crewkerne
Yeovil
Sherborne
Ilminster
Beaminster
Bridport
Lyme Regis
Lyme Bay
Axminster
Seaton
Dorchester
Weymouth
Wareham
Shaftesbury
Gillingham
Mere
Wincanton
Bristol Channel
Cardigan Bay
St. George's Channel
ENGLISH
WALES
Isles of Scilly
Rosslare
Dublin
Roscoff
Santander
Dalkey
Bray
Greystones
Rathnew
Wicklow
40
41
42
43
32
33
34
22
23
24
25
26
14
15
16
2
3
4
5
6
7
8
9

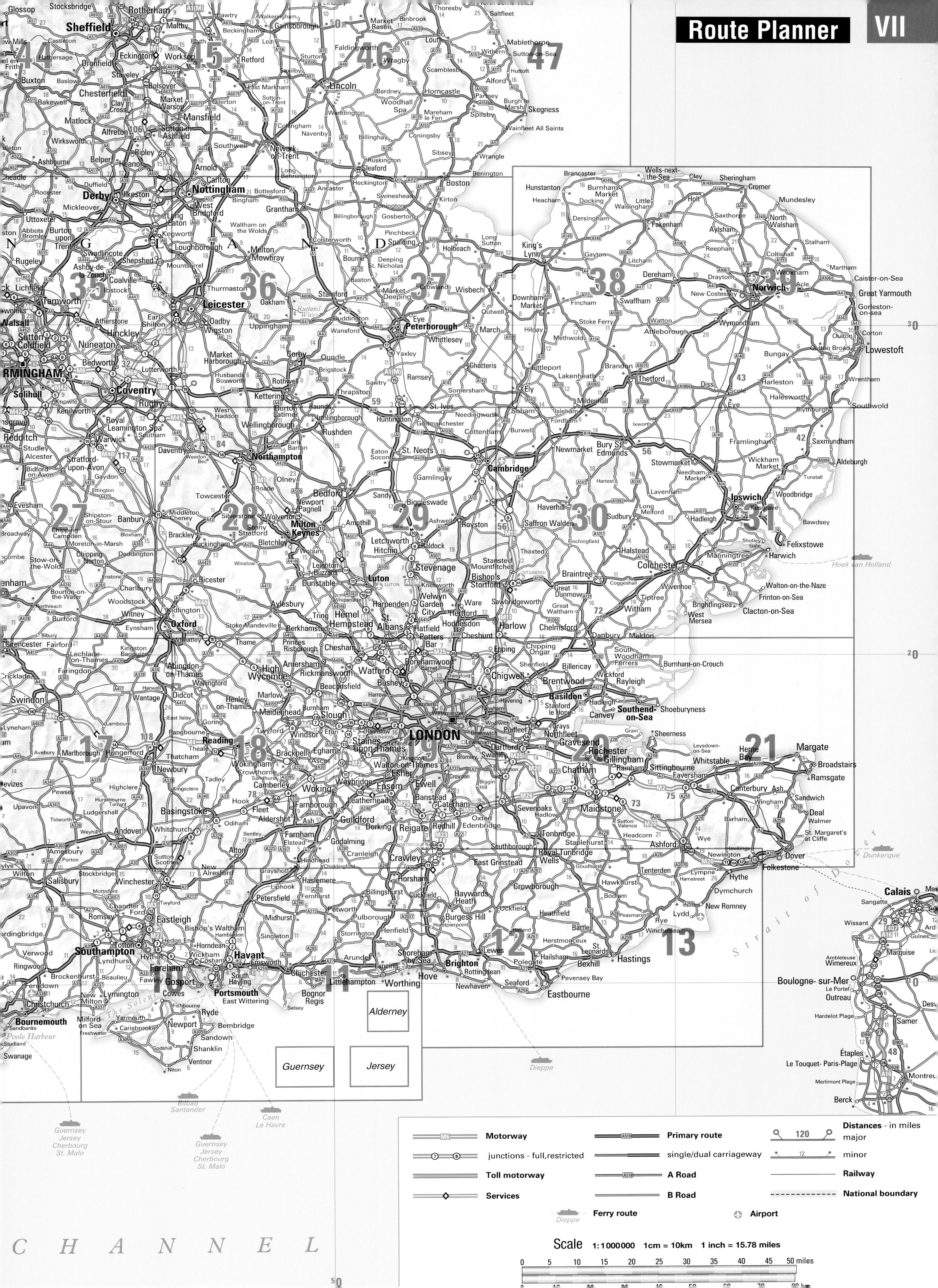

Legend

Motorway	Primary route	**Distances** - in miles
junctions - full, restricted	single/dual carriageway	major
Toll motorway	A Road	minor
Services	B Road	Railway
Ferry route		National boundary
	Airport	

Scale

Scale 1:1000000 1cm = 10km 1 inch = 15.78 miles

0 5 10 15 20 25 30 35 40 45 50 miles

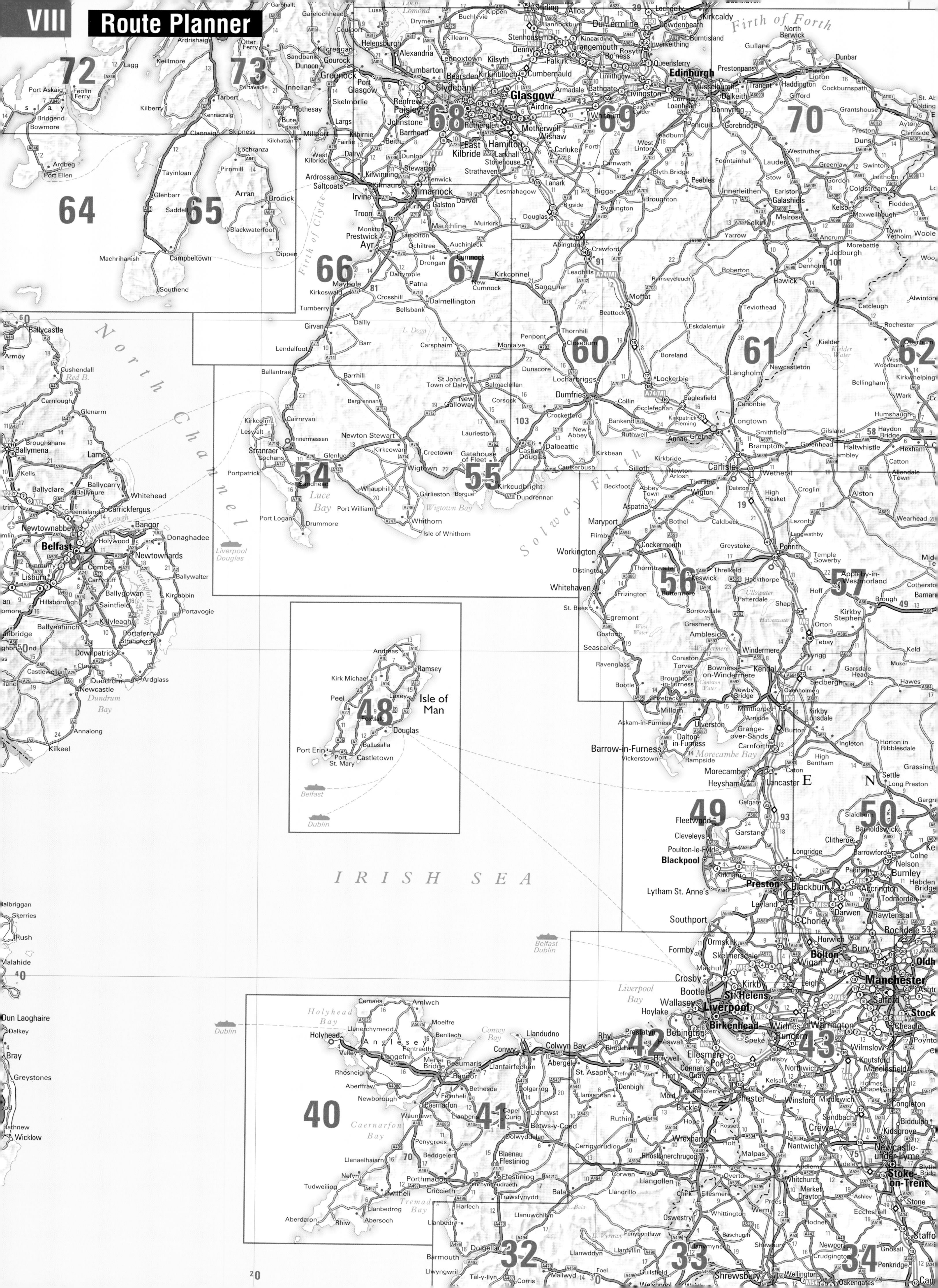
Firth of Forth
North Channel
IRISH SEA
Solway Firth
Firth of Clyde
Isle of Man
Anglesey
Luce Bay
Wigtown Bay
Morecambe Bay
Liverpool Bay
Caernarfon Bay
Tremadog Bay
Holyhead Bay
Conwy Bay
Dundrum Bay
Belfast Lough
Strangford Lough
Islay
Arran
Glasgow
Edinburgh
Stirling
Dunfermline
Kirkcaldy
Falkirk
Paisley
Greenock
Kilmarnock
Ayr
Hamilton
Motherwell
East Kilbride
Livingston
Dumfries
Stranraer
Carlisle
Penrith
Kendal
Keswick
Windermere
Workington
Whitehaven
Barrow-in-Furness
Lancaster
Morecambe
Blackpool
Preston
Blackburn
Bolton
Wigan
Southport
Liverpool
Birkenhead
St. Helens
Manchester
Warrington
Chester
Wrexham
Crewe
Stoke-on-Trent
Bangor
Holyhead
Llandudno
Caernarfon
Belfast
Larne
Bangor
Newtownards
Lisburn
Ballymena
Douglas
Ramsey
Peel
Castletown
Dun Laoghaire
Bray
Wicklow
Shrewsbury
72
73
64
65
66
67
68
69
70
54
55
60
61
62
56
57
48
49
50
40
41
42
43
32
33
34

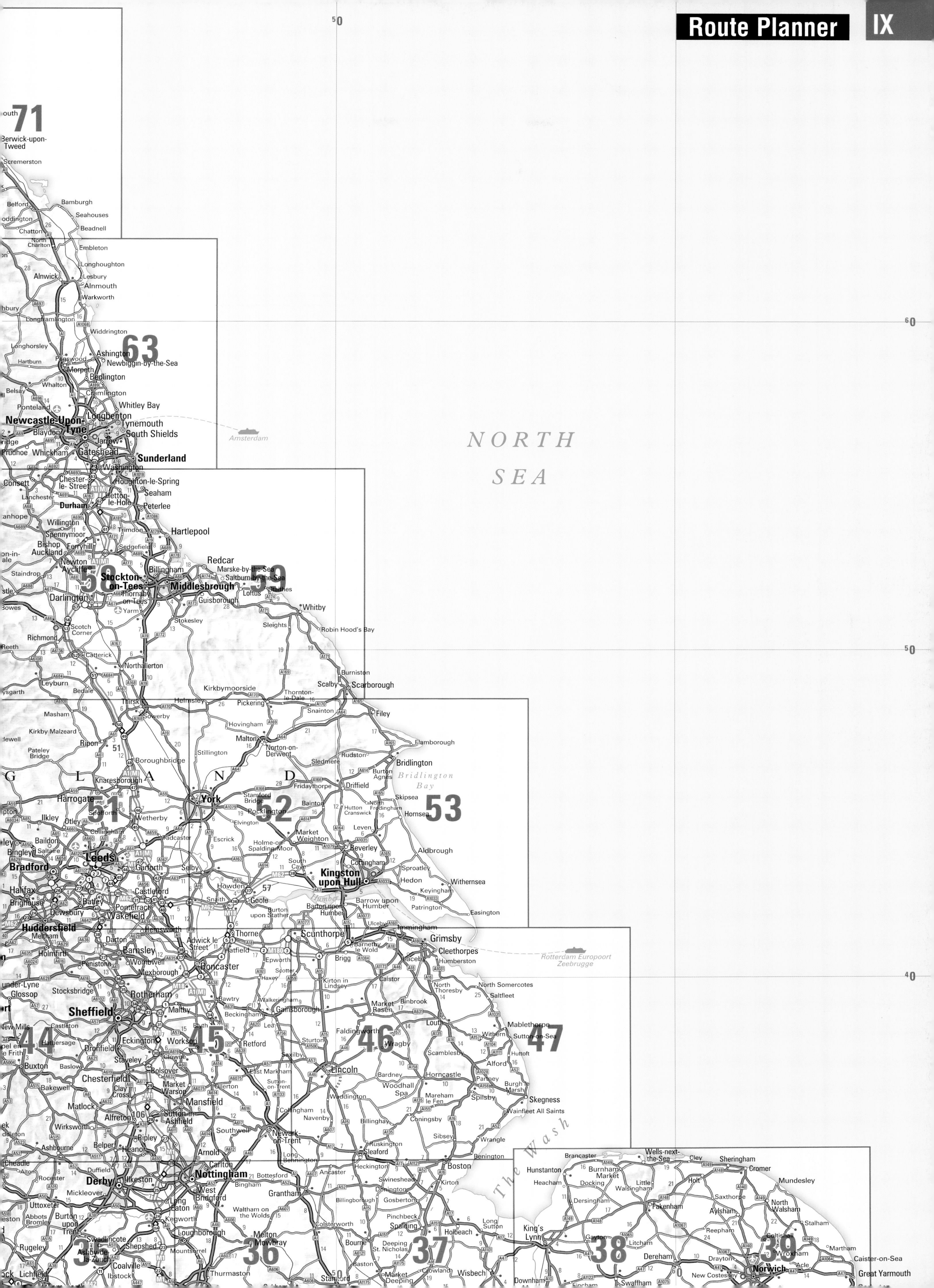
NORTH
SEA
71
63
58
59
51
52
53
44
45
46
47
35
36
37
38
39
Berwick-upon-Tweed
Scremerston
Belford
Bamburgh
Seahouses
Beadnell
Chatton
North Charlton
Embleton
Longhoughton
Alnwick
Lesbury
Alnmouth
Warkworth
Longframlington
Widdrington
Longhorsley
Hartburn
Ashington
Newbiggin-by-the-Sea
Morpeth
Bedlington
Whalton
Cramlington
Belsay
Ponteland
Whitley Bay
Newcastle-Upon-Tyne
Longbenton
Tynemouth
South Shields
Blaydon
Jarrow
Amsterdam
Prudhoe
Whickham
Gateshead
Sunderland
Washington
Consett
Chester-le-Street
Houghton-le-Spring
Seaham
Lanchester
Durham
Hetton-le-Hole
Peterlee
Willington
Trimdon
Hartlepool
Spennymoor
Bishop Auckland
Ferryhill
Sedgefield
Newton Aycliffe
Redcar
Marske-by-the-Sea
Saltburn-by-the-Sea
Staindrop
Stockton-on-Tees
Billingham
Middlesbrough
Darlington
Thornaby on Tees
Guisborough
Loftus
Staithes
Whitby
Yarm
Bowes
Scotch Corner
Stokesley
Sleights
Robin Hood's Bay
Richmond
Reeth
Catterick
Northallerton
Burniston
Scalby
Scarborough
Leyburn
Bedale
Kirkbymoorside
Thornton-le-Dale
Thirsk
Helmsley
Pickering
Snainton
Filey
Masham
Sowerby
Hovingham
Kirkby Malzeard
Malton
Norton-on-Derwent
Flamborough
Ripon
Pateley Bridge
Boroughbridge
Stillington
Sledmere
Rudston
Bridlington
Bridlington Bay
Knaresborough
Fridaythorpe
Driffield
Burton Agnes
Skipsea
Harrogate
York
Stamford Bridge
Bainton
Hutton Cranswick
North Frodingham
Hornsea
Ilkley
Otley
Spofforth
Wetherby
Pocklington
Elvington
Leven
Baildon
Bingley
Saltaire
Collingham
Tadcaster
Escrick
Market Weighton
Beverley
Aldbrough
Leeds
Holme-on-Spalding-Moor
Bradford
Garforth
Selby
South Cave
Cottingham
Sproatley
Kingston upon Hull
Hedon
Withernsea
Halifax
Howden
Keyingham
Brighouse
Batley
Castleford
Snaith
Goole
Barrow upon Humber
Patrington
Dewsbury
Pontefract
Wakefield
Burton upon Stather
Barton-upon-Humber
Easington
Huddersfield
Hemsworth
Thorne
Scunthorpe
Immingham
Meltham
Grimsby
Holmfirth
Darton
Barnsley
Adwick le Street
Hatfield
Barnetby le Wold
Cleethorpes
Penistone
Wombwell
Doncaster
Epworth
Brigg
Laceby
Humberston
Rotterdam Europoort Zeebrugge
Mexborough
Scotter
Haxey
Kirton in Lindsey
Caistor
North Somercotes
Stocksbridge
Rotherham
Bawtry
Walkeringham
North Thoresby
Saltfleet
Glossop
Sheffield
Maltby
Beckingham
Gainsborough
Market Rasen
Binbrook
Castleton
Blyth
Lea
Sturton
Louth
Mablethorpe
Hathersage
Eckington
Worksop
Retford
Faldingworth
Withern
Sutton-on-Sea
Buxton
Baslow
Staveley
Clowne
Saxilby
Wragby
Huttoft
Chesterfield
Bolsover
East Markham
Lincoln
Scamblesby
Alford
Bakewell
Market Warsop
Sutton-on-Trent
Bardney
Horncastle
Partney
Burgh le Marsh
Clay Cross
Ollerton
Woodhall Spa
Skegness
Matlock
Mansfield
Waddington
Mareham le Fen
Spilsby
Wainfleet All Saints
Wirksworth
Alfreton
Sutton-in-Ashfield
Collingham
Navenby
Billinghay
Coningsby
Southwell
Newark-on-Trent
Sibsey
Wrangle
Ashbourne
Belper
Heanor
Ripley
Ruskington
Sleaford
The Wash
Arnold
Long Bennington
Benington
Brancaster
Wells-next-the-Sea
Cley
Sheringham
Cromer
Cheadle
Nottingham
Carlton
Bottesford
Ancaster
Heckington
Boston
Hunstanton
Burnham Market
Alton
Rocester
Duffield
Derby
Ilkeston
West Bridgford
Bingham
Grantham
Swineshead
Donington
Kirton
Heacham
Docking
Little Walsingham
Holt
Mundesley
Mickleover
Uttoxeter
Long Eaton
Billingborough
Gosberton
Dersingham
Fakenham
Saxthorpe
North Walsham
Abbots Bromley
Burton upon Trent
Kegworth
Waltham on the Wolds
Colsterworth
Pinchbeck
Spalding
Long Sutton
Aylsham
Stalham
Swadlincote
Loughborough
Melton Mowbray
Bourne
Holbeach
King's Lynn
Gayton
Litcham
Reepham
Coltishall
Rugeley
Ashby de la Zouch
Shepshed
Mountsorrel
Deeping St. Nicholas
Wroxham
Martham
Lichfield
Coalville
Ibstock
Thurmaston
Stamford
Baston
Market Deeping
Crowland
Wisbech
Downham Market
Dereham
Drayton
Norwich
Acle
Caister-on-Sea
Great Yarmouth
Swaffham
New Costessey

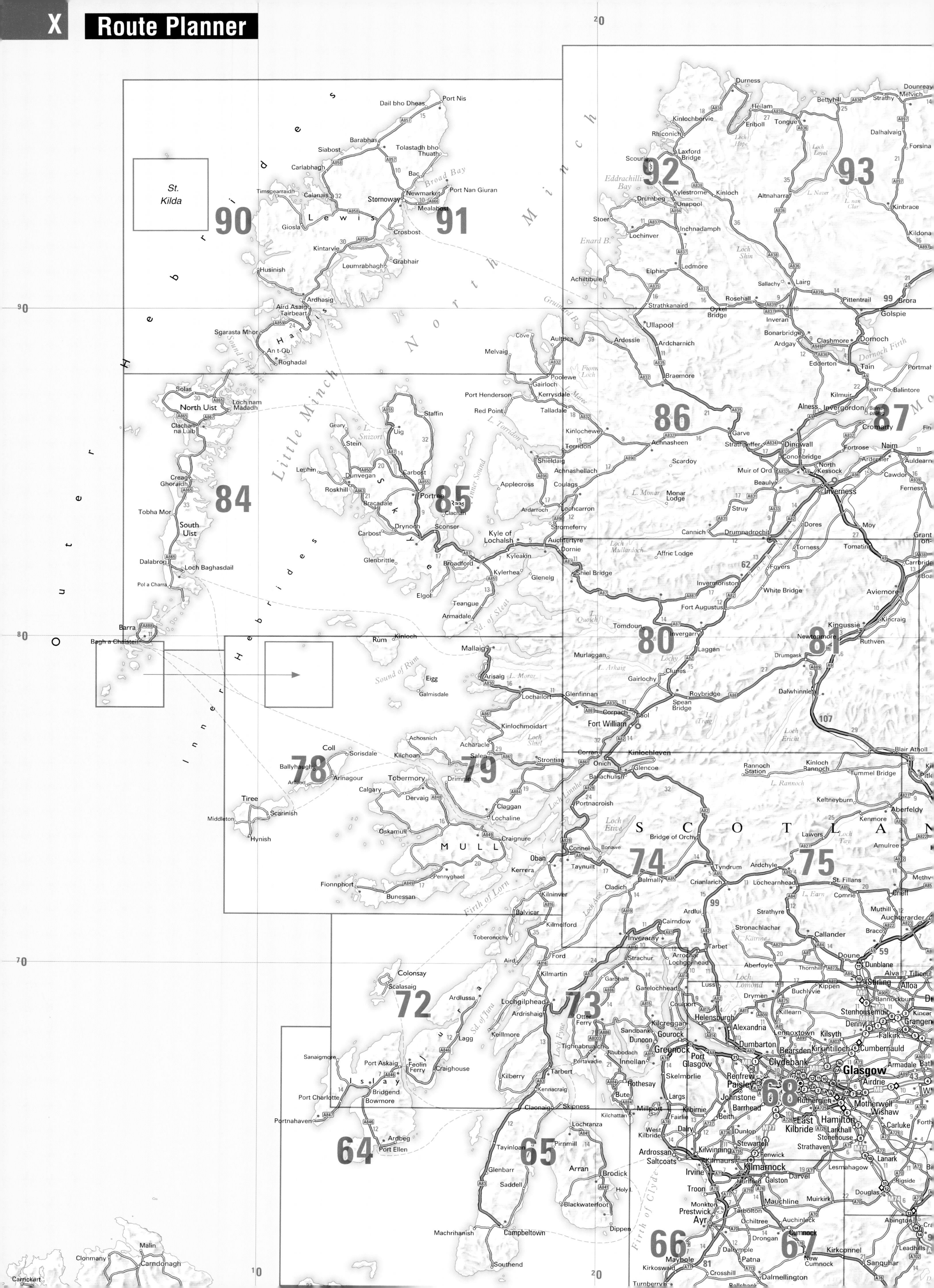

Outer Hebrides
Inner Hebrides
North Minch
Little Minch
St. Kilda
90
91
92
93
84
85
86
87
80
81
78
79
74
75
72
73
64
65
66
67
68
99
SCOTLAND
Port Nis
Dail bho Dheas
Barabhas
Siabost
Tolastadh bho Thuath
Carlabhagh
Bac
Broad Bay
Port Nan Giuran
Timsgearraidh
Calanais
Stornoway
Newmarket
Mealabost
Lewis
Giosla
Crosbost
Kintarvie
Grabhair
Leumrabhagh
Husinish
Ardhasig
Aird Asaig
Tairbeart
Sgarasta Mhor
Harris
An t-Ob
Roghadal
Sound of Harris
Solas
North Uist
Loch nam Madadh
Clachan na Luib
Creag Ghoraidh
Tobha Mor
South Uist
Dalabrog
Loch Baghasdail
Pol a Charra
Barra
Bagh a Chaisteil
Staffin
Geary
Uig
Stein
Snizort
Lephin
Dunvegan
Carbost
Roskhill
Bracadale
Portree
Raasay
Clachan
Skye
Drynoch
Sconser
Glenbrittle
Broadford
Kylerhea
Glenelg
Elgol
Teangue
Armadale
Sd. of Sleat
Inner Sound
Applecross
Ardarroch
Kyle of Lochalsh
Kyleakin
Rum
Kinloch
Sound of Rum
Eigg
Galmisdale
Mallaig
Arisaig
Lochailort
Glenfinnan
Kinlochmoidart
Acharacle
Salen
Strontian
Coll
Sorisdale
Arinagour
Ballyhaugh
Arileod
Tiree
Scarinish
Middleton
Hynish
Achosnich
Kilchoan
Tobermory
Calgary
Dervaig
Drimnin
Claggan
Lochaline
Oskamull
Craignure
MULL
Pennyghael
Fionnphort
Bunessan
Oban
Kerrera
Firth of Lorn
Kilninver
Balvicar
Toberonochy
Kilmelford
Colonsay
Scalasaig
Ardlussa
Jura
Sd. of Jura
Lagg
Craighouse
Sanaigmore
Port Askaig
Feolin Ferry
Islay
Bridgend
Bowmore
Port Charlotte
Portnahaven
Ardbeg
Port Ellen
Aird
Ford
Kilmartin
Lochgilphead
Ardrishaig
Kilmore
Kilberry
Tarbert
Kennacraig
Claonaig
Skipness
Lochranza
Pirnmill
Tayinloan
Arran
Brodick
Holy I.
Glenbarr
Saddell
Blackwaterfoot
Machrihanish
Campbeltown
Southend
Dippen
Firth of Clyde
Malin
Clonmany
Carndonagh
Carrickart
Durness
Heilam
Eriboll
Tongue
Kinlochbervie
Rhiconich
Scourie
Laxford Bridge
Eddrachillis Bay
Drumbeg
Kylestrome
Unapool
Kinloch
Altnaharra
Stoer
Lochinver
Inchnadamph
Enard B.
Loch Shin
Elphin
Ledmore
Achiltibuie
Sallachy
Lairg
Rosehall
Oykel Bridge
Strathkanaird
Ullapool
Ardcharnich
Ardessie
Inveran
Bonarbridge
Ardgay
Clashmore
Dornoch
Dornoch Firth
Edderton
Tain
Portmahomack
Bettyhill
Strathy
Dounreay
Melvich
Dalhalvaig
Forsinard
Kinbrace
Kildonan
Pittentrail
Brora
Golspie
Loch Naver
Cove
Aultbea
Melvaig
Poolewe
Gairloch
Kerrysdale
Talladale
Loch Maree
Port Henderson
Red Point
L. Torridon
Kinlochewe
Torridon
Shieldaig
Achnashellach
Coulags
Lochcarron
Stromeferry
Auchtertyre
Dornie
Shiel Bridge
Braemore
Achnasheen
Garve
Strathpeffer
Dingwall
Conon Bridge
Muir of Ord
Beauly
North Kessock
Inverness
Alness
Invergordon
Cromarty
Kilmuir
Fearn
Balintore
Fortrose
Nairn
Ardersier
Cawdor
Auldearn
Ferness
Scardoy
L. Monar
Monar Lodge
Struy
Cannich
Drumnadrochit
Dores
Moy
Tomatin
Grantown-on-Spey
Carrbridge
Loch Mullardoch
Affric Lodge
Torness
Foyers
Invermoriston
White Bridge
Aviemore
Fort Augustus
Loch Quoich
Tomdoun
Invergarry
Laggan
Kincraig
Kingussie
Newtonmore
Ruthven
Drumgask
Loch Lochy
Murlaggan
L. Arkaig
Clunes
Gairlochy
Roybridge
Spean Bridge
Dalwhinnie
Corpach
Caol
Fort William
L. Treig
Loch Ericht
Blair Atholl
Kinlochleven
Corran
Onich
Glencoe
Ballachulish
Portnacroish
Loch Linnhe
Rannoch Station
Kinloch Rannoch
L. Rannoch
Tummel Bridge
Keltneyburn
Aberfeldy
Kenmore
Loch Etive
Bridge of Orchy
Lawers
Loch Tay
Amulree
Connel
Bonawe
Taynuilt
Tyndrum
Ardchyle
Crianlarich
Lochearnhead
St. Fillans
Comrie
Crieff
Dalmally
Cladich
Loch Awe
L. Earn
Ardlui
Strathyre
Muthill
Auchterarder
Cairndow
Stronachlachar
Inveraray
Callander
Braco
Strachur
Arrochar
Lochgoilhead
Tarbet
L. Katrine
Aberfoyle
Thornhill
Doune
Dunblane
Stirling
Alloa
Tillicoultry
Garbhallt
Garelochhead
Loch Fyne
Luss
Loch Lomond
Drymen
Kippen
Buchlyvie
Bannockburn
Stenhousemuir
Kincardine
Grangemouth
Denny
Falkirk
Killearn
Coulport
Helensburgh
Alexandria
Kilcreggan
Gourock
Greenock
Dunoon
Sandbank
Tighnabruaich
Otter Ferry
Portavadie
Innellan
Rothesay
Bute
Millport
Port Glasgow
Dumbarton
Lennoxtown
Kilsyth
Bearsden
Kirkintilloch
Cumbernauld
Clydebank
Glasgow
Airdrie
Renfrew
Paisley
Johnstone
Rutherglen
Motherwell
Wishaw
Barrhead
East Kilbride
Hamilton
Larkhall
Carluke
Stonehouse
Strathaven
Skelmorlie
Largs
Fairlie
Kilbirnie
Beith
Dalry
West Kilbride
Dunlop
Stewarton
Ardrossan
Saltcoats
Kilwinning
Kilmaurs
Fenwick
Irvine
Kilmarnock
Hurlford
Galston
Darvel
Lesmahagow
Lanark
Douglas
Troon
Monkton
Prestwick
Ayr
Tarbolton
Mauchline
Muirkirk
Ochiltree
Auchinleck
Cumnock
New Cumnock
Abington
Drongan
Kirkconnel
Sanquhar
Leadhills
Maybole
Dalrymple
Patna
Kirkoswald
Crosshill
Dalmellington
Turnberry
Ballantrae
Glasgow

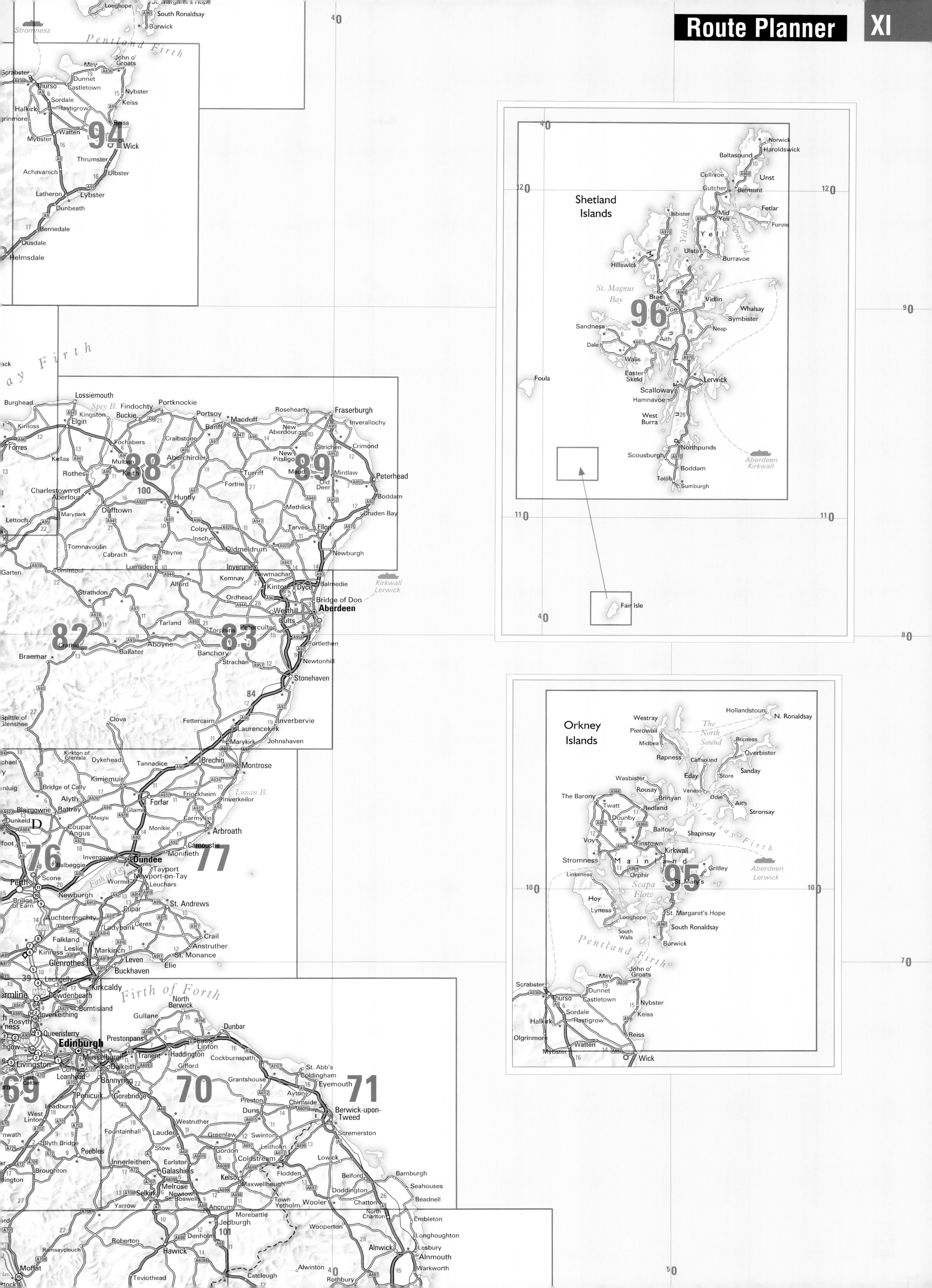
Shetland Islands
Norwick
Haroldswick
Baltasound
Unst
Cullivoe
Gutcher
Belmont
Fetlar
Funzie
Mid Yell
Yell
Isbister
Ulsta
Burravoe
Hillswick
St. Magnus Bay
Brae
Vidlin
Whalsay
Symbister
Voe
Sandness
Dale
Aith
Neap
Walls
Easter Skeld
Foula
Lerwick
Scalloway
Hamnavoe
West Burra
Scousburgh
Northpunds
Boddam
Toab
Sumburgh
Aberdeen Kirkwall
Fair Isle
96
Orkney Islands
Westray
Pierowall
Midbea
Hollandstoun
N. Ronaldsay
The North Sound
Burness
Overbister
Sanday
Rapness
Calfsound
Eday
Store
Wasbister
Rousay
The Barony
Brinyan
Twatt
Redland
Dounby
Veness
Odie
Aith
Stronsay
Balfour
Shapinsay
Voy
Finstown
Kirkwall
Stromness
Mainland
Orphir
Gritley
Linksness
Scapa Flow
St. Mary's
Aberdeen Lerwick
Hoy
Lyness
Longhope
St. Margaret's Hope
South Ronaldsay
South Walls
Burwick
Pentland Firth
Mey
John o' Groats
Scrabster
Dunnet
Thurso
Castletown
Nybster
Keiss
Halkirk
Sordale
Hastigrow
Reiss
Olgrinmore
Watten
Mybster
Wick
95
Stromness
Pentland Firth
Thurso
Halkirk
Watten
Thrumster
Ulbster
Achavanich
Latheron
Lybster
Dunbeath
Berriedale
Ousdale
Helmsdale
94
Lossiemouth
Burghead
Portknockie
Findochty
Buckie
Portsoy
Kingston
Elgin
Kinloss
Forres
Fochabers
Banff
Macduff
Rosehearty
Fraserburgh
Inverallochy
New Aberdour
Crimond
Cairnbulg
Aberchirder
Strichen
New Pitsligo
Maud
Mintlaw
Peterhead
Old Deer
Boddam
Kellas
Rothes
Mulben
Keith
Turriff
Fortrie
Charlestown of Aberlour
Dufftown
Huntly
Methlick
Cruden Bay
Ellon
Tarves
Colpy
Insch
Oldmeldrum
Newburgh
Tomnavoulin
Cabrach
Rhynie
Lumsden
Inverurie
Tomintoul
Alford
Kemnay
Newmachar
Kintore
Dyce
Balmedie
Strathdon
Ordhead
Bridge of Don
Westhill
Aberdeen
Cults
Tarland
Torphins
Peterculter
Portlethen
Crathie
Ballater
Aboyne
Banchory
Braemar
Strachan
Newtonhill
Stonehaven
Clova
Fettercairn
Laurencekirk
Inverbervie
Marykirk
Johnshaven
88
89
82
83
84
100
Kirkwall Lerwick
Kirkton of Glenisla
Dykehead
Tannadice
Brechin
Montrose
Kirriemuir
Bridge of Cally
Alyth
Friockheim
Lunan B.
Inverkeilor
Forfar
Blairgowrie
Rattray
Glamis
Meigle
Carmyllie
Coupar Angus
Monikie
Arbroath
Carnoustie
Invergowrie
Monifieth
Dundee
Balbeggie
Tayport
Newport-on-Tay
Scone
Perth
Wormit
Leuchars
Newburgh
St. Andrews
Cupar
Auchtermuchty
Ceres
Ladybank
Falkland
Crail
Leslie
Markinch
Kinross
Anstruther
Glenrothes
Leven
St. Monance
Elie
Buckhaven
Lochgelly
Kirkcaldy
Cowdenbeath
Burntisland
Inverkeithing
Firth of Forth
76
77
North Berwick
Gullane
Dunbar
Prestonpans
East Linton
Edinburgh
Musselburgh
Tranent
Haddington
Cockburnspath
Dalkeith
Gifford
St. Abb's
Coldingham
Livingston
Loanhead
Bonnyrigg
Grantshouse
Eyemouth
Penicuik
Gorebridge
Preston
Ayton
Chirnside
Duns
Berwick-upon-Tweed
West Linton
Westruther
Fountainhall
Lauder
Greenlaw
Swinton
Scremerston
Blyth Bridge
Stow
Gordon
Coldstream
Leitholm
Peebles
Earlston
Lowick
Broughton
Innerleithen
Galashiels
Kelso
Flodden
Belford
Bamburgh
Melrose
Maxwellheugh
Seahouses
Selkirk
Newtown St. Boswells
Doddington
Yarrow
Ancrum
Town Yetholm
Wooler
Chatton
Beadnell
Jedburgh
Morebattle
North Charlton
Embleton
Denholm
Wooperton
Robertson
Longhoughton
Hawick
Alnwick
Lesbury
Alnmouth
Warkworth
Alwinton
Rothbury
Catcleugh
Teviothead
Moffat
69
70
71
101

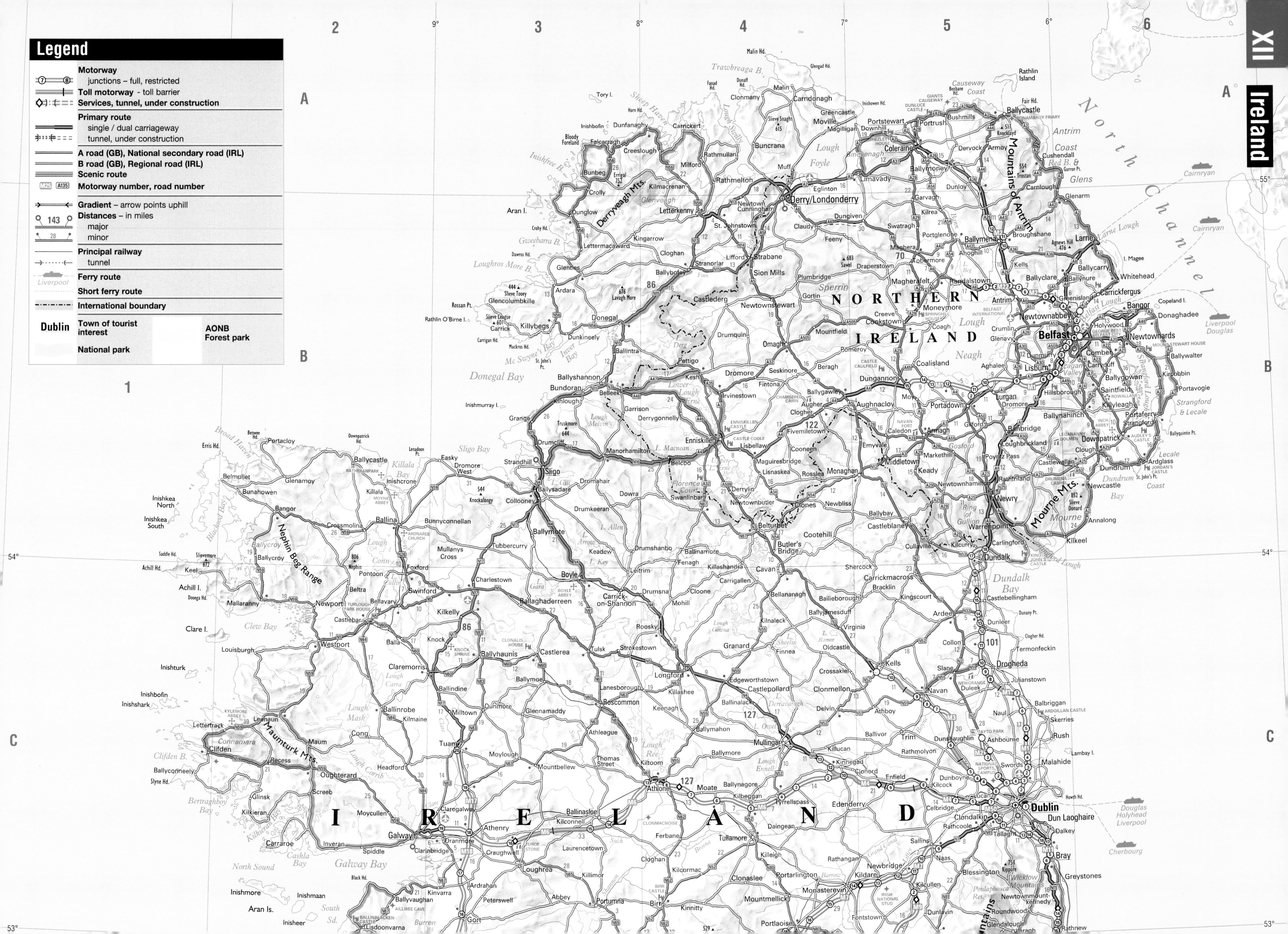

Legend
Motorway
junctions – full, restricted
Toll motorway - toll barrier
Services, tunnel, under construction
Primary route
single / dual carriageway
tunnel, under construction
A road (GB), National secondary road (IRL)
B road (GB), Regional road (IRL)
Scenic route
Motorway number, road number
Gradient – arrow points uphill
Distances – in miles
major
minor
Principal railway
tunnel
Ferry route
Short ferry route
International boundary
Dublin
Town of tourist interest
National park
AONB
Forest park
NORTHERN IRELAND
IRELAND
North Channel
Mountains of Antrim
Derryveagh Mts.
Mourne Mts.
Nephin Beg Range
Maumturk Mts.
Donegal Bay
Sligo Bay
Galway Bay
Clew Bay
Dundalk Bay
Belfast
Derry/Londonderry
Dublin
Dun Laoghaire
Galway
Sligo
Donegal
Letterkenny
Enniskillen
Armagh
Newry
Dundalk
Drogheda
Athlone
Mullingar
Longford
Castlebar
Westport
Ballina
Tuam
Cavan
Monaghan
Omagh
Coleraine
Ballymena
Larne
Bangor
Lisburn
Portadown
Downpatrick

St. George's Channel

Wicklow Mts.

Knockmealdown Mts.

Macgillicuddy's Reeks

Boggeragh Mts.

Scale · 1 : 1000000

1cm = 10km   1 inch = 16 miles

```
0        10        20        30 miles
0    10   20    30    40   50 km
```

Tourism

- National Park
- Area of Outstanding Natural Beauty
- National Scenic Area
- Built-up area
- —— Long distance footpath
- ● Town of tourist interest
- ◆ Other tourist attraction
- ○ Other town

Top Ireland Tourist Attractions

		Visitors in millions (2018)
1.	Guinness Storehouse, Dublin	1.7
2.	Cliffs of Moher Visitor Experience, Clare	1.6
3.	Dublin Zoo	1.2
4.	Book of Kells, Dublin	1.1
5.	National Gallery of Ireland, Dublin	0.8
6.	Glendalough Site, Wicklow	0.7
7.	Tayto Park, Dublin	0.7
8.	National Botanic Gardens, Dublin	0.7
9.	St Patrick's Cathedral, Dublin	0.6
10.	Kylemore Abbey & Gardens, Galway	0.6

Top UK Tourist Attractions

		Visitors in millions (2018)
1.	Tate Modern, London	5.9
2.	British Museum, London	5.8
3.	National Gallery, London	5.7
4.	Natural History Museum, London	5.2
5.	Southbank Centre, London	4.5
6.	Victoria & Albert Museum, London	4.0
7.	Science Museum, London	3.2
8.	Somerset House, London	3.1
9.	Tower of London	2.9
10.	Royal Museums, Greenwich	2.5
11.	National Museum of Scotland, Edinburgh	2.2
12.	Edinburgh Castle	2.1
13.	Chester Zoo	2.0
14.	Royal Botanic Gardens, Kew	1.9
15.	Royal Albert Hall, London	1.8
16.	Scottish National Gallery, Edinburgh	1.7
17.	St Paul's Cathedral, London	1.7
18.	Royal Academy, London	1.6
19.	National Portrait Gallery, London	1.6
20.	Stonehenge, Wiltshire	1.6

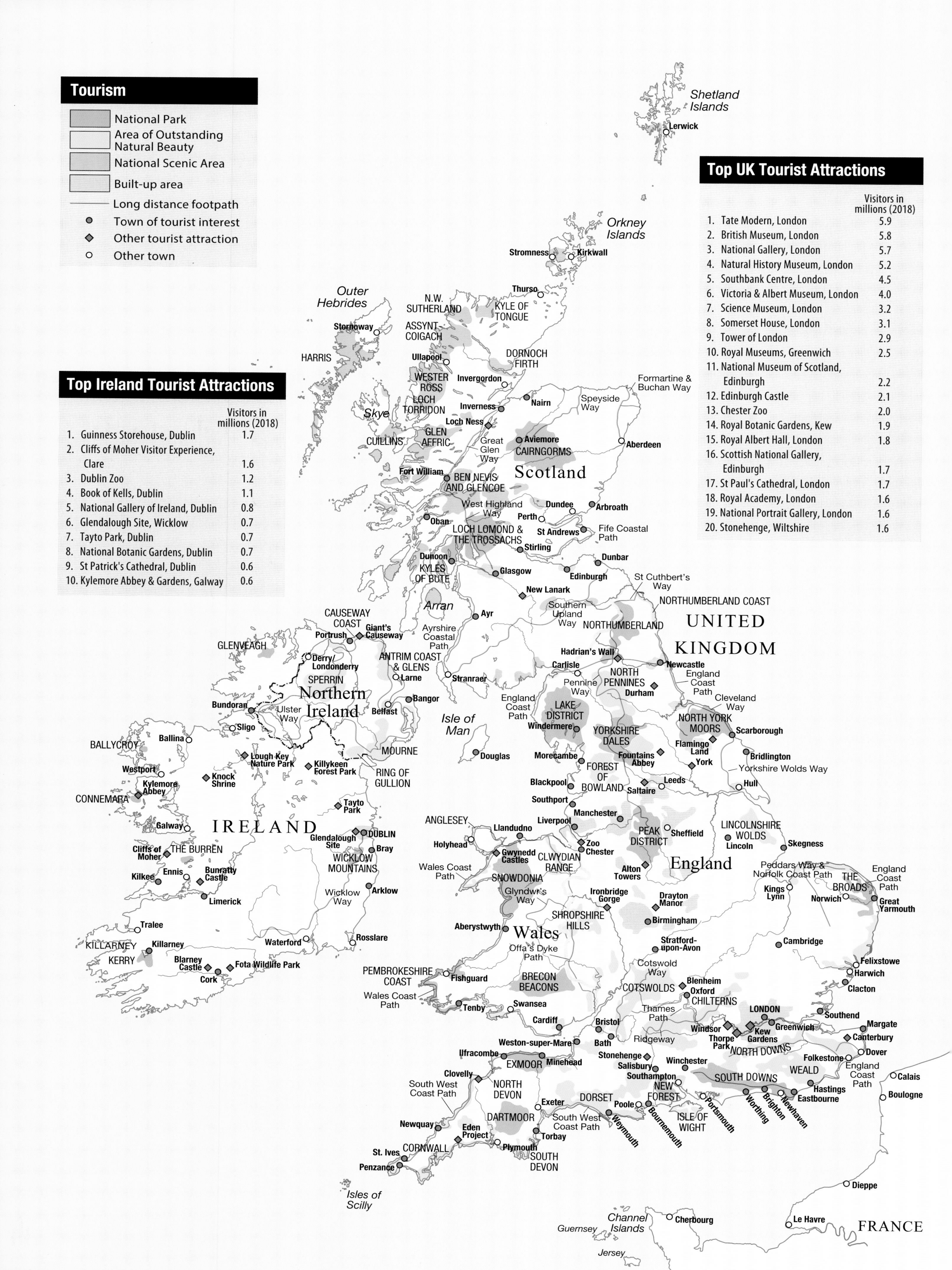

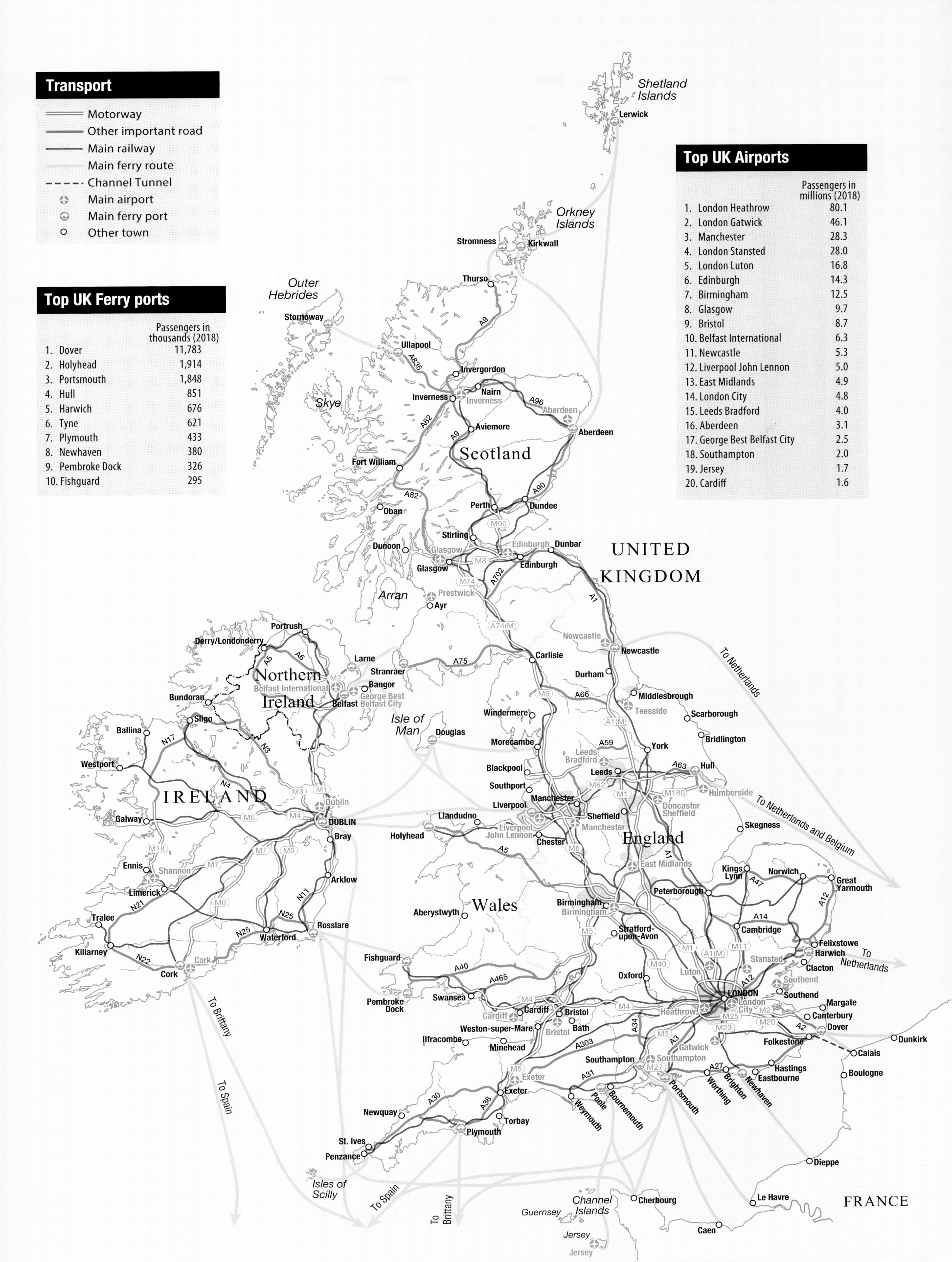

Transport

- ———— Motorway
- ———— Other important road
- ———— Main railway
- ———— Main ferry route
- – – – – Channel Tunnel
- ✈ Main airport
- ⚓ Main ferry port
- ○ Other town

Top UK Ferry ports

		Passengers in thousands (2018)
1.	Dover	11,783
2.	Holyhead	1,914
3.	Portsmouth	1,848
4.	Hull	851
5.	Harwich	676
6.	Tyne	621
7.	Plymouth	433
8.	Newhaven	380
9.	Pembroke Dock	326
10.	Fishguard	295

Top UK Airports

		Passengers in millions (2018)
1.	London Heathrow	80.1
2.	London Gatwick	46.1
3.	Manchester	28.3
4.	London Stansted	28.0
5.	London Luton	16.8
6.	Edinburgh	14.3
7.	Birmingham	12.5
8.	Glasgow	9.7
9.	Bristol	8.7
10.	Belfast International	6.3
11.	Newcastle	5.3
12.	Liverpool John Lennon	5.0
13.	East Midlands	4.9
14.	London City	4.8
15.	Leeds Bradford	4.0
16.	Aberdeen	3.1
17.	George Best Belfast City	2.5
18.	Southampton	2.0
19.	Jersey	1.7
20.	Cardiff	1.6

Distance table

John o' Groats, Kyle of Lochalsh, Inverness, Aberdeen, Braemar, Fort William, Dundee, Oban, Edinburgh, Glasgow, Berwick-upon-Tweed, Ayr, Stranraer, Newcastle upon Tyne, Carlisle, York, Kingston upon Hull, Leeds, Blackpool, Manchester, Doncaster, Holyhead, Liverpool, Sheffield, Lincoln, Nottingham, Norwich, Great Yarmouth, Shrewsbury, Leicester, Birmingham, Aberystwyth, Cambridge, Fishguard, Gloucester, Harwich, Swansea, Oxford, Cardiff, Bristol, London, Dover, Southampton, Brighton, Exeter, Bournemouth, Portsmouth, Plymouth, Land's End

How to use this table

Distances are shown in miles and kilometres with estimated journey times in hours and minutes.

For example: the distance between Dover and Fishguard is 331 miles or 533 kilometres with an estimated journey time of 6 hours, 20 minutes.

Estimated driving times are based on an average speed of 60mph on Motorways and 40mph on other roads. Drivers should allow extra time when driving at peak periods or through areas likely to be congested.

	Fishguard	Exeter	Edinburgh	Dundee	Dover
Dundee					523 / 842 / 9:10
Edinburgh				56 / 90 / 1:30	462 / 744 / 8:10
Exeter			450 / 724 / 8:00	518 / 834 / 9:10	248 / 399 / 4:40
Fishguard		230 / 370 / 4:30	399 / 642 / 7:30	460 / 740 / 8:30	331 / 533 / 6:20
Fort William	486 / 782 / 9:30	560 / 901 / 10:20	144 / 232 / 3:30	127 / 204 / 3:10	596 / 959 / 11:00

	London	Aberdeen	Aberystwyth	Ayr	Berwick-upon-Tweed	Birmingham	Blackpool	Bournemouth	Braemar	Brighton	Bristol	Cambridge	Cardiff	Carlisle	Doncaster	Dover	Dundee	Edinburgh	Exeter	Fishguard	Fort William	Glasgow	Gloucester	Great Yarmouth	Harwich	Holyhead	Inverness	John o' Groats	Kingston upon Hull	Kyle of Lochalsh	Land's End	Leeds	Leicester	Lincoln	Liverpool	Manchester	Newcastle upon Tyne	Norwich	Nottingham	Oban	Oxford	Plymouth	Portsmouth	Sheffield	Shrewsbury	Southampton	Stranraer	Swansea
London																																																
Aberdeen	517 / 832 / 11:20
Aberystwyth	211 / 340 / 4:40	445 / 716 / 8:40
Ayr	394 / 634 / 7:20	183 / 295 / 4:20	317 / 510 / 6:10
Berwick-upon-Tweed	352 / 567 / 7:30	182 / 293 / 4:40	311 / 501 / 6:20	134 / 216 / 3:00
Birmingham	117 / 188 / 2:50	420 / 676 / 8:30	114 / 183 / 2:50	289 / 465 / 5:30	274 / 441 / 5:30
Blackpool	226 / 364 / 4:30	308 / 496 / 6:20	153 / 246 / 3:20	180 / 290 / 3:30	181 / 291 / 3:50	123 / 198 / 2:40
Bournemouth	107 / 172 / 2:40	564 / 908 / 10:20	207 / 333 / 4:30	436 / 702 / 8:00	412 / 663 / 7:50	147 / 237 / 3:10	270 / 435 / 5:00
Braemar	482 / 776 / 10:30	59 / 95 / 1:30	405 / 652 / 7:50	143 / 230 / 3:00	148 / 238 / 3:20	385 / 620 / 7:10	281 / 452 / 5:20	524 / 843 / 9:30
Brighton	52 / 84 / 1:50	573 / 922 / 10:30	253 / 407 / 5:10	446 / 718 / 8:00	409 / 658 / 7:40	163 / 262 / 3:20	286 / 460 / 5:20	92 / 148 / 2:10	534 / 859 / 9:40
Bristol	122 / 196 / 2:50	493 / 793 / 9:10	125 / 201 / 3:00	370 / 595 / 6:40	362 / 583 / 6:50	81 / 130 / 2:00	204 / 328 / 3:50	82 / 132 / 2:30	477 / 768 / 8:40	147 / 237 / 4:10
Cambridge	54 / 87 / 1:30	471 / 758 / 10:00	214 / 344 / 4:20	357 / 575 / 6:20	306 / 493 / 5:40	100 / 161 / 2:10	208 / 335 / 3:50	154 / 248 / 3:00	438 / 705 / 7:50	116 / 187 / 2:20	169 / 272 / 3:10
Cardiff	157 / 253 / 3:20	505 / 813 / 9:20	105 / 169 / 2:40	382 / 615 / 7:00	368 / 592 / 7:00	103 / 166 / 2:20	209 / 336 / 4:00	117 / 188 / 3:00	483 / 778 / 8:40	182 / 293 / 3:40	45 / 72 / 1:20	190 / 306 / 3:30
Carlisle	301 / 484 / 5:40	221 / 356 / 4:30	224 / 360 / 4:30	93 / 150 / 2:00	87 / 140 / 2:10	196 / 315 / 3:50	87 / 140 / 1:50	343 / 552 / 6:20	196 / 316 / 3:50	370 / 596 / 6:40	277 / 446 / 5:00	264 / 425 / 4:40	289 / 465 / 5:20
Doncaster	171 / 275 / 3:30	344 / 554 / 6:50	176 / 283 / 3:40	235 / 378 / 4:20	184 / 296 / 3:50	94 / 151 / 2:00	94 / 151 / 1:50	235 / 378 / 4:20	310 / 499 / 5:40	236 / 380 / 4:30	175 / 282 / 3:20	116 / 187 / 2:10	209 / 336 / 4:00	142 / 229 / 3:00
Dover	71 / 114 / 2:00	588 / 947 / 10:40	297 / 478 / 5:50	478 / 769 / 8:30	424 / 683 / 7:50	194 / 312 / 3:50	312 / 502 / 5:40	174 / 280 / 4:30	553 / 890 / 9:50	82 / 132 / 2:20	202 / 325 / 3:50	125 / 201 / 2:30	238 / 383 / 4:30	389 / 626 / 7:00	242 / 390 / 4:30
Dundee	448 / 721 / 8:40	67 / 108 / 1:50	376 / 605 / 7:10	117 / 188 / 2:30	113 / 182 / 2:40	349 / 562 / 6:20	239 / 385 / 4:30	495 / 797 / 8:50	52 / 84 / 1:20	517 / 832 / 9:10	430 / 692 / 7:40	406 / 654 / 7:10	441 / 710 / 8:00	152 / 245 / 3:00	275 / 443 / 5:00	523 / 842 / 9:10
Edinburgh	390 / 628 / 7:20	125 / 201 / 3:10	320 / 515 / 6:20	73 / 117 / 1:50	57 / 92 / 1:40	292 / 470 / 5:30	183 / 295 / 3:30	439 / 707 / 8:00	91 / 146 / 2:10	456 / 734 / 8:20	373 / 600 / 6:50	345 / 555 / 6:10	385 / 620 / 7:00	96 / 154 / 2:00	219 / 352 / 4:00	462 / 744 / 8:10	56 / 90 / 1:30
Exeter	181 / 291 / 3:40	569 / 916 / 10:20	201 / 323 / 4:10	446 / 718 / 7:50	428 / 689 / 7:50	157 / 253 / 3:10	282 / 454 / 5:10	82 / 132 / 2:20	550 / 885 / 9:40	184 / 296 / 5:00	76 / 122 / 1:40	249 / 401 / 4:30	121 / 195 / 2:30	353 / 568 / 6:20	251 / 404 / 4:30	248 / 399 / 4:40	518 / 834 / 9:10	450 / 724 / 8:00
Fishguard	260 / 418 / 5:20	504 / 811 / 10:10	56 / 90 / 1:30	373 / 600 / 7:00	371 / 597 / 7:20	170 / 274 / 3:40	209 / 336 / 4:10	222 / 357 / 4:40	493 / 794 / 9:10	291 / 468 / 5:40	154 / 248 / 3:20	270 / 435 / 5:10	112 / 180 / 2:40	297 / 478 / 5:40	247 / 398 / 4:50	331 / 533 / 6:20	460 / 740 / 8:30	399 / 642 / 7:30	230 / 370 / 4:30
Fort William	510 / 821 / 9:50	149 / 240 / 3:50	430 / 692 / 8:40	133 / 214 / 3:20	190 / 306 / 4:40	392 / 631 / 7:40	296 / 476 / 6:00	539 / 867 / 10:10	125 / 201 / 3:10	575 / 926 / 10:50	486 / 782 / 9:10	479 / 771 / 9:00	485 / 781 / 9:10	206 / 332 / 4:30	357 / 575 / 7:00	596 / 959 / 11:00	127 / 204 / 3:10	144 / 232 / 3:30	560 / 901 / 10:20	486 / 782 / 9:30
Glasgow	397 / 639 / 7:30	145 / 233 / 3:30	320 / 515 / 6:20	33 / 53 / 1:10	101 / 163 / 2:40	292 / 470 / 5:30	183 / 295 / 3:40	439 / 707 / 8:00	110 / 177 / 2:30	468 / 753 / 8:30	373 / 600 / 6:50	372 / 599 / 6:40	385 / 620 / 7:00	96 / 154 / 2:10	249 / 401 / 4:40	488 / 786 / 8:40	83 / 134 / 2:00	44 / 71 / 1:20	449 / 723 / 8:00	376 / 605 / 7:10	101 / 163 / 2:50
Gloucester	109 / 175 / 2:30	468 / 753 / 8:30	102 / 164 / 2:30	330 / 531 / 5:50	318 / 512 / 6:00	56 / 90 / 1:20	174 / 280 / 3:10	99 / 159 / 2:40	443 / 713 / 8:00	159 / 256 / 3:10	35 / 56 / 1:00	123 / 198 / 2:20	56 / 90 / 1:20	247 / 398 / 4:20	150 / 241 / 2:50	191 / 307 / 3:30	410 / 660 / 7:10	349 / 562 / 6:10	111 / 179 / 2:10	153 / 246 / 3:10	454 / 731 / 8:30	346 / 557 / 6:10
Great Yarmouth	128 / 206 / 3:40	517 / 832 / 10:50	294 / 473 / 6:20	402 / 647 / 7:40	345 / 555 / 7:00	180 / 290 / 4:10	252 / 406 / 5:10	240 / 386 / 5:00	477 / 768 / 9:10	180 / 290 / 4:10	275 / 443 / 5:40	82 / 132 / 2:10	284 / 457 / 5:50	320 / 515 / 6:20	167 / 269 / 3:40	185 / 298 / 4:00	484 / 779 / 9:00	386 / 621 / 7:30	335 / 539 / 6:30	366 / 589 / 7:20	527 / 848 / 10:20	419 / 674 / 8:00	225 / 362 / 4:40
Harwich	76 / 122 / 2:20	535 / 861 / 11:20	281 / 452 / 5:50	425 / 684 / 8:00	372 / 599 / 7:20	167 / 269 / 3:40	275 / 443 / 5:20	187 / 301 / 4:00	504 / 811 / 9:20	128 / 206 / 3:00	217 / 349 / 4:30	67 / 108 / 1:50	246 / 396 / 5:00	336 / 541 / 6:20	194 / 312 / 4:00	125 / 201 / 2:50	469 / 755 / 8:40	413 / 665 / 7:40	279 / 449 / 5:20	337 / 542 / 6:40	543 / 874 / 10:30	432 / 695 / 8:10	196 / 316 / 4:00	82 / 132 / 2:10
Holyhead	269 / 433 / 5:40	439 / 707 / 8:40	111 / 179 / 2:50	305 / 491 / 6:10	311 / 501 / 6:30	148 / 238 / 3:30	141 / 227 / 3:20	288 / 463 / 5:50	426 / 686 / 8:20	334 / 538 / 6:40	206 / 332 / 4:30	270 / 435 / 5:20	216 / 348 / 5:40	231 / 372 / 4:50	181 / 291 / 3:50	360 / 580 / 7:00	394 / 634 / 7:30	333 / 536 / 6:40	282 / 454 / 5:40	167 / 269 / 4:00	438 / 705 / 8:50	330 / 531 / 6:40	191 / 307 / 4:00	334 / 538 / 7:00	349 / 562 / 7:10
Inverness	550 / 885 / 10:40	105 / 169 / 2:50	486 / 782 / 9:40	199 / 320 / 4:30	215 / 346 / 5:10	458 / 737 / 9:00	348 / 560 / 7:00	597 / 961 / 11:20	75 / 121 / 2:00	617 / 993 / 11:30	539 / 867 / 10:10	505 / 813 / 9:30	549 / 884 / 10:20	262 / 422 / 5:30	383 / 617 / 7:30	622 / 1001 / 11:30	132 / 212 / 3:20	158 / 254 / 3:50	618 / 995 / 11:30	542 / 872 / 10:30	66 / 106 / 1:40	166 / 267 / 4:00	504 / 811 / 9:30	553 / 890 / 11:00	569 / 916 / 11:00	474 / 763 / 9:40
John o' Groats	663 / 1067 / 13:30	232 / 373 / 5:50	601 / 967 / 12:40	328 / 528 / 7:40	342 / 550 / 8:10	574 / 924 / 11:50	478 / 769 / 10:00	724 / 1165 / 14:20	202 / 325 / 5:00	741 / 1193 / 14:40	668 / 1075 / 13:20	630 / 1014 / 12:30	680 / 1094 / 13:30	391 / 629 / 8:40	507 / 816 / 10:30	746 / 1201 / 14:40	259 / 417 / 6:30	285 / 459 / 7:00	744 / 1197 / 14:30	671 / 1080 / 13:40	195 / 314 / 5:00	295 / 475 / 7:10	628 / 1011 / 12:30	677 / 1090 / 14:00	693 / 1116 / 14:00	603 / 970 / 12:40	129 / 208 / 3:20
Kingston upon Hull	184 / 296 / 3:50	364 / 586 / 7:20	223 / 359 / 4:40	251 / 404 / 4:40	185 / 298 / 3:50	134 / 216 / 2:50	127 / 204 / 2:30	264 / 425 / 5:00	327 / 526 / 6:10	245 / 394 / 4:40	233 / 375 / 4:20	139 / 224 / 3:10	244 / 393 / 4:40	158 / 254 / 3:00	47 / 76 / 1:10	256 / 412 / 4:50	295 / 475 / 5:30	234 / 377 / 4:30	309 / 497 / 5:40	280 / 451 / 5:30	369 / 594 / 7:20	254 / 409 / 4:50	169 / 272 / 3:10	207 / 333 / 5:20	196 / 316 / 4:10	231 / 372 / 4:50	394 / 634 / 7:50	518 / 834 / 10:50
Kyle of Lochalsh	586 / 943 / 11:40	189 / 304 / 4:50	499 / 803 / 10:20	212 / 341 / 5:10	263 / 423 / 6:20	471 / 758 / 9:40	372 / 599 / 7:50	618 / 995 / 12:10	159 / 256 / 4:00	651 / 1048 / 12:40	552 / 888 / 10:50	555 / 893 / 10:50	564 / 908 / 11:10	275 / 443 / 6:10	432 / 695 / 8:40	671 / 1080 / 12:50	186 / 299 / 4:40	216 / 348 / 5:20	628 / 1011 / 12:00	567 / 913 / 11:20	76 / 122 / 1:50	179 / 288 / 4:40	528 / 850 / 10:20	602 / 969 / 12:10	611 / 983 / 12:10	514 / 827 / 10:40	84 / 135 / 2:10	189 / 304 / 4:40	445 / 716 / 9:00
Land's End	297 / 478 / 6:30	692 / 1114 / 13:10	313 / 504 / 6:50	570 / 917 / 10:50	552 / 888 / 10:40	281 / 452 / 6:00	405 / 652 / 8:00	205 / 330 / 5:20	665 / 1070 / 12:30	308 / 496 / 7:50	200 / 322 / 4:40	374 / 602 / 7:20	245 / 394 / 5:20	477 / 768 / 9:10	374 / 602 / 7:20	381 / 613 / 7:40	642 / 1033 / 12:00	574 / 924 / 10:50	123 / 198 / 3:20	353 / 568 / 7:20	686 / 1104 / 13:20	573 / 922 / 10:50	235 / 378 / 5:00	446 / 718 / 9:10	390 / 628 / 8:00	405 / 652 / 8:30	741 / 1193 / 14:20	868 / 1397 / 17:20	421 / 678 / 8:20	763 / 1228 / 15:10
Leeds	189 / 304 / 3:50	327 / 526 / 6:50	169 / 272 / 3:40	212 / 341 / 4:00	156 / 251 / 3:20	113 / 182 / 2:30	72 / 116 / 1:40	255 / 410 / 4:50	293 / 472 / 5:30	260 / 419 / 5:00	194 / 312 / 3:50	145 / 233 / 2:50	232 / 373 / 4:20	119 / 192 / 2:30	29 / 47 / 0:50	260 / 418 / 4:50	258 / 415 / 4:50	202 / 325 / 4:00	270 / 435 / 5:00	237 / 381 / 4:40	329 / 530 / 6:40	215 / 346 / 4:10	174 / 280 / 3:20	196 / 315 / 4:20	223 / 359 / 4:30	176 / 283 / 4:00	360 / 579 / 7:10	487 / 784 / 10:20	55 / 89 / 1:30	394 / 634 / 8:20	405 / 652 / 8:00
Leicester	97 / 156 / 2:20	414 / 666 / 7:40	153 / 246 / 3:20	299 / 481 / 5:20	252 / 406 / 5:00	39 / 63 / 1:10	140 / 225 / 2:40	158 / 254 / 3:10	389 / 626 / 7:00	166 / 267 / 3:20	120 / 193 / 2:30	68 / 109 / 1:20	154 / 248 / 3:00	206 / 332 / 3:50	74 / 119 / 1:30	185 / 298 / 3:30	349 / 562 / 6:20	296 / 476 / 5:20	196 / 315 / 3:40	209 / 336 / 4:10	422 / 679 / 8:00	314 / 505 / 5:40	85 / 137 / 1:40	140 / 225 / 3:20	147 / 237 / 3:10	190 / 306 / 4:00	461 / 742 / 8:50	588 / 947 / 11:50	102 / 164 / 2:10	500 / 805 / 9:50	320 / 515 / 6:30	95 / 153 / 2:00
Lincoln	131 / 211 / 3:10	383 / 616 / 7:20	199 / 320 / 4:20	274 / 441 / 5:10	224 / 360 / 4:40	90 / 145 / 2:10	128 / 206 / 2:40	209 / 336 / 4:10	357 / 575 / 6:40	197 / 317 / 4:00	183 / 295 / 3:40	85 / 137 / 2:20	208 / 335 / 4:10	191 / 307 / 3:40	39 / 63 / 1:10	202 / 325 / 4:00	314 / 505 / 5:50	258 / 415 / 5:00	247 / 398 / 4:40	272 / 438 / 5:30	399 / 642 / 7:50	291 / 468 / 5:30	159 / 256 / 3:10	128 / 206 / 3:20	155 / 249 / 3:30	216 / 348 / 4:40	427 / 687 / 8:30	554 / 892 / 11:30	44 / 71 / 1:20	476 / 766 / 9:40	371 / 597 / 7:30	68 / 109 / 1:50	51 / 82 / 1:20
Liverpool	202 / 325 / 4:10	341 / 549 / 6:40	104 / 167 / 2:40	213 / 343 / 4:10	219 / 352 / 4:30	93 / 150 / 2:10	49 / 79 / 1:20	234 / 377 / 4:30	318 / 512 / 6:00	272 / 438 / 5:10	161 / 259 / 3:10	194 / 312 / 3:40	169 / 272 / 3:20	120 / 193 / 2:30	86 / 138 / 1:50	299 / 481 / 5:30	286 / 460 / 5:20	216 / 348 / 4:10	237 / 381 / 4:30	160 / 257 / 3:30	329 / 530 / 6:40	216 / 348 / 4:10	140 / 225 / 2:40	240 / 386 / 5:00	265 / 427 / 5:20	102 / 164 / 2:40	382 / 615 / 7:40	511 / 822 / 10:40	130 / 209 / 2:40	407 / 655 / 8:30	361 / 581 / 7:20	75 / 121 / 1:50	130 / 209 / 2:40	129 / 208 / 2:50
Manchester	185 / 298 / 3:50	340 / 547 / 6:30	129 / 208 / 3:00	212 / 341 / 4:00	196 / 315 / 4:00	80 / 129 / 2:00	48 / 77 / 1:20	227 / 365 / 4:20	318 / 512 / 6:00	257 / 414 / 4:50	161 / 259 / 3:10	165 / 266 / 3:10	183 / 295 / 3:40	119 / 192 / 2:30	61 / 98 / 1:30	276 / 444 / 5:10	285 / 459 / 5:20	215 / 346 / 4:10	236 / 380 / 4:20	197 / 317 / 4:00	329 / 530 / 6:40	215 / 346 / 4:10	126 / 203 / 2:30	212 / 341 / 4:30	228 / 367 / 4:40	124 / 200 / 3:00	373 / 600 / 7:30	500 / 805 / 10:30	95 / 153 / 2:10	406 / 654 / 8:30	361 / 581 / 7:20	40 / 64 / 1:10	92 / 148 / 2:00	84 / 135 / 2:00	35 / 56 / 1:10
Newcastle upon Tyne	286 / 460 / 5:40	235 / 378 / 4:50	257 / 414 / 5:20	149 / 240 / 3:00	64 / 103 / 1:50	207 / 333 / 4:10	129 / 208 / 2:40	347 / 558 / 6:30	201 / 323 / 4:00	352 / 567 / 6:30	299 / 481 / 5:30	241 / 388 / 4:20	325 / 523 / 6:00	57 / 92 / 1:50	114 / 183 / 2:20	358 / 576 / 6:30	166 / 267 / 3:20	110 / 177 / 2:20	364 / 586 / 6:30	329 / 529 / 6:20	253 / 407 / 5:20	148 / 238 / 3:10	266 / 428 / 4:50	281 / 452 / 5:40	308 / 496 / 6:00	272 / 438 / 5:40	268 / 431 / 5:40	395 / 636 / 8:50	132 / 212 / 2:50	318 / 512 / 7:00	498 / 802 / 9:40	92 / 148 / 2:10	187 / 301 / 3:40	159 / 256 / 3:20	168 / 270 / 3:20	132 / 212 / 2:50
Norwich	114 / 183 / 3:30	496 / 798 / 9:40	276 / 444 / 6:00	382 / 615 / 7:20	328 / 528 / 6:40	166 / 267 / 3:50	232 / 373 / 4:50	214 / 344 / 4:40	457 / 735 / 8:40	175 / 282 / 4:00	252 / 406 / 5:10	62 / 100 / 1:50	262 / 422 / 5:20	289 / 465 / 5:40	147 / 237 / 3:20	174 / 280 / 3:50	422 / 679 / 8:00	366 / 589 / 7:00	308 / 496 / 6:00	343 / 552 / 7:00	504 / 811 / 10:00	385 / 620 / 9:00	204 / 328 / 4:10	20 / 32 / 0:40	73 / 117 / 2:00	311 / 501 / 6:40	529 / 852 / 10:30	654 / 1053 / 13:30	149 / 240 / 4:00	582 / 937 / 11:50	421 / 678 / 8:40	176 / 283 / 3:50	119 / 192 / 3:20	105 / 169 / 2:50	220 / 354 / 4:40	185 / 298 / 4:30	264 / 425 / 5:20
Nottingham	122 / 196 / 2:40	393 / 633 / 7:30	164 / 264 / 3:40	274 / 441 / 5:10	221 / 356 / 4:30	50 / 80 / 1:20	111 / 179 / 2:20	183 / 295 / 3:40	353 / 568 / 6:30	193 / 311 / 3:50	145 / 233 / 3:00	83 / 134 / 1:40	172 / 277 / 3:20	194 / 312 / 3:40	43 / 69 / 1:10	205 / 330 / 3:50	328 / 528 / 6:00	262 / 422 / 4:50	221 / 356 / 4:10	220 / 354 / 4:30	401 / 646 / 7:50	293 / 472 / 5:30	110 / 177 / 2:10	153 / 246 / 3:30	150 / 241 / 3:20	185 / 298 / 4:00	430 / 692 / 8:20	557 / 896 / 11:30	90 / 145 / 2:00	479 / 771 / 9:40	345 / 555 / 7:00	70 / 113 / 1:40	25 / 40 / 0:50	35 / 56 / 1:10	98 / 158 / 2:10	73 / 118 / 1:40	157 / 253 / 3:10	130 / 209 / 3:40
Oban	499 / 803 / 9:30	178 / 286 / 4:20	412 / 663 / 8:10	94 / 151 / 2:20	180 / 290 / 4:20	384 / 618 / 7:30	285 / 459 / 5:40	530 / 853 / 9:50	141 / 227 / 3:30	565 / 910 / 10:30	465 / 748 / 8:40	468 / 753 / 8:40	477 / 768 / 9:00	188 / 303 / 4:00	346 / 557 / 6:40	585 / 942 / 10:40	117 / 188 / 2:50	123 / 198 / 3:00	549 / 884 / 10:00	481 / 774 / 9:10	49 / 79 / 1:20	92 / 148 / 2:30	441 / 710 / 8:10	515 / 829 / 10:00	524 / 843 / 10:00	427 / 687 / 8:30	117 / 188 / 3:00	244 / 393 / 6:10	346 / 557 / 6:40	128 / 206 / 3:10	665 / 1070 / 12:50	307 / 494 / 6:00	419 / 674 / 7:50	387 / 623 / 7:30	308 / 496 / 6:10	307 / 494 / 6:00	233 / 375 / 4:50	492 / 792 / 9:40	390 / 628 / 7:30
Oxford	57 / 92 / 1:40	483 / 777 / 8:50	154 / 248 / 3:20	353 / 568 / 6:20	324 / 521 / 6:10	64 / 103 / 1:30	187 / 301 / 3:30	90 / 145 / 2:00	465 / 749 / 8:20	108 / 174 / 2:20	74 / 119 / 1:40	83 / 134 / 1:40	108 / 174 / 2:20	260 / 418 / 4:40	145 / 233 / 2:40	141 / 227 / 2:50	433 / 697 / 7:40	372 / 599 / 6:40	156 / 251 / 3:00	205 / 330 / 4:10	472 / 760 / 9:00	356 / 573 / 6:30	52 / 84 / 1:30	200 / 322 / 4:20	145 / 233 / 3:10	238 / 383 / 4:50	532 / 856 / 10:00	656 / 1056 / 13:00	192 / 309 / 3:40	550 / 885 / 10:40	274 / 441 / 5:40	168 / 270 / 3:10	73 / 117 / 1:30	137 / 221 / 2:50	172 / 277 / 3:20	144 / 232 / 2:50	260 / 418 / 4:50	145 / 233 / 3:50	109 / 175 / 2:10	462 / 744 / 8:30
Plymouth	218 / 351 / 4:40	615 / 990 / 11:20	237 / 382 / 5:10	492 / 792 / 9:00	474 / 763 / 9:00	203 / 327 / 4:20	328 / 528 / 6:10	128 / 206 / 3:30	587 / 945 / 10:40	224 / 361 / 6:00	122 / 196 / 2:50	293 / 472 / 5:30	167 / 269 / 3:40	399 / 642 / 7:20	297 / 478 / 5:40	300 / 483 / 5:50	552 / 888 / 10:00	496 / 798 / 9:00	46 / 74 / 1:30	264 / 425 / 5:30	595 / 958 / 11:20	495 / 797 / 9:10	157 / 253 / 3:20	365 / 588 / 7:20	309 / 497 / 6:10	328 / 528 / 6:40	664 / 1069 / 12:30	790 / 1271 / 15:40	355 / 571 / 6:40	674 / 1085 / 13:10	89 / 143 / 2:20	316 / 509 / 6:00	242 / 389 / 4:40	293 / 472 / 5:50	283 / 455 / 5:30	283 / 455 / 5:30	410 / 660 / 7:40	343 / 552 / 7:00	267 / 430 / 5:10	587 / 945 / 11:00	199 / 320 / 4:00
Portsmouth	70 / 113 / 2:00	560 / 901 / 10:10	222 / 357 / 4:40	430 / 692 / 7:40	401 / 645 / 7:30	141 / 227 / 3:00	264 / 425 / 4:50	52 / 84 / 1:30	547 / 881 / 9:50	48 / 77 / 1:40	97 / 156 / 2:10	144 / 232 / 2:50	142 / 229 / 3:00	348 / 560 / 6:10	234 / 377 / 4:20	130 / 209 / 2:50	514 / 827 / 9:00	453 / 729 / 8:10	135 / 217 / 2:40	251 / 404 / 5:00	555 / 893 / 10:20	448 / 721 / 8:10	119 / 192 / 3:00	221 / 356 / 4:40	166 / 267 / 3:40	311 / 501 / 6:10	613 / 987 / 11:30	737 / 1186 / 14:30	269 / 433 / 5:00	633 / 1019 / 12:10	259 / 417 / 5:40	257 / 414 / 4:50	162 / 261 / 3:10	201 / 323 / 4:00	254 / 409 / 4:50	236 / 380 / 4:30	337 / 542 / 6:10	207 / 333 / 4:20	191 / 307 / 3:40	545 / 877 / 10:00	77 / 124 / 1:40	176 / 283 / 4:50
Sheffield	159 / 256 / 3:20	360 / 579 / 6:50	159 / 256 / 3:30	245 / 394 / 4:30	190 / 306 / 4:00	76 / 122 / 1:50	86 / 138 / 1:50	216 / 348 / 4:10	320 / 515 / 6:00	226 / 364 / 4:20	161 / 259 / 3:10	120 / 193 / 2:20	194 / 312 / 3:40	152 / 245 / 3:00	18 / 29 / 0:40	245 / 394 / 4:30	291 / 468 / 5:20	235 / 378 / 4:20	237 / 381 / 4:20	215 / 346 / 4:20	348 / 560 / 6:50	248 / 399 / 4:40	126 / 203 / 2:20	166 / 267 / 3:40	187 / 301 / 3:50	168 / 270 / 3:40	393 / 632 / 7:40	520 / 837 / 10:50	65 / 105 / 1:30	427 / 687 / 8:40	361 / 581 / 7:10	33 / 53 / 1:00	62 / 100 / 1:20	46 / 74 / 1:20	72 / 116 / 1:40	38 / 61 / 1:00	125 / 201 / 2:40	146 / 235 / 3:20	37 / 60 / 1:00	339 / 546 / 6:30	135 / 217 / 2:40	283 / 455 / 5:30	230 / 370 / 4:20
Shrewsbury	160 / 258 / 3:20	399 / 642 / 7:30	77 / 124 / 2:10	269 / 433 / 5:00	265 / 426 / 5:10	45 / 72 / 1:20	98 / 158 / 2:00	185 / 298 / 3:40	371 / 597 / 6:50	226 / 364 / 4:20	103 / 166 / 2:50	159 / 256 / 3:00	111 / 179 / 2:20	176 / 283 / 3:20	109 / 175 / 2:10	251 / 404 / 4:30	330 / 531 / 6:00	274 / 441 / 5:00	179 / 288 / 3:20	145 / 233 / 3:10	382 / 615 / 7:20	272 / 438 / 5:00	77 / 124 / 1:30	225 / 362 / 4:40	240 / 386 / 4:40	113 / 182 / 2:50	438 / 705 / 8:20	567 / 912 / 11:30	169 / 272 / 3:10	451 / 726 / 9:00	303 / 488 / 6:10	109 / 175 / 2:20	84 / 135 / 1:40	133 / 214 / 2:50	58 / 93 / 1:50	69 / 111 / 1:40	201 / 323 / 3:50	205 / 330 / 4:20	93 / 150 / 2:00	364 / 586 / 7:00	106 / 171 / 2:10	225 / 362 / 4:40	207 / 333 / 3:50	82 / 132 / 2:10
Southampton	77 / 124 / 2:00	547 / 880 / 10:00	201 / 323 / 4:10	417 / 671 / 7:30	388 / 624 / 7:10	128 / 206 / 2:40	251 / 404 / 4:40	31 / 50 / 1:00	532 / 856 / 9:30	61 / 98 / 1:50	76 / 122 / 2:20	148 / 238 / 2:50	121 / 195 / 2:30	324 / 521 / 5:50	209 / 336 / 3:50	143 / 230 / 2:50	500 / 805 / 8:50	438 / 705 / 7:50	105 / 169 / 3:00	233 / 375 / 4:40	541 / 871 / 10:00	433 / 697 / 7:40	105 / 169 / 2:40	220 / 354 / 4:40	164 / 264 / 3:30	293 / 472 / 5:50	598 / 963 / 11:10	723 / 1164 / 14:10	256 / 412 / 4:40	618 / 995 / 12:00	228 / 367 / 5:00	232 / 373 / 4:20	137 / 220 / 2:40	204 / 328 / 4:00	239 / 385 / 4:30	221 / 356 / 4:10	324 / 521 / 5:50	206 / 332 / 4:20	176 / 283 / 3:20	530 / 853 / 9:40	64 / 103 / 1:30	151 / 243 / 4:10	21 / 34 / 0:50	199 / 320 / 3:40	185 / 298 / 4:10
Stranraer	402 / 647 / 7:50	228 / 367 / 5:10	325 / 523 / 6:50	51 / 82 / 1:20	170 / 274 / 4:10	297 / 478 / 6:00	188 / 303 / 4:00	444 / 715 / 8:30	194 / 312 / 4:20	475 / 765 / 9:00	378 / 608 / 7:20	379 / 610 / 7:10	390 / 628 / 7:30	101 / 163 / 2:40	257 / 414 / 5:10	496 / 798 / 9:10	167 / 269 / 3:40	124 / 200 / 3:00	454 / 731 / 8:30	392 / 631 / 7:50	195 / 314 / 4:50	84 / 135 / 2:30	343 / 552 / 6:30	426 / 686 / 8:40	410 / 660 / 8:10	338 / 544 / 7:00	262 / 422 / 6:00	379 / 610 / 9:00	259 / 417 / 5:20	263 / 423 / 6:30	585 / 942 / 11:30	220 / 354 / 4:40	330 / 531 / 6:20	298 / 480 / 6:00	221 / 356 / 4:40	220 / 354 / 4:40	158 / 254 / 3:40	403 / 649 / 8:10	290 / 467 / 5:50	148 / 238 / 3:40	379 / 610 / 7:10	500 / 805 / 9:40	461 / 742 / 8:40	263 / 423 / 5:20	277 / 446 / 5:30	445 / 716 / 8:20
Swansea	194 / 312 / 4:00	507 / 816 / 9:20	73 / 117 / 2:00	379 / 610 / 6:50	383 / 616 / 7:10	119 / 192 / 2:30	216 / 348 / 4:00	167 / 269 / 3:20	505 / 813 / 9:00	222 / 357 / 4:20	85 / 137 / 1:50	227 / 365 / 4:10	41 / 66 / 1:10	309 / 497 / 5:30	232 / 373 / 4:10	274 / 441 / 5:00	473 / 761 / 8:20	412 / 663 / 7:20	161 / 259 / 3:00	67 / 108 / 1:50	496 / 798 / 9:20	409 / 658 / 7:20	89 / 143 / 1:50	329 / 530 / 6:30	267 / 430 / 5:10	184 / 296 / 4:50	572 / 921 / 10:40	696 / 1120 / 13:40	264 / 425 / 4:50	594 / 956 / 11:30	285 / 459 / 6:00	248 / 399 / 4:40	177 / 285 / 3:20	233 / 375 / 4:30	195 / 314 / 3:40	187 / 301 / 3:30	347 / 559 / 6:20	301 / 485 / 6:00	192 / 309 / 3:40	506 / 815 / 9:20	141 / 227 / 2:40	206 / 332 / 4:10	182 / 293 / 3:30	217 / 349 / 4:00	118 / 190 / 2:20	161 / 259 / 3:00	417 / 671 / 7:50
York	207 / 333 / 4:10	319 / 513 / 6:10	195 / 314 / 4:10	214 / 344 / 4:00	148 / 238 / 3:10	130 / 209 / 2:40	96 / 154 / 2:00	269 / 433 / 5:00	285 / 459 / 5:20	275 / 443 / 5:10	222 / 357 / 4:10	165 / 266 / 3:10	244 / 393 / 4:40	121 / 195 / 2:30	34 / 55 / 1:00	282 / 454 / 5:10	250 / 402 / 4:40	194 / 312 / 3:40	287 / 462 / 5:10	261 / 420 / 5:10	330 / 531 / 6:30	217 / 349 / 4:10	189 / 304 / 3:30	201 / 323 / 4:20	228 / 367 / 4:40	204 / 328 / 4:20	352 / 566 / 7:00	479 / 771 / 10:10	37 / 60 / 1:10	407 / 655 / 8:20	411 / 661 / 8:00	24 / 39 / 0:50	108 / 174 / 2:10	75 / 121 / 1:50	99 / 159 / 2:10	64 / 103 / 1:30	84 / 135 / 2:20	181 / 291 / 4:20	77 / 124 / 1:40	309 / 497 / 6:00	181 / 291 / 3:20	333 / 536 / 6:20	278 / 448 / 5:10	52 / 84 / 1:20	133 / 214 / 2:40	258 / 415 / 5:10	222 / 357 / 4:40	272 / 438 / 5:10

Key to road map pages

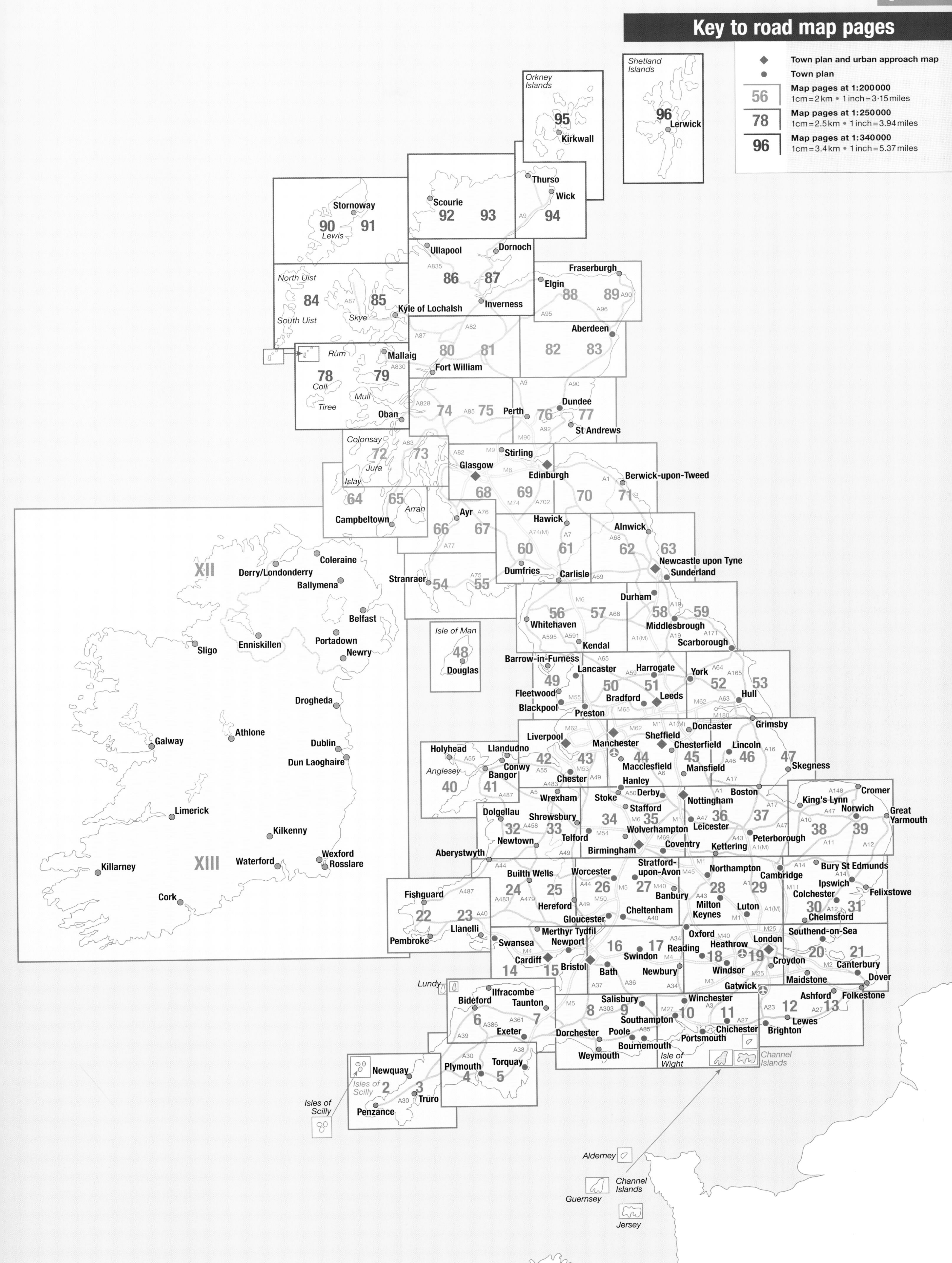

Town plan and urban approach map
Town plan
56 Map pages at 1:200000
1cm=2km • 1inch=3·15miles
78 Map pages at 1:250000
1cm=2.5km • 1inch=3.94miles
96 Map pages at 1:340000
1cm=3.4km • 1inch=5.37miles
Shetland Islands
96 Lerwick
Orkney Islands
95 Kirkwall
Thurso
Wick
94
Scourie
92 93
Stornoway
90 91
Lewis
Ullapool
Dornoch
86 87
Inverness
North Uist
84 85
South Uist
Skye
Kyle of Lochalsh
Fraserburgh
Elgin
88 89
Aberdeen
82 83
80 81
Fort William
Rùm
Mallaig
78 79
Coll
Tiree
Mull
Oban
74 75
Perth
76 77
Dundee
St Andrews
Colonsay
72 73
Jura
Islay
Stirling
Glasgow
Edinburgh
68 69
70 71
Berwick-upon-Tweed
64 65
Arran
Campbeltown
Ayr
66 67
Hawick
60 61
Alnwick
62 63
Newcastle upon Tyne
Sunderland
Dumfries
Carlisle
Stranraer
54 55
XII
Coleraine
Derry/Londonderry
Ballymena
Belfast
Sligo
Enniskillen
Portadown
Newry
Drogheda
Galway
Athlone
Dublin
Dun Laoghaire
Limerick
Kilkenny
Killarney
XIII
Waterford
Wexford
Rosslare
Cork
Durham
56 57
58 59
Whitehaven
Middlesbrough
Kendal
Scarborough
Isle of Man
48
Douglas
Barrow-in-Furness
Lancaster
Harrogate
York
49
50 51
52 53
Fleetwood
Blackpool
Bradford
Leeds
Hull
Preston
Doncaster
Grimsby
Liverpool
Manchester
Sheffield
Chesterfield
Lincoln
42 43
44 45
46 47
Macclesfield
Mansfield
Skegness
Holyhead
Llandudno
Conwy
Bangor
Anglesey
40 41
Chester
Hanley
Wrexham
Stoke
Derby
Nottingham
Boston
King's Lynn
Cromer
Norwich
Great Yarmouth
Dolgellau
Shrewsbury
Stafford
32 33
34 35
36 37
38 39
Newtown
Telford
Wolverhampton
Leicester
Peterborough
Birmingham
Coventry
Kettering
Aberystwyth
Builth Wells
Worcester
Stratford-upon-Avon
Northampton
Cambridge
Bury St Edmunds
Ipswich
Felixstowe
Fishguard
24 25
26 27
28 29
Banbury
Colchester
Hereford
Milton Keynes
Luton
30 31
Chelmsford
22 23
Llanelli
Pembroke
Gloucester
Cheltenham
Merthyr Tydfil
Newport
Oxford
Southend-on-Sea
Swansea
16 17
Swindon
Reading
Heathrow
London
20 21
18 19
Cardiff
14 15
Bristol
Bath
Newbury
Windsor
Croydon
Canterbury
Maidstone
Dover
Gatwick
Lundy
Ilfracombe
Bideford
Taunton
Salisbury
Winchester
Ashford
Folkestone
6 7
8 9
10 11
12 13
Southampton
Chichester
Lewes
Brighton
Exeter
Dorchester
Poole
Portsmouth
Bournemouth
Weymouth
Isle of Wight
Channel Islands
Newquay
Plymouth
Torquay
Isles of Scilly
2 3
4 5
Truro
Penzance
Alderney
Guernsey
Jersey

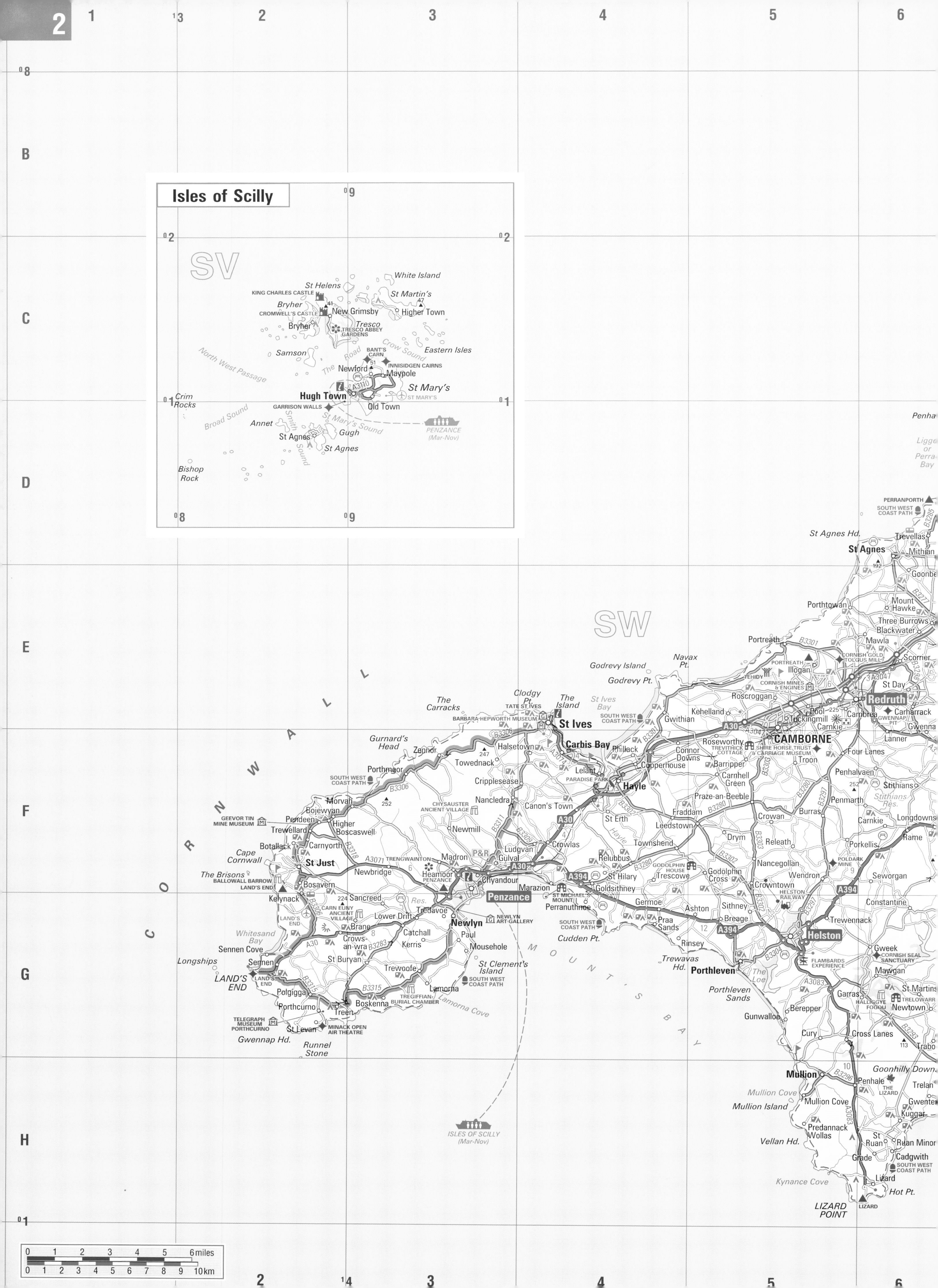

Isles of Scilly

SV

SW

White Island

St Helens

KING CHARLES CASTLE
Bryher
CROMWELL'S CASTLE
New Grimsby
St Martin's
Higher Town

Tresco
TRESCO ABBEY GARDENS
Bryher

Eastern Isles

North West Passage

The Road

Crow Sound

Samson

BANT'S CARN
Newford
INNISIDGEN CAIRNS
Maypole

Crim Rocks

Broad Sound

Hugh Town
A3110
St Mary's
ST MARY'S

Old Town

GARRISON WALLS

St Mary's Sound

PENZANCE
(Mar-Nov)

Annet
St Agnes
Gugh
Smith Sound

St Agnes

Bishop Rock

CORNWALL

Penha

Ligge or Perra Bay

PERRANPORTH
SOUTH WEST COAST PATH

St Agnes Hd.
Trevellas

St Agnes
Mithian
Goonbe

Porthtowan
Mount Hawke

Three Burrows
Blackwater

Mawla

Portreath
CORNISH GOLD TOLGUS MILL
Scorrier

Navax Pt.
PORTREATH
Illogan
CORNISH MINES & ENGINES
St Day
A3047

Godrevy Island
Godrevy Pt.
Redruth

The Carracks
Clodgy Pt.
TATE ST IVES
The Island
St Ives Bay
Roscroggan
Tuckingmill
Pool—225
Cambree
Carharrack

Gwithian
SOUTH WEST COAST PATH
Kehelland
A30
A3047
CAMBORNE
Carnkie
Gwenna

Gurnard's Head
BARBARA HEPWORTH MUSEUM
St Ives
Roseworthy
TREVITHICK COTTAGE
SHIRE HORSE TRUST & CARRIAGE MUSEUM
Four Lanes

Zennor
Halsetown
Carbis Bay
Phillack
Connor Downs
Barripper
Troon
Lanner

247
Towednack
Lelant
Copperhouse
Carnhell Green
Penhalvaen

Porthmeor
Cripplesease
PARADISE PARK
Hayle
Praze-an-Beeble
Penmarth
Burras

SOUTH WEST COAST PATH
Nancledra
Fraddam
Crowan
Carnkie
Longdon

Morvah
B3306
252
Canon's Town
Leedstown
Drym
Releath
B3303
Porkellis
Rame

Bojewyan
CHYSAUSTER ANCIENT VILLAGE
Newmill
St Erth
Townshend
B3280
Nancegollan
Stithians Res.

GEEVOR TIN MINE MUSEUM
Pendeen
Higher Boscaswell
B3311
A30
Crowlas
Relubbus
GODOLPHIN HOUSE
Wendron

Trewellard
Nancledra
Ludgvan
St Hilary
Godolphin Cross
POLDARK MINE

Botallack
Carnyorth
A3071
TRENGWAINTON
Madron
P&R
Gulval
Marazion
Goldsithney
Crowntown
HELSTON RAILWAY
A394

Cape Cornwall
St Just
Newbridge
HEAMOOR
Chyandour
ST MICHAEL'S MOUNT
Germoe
Ashton
Sithney
Constantine

The Brisons
BALLOWALL BARROW
LAND'S END
Bosavern
Sancreed
PENZANCE
Marazion
A30
A394
Breage
Trewennack

Kelynack
224
CARN EUNY ANCIENT VILLAGE
Tredavoe
Penzance
Perranuthnoe
Praa Sands
A394

LAND'S END
Brane
Lower Drift
NEWLYN ART GALLERY
SOUTH WEST COAST PATH
Rinsey
Helston

Whitesand Bay
Crows-an-wra
Catchall
Newlyn
Cudden Pt.
FLAMBARDS EXPERIENCE

Sennen Cove
B3283
Kerris
Paul
Gweek
CORNISH SEAL SANCTUARY

Longships
Sennen
St Buryan
Mousehole
The Loe
Mawgan

LAND'S END
Trewoofe
St Clement's Island
Trewavas Hd.
A3083
Garras
St Martins

B3315
Lamorna
SOUTH WEST COAST PATH
Porthleven
HALLIGGYE FOGOU
TRELOWARE
Newtown

Polgigga
Boskenna
TREGIFFIAN BURIAL CHAMBER
Porthleven Sands
Gunwalloe
Berepper
Cross Lanes

Porthcurno
Treen
Lamorna Cove
113
Trabo

TELEGRAPH MUSEUM PORTHCURNO
St Levan
MINACK OPEN AIR THEATRE
MOUNT'S BAY
Cury
Trelan

Gwennap Hd.
Runnel Stone
Goonhilly Down

Mullion
THE LIZARD
Penhale
Gwenter
Kuggar

Mullion Cove
Mullion Cove

Mullion Island
Predannack Wollas
St Ruan
Ruan Minor

ISLES OF SCILLY
(Mar-Nov)

Vellan Hd.
Grade
Cadgwith

Lizard
Hot Pt.

Kynance Cove
LIZARD

LIZARD POINT

SOUTH WEST COAST PATH

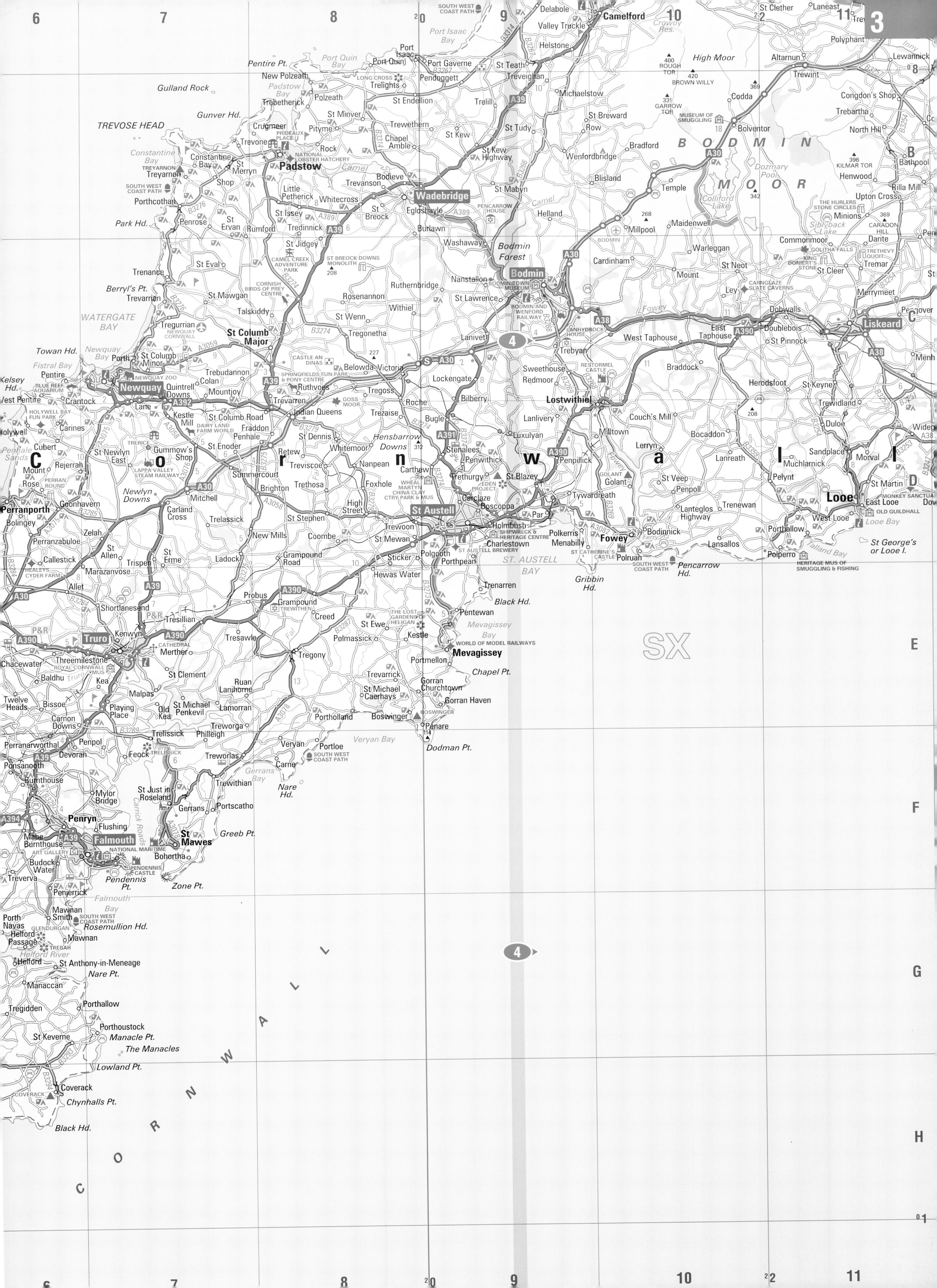

6
7
8
9
10
11
C
D
E
F
G
H
SX
C o r n w a l l
C O R N W A L L
B O D M I N
M O O R
Camelford
Delabole
Valley Truckle
Helstone
St Teath
Treveighan
Michaelstow
Port Isaac Bay
Port Isaac
Port Quin
Port Gaverne
Pendoggett
Pentire Pt.
Port Quin Bay
New Polzeath
Polzeath
Trebetherick
Padstow Bay
Gulland Rock
Gunver Hd.
TREVOSE HEAD
Trelights
Long Cross
St Endellion
Trelill
St Minver
Trewethern
St Kew
St Tudy
Chapel Amble
Pityme
Crugmeer
Trevone
Prideaux Place
Rock
National Lobster Hatchery
Padstow
Camel
Constantine Bay
Treyarnon
St Merryn
Shop
South West Coast Path
Porthcothan
Little Petherick
Trevanson
Bodieve
Wadebridge
Whitecross
St Breock
Egloshayle
St Issey
Tredinnick
Penrose
St Ervan
Rumford
Park Hd.
Burlawn
Washaway
Pencarrow House
St Jidgey
Camel Creek Adventure Park
St Breock Downs Monolith
St Eval
Trenance
Berryl's Pt.
Trevarrian
Cornish Birds of Prey Centre
St Mawgan
Talskiddy
Watergate Bay
Tregurrian
Newquay Cornwall
St Columb Major
Rosenannon
Ruthernbridge
Withiel
St Wenn
Tregonetha
Towan Hd.
Newquay Bay
Fistral Bay
Pentire
Porth
St Columb Minor
Trebudannon
Colan
Castle an Dinas
Springfields Fun Park & Pony Centre
Belowda
Victoria
Kelsey Hd.
West Pentire
Blue Reef Aquarium
Newquay
Newquay Zoo
Quintrell Downs
Mountjoy
Ruthvoes
Trevarren
Indian Queens
Goss Moor
Tregoss
Crantock
Lane
Holywell Bay Fun Park
Holywell
Carines
Kestle Mill
Dairy Land Farm World
St Columb Road
Fraddon
Penhale
St Dennis
Trezaise
Roche
Lockengate
Bilberry
Bugle
Hensbarrow Downs
Whitemoor
Cubert
Penhale Sands
St Newlyn East
Trerice
Gummow's Shop
St Enoder
Retew
Treviscoe
Nanpean
Rejerrah
Mount
Rose
Perran Round
Lappa Valley Steam Railway
Summercourt
Trethosa
Foxhole
Carthew
Wheal Martyn China Clay Ctry Park & Mus
Newlyn Downs
Brighton
Mitchell
Goonhavern
Perranporth
Bolingey
Carland Cross
Trelassick
St Stephen
High Street
St Austell
Stenalees
Penwithick
Trethurgy
Eden Project
St Blazey
Carclaze
Boscoppa
Par
Holmbush
Shipwreck & Heritage Centre
Charlestown
St Austell Brewery
Polgooth
Porthpean
St Austell Bay
Trewoon
St Mewan
Sticker
New Mills
Coombe
Zelah
St Allen
Perranzabuloe
Callestick
Healeys Cyder Farm
Trispen
St Erme
Ladock
Grampound Road
Marazanvose
Allet
Hewas Water
Tresillian
Probus
Grampound
Trewithen
Creed
Shortlanesend
Kenwyn
Truro
Cathedral
Merther
Tresawle
Tregony
St Ewe
The Lost Gardens of Heligan
Kestle
Polmassick
Pentewan
Mevagissey Bay
Mevagissey
World of Model Railways
Portmellon
Chacewater
Threemilestone
Royal Cornwall Mus
Baldhu
Kea
St Clement
Ruan Lanihorne
Trevarrick
St Michael Caerhays
Gorran Churchtown
Gorran Haven
Chapel Pt.
Twelve Heads
Bissoe
Carnon Downs
Malpas
Playing Place
Old Kea
St Michael Penkevil
Lamorran
Treworga
Philleigh
Portholland
Boswinger
Penare
Dodman Pt.
Veryan Bay
Perranarworthal
Penpol
Devoran
Feock
Trelissick
Veryan
Portloe
Carne
Treworlas
Ponsanooth
Burnthouse
Mylor Bridge
St Just in Roseland
Trewithian
Gerrans Bay
Gerrans
Portscatho
Nare Hd.
Carrick Roads
Penryn
Flushing
Falmouth
Mabe Burnthouse
National Maritime
St Mawes
Bohortha
Greeb Pt.
Art Gallery
Budock Water
Pendennis Castle
Pendennis Pt.
Zone Pt.
Treverva
Penjerrick
Falmouth Bay
Mawnan Smith
South West Coast Path
Rosemullion Hd.
Port Navas
Helford Passage
Glendurgan
Trebah
Mawnan
Helford River
Helford
St Anthony-in-Meneage
Nare Pt.
Manaccan
Tregidden
Porthallow
Porthoustock
St Keverne
Manacle Pt.
The Manacles
Lowland Pt.
Coverack
Chynhalls Pt.
Black Hd.
Black Hd.
Trenarren
St Clether
Laneast
Polyphant
Altarnun
Trewint
Lewannick
Crowdy Res.
High Moor
Rough Tor
Brown Willy
Garrow Tor
Codda
Museum of Smuggling
Bolventor
Congdon's Shop
Trebartha
North Hill
Bathpool
Kilmar Tor
Henwood
Rilla Mill
Upton Cross
St Breward
Row
Wenfordbridge
Bradford
Blisland
Temple
Dozmary Pool
Colliford Lake
The Hurlers Stone Circles
Minions
Caradon Hill
St Mabyn
St Kew Highway
Helland
Camel
Bodmin Forest
Millpool
Maidenwell
Siblyback Lake
Commonmoor
Golitha Falls
Trethevy Quoit
Darite
Bodmin
Cardinham
Warleggan
St Neot
King Doniert's Stone
St Cleer
Tremar
Nanstallon
Bodmin Town Museum
Bodmin and Wenford Railway
St Lawrence
Mount
Carnglaze Slate Caverns
Ley
Merrymeet
Pengover
Fowey
Dobwalls
Doublebois
Liskeard
Lanivet
Lanhydrock House
Trebyan
West Taphouse
East Taphouse
St Pinnock
Menheniot
Sweethouse
Redmoor
Restormel Castle
Braddock
Herodsfoot
St Keyne
Lostwithiel
Lanlivery
Luxulyan
Couch's Mill
Milltown
Trewidland
Duloe
Widegates
Bocaddon
Lerryn
Penpillick
Golant
Lanreath
Sandplace
Morval
Muchlarnick
Pelynt
St Veep
Penpoll
St Martin
Tywardreath
Lanteglos Highway
Trenewan
Looe
East Looe
West Looe
Monkey Sanctuary
Old Guildhall
Looe Bay
Polkerris
Menabilly
Fowey
Bodinnick
Lansallos
Porthallow
Talland Bay
St George's or Looe I.
St Catherine's Castle
Polruan
South West Coast Path
Pencarrow Hd.
Polperro
Heritage Mus of Smuggling & Fishing
Gribbin Hd.
A30
A39
A38
A390
A391
A392
A394
A389
A3058
A3059
A3075
A3076
A3078
A3082
B3314
B3267
B3266
B3274
B3276
B3275
B3279
B3287
B3268
B3269
B3284
B3285
B3289
B3291
B3293
B3294
B3254
B3257
B3252
B3253
B3359
B3273
B3374
P&R
4

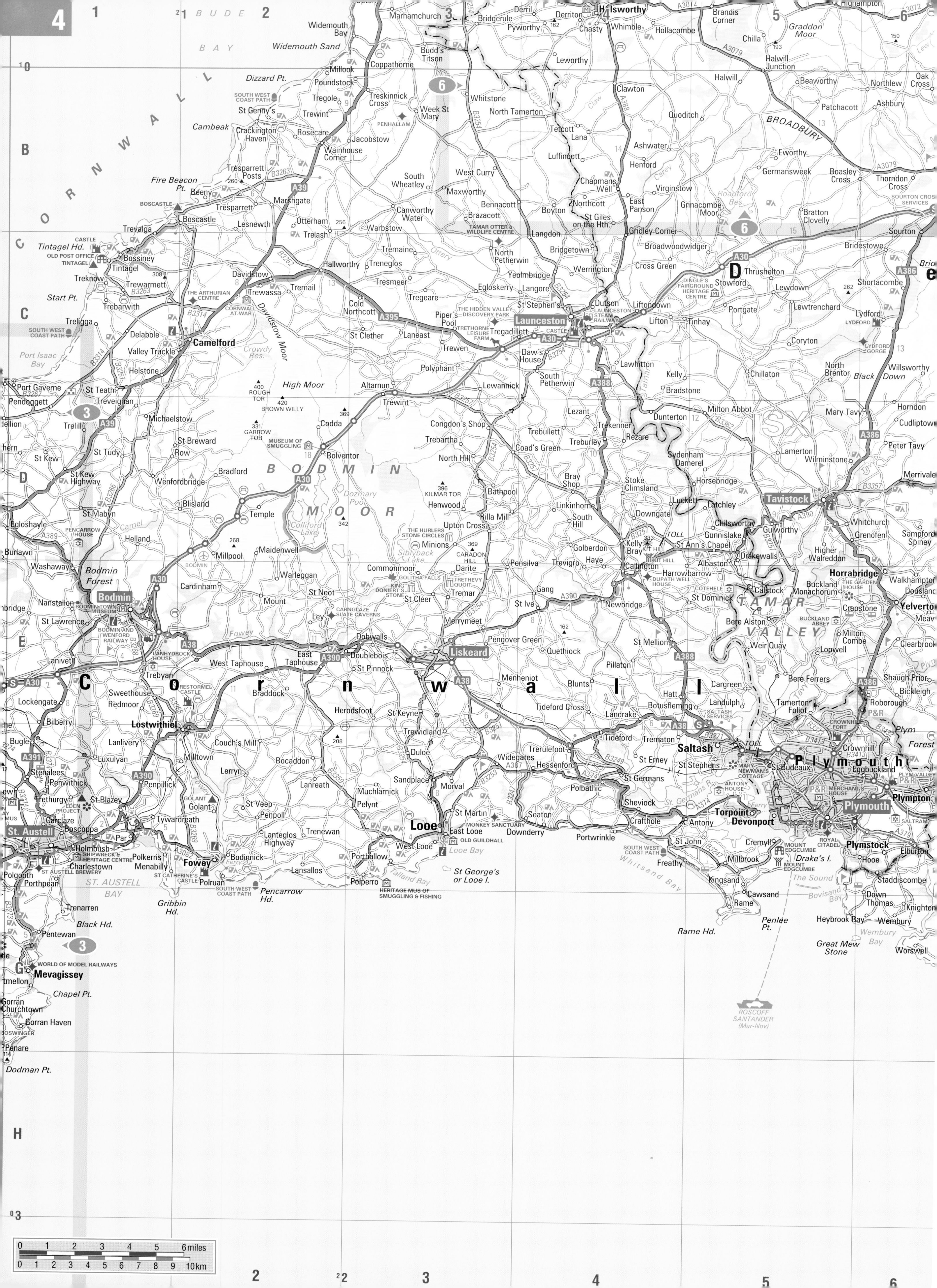
BUDE
BAY
Widemouth Bay
Widemouth Sand
Marhamchurch
Bridgerule
Derril
Pyworthy
Derriton
Holsworthy
Chasty
Whimble
Hollacombe
Brandis Corner
Graddon Moor
Chilla
Halwill Junction
Highampton
Budd's Titson
Millook
Coppathorne
Dizzard Pt.
Poundstock
Treskinnick Cross
Whitstone
Lewtorthy
Clawton
Halwill
Beaworthy
Northlew
Oak Cross
SOUTH WEST COAST PATH
St Gennys
Tregole
Trewint
Week St Mary
PENHALLAM
North Tamerton
Quoditch
Patchacott
Ashbury
BROADBURY
Cambeak
Crackington Haven
Rosecare
Jacobstow
Tetcott
Lana
Wainhouse Corner
Luffincott
Ashwater
Eworthy
Henford
Germansweek
Boasley Cross
Thorndon Cross
SOURTON CROSS SERVICES
Fire Beacon Pt.
Tresparrett Posts
South Wheatley
West Curry
Chapmans Well
Virginstow
Maxworthy
Beeny
BOSCASTLE
Marshgate
Tresparrett
Bennacott
Northcott
East Panson
Grinacombe Moor
Roadford Res.
Bratton Clovelly
Canworthy Water
Boyton
Boscastle
Otterham
Brazacott
St Giles on the Hth.
Lesnewth
Warbstow
TAMAR OTTER & WILDLIFE CENTRE
Langdon
Gridley Corner
Sourton
Trevalga
Trelash
CASTLE
Tintagel Hd.
OLD POST OFFICE TINTAGEL
Bossiney
Tintagel
Tremaine
North Petherwin
Bridgetown
Broadwoodwidger
Bridestowe
Hallworthy
Treneglos
Werrington
Cross Green
Thrushelton
Trewarmett
Davidstow
Tresmeer
Yeolmbridge
DINGLE'S FAIRGROUND HERITAGE CENTRE
Stowford
Shortacombe
Treknow
Start Pt.
THE ARTHURIAN CENTRE
Trewassa
Tremail
Egloskerry
Langore
Lewdown
Trebarwith
CORNWALL AT WAR
Davidstow Moor
Cold Northcott
Tregeare
Dutson
LAUNCESTON STEAM RAILWAY
Liftondown
Portgate
Lewtrenchard
Lydford
LYDFORD
Treligga
THE HIDDEN VALLEY DISCOVERY PARK
Piper's Pool
St Stephen's
Launceston
CASTLE
Lifton
Tinhay
SOUTH WEST COAST PATH
Delabole
Camelford
Crowdy Res.
St Clether
Laneast
TRETHORNE LEISURE FARM
Tregadillett
Coryton
Trewen
Daw's House
LYDFORD GORGE
Port Isaac Bay
Valley Truckle
Polyphant
Lawhitton
Helstone
South Petherwin
Kelly
Chillaton
North Brentor
Black Down
Willsworthy
Port Gaverne
St Teath
ROUGH TOR
BROWN WILLY
High Moor
Altarnun
Lewannick
Bradstone
Pendoggett
Treveighan
Trewint
Milton Abbot
Horndon
Mary Tavy
Trelill
Michaelstow
Codda
Congdon's Shop
Lezant
Trekenner
Dunterton
Cudliptown
GARROW TOR
Trebullett
Rezare
St Breward
MUSEUM OF SMUGGLING
Trebartha
Treburley
Peter Tavy
St Tudy
Row
Bolventor
Coad's Green
Sydenham Damerel
Lamerton
St Kew
North Hill
Wilminstone
BODMIN
St Kew Highway
Bradford
MOOR
Bray Shop
Stoke Climsland
Horsebridge
Merrivale
Wenfordbridge
KILMAR TOR
Bathpool
Dozmary Pool
Henwood
Blisland
Linkinhorne
Luckett
Latchley
Tavistock
St Mabyn
Temple
Rilla Mill
South Hill
Downgate
Whitchurch
Egloshayle
PENCARROW HOUSE
Colliford Lake
THE HURLERS STONE CIRCLES
Upton Cross
Chilsworthy
Gulworthy
Grenofen
Sampford Spiney
Helland
Minions
CARADON HILL
Kelly Bray
KIT HILL
TOLL
Gunnislake
Burlawn
Millpool
Maidenwell
Siblyback Lake
Golberdon
St Ann's Chapel
Drakewalls
Higher Walreddon
Washaway
Bodmin Forest
Darite
Pensilva
Trevigro
Haye
Callington
Albaston
Commonmoor
GOLITHA FALLS
TRETHEVY QUOIT
Harrowbarrow
DUPATH WELL HOUSE
Horrabridge
THE GARDEN HOUSE
Walkhampton
Cardinham
Warleggan
KING DONIERT'S STONE
Tremar
COTEHELE
Calstock
Buckland Monachorum
Dousland
Bodmin
Nanstallon
BODMIN TOWN MUSEUM
Mount
St Neot
St Cleer
Gang
St Ive
Newbridge
St Dominick
TAMAR
Crapstone
Yelverton
St Lawrence
BODMIN AND WENFORD RAILWAY
Ley
CARNGLAZE SLATE CAVERNS
Merrymeet
Bere Alston
BUCKLAND ABBEY
VALLEY
Meavy
Fowey
Dobwalls
Pengover Green
St Mellion
Milton Combe
Clearbrook
LANHYDROCK HOUSE
East Taphouse
Doublebois
Liskeard
Quethiock
Weir Quay
Lopwell
Lanivet
West Taphouse
St Pinnock
Pillaton
Trebyan
Menheniot
Blunts
Cargreen
Bere Ferrers
Shaugh Prior
RESTORMEL CASTLE
Sweetshouse
Braddock
C o r n w a l l
Hatt
Bickleigh
Lockengate
Redmoor
Tideford Cross
Landulph
Tamerton Foliot
Roborough
Herodsfoot
St Keyne
Landrake
Botusfleming
SALTASH SERVICES
P&R
CROWNHILL FORT
Plym
Bilberry
Lostwithiel
Trewidland
Forest
Bugle
Lanlivery
Couch's Mill
Trerulefoot
Tideford
Trematon
Saltash
TOLL
Crownhill
Luxulyan
Milltown
Duloe
Widegates
Hessenford
St Erney
St Stephens
St Budeaux
Plymouth
Eggbuckland
Stenalees
Bocaddon
MARY NEWMAN'S COTTAGE
PLYM VALLEY
Penwithick
Penpillick
Lerryn
Lanreath
Sandplace
Morval
St Germans
Trethurgy
Golant
Muchlarnick
Polbathic
ANTONY HOUSE
MERCHANT'S HOUSE
Plympton
St Blazey
EDEN PROJECT
St Veep
Pelynt
St Martin
Seaton
Sheviock
Plymouth
Carclaze
Tywardreath
Penpoll
MONKEY SANCTUARY
Crafthole
Torpoint
Devonport
SALTRAM
St. Austell
Boscoppa
Par
Lanteglos Highway
Trenewan
Looe
East Looe
Downderry
Portwrinkle
Antony
ROYAL CITADEL
Plymstock
Elburton
Holmbush
SHIPWRECK & HERITAGE CENTRE
Polkerris
Menabilly
Bodinnick
West Looe
OLD GUILDHALL
Looe Bay
St John
Cremyll
MOUNT EDGCUMBE
Drake's I.
Hooe
ST AUSTELL BREWERY
Charlestown
Fowey
St George's or Looe I.
SOUTH WEST COAST PATH
Freathy
Millbrook
Polgooth
Porthpean
ST CATHERINE'S CASTLE
Polruan
Lansallos
Porthallow
Talland Bay
Whitsand Bay
MOUNT EDGCUMBE
The Sound
Staddiscombe
ST. AUSTELL BAY
SOUTH WEST COAST PATH
Pencarrow Hd.
Polperro
HERITAGE MUS OF SMUGGLING & FISHING
Kingsand
Cawsand
Bovisand Bay
Down Thomas
Gribbin Hd.
Trenarren
Rame
Knighton
Black Hd.
Penlee Pt.
Heybrook Bay
Wembury
Rame Hd.
Wembury Bay
Great Mew Stone
Worswell
Pentewan
WORLD OF MODEL RAILWAYS
Mevagissey
Chapel Pt.
Gorran Churchtown
Gorran Haven
BOSWINGER
Penare
Dodman Pt.
ROSCOFF SANTANDER (Mar-Nov)
H
0 1 2 3 4 5 6 miles
0 1 2 3 4 5 6 7 8 9 10 km

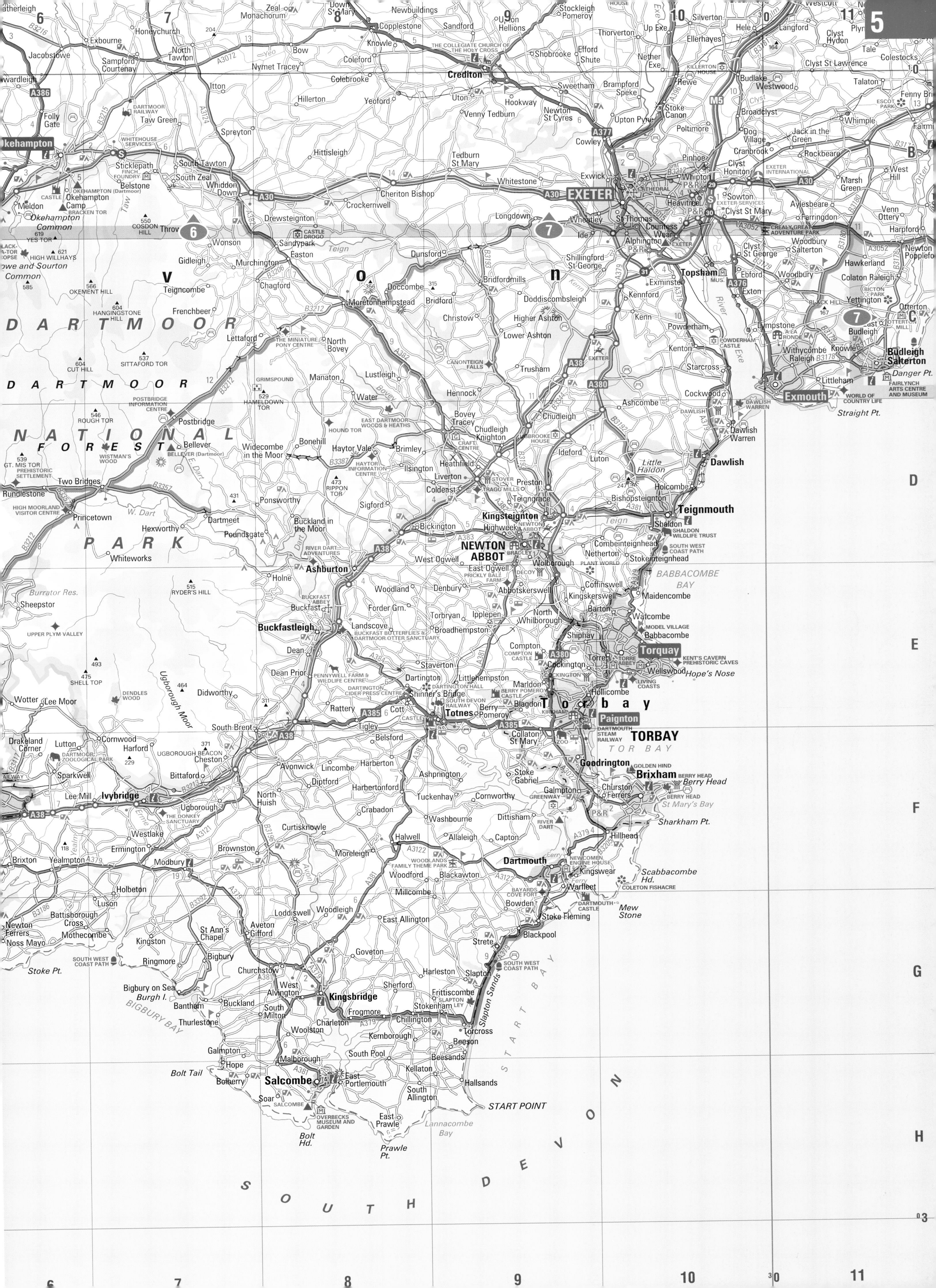

Okehampton
Exbourne
Jacobstowe
Sampford Courtenay
Honeychurch
North Tawton
Bow
Zeal Monachorum
Down St Mary
Copplestone
Newbuildings
Sandford
Knowle
Coleford
Nymet Tracey
Colebrooke
Crediton
Yeoford
Hillerton
Uton
Venny Tedburn
Hookway
Shobrooke
Efford
Shute
Stockleigh Pomeroy
Upton Hellions
Thorverton
Up Exe
Nether Exe
Silverton
Ellerhayes
Hele
Langford
Clyst Hydon
Plymtree
Tale
Colestocks
Clyst St Lawrence
Talaton
Killerton House
Rewe
Bramford Speke
Sweetham
Newton St Cyres
Upton Pyne
Stoke Canon
Poltimore
Cowley
Budlake
Westwood
Broadclyst
Whimple
Dog Village
Jack in the Green
Cranbrook
Rockbeare
Pinhoe
Clyst Honiton
Exeter International
West Hill
Marsh Green
Aylesbeare
Farringdon
Venn Ottery
Harpford
Whipton
Heavitree
Sowton
Exeter Services
Clyst St Mary
Crealy Great Adventure Park
Woodbury Salterton
Clyst St George
Newton Poppleford
Hawkerland
Colaton Raleigh
Ebford
Woodbury
Exton
Bicton Park
Yettington
Black Hill
Otterton
East Budleigh
Lympstone
A La Ronde
Withycombe Raleigh
Knowle
Budleigh Salterton
Danger Pt.
Littleham
Exmouth
World of Country Life
Fairlynch Arts Centre and Museum
Straight Pt.
Dawlish Warren
EXETER
Exwick
Whitestone
St Thomas
Countess Wear
Alphington
Ide
Wheatley
Longdown
Shillingford St George
Topsham
Exminster
Kennford
Kenn
Powderham
Powderham Castle
Kenton
Starcross
Cockwood
Ashcombe
Dawlish
Dawlish Warren
Little Haldon
Holcombe
Bishopsteignton
Teignmouth
Shaldon
Shaldon Wildlife Trust
South West Coast Path
Combeinteignhead
Netherton
Stokeinteignhead
Babbacombe Bay
Maidencombe
Watcombe
Model Village
Babbacombe
Torquay
Kent's Cavern Prehistoric Caves
Wellswood
Hope's Nose
Living Coasts
Hollicombe
Torre
Torre Abbey
Torbay
Paignton
Dartmouth Steam Railway
TORBAY
Tor Bay
Goodrington
Golden Hind
Brixham
Berry Head
Churston Ferrers
St Mary's Bay
Sharkham Pt.
Galmpton
Greenway
Hillhead
Kingswear
Newcomen Engine House
Scabbacombe Hd.
Coleton Fishacre
Dartmouth
Dartmouth Castle
Warfleet
Mew Stone
Stoke Fleming
Bayards Cove Fort
Bowden
Blackpool
Strete
Slapton
Slapton Sands
Slapton Ley
Start Bay
Torcross
Beeson
Beesands
Hallsands
Start Point
Kellaton
South Allington
East Prawle
Prawle Pt.
Lannacombe Bay
East Portlemouth
Salcombe
Overbecks Museum and Garden
Bolt Hd.
Soar
Bolberry
Bolt Tail
Hope
Malborough
Galmpton
South Pool
Kernborough
Chillington
Frogmore
Stokenham
Charleton
Woolston
Kingsbridge
West Alvington
South Milton
Thurlestone
Bantham
Buckland
Bigbury Bay
Bigbury on Sea
Burgh I.
Bigbury
Churchstow
Ringmore
Kingston
St Ann's Chapel
Aveton Gifford
Loddiswell
Woodleigh
East Allington
Goveton
Harleston
Sherford
Frittiscombe
Millcombe
Woodford
Blackawton
Woodlands Family Theme Park
Halwell
Moreleigh
Washbourne
Allaleigh
Capton
Dittisham
Cornworthy
Tuckenhay
Ashprington
Stoke Gabriel
Harbertonford
Harberton
Crabadon
Diptford
Curtisknowle
North Huish
Avonwick
Lincombe
Belsford
Tigley
Rattery
Cott
Totnes
Berry Pomeroy
Berry Pomeroy Castle
Blagdon
Collaton St Mary
Marldon
Compton
Compton Castle
Cockington
Littlehempston
Dartington
Dartington Hall
Dartington Cider Press Centre
Shinner's Bridge
Staverton
Dean Prior
Dean
Pennywell Farm & Wildlife Centre
Buckfastleigh
Buckfast
Buckfast Abbey
Buckfast Butterflies & Dartmoor Otter Sanctuary
Landscove
Broadhempston
Torbryan
Forder Grn.
Ipplepen
North Whilborough
Kingskerswell
Coffinswell
Barton
Shiphay
Abbotskerswell
Denbury
Woodland
East Ogwell
West Ogwell
Prickly Ball Farm
Decoy
Wolborough
NEWTON ABBOT
Bradley
Highweek
Kingsteignton
Teigngrace
Preston
Bickington
Coldeast
Liverton
Heathfield
Stover
Trago Mills
Ilsington
Haytor Vale
Haytor Information Centre
Brimley
Bovey Tracey
Chudleigh Knighton
Chudleigh
Ugbrooke House
Ideford
Luton
Hennock
Trusham
Canonteign Falls
Lower Ashton
Higher Ashton
Christow
Doddiscombsleigh
Bridford
Bridfordmills
Dunsford
Doccombe
Moretonhampstead
North Bovey
Lustleigh
Manaton
Water
East Dartmoor Woods & Heaths
Hound Tor
Widecombe in the Moor
Bonehill
Rippon Tor
Sigford
Ponsworthy
Buckland in the Moor
River Dart Adventures
Ashburton
Holne
Poundsgate
Dartmeet
Hexworthy
Whiteworks
Princetown
Two Bridges
Rundlestone
High Moorland Visitor Centre
Gt. Mis Tor
Prehistoric Settlement
Wistman's Wood
Bellever
Postbridge
Postbridge Information Centre
Rough Tor
Hameldown Tor
Grimspound
The Miniature Pony Centre
Lettaford
Chagford
Murchington
Gidleigh
Teigncombe
Frenchbeer
Sittaford Tor
Cut Hill
Hangingstone Hill
Okement Hill
Yes Tor
High Willhays
Sourton Common
Okehampton Common
Cosdon Hill
Throwleigh
Wonson
Drewsteignton
Castle Drogo
Sandypark
Easton
Crockernwell
Cheriton Bishop
Tedburn St Mary
Hittisleigh
Spreyton
Taw Green
Folly Gate
Itton
Dartmoor Railway
Whitehouse Services
Sticklepath
Finch Foundry
Belstone
South Tawton
South Zeal
Whiddon Down
Okehampton Camp
Bracken Tor
Meldon
Okehampton Castle
DARTMOOR
DARTMOOR NATIONAL FOREST PARK
DEVON
SOUTH DEVON
Burrator Res.
Sheepstor
Upper Plym Valley
Shell Top
Ryder's Hill
Dendles Wood
Ugborough Moor
Didworthy
South Brent
Lee Moor
Wotter
Drakeland Corner
Lutton
Cornwood
Harford
Dartmoor Zoological Park
Ugborough Beacon
Cheston
Bittaford
Sparkwell
Lee Mill
Ivybridge
Ugborough
The Donkey Sanctuary
Westlake
Ermington
Brownston
Modbury
Yealmpton
Brixton
Holbeton
Luson
Battisborough Cross
Mothecombe
Newton Ferrers
Noss Mayo
Stoke Pt.
Teign
Exe
Dart
A30
A38
A380
A381
A385
A386
A3072
A377
A379
A376
A3052
A3122
A3121
A382
A383
B3212
B3357
B3387
B3193
B3213
B3392
B3197
M5

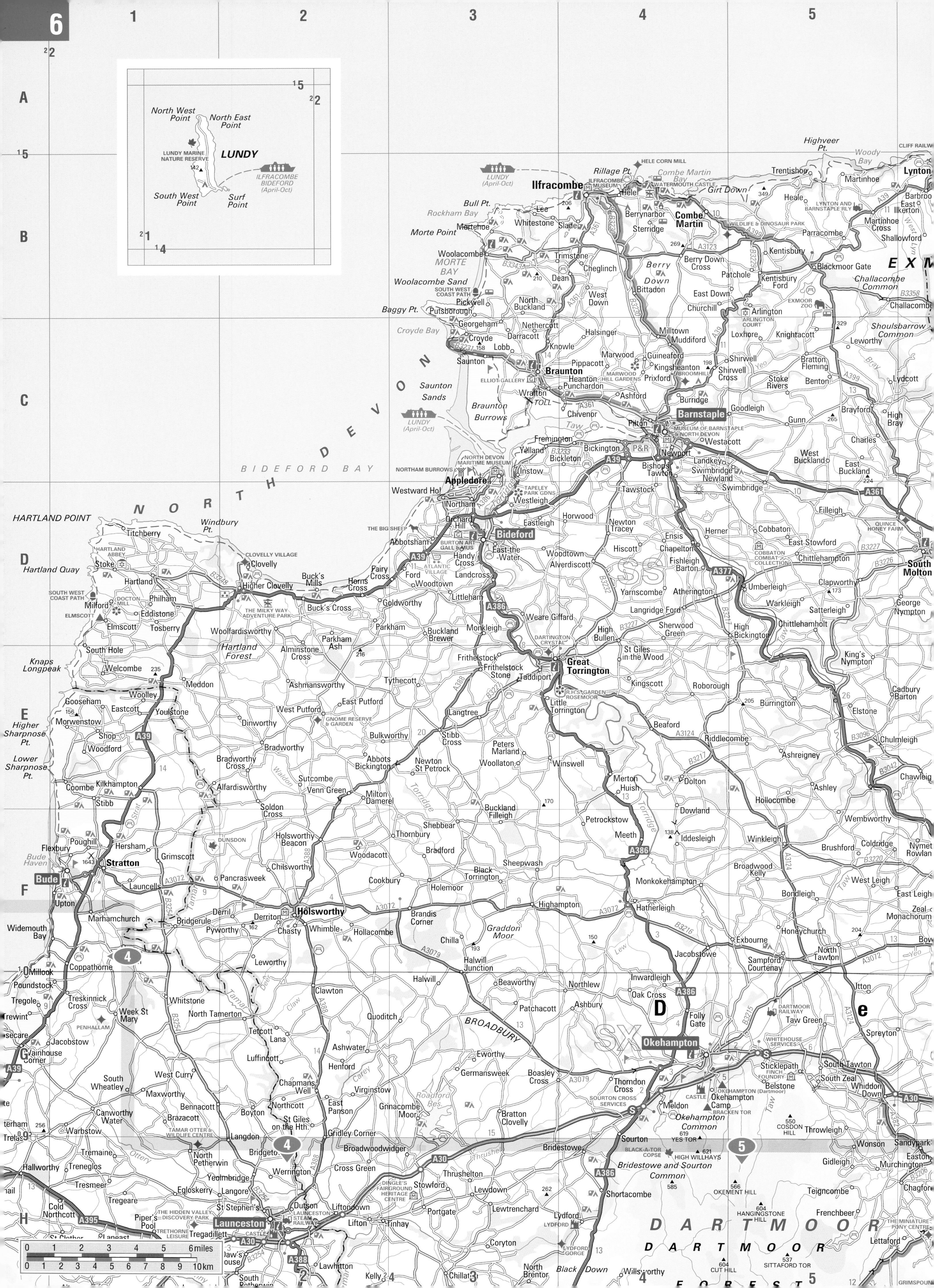

1
2
3
4
5
A
B
C
D
E
F
G
H
North West Point
North East Point
LUNDY
LUNDY MARINE NATURE RESERVE
142
South West Point
Surf Point
ILFRACOMBE BIDEFORD (April-Oct)
LUNDY (April-Oct)
Highveer Pt.
Woody Bay
CLIFF RAILWAY
Lynton
HELE CORN MILL
Rillage Pt.
Combe Martin Bay
Ilfracombe
ILFRACOMBE MUSEUM
Hele
WATERMOUTH CASTLE
Girt Down
Trentishoe
Martinhoe
Barbrook
Bull Pt.
Rockham Bay
Lee
Whitestone
Slade
Berrynarbor
Combe Martin
Heale
LYNTON AND BARNSTAPLE RLY
East Ilkerton
Morte Point
Mortehoe
Sterridge
WILDLIFE & DINOSAUR PARK
Parracombe
Martinhoe Cross
Shallowford
Woolacombe
MORTE BAY
Trimstone
Cheglinch
Berry Down
Berry Down Cross
Kentisbury
Blackmoor Gate
EXM
Woolacombe Sand
SOUTH WEST COAST PATH
Dean
West Down
Bittadon
Patchole
Kentisbury Ford
Challacombe Common
Pickwell
North Buckland
East Down
EXMOOR ZOO
Challacombe
Baggy Pt.
Putsborough
Churchill
Arlington
ARLINGTON COURT
Georgeham
Nethercott
Croyde Bay
Croyde
Darracott
Halsinger
Milltown
Muddiford
Loxhore
Knightacott
Shoulsbarrow Common
Leworthy
Lobb
Knowle
Marwood
Guineaford
Saunton
Braunton
Pippacott
Kingsheanton
Shirwell
Shirwell Cross
Bratton Fleming
Lydcott
ELLIOT GALLERY
Heanton Punchardon
MARWOOD HILL GARDENS
Prixford
BROOMHILL
Stoke Rivers
Benton
Saunton Sands
Braunton Burrows
Wrafton
TOLL
Ashford
Burridge
Barnstaple
Goodleigh
Brayford
High Bray
Chivenor
Taw
Pilton
MUSEUM OF BARNSTAPLE & NORTH DEVON
Gunn
Fremington
Westacott
Charles
Yelland
Bickington
Bickleton
P&R
Newport
Landkey
West Buckland
Bishops Tawton
Swimbridge Newland
East Buckland
BIDEFORD BAY
NORTHAM BURROWS
NORTH DEVON MARITIME MUSEUM
Instow
Appledore
Swimbridge
NORTH DEVON
Westward Ho!
Tawstock
TAPELEY PARK GDNS
Northam
Westleigh
Filleigh
HARTLAND POINT
Windbury Pt.
THE BIG SHEEP
Orchard Hill
Eastleigh
Horwood
Newton Tracey
Herner
Cobbaton
QUINCEY HONEY FARM
Titchberry
Abbotsham
BURTON ART GALLERY
Bideford
Hiscott
Ensis
Chapelton
East Stowford
HARTLAND ABBEY
CLOVELLY VILLAGE
Clovelly
East-the-Water
Woodtown
Alverdiscott
COBBATON COMBAT COLLECTION
Chittlehampton
South Molton
Hartland Quay
Stoke
Hartland
ATLANTIC VILLAGE
Handy Cross
Fishleigh Barton
Buck's Mills
Fairy Cross
Horns Cross
Ford
Landcross
Umberleigh
Clapworthy
SOUTH WEST COAST PATH
Higher Clovelly
Woodtown
Littleham
Yarnscombe
Atherington
Philham
DOCTON MILL
Goldworthy
Warkleigh
George Nympton
Milford
Eddistone
THE MILKY WAY ADVENTURE PARK
Buck's Cross
ELMSCOTT
Langridge Ford
Satterleigh
Elmscott
Tosberry
Woolfardisworthy
Parkham
Buckland Brewer
Monkleigh
Weare Giffard
Chittlehamholt
Sherwood Green
High Bickington
Hartland Forest
Parkham Ash
DARTINGTON CRYSTAL
High Bullen
South Hole
Alminstone Cross
St Giles in the Wood
King's Nympton
Knaps Longpeak
Welcombe
Frithelstock
Frithelstock Stone
Great Torrington
Taddiport
Meddon
Tythecott
Kingscott
Roborough
Ashmansworthy
R.H.S. GARDEN ROSEMOOR
Cadbury Barton
Woolley
Little Torrington
Gooseham
Eastcott
West Putford
East Putford
Burrington
Elstone
Youlstone
Langtree
Higher Sharpnose Pt.
Morwenstow
Dinworthy
GNOME RESERVE & GARDEN
Beaford
Shop
Bulkworthy
Stibb Cross
Riddlecombe
Chulmleigh
Woodford
Bradworthy
Peters Marland
Ashreigney
Lower Sharpnose Pt.
Bradworthy Cross
Abbots Bickington
Newton St Petrock
Woollaton
Winswell
Chawleigh
Coombe
Kilkhampton
Sutcombe
Merton
Huish
Dolton
Stibb
Alfardisworthy
Venn Green
Milton Damerel
Torridge
Ashley
Hollocombe
Soldon Cross
Buckland Filleigh
Dowland
Wembworthy
Poughill
DUNSDON
Holsworthy Beacon
Thornbury
Shebbear
Petrockstow
Iddesleigh
Winkleigh
Coldridge
Nymet Rowland
Flexbury
Hersham
Meeth
Brushford
Bude Haven
Stratton
Grimscott
Woodacott
Bradford
Sheepwash
Bude
Chilsworthy
Black Torrington
Broadwood Kelly
Launcells
Pancrasweek
Cookbury
Monkokehampton
West Leigh
Upton
Holemoor
Bondleigh
East Leigh
Derril
Highampton
Hatherleigh
Zeal Monachorum
Marhamchurch
Bridgerule
Derriton
Holsworthy
Brandis Corner
Widemouth Bay
Pyworthy
Chasty
Whimble
Hollacombe
Graddon Moor
Honeychurch
Chilla
Exbourne
Jacobstowe
North Tawton
Coppathorne
Leworthy
Halwill Junction
Sampford Courtenay
Millook
Poundstock
Halwill
Beaworthy
Inwardleigh
Itton
Tregole
Treskinnick Cross
Clawton
Northlew
Oak Cross
Whitstone
Week St Mary
PENHALLAM
North Tamerton
Quoditch
Patchacott
Ashbury
DARTMOOR RAILWAY
Folly Gate
Taw Green
Spreyton
BROADBURY
Tetcott
Lana
Jacobstow
Ashwater
Okehampton
WHITEHOUSE SERVICES
Vainhouse Corner
Luffincott
Henford
Eworthy
Sticklepath
South Tawton
FINCH FOUNDRY
South Wheatley
West Curry
Germansweek
Boasley Cross
Thorndon Cross
Belstone
South Zeal
Whiddon Down
Maxworthy
Chapmans Well
Virginstow
OKEHAMPTON (Dartmoor)
Okehampton Camp
CASTLE
Bennacott
Northcott
East Panson
Grinacombe Moor
Roadford Res.
Bratton Clovelly
Meldon
BRACKEN TOR
Canworthy Water
SOURTON CROSS SERVICES
Okehampton Common
Brazacott
Boyton
St Giles on the Hth.
COSDON HILL
Throwleigh
Warbstow
TAMAR OTTER & WILDLIFE CENTRE
Gridley Corner
YES TOR
Sourton
Wonson
Sandypark
Langdon
Bridestowe
BLACK-A-TOR COPSE
HIGH WILLHAYS
Gidleigh
Eastontown
Tremaine
Bridgetown
Broadwoodwidger
North Petherwin
Thrushelton
Bridestowe and Sourton Common
Murchington
Hallworthy
Treneglos
Werrington
Cross Green
Tresmeer
Yeolmbridge
Egloskerry
Langore
DINGLE'S FAIRGROUND HERITAGE CENTRE
Stowford
Lewdown
Shortacombe
OKEMENT HILL
Teigncombe
Chagford
Tregeare
Dutson
Liftondown
Cold Northcott
St Stephen's
THE HIDDEN VALLEY DISCOVERY PARK
LAUNCESTON STEAM RAILWAY
Lewtrenchard
HANGINGSTONE HILL
Frenchbeer
Piper's Pool
Launceston
Lifton
Tinhay
Portgate
Lydford
LYDFORD
DARTMOOR
THE MINIATURE PONY CENTRE
TRETHORNE LEISURE
Tregadillett
CASTLE
Coryton
LYDFORD GORGE
Lettaford
Daw's House
Lawhitton
North Brentor
Black Down
Willsworthy
CUT HILL
SITTAFORD TOR
South
Kelly
Chillaton
FOREST
GRIMSPOUND
0 1 2 3 4 5 6 miles
0 1 2 3 4 5 6 7 8 9 10km
A39
A361
A399
A3123
B3230
B3343
B3231
B3233
B3358
B3226
B3227
B3232
B3217
B3096
B3042
B3220
B3216
B3215
B3248
B3254
A386
A388
A377
A3124
A3072
A3079
A30
A395
A382
SS
SX
D
e
4
5

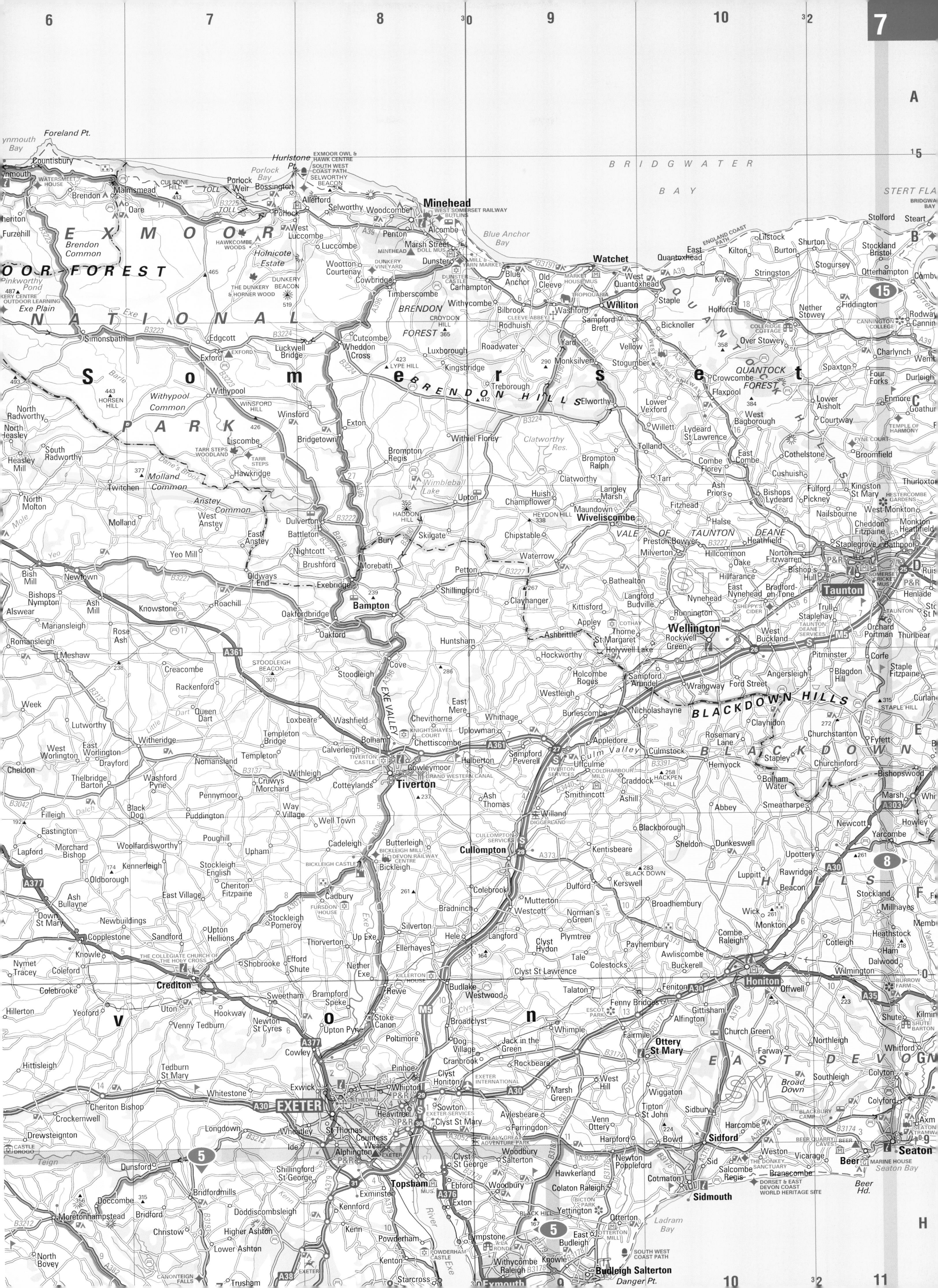

6
7
8
9
10
A
B
C
D
E
F
H
11
Foreland Pt.
Countisbury
Hurlstone Pt.
EXMOOR OWL & HAWK CENTRE
SOUTH WEST COAST PATH
SELWORTHY BEACON
B R I D G W A T E R
B A Y
STERT FLA
Porlock Bay
Porlock
Porlock Weir
Bossington
Allerford
Selworthy
Minehead
Woodcombe
WEST SOMERSET RAILWAY
BUTLINS
Alcombe
Brendon
Malmsmead
Oare
Brendon Common
E X M O O R
OOR FOREST
Holnicote Estate
West Luccombe
Luccombe
Wootton Courtenay
Cowbridge
Dunster
Marsh Street
Periton
Blue Anchor Bay
Watchet
Blue Anchor
Old Cleeve
Carhampton
Withycombe
Washford
Williton
West Quantoxhead
East Quantoxhead
Kilve
Kilton
Lilstock
Burton
Shurton
Stolford
Steart
Stogursey
Stockland Bristol
Otterhampton
Stringston
Holford
Nether Stowey
Fiddington
Timberscombe
BRENDON FOREST
DUNKERY BEACON
Exe Plain
Pinkworthy Pond
N A T I O N A L
P A R K
S o m e r s e t
Simonsbath
Edgcott
Exford
Cutcombe
Wheddon Cross
Luckwell Bridge
Luxborough
Roadwater
Rodhuish
Bilbrook
Sampford Brett
Bicknoller
Stogumber
Monksilver
Yard
Vellow
Over Stowey
QUANTOCK FOREST
Crowcombe
Flaxpool
Spaxton
Charlynch
Four Forks
Durleigh
Kingsbridge
Treborough
B R E N D O N   H I L L S
Elworthy
Withypool
Withypool Common
Winsford
Exton
Bridgetown
Liscombe
TARR STEPS
Hawkridge
Molland Common
North Radworthy
North Heasley
South Radworthy
Heasley Mill
Twitchen
North Molton
Molland
Anstey Common
West Anstey
East Anstey
Dulverton
Battleton
Wimbleball Lake
Upton
Brompton Regis
Withiel Florey
Clatworthy Res.
Clatworthy
Brompton Ralph
Huish Champflower
Langley Marsh
Wiveliscombe
Lower Vexford
Willett
Lydeard St Lawrence
Tolland
Combe Florey
East Combe
Cothelstone
West Bagborough
Lower Aisholt
Courtway
Broomfield
Enmore
Goathurst
Kingston St Mary
Cushuish
Ash Priors
Tarr
Fitzhead
Bishops Lydeard
Fulford
Pickney
Nailsbourne
West Monkton
Cheddon Fitzpaine
Monkton Heathfield
Halse
VALE OF TAUNTON DEANE
Preston Bowyer
Heathfield
Milverton
Hillcommon
Norton Fitzwarren
Staplegrove
Bathpool
Oake
Bishop's Hull
Taunton
Hillfarrance
East Nynehead
Nynehead
Bradford-on-Tone
Henlade
Langford Budville
Bathealton
Skilgate
Bury
Chipstable
Waterrow
Petton
Shillingford
Clayhanger
Kittisford
Appley
Thorne St Margaret
Holywell Lake
Runnington
Wellington
Rockwell Green
West Buckland
Stoplehay
Trull
Orchard Portman
Thurlbear
Ashbrittle
Nightcott
Brushford
Morebath
Exebridge
Oldways End
Bampton
Yeo Mill
Bish Mill
Newtown
Bishops Nympton
Ash Mill
Alswear
Knowstone
Roachill
Oakfordbridge
Oakford
Mariansleigh
Rose Ash
Romansleigh
Meshaw
Creacombe
Rackenford
Stoodleigh
Cove
Huntsham
Hockworthy
Holcombe Rogus
Sampford Arundel
Wrangway
Ford Street
Angersleigh
Pitminster
Blagdon Hill
Corfe
Staple Fitzpaine
BLACKDOWN HILLS
Westleigh
Burlescombe
Nicholashayne
Clayhidon
Churchstanton
Fyfett
Week
Lutworthy
Queen Dart
Loxbeare
Washfield
EXE VALLEY
East Mere
Chevithorne
Whitnage
Uplowman
Appledore
Culm Valley
Culmstock
Hemyock
Stapley
Churchinford
Bishopswood
Rosemary Lane
West Worlington
East Worlington
Witheridge
Templeton Bridge
Templeton
Calverleigh
Bolham
Chettiscombe
Halberton
Sampford Peverell
Uffculme
Craddock
Ashill
Smithincott
Bolham Water
Smeatharpe
Marsh
Cheldon
Drayford
Nomansland
Thelbridge Barton
Washford Pyne
Cruwys Morchard
Withleigh
Cotteylands
Cowleymoor
Tiverton
GRAND WESTERN CANAL
Ash Thomas
Willand
Abbey
Newcott
Howley
Yarcombe
Pennymoor
Way Village
Well Town
Filleigh
Black Dog
Puddington
Eastington
Poughill
Lapford
Morchard Bishop
Woolfardisworthy
Upham
Cadeleigh
Butterleigh
Bickleigh
Cullompton
Kentisbeare
Blackborough
Sheldon
Dunkeswell
Upottery
Luppitt
Rawridge
Beacon
Stockland
Millhayes
Kennerleigh
Oldborough
Stockleigh English
Cheriton Fitzpaine
Cadbury
Colebrook
Mutterton
Westcott
Dulford
Kerswell
Broadhembury
Norman's Green
Wick
Monkton
Heathstock
Ash Bullayne
Down St Mary
East Village
Newbuildings
Stockleigh Pomeroy
Bradninch
Silverton
Up Exe
Hele
Langford
Plymtree
Payhembury
Combe Raleigh
Cotleigh
Ham
Dalwood
Copplestone
Sandford
Upton Hellions
Thorverton
Ellerhayes
Clyst Hydon
Tale
Colestocks
Awliscombe
Buckerell
Wilmington
Nymet Tracey
Knowle
Coleford
Shobrooke
Efford Shute
Nether Exe
Clyst St Lawrence
Crediton
Colebrooke
Sweetham
Brampford Speke
Rewe
Budlake
Westwood
Talaton
Feniton
Honiton
Offwell
Shute
Hillerton
Yeoford
Uton
Hookway
Newton St Cyres
Stoke Canon
Upton Pyne
Broadclyst
Fenny Bridges
Gittisham
Alfington
Whimple
Fairmile
Ottery St Mary
Church Green
Northleigh
Whitford
Venny Tedburn
Poltimore
Dog Village
Jack in the Green
Rockbeare
Cranbrook
Farway
Cowley
Hittisleigh
Tedburn St Mary
Pinhoe
Clyst Honiton
EXETER INTERNATIONAL
West Hill
Marsh Green
Wiggaton
E A S T   D E V O N
Broad Down
Southleigh
Colyton
Colyford
Whitestone
Exwick
Whipton
EXETER
Heavitree
Sowton
Clyst St Mary
Aylesbeare
Farringdon
Tipton St John
Sidbury
Venn Ottery
Harpford
Bowd
Sidford
Harcombe
Axmouth
Seaton
Cheriton Bishop
Crockernwell
Longdown
Whitestone
Drewsteignton
Whiteley
St Thomas
Countess Wear
Alphington
Ide
Clyst St George
Woodbury Salterton
Newton Poppleford
Hawkerland
Colaton Raleigh
Sid
Salcombe Regis
Branscombe
Weston
Vicarage
Beer
Beer Hd.
Seaton Bay
Dunsford
Shillingford St George
Topsham
Ebford
Woodbury
Exton
Exminster
Cotmaton
Sidmouth
DORSET & EAST DEVON COAST WORLD HERITAGE SITE
Teign
Bridfordmills
Doccombe
Moretonhampstead
Bridford
Christow
Doddiscombsleigh
Higher Ashton
Lower Ashton
Kennford
Kenn
Powderham
Lympstone
Yettington
Otterton
Ladram Bay
East Budleigh
North Bovey
Canonteign Falls
Trusham
Kenton
Starcross
Exmouth
Withycombe Raleigh
Knowle
Budleigh Salterton
Danger Pt.
SOUTH WEST COAST PATH

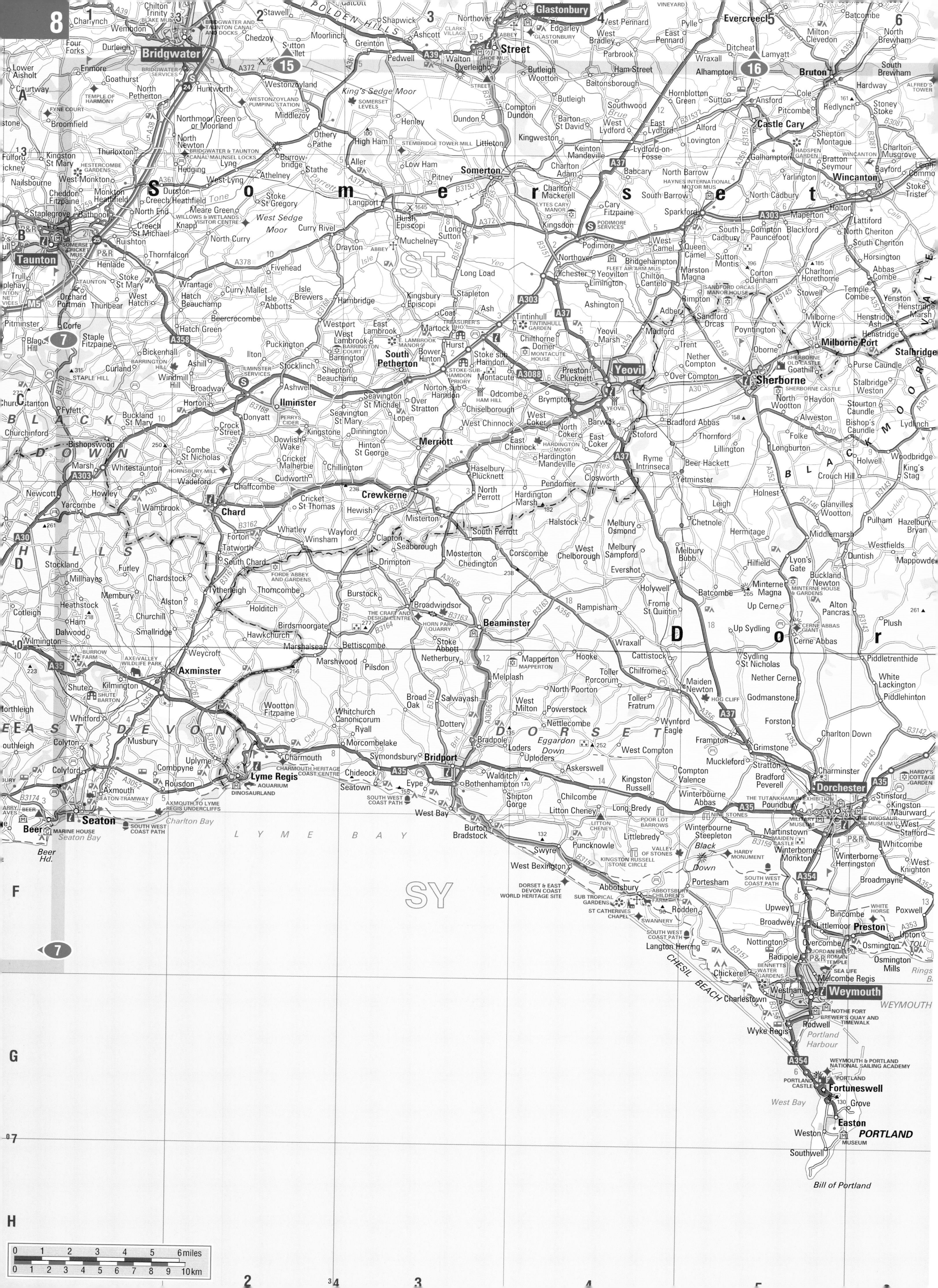
Glastonbury
Street
Bridgwater
Taunton
Somerton
Yeovil
Sherborne
Wincanton
Bruton
Castle Cary
Evercreech
Ilminster
Chard
Crewkerne
South Petherton
Merriott
Beaminster
Axminster
Bridport
Lyme Regis
Seaton
Beer
Dorchester
Weymouth
Fortuneswell
PORTLAND
Bill of Portland
Milborne Port
Stalbridge
Langport
Ilchester
Martock
Montacute
Charmouth
Chideock
Symondsbury
Abbotsbury
Chickerell
Preston
Upwey
Broadmayne
Cerne Abbas
Maiden Newton
Frampton
Yetminster
Halstock
Evershot
Broadwindsor
Drimpton
Mosterton
Misterton
Hewish
Winsham
Tatworth
Forton
Thorncombe
Hawkchurch
Kilmington
Shute
Colyton
Colyford
Axmouth
Uplyme
Musbury
Whitford
Wilmington
Stockland
Membury
Yarcombe
Whitestaunton
Buckland St Mary
Combe St Nicholas
Donyatt
Broadway
Ashill
Curry Rivel
Drayton
Muchelney
Long Sutton
Kingsdon
Podimore
Yeovilton
Limington
Tintinhull
Stoke sub Hamdon
Odcombe
Brympton
Barwick
Stoford
Bradford Abbas
Thornford
West Coker
East Coker
North Coker
Hardington Mandeville
Closworth
Chiselborough
West Chinnock
East Chinnock
Haselbury Plucknett
North Perrott
South Perrott
Corscombe
Melbury Osmond
Rampisham
Hooke
Toller Porcorum
Powerstock
Loders
Bradpole
Walditch
Bothenhampton
Shipton Gorge
Burton Bradstock
West Bay
Eype
Seatown
Morcombelake
Whitchurch Canonicorum
Litton Cheney
Long Bredy
Puncknowle
Swyre
West Bexington
Portesham
Winterborne Steepleton
Martinstown
Winterborne Monkton
Charminster
Poundbury
Stinsford
Kingston Maurward
West Stafford
Whitcombe
Osmington
Poxwell
Radipole
Melcombe Regis
Wyke Regis
Rodwell
Westham
Charlestown
Easton
Weston
Southwell
Grove
L Y M E   B A Y
SY
ST
CHESIL BEACH
Portland Harbour
West Bay
Charlton Bay
Seaton Bay
Beer Hd.
S o m e r s e t
D o r s e t
E A S T   D E V O N
B L A C K D O W N   H I L L S
B L A C K M O O R   V A L E
King's Sedge Moor
West Sedge Moor
POLDEN HILLS
Eggardon Down
Black Down
A39
A372
A361
A303
A37
A358
A30
A35
A3088
A356
A352
A354
A357
A371
A359
B3151
B3153
B3157
B3162
B3163
B3165
M5
15
16
7
A
B
C
D
E
F
G
H
1
2
3
4
5
6
0 1 2 3 4 5 6 miles
0 1 2 3 4 5 6 7 8 9 10 km

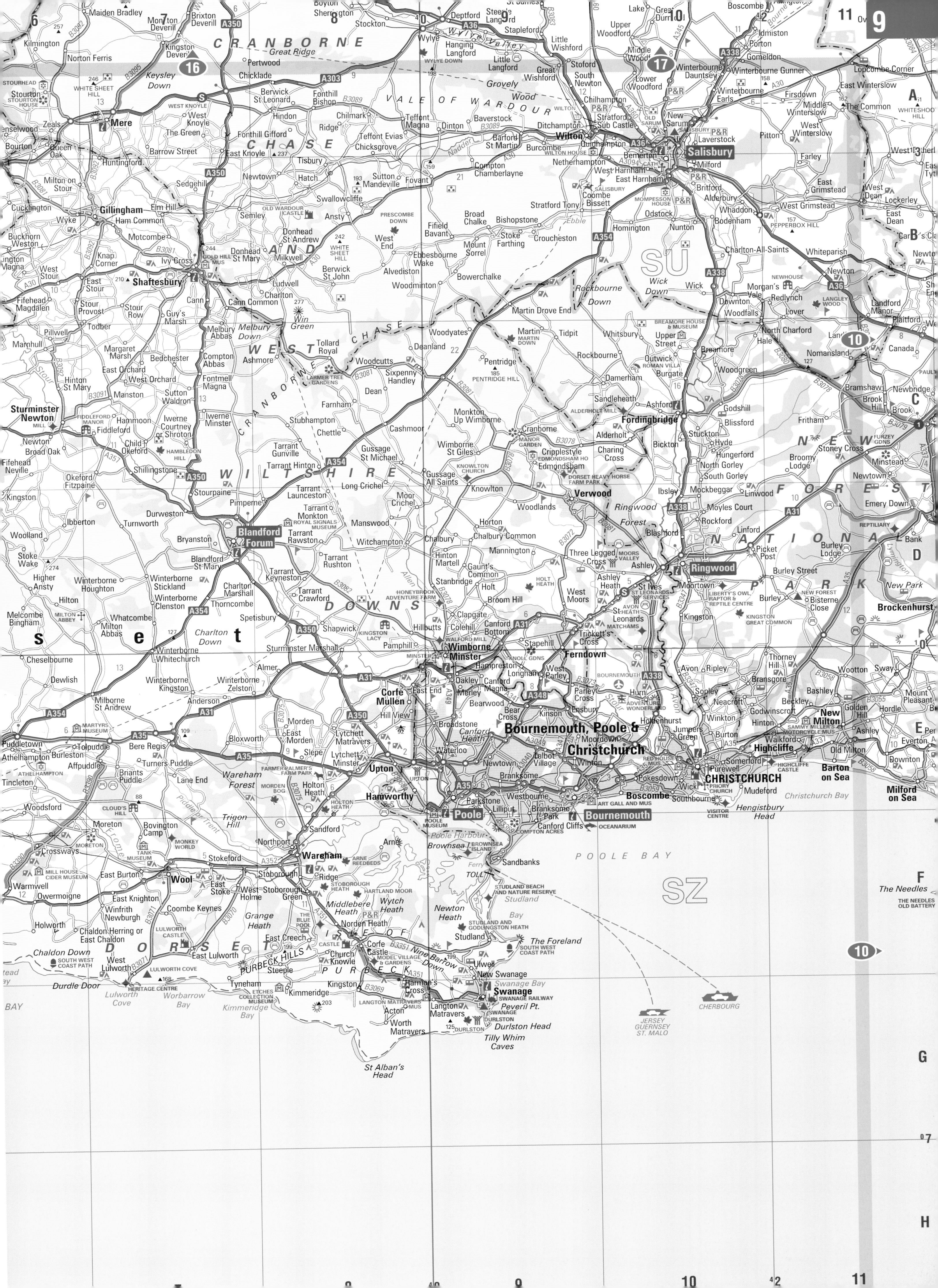

9
6
7
8
9
10
11
A
B
C
D
E
F
G
H
16
17
10
CRANBORNE CHASE
VALE OF WARDOUR
CHASE
AND
WEST CHASE
CRANBORNE
WILTSHIRE
DOWNS
DORSET
PURBECK HILLS
ISLE OF PURBECK
NEW FOREST NATIONAL PARK
SU
SZ
POOLE BAY
Maiden Bradley
Monkton Deverill
Brixton Deverill
Kingston Deverill
Kilmington
Norton Ferris
Great Ridge
Pertwood
Chicklade
Keysley Down
Stourhead
Stourton
Stourton House
White Sheet Hill
Zeals
Mere
West Knoyle
The Green
Fonthill Gifford
Hindon
Berwick St Leonard
Fonthill Bishop
Chilmark
Ridge
Teffont Magna
Teffont Evias
Dinton
Baverstock
Barford St Martin
Burcombe
Wilton
Wilton House
Chicksgrove
East Knoyle
Barrow Street
Queen Oak
Bourton
Huntingford
Milton on Stour
Sedgehill
Newtown
Tisbury
Hatch
Sutton Mandeville
Fovant
Compton Chamberlayne
Swallowcliffe
Semley
Old Wardour Castle
Ansty
Prescombe Down
Donhead St Andrew
Donhead St Mary
West End
White Sheet Hill
Ebbesbourne Wake
Fifield Bavant
Broad Chalke
Bishopstone
Stoke Farthing
Croucheston
Mount Sorrel
Alvediston
Berwick St John
Bowerchalke
Woodminton
Cucklington
Gillingham
Elm Hill
Ham Common
Wyke
Motcombe
Buckhorn Weston
Knap Corner
Ivy Cross
Gold Hill Mus
Milkwell
Shaftesbury
West Stour
East Stour
Fifehead Magdalen
Stour Provost
Stour Row
Cann
Cann Common
Ludwell
Charlton
Guy's Marsh
Todber
Pillwell
Marnhull
Melbury Abbas
Melbury Down
Win Green
Tollard Royal
Compton Abbas
Ashmore
Margaret Marsh
Bedchester
East Orchard
West Orchard
Fontmell Magna
Hinton St Mary
Manston
Sutton Waldron
Sturminster Newton
Fiddleford Manor
Fiddleford
Hammoon
Iwerne Minster
Iwerne Courtney or Shroton
Child Okeford
Hambledon Hill
Newton
Broad Oak
Fifehead Neville
Okeford Fitzpaine
Shillingstone
Stourpaine
Pimperne
Kingston
Ibberton
Turnworth
Durweston
Woolland
Bryanston
Blandford Forum
Blandford St Mary
Stoke Wake
Higher Ansty
Winterborne Houghton
Winterborne Stickland
Winterborne Clenston
Charlton Marshall
Thorncombe
Hilton
Milton Abbey
Milton Abbas
Melcombe Bingham
Whatcombe
Spetisbury
Charlton Down
Winterborne Whitechurch
Cheselbourne
Dewlish
Winterborne Kingston
Winterborne Zelston
Milborne St Andrew
Anderson
Almer
Sturminster Marshall
Shapwick
Kingston Lacy
Pamphill
Woodcutts
Larmer Tree Gardens
Sixpenny Handley
Dean
Deanland
Woodyates
Farnham
Stubhampton
Chettle
Cashmoor
Tarrant Gunville
Tarrant Hinton
Gussage St Michael
Long Crichel
Moor Crichel
Tarrant Launceston
Tarrant Monkton
Royal Signals Museum
Tarrant Rawston
Tarrant Rushton
Manswood
Witchampton
Tarrant Keyneston
Tarrant Crawford
Honeybrook Adventure Farm
Hillbutts
Colehill
Wimborne Minster
Deptford
Steeple Langford
Stapleford
Wylye
Wylye Valley
Wylye Down
Hanging Langford
Little Langford
Little Wishford
Great Wishford
Grovely Wood
Stockton
Boyton
Sherrington
Stoford
South Newton
Chilhampton
Stratford sub Castle
Old Sarum
Upper Woodford
Middle Woodford
Lower Woodford
Lake
Great Durnford
Winterbourne Dauntsey
Winterbourne Earls
Winterbourne Gunner
Gomeldon
Porton
Idmiston
Boscombe
Lopcombe Corner
East Winterslow
Firsdown
Middle Winterslow
West Winterslow
The Common
Whiteshoot Hill
Pitton
Farley
West Tytherley
New Sarum
Laverstock
Salisbury
Quidhampton
Bemerton
Netherhampton
Milford
West Harnham
East Harnham
Salisbury Cathedral
Coombe Bissett
Britford
Alderbury
Mompesson House
Stratford Tony
Odstock
Whaddon
Bodenham
Nunton
Homington
East Grimstead
West Grimstead
West Dean
Lockerley
East Dean
Pepperbox Hill
Charlton-All-Saints
Whiteparish
Newton
Wick
Wick Down
Rockbourne Down
Martin Drove End
Martin
Martin Down
Tidpit
Whitsbury
Upper Street
Breamore House & Museum
Outwick
Burgate
Breamore
Rockbourne
Rockbourne Roman Villa
Morgan's Vale
Redlynch
Newhouse
Downton
Woodfalls
Lover
Langley Wood
Landford Manor
Plaitford
North Charford
Hale
Nomansland
Canada
Pentridge
Pentridge Hill
Damerham
Woodgreen
Sandleheath
Alderholt Mill
Ashford
Fordingbridge
Godshill
Blissford
Bramshaw
Brook
Brook Hill
Newbridge
Fritham
Monkton Up Wimborne
Cranborne
Manor Garden
Wimborne St Giles
Cripplestyle
Edmondsham
Edmondsham Ho
Alderholt
Charing Cross
Stuckton
Hyde
Bickton
Hungerford
North Gorley
South Gorley
Broomy Lodge
Stoney Cross
Furzey Gdns
Minstead
Newtown
Emery Down
Gussage All Saints
Knowlton Church
Knowlton
Dorset Heavy Horse Farm Park
Verwood
Ibsley
Mockbeggar
Linwood
Moyles Court
Rockford
Ringwood Forest
Woodlands
Horton
Chalbury
Chalbury Common
Mannington
Three Legged Cross
Moors Valley
Ashley
Blashford
Ringwood
Linford
Picket Post
Burley Lodge
Burley Street
Burley
Reptiliary
Bank
Hinton Martell
Gaunt's Common
Holt Heath
Holt
Stanbridge
Broom Hill
West Moors
Ashley Heath
St Ives
St Leonards Services
Moortown
Liberty's Owl, Raptor & Reptile Centre
New Forest Bisterne Close
Kingston
Kingston Great Common
Brockenhurst
New Park
Clapgate
Canford Bottom
St Leonards
Matchams
Avon Heath
Trickett's Cross
Stapehill
Ferndown
Hampreston
Knoll Gdns
Longham
West Parley
Avon
Ripley
Thorney Hill
Wootton
Sway
Bransgore
Bashley
Mount Pleasant
Oakley
Merley
Canford Magna
Parley Cross
Bournemouth Airport
Hurn
Adventure Wonderland
Sopley
Neacroft
Godwinscroft
Hinton
Golden Hill
Hordle
Beckley
Corfe Mullen
East End
Hill View
Bearwood
Bear Cross
Kinson
Ensbury
Holdenhurst
Winkton
Jumpers Green
Burton
New Milton
Sammy Miller's Motorcycle Mus
Ashley
Walkford
Highcliffe
Highcliffe Castle
Everton
Old Milton
Downton
Broadstone
Canford Heath
Bournemouth, Poole & Christchurch
Moordown
Talbot Village
Winton
Red House Mus
Christchurch
Somerford
Purewell
Priory Church
Mudeford
Barton on Sea
Milford on Sea
Christchurch Bay
Hengistbury Head
Visitor Centre
Southbourne
Wick
Pokesdown
Boscombe
Westbourne
Branksome
Branksome Park
Canford Cliffs
Bournemouth
Oceanarium
Art Gall and Mus
Compton Acres
Lilliput
Parkstone
Poole
Poole Museum
Newtown
Waterloo
Upton
Hamworthy
Lytchett Matravers
Lytchett Minster
Morden
East Morden
Slepe
Bloxworth
Bere Regis
Turners Puddle
Lane End
Wareham Forest
Farmer Palmer's Farm Park
Morden Bog
Holton Heath
Puddletown
Tolpuddle
Martyrs Museum
Athelhampton
Burleston
Affpuddle
Briantspuddle
Tincleton
Woodsford
Cloud's Hill
Bovington Camp
Tank Museum
Monkey World
Moreton
Trigon Hill
Northport
Sandford
Wareham
Arne
Arne Reedbeds
Poole Harbour
Brownsea Island
Sandbanks
Ferry
Toll
Studland Beach and Nature Reserve
Studland
Studland Bay
Stoborough
Stoborough Heath
Ridge
West Stoborough
Stoborough Green
Hartland Moor
Crossways
Mill House Cider Museum
Stokeford
Wool
East Burton
East Stoke
West Holme
Warmwell
Owermoigne
East Knighton
Winfrith Newburgh
Coombe Keynes
Grange Heath
Middlebere Heath
Wytch Heath
Norden Heath
Newton Heath
The Blue Pool
Studland and Godlingston Heath
Holworth
Chaldon Herring or East Chaldon
Lulworth Castle
East Creech
Corfe Castle
Nine Barrow Down
Model Village & Gardens
Church Knowle
Ulwell
The Foreland
South West Coast Path
Chaldon Down
West Lulworth
East Lulworth
Steeple
New Swanage
Swanage Bay
Swanage
Swanage Railway
Durdle Door
Lulworth Cove
Heritage Centre
Worbarrow Bay
Tyneham
Kimmeridge
Kimmeridge Bay
Etches Collection Museum
Kingston
Harman's Cross
Langton Matravers Mus
Langton Matravers
Acton
Worth Matravers
Peveril Pt.
Durlston
Durlston Head
Tilly Whim Caves
St Alban's Head
The Needles
The Needles Old Battery
Jersey Guernsey St. Malo
Cherbourg
A350
A303
A36
A30
A354
A338
A345
A357
A31
A35
A348
A349
A3049
A341
A352
A351
A3066
A337
A338
B3089
B3081
B3082
B3075
B3078
B3072
B3073
B3074
B3092
B3095
B3091
B3390
B3070
B3071
B3069
B3351
B3059
B3058
B3055
B3347
B3080
B3079
B3054
B3083
B3084
P&R

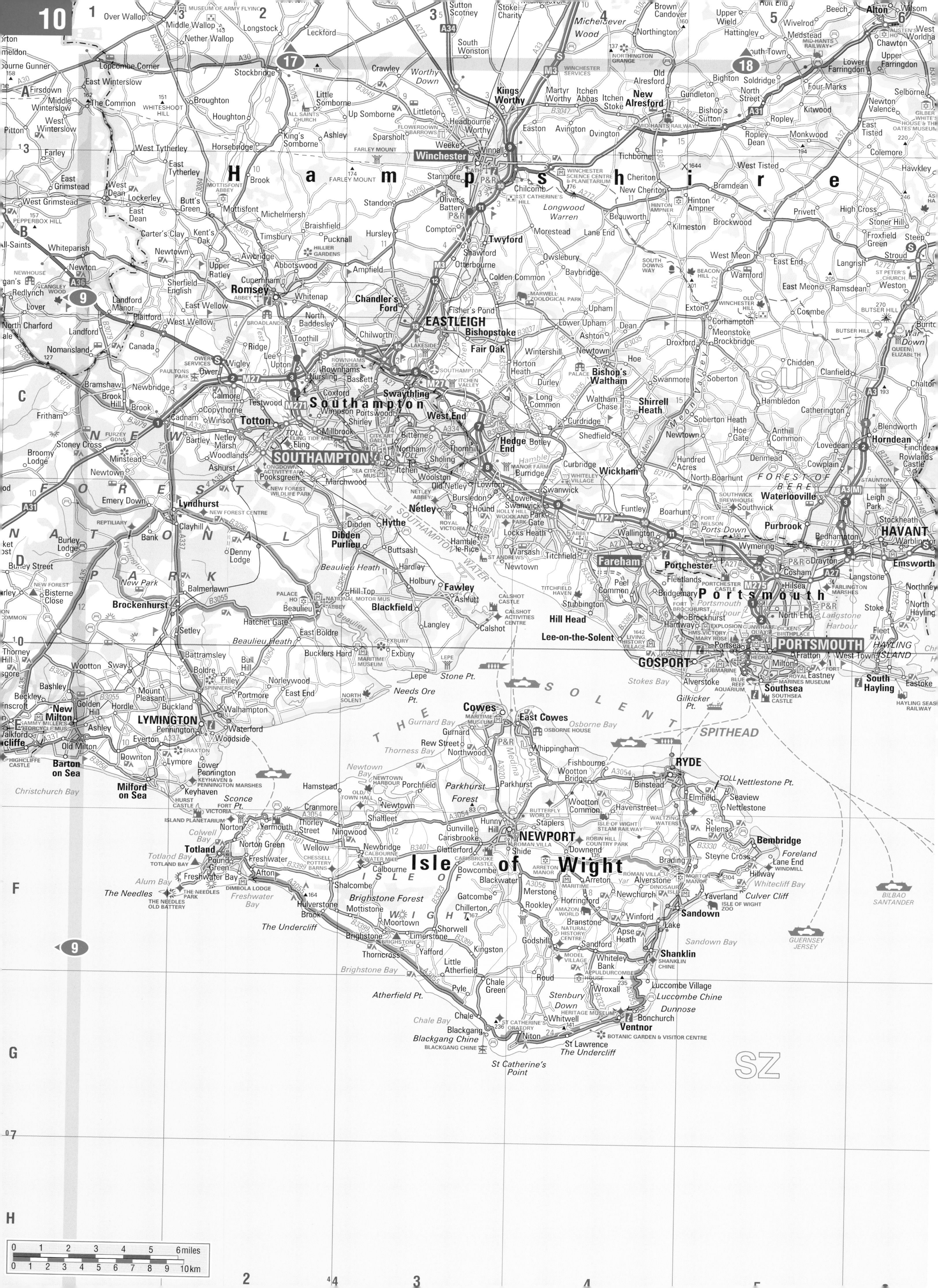

Hampshire
Over Wallop
Middle Wallop
Nether Wallop
Museum of Army Flying
Longstock
Leckford
Sutton Scotney
South Wonston
Stoke Charity
Micheldever Wood
Northington
Brown Candover
Upper Wield
Hattingley
Medstead
Wivelrod
Beech
Alton
Wilsom
Worldham
Chawton
Upper Farringdon
Lower Farringdon
Four Marks
Selborne
Newton Valence
Gilbert White's House & The Oates Museum
East Tisted
Colemore
Hawkley
Ropley
Ropley Dean
Kitwood
Monkwood
West Tisted
Bishop's Sutton
Mid-Hants Railway
North Street
Soldridge
Bighton
Gundleton
South Town
New Alresford
Old Alresford
Northington Grange
Itchen Stoke
Itchen Abbas
Martyr Worthy
Kings Worthy
Winchester Services
Worthy Down
Crawley
Little Somborne
Up Somborne
All Saints Church
Littleton
Headbourne Worthy
Flowerdown Barrows
Sparsholt
Farley Mount
Ashley
King's Somborne
Stockbridge
Lopcombe Corner
East Winterslow
Middle Winterslow
West Winterslow
Firsdown
The Common
Whiteshoot Hill
Broughton
Houghton
Horsebridge
West Tytherley
East Tytherley
Farley
Pitton
West Dean
East Dean
East Grimstead
West Grimstead
Lockerley
Butt's Green
Mottisfont
Mottisfont Abbey
Brook
Pepperbox Hill
Whiteparish
Carter's Clay
Kent's Oak
Newtown
Awbridge
Michelmersh
Timsbury
Braishfield
Pucknall
Hillier Gardens
Hursley
Ampfield
Abbotswood
Newton
Upper Ratley
Sherfield English
Cupernham
Romsey
Romsey Abbey
Whitenap
Landford Manor
Plaitford
East Wellow
West Wellow
Lover
Redlynch
Langley Wood
North Charford
Landford
Nomansland
Canada
Broadlands
North Baddesley
Chandler's Ford
Chilworth
Toothill
Ridge
Lee
Upton
Rownhams
Rownhams Services
Nursling
Bassett
Swaythling
Southampton
SOUTHAMPTON
Wigley
Ower
Ower Services
Paultons Park
Bramshaw
Brook Hill
Newbridge
Calmore
Testwood
Totton
Copythorne
Cadnam
Winsor
Fritham
Furzey Gdns
Stoney Cross
Broomy Lodge
Minstead
Bartley
Netley Marsh
Woodlands
Ashurst
Longdown Activity Farm
Pooksgreen
New Forest Wildlife Park
Marchwood
Eling
Millbrook
Shirley
Portswood
Coxford
Wimpson
Bitterne
Northam
Itchen
Sholing
Woolston
Old Netley
Netley
Netley Abbey
Royal Victoria
West End
Thornhill
Hedge End
Botley
Burridge
Manor Farm
Bursledon
Lowford
Hound
Hamble-le-Rice
Holly Hill Woodland Park
Sarisbury
Swanwick
Lower Swanwick
Park Gate
Locks Heath
Warsash
St Andrews
Newtown
Titchfield
Titchfield Abbey
Titchfield Haven
Stubbington
Hill Head
Lee-on-the-Solent
Fareham
Portchester
Portchester Castle
Fleetlands
Peel Common
Bridgemary
Brockhurst
Fort Brockhurst
Hardway
Gosport
Alverstoke
Stokes Bay
Gilkicker Pt.
Portsmouth
PORTSMOUTH
Portsmouth Harbour
HMS Victory
Mary Rose
Gunwharf Quays
Dickens Birthplace
North End
Hilsea
Cosham
Drayton
Fratton
Milton
Southsea
Southsea Castle
Royal Marines Museum
Eastney
Langstone Harbour
Langstone
Hayling Island
West Town
South Hayling
Eastoke
Hayling Seaside Railway
Stoke
North Hayling
Northney
Fleet
Emsworth
Havant
Warblington
Bedhampton
Stockheath
Leigh Park
Purbrook
Waterlooville
Cowplain
Lovedean
Horndean
Finchdean
Rowlands Castle
Blendworth
Catherington
Hambledon
Clanfield
Chalton
Chidden
Denmead
Anthill Common
Forest of Bere
Southwick
Southwick Brewhouse
Fort Nelson
Ports Down
Wymering
Boarhunt
North Boarhunt
Hundred Acres
Wickham
Soberton
Soberton Heath
Newtown
Hoe Gate
Shedfield
Curdridge
Shirrell Heath
Waltham Chase
Swanmore
Bishop's Waltham
Palace
Durley
Long Common
Horton Heath
Fair Oak
Bishopstoke
Eastleigh
EASTLEIGH
Fisher's Pond
Colden Common
Otterbourne
Shawford
Compton
Twyford
Oliver's Battery
Winchester
Winnall
Stanmore
Weeke
Chilcomb
St Catherine's Hill
Winchester Science Centre & Planetarium
Easton
Avington
Ovington
Tichborne
Cheriton
New Cheriton
Hinton Ampner
Longwood Warren
Morestead
Owslebury
Baybridge
Marwell Zoological Park
Beauworth
Lane End
Kilmeston
Bramdean
Brockwood
Privett
High Cross
Stoner Hill
Froxfield Green
Steep
Stroud
Langrish
East Meon
Ramsdean
Westbury
West Meon
Warnford
Beacon Hill
South Downs Way
Old Winchester Hill
Exton
Corhampton
Meonstoke
Brockbridge
Droxford
Meon Valley
Upham
Lower Upham
Ashton
Dean
Wintershill
Hoe
Butser Hill
Queen Elizabeth
War Down
Buriton
St Peter's Church
Coombe
Upham
Ditden
Hythe
Dibden Purlieu
Buttsash
Beaulieu Heath
Hardley
Holbury
Fawley
Ashlett
Calshot
Calshot Castle
Calshot Activities Centre
Blackfield
Langley
Hill Top
National Motor Mus
Beaulieu
Palace Ho
Abbey
East Boldre
Hatchet Gate
Bucklers Hard
Maritime Museum
Exbury
Lepe
Stone Pt.
Needs Ore Pt.
North Solent
Lyndhurst
New Forest Centre
Reptiliary
Emery Down
Clayhill
Bank
Burley Lodge
Denny Lodge
Bishop's Dale
New Park
Balmerlawn
Brockenhurst
Setley
Bisterne Close
New Forest
Burley Street
Battramsley
Bull Hill
Boldre
Pilley
Spinners
Norleywood
East End
Portmore
Walhampton
Lymington
LYMINGTON
Pennington
Buckland
Waterford
Woodside
Mount Pleasant
Sway
Wootton
Bashley
Golden Hill
Hordle
Everton
Ashley
Old Milton
New Milton
Sammy Miller's Motorcycle Mus
Barton on Sea
Downton
Lymore
Braxton
Lower Pennington
Keyhaven & Pennington Marshes
Keyhaven
Milford on Sea
Hurst Castle
Christchurch Bay
Highcliffe Castle
Bisterne
New Forest National Park
The Solent
Spithead
Cowes
East Cowes
Osborne House
Osborne Bay
Gurnard Bay
Gurnard
Rew Street
Northwood
Thorness Bay
Whippingham
Fishbourne
Wootton Bridge
Ryde
RYDE
Binstead
Nettlestone Pt.
Seaview
Nettlestone
Elmfield
St Helens
Bembridge
Foreland
Lane End
Bembridge Windmill
Hillway
Whitecliff Bay
Culver Cliff
Yaverland
Isle of Wight Zoo
Sandown
Sandown Bay
Lake
Shanklin
Shanklin Chine
Apse Heath
Winford
Newchurch
Brading
Roman Villa
Alverstone
Dinosaur Isle
Morton Manor
Steyne Cross
Havenstreet
Isle of Wight Steam Railway
Waltzing Waters
Wootton Common
Staplers
Newport
NEWPORT
Roman Villa
Robin Hill Country Park
Downend
Arreton
Arreton Manor
Merstone
Rookley
Horringford
Amazon World
Branstone
Natural History Centre
Godshill
Model Village
Sandford
Whiteley Bank
Appuldurcombe House
Wroxall
Luccombe Village
Luccombe Chine
Dunnose
Bonchurch
Ventnor
Botanic Garden & Visitor Centre
St Lawrence
The Undercliff
Stenbury Down
Heritage Museum
Whitwell
Niton
St Catherine's Oratory
St Catherine's Point
Blackgang
Blackgang Chine
Chale
Chale Bay
Chale Green
Pyle
Atherfield Pt.
Little Atherfield
Kingston
Shorwell
Yafford
Limerstone
Brighstone
Brighstone Bay
Brighstone Forest
Thorncross
Moortown
Mottistone
Chillerton
Gatcombe
Carisbrooke
Carisbrooke Castle
Gunville
Bowcombe
Blackwater
Shide
Hunny Hill
Parkhurst
Parkhurst Forest
Isle of Wight
Newtown Bay
Newtown
Old Town Hall
Porchfield
Hamstead
Shalfleet
Cranmore
Thorley Street
Ningwood
Newbridge
Calbourne Water Mill
Calbourne
Wellow
Chessell Pottery Barns
Shalcombe
Yarmouth
Norton
Norton Green
Fort Victoria
Island Planetarium
Sconce Pt.
Colwell Bay
Totland
Totland Bay
Pound Green
Freshwater
Freshwater Bay
Afton
Dimbola Lodge
Alum Bay
The Needles
The Needles Old Battery
The Needles Park
Hulverstone
Brook
The Undercliff
Winchester
Southampton Water
Hamble
Medina
Bilbao Santander
Guernsey Jersey
SU
SZ
M27
M3
M271
M275
A27
A31
A3(M)
A34
0 1 2 3 4 5 6 miles
0 1 2 3 4 5 6 7 8 9 10 km

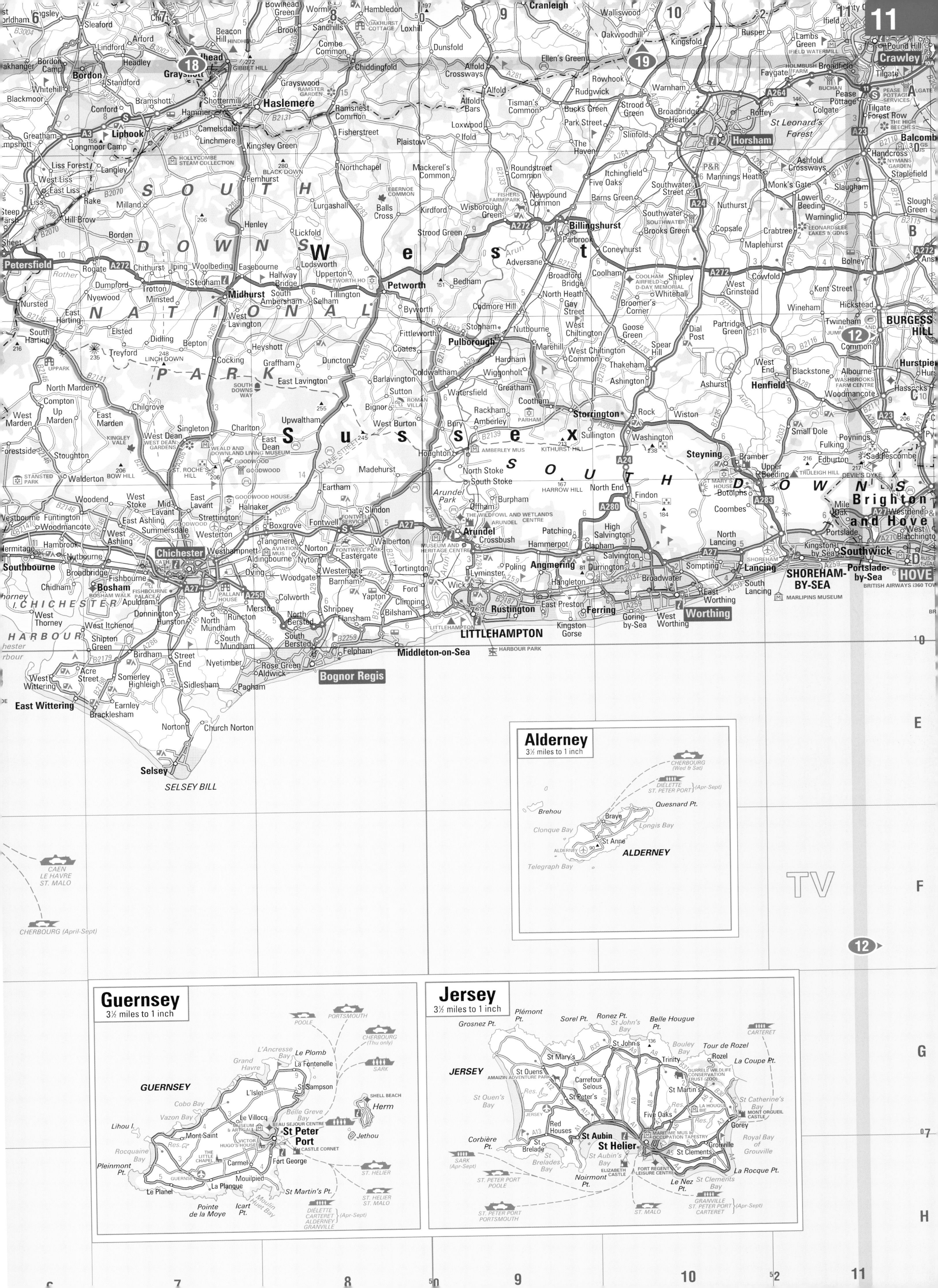

Haslemere
Liphook
Bordon
Grayshott
Petersfield
Midhurst
Petworth
Pulborough
Billingshurst
Horsham
Crawley
Chichester
Bosham
Bognor Regis
Littlehampton
Arundel
Rustington
Angmering
Worthing
Lancing
SHOREHAM-BY-SEA
Southwick
Portslade-by-Sea
HOVE
Brighton and Hove
BURGESS HILL
Henfield
Steyning
Storrington
Selsey
SELSEY BILL
East Wittering
Southbourne
Middleton-on-Sea
West Sussex
SOUTH DOWNS NATIONAL PARK
SOUTH DOWNS
CHICHESTER HARBOUR
Alderney
3½ miles to 1 inch
ALDERNEY
Braye
St Anne
Quesnard Pt.
Longis Bay
Clonque Bay
Telegraph Bay
Brehou
CHERBOURG (Wed & Sat)
DIELETTE ST. PETER PORT (Apr-Sept)
Guernsey
3½ miles to 1 inch
GUERNSEY
St Peter Port
St Sampson
L'Islet
Le Villocq
Mont Saint
Carmel
Fort George
La Planque
Le Planel
Herm
Jethou
Grand Havre
L'Ancresse Bay
Le Plomb
La Fontenelle
Cobo Bay
Vazon Bay
Lihou I.
Rocquaine Bay
Pleinmont Pt.
Pointe de la Moye
Icart Pt.
Moulin Huet Bay
St Martin's Pt.
Belle Greve Bay
POOLE
PORTSMOUTH
CHERBOURG (Thu only)
SARK
ST. HELIER
ST. HELIER ST. MALO
DIELETTE CARTERET ALDERNEY GRANVILLE (Apr-Sept)
Jersey
3½ miles to 1 inch
JERSEY
St Helier
St Aubin
St Ouens
St Mary's
St John's
Trinity
Rozel
St Martin's
Gorey
St Clements
St Peter's
Carrefour Selous
Five Oaks
Red Houses
St Brelade
Plémont Pt.
Grosnez Pt.
Sorel Pt.
Ronez Pt.
Belle Hougue Pt.
Bouley Bay
Tour de Rozel
La Coupe Pt.
St Catherine's Bay
St Ouen's Bay
Corbière Pt.
St Brelades Bay
St Aubin's Bay
Noirmont Pt.
Le Nez Pt.
La Rocque Pt.
St Clements Bay
Royal Bay of Grouville
Grouville
CARTERET
SARK (Apr-Sept)
ST. PETER PORT POOLE
ST. PETER PORT PORTSMOUTH
ST. MALO
GRANVILLE ST. PETER PORT CARTERET (Apr-Sept)
CAEN LE HAVRE ST. MALO
CHERBOURG (April-Sept)
TV
TQ

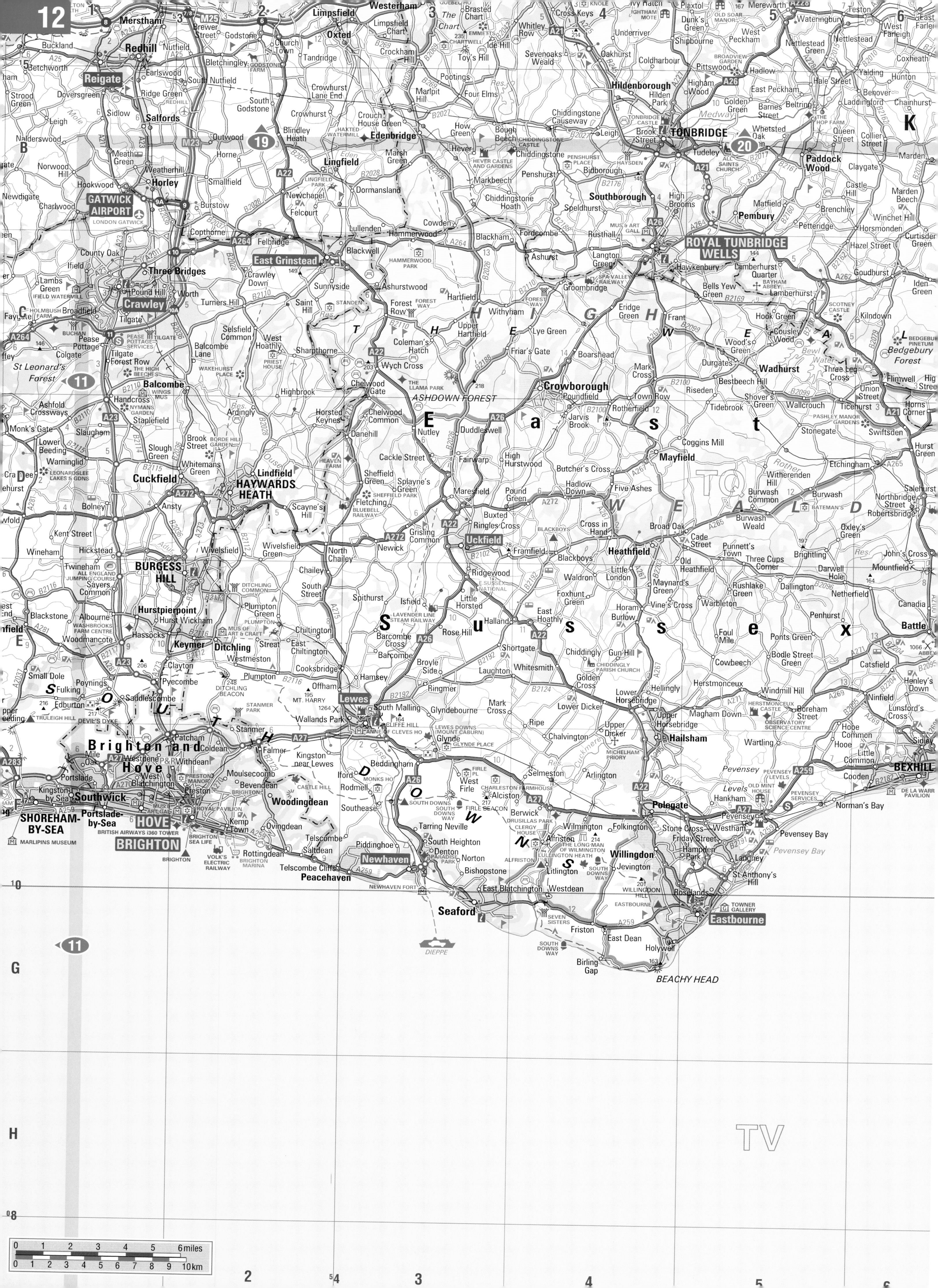

Merstham
Brewer Street
Godstone
Limpsfield
Oxted
Westerham
Limpsfield Chart
The Chart
Brasted Chart
Cross Keys
Ightham Mote
Plaxtol
Mereworth
Teston
Wateringbury
West Farleigh
East Farleigh
Buckland
Redhill
Nutfield
Church Town
Tandridge
Crockham Hill
Toy's Hill
Ide Hill
Whitley Row
Sevenoaks Weald
Underriver
Oakhurst
Coldharbour
Dunk's Green
Shipbourne
West Peckham
Nettlestead Green
Nettlestead
Coxheath
Betchworth
Reigate
Earlswood
Bletchingley
South Nutfield
Marlpit Hill
Pootings
Four Elms
Hildenborough
Hilden Park
Pittswood
Hadlow
Higham Wood
East Peckham
Hale Street
Yalding
Hunton
Strood Green
Doversgreen
Ridge Green
Crowhurst Lane End
Crowhurst
South Godstone
Sidlow
Salfords
Chiddingstone Causeway
Golden Green
Barnes Street
Beltring
Laddingford
Benover
Chainhurst
Leigh
Outwood
Blindley Heath
Crouch House Green
Haxted Watermill
Edenbridge
How Green
Bough Beech
Chiddingstone Castle
Brook Street
TONBRIDGE
Medway
Whetsted
Oak
Queen Street
Collier Street
K
Nalderswood
B
Norwood Hill
Meath Green
Horne
Weatherhill
Marsh Green
Lingfield
Hever
Hever Castle and Gardens
Chiddingstone
Penshurst Place
Haysden
Tudeley
All Saints Church
Paddock Wood
Claygate
Marden
Hookwood
Horley
Smallfield
Lingfield Park
Dormansland
Markbeech
Penshurst
Bidborough
Castle Hill
Marden Beech
Newdigate
Charlwood
GATWICK AIRPORT
London Gatwick
Burstow
Newchapel
Felcourt
Chiddingstone Hoath
Southborough
High Brooms
Matfield
Pembury
Brenchley
Winchet Hill
Copthorne
Lullenden
Hammerwood
Cowden
Blackham
Fordcombe
Speldhurst
Rusthall
Petteridge
Horsmonden
Curtisder Green
County Oak
Felbridge
East Grinstead
Blackwell
Hammerwood Park
Ashurst
Langton Green
ROYAL TUNBRIDGE WELLS
Hawkenbury
Lamberhurst Quarter
Hazel Street
Ifield
Three Bridges
Crawley Down
Sunnyside
Spa Valley Railway
Groombridge
Bayham Abbey
Lamberhurst
Goudhurst
Lambs Green
Ifield Watermill
Pound Hill
Worth
Crawley
Ashurstwood
Hartfield
Bells Yew Green
Iden Green
C
Holmbush Farm
Broadfield
Turners Hill
Saint Hill
Standen
Forest Row
Forest Way
Withyham
Eridge Green
Frant
Hook Green
Scotney Castle
Kilndown
Faygate
Tilgate
Buchan
Pease Pottage
Selsfield Common
West Hoathly
Coleman's Hatch
Upper Hartfield
Lye Green
Wood's Green
Cousley Wood
Bedgebury Pinetum
Bedgebury Forest
Colgate
Forest Row
The High Beeches
Balcombe Lane
Priest House
Sharpthorne
Wych Cross
Friar's Gate
Boarshead
Durgates
Wadhurst
Bewl Water
Three Leg Cross
Flimwell
St Leonard's Forest
Wakehurst Place
The Llama Park
Crowborough
Poundfield
Mark Cross
Bestbeech Hill
Balcombe
Highbrook
Chelwood Gate
ASHDOWN FOREST
Town Row
Riseden
Shover's Green
Union Street
Ashfold Crossways
Handcross
Nymans Garden
Ardingly
Horsted Keynes
Chelwood Common
Jarvis Brook
Rotherfield
Tidebrook
Wallcrouch
Ticehurst
Horns Corner
Staplefield
E
Nutley
Duddleswell
a
s
t
Pashley Manor Gardens
Stonegate
Swiftsden
Monk's Gate
Slaughan
Lower Beeding
Borde Hill Garden
Danehill
Coggins Mill
Hurst Green
Brook Street
Slough Green
Warninglid
Leonardslee Lakes & Gdns
Cuckfield
Whitemans Green
Lindfield
HAYWARDS HEATH
Heaven Farm
Cackle Street
Fairwarp
High Hurstwood
Butcher's Cross
Mayfield
Witherenden Hill
Etchingham
TQ
Sheffield Green
Splayne's Green
Sheffield Park
Fletching
Bluebell Railway
Hadlow Down
Five Ashes
Burwash Common
Burwash
Salehurst
Bolney
Ansty
Scayne's Hill
Maresfield
Pound Green
W
E
A
L
D
Bateman's
Northbridge Street
Robertsbridge
Kent Street
Buxted
Ringles Cross
Grisling Common
Cross in Hand
Broad Oak
Burwash Weald
Oxley's Green
Wineham
Hickstead
Wivelsfield
Wivelsfield Green
North Chailey
Newick
Uckfield
Framfield
Blackboys
Heathfield
Cade Street
Punnett's Town
Three Cups Corner
Brightling
John's Cross
Twineham
BURGESS HILL
All England Jumping Course
Sayers Common
Chailey
South Street
Ditchling Common
Ridgewood
Little London
Old Heathfield
Darwell Hole
Mountfield
Waldron
Maynard's Green
Dallington
Netherfield
Rushlake Green
Foxhunt Green
Vine's Cross
Warbleton
Canadia
Blackstone
Albourne
Washbrooks Farm Centre
Hurstpierpoint
Hurst Wickham
Plumpton Green
Spithurst
Isfield
Little Horsted
Lavender Line Steam Railway
Halland
East Hoathly
Horam
Burlow
Penhurst
Battle
Hassocks
Woodmancote
Mus of Art & Craft
Keymer
Ditchling
Streat
Chiltington
East Chiltington
S
u
s
s
e
x
Barcombe Cross
Rose Hill
Foul Mile
Ponts Green
Bodle Street Green
Catsfield
Westmeston
Cooksbridge
Barcombe
Shortgate
Chiddingly
Gun Hill
Chiddingly Parish Church
Cowbeech
Small Dole
Clayton
Pyecombe
Plumpton
Offham
Hamsey
Broyle Side
Laughton
Whitesmith
Golden Cross
Herstmonceux
Henley's Down
Poynings
Fulking
Saddlescombe
Ditchling Beacon
Mt. Harry
Lewes
Ringmer
Hellingly
Windmill Hill
Ninfield
Edburton
Truleigh Hill
Devil's Dyke
Stanmer Park
South Malling
Cliffe Hill
Glyndebourne
Mark Cross
Lower Dicker
Lower Horsebridge
Upper Horsebridge
Magham Down
Herstmonceux Castle
Observatory Science Centre
Boreham Street
Lunsford's Cross
Wallands Park
Anne of Cleves Ho
Lewes Downs (Mount Caburn)
Glynde
Glynde Place
Ripe
Chalvington
Upper Dicker
Hailsham
Hooe Common
Hooe
Sidley
Stanmer
Patcham
Coldean
Falmer
Kingston near Lewes
Beddingham
Michelham Priory
Selmeston
Arlington
Wartling
Little Common
Brighton and Hove
Withdean
Mile Oak
Westdene
Portslade
West Blatchington
Preston Manor
Moulsecoomb
Bevendean
Castle Hill
Iford
Rodmell
Monks Ho
Firle Pl
West Firle
Charleston Farmhouse
Pevensey
Pevensey Levels
Levels
Old Mint House
Cooden
BEXHILL
De La Warr Pavilion
Kingston by Sea
Southwick
Brighton
Preston
Royal Pavilion
Woodingdean
Southease
Alciston
Firle Beacon
Berwick
Polegate
Hankham
Pevensey Services
Norman's Bay
SHOREHAM-BY-SEA
Portslade-by-Sea
HOVE
British Airways i360 Tower
Kemp Town
Ovingdean
Tarring Neville
Drusillas Park
Clergy House
Wilmington
The Long Man of Wilmington
Folkington
Stone Cross
Westham
Pevensey Bay
Marlipins Museum
BRIGHTON
Brighton Sea Life
Volk's Electric Railway
Brighton Marina
Rottingdean
Telscombe
Saltdean
Piddinghoe
South Heighton
Denton
Paradise Park
Newhaven
Norton
Alfriston
Lullington Heath
Willingdon
Friday Street
Hampden Park
Langney
Telscombe Cliffs
Peacehaven
Bishopstone
Litlington
Jevington
St Anthony's Hill
Newhaven Fort
East Blatchington
Westdean
Willingdon Hill
Roselands
Eastbourne
Towner Gallery
Seaford
Seven Sisters
Friston
East Dean
South Downs Way
Holywell
Dieppe
Birling Gap
BEACHY HEAD
G
H
TV
0 1 2 3 4 5 6 miles
0 1 2 3 4 5 6 7 8 9 10 km

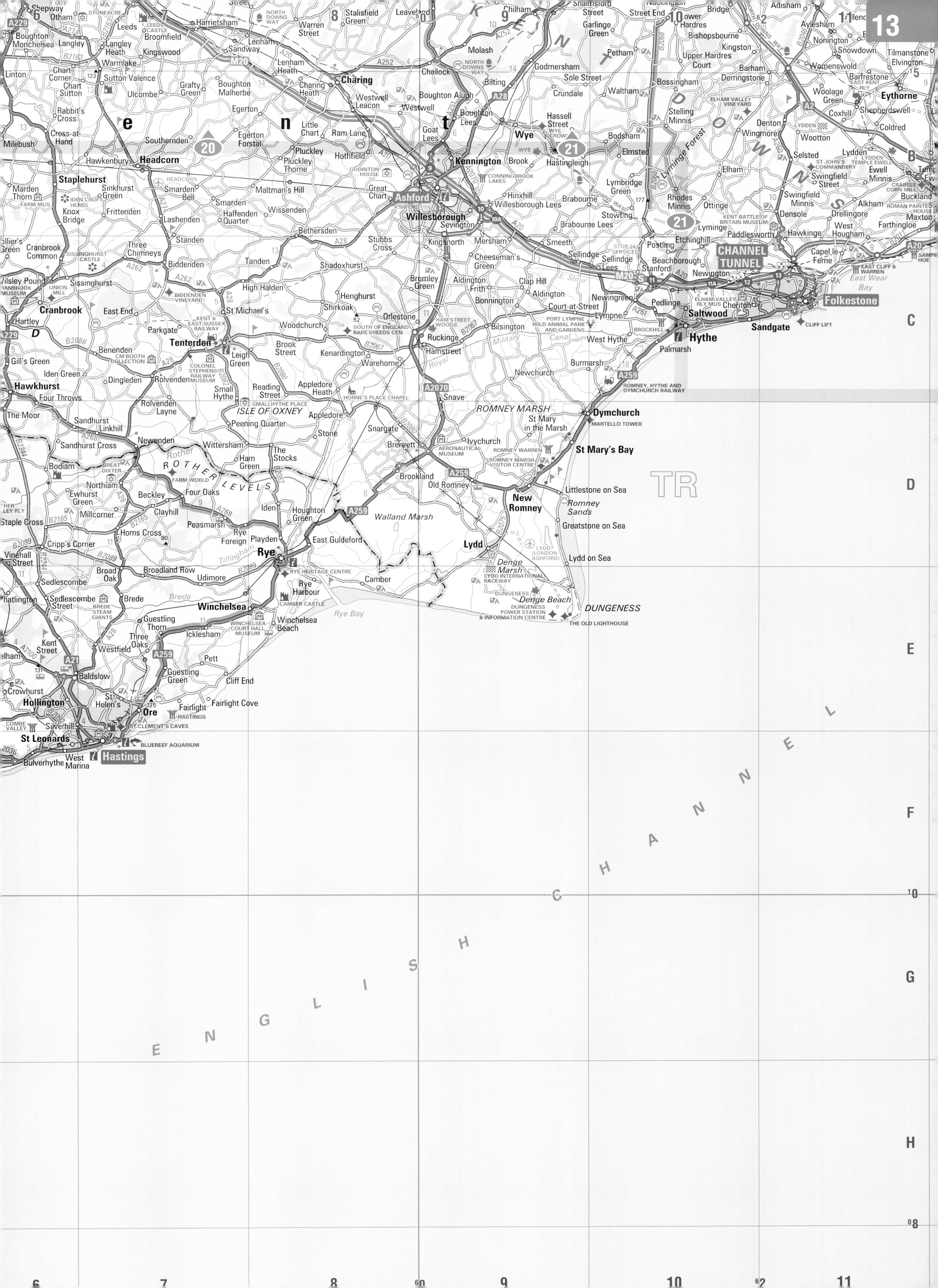
Kent
Charing
Headcorn
Staplehurst
Ashford
Willesborough
Kennington
Wye
Folkestone
Hythe
Saltwood
Sandgate
Newington
Cheriton
CHANNEL TUNNEL
Tenterden
Cranbrook
Hawkhurst
Biddenden
Sissinghurst
Rolvenden
Benenden
Appledore
ISLE OF OXNEY
ROTHER LEVELS
ROMNEY MARSH
Walland Marsh
Dymchurch
St Mary's Bay
New Romney
Littlestone on Sea
Greatstone on Sea
Lydd
Lydd on Sea
Denge Marsh
Denge Beach
DUNGENESS
THE OLD LIGHTHOUSE
Camber
Rye
Rye Harbour
Rye Bay
Winchelsea
Winchelsea Beach
Brookland
Brenzett
Ivychurch
Snargate
Old Romney
Northiam
Bodiam
Beckley
Peasmarsh
Iden
Playden
Udimore
Brede
Sedlescombe
Westfield
Guestling Green
Icklesham
Pett
Cliff End
Fairlight
Fairlight Cove
Ore
Hollington
St Leonards
Hastings
Bulverhythe
West Marina
Baldslow
Crowhurst
Silverhill
BLUEREEF AQUARIUM
Woodchurch
Shadoxhurst
Kingsnorth
Hamstreet
Ruckinge
Bilsington
Aldington
Mersham
Smeeth
Sellindge
Lympne
West Hythe
Burmarsh
Newchurch
Elham
Lyminge
Etchinghill
Hawkinge
Capel le Ferne
Densole
Swingfield Minnis
Lydden
Denton
Barham
Bossingham
Eythorne
Shepherdswell
Coldred
Pluckley
Smarden
High Halden
St Michael's
Egerton
Westwell
Boughton Aluph
Challock
Molash
Crundale
Waltham
Brabourne
Stowting
Postling
E N G L I S H C H A N N E L
TR
A20
A28
A259
A2070
A268
A21
M20
A2
20
21

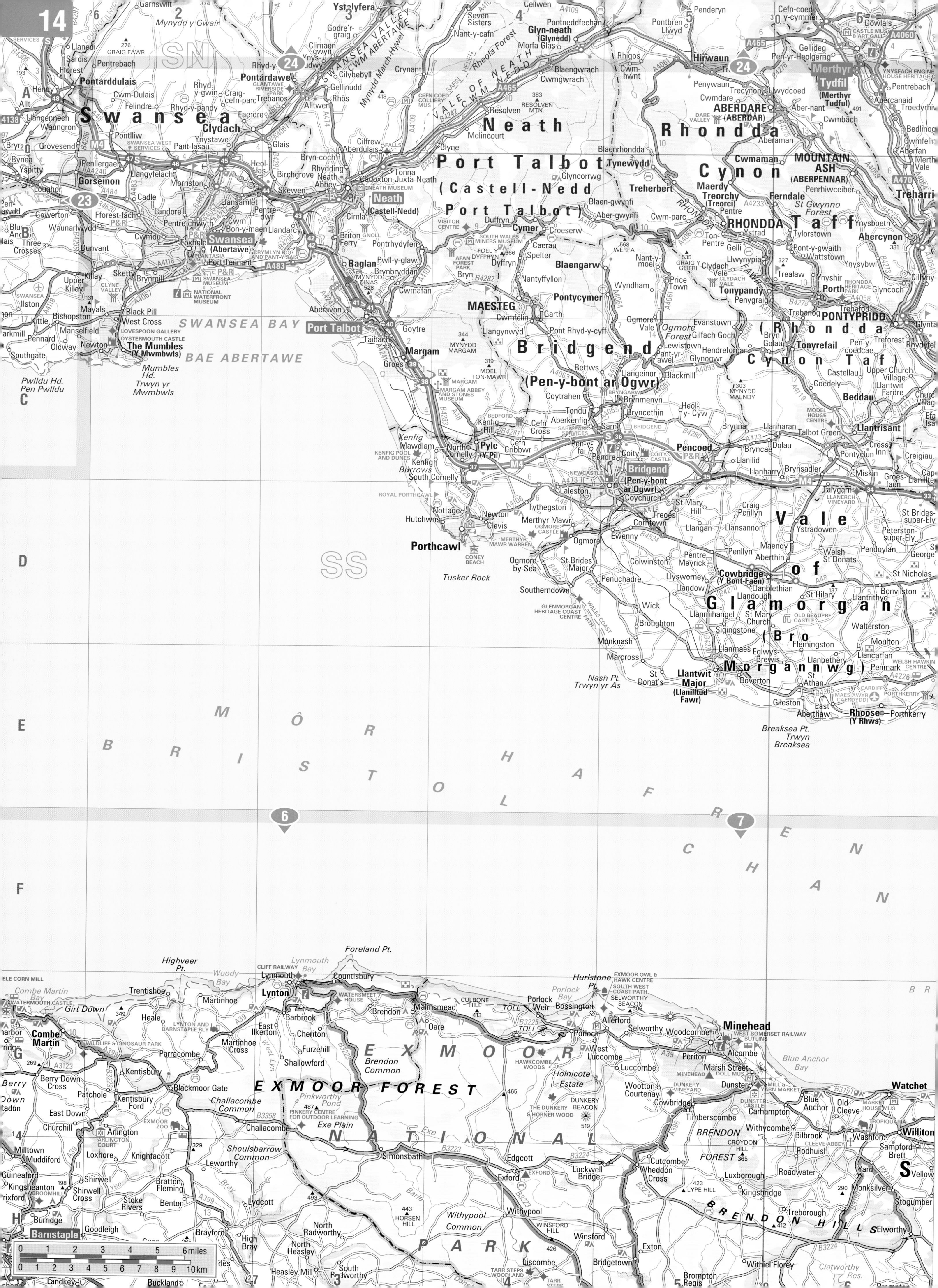
Swansea
Clydach
Pontarddulais
Gorseinon
Pontardawe
Ystalyfera
Neath
Port Talbot
(Castell-Nedd
Port Talbot)
Rhondda
Cynon
Taf
Merthyr Tydfil
(Merthyr Tudful)
Aberdare
(Aberdâr)
Mountain Ash
(Aberpennar)
Hirwaun
Glyn-neath
(Glynedd)
Maesteg
Bridgend
(Pen-y-bont ar Ogwr)
Pyle
(Y Pîl)
Porthcawl
Pontypridd
Llantrisant
Tonyrefail
Pencoed
Cowbridge
(Y Bont-Faen)
Llantwit Major
(Llanilltud Fawr)
Rhoose
(Y Rhws)
Vale of Glamorgan
(Bro Morgannwg)
Swansea Bay
Bae Abertawe
The Mumbles
(Y Mwmbwls)
Mumbles Hd.
Trwyn yr Mwmbwls
Pwlldu Hd.
Pen Pwlldu
Tusker Rock
Nash Pt.
Trwyn yr As
Breaksea Pt.
Trwyn Breaksea
SN
SS
Môr Hafren
Bristol Channel
Vale of Neath
Cwm Nedd
Swansea Valley
Cwm Abertawe
Rheola Forest
Mynydd y Gwair
Mynydd March-Hywel
Foreland Pt.
Highveer Pt.
Hurlstone Pt.
Lynmouth
Lynton
Countisbury
Combe Martin
Porlock
Porlock Weir
Minehead
Dunster
Watchet
Williton
Blue Anchor Bay
Exmoor
Exmoor Forest
Exmoor National Park
Brendon Common
Brendon Hills
Brendon Forest
Simonsbath
Exford
Withypool
Winsford
Dulverton
Barnstaple
Challacombe
Shoulsbarrow Common
Withypool Common
Pinkworthy Pond
Exe Plain
Holnicote Estate
Dunkery Beacon
Wheddon Cross
Luxborough
Clatworthy Res.
Brompton Regis
Liscombe
Tarr Steps
0 1 2 3 4 5 6 miles
0 1 2 3 4 5 6 7 8 9 10 km

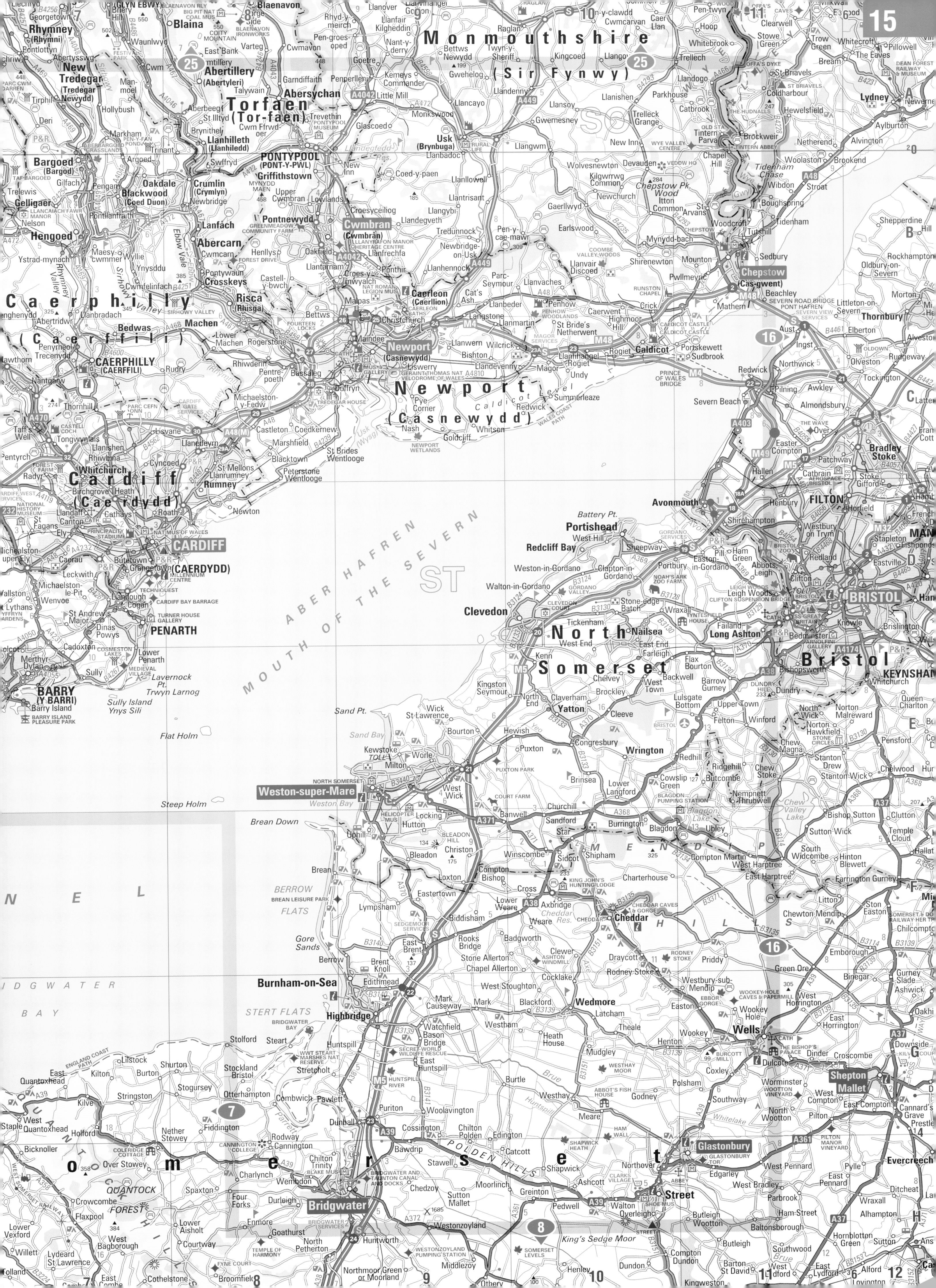

Monmouthshire
(Sir Fynwy)
Torfaen
(Tor-faen)
Caerphilly
(Caerffili)
Newport
(Casnewydd)
Cardiff
(Caerdydd)
North
Somerset
Bristol
Somerset
ABER HAFREN
MOUTH OF THE SEVERN
ST
Blaenavon
Blaina
Rhymney
(Rhymni)
Abertillery
(Abertyleri)
New
Tredegar
(Tredegar
Newydd)
Abersychan
Raglan
Usk
(Brynbuga)
PONTYPOOL
(PONT-Y-PWL)
Griffithstown
Bargoed
(Bargod)
Oakdale
Blackwood
(Coed Duon)
Crumlin
(Crymlyn)
Gelligaer
Hengoed
Pontnewydd
Cwmbran
(Cwmbrân)
Abercarn
Crosskeys
Risca
(Rhisga)
Caerleon
(Caerllion)
Machen
Bedwas
CAERPHILLY
(CAERFFILI)
Trellech
Chepstow
(Cas-gwent)
Chepstow Pk. Wood
Caldicot
Magor
Langstone
Lydney
Thornbury
Avonmouth
FILTON
Portishead
Redcliff Bay
Clevedon
Nailsea
Long Ashton
BRISTOL
Keynsham
Whitchurch
Cardiff
CARDIFF
(CAERDYDD)
PENARTH
BARRY
(Y BARRI)
Barry Island
Lavernock Pt.
Trwyn Larnog
Sully Island
Ynys Sili
Flat Holm
Steep Holm
Sand Pt.
Weston-super-Mare
Weston Bay
Brean Down
Yatton
Wrington
Congresbury
Banwell
Churchill
Blagdon
Axbridge
Cheddar
Cheddar Res.
BERROW FLATS
Burnham-on-Sea
Highbridge
STERT FLATS
BRIDGWATER BAY
Wedmore
Wells
Shepton Mallet
Glastonbury
Street
Bridgwater
POLDEN HILLS
QUANTOCK FOREST
King's Sedge Moor
Westonzoyland
North Petherton
Nether Stowey
Kilve
Stogursey
Cannington
Chew Magna
Compton Martin
West Harptree
East Harptree
Chewton Mendip
Evercreech
Pilton
Croscombe
Dinder
Wookey Hole
Westbury-sub-Mendip
Priddy
Rodney Stoke
Meare
Godney
Butleigh
Compton Dundon
M4
M48
M49
M5
M32
A48
A449
A4042
A38
A39
A37
A361
A371
A368
A370
A369
A403

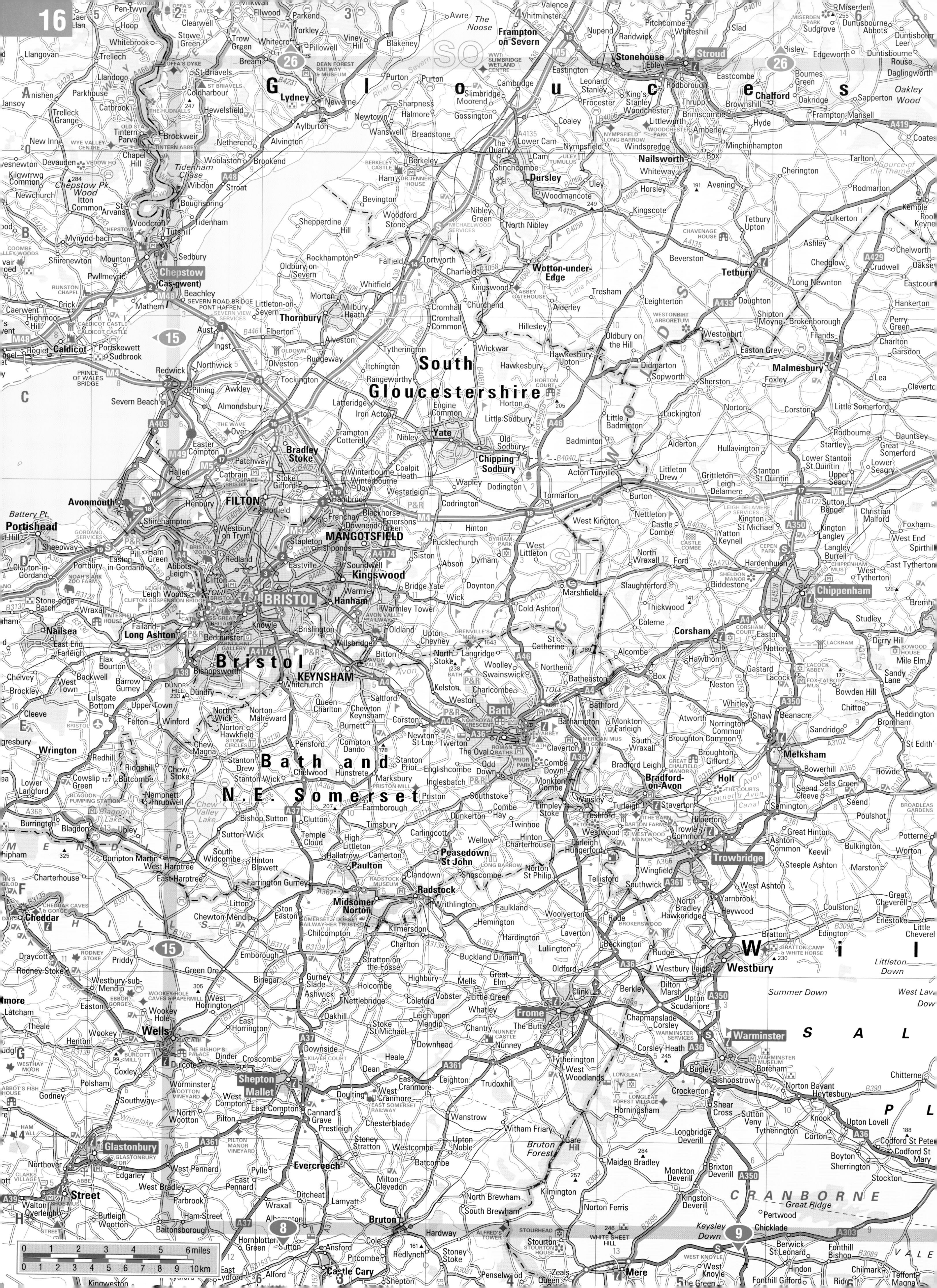

Gloucestershire
South Gloucestershire
Bristol
Bath and N.E. Somerset
Wiltshire
Mendip Hills
Cotswolds
Cranborne Chase
Salisbury Plain
Vale
Chepstow (Cas-gwent)
Lydney
Stroud
Stonehouse
Nailsworth
Dursley
Wotton-under-Edge
Tetbury
Malmesbury
Thornbury
Yate
Chipping Sodbury
Chippenham
Corsham
Melksham
Trowbridge
Bradford-on-Avon
Westbury
Warminster
Frome
Radstock
Midsomer Norton
Peasedown St John
Paulton
Keynsham
Bath
Kingswood
Mangotsfield
Filton
Avonmouth
Portishead
Nailsea
Long Ashton
Cheddar
Wells
Shepton Mallet
Glastonbury
Street
Bruton
Castle Cary
Mere
Evercreech
Caldicot
Frampton on Severn
Chalford
Severn Beach
Hanham
Holt
Tidenham Chase
Chepstow Pk. Wood
Oakley Wood
Bruton Forest
Great Ridge
Summer Down
Littleton Down
West Lavington Down
Keysley Down
The Noose
Battery Pt.
Blagdon Lake
Chew Valley Lake
Kennet & Avon Canal
15
26
8
9
0 1 2 3 4 5 6 miles
0 1 2 3 4 5 6 7 8 9 10 km

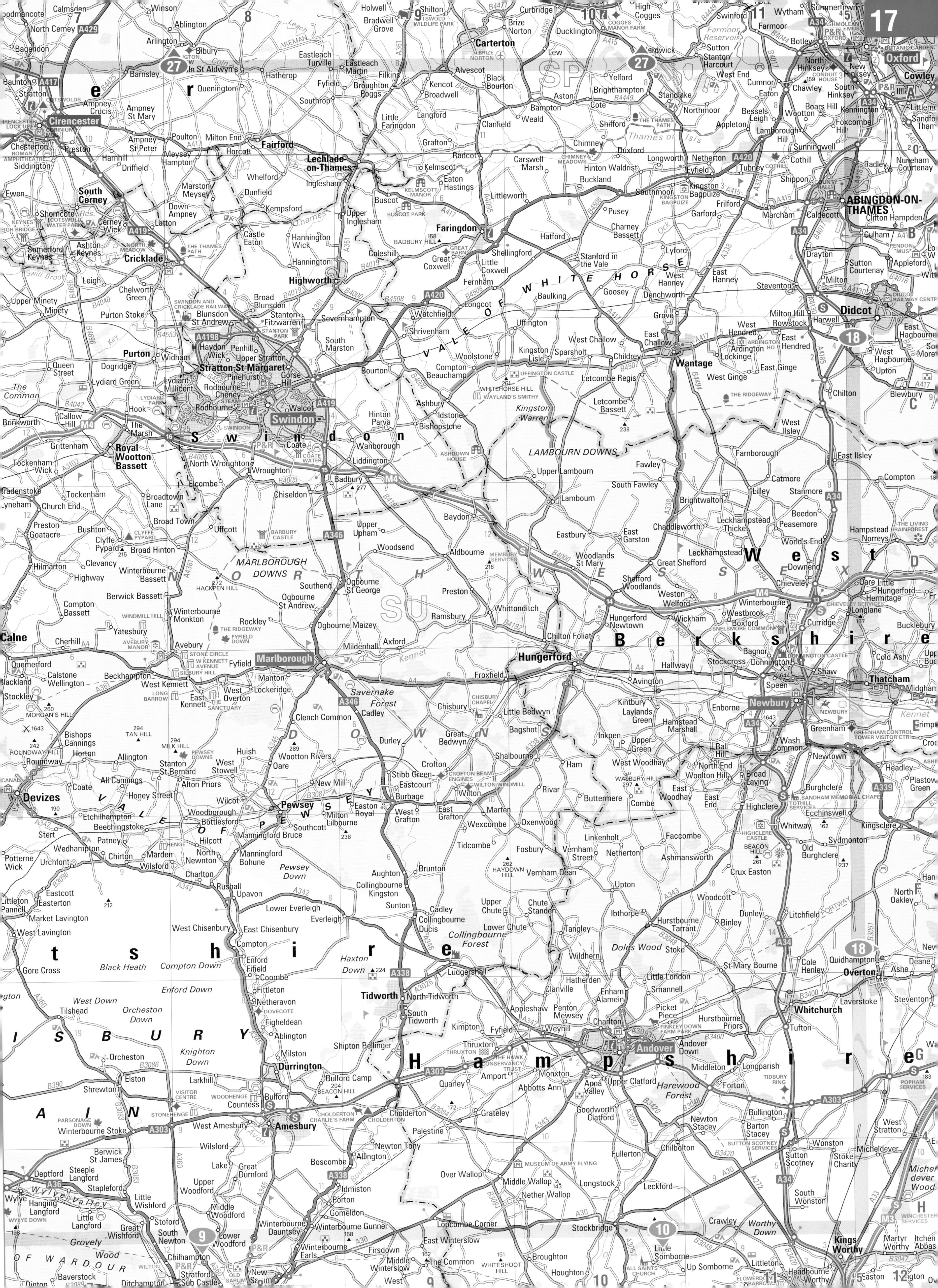
Calmsden
Winson
Ablington
North Cerney
Bagendon
Arlington
Bibury
Barnsley
Coln St Aldwyn's
Hatherop
Quenington
Baunton
Stratton
Cirencester
Ampney Crucis
Ampney St Mary
Ampney St Peter
Poulton
Milton End
Fairford
Horcott
Meysey Hampton
Chesterton
Preston
Harnhill
Driffield
Siddington
South Cerney
Marston Meysey
Dunfield
Whelford
Kempsford
Down Ampney
Latton
Ewen
Shorncote
Cerney Wick
Ashton Keynes
Somerford Keynes
Cricklade
Leigh
Chelworth Green
Upper Minety
Minety
Purton Stoke
Blunsdon St Andrew
Broad Blunsdon
Castle Eaton
Hannington Wick
Hannington
Highworth
Stanton Fitzwarren
Sevenhampton
Purton
Widham
Haydon Wick
Penhill
Upper Stratton
Stratton St Margaret
Queen Street
Dogridge
Lydiard Green
Lydiard Millicent
Pinehurst
Gorse Hill
Rodbourne Cheney
Rodbourne
The Common
Hook
Callow Hill
Walcot
Swindon
Brinkworth
The Marsh
Grittenham
Royal Wootton Bassett
Tockenham Wick
Coate
Wanborough
Liddington
North Wroughton
Wroughton
Elcombe
Badbury
Chiseldon
Tockenham
Church End
Broadtown Lane
Broad Town
Uffcott
Preston
Goatacre
Bushton
Clyffe Pypard
Broad Hinton
Hilmarton
Clevancy
Highway
Winterbourne Bassett
Marlborough Downs
Hackpen Hill
Compton Bassett
Berwick Bassett
Winterbourne Monkton
Rockley
Yatesbury
Calne
Cherhill
Avebury
Quemerford
Calstone Wellington
Beckhampton
West Kennett
East Kennett
West Overton
Lockeridge
Fyfield
Marlborough
Manton
Stockley
Morgan's Hill
Tan Hill
Milk Hill
Bishops Cannings
Roundway
Horton
Allington
Stanton St Bernard
West Stowell
Huish
Oare
Wootton Rivers
All Cannings
Alton Priors
Coate
Honey Street
Wilcot
Devizes
Vale of Pewsey
Woodborough
Bottlesford
Pewsey
Etchilhampton
Beechingstoke
Manningford Bruce
Southcott
Milton Lilbourne
Easton Royal
Stert
Patney
Hilcott
Chirton
Marden
North Newnton
Wedhampton
Manningford Bohune
Potterne Wick
Urchfont
Wilsford
Charlton
Rushall
Upavon
Pewsey Down
Eastcott
Easterton
Littleton Pannell
Market Lavington
West Lavington
West Chisenbury
East Chisenbury
Compton
Enford
Fifield
Coombe
Black Heath
Compton Down
Gore Cross
Enford Down
Fittleton
Netheravon
West Down
Tilshead
Orcheston Down
Figheldean
Ablington
Knighton Down
Orcheston
Milston
Durrington
Elston
Larkhill
Shrewton
Bulford Camp
Bulford
Countess
Stonehenge
Amesbury
West Amesbury
Winterbourne Stoke
Wilsford
Berwick St James
Lake
Great Durnford
Upper Woodford
Middle Woodford
Lower Woodford
Deptford
Steeple Langford
Stapleford
Wylye
Wylye Valley
Hanging Langford
Little Wishford
Little Langford
Great Wishford
Stoford
South Newton
Grovely Wood
Chilhampton
Stratford sub Castle
Baverstock
Ditchampton
Old Sarum
Holwell
Bradwell Grove
Shilton
Cotswold Wildlife Park
Curbridge
Brize Norton
Carterton
Ducklington
High Cogges
Swinford
Wytham
Farmoor
Farmoor Reservoir
Sutton
Stanton Harcourt
Hardwick
Eastleach Turville
Eastleach Martin
Filkins
Alvescot
Kencot
Broadwell
Black Bourton
Fyfield
Broughton Poggs
Southrop
Little Faringdon
Langford
Grafton
Clanfield
Weald
Bampton
Aston
Cote
Yelford
Brighthampton
Standlake
Northmoor
Shifford
Chimney
Duxford
Thames or Isis
Lechlade-on-Thames
Inglesham
Kelmscott
Radcot
Eaton Hastings
Buscot
Carswell Marsh
Hinton Waldrist
Buckland
Longworth
Netherton
Fyfield
Tubney
Kingston Bagpuize
Southmoor
Upper Inglesham
Littleworth
Faringdon
Coleshill
Great Coxwell
Little Coxwell
Shellingford
Hatford
Pusey
Charney Bassett
Garford
Frilford
Marcham
Stanford in the Vale
Lyford
Fernham
Baulking
Goosey
West Hanney
East Hanney
Denchworth
Longcot
Watchfield
Shrivenham
Uffington
Vale of White Horse
South Marston
Bourton
Compton Beauchamp
Woolstone
Kingston Lisle
Sparsholt
West Challow
East Challow
Childrey
Grove
Wantage
Letcombe Regis
Letcombe Bassett
Uffington Castle
Whitehorse Hill
Wayland's Smithy
Kingston Warren
Ashbury
Idstone
Bishopstone
Hinton Parva
Ashdown House
Lambourn Downs
Upper Lambourn
Lambourn
Fawley
South Fawley
Baydon
Upper Upham
Woodsend
Aldbourne
Membury Services
Eastbury
East Garston
Woodlands St Mary
Great Shefford
Shefford Woodlands
Weston
Welford
Ogbourne St George
Ogbourne St Andrew
Southend
Ogbourne Maizey
Preston
Ramsbury
Whittonditch
Chilton Foliat
Hungerford
Hungerford Newtown
Axford
Mildenhall
Froxfield
Savernake Forest
Cadley
Chisbury
Little Bedwyn
Great Bedwyn
Bagshot
Durley
Clench Common
Crofton
Shalbourne
Ham
Stibb Green
Eastcourt
Burbage
Wilton
West Grafton
East Grafton
Marten
Wexcombe
Oxenwood
Tidcombe
Fosbury
Vernham Street
Vernham Dean
Haydown Hill
Linkenholt
Netherton
Faccombe
Ashmansworth
Crux Easton
Upton
Aughton
Collingbourne Kingston
Brunton
Sunton
Cadley
Collingbourne Ducis
Collingbourne Forest
Upper Chute
Chute Standen
Lower Chute
Tangley
Ibthorpe
Hurstbourne Tarrant
Doles Wood
Stoke
Haxton Down
Ludgershall
Wildhern
Hatherden
Clanville
Tidworth
North Tidworth
South Tidworth
Penton Mewsey
Appleshaw
Enham Alamein
Smannell
Kimpton
Fyfield
Weyhill
Charlton
Andover
Thruxton
Shipton Bellinger
Quarley
Amport
Monxton
Abbotts Ann
Anna Valley
Upper Clatford
Goodworth Clatford
Grateley
Cholderton
Palestine
Newton Tony
Allington
Boscombe
Idmiston
Porton
Gomeldon
Winterbourne Dauntsey
Winterbourne Gunner
Winterbourne Earls
Over Wallop
Middle Wallop
Nether Wallop
Fullerton
Longstock
Leckford
Lopcombe Corner
Stockbridge
East Winterslow
Firsdown
Middle Winterslow
The Common
Broughton
Houghton
Little Somborne
Up Somborne
Oxford
Cowley
Botley
North Hinksey
New Hinksey
Cumnor
Chawley
Eaton
South Hinksey
Boars Hill
Kennington
Wootton
Bessels Leigh
Appleton
Foxcombe Hill
Sunningwell
Radley
Nuneham Courtenay
Shippon
Abingdon-on-Thames
Caldecott
Clifton Hampden
Culham
Drayton
Sutton Courtenay
Appleford
Milton
Steventon
Didcot
Milton Hill
Rowstock
Harwell
West Hendred
East Hendred
Ardington
Lockinge
West Ginge
East Ginge
West Hagbourne
East Hagbourne
Upton
Chilton
Blewbury
The Ridgeway
West Ilsley
East Ilsley
Farnborough
Catmore
Compton
Lilley
Stanmore
Brightwalton
Beedon
Peasemore
Leckhampstead Thicket
Chaddleworth
Leckhampstead
World's End
Downend
Hampstead Norreys
Chieveley
Oare
Hermitage
Little Hungerford
Winterbourne
Westbrook
Boxford
Longlane
Wickham
Curridge
Bucklebury
Berkshire
West
Bagnor
Donnington
Stockcross
Halfway
Cold Ash
Avington
Speen
Shaw
Thatcham
Midgham
Newbury
Kintbury
Laylands Green
Enborne
Hamstead Marshall
Inkpen
Upper Green
Greenham
Ball Hill
Wash Common
Newtown
West Woodhay
North End
Woolton Hill
Broad Laying
East Woodhay
Headley
Burghclere
Plastow Green
Rivar
Buttermere
Combe
East End
Highclere
Ecchinswell
Whitway
Kingsclere
Sydmonton
Old Burghclere
Beacon Hill
Woodcott
Dunley
Litchfield
Binley
North Oakley
St Mary Bourne
Little London
Cole Henley
Quidhampton
Overton
Deane
Ashe
Laverstoke
Freefolk
Whitchurch
Picket Piece
Hurstbourne Priors
Tufton
Andover Down
Middleton
Longparish
Harewood Forest
Forton
Bullington
Barton Stacey
Newton Stacey
Chilbolton
Wonston
Sutton Scotney
Micheldever
Stoke Charity
West Stratton
South Wonston
Crawley
Worthy Down
Kings Worthy
Headbourne Worthy
Littleton
Martyr Worthy
Itchen Abbas
Easton
Hampshire
Swindon
Wiltshire
Salisbury Plain
Marlborough Downs

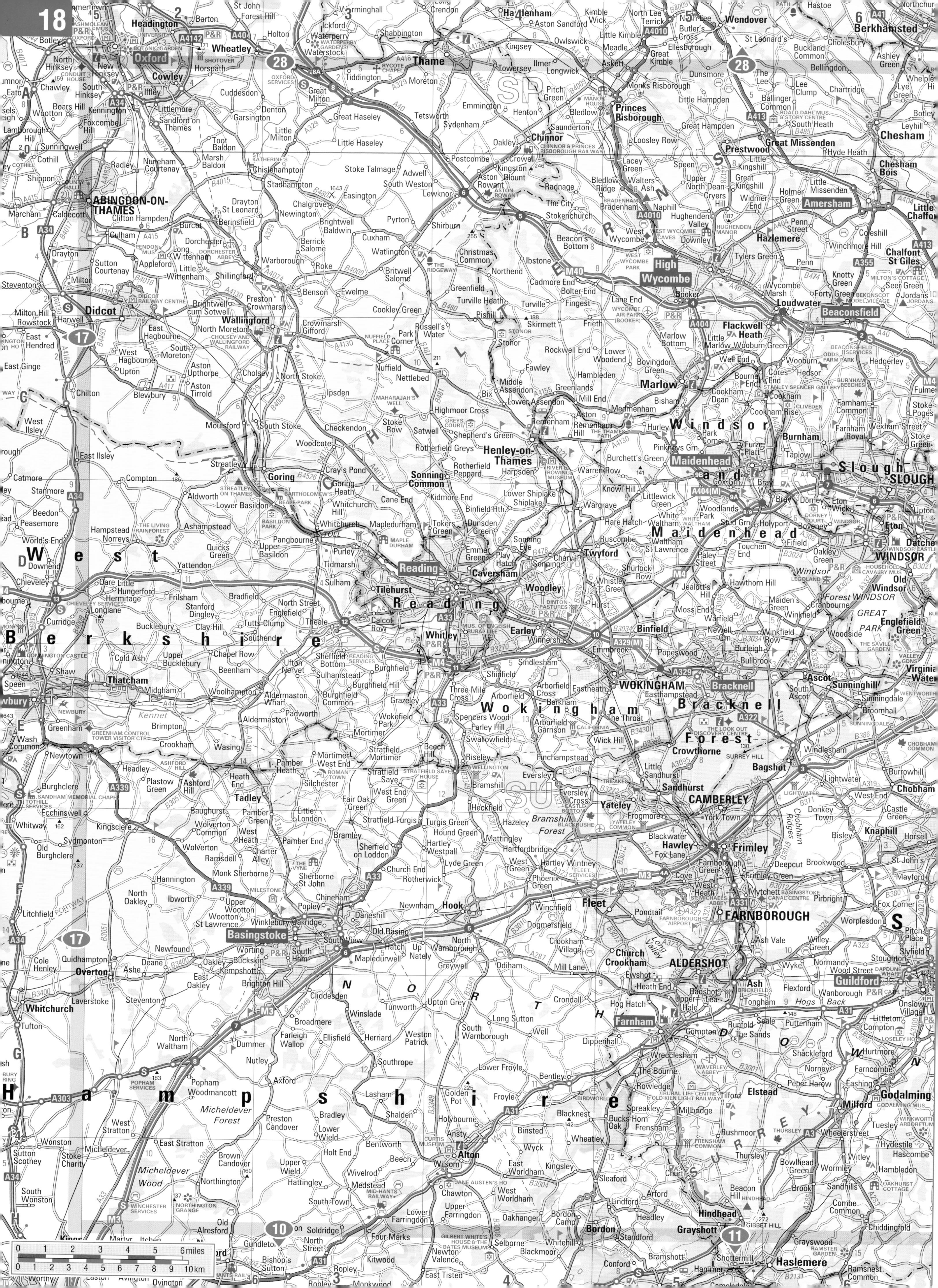

18
Oxford
Headington
Wheatley
Cowley
Thame
Wendover
Berkhamsted
Princes Risborough
Chinnor
Chesham
Great Missenden
Amersham
ABINGDON-ON-THAMES
Didcot
Wallingford
High Wycombe
Beaconsfield
Marlow
Henley-on-Thames
Maidenhead
Slough
SLOUGH
WINDSOR
Reading
Caversham
Woodley
Twyford
Goring
Pangbourne
West Berkshire
Thatcham
Newbury
WOKINGHAM
Bracknell
Wokingham
Bracknell Forest
Windsor and Maidenhead
Ascot
Sandhurst
CAMBERLEY
Frimley
Yateley
Fleet
Hook
FARNBOROUGH
ALDERSHOT
Farnham
Basingstoke
Tadley
Overton
Whitchurch
Alton
Bordon
Hindhead
Haslemere
Godalming
Guildford
Hampshire
SURREY
NORTH DOWNS
CHILTERN HILLS
SP
SU
28
17
10
11
0 1 2 3 4 5 6 miles
0 1 2 3 4 5 6 7 8 9 10 km

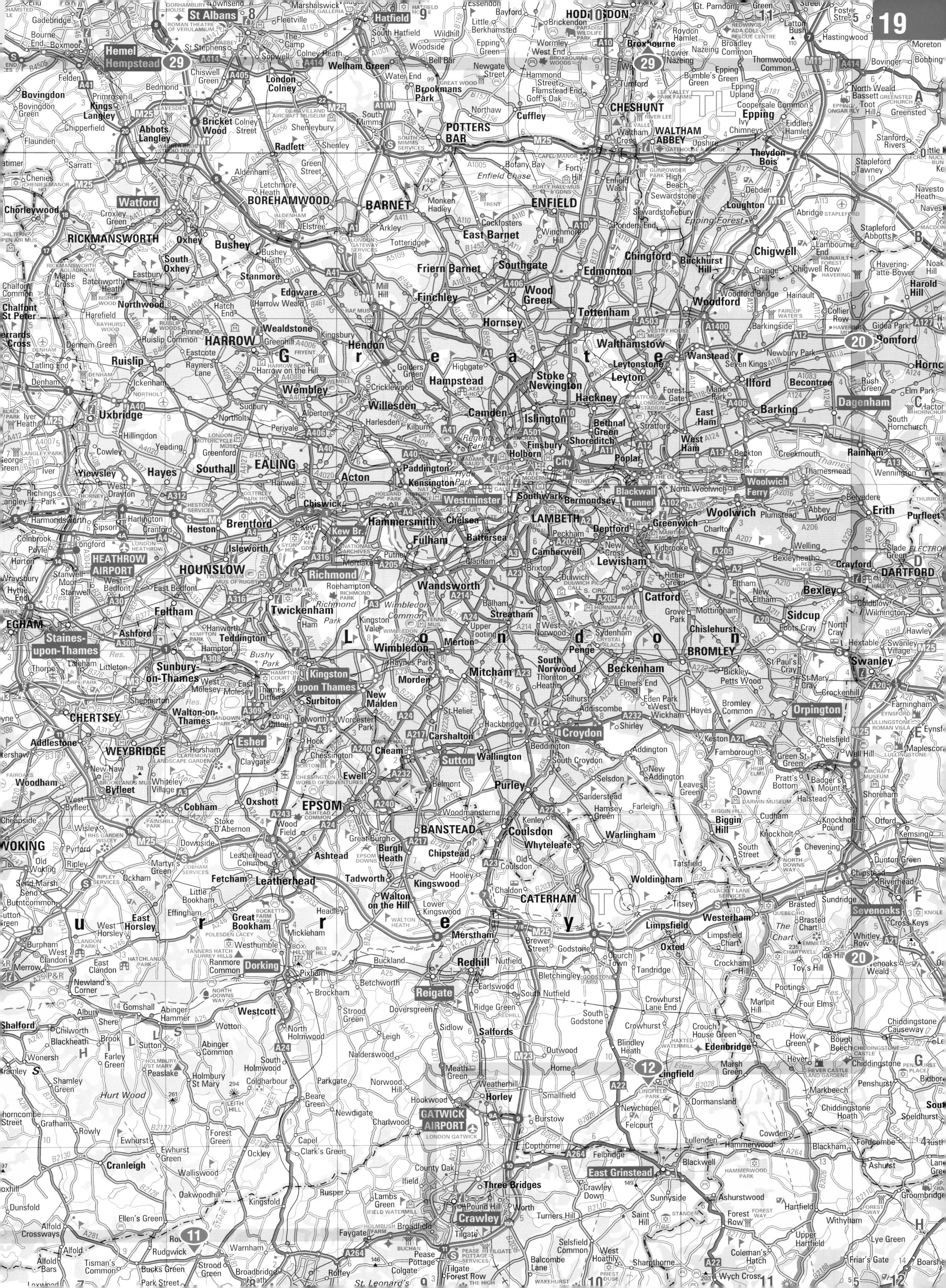
St Albans
Hatfield
Hemel Hempstead
HODDESDON
Broxbourne
Cheshunt
WALTHAM ABBEY
POTTERS BAR
Watford
RICKMANSWORTH
BOREHAMWOOD
BARNET
ENFIELD
Epping
Loughton
Chigwell
Chingford
Edmonton
Southgate
Friern Barnet
Finchley
Wood Green
Tottenham
Walthamstow
Woodford
Romford
Ilford
Barking
Dagenham
HARROW
Wealdstone
Hendon
Hornsey
Stoke Newington
Hackney
Leytonstone
Leyton
Ruislip
Uxbridge
Wembley
Willesden
Hampstead
Camden
Islington
Bethnal Green
Shoreditch
Stratford
East Ham
West Ham
Poplar
City
Holborn
Finsbury
Paddington
Kensington
Westminster
Southwark
Bermondsey
LAMBETH
Chelsea
Hammersmith
Fulham
Battersea
Camberwell
Peckham
Deptford
Greenwich
Woolwich
Lewisham
Catford
Erith
DARTFORD
Bexley
Sidcup
Chislehurst
BROMLEY
Beckenham
Penge
Sydenham
Streatham
Brixton
Clapham
Wandsworth
Wimbledon
Merton
Mitcham
Morden
Richmond
Twickenham
HOUNSLOW
HEATHROW AIRPORT
Feltham
Hayes
Southall
EALING
Acton
Chiswick
Brentford
Isleworth
Kew Br.
Kingston upon Thames
Surbiton
New Malden
Sutton
Carshalton
Croydon
Purley
Coulsdon
Caterham
Orpington
Swanley
Sevenoaks
Westerham
Oxted
Edenbridge
Lingfield
East Grinstead
Crawley
Three Bridges
GATWICK AIRPORT
Horley
Redhill
Reigate
Merstham
BANSTEAD
EPSOM
Ewell
Cheam
Leatherhead
Ashtead
Dorking
Esher
Cobham
WEYBRIDGE
CHERTSEY
Addlestone
Byfleet
WOKING
EGHAM
Staines-upon-Thames
Ashford
Sunbury-on-Thames
Walton-on-Thames
Cranleigh
Horsham
Great Bookham
East Horsley
Greater London
Surrey
Blackwall Tunnel
Woolwich Ferry
M25
M1
M4
M3
M23
M20
M11
A1(M)
TL
TQ

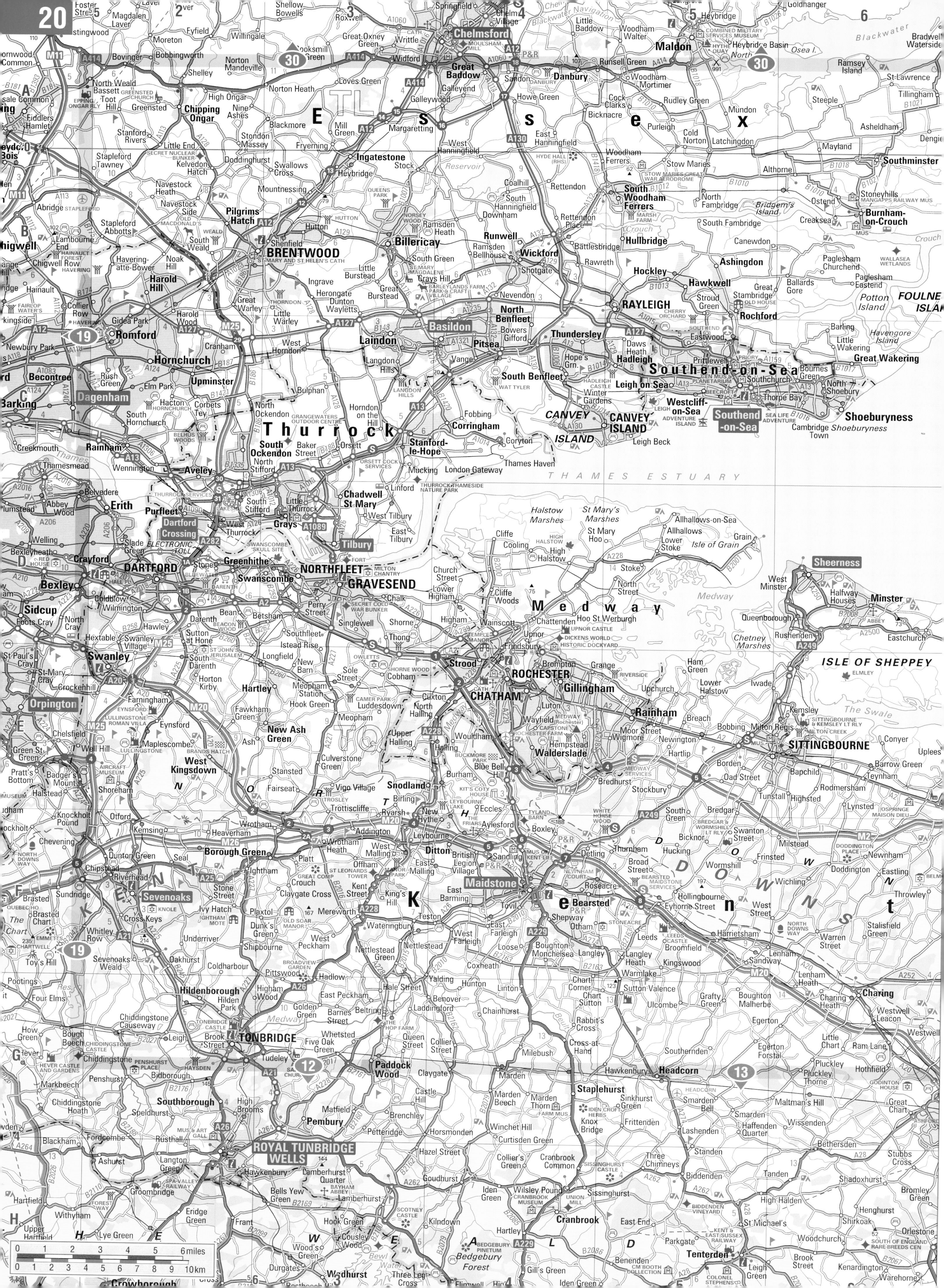
Chelmsford
Great Baddow
Maldon
Heybridge
Heybridge Basin
Danbury
Little Baddow
Woodham Walter
Writtle
Widford
Galleyend
Galleywood
Sandon
Howe Green
Margaretting
Ingatestone
Fryerning
Mill Green
Blackmore
Stock
West Hanningfield
East Hanningfield
Woodham Mortimer
Cock Clarks
Rudley Green
Bicknacre
Purleigh
Cold Norton
Latchingdon
Mundon
Steeple
Mayland
Asheldham
Southminster
Althorne
Stow Maries
Woodham Ferrers
Rettendon
South Woodham Ferrers
North Fambridge
South Fambridge
Burnham-on-Crouch
Creeksea
Ostend
Stoneyhills
Bradwell Waterside
Ramsey Island
St Lawrence
Tillingham
Dengie
Osea I.
Blackwater
Essex
Chipping Ongar
Greensted
High Ongar
Norton Mandeville
Norton Heath
Bovinger
Bobbingworth
Moreton
Fyfield
Willingale
Magdalen Laver
Shelley
North Weald Bassett
Toot Hill
Epping
Nine Ashes
Stondon Massey
Stanford Rivers
Little End
Kelvedon Hatch
Stapleford Tawney
Doddinghurst
Navestock Heath
Navestock Side
Swallows Cross
Mountnessing
Pilgrims Hatch
Stapleford Abbotts
Abridge
Lambourne End
Chigwell Row
Havering-atte-Bower
Noak Hill
Harold Hill
Harold Wood
Hainault
Collier Row
Gidea Park
Romford
South Weald
Shenfield
BRENTWOOD
Hutton
Billericay
Ramsden Heath
South Green
Little Burstead
Great Burstead
Ingrave
Herongate
Dunton Wayletts
Great Warley
Little Warley
Downham
South Hanningfield
Coalhill
Runwell
Ramsden Bellhouse
Wickford
Shotgate
Battlesbridge
Rawreth
Hullbridge
Hockley
Hawkwell
Ashingdon
Canewdon
Paglesham Churchend
Paglesham Eastend
Ballards Gore
Great Stambridge
Stroud Green
Rochford
RAYLEIGH
Nevendon
North Benfleet
Bowers Gifford
Basildon
Laindon
Pitsea
Vange
Thundersley
Daws Heath
Hadleigh
South Benfleet
Hope's Grn.
Eastwood
Southend-on-Sea
Prittlewell
Leigh on Sea
Westcliff-on-Sea
Southchurch
Thorpe Bay
Bournes Green
North Shoebury
Shoeburyness
Great Wakering
Little Wakering
Barling
Potton Island
Havengore Island
FOULNESS ISLAND
Canvey Island
Leigh Beck
Cranham
Hornchurch
Upminster
Elm Park
Rush Green
Becontree
Dagenham
Barking
Hacton
Corbets Tey
South Hornchurch
Rainham
Creekmouth
Wennington
Aveley
North Ockendon
South Ockendon
Bulphan
West Horndon
Langdon Hills
Horndon on the Hill
Orsett
Baker Street
North Stifford
South Stifford
Thurrock
Stanford-le-Hope
Corringham
Fobbing
Coryton
Thames Haven
Mucking
London Gateway
Linford
Chadwell St Mary
Little Thurrock
Grays
West Thurrock
Purfleet
Tilbury
West Tilbury
East Tilbury
Thamesmead
Belvedere
Erith
Abbey Wood
Welling
Bexleyheath
Bexley
Crayford
DARTFORD
Dartford Crossing
Stone
Greenhithe
Swanscombe
NORTHFLEET
GRAVESEND
THAMES ESTUARY
Sidcup
Foots Cray
North Cray
Swanley
Hextable
Swanley Village
Wilmington
Darenth
Sutton at Hone
South Darenth
Horton Kirby
Bean
Betsham
Southfleet
Istead Rise
Perry Street
Singlewell
Longfield
Hartley
New Barn
Chalk
Shorne
Thong
Higham
Cobham
Sole Street
Meopham
Meopham Station
Hook Green
Luddesdown
Strood
Rochester
Chatham
Gillingham
Frindsbury
Upnor
Wainscott
Chattenden
Hoo St Werburgh
Cliffe
Cliffe Woods
Cooling
High Halstow
Lower Stoke
Stoke
Allhallows
Allhallows-on-Sea
Grain
Isle of Grain
Medway
Halstow Marshes
St Mary's Marshes
St Mary Hoo
Church Street
Lower Higham
Sheerness
West Minster
Minster
Halfway Houses
Queenborough
Rushenden
Eastchurch
ISLE OF SHEPPEY
Chetney Marshes
Iwade
Lower Halstow
Upchurch
Rainham
Brompton
Grange
Luton
Wayfield
Walderslade
Hempstead
Wigmore
Moor Street
Newington
Hartlip
Bobbing
Kemsley
Milton Regis
SITTINGBOURNE
Borden
Bapchild
Conyer
Teynham
Barrow Green
Uplees
Oad Street
Stockbury
Bredhurst
Rodmersham
Tunstall
Highsted
Lynsted
Bredgar
Bicknor
Hucking
Wormshill
Milstead
Frinsted
Newnham
Doddington
Eastling
Wichling
Throwley
Orpington
Chelsfield
Well Hill
Halstead
Shoreham
Eynsford
Farningham
Crockenhill
St Paul's Cray
St Mary Cray
Badger's Mount
Pratt's Bottom
Knockholt Pound
Otford
Kemsing
Chevening
Dunton Green
Riverhead
Sevenoaks
Seal
Heaverham
Borough Green
Ightham
Wrotham
Wrotham Heath
West Kingsdown
Fawkham Green
New Ash Green
Ash
Maplescombe
Culverstone Green
Stansted
Fairseat
Vigo Village
Trottiscliffe
Addington
Ryarsh
Birling
Snodland
Halling
Upper Halling
North Halling
Cuxton
Wouldham
Burham
Blue Bell Hill
Eccles
Aylesford
New Hythe
Leybourne
Ditton
West Malling
East Malling
Offham
Larkfield
Sandling
Boxley
Detling
Thurnham
Maidstone
Bearsted
Roseacre
Hollingbourne
Eyhorne Street
Broad Street
Harrietsham
Lenham
Platt
Crouch
Claygate Cross
Stone Street
Ivy Hatch
Plaxtol
Mereworth
Kings Hill
Teston
East Barming
Tovil
Shepway
Otham
Leeds
Langley
Boughton Monchelsea
Loose
East Farleigh
West Farleigh
Wateringbury
Dunk's Green
West Peckham
Nettlestead
Nettlestead Green
Shipbourne
Underriver
Sundridge
Brasted
Brasted Chart
The Chart
Cross Keys
Whitley Row
Sevenoaks Weald
Toy's Hill
Four Elms
Pootings
Hildenborough
Hilden Park
Higham Wood
Hadlow
Golden Green
East Peckham
Barnes Street
Beltring
Yalding
Hunton
Coxheath
Linton
Chart Corner
Chart Sutton
Sutton Valence
Kingswood
Broomfield
Warmlake
Langley Heath
Ulcombe
Grafty Green
Boughton Malherbe
Charing
Charing Heath
Westwell
Westwell Leacon
Lenham Heath
Egerton
Egerton Forstal
Little Chart
Rabbit's Cross
Chainhurst
Benover
Laddingford
Cross-at-Hand
Milebush
Headcorn
Hawkenbury
Southernden
Pluckley
Pluckley Thorne
Hothfield
Great Chart
Smarden
Smarden Bell
Haffenden Quarter
Wissenden
Bethersden
Staplehurst
Sinkhurst Green
Frittenden
Marden
Marden Beech
Marden Thorn
Knox Bridge
Lashenden
Standen
Three Chimneys
Biddenden
Tonbridge
Chiddingstone Causeway
Leigh
Brook Street
Tudeley
Five Oak Green
Whetsted
Queen Street
Collier Street
Paddock Wood
Claygate
Castle Hill
Matfield
Brenchley
Pembury
Petteridge
Horsmonden
Winchet Hill
Curtisden Green
Collier's Green
Cranbrook Common
Hazel Street
Goudhurst
Iden Green
Wilsley Pound
Sissinghurst
Cranbrook
Hartley
Kilndown
Bedgebury Forest
Southborough
High Brooms
Speldhurst
Rusthall
ROYAL TUNBRIDGE WELLS
Langton Green
Hawkenbury
Lamberhurst Quarter
Lamberhurst
Bells Yew Green
Frant
Hook Green
Cousley Wood
Wood's Green
Wadhurst
Durgates
Three Leg Cross
Gill's Green
Iden Green
Benenden
East End
Tenterden
Leigh Green
Parkgate
St Michael's
High Halden
Woodchurch
Shirkoak
Henhurst
Orlestone
Kenardington
Warehorne
Brook Street
Shadoxhurst
Bromley Green
Tanden
Stubbs Cross
Hever
How Green
Bough Beech
Chiddingstone
Penshurst
Markbeech
Bidborough
Chiddingstone Hoath
Fordcombe
Blackham
Ashurst
Groombridge
Hartfield
Withyham
Upper Hartfield
Lye Green
Eridge Green
Crowborough
Medway
The Swale
KENT DOWNS
0 1 2 3 4 5 6 miles
0 1 2 3 4 5 6 7 8 9 10 km

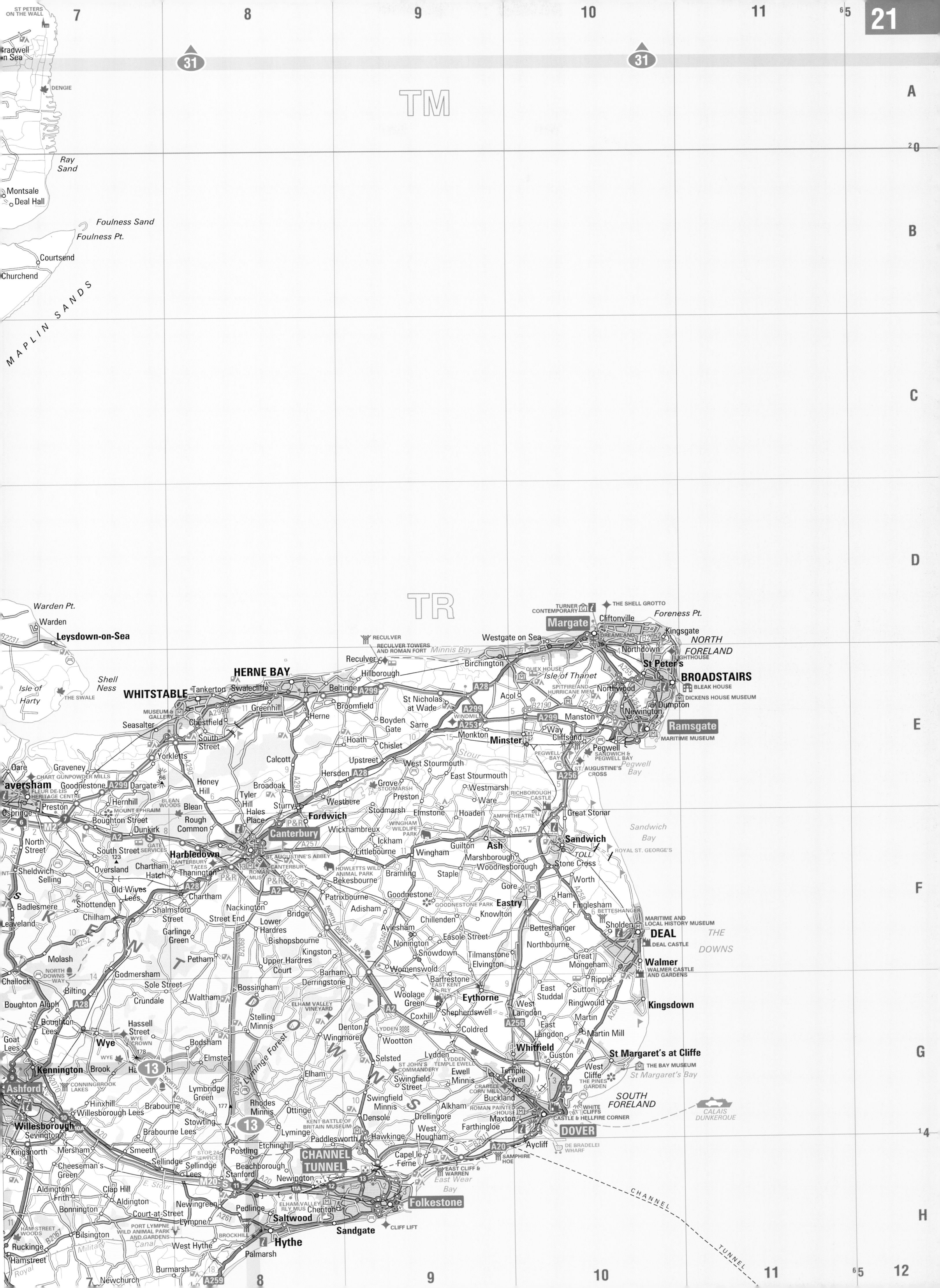

7　　　　8　　　　9　　　　10　　　　11　　6 5

31　　　　　　　　　31

TM

A

2 0

B

Ray Sand

Foulness Sand
Foulness Pt.

MAPLIN SANDS

C

D

TR

Warden Pt.
Warden

Leysdown-on-Sea

TURNER
CONTEMPORARY
THE SHELL GROTTO

Margate
Cliftonville
Foreness Pt.

RECULVER
RECULVER TOWERS
AND ROMAN FORT
Minnis Bay
Westgate on Sea
DREAMLAND
Kingsgate
NORTH
FORELAND
LIGHTHOUSE

Shell
Ness
THE SWALE

Isle
of Harty

HERNE BAY
Swalecliffe
Tankerton
Reculver
Beltinge
Hillborough
Birchington
QUEX HOUSE
Isle of Thanet
Northdown
St Peter's
BROADSTAIRS

WHITSTABLE
MUSEUM &
GALLERY
Chestfield
Greenhill
Herne
Broomfield
St Nicholas
at Wade
Sarre
SPITFIRE AND
HURRICANE MEM
Acol
Northwood
DICKENS HOUSE MUSEUM

E

Seasalter
South
Street
Yorkletts
Hoath
Boyden
Gate
Hoath
Chislet
WINDMILL
Monkton
Minster
Cliffsend
Way
Newington
Manston
Ramsgate
MARITIME MUSEUM

Calcott
Upstreet
West Stourmouth
Stour
Pegwell
Pegwell
Bay
SANDWICH &
PEGWELL BAY
ST AUGUSTINE'S
CROSS

aversham
CHART GUNPOWDER MILLS
Oare
Graveney
Goodnestone
Dargate
FLEUR-DE-LIS
HERITAGE CENTRE
Honey
Hill
Tyler
Hill
Broadoak
Hersden
Grove
STODMARSH
East Stourmouth
Westmarsh
Ware
RICHBOROUGH
CASTLE
Sandwich
Bay

Ospringe
Preston
Hernhill
MOUNT EPHRAIM
BLEAN
WOODS
Blean
Sturry
Preston
Stodmarsh
Hoaden
AMPHITHEATRE
Great Stonar

North
Street
Boughton Street
Dunkirk
Rough
Common
Hales
Place
Fordwich
Wickhambreux
Ickham
WINGHAM
WILDLIFE
PARK
Guilton
Ash
A257
TOLL

F

Sheldwich
Selling
South Street
SERVICES
Harbledown
Canterbury
ST AUGUSTINE'S ABBEY
Littlebourne
Wingham
Marshborough
Woodnesborough
Stone Cross
Royal St. George's

Oversland
Chartham
Hatch
Thanington
ROMAN
MUS
Bekesbourne
HOWLETTS WILD
ANIMAL PARK
Bramling
Staple
Worth

Old Wives
Lees
Chartham
Patrixbourne
Goodnestone
Eastry
Gore
Ham

Badlesmere
Shottenden
Chilham
Nackington
Bridge
Adisham
GOODNESTONE
PARK
Knowlton
Finglesham

Leaveland
Shalmsford
Street
Street End
Lower
Hardres
Chillenden
Betteshanger
MARITIME AND
LOCAL HISTORY MUSEUM

Molash
Garlinge
Green
Bishopsbourne
Aylesham
Nonington
Easole Street
Northbourne
Sholden
DEAL
DEAL CASTLE

NORTH
DOWNS
WAY
Petham
Kingston
Snowdown
Tilmanstone
Great
Mongeham
THE
DOWNS

Challock
Godmersham
Sole Street
Upper Hardres
Court
Barham
Womenswold
Elvington
Ripple
Walmer
WALMER CASTLE
AND GARDENS

Boughton Aluph
Bilting
Crundale
Waltham
Derringstone
Barfrestone
EAST KENT
RLY
East
Studdal
Sutton
Ringwould

Goat
Lees
Bossingham
Woolage
Green
Shepherdswell
West
Langdon
Martin
Kingsdown

Wye
WYE
CROWN
Hassell
Street
Stelling
Minnis
Denton
Coxhill
Eythorne
East
Langdon
Martin Mill

G

Kennington
Brook
Bodsham
Elmsted
Wingmore
LYDDEN
Wootton
Lydden
TEMPLE EWELL
Whitfield
Guston
West
Cliffe
St Margaret's at Cliffe
THE BAY MUSEUM

Ashford
CONNINGBROOK
LAKES
Lymbridge
Green
Rhodes
Minnis
Selsted
ST JOHN'S
COMMANDERY
Ewell
Minnis
Temple
Ewell
THE PINES
GARDEN
St Margaret's Bay

Willesborough
Brabourne
Swingfield
Minnis
Ottinge
Swingfield
Street
Alkham
Buckland
CRABBLE
CORN MILL
ROMAN PAINTED
HOUSE
WHITE
CLIFFS
SOUTH
FORELAND

Sevington
Brabourne Lees
Stowting
Lyminge
Drellingore
Densole
West
Hougham
Farthingloe
CASTLE & HELLFIRE CORNER
DOVER
CALAIS
DUNKERQUE

Kingsnorth
Mersham
Smeeth
Sellindge
Lees
Postling
LYMINGE FOREST
Etchinghill
Paddlesworth
Hawkinge
KENT BATTLE
OF BRITAIN MUSEUM
West
Houghton
Aycliff
DE BRADELEI
WHARF

H

Cheeseman's
Green
Sellindge
Beachborough
Stanford
Newington
CHANNEL
TUNNEL
Capel le
Ferne
EAST CLIFF &
WARREN
SAMPHIRE
HOE

Aldington
Frith
Clap Hill
Aldington
Stowting
STOP 24
SERVICES
Lyminge
Newingreen
ELHAM VALLEY
RLY MUS
Cheriton
Folkestone
East Wear
Bay

Bonnington
HAM STREET
WOODS
Ruckinge
Bilsington
PORT LYMPNE
WILD ANIMAL PARK
AND GARDENS
Lympne
BROCKHILL
Saltwood
Sandgate
CLIFF LIFT

Hamstreet
Burmarsh
West Hythe
Military
Canal
Palmarsh
Hythe

Newchurch

7　　　　8　　　　9　　　　10　　　　11　　6 5　　12

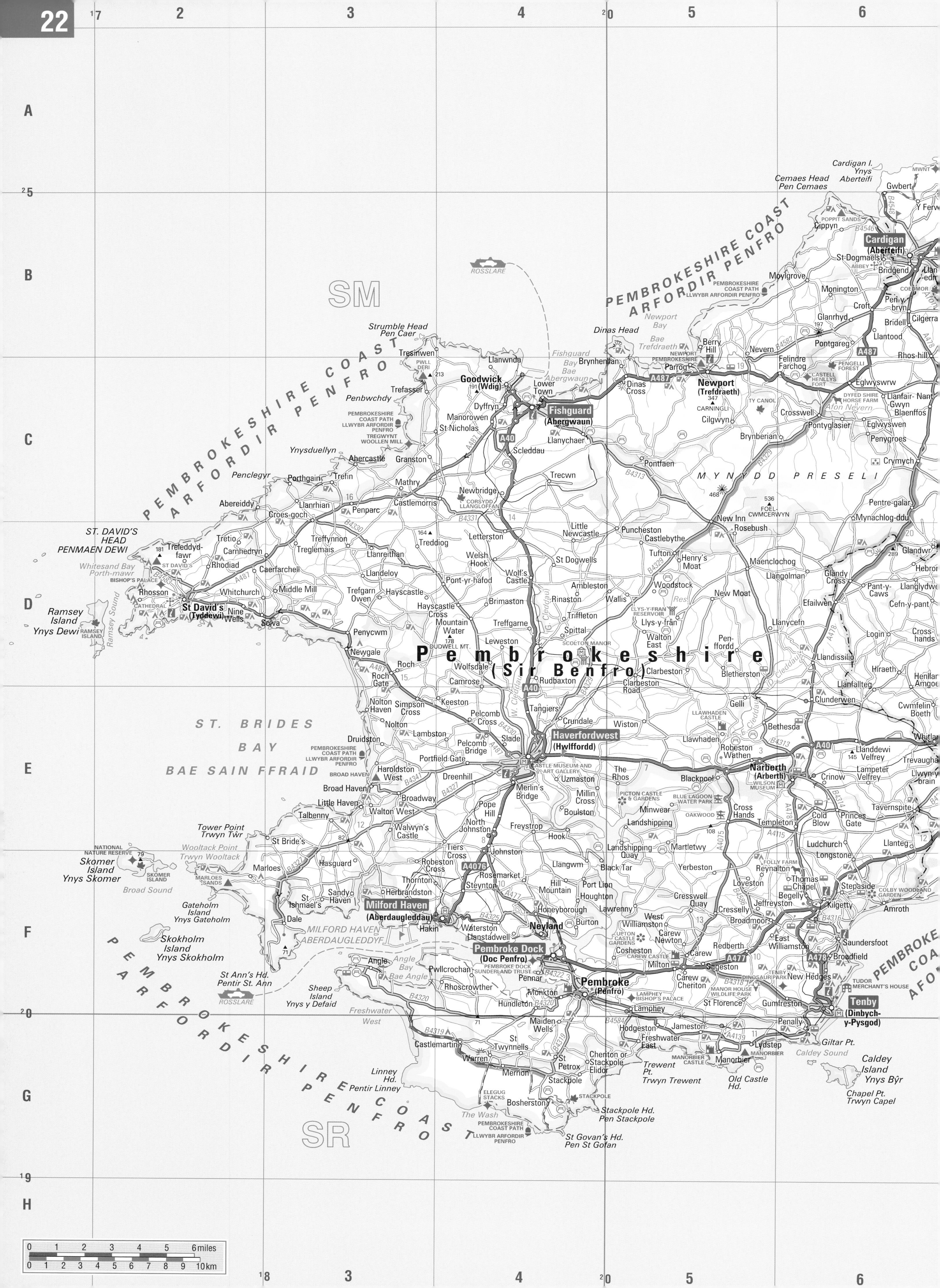
SM
SR
ROSSLARE
PEMBROKESHIRE COAST
ARFORDIR PENFRO
Pembrokeshire
(Sir Benfro)
MYNYDD PRESELI
ST. BRIDES
BAY
BAE SAIN FFRAID
Cardigan I.
Ynys Aberteifi
Cemaes Head
Pen Cemaes
Gwbert
Y Ferwig
Cippyn
POPPIT SANDS
Cardigan
(Aberteifi)
St Dogmaels
ABBEY
Bridgend
Moylgrove
Monington
Pen-y-bryn
Croft
Glanrhyd
Bridell
Cilgerran
Llantood
Pontgarreg
Rhos-hill
PEMBROKESHIRE COAST PATH
LLWYBR ARFORDIR PENFRO
Newport Bay
Bae Trefdraeth
Dinas Head
Berry Hill
Nevern
Felindre Farchog
CASTELL HENLLYS FORT
PENGELLI FOREST
Eglwyswrw
Llanfair-Nant-Gwyn
Blaenffos
DYFED SHIRE HORSE FARM
Afon Nevern
NEWPORT PEMBROKESHIRE
Parrog
Newport
(Trefdraeth)
CARNINGLI
347
Cilgwyn
TY CANOL
Crosswell
Pontyglasier
Eglwyswen
Penygroes
Crymych
Brynberian
Dinas Cross
A487
Fishguard Bay
Bae Abergwaun
Brynhenllan
Strumble Head
Pen Caer
Tresinwen
PWLL DERI
213
Llanwnda
Goodwick
(Wdig)
191
Lower Town
Fishguard
(Abergwaun)
Trefasser
Penbwchdy
Dyffryn
Manorowen
St Nicholas
TREGWYNT WOOLLEN MILL
Llanychaer
A40
Scleddau
Ynysduellyn
Abercastle
Granston
Pontfaen
Trecwn
B4313
Penclegyr
Porthgain
Trefin
Mathry
Newbridge
Castlemorris
CORSYDD LLANGLOFFAN
Abereiddy
Llanrhian
Penparc
Croes-goch
B4330
B4331
468
536
FOEL CWMCERWYN
New Inn
Rosebush
Mynachlog-ddu
Pentre-galar
ST. DAVID'S HEAD
PENMAEN DEWI
Treleddyd-fawr
181
Tretio
Carnhedryn
Treffynnon
Treglemais
164
Treddiog
Llanreithan
Letterston
Little Newcastle
Puncheston
Castlebythe
Tufton
Henry's Moat
Glandwr
Whitesand Bay
Porth-mawr
ST DAVID'S
BISHOP'S PALACE
Rhodiad
Caerfarchell
Llandeloy
Welsh Hook
Wolf's Castle
St Dogwells
Maenclochog
Llangolman
Glandy Cross
Pant-y-Caws
Llanglydwen
Hebron
Cefn-y-pant
Rhosson
CATHEDRAL
St David's
(Tyddewi)
Whitchurch
Middle Mill
Trefgarn Owen
Hayscastle
Pont-yr-hafod
Ambleston
Woodstock
Rinaston
Wallis
New Moat
Efailwen
Ramsey Island
Ynys Dewi
RAMSEY ISLAND
Ramsey Sound
Nine Wells
Solva
Hayscastle Cross
Brimaston
Mountain Water
Treffgarne
Triffleton
LLYS-Y-FRAN RESERVOIR
Llys-y-fran
Llanycefn
Penycwm
178
DUDWELL MT.
Leweston
Spittal
Walton East
Pen-ffordd
Login
Cross-hands
Newgale
Roch
Wolfsdale
SCOLTON MANOR
Clarbeston
Bletherston
Llandissilio
Roch Gate
Camrose
Rudbaxton
Clarbeston Road
Hiraeth
Henllan Amgoed
Llanfallteg
Nolton Haven
Simpson Cross
Keeston
Gelli
Clunderwen
Cwmfelin Boeth
Nolton
Pelcomb Cross
Tangiers
Crundale
Wiston
LLAWHADEN CASTLE
Bethesda
Druidston
Lambston
Pelcomb Bridge
Slade
Haverfordwest
(Hwlffordd)
Llawhaden
Robeston Wathen
Llanddewi Velfrey
145
Whitland
Haroldston West
Portfield Gate
CASTLE MUSEUM AND ART GALLERY
Uzmaston
The Rhos
Blackpool
Narberth
(Arberth)
WILSON MUSEUM
Crinow
Lampeter Velfrey
Trevaughan
Llwyn-y-brain
BROAD HAVEN
Broad Haven
Dreenhill
Merlin's Bridge
Millin Cross
PICTON CASTLE & GARDENS
BLUE LAGOON WATER PARK
Cross Hands
Taverspite
Little Haven
Broadway
Walton West
Pope Hill
Boulston
Minwear
OAKWOOD
Templeton
Cold Blow
Princes Gate
Talbenny
Landshipping
108
A4115
Tower Point
Trwyn Twr
Walwyn's Castle
North Johnston
Freystrop
Hook
Ludchurch
Llanteg
St Bride's
82
Longstone
NATIONAL NATURE RESERVE
79
Wooltack Point
Trwyn Wooltack
Skomer Island
Ynys Skomer
SKOMER ISLAND
Marloes
Hasguard
Tiers Cross
Johnston
Landshipping Quay
Martletwy
Robeston Cross
Llangwm
Black Tar
Yerbeston
FOLLY FARM
Reynalton
MARLOES SANDS
Broad Sound
Thornton
A4076
Rosemarket
Hill Mountain
Port Lion
Loveston
Thomas Chapel
Stepaside
COLBY WOODLAND GARDEN
Gateholm Island
Ynys Gateholm
St Ishmael's
Sandy Haven
Herbrandston
Steynton
Houghton
Cresswell Quay
Begelly
Jeffreyston
Kilgetty
Milford Haven
(Aberdaugleddau)
Honeyborough
Lawrenny
Cresselly
Amroth
Dale
Hakin
Waterston
Neyland
Burton
Williamston
West Williamston
Broadmoor
B4316
MILFORD HAVEN
ABERDAUGLEDDYF
Llanstadwell
Carew Newton
UPTON CASTLE GARDENS
East Williamston
Saundersfoot
Skokholm Island
Ynys Skokholm
71
Pembroke Dock
(Doc Penfro)
Cosheston
Carew
Redberth
Angle
Angle Bay
Bae Angle
Pwllcrochan
PEMBROKE DOCK SUNDERLAND TRUST
Pennar
CAREW CASTLE
Milton
A477
Sageston
Broadfield
St Ann's Hd.
Pentir St. Ann
ROSSLARE
Rhoscrowther
Pembroke
(Penfro)
Carew Cheriton
TENBY DINOSAUR PARK
New Hedges
TUDOR MERCHANT'S HOUSE
Sheep Island
Ynys y Defaid
Monkton
LAMPHEY BISHOP'S PALACE
MANOR HOUSE WILDLIFE PARK
Hundleton
St Florence
Gumfreston
Tenby
(Dinbych-y-Pysgod)
Freshwater West
B4320
Lamphey
Maiden Wells
Hodgeston
Jameston
Penally
Castlemartin
St Twynnells
Freshwater East
Lydstep
MANORBIER
Giltar Pt.
Caldey Sound
Caldey Island
Ynys Bŷr
Warren
St Petrox
Chenton or Stackpole Elidor
Trewent Pt.
Trwyn Trewent
MANORBIER CASTLE
Manorbier
Old Castle Hd.
Linney Hd.
Pentir Linney
Merrion
Stackpole
ELEGUG STACKS
STACKPOLE
Chapel Pt.
Trwyn Capel
Bosherston
The Wash
Stackpole Hd.
Pen Stackpole
St Govan's Hd.
Pen St Gofan
0 1 2 3 4 5 6 miles
0 1 2 3 4 5 6 7 8 9 10 km
A B C D E F G H
1 2 3 4 5 6

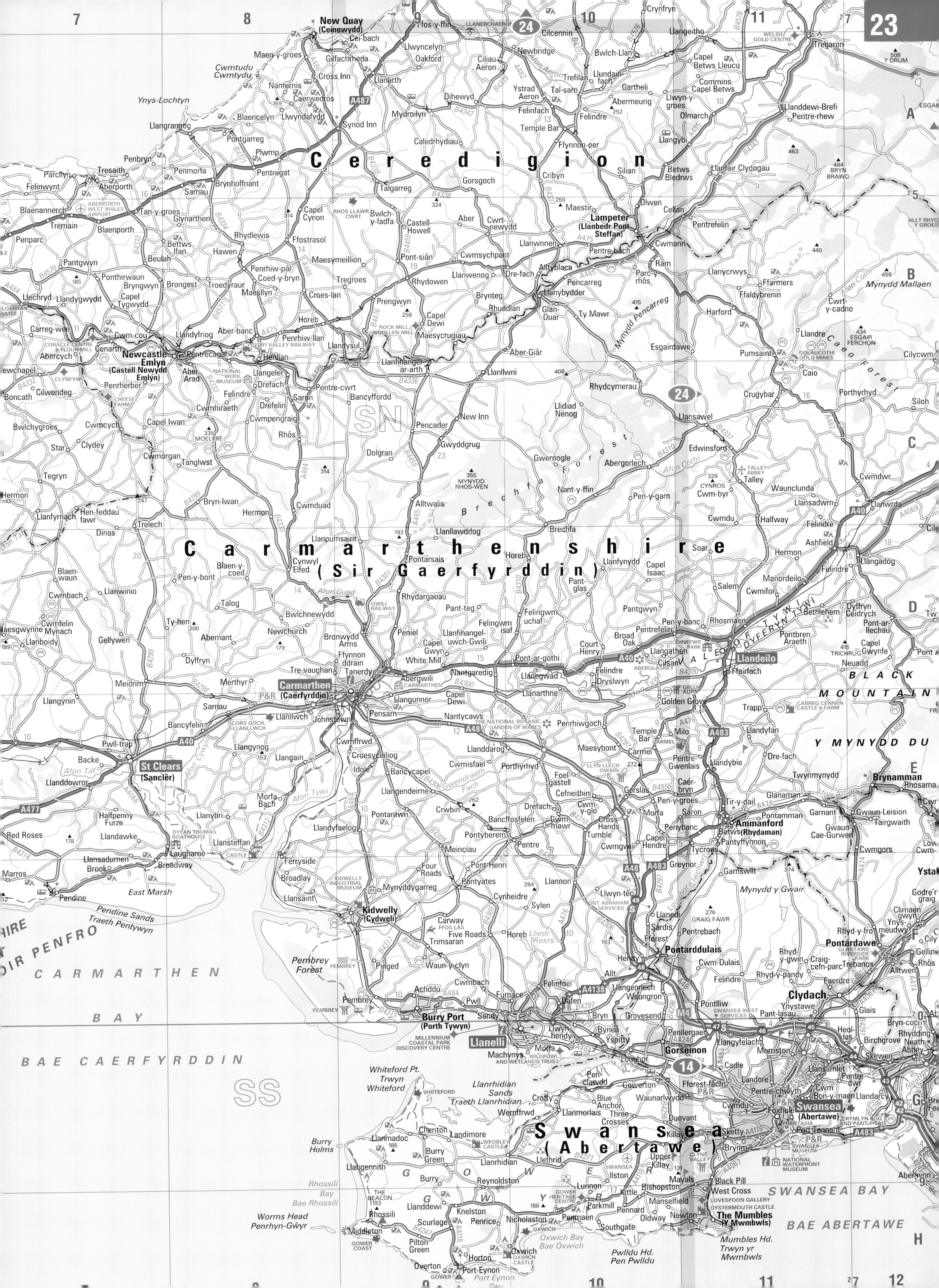
Ceredigion
Carmarthenshire
(Sir Gaerfyrddin)
Swansea
(Abertawe)
New Quay
(Ceinewydd)
Cei-bach
Gilfachrheda
Llanarth
Cross Inn
Synod Inn
Cwmtudu
Cwmtydu
Ynys-Lochtyn
Llangrannog
Penbryn
Tresaith
Aberporth
Parcllyn
Felinwynt
Blaenannerch
Tremain
Penparc
Aberaeron
Ciliau Aeron
Newbridge
Cilcennin
Oakford
Llwyncelyn
Ffos-y-ffin
Dihewyd
Mydroilyn
Ystrad Aeron
Felinfach
Temple Bar
Tal-sarn
Trefilan
Llundain-fach
Gartheli
Abermeurig
Llwyn-y-groes
Olmarch
Llangeitho
Capel Betws Lleucu
Commins Capel Betws
Tregaron
Welsh Gold Centre
Llanddewi-Brefi
Pentre-rhew
Llangybi
Betws Bledrws
Llanfair Clydogau
Cellan
Olwen
Silian
Cribyn
Ffynnon-oer
Felindre
Lampeter
(Llanbedr Pont Steffan)
Maestir
Cwmann
Pentrefelin
Pentre-bach
Llanwnnen
Gorsgoch
Talgarreg
Capel Cynon
Ffostrasol
Rhydlewis
Hawen
Bettws Ifan
Beulah
Brongest
Troedyraur
Maesllyn
Penrhiw-pal
Coed-y-bryn
Pentregat
Brynhoffnant
Sarnau
Penmorfa
Plwmp
Pontgarreg
Blaencelyn
Nanternis
Caerwedros
Llwyndafydd
Maen-y-groes
Glynarthen
Tan-y-groes
Blaenporth
Aberporth West Wales Airport
Pantgwyn
Ponthirwaun
Bryngwyn
Capel Tygwydd
Llechryd
Llandygwydd
Carreg-wen
Cwm-cou
Cenarth
Abercych
Newcastle Emlyn
(Castell Newydd Emlyn)
Adpar
Pentrecagal
Llandyfriog
Aber-banc
Henllan
Llandysul
Horeb
Penrhiw-llan
Croes-lan
Maesymeillion
Tregroes
Pont-siân
Rhydowen
Prengwyn
Capel Dewi
Maesycrugiau
Llanfihangel-ar-arth
Llanllwni
Aber-Giâr
Llanybydder
Glan-Duar
Ty Mawr
Mynydd Pencarreg
Pencarreg
Alltyblaca
Dre-fach
Llanwenog
Cwmsychpant
Cwrt-newydd
Aber
Castell-Howell
Bwlch-y-fadfa
Rhuddlan
Brynteg
Parc-y-rhôs
Ram
Llanycrwys
Ffarmers
Ffaldybrenin
Cwrt-y-cadno
Mynydd Mallaen
Harford
Esgairdawe
Pumsaint
Dolaucothi Gold Mines
Caio
Llandre
Cilycwm
Caeo Forest
Crugybar
Porthyrhyd
Siloh
Rhydcymerau
Llansawel
Edwinsford
Talley Abbey
Talley
Cynros
Cwm-byr
Wauncluda
Llansadwrn
Cwmdwr
Llanwrda
Halfway
Felindre
Ashfield
Llangadog
Abergorlech
Brechfa Forest
Nant-y-ffin
Pen-y-garn
Cwmdu
Brechfa
Lliidiad Nenog
Gwernogle
New Inn
Pencader
Gwyddgrug
Alltwalis
Mynydd Rhos-wen
Llanllawddog
Llanpumsaint
Cynwyl Elfed
Horeb
Pontarsais
Llanfynydd
Capel Isaac
Pant-glas
Soar
Hermon
Salem
Manordeilo
Cwmifor
Rhosmaen
Dyffryn Ceidrych
Bethlehem
Pont-ar-llechau
Pontbren Araeth
Capel Gwynfe
Trichrug
Neuadd
Black Mountain
Y Mynydd Du
Llandeilo
Ffairfach
Dyffryn Tywi
Vale of Tywi
Pen-y-banc
Llangathen
Cilsan
Broad Oak
Court Henry
Pentrefelin
Dinefwr Park
Aberglasney
Pont-ar-gothi
Felindre
Dryslwyn
Llanegwad
Nantgaredig
Llanarthne
Golden Grove
Gelli Aur
Carreg Cennen Castle & Farm
Trapp
Llandyfan
Dre-fach
Temple Bar
Milo
Carmel
Pentre-Gwenlais
Llandybie
Caer-bryn
Twynmynydd
Brynamman
Glanaman
Garnant
Gwaun-Cae-Gurwen
Tairgwaith
Gwaun-Leision
Cwmgors
Ammanford
(Rhydaman)
Betws
Pantyffynnon
Tir-y-dail
Pen-y-groes
Saron
Penybanc
Capel Hendre
Tycroes
Gorslas
Cross Hands
Tumble
Cwmgwili
Cefneithin
Foel-gastell
Maesybont
Llyn Llech Owain
Porthyrhyd
Llanddarog
The National Botanic Garden of Wales
Penrhiwgoch
Nantycaws
Capel Dewi
Llangunnor
Abergwili
Carmarthen
(Caerfyrddin)
Johnstown
Pensarn
Tanerdy
Tre-vaughan
Ffynnon ddrain
Bronwydd Arms
Gwili Railway
Rhydargaeau
Pant-teg
Felingwm isaf
Felingwm uchaf
Llanfihangel-uwch-Gwili
Capel Gwyn
White Mill
Peniel
Newchurch
Bwlchnewydd
Cwmduad
Dolgran
Rhôs
Cwmpengraig
Drefelin
Drefach
Saron
Pentre-cwrt
Bancyffordd
Llangeler
National Wool Museum
Felindre
Cwmhiraeth
Capel Iwan
Penrherber
Cwmcych
Bwlchygroes
Cilwendeg
Boncath
Star
Clydey
Cwmorgan
Tanglwst
Moelfre
Hermon
Tegryn
Bryn-Iwan
Llanfyrnach
Hen-feddau fawr
Dinas
Trelech
Blaen-waun
Pen-y-bont
Blaen-y-coed
Talog
Cwmbach
Llanwinio
Cwmfelin Mynach
Llanboidy
Gellywen
Ty-hen
Abernant
Dyffryn
Merthyr
Meidrim
Llangynin
Sarnau
Bancyfelin
Cors Goch Llanllwch
Llanllwch
Pwll-trap
St Clears
(Sanclêr)
Backe
Afon Tâf
Llanddowror
Llangynog
Llangain
Cwmffrwd
Croesyceiliog
Idole
Bancycapel
Cwmisfael
Llangendeirne
Crwbin
Pontantwn
Llandyfaelog
Pontyberem
Bancffosfelen
Drefach
Cwm-y-glo
Cwm-mawr
Pentre
Meinciau
Pont-Henri
Pontyates
Four Roads
Llannon
Cynheidre
Sylen
Llwyn-teg
Pont Abraham Services
Mynyddygarreg
Kidwelly
(Cydweli)
Kidwelly Industrial Museum
Ferryside
Broadlay
Llansaint
Carway
Ffos Las
Five Roads
Trimsaran
Horeb
Lliedi Resrs.
Pinged
Waun-y-clyn
Cwmbach
Pembrey Forest
Pembrey
Achddu
Pwll
Burry Port
(Porth Tywyn)
Millennium Coastal Park Discovery Centre
Llanelli
Sandy
Furnace
Felinfoel
Dafen
Llwynhendy
Bynea
Machynys
Morfa
Wildfowl and Wetlands Trust
Bryn
Yspitty
Llangennech
Waungron
Grovesend
Hendy
Pontarddulais
Llanedi
Sardis
Fforest
Allt
Cwm-Dulais
Pentrebach
Craig Fawr
Garnswllt
Mynydd y Gwair
Felindre
Rhyd-y-pandy
Pontlliw
Swansea West Services
Penllergaer
Gorseinon
Loughor
Llangyfelach
Morriston
Clydach
Ynystawe
Pant-lasau
Glais
Pontardawe
Glantawe Riverside Park
Trebanos
Alltwen
Rhyd-y-gwin
Craig-cefn-parc
Faerdre
Rhyd-y-fro
Ynysmeudwy
Rhydding
Neath Abbey
Skewen
Birchgrove
Llansamlet
Heol-las
Cadle
Landore
Pentre-chwyth
Fforest-fach
Cwmdu
Swansea
(Abertawe)
Port Tennant
Swansea Museum
National Waterfront Museum
Foxhole
Bon-y-maen
Landarcy
Crymlyn Bog and Pant-y-Sais
Sketty
Brynmill
Killay
Dunvant
Upper Killay
Gowerton
Waunarlwydd
Three Crosses
Blue Anchor
Llanmorlais
Crofty
Pen-clawdd
Llethrid
Ilston
Clyne Valley
Mayals
Black Pill
West Cross
Bishopston
Kittle
Mansel Field
Lovespoon Gallery
Oystermouth Castle
Newton
The Mumbles
(Y Mwmbwls)
Oldway
Pennard
Parkmill
Penmaen
Gower Heritage Centre
Southgate
Pwlldu Hd.
Pen Pwlldu
Mumbles Hd.
Trwyn yr Mwmbwls
Swansea Bay
Bae Abertawe
Whiteford Pt.
Trwyn Whiteford
Llanrhidian Sands
Traeth Llanrhidian
Wernffrwd
Llanrhidian
Weobley Castle
Landimore
Cheriton
Llanmadoc
Burry Green
Burry
Llangennith
Reynoldston
Knelston
Penrice
Nicholaston
Oxwich Bay
Bae Oxwich
Oxwich
Oxwich Castle
Horton
Port-Eynon
Overton
Gower
Pilton Green
Scurlage
Llanddewi
Rhossili
The Beacon
Middleton
Gower Coast
Rhossili Bay
Bae Rhossili
Worms Head
Penrhyn-Gŵyr
Burry Holms
Gower
Carmarthen Bay
Bae Caerfyrddin
Pendine Sands
Traeth Pentywyn
Pendine
East Marsh
Marros
Red Roses
Llanddawke
Llansadurnen
Brook
Broadway
Laugharne
Dylan Thomas Boathouse
Llansteffan
Castle
Llanybri
Morfa Bach
Halfpenny Furze
Afon Tywi
Afon Cothi
Afon Duad
Gwendraeth Fach
SN
SS

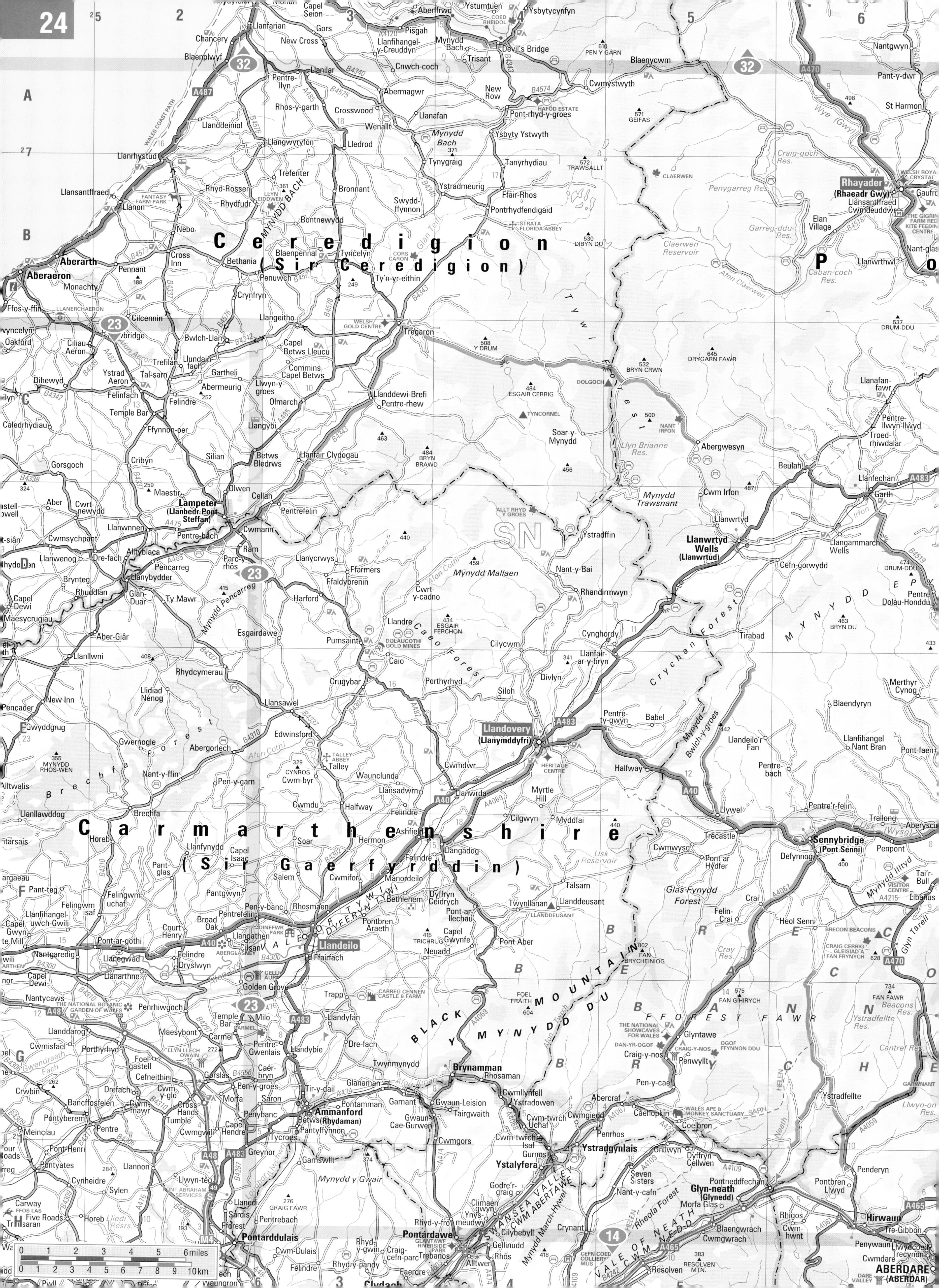
Ceredigion
(Sir Ceredigion)
Carmarthenshire
(Sir Gaerfyrddin)
Llanfarian
Chancery
Blaenplwyf
Gors
New Cross
Pisgah
Llanfihangel-y-Creuddyn
Aberffrwd
Ystumtuen
Ysbytycynfyn
Devil's Bridge
Mynydd Bach
Trisant
Cnwch-coch
Llanilar
Pentre-llyn
Abermagwr
Rhos-y-garth
Crosswood
Wenallt
Llanafan
Llanddeiniol
Llangwyryfon
Lledrod
Mynydd Bach
Llanrhystud
Llansantffraed
Llanon
Trefenter
Rhyd-Rosser
Rhydfudr
Bronnant
Tynygraig
Ystradmeurig
Swydd-ffynnon
Nebo
Bontnewydd
Aberarth
Aberaeron
Pennant
Monachty
Cross Inn
Bethania
Blaenpennal
Tyncelyn
Penuwch
Ty'n-yr-eithin
Cryntryn
Cilcennin
Llangeitho
Tregaron
Bwlch-Llan
Capel Betws Lleucu
Commins Capel Betws
Trefilan
Llundain-fach
Gartheli
Ystrad Aeron
Tal-sarn
Llwyn-y-groes
Abermeurig
Dihewyd
Felinfach
Felindre
Olmarch
Llanddewi-Brefi
Pentre-rhew
Temple Bar
Ffynnon-oer
Llangybi
Llanfair Clydogau
Silian
Betws Bledrws
Cribyn
Gorsgoch
Maestir
Olwen
Cellan
Lampeter
(Llanbedr Pont Steffan)
Pentrefelin
Cwmann
Llanwnnen
Pentre-bach
Cwmsychpant
Alltyblaca
Llanwenog
Dre-fach
Pencarreg
Parc-y-rhôs
Llanybydder
Brynteg
Rhuddlan
Glan-Duar
Ty Mawr
Capel Dewi
Maesycrugiau
Aber-Giâr
Llanllwni
Llanycrwys
Ffarmers
Ffaldybrenin
Harford
Cwrt-y-cadno
Mynydd Mallaen
Llandre
Caeo Forest
Pumsaint
Caio
Esgairdawe
Rhydcymerau
Crugybar
Llansawel
Porthyrhyd
Siloh
Cilycwm
Divlyn
Llanfair-ar-y-bryn
Cynghordy
Rhandirmwyn
Nant-y-Bai
Ystradffin
Soar-y-Mynydd
Llyn Brianne Res.
Abergwesyn
Llanwrtyd
Llanwrtyd Wells
(Llanwrtud)
Cwm Irfon
Beulah
Llanfechan
Garth
Llangammarch Wells
Cefn-gorwydd
Mynydd Trawsnant
Crychan Forest
Tirabad
Llandovery
(Llanymddyfri)
Pentre-ty-gwyn
Babel
Edwinsford
Abergorlech
Brechfa Forest
Gwernogle
Talley
Cwm-byr
Wauncluda
Cwmdwr
Llansadwrn
Llanwrda
Halfway
Nant-y-ffin
Pen-y-garn
Cwmdu
Myrtle Hill
Cilgwyn
Myddfai
Brechfa
Horeb
Soar
Hermon
Ashfield
Llangadog
Llanfynydd
Capel Isaac
Pant-glas
Salem
Cwmifor
Manordeilo
Felindre
Dyffryn Ceidrych
Bethlehem
Pentrefelin
Pen-y-banc
Rhosmaen
Broad Oak
Court Henry
Llangathen
Cilsan
Llandeilo
Ffairfach
Pontbren Araeth
Capel Gwynfe
Pont-ar-llechau
Twynllanan
Llanddeusant
Talsarn
Pont Aber
Usk Reservoir
Trecastle
Cwmwysg
Pont ar Hydfer
Sennybridge
(Pont Senni)
Defynnog
Glas Fynydd Forest
Crai
Felin-Crai
Heol Senni
Black Mountain
Y Mynydd Du
Fforest Fawr
Brecon Beacons
Glyntawe
Craig-y-nos
Penwyllt
Pen-y-cae
Abercraf
Caehopkin
Coelbren
Ystradgynlais
Ystalyfera
Brynamman
Rhosaman
Cwmllynfell
Ystradowen
Gwaun-Leision
Tairgwaith
Garnant
Glanaman
Ammanford
(Rhydaman)
Pantyffynnon
Betws
Tycroes
Cwmgors
Gwaun-Cae-Gurwen
Llandybie
Dre-fach
Twynmynydd
Llandyfan
Trapp
Golden Grove
Dryslwyn
Llangwad
Llanarthne
Nantgaredig
Pont-ar-gothi
Felindre
Penrhiwgoch
Temple Bar
Milo
Carmel
Pentre-Gwenlais
Maesybont
Porthyrhyd
Llanddarog
Cwmisfael
Foel-gastell
Cefneithin
Gorslas
Cross Hands
Drefach
Cwm-y-glo
Caer-bryn
Pen-y-groes
Saron
Penybanc
Tir-y-dail
Pontamman
Capel Hendre
Cwmgwili
Tumble
Pontyberem
Meinciau
Pentre
Bancffosfelen
Crwbin
Garnswllt
Mynydd y Gwair
Llannon
Sylen
Llwyn-teg
Cynheidre
Pontyates
Pont-Henri
Carway
Five Roads
Horeb
Llanedi
Sardis
Pentrebach
Pontarddulais
Cwm-Dulais
Felindre
Rhyd-y-pandy
Pontardawe
Rhyd-y-fro
Trebanos
Craig-cefn-parc
Alltwen
Rhôs
Gellinudd
Cilybebyll
Godre'r-graig
Swansea Valley
Cwm Abertawe
Ystradfellte
Penderyn
Pontbren Llwyd
Hirwaun
Glyn-neath
(Glynedd)
Pontneddfechan
Morfa Glas
Blaengwrach
Cwmgwrach
Rhigos
Cwm-hwnt
Seven Sisters
Nant-y-cafn
Onllwyn
Dyffryn Cellwen
Crynant
Resolven
Vale of Neath
Cwm Nedd
Aberdare
(Aberdâr)
Rhayader
(Rhaeadr Gwy)
Llansantffraed Cwmdeuddwr
Elan Village
Nantgwyn
Pant-y-dwr
St Harmon
Llanwrthwl
Claerwen Reservoir
Llanafan-fawr
Pentre-llwyn-llwyd
Troed-rhiwdalar
Blaenycwm
Cwmystwyth
Pont-rhyd-y-groes
Ysbyty Ystwyth
Tanyrhydiau
Ffair-Rhos
Pontrhydfendigaid
Tywi Forest
Mynydd Epynt
Merthyr Cynog
Blaendyryn
Llanfihangel Nant Bran
Llandeilo'r Fan
Pentre-bach
Llywel
Pentre'r-felin
Trallong
0 1 2 3 4 5 6 miles
0 1 2 3 4 5 6 7 8 9 10 km

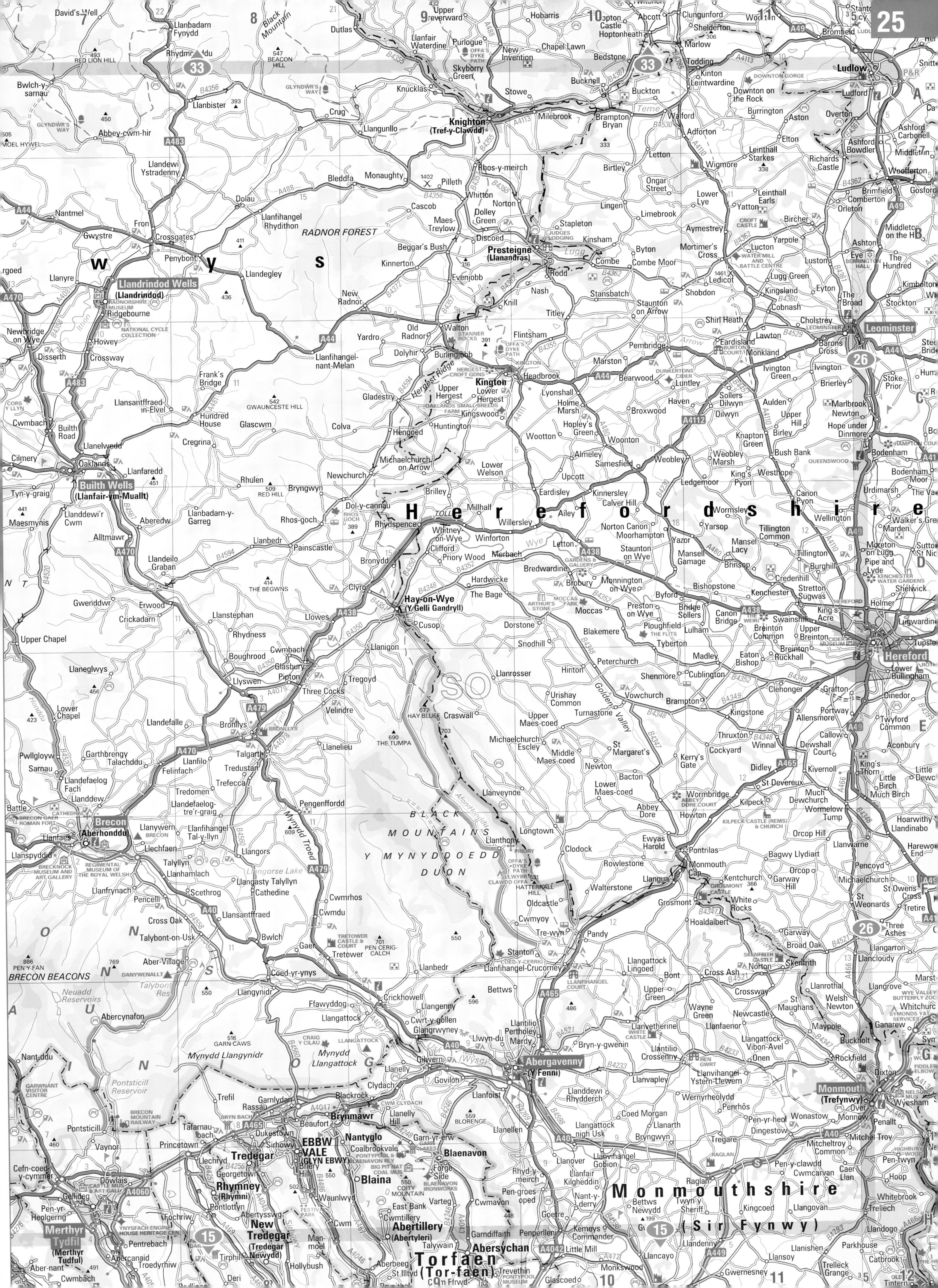

David's Well
Llanbadarn Fynydd
Black Mountain
Dutlas
Upper Treverward
Hobarris
Bucknell
Clungunford
Abcott
Hopton Castle
Hoptonheath
Shelderton
Marlow
Bromfield
Ludlow
Red Lion Hill
Rhydmeddu
Beacon Hill
Llanfair Waterdine
Purlogue
New Invention
Chapel Lawn
Bedstone
Skyborry Green
Knucklas
Stowe
Buckton
Brampton Bryan
Todding
Kinton
Leintwardine
Downton on the Rock
Downton Gorge
Bwlch-y-sarnau
Llanbister
Crug
Knighton
(Tref-y-Clawdd)
Milebrook
Walford
Burrington
Aston
Overton
Glyndwr's Way
Abbey-cwm-hir
Llangunllo
Adforton
Elton
Ashford Carbonell
Ashford Bowdler
Moel Hywel
Llandewi Ystradenny
Monaughty
Pilleth
Bleddfa
Rhos-y-meirch
Letton
Birtley
Wigmore
Leinthall Starkes
Richards Castle
Middleton
Woofferton
Dolau
Whitton
Norton
Dolley Green
Cascob
Maes-Treylow
Ongar Street
Lingen
Lower Lye
Leinthall Earls
Yatton
Brimfield
Comberton
Orleton
Nantmel
Fron
Gwystre
Crossgates
Llanfihangel Rhydithon
Radnor Forest
Discoed
Stapleton
Limebrook
Judges Lodging
Croft Castle
Bircher
Aymestrey
Middleton on the Hill
Penybont
Beggar's Bush
Presteigne
(Llanandras)
Kinsham
Byton
Mortimer's Cross
Lucton
Yarpole
Ashton
Eye
Berrington Hall
Llandegley
Kinnerton
Evenjobb
Combe
Combe Moor
Lugg
Luston
The Hundred
Llanyre
Llandrindod Wells
(Llandrindod)
Radnorshire Museum
Ridgebourne
Rodd
Nash
Ledicot
Lugg Green
Shobdon
Kingsland
Eyton
Kimbolton
Stansbatch
Staunton on Arrow
Cobnash
The Broad
Stockton
New Radnor
Knill
Titley
Shirl Heath
Cholstrey
Newbridge on Wye
National Cycle Collection
Howey
Disserth
Walton
Stanner Rocks
Old Radnor
Yardro
Flintsham
Eardisland
Burton Court
Monkland
Leominster
Barons Cross
Crossway
Llanfihangel-nant-Melan
Dolyhir
Burlingjobb
Offa's Dyke Path
Pembridge
Lawton
Arrow
Frank's Bridge
Hergest Croft Gdns
Hergest Ridge
Kington
Headbrook
Lower Hergest
Upper Hergest
Marston
Bearwood
Dunkertons Cider
Luntley
Ivington Green
Ivington
Stoke Prior
Llansantffraed-in-Elvel
Gwaunceste Hill
Gladestry
Oaklands Small Breeds Farm
Kingswood
Lyonshall
Holme Marsh
Broxwood
Sollers Dilwyn
Dilwyn
Haven
Brierley
Aulden
Marlbrook
Newton
Hope under Dinmore
Cwmbach
Builth Road
Hundred House
Glascwm
Colva
Hengoed
Huntington
Hopley's Green
Wootton
Woonton
Upper Hill
Birley
Knapton Green
Llanelwedd
Cregrina
Michaelchurch on Arrow
Lower Welson
Almeley
Sarnesfield
Weobley
Weobley Marsh
Bush Bank
Queenswood
Bodenham
Cilmery
Oaklands
Llanfaredd
Builth Wells
(Llanfair-ym-Muallt)
Rhulen
Newchurch
Bryngwyn
Red Hill
Upcott
King's Pyon
Westhope
Bodenham Moor
Tyn-y-graig
Brilley
Eardisley
Kinnersley
Ledgemoor
Canon Pyon
Urdimarsh
Maesmynis
Llanddewi'r Cwm
Aberedw
Llanbadarn-y-Garreg
Rhos-goch
Doly-cannau
Rhydspence
Millhalf
Calver Hill
Ailey
Willersley
Herefordshire
Wormsley
Yarsop
Wellington
Walker's Green
Alltmawr
Whitney-on-Wye
Winforton
Norton Canon
Moorhampton
Yazor
Mansel Lacy
Tillington Common
Marden
Llanbedr
Painscastle
Clifford
Letton
Staunton on Wye
Mansell Gamage
Brinsop
Tillington
Moreton on Lugg
Pipe and Lyde
Llandeilo Graban
Bronydd
Priory Wood
Merbach
Wye
Bredwardine
Burghill
Credenhill
The Begwns
Clyro
Hardwicke
Brobury
Monnington on Wye
Bishopstone
Kenchester
Stretton Sugwas
Shelwick
Gwenddwr
Erwood
Hay-on-Wye
(Y Gelli Gandryll)
The Bage
Arthur's Stone
Moccas Park
Moccas
Byford
Preston on Wye
Bridge Sollers
Canon Bridge
Swainshill
King's Acre
Holmer
Crickadarn
Llanstephan
Llowes
Cusop
Dorstone
Blakemere
The Weir
Breinton Common
Upper Breinton
Lugwardine
Upper Chapel
Rhydness
Llanigon
Snodhill
Tyberton
Lulham
Cider Museum
Hereford
Tupsley
Boughrood
Cwmbach
Glasbury
Pipton
Peterchurch
Madley
Eaton Bishop
Breinton
Ruckhall
Lower Bullingham
Llaneglwys
Llyswen
Tregoyd
Llanrosser
Hinton
Shenmore
Cublington
Clehonger
Grafton
Dinedor
Three Cocks
Velindre
Urishay Common
Vowchurch
Brampton
Kingstone
Portway
Twyford Common
Lower Chapel
Llandefalle
Bronllys
Hay Bluff
Craswall
Golden Valley
Turnastone
Upper Maes-coed
Allensmore
Callow
Garthbrengy
Talachddu
Llanfilo
The Tumpa
Llanelieu
Michaelchurch Escley
Middle Maes-coed
St Margaret's
Thruxton
Winnal
Dewshall Court
Aconbury
Pwllgloyw
Sarnau
Felinfach
Talgarth
Tredustan
Trefecca
Newton
Kerry's Gate
Cockyard
Didley
Kivernoll
King's Thorn
Llandefaelog Fach
Llanddew
Tredomen
Llandefaelog-tre'r-graig
Llanveynoe
Lower Maes-coed
Bacton
St Devereux
Little Birch
Much Birch
Battle
Brecon Gaer Roman Fort
Cathedral
Brecon
(Aberhonddu)
Llanywern
Llanfihangel Tal-y-llyn
Pengenffordd
Mynydd Troed
Black Mountains
Y Mynyddoedd Duon
Longtown
Abbey Dore
Wormbridge
Howton
Kilpeck
Much Dewchurch
Wormelow Tump
Hoarwithy
Llandinabo
Llanfaes
Llanspyddid
Brecknock Museum and Art Gallery
Regimental Museum of the Royal Welsh
Llechfaen
Llangors
Llanthony
Priory
Clodock
Ewyas Harold
Pontrilas
Orcop Hill
Llanwarne
Harewood End
Talyllyn
Llanhamlach
Llangorse Lake
Llangasty Talyllyn
Cathedine
Llanfrynach
Scethrog
Hatterrall Hill
Rowlestone
Walterstone
Llangua
Monmouth Cap
Kentchurch
Grosmont
Garway Hill
Bagwy Llydiart
Orcop
Pencoyd
Michaelchurch
St Owens Cross
St Weonards
Tretire
Pencelli
Cross Oak
Talybont-on-Usk
Llansantffraed
Cwmrhos
Cwmdu
Oldcastle
Cwmyoy
Tre-wyn
Pandy
White Rocks
Hoaldalbert
Garway
Broad Oak
Three Ashes
Pen y Fan
Aber-Village
Danywenallt
Brecon Beacons
Bwlch
Tretower Castle & Court
Pen Cerig-calch
Tretower
Gaer
Llanbedr
Stanton
Coed-y-Cerrig
Llanfihangel-Crucorney
Llangattock Lingoed
Skenfrith
Llangarron
Llancloudy
Neuadd Reservoirs
Talybont Res.
Coed-yr-ynys
Llangynidr
Crickhowell
Bettws
Llanfihangel Court
Bont
Upper Green
Cross Ash
Crossway
Llanrothal
Welsh Newton
Llangrove
Whitchurch
Abercynafon
Ffawyddog
Llangattock
Llangenny
Cwrt-y-gollen
Glangrwyney
Llantilio Pertholey
Mardy
Wayne Green
Newcastle
Llanvetherine
Llanfaenor
St Maughans
Maypole
Ganarew
Buckholt
Garn Caws
Mynydd Llangynidr
Craig y Cilau
Mynydd Llangattock
Llwyn-du
Bryn-y-gwenin
Llantilio Crossenny
Llangattock-Vibon-Avel
Onen
Rockfield
Nant-ddu
Pontsticill Reservoir
Garwnant Visitor Centre
Gilwern
Llanelly
Govilon
Abergavenny
(Y Fenni)
Llanvapley
Llanvihangel Ystern-Llewern
Dixton
Clydach
Blackrock
Llanfoist
Llanddewi Rhydderch
Wernyrheolydd
Penrhôs
Monmouth
(Trefynwy)
Wyesham
Trefil
Rassau
Garnlydan
Brynmawr
Llanelly Hill
Blorenge
Coed Morgan
Llanarth
Wonastow
Monnow
Penallt
Pontsticill
Brecon Mountain Railway
Tafarnau-bach
Beaufort
Dukestown
Sirhowy
Ebbw Vale
(Glyn Ebwy)
Nantyglo
Garn-yr-erw
Llanellen
Llangattock nigh Usk
Bryngwyn
Pen-yr-heol
Dingestow
Tregare
Mitchel Troy
Mitcheltroy Common
Vaynor
Princetown
Tredegar
Coalbrookvale
Blaenavon
Llanover
Llanvihangel Gobion
Raglan
Pen-y-clawdd
Cwmcarvan
Pen-twyn
Cefn-coed-y-cymmer
Dowlais
Llechryd
Georgetown
Forge Side
Blaina
Rhyd-y-meirch
Llanfair Kilgheddin
Caer Llan
Hoop
Gellideg
Rhymney
(Rhymni)
Pontlottyn
Waunlwyd
Cwmavon
Pen-groes-oped
Nant-y-derry
Monmouthshire
(Sir Fynwy)
Bettws Newydd
Twyn-y-Sheriff
Kingcoed
Llangovan
Trellech
Whitebrook
Pen-yr-Heolgerrig
Fochriw
Abertysswg
New Tredegar
East Bank
Varteg
Cwmtillery
Abertillery
(Abertyleri)
Goetre
Kemeys Commander
Llandogo
Merthyr Tydfil
Pentrebach
Garndiffaith
Penperlleni
Llandenny
Parkhouse
Abercanaid
Troedyrhiw
Tirphil
Man-moel
Talywain
Abersychan
Little Mill
Llancayo
Llanishen
Catbrook
Aber-nant
Cwmbach
Hollybush
Aberbeeg
Torfaen
(Tor-faen)
Trevethin
Monkswood
Llansoy
Trelleck Grange
Deri
Glascoed
Gwernesney

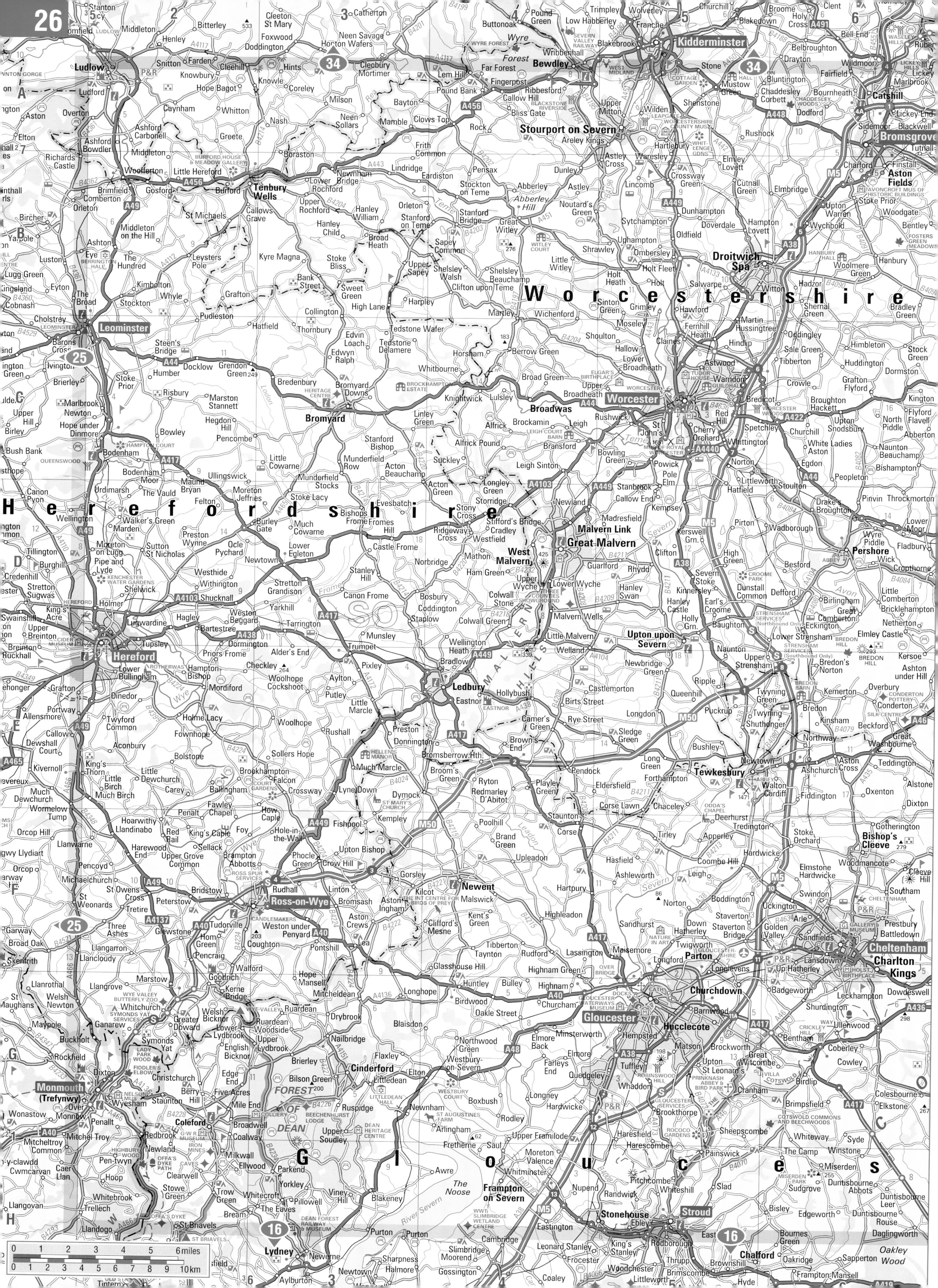
Herefordshire
Worcestershire
Gloucester
Ludlow
Leominster
Kidderminster
Bewdley
Stourport on Severn
Bromsgrove
Tenbury Wells
Bromyard
Worcester
Droitwich Spa
Malvern Link
Great Malvern
West Malvern
Hereford
Ledbury
Upton upon Severn
Pershore
Tewkesbury
Ross-on-Wye
Newent
Cheltenham
Charlton Kings
Gloucester
Hucclecote
Churchdown
Monmouth
(Trefynwy)
Coleford
Cinderford
Lydney
Stroud
Stonehouse
Frampton on Severn
Chalford
Bishop's Cleeve
Broadwas
Catshill
Aston Fields
Forest of Dean
Wyre Forest
Malvern Hills
River Severn
The Noose
Cleobury Mortimer
Abberley Hill
Bredon Hill
Oakley Wood
M5
M50
A49
A44
A417
A449
A38
A40
A456
A4103
A438
A48
A466
A4137
A443
A451
A448
A4440
A422
A46
25
34
16
0 1 2 3 4 5 6 miles
0 1 2 3 4 5 6 7 8 9 10km

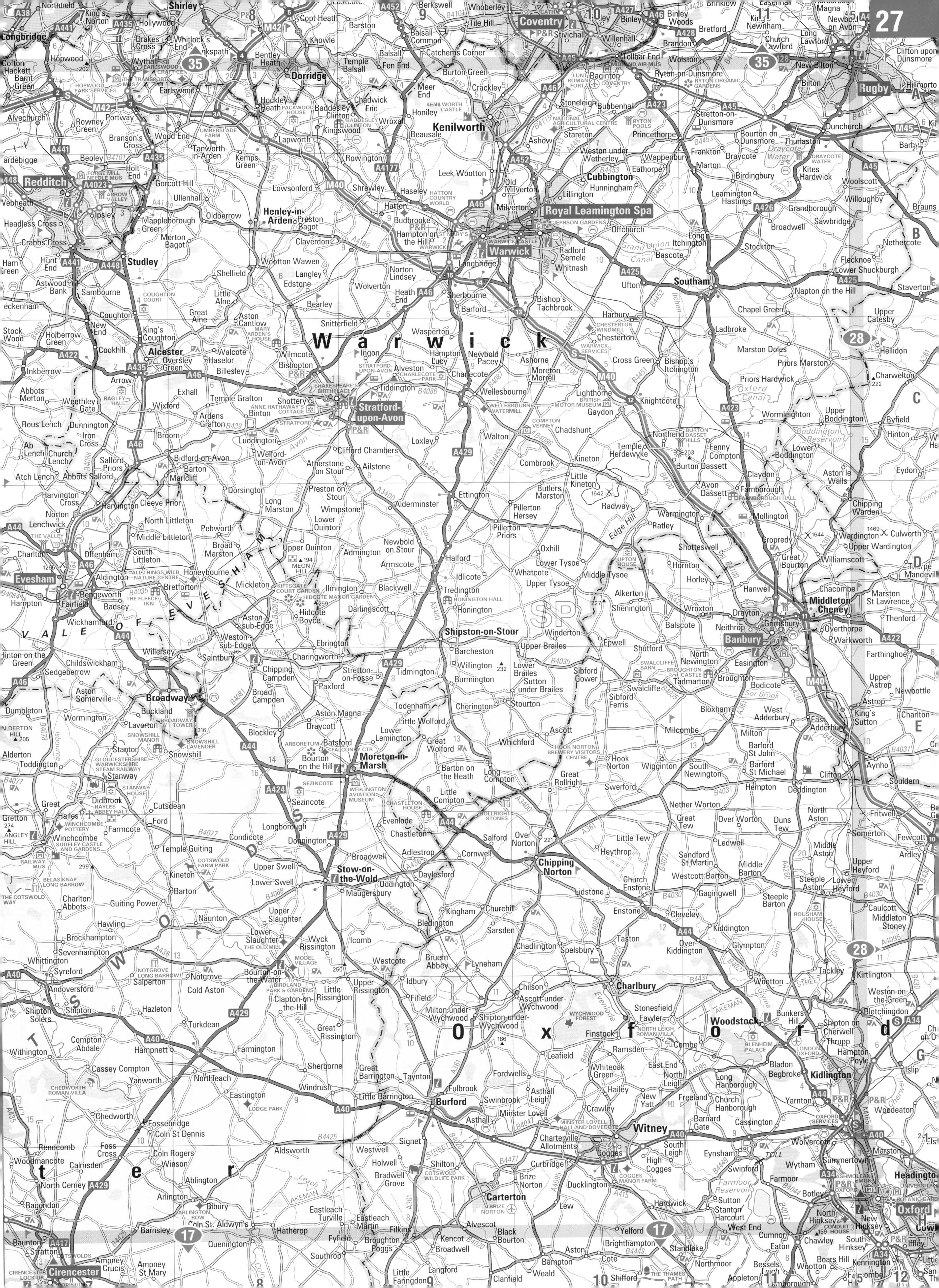
27
Warwick
Oxford
Vale of Evesham
Cotswolds
SP
Coventry
Royal Leamington Spa
Warwick
Kenilworth
Rugby
Redditch
Studley
Alcester
Stratford-upon-Avon
Evesham
Broadway
Chipping Campden
Shipston-on-Stour
Moreton-in-Marsh
Stow-on-the-Wold
Chipping Norton
Banbury
Southam
Middleton Cheney
Woodstock
Kidlington
Charlbury
Burford
Witney
Carterton
Oxford
Cirencester
Winchcombe
Bourton-on-the-Water
Henley-in-Arden
Dorridge
Shirley
Longbridge
Wellesbourne
Kineton
Deddington
Headington
Botley
Eynsham
Northleach
Fairford
Lechlade
M42
M40
M45
A44
A46
A429
A424
A40
A361
A3400
A422
A423
A425
A435
A45
A452
A34
A4260
A417
A436
A4177
A4023
A441
35
28
17
Coleshill
Balsall Common
Kingswood
Lapworth
Hatton
Claverdon
Wootton Wawen
Snitterfield
Hampton Lucy
Charlecote
Barford
Bishop's Tachbrook
Harbury
Ufton
Long Itchington
Stockton
Napton on the Hill
Fenny Compton
Farnborough
Mollington
Cropredy
Wardington
Ettington
Halford
Tredington
Ilmington
Mickleton
Honeybourne
Bretforton
Badsey
Willersey
Saintbury
Snowshill
Stanton
Stanway
Blockley
Batsford
Bourton on the Hill
Long Compton
Little Compton
Hook Norton
Great Rollright
Enstone
Kingham
Churchill
Bledington
Milton under Wychwood
Shipton-under-Wychwood
Ascott-under-Wychwood
Leafield
Finstock
Ramsden
Stonesfield
Bladon
Yarnton
Cassington
Hanborough
Minster Lovell
Asthall
Swinbrook
Fulbrook
Taynton
Great Barrington
Little Barrington
Windrush
Sherborne
Farmington
Aldsworth
Bibury
Coln St Aldwyn's
Hatherop
Quenington
Southrop
Filkins
Kencot
Broadwell
Alvescot
Black Bourton
Bampton
Aston
Standlake
Northmoor
Stanton Harcourt
Sutton
Cumnor
Wytham
Wolvercote
Summertown
Marston
Kennington
Iffley
Cowley
Ampney Crucis
Barnsley
Rendcomb
North Cerney
Bagendon
Baunton
Stratton
Chedworth
Withington
Compton Abdale
Hampnett
Turkdean
Hazleton
Notgrove
Cold Aston
Salperton
Sevenhampton
Syreford
Andoversford
Whittington
Brockhampton
Hawling
Guiting Power
Naunton
Upper Slaughter
Lower Slaughter
Upper Swell
Lower Swell
Broadwell
Donnington
Longborough
Condicote
Temple Guiting
Kineton
Barton
Ford
Cutsdean
Farmcote
Didbrook
Hailes
Toddington
Alderton
Dumbleton
Wormington
Laverton
Buckland
Aston Somerville
Childswickham
Sedgeberrow
Hinton on the Green
Wickhamford
Bengeworth
Hampton
Aldington
Offenham
Charlton
Cropthorne
Harvington
Norton
Lenchwick
Salford Priors
Abbots Salford
Bidford-on-Avon
Marcliff
Welford-on-Avon
Luddington
Binton
Temple Grafton
Ardens Grafton
Exhall
Wixford
Broom
Dunnington
Rous Lench
Weethley Gate
Arrow
Abbots Morton
Inkberrow
Oversley Green
Haselor
Walcote
Billesley
Great Alne
Aston Cantlow
Wilmcote
Bishopton
Shottery
Tiddington
Alveston
Loxley
Walton
Wellesbourne
Combrook
Butlers Marston
Pillerton Hersey
Pillerton Priors
Oxhill
Whatcote
Idlicote
Honington
Barcheston
Willington
Burmington
Cherington
Stourton
Whichford
Ascott
Todenham
Lower Lemington
Great Wolford
Little Wolford
Barton on the Heath
Evenlode
Chastleton
Adlestrop
Cornwell
Salford
Over Norton
Heythrop
Little Tew
Great Tew
Nether Worton
Over Worton
Duns Tew
North Aston
Middle Aston
Steeple Aston
Lower Heyford
Upper Heyford
Somerton
Fewcott
Ardley
Souldern
Aynho
Clifton
Hempton
Barford St John
Barford St Michael
Milcombe
Bloxham
Wigginton
Swerford
South Newington
Milton
Adderbury
Bodicote
Broughton
Tadmarton
Swalcliffe
Sibford Ferris
Sibford Gower
Shutford
North Newington
Epwell
Winderton
Upper Brailes
Lower Brailes
Sutton under Brailes
Alkerton
Shenington
Wroxton
Balscote
Drayton
Hanwell
Horley
Hornton
Shotteswell
Ratley
Radway
Warmington
Avon Dassett
Burton Dassett
Northend
Gaydon
Lighthorne
Chadshunt
Moreton Morrell
Ashorne
Newbold Pacey
Wasperton
Sherbourne
Chesterton
Bishop's Itchington
Cross Green
Ladbroke
Marston Doles
Priors Marston
Priors Hardwick
Wormleighton
Claydon
Hellidon
Charwelton
Byfield
Boddington
Aston le Walls
Eydon
Chipping Warden
Culworth
Thenford
Warkworth
Farthinghoe
Astrop
King's Sutton
Charlton
Newbottle
Chacombe
Marston St Lawrence
Overthorpe
Grimsbury
Neithrop
Easington
Hinton
Bascote
Offchurch
Radford Semele
Whitnash
Lillington
Cubbington
Hunningham
Weston under Wetherley
Eathorpe
Wappenbury
Marton
Frankton
Birdingbury
Leamington Hastings
Grandborough
Broadwell
Sawbridge
Willoughby
Woolscott
Kites Hardwick
Draycote
Thurlaston
Bourton on Dunsmore
Princethorpe
Stretton-on-Dunsmore
Dunchurch
Bilton
New Bilton
Hillmorton
Barby
Clifton upon Dunsmore
Newbold on Avon
Long Lawford
Church Lawford
King's Newnham
Bretford
Brandon
Wolston
Ryton-on-Dunsmore
Bubbenhall
Stoneleigh
Stareton
Ashow
Baginton
Willenhall
Binley
Binley Woods
Stivichall
Tile Hill
Whoberley
Berkswell
Balsall Common
Burton Green
Crackley
Honiley
Beausale
Haseley
Rowington
Shrewley
Leek Wootton
Old Milverton
Milverton
Budbrooke
Hampton on the Hill
Longbridge
Norton Lindsey
Wolverton
Langley
Edstone
Bearley
Heath End
Preston Bagot
Lowsonford
Wroxall
Chadwick End
Baddesley Clinton
Hockley Heath
Temple Balsall
Knowle
Barston
Bentley Heath
Copt Heath
Catchems Corner
Meer End
Fen End
Balsall
Earlswood
Wythall
Drakes Cross
Hollywood
Whitlock's End
King's Norton
Northfield
Hopwood
Cofton Hackett
Barnt Green
Alvechurch
Rowney Green
Portway
Branson's Cross
Wood End
Tanworth-in-Arden
Beoley
Holt End
Gorcott Hill
Ullenhall
Oldberrow
Mappleborough Green
Morton Bagot
Ipsley
Headless Cross
Webheath
Crabbs Cross
Hunt End
Astwood Bank
Sambourne
Coughton
Kings Coughton
Cookhill
Holberrow Green
New End
Stock Wood
Shelfield
Little Alne
Ullenhall
Kemps Green
Lapworth
Dorsington
Long Marston
Pebworth
Broad Marston
Cleeve Prior
North Littleton
Middle Littleton
South Littleton
Atherstone on Stour
Preston on Stour
Clifford Chambers
Ailstone
Wimpstone
Alderminster
Lower Quinton
Upper Quinton
Admington
Newbold on Stour
Armscote
Blackwell
Darlingscott
Hidcote Boyce
Aston sub-Edge
Weston sub-Edge
Ebrington
Charingworth
Stretton-on-Fosse
Tidmington
Paxford
Broad Campden
Aston Magna
Draycott
Sezincote
Oddington
Daylesford
Maugersbury
Icomb
Wyck Rissington
Little Rissington
Great Rissington
Upper Rissington
Westcote
Idbury
Fifield
Bruern Abbey
Lyneham
Sarsden
Chadlington
Spelsbury
Taston
Chilson
Clapton-on-the-Hill
Eastington
Yanworth
Cassey Compton
Fossebridge
Coln St Dennis
Coln Rogers
Winson
Ablington
Arlington
Foss Cross
Calmsden
Woodmancote
Eastleach Turville
Eastleach Martin
Holwell
Westwell
Signet
Shilton
Bradwell Grove
Brize Norton
Curbridge
Charterville Allotments
Ducklington
Hardwick
Cogges
Coombe
Long Hanborough
Freeland
Church Hanborough
Barnard Gate
North Leigh
East End
New Yatt
Hailey
Crawley
Whiteoak Green
Fawler
Fordwells
Worsham
Kiddington
Over Kiddington
Glympton
Wootton
Tackley
Kirtlington
Weston-on-the-Green
Bletchingdon
Shipton on Cherwell
Thrupp
Hampton Poyle
Islip
Begbroke
Woodeaton
Steeple Barton
Middle Barton
Westcott Barton
Sandford St Martin
Ledwell
Gagingwell
Church Enstone
Lidstone
Cleveley
Rousham
Caulcott
Middleton Stoney
Broughton Poggs
Langford
Little Faringdon
Clanfield
Weald
Cote
Shifford
Brighthampton
Yelford
Appleton
Bessels Leigh
Eaton
Wootton
Boars Hill
Chawley
North Hinkley
New Hinksey
South Hinksey
Farmoor
Sutton
Upper Boddington
Lower Boddington
Upper Catesby
Stourton
Whitnash
Frankton
Bourton
Great Bourton
Williamscott
Upper Wardington
Grimsbury
Flecknoe
Lower Shuckburgh
Staverton
Nethercote
Chapel Green
Ufton
Thorpe Mandeville
Wardington
Little Kineton
Edge Hill
Stanway
Gretton
Greet
Langley Hill
Sudeley Castle and Gardens
Hailes Abbey
Kiftsgate Court Garden
Hidcote Manor Garden
Meon Hill
Upton House
Compton Verney
Charlecote Park
Warwick Castle
Kenilworth Castle
Coventry Airport
Ryton Organic Gardens
National Agricultural Centre
British Motor Museum
Burton Dassett Hills
Broughton Castle
Swalcliffe Barn
Farnborough Hall
Chastleton House
Rollright Stones
Wellington Aviation Museum
Cotswold Farm Park
Cotswold Wildlife Park
Blenheim Palace
North Leigh Roman Villa
Minster Lovell Hall and Dovecote
Cogges Manor Farm
Wychwood Forest
Chedworth Roman Villa
Lodge Park
Belas Knap Long Barrow
Notgrove Long Barrow
Snowshill Manor
Broadway Tower
Gloucestershire Warwickshire Steam Railway
Anne Hathaway's Cottage
Shakespeare's Birthplace
Mary Arden's House
Ragley Hall
Coughton Court
Forge Mill Needle Mus
Arrow Valley
Packwood House
Baddesley Clinton
Umberslade Farm
Hatton Country World
Jephson Gardens
Draycote Water
Oxford Canal
Grand Union Canal
Farmoor Reservoir
Boddington Reservoir
The Thames Path
Avon
Stour
Windrush
Evenlode
Leach
Coln
Churn
Cherwell
Leam
Itchen
Glyme
Dorn
Isbourne
Sor Brook

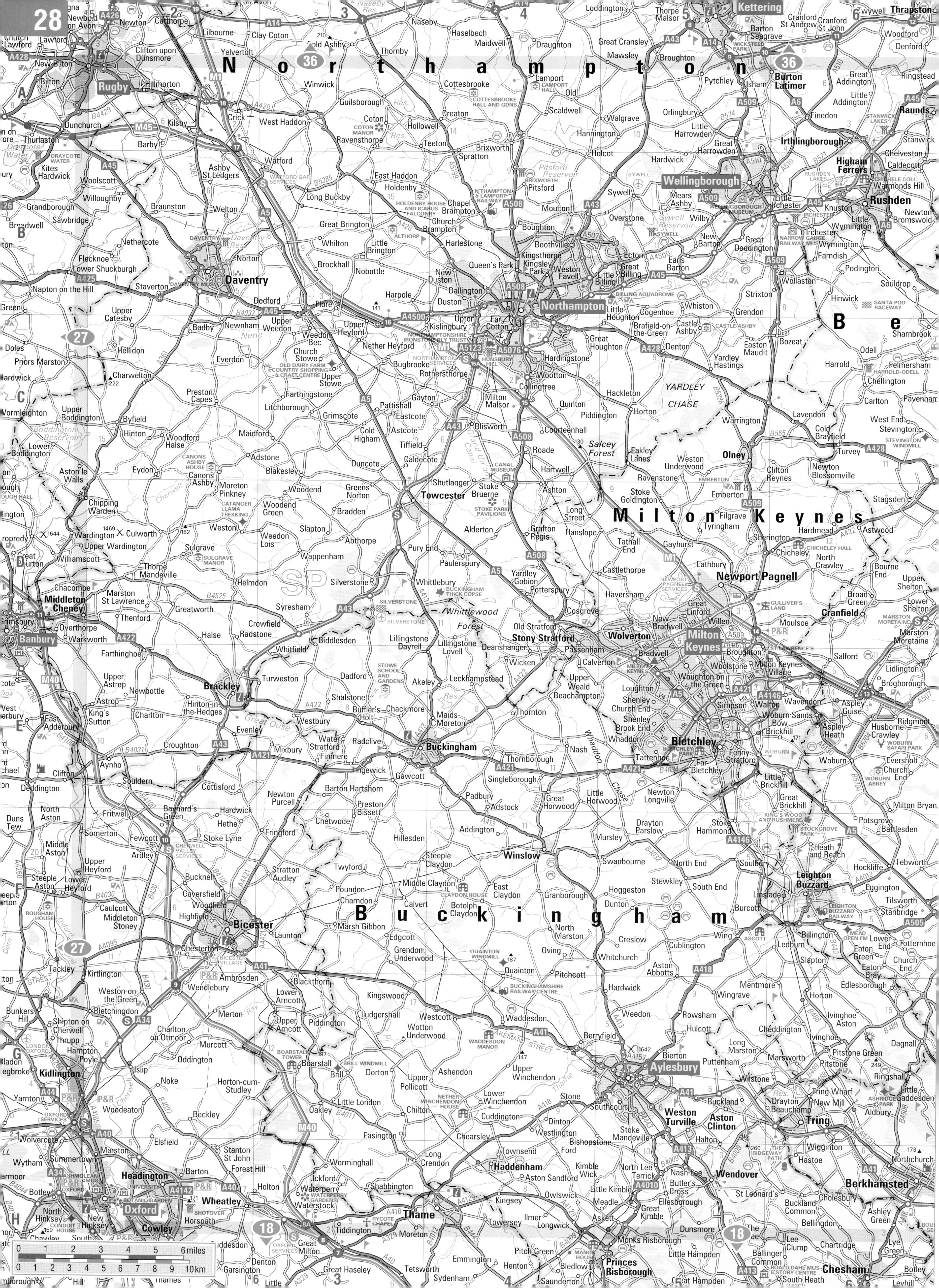
Northampton
Milton Keynes
Buckingham
Be
Rugby
Daventry
Kettering
Wellingborough
Northampton
Rushden
Higham Ferrers
Irthlingborough
Raunds
Thrapston
Burton Latimer
Towcester
Brackley
Banbury
Bicester
Buckingham
Newport Pagnell
Olney
Wolverton
Stony Stratford
Milton Keynes
Bletchley
Winslow
Leighton Buzzard
Aylesbury
Tring
Berkhamsted
Wendover
Princes Risborough
Chesham
Thame
Haddenham
Oxford
Kidlington
Wheatley
Cowley
Headington
Middleton Cheney
Cranfield
Dunchurch
Crick
Long Buckby
Brixworth
Moulton
Earls Barton
Silverstone
Whittlewood Forest
Salcey Forest
Yardley Chase
Deanshanger
Steeple Claydon
Waddesdon
Stoke Mandeville
Weston Turville
Aston Clinton
Long Crendon
Great Milton
Tetsworth
Pitsford Reservoir
Sywell Reservoir
Daventry Res.
Draycote Water
36
27
18
M1
M40
M45
A5
A43
A41
A421
A413
A418
0 1 2 3 4 5 6 miles
0 1 2 3 4 5 6 7 8 9 10 km

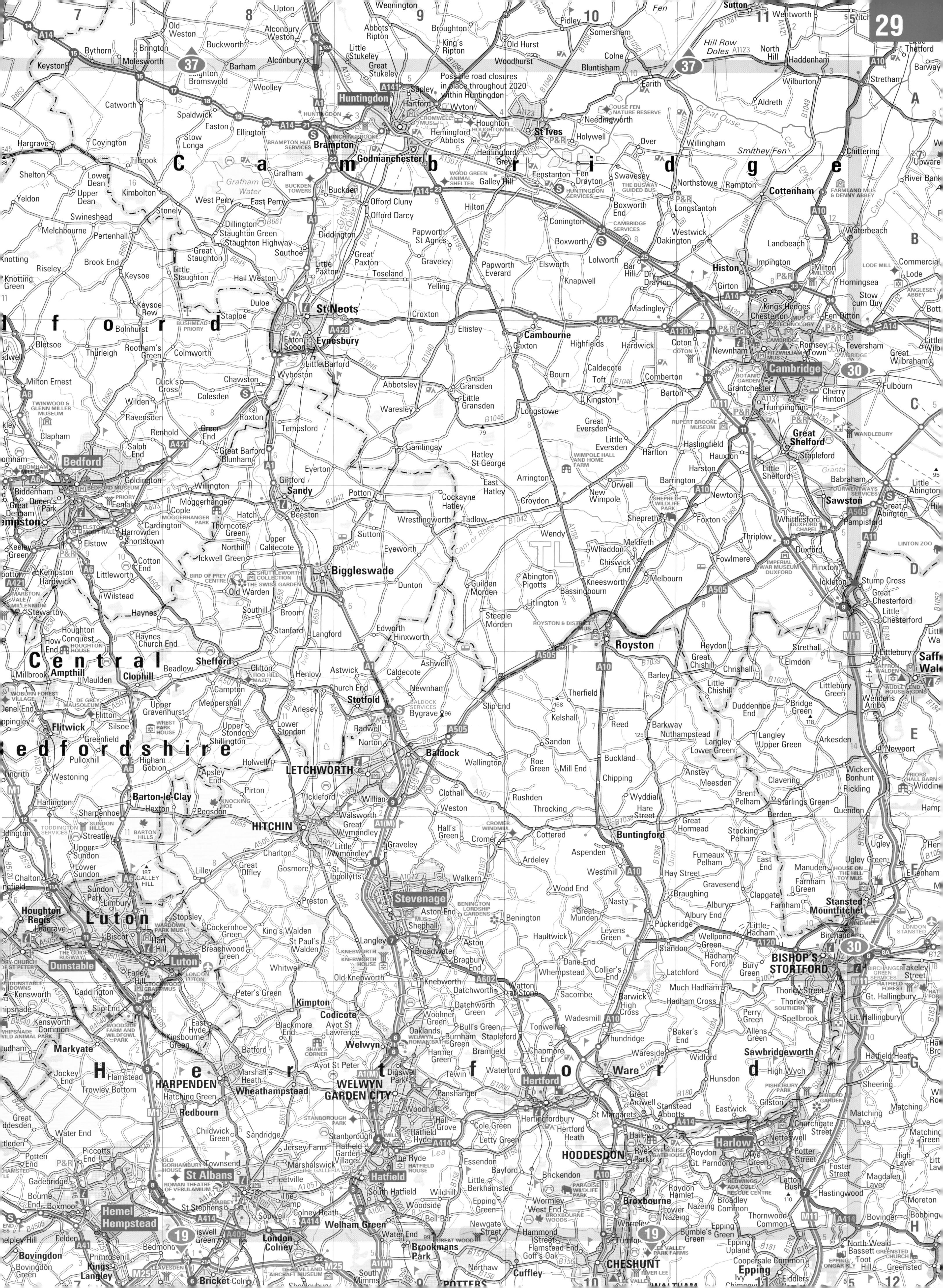
Cambridge
Bedford
Hertford
Central Bedfordshire
Luton
Huntingdon
Possible road closures in place throughout 2020 within Huntingdon
St Ives
Brampton
Godmanchester
St Neots
Eynesbury
Eaton Socon
Cambourne
Cambridge
Histon
Cottenham
Chesterton
Sandy
Biggleswade
Royston
Shefford
Ampthill
Flitwick
Stotfold
Baldock
Letchworth
Hitchin
Stevenage
Luton
Dunstable
Houghton Regis
Harpenden
Welwyn Garden City
Hertford
Ware
Bishop's Stortford
Stansted Mountfitchet
Sawbridgeworth
Harlow
Hoddesdon
Broxbourne
Cheshunt
Hatfield
St Albans
Hemel Hempstead
London Colney
Welham Green
Brookmans Park
Buntingford
Great Shelford
Sawston
Kempston
Barton-le-Clay
Wheathampstead
Redbourn
Welwyn
Codicote
Kimpton
Newport
Saffron Walden
37
30
19
TL
Fen
Great Ouse
Grafham Water
Smithey Fen
Cam or Rhee
Ivel
Lea
Stort
Granta
Rib
Quin

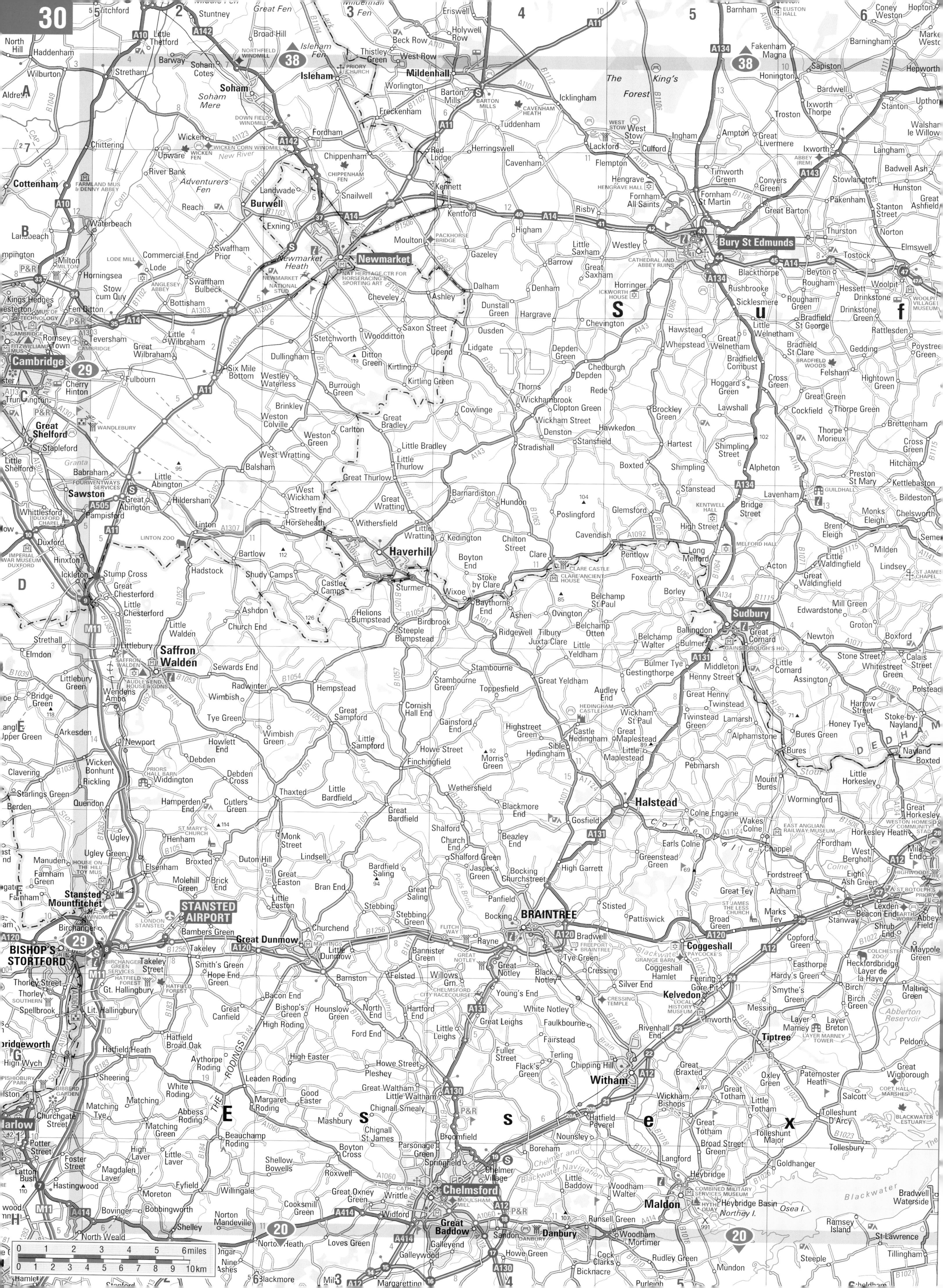
Littleport
Stuntney
Great Fen
Isleham Fen
Mildenhall Fen
Eriswell
Barnham
Coney Weston
Hopton
North Hill
Haddenham
Little Thetford
Broad Hill
Northfield Windmill
Beck Row
Holywell Row
Barningham
Market Weston
Wilburton
Stretham
Barway
Soham Cotes
Isleham
Thistley Green
West Row
Fakenham Magna
Sapiston
Hepworth
Priory Church
Mildenhall
The King's Forest
Honington
Soham
Soham Mere
Worlington
Barton Mills
Icklingham
Bardwell
Upthorpe
Aldreth
Freckenham
Cavenham Heath
Troston
Ixworth Thorpe
Stanton
Down Field Windmill
Tuddenham
West Stow
Walsham le Willows
Wicken
Fordham
Red Lodge
Ingham
Ampton
Great Livermere
Chittering
Wicken Corn Windmill
Upware
Wicken Fen
New River
Chippenham
Herringswell
Lackford
Culford
Ixworth
Langham
Cavenham
Flempton
Timworth Green
Abbey (Rem)
Badwell Ash
River Bank
Chippenham Fen
Kennett
Hengrave
Hengrave Hall
Conyers Green
Stowlangtoft
Cottenham
Farmland Mus & Denny Abbey
Adventurers' Fen
Landwade
Snailwell
Fornham All Saints
Fornham St Martin
Pakenham
Hunston
Great Ashfield
Reach
Burwell
Kentford
Risby
Great Barton
Stanton Street
Waterbeach
Exning
Higham
Thurston
Norton
Landbeach
Moulton
Packhorse Bridge
Little Saxham
Westley
Bury St Edmunds
Tostock
Lode Mill
Commercial End
Swaffham Prior
Newmarket Heath
Newmarket
Gazeley
Barrow
Cathedral and Abbey Ruins
Elmswell
Histon
Milton
Horningsea
Lode
Nat Heritage Ctr for Horseracing & Sporting Art
Great Saxham
Blackthorpe
Beyton
Woolpit
Kings Hedges
Stow cum Quy
Swaffham Bulbeck
Anglesey Abbey
Newmarket National Stud
Dalham
Denham
Horringer
Rougham
Hessett
Drinkstone
Woolpit Village Museum
Chesterton
Fen Ditton
Bottisham
Cheveley
Ashley
Ickworth House
Rushbrooke
Sicklesmere
Rougham Green
Drinkstone Green
Mus of Technology
Dunstall Green
Hargrave
Bradfield St George
Cambridge
Teversham
Romsey Town
Saxon Street
Ousden
Chevington
Little Welnetham
Rattlesden
Fitzwilliam Mus
Stetchworth
Woodditton
Hawstead
Great Welnetham
Great Wilbraham
Little Wilbraham
Ditton Green
Lidgate
Whepstead
Bradfield St Clare
Gedding
Poystreet Green
Dullingham
Kirtling
Upend
Depden Green
Chedburgh
Depden
Bradfield Combust
Bradfield Woods
Felsham
Cherry Hinton
Six Mile Bottom
Fulbourn
Westley Waterless
Burrough Green
Kirtling Green
Thorns
Rede
Hoggard's Green
Cross Green
Hightown Green
Trumpington
Wickhambrook
Clopton Green
Lawshall
Great Green
Cockfield
Thorpe Green
Wandlebury
Brinkley
Great Bradley
Cowlinge
Wickham Street
Brockley Green
Great Shelford
Stapleford
Weston Colville
Carlton
Weston Green
Denston
Hawkedon
Stansfield
Brettenham
Thorpe Morieux
Little Bradley
Stradishall
Hartest
Shimpling Street
Cross Green
West Wratting
Balsham
Little Thurlow
Boxted
Shimpling
Alpheton
Hitcham
Little Shelford
Granta
Babraham
Great Thurlow
Preston St Mary
Little Abington
Barnardiston
Stanstead
Kettlebaston
Sawston
Fourwentways Services
Great Abington
West Wickham
Great Wratting
Hundon
Poslingford
Glemsford
Guildhall
Lavenham
Bildeston
Whittlesford
Hildersham
Streetly End
Kentwell Hall
Bridge Street
Monks Eleigh
Duxford Chapel
Pampisford
Horseheath
Withersfield
Chilton Street
Cavendish
High Street
Chelsworth
Duxford
Linton
Linton Zoo
Little Wratting
Kedington
Brent Eleigh
Semer
Imperial War Museum Duxford
Hinxton
Bartlow
Haverhill
Boyton End
Clare
Pentlow
Long Melford
Melford Hall
Milden
Ickleton
Stump Cross
Hadstock
Shudy Camps
Stoke by Clare
Clare Castle
Clare Ancient House
Little Waldingfield
Acton
Lindsey
St James Chapel
Great Chesterford
Castle Camps
Sturmer
Foxearth
Great Waldingfield
Little Chesterford
Ashdon
Helions Bumpstead
Wixoe
Baythorne End
Belchamp St Paul
Borley
Ashen
Ovington
Mill Green
Edwardstone
Strethall
Little Walden
Church End
Steeple Bumpstead
Birdbrook
Ridgewell
Tilbury Juxta Clare
Belchamp Otten
Sudbury
Great Cornard
Groton
Elmdon
Littlebury
Saffron Walden
Sewards End
Little Yeldham
Belchamp Walter
Ballingdon
Bulmer
Newton
Boxford
Gainsborough's Ho
Audley End House & Gdns
Radwinter
Hempstead
Stambourne
Stambourne Green
Toppesfield
Great Yeldham
Bulmer Tye
Gestingthorpe
Middleton
Henny Street
Little Cornard
Assington
Stone Street
Whitestreet Green
Calais Street
Littlebury Green
Wendens Ambo
Wimbish
Cornish Hall End
Audley End
Hedingham Castle
Wickham St Paul
Great Henny
Twinstead
Polstead
Bridge Green
Great Sampford
Gainsford End
Highstreet Green
Twinstead Green
Lamarsh
Harrow Street
Honey Tye
Stoke-by-Nayland
Arkesden
Tye Green
Wimbish Green
Little Sampford
Castle Hedingham
Great Maplestead
Alphamstone
Bures Green
Upper Green
Newport
Howlett End
Howe Street
Morris Green
Sible Hedingham
Little Maplestead
Bures
Nayland
Boxted
Wicken Bonhunt
Debden
Finchingfield
Pebmarsh
Dedham
Clavering
Rickling
Priors Hall Barn
Widdington
Debden Cross
Mount Bures
Little Horkesley
Starlings Green
Thaxted
Little Bardfield
Wethersfield
Halstead
Stour
Berden
Quendon
Hamperden End
Cutlers Green
Blackmore End
Colne Engaine
Wormingford
Great Horkesley
Great Bardfield
Gosfield
Wakes Colne
East Anglian Railway Museum
St Mary's Church
Henham
Ugley
Monk Street
Shalford
Beazley End
Earls Colne
Chappel
Horkesley Heath
Manuden
Ugley Green
Lindsell
Church End
Shalford Green
Greenstead Green
Fordham
West Bergholt
House on the Hill Toy Mus
Broxted
Duton Hill
Bardfield Saling
Jasper's Green
Bocking Churchstreet
High Garrett
Mile End
Farnham Green
Elsenham
Great Easton
Molehill Green
Brick End
Bran End
Great Saling
Fordstreet
Aldham
Eight Ash Green
Farnham
Stansted Mountfitchet
Stansted Airport
Little Easton
Stebbing
Stebbing Green
Panfield
Great Tey
Stisted
Marks Tey
Lexden
Bocking
Braintree
Pattiswick
Stanway
Broad Green
Beacon End
London Stansted
Birchanger
Bambers Green
Churchend
Flitch Way
Shrub End
Bishop's Stortford
Takeley
Great Dunmow
Rayne
Bradwell
Coggeshall
Copford Green
Maypole Green
Freeport Braintree
Birchanger Green Services
Takeley Street
Little Dunmow
Bannister Green
Great Notley
Tye Green
Paycocke's
Colchester Zoo
Heckfordbridge
Layer de la Haye
Eastthorpe
Smith's Green
Hope End Green
Felsted
Willows Grn
Black Notley
Cressing
Coggeshall Hamlet
Grange Barn
Thorley Street
Hatfield Forest
Barnston
Hardy's Green
Thorley
Gt. Hallingbury
Chelmsford City Racecourse
Young's End
Silver End
Feering
Gore Pit
Birch
Malting Green
Southern
Spellbrook
Bacon End
Bishop's Green
Hounslow Green
North End
Hartford End
White Notley
Cressing Temple
Kelvedon
Local History Museum
Smythe's Green
Birch Green
Lit. Hallingbury
Great Canfield
High Roding
Ford End
Great Leighs
Faulkbourne
Inworth
Messing
Abberton Reservoir
Hatfield Broad Oak
Little Leighs
Fairstead
Rivenhall End
Layer Marney
Layer Breton
Layer Marney Tower
Tiptree
Sawbridgeworth
Hatfield Heath
Aythorpe Roding
The Rodings
High Easter
Fuller Street
Terling
Flack's Green
Chipping Hill
Peldon
High Wych
Howe Street
Pleshey
Witham
Great Braxted
Great Wigborough
Gibberd Garden
Sheering
White Roding
Leaden Roding
Great Waltham
Little Waltham
Oxley Green
Paternoster Heath
Copt Hall Marshes
Matching
Margaret Roding
Good Easter
Great Totham
Salcott
Harlow
Churchgate Street
Matching Tye
Abbess Roding
Mashbury
Chignall Smealy
Wickham Bishops
Little Totham
Tolleshunt D'Arcy
Blackwater Estuary
Essex
Chignall St James
Hatfield Peverel
Potter Street
Matching Green
Beauchamp Roding
Broomfield
Nounsley
Great Totham
Tolleshunt Major
Boreham
Broad Street Green
Tollesbury
High Laver
Little Laver
Boyton Cross
Parsonage Green
Springfield
Chelmer Village
Chelmer and Blackwater Navigation
Langford
Goldhanger
Foster Street
Latton Bush
Shellow Bowells
Magdalen Laver
Roxwell
Heybridge
Little Baddow
Woodham Walter
Blackwater
Bradwell Waterside
Hastingwood
Fyfield
Willingale
Moreton
Great Oxney Green
Writtle
Chelmsford
Maldon
Combined Military Services Museum
Hythe Quay
Heybridge Basin
Osea I.
Northey I.
North Weald
Bovinger
Bobbingworth
Norton Mandeville
Cooksmill Green
Widford
Moulsham Mill
Great Baddow
Sandon
Danbury
Russell Green
Ramsey Island
Shelley
Galleyend
Woodham Mortimer
St Lawrence
Norton Heath
Loves Green
Howe Green
Rudley Green
Tillingham
Nine Ashes
Galleywood
Cock Clarks
Steeple
Blackmore
Margaretting
Bicknacre
Mundon
Purleigh
Chelmsford
TL
Suffolk
Essex
0 1 2 3 4 5 6 miles
0 1 2 3 4 5 6 7 8 9 10 km
38
29
20

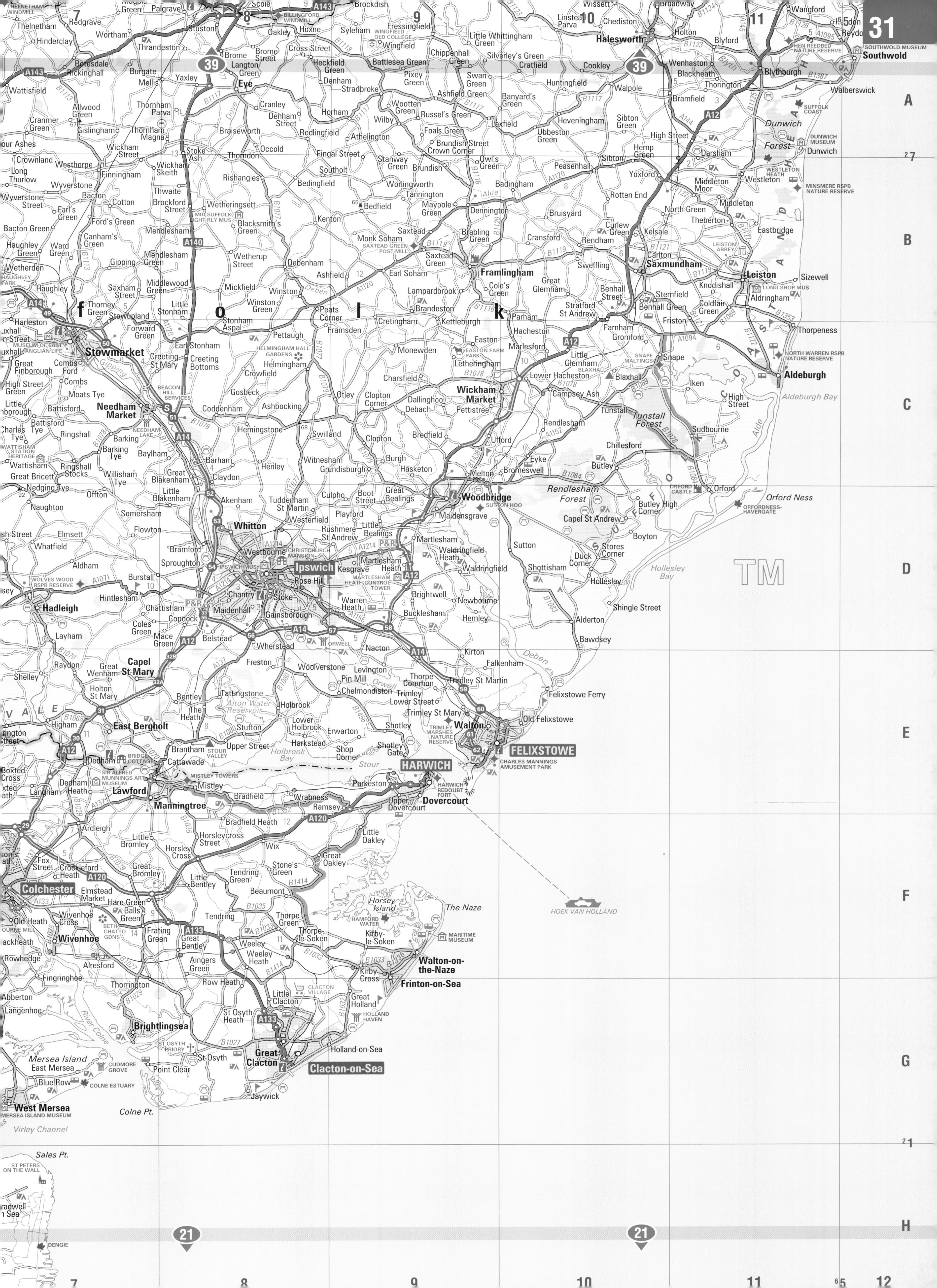

Thelnetham
Redgrave
Palgrave
Scole
A143
Brockdish
Wissett
Broadway
Wangford
Hinderclay
Wortham
Stuston
Oakley
Hoxne
Syleham
Fressingfield
Linstead Parva
Chediston
Halesworth
Holton
Blyford
Southwold
Southwold Museum
Hen Reedbed Nature Reserve
Thrandeston
Brome
Brome Street
Cross Street
Wingfield
Little Whittingham Green
Botesdale
Rickinghall
Burgate
Yaxley
Langton Green
Eye
Heckfield Green
Battlesea Green
Chippenhall Green
Silverley's Green
Cratfield
Cookley
Wenhaston
Blackheath
Blythburgh
Thorington
Walberswick
Wattisfield
Mellis
Denham
Stradbroke
Pixey Green
Swan Green
Huntingfield
Walpole
Bramfield
Allwood Green
Thornham Parva
Cranley
Wootten Green
Ashfield Green
Banyard's Green
Suffolk Coast
Cranmer Green
Gislingham
Thornham Magna
Braiseworth
Denham Street
Horham
Wilby
Russel's Green
Laxfield
Heveningham
Sibton Green
Dunwich
Dunwich Forest
Dunwich Museum
Ubbeston Green
High Street
Redlingfield
Athelington
Foals Green
Brundish Street
Crown Corner
Hemp Green
Darsham
Wickham Street
Stoke Ash
Thorndon
Occold
Fingal Street
Stanway Green
Brundish
Owl's Green
Peasenhall
Sibton
Yoxford
Crowland
Westhorpe
Wickham Skeith
Southolt
Westleton Heath
Westleton
Long Thurlow
Finningham
Rishangles
Bedingfield
Worlingworth
Badingham
Middleton Moor
Minsmere RSPB Nature Reserve
Wyverstone
Thwaite
Tannington
Rotten End
Middleton
Wyverstone Street
Bacton
Cotton
Brockford Street
Wetheringsett
Maypole Green
Dennington
Bruisyard
North Green
Theberton
Earl's Green
Ford's Green
Mid Suffolk Light Rly Mus
Blacksmith's Green
Kenton
Bedfield
Curlew Green
Kelsale
Eastbridge
Bacton Green
Mendlesham
Saxtead
Brabling Green
Cransford
Rendham
Carlton
Leiston Abbey
Haughley Green
Ward Green
Canham's Green
Monk Soham
Saxtead Green Post Mill
Framlingham
Sweffling
Saxmundham
Leiston
Sizewell
Wetherden
Haughley Park
Gipping
Mendlesham Green
Wetherup Street
Debenham
Saxtead Green
Earl Soham
Great Glemham
Benhall Street
Knodishall
Haughley
Saxham Street
Middlewood Green
Mickfield
Winston
Ashfield
Lampardbrook
Cole's Green
Sternfield
Long Shop Mus
Aldringham
Thorney Green
Stowupland
Little Stonham
Winston Green
Peats Corner
Brandeston
Stratford St Andrew
Benhall Green
Coldfair Green
Harleston
Stonham Aspal
Kettleburgh
Parham
Hacheston
Friston
Farnham
Thorpeness
Forward Green
Pettaugh
Framsden
Cretingham
Easton
Gromford
Stowmarket
Museum of East Anglian Life
Earl Stonham
Helmingham Hall Gardens
Monewden
Easton Farm Park
Marlesford
Little Glemham
Snape Maltings
Snape
North Warren RSPB Nature Reserve
Great Finborough
Combs
Combs Ford
Creeting St Mary
Creeting Bottoms
Helmingham
Letheringham
Blaxhall
Blaxhall
Aldeburgh
Crowfield
Charsfield
Lower Hacheston
High Street
Moats Tye
Gosbeck
Otley
Clopton Corner
Dallinghoo
Debach
Wickham Market
Pettistree
Campsey Ash
Iken
Aldeburgh Bay
Battisford
Needham Market
Beacon Hill Services
Coddenham
Ashbocking
Tunstall
Tunstall Forest
High Street
Battisford Tye
Ringshall
Needham Lake
Barking
Hemingstone
Swilland
Clopton
Bredfield
Rendlesham
Sudbourne
Wattisham Station Heritage
Barking Tye
Baylham
Ufford
Chillesford
Wattisham
Ringshall Stocks
Barham
Henley
Witnesham
Burgh
Grundisburgh
Hasketon
Melton
Eyke
Bromeswell
Butley
Alde
Great Bricett
Willisham Tye
Great Blakenham
Claydon
Nedging Tye
Offton
Little Blakenham
Akenham
Tuddenham St Martin
Culpho
Boot Street
Great Bealings
Woodbridge
Sutton Hoo
Rendlesham Forest
Orford Castle
Orford
Orford Ness
Orfordness-Havergate
Naughton
Somersham
Westerfield
Playford
Maidensgrave
Butley High Corner
Capel St Andrew
Whitton
Little Bealings
Rushmere St Andrew
Martlesham
Flowton
Elmsett
Bramford
Westbourne
Christchurch Mansion
Waldringfield Heath
Waldringfield
Sutton
Boyton
Whatfield
Sproughton
Ipswich
Ipswichmus
Kesgrave
Martlesham Heath
Martlesham Heath Control Tower
Stores Corner
Duck Corner
Shottisham
Hollesley Bay
Hollesley
TM
Aldham
Wolves Wood RSPB Reserve
Burstall
Rose Hill
Hintlesham
Chantry
Stoke
Warren Heath
Brightwell
Newbourne
Hadleigh
Chattisham
Copdock
Maidenhall
Gainsborough
Bucklesham
Hemley
Alderton
Shingle Street
Layham
Coles Green
Mace Green
Belstead
Wherstead
Orwell
Nacton
Kirton
Bawdsey
Falkenham
Deben
Raydon
Great Wenham
Capel St Mary
Freston
Woolverstone
Levington
Pin Mill
Thorpe Common
Trimley St Martin
Shelley
Holton St Mary
Bentley
Tattingstone
Alton Water Reservoir
Holbrook
Chelmondiston
Trimley Lower Street
Felixstowe Ferry
Vale
Higham
The Heath
East Bergholt
Stutton
Lower Holbrook
Erwarton
Shotley
Trimley St Mary
Walton
Trimley Marshes Nature Reserve
Old Felixstowe
Dedham
Bridge Cottage
Brantham
Stour Valley
Upper Street
Harkstead
Holbrook Bay
Shop Corner
Shotley Gate
Felixstowe
Charles Mannings Amusement Park
Cattawade
Stour
Harwich
Sir Alfred Munnings Art Museum
Dedham Heath
Langham
Lawford
Mistley Towers
Mistley
Parkeston
Harwich Redoubt Fort
Bradfield
Wrabness
Ramsey
Upper Dovercourt
Dovercourt
Manningtree
Bradfield Heath
Ardleigh
Horsleycross Street
Little Bromley
Little Oakley
Horsley Cross
Wix
Great Oakley
Fox Street
Crockleford Heath
Great Bromley
Stone's Green
Tendring Green
Little Bentley
Colchester
Elmstead Market
Beaumont
Hare Green
Balls Green
Horsey Island
The Naze
Old Heath
Wivenhoe Cross
Beth Chatto Gdns
Tendring
Thorpe Green
Hamford Water
Thorpe-le-Soken
Kirby-le-Soken
Maritime Museum
Hoek van Holland
Wivenhoe
Frating Green
Great Bentley
Weeley
Weeley Heath
Walton-on-the-Naze
Rowhedge
Alresford
Aingers Green
Kirby Cross
Frinton-on-Sea
Fingringhoe
Thorrington
Row Heath
Little Clacton
Clacton Village
Great Holland
Holland Haven
Abberton
Langenhoe
River Colne
St Osyth Heath
Brightlingsea
St Osyth Priory
St Osyth
Holland-on-Sea
Great Clacton
Mersea Island
East Mersea
Cudmore Grove
Point Clear
Clacton-on-Sea
Blue Row
Colne Estuary
Jaywick
West Mersea
Mersea Island Museum
Colne Pt.
Virley Channel
Sales Pt.
St Peters on the Wall
Bradwell on Sea
Dengie
39
21
7
8
9
10
11
12
A
B
C
D
E
F
G
H

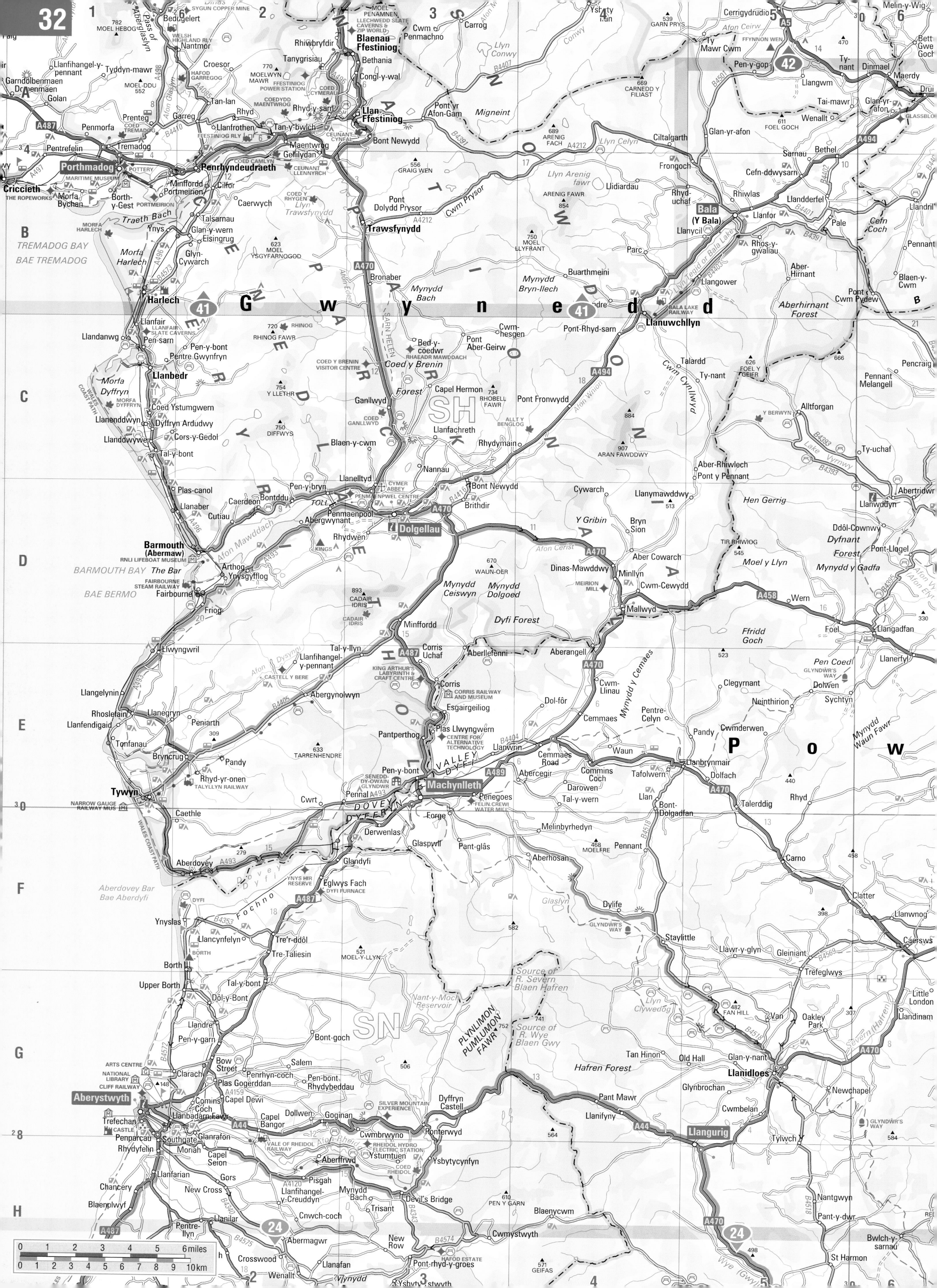
Beddgelert
Nantmor
Blaenau Ffestiniog
Cwm Penmachno
Carrog
Cerrigydrudion
Melin-y-Wig
Rhiwbryfdir
Tanygrisiau
Bethania
Congl-y-wal
Llanfihangel-y-pennant
Tyddyn-mawr
Garndolbenmaen
Dolbenmaen
Golan
Croesor
Tan-lan
Rhyd
Llan Ffestiniog
Rhyd-y-sarn
Pont yr Afon-Gam
Migneint
Penmorfa
Prenteg
Garreg
Llanfrothen
Tan-y-bwlch
Maentwrog
Gellilydan
Bont Newydd
Pentrefelin
Tremadog
Porthmadog
Penrhyndeudraeth
Criccieth
Minffordd
Portmeirion
Cilfor
Morfa Bychan
Borth-y-Gest
Caerwych
Pont Dolydd Prysor
Cwm Prysor
Trawsfynydd
Talsarnau
Ynys
Glan-y-wern
Eisingrug
Tremadog Bay
Bae Tremadog
Morfa Harlech
Glyn-Cywarch
Traeth Bach
Harlech
Llanfair
Llandanwg
Pen-sarn
Pen-y-bont
Pentre Gwynfryn
Llanbedr
Morfa Dyffryn
Coed Ystumgwern
Llanenddwyn
Dyffryn Ardudwy
Llanddwywe
Cors-y-Gedol
Tal-y-bont
Plas-canol
Llanaber
Caerdeon
Bontddu
Cutiau
Barmouth (Abermaw)
Barmouth Bay
Bae Bermo
The Bar
Arthog
Ynysgyfflog
Fairbourne
Friog
Llwyngwril
Llangelynin
Rhoslefain
Llanegryn
Llanfendigaid
Peniarth
Tonfanau
Bryncrug
Pandy
Rhyd-yr-onen
Tywyn
Caethle
Aberdovey
Aberdovey Bar
Bae Aberdyfi
Ynyslas
Llancynfelyn
Borth
Upper Borth
Tal-y-bont
Dôl-y-Bont
Llandre
Pen-y-garn
Bow Street
Clarach
Aberystwyth
Trefechan
Penparcau
Rhydyfelin
Llanfarian
Chancery
Blaenplwyf
Pentre-llyn
Crosswood
Wenallt
Llanafan
Abermagwr
Llanilar
New Cross
Gors
Capel Seion
Moriah
Southgate
Glanrafon
Llanbadarn Fawr
Comins Coch
Capel Dewi
Plas Gogerddan
Penrhyn-coch
Pen-bont Rhydybeddau
Salem
Capel Bangor
Dollwen
Goginan
Cwmbrwyno
Aberffrwd
Ystumtuen
Pisgah
Llanfihangel-y-Creuddyn
Mynydd Bach
Trisant
Cnwch-coch
Devil's Bridge
Ysbyty Ystwyth
Pont-rhyd-y-groes
New Row
Cwmystwyth
Blaenycwm
Ysbytycyfnyw
Ponterwyd
Dyffryn Castell
Pant Mawr
Llanifyny
Llangurig
Tan Hinon
Old Hall
Glan-y-nant
Llanidloes
Glynbrochan
Cwmbelan
Newchapel
Tylwch
Nantgwyn
Pant-y-dwr
Bwlch-y-sarnau
St Harmon
Hafren Forest
Plynlimon Pumlumon Fawr
Source of R. Severn Blaen Hafren
Source of R. Wye Blaen Gwy
Nant-y-Moch Reservoir
Bont-goch
Tre'r-ddôl
Tre-Taliesin
Eglwys Fach
Glandyfi
Derwenlas
Glaspwll
Pant-glâs
Forge
Machynlleth
Penegoes
Cwrt
Pennal
Pen-y-bont
Pantperthog
Plas Llwyngwern
Esgairgeiliog
Corris
Corris Uchaf
Aberllefenni
Tal-y-llyn
Minffordd
Abergynolwyn
Llanfihangel-y-pennant
Mynydd Ceiswyn
Mynydd Dolgoed
Dyfi Forest
Aberangell
Mallwyd
Cwm-Cewydd
Minllyn
Dinas-Mawddwy
Aber Cowarch
Bryn Sion
Y Gribin
Cywarch
Llanymawddwy
Cwm-Llinau
Dol-fôr
Cemmaes
Pentre-Celyn
Cemmaes Road
Llanwrin
Abercegir
Commins Coch
Waun
Darowen
Tafolwern
Llanbrynmair
Dolfach
Llan
Tal-y-wern
Bont-Dolgadfan
Talerddig
Melinbyrhedyn
Pennant
Aberhosan
Dylife
Staylittle
Carno
Clatter
Llawr-y-glyn
Gleiniant
Trefeglwys
Van
Oakley Park
Llandinam
Little London
Caersws
Llanwnog
Pandy
Cwmderwen
Neinthirion
Clegyrnant
Dolwen
Sychtyn
Llanerfyl
Pen Coed
Fridd Goch
Foel
Llangadfan
Wern
Moel y Llyn
Mynydd y Gadfa
Dyfnant Forest
Pont-Llogel
Ddôl-Cownwy
Hen Gerrig
Llanwddyn
Abertridwr
Ty-uchaf
Lake Vyrnwy
Alltforgan
Pennant Melangell
Pencraig
Aber-Rhiwlech
Pont y Pennant
Talardd
Ty-nant
Cwm Cynllwyd
Aran Fawddwy
Pont-Rhyd-sarn
Llanuwchllyn
Buarthmeini
Mynydd Bryn-llech
Parc
Llangower
Llyn Tegid or Bala Lake
Llanycil
Bala (Y Bala)
Rhyd-uchaf
Llanfor
Rhiwlas
Llandderfel
Pale
Cefn Coch
Llandrillo
Rhos-y-gwaliau
Aber-Hirnant
Aberhirnant Forest
Blaen-y-Cwm
Pont Cwm Pydew
Pennant
Frongoch
Llidiardau
Llyn Arenig fawr
Llyn Celyn
Ciltalgarth
Sarnau
Bethel
Cefn-ddwysarn
Glan-yr-afon
Glan-yr-afon
Wenallt
Tai-mawr
Llangwm
Maerdy
Dinmael
Ty-nant
Pen-y-gop
Ty Mawr Cwm
Bettws Gwerfil Goch
Ysbyty Ifan
Llyn Conwy
Mynydd Bach
Bronaber
Bed-y-coedwr
Coed y Brenin Forest
Pont Aber-Geirw
Cwm-hesgen
Capel Hermon
Ganllwyd
Pont Fronwydd
Llanfachreth
Rhydymain
Blaen-y-cwm
Nannau
Llanelltyd
Pen-y-bryn
Bont Newydd
Brithdir
Penmaenpool
Abergwynant
Dolgellau
Rhydwen
Afon Mawddach
Gwynedd
Powys
SH
SN
0 1 2 3 4 5 6 miles
0 1 2 3 4 5 6 7 8 9 10 km

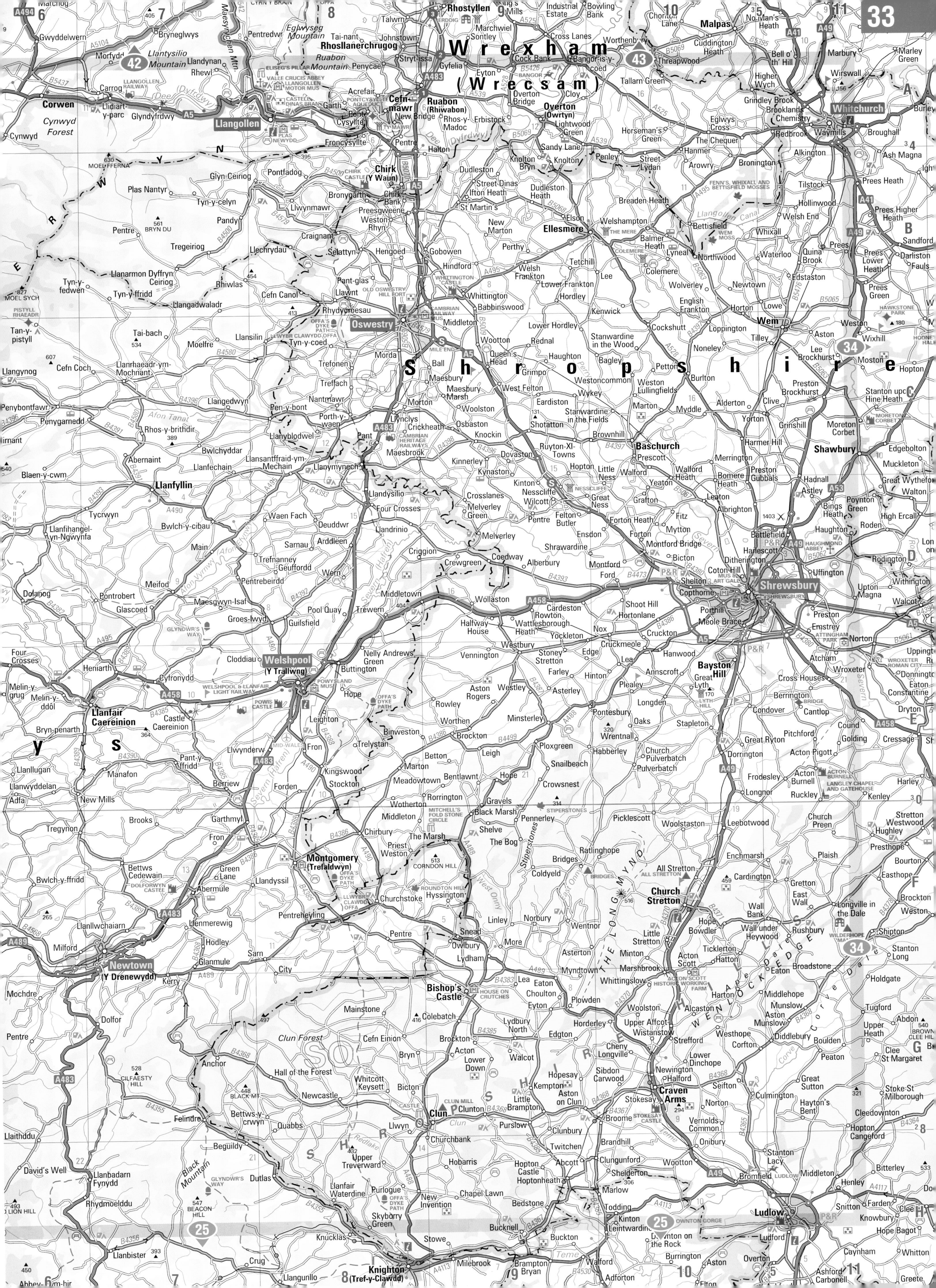
Wrexham
(Wrecsam)
Shropshire
Rhostyllen
Rhosllanerchrugog
Ruabon
(Rhiwabon)
Cefn-mawr
Llangollen
Corwen
Cynwyd Forest
Chirk
(Y Waun)
Oswestry
Whittington
Gobowen
Ellesmere
Overton
(Owrtyn)
Bangor-is-y-coed
Malpas
Whitchurch
Wem
Shawbury
Baschurch
Shrewsbury
Welshpool
(Y Trallwng)
Llanfyllin
Llanfair Caereinion
Newtown
(Y Drenewydd)
Montgomery
(Trefaldwyn)
Bishop's Castle
Church Stretton
Craven Arms
Clun
Clun Forest
Ludlow
Knighton
(Tref-y-Clawdd)
Pontesbury
Bayston Hill
Four Crosses
Llanymynech
Pant
Middletown
Minsterley
Lydham
Lydbury North
Bucknell
Leintwardine
Brampton Bryan
Llanbister
Dolfor
Kerry
Felindre
Beguildy
Black Mountain
Offa's Dyke Path
The Long Mynd
Wenlock Edge
Stiperstones
Corndon Hill
Dee
Severn
Teme
Clun
Llangollen Canal
42
43
34
25

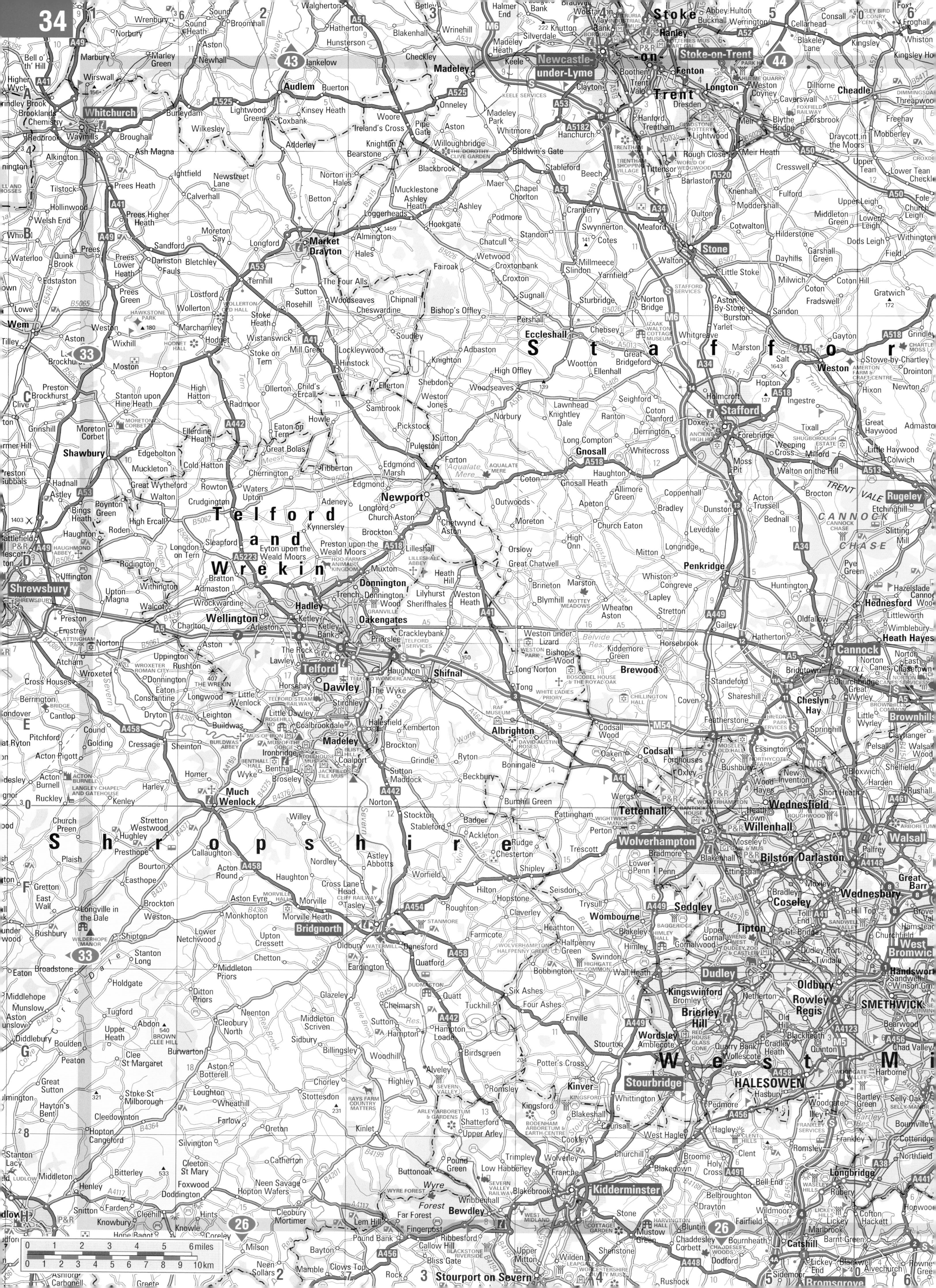

Whitchurch
Wem
Shrewsbury
Audlem
Market Drayton
Madeley
Newcastle-under-Lyme
Stoke-on-Trent
Hanley
Fenton
Longton
Cheadle
Stone
Eccleshall
Stafford
Weston
Rugeley
Newport
Telford and Wrekin
Wellington
Hadley
Oakengates
Donnington
Telford
Dawley
Madeley
Ironbridge
Much Wenlock
Shifnal
Albrighton
Gnosall
Penkridge
Cannock
Hednesford
Brewood
Codsall
Tettenhall
Wolverhampton
Wednesfield
Willenhall
Walsall
Bilston
Darlaston
Wednesbury
Coseley
Sedgley
Tipton
Dudley
Oldbury
Rowley Regis
Smethwick
Brierley Hill
Kingswinford
Wordsley
Stourbridge
Halesowen
Wombourne
Bridgnorth
Kinver
Kidderminster
Bewdley
Stourport on Severn
Cleobury Mortimer
Longbridge
Bromsgrove
Shropshire
Stafford
West Mi
Cannock Chase
Trent Vale
Shawbury
Prees
Hodnet
Stanton upon Hine Heath
Hinstock
Woore
Keele
Barlaston
Trentham
Meir
Blythe Bridge
Sandon
Ingestre
Milford
Huntington
Cheslyn Hay
Brownhills
Great Wyrley
Harborne
Quinton
Hagley
Blakedown
Chaddesley Corbett
Wolverley
Stourton
Enville
Quatt
Alveley
Highley
Kinlet
Tasley
Morville
Astley Abbotts
Worfield
Pattingham
Perton
Trysull
Swindon
Himley
Acton Burnell
Cressage
Broseley
Coalport
Kemberton
Sutton Maddock
Beckbury
Tong
Weston under Lizard
Lilleshall
Muxton
Edgmond
Chetwynd Aston
Forton
Norbury
High Offley
Adbaston
Cheswardine
Ternhill
Hodnet
Marchamley
Weston
Wixhill
Moreton Corbet
Upton Magna
Atcham
Cross Houses
Condover
Acton Pigott
Kenley
Harley
Sheinton
Buildwas
Leighton
Wroxeter
Eaton Constantine
Rodington
Withington
High Ercall
Crudgington
Waters Upton
Rowton
Kynnersley
Preston upon the Weald Moors
Eyton upon the Weald Moors
Sleapford
Longdon on Tern
Stretton Westwood
Bourton
Easthope
Brockton
Shipton
Monkhopton
Upton Cressett
Middleton Priors
Ditton Priors
Neenton
Cleobury North
Burwarton
Aston Botterell
Loughton
Wheathill
Farlow
Silvington
Oreton
Stottesdon
Chorley
Billingsley
Middleton Scriven
Sidbury
Glazeley
Chelmarsh
Sutton
Hampton Loade
Eardington
Oldbury
Danesford
Quatford
Farmcote
Claverley
Hopstone
Roughton
Rudge
Chesterton
Ackleton
Badger
Stockton
Stableford
Norton
Nordley
Willey
Upper Arley
Shatterford
Trimpley
Low Habberley
Wribbenhall
Far Forest
Callow Hill
Rock
Bliss Gate
Clows Top
Mamble
Bayton
Neen Sollars
Milson
Hopton Wafers
Doddington
Cleehill
Knowbury
Hints
Coreley
Neen Savage
Catherton
Cleeton St Mary
Bitterley
Hopton Cangeford
Cleedownton
Stoke St Milborough
Clee St Margaret
Abdon
Tugford
Holdgate
Broadstone
Munslow
Diddlebury
Peaton
Great Sutton
Hayton's Bent
Middleton
Henley
Snitton
Farden
Ludlow
Stanton Lacy
Wyre Forest
Dudmaston
Kingsford
Blakeshall
Cookley
Caunsall
Churchill
Broome
Clent
Romsley
Frankley
Belbroughton
Fairfield
Bournheath
Catshill
Dodford
Shenstone
Mustow Green
Stone
Harvington Hall
Bluntington
Drayton
Wildmoor
Cofton Hackett
Lickey
Barnt Green
Marlbrook
Blackwell
Alvechurch

0 1 2 3 4 5 6 miles
0 1 2 3 4 5 6 7 8 9 10 km

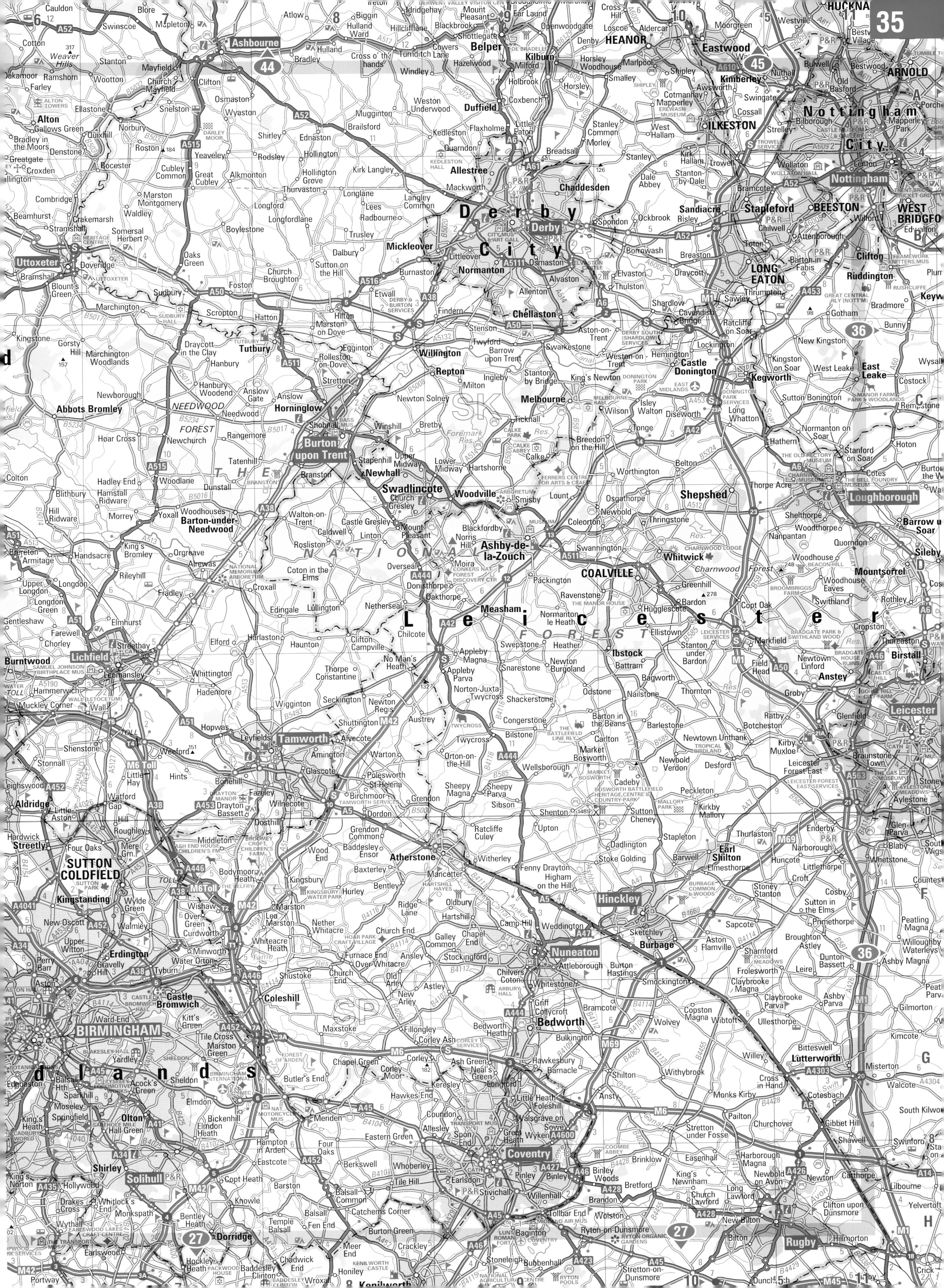
Ashbourne
Belper
Heanor
Eastwood
Hucknall
Arnold
Nottingham
City
Kimberley
Ilkeston
Duffield
Allestree
Chaddesden
Derby
Derby
City
Mickleover
Normanton
Spondon
Borrowash
Sandiacre
Stapleford
Beeston
West Bridgford
Long Eaton
Clifton
Ruddington
Uttoxeter
Sudbury
Tutbury
Chellaston
Castle Donington
Kegworth
Melbourne
Repton
Willington
Horninglow
Burton upon Trent
Abbots Bromley
Needwood Forest
Swadlincote
Woodville
Ashby-de-la-Zouch
Shepshed
Loughborough
Whitwick
Coalville
Measham
Leicester
Mountsorrel
Barton-under-Needwood
Lichfield
Tamworth
Ibstock
Anstey
Birstall
National Forest
Charnwood Forest
Atherstone
Hinckley
Nuneaton
Bedworth
Sutton Coldfield
Birmingham
Coleshill
Castle Bromwich
Erdington
Solihull
Coventry
Rugby
Lutterworth
Earl Shilton
Market Bosworth
Kenilworth
Dorridge
Shirley
Olton
Meriden
Sileby
Blaby
Wigston
Broughton Astley
Ullesthorpe
Brandon
Wolston
Binley
SK
SP
Leicester
West Midlands
M1
M6
M6 Toll
M42
M69
A38
A50
A52
A6
A42
A5
A444
A46
A45
44
45
36
27

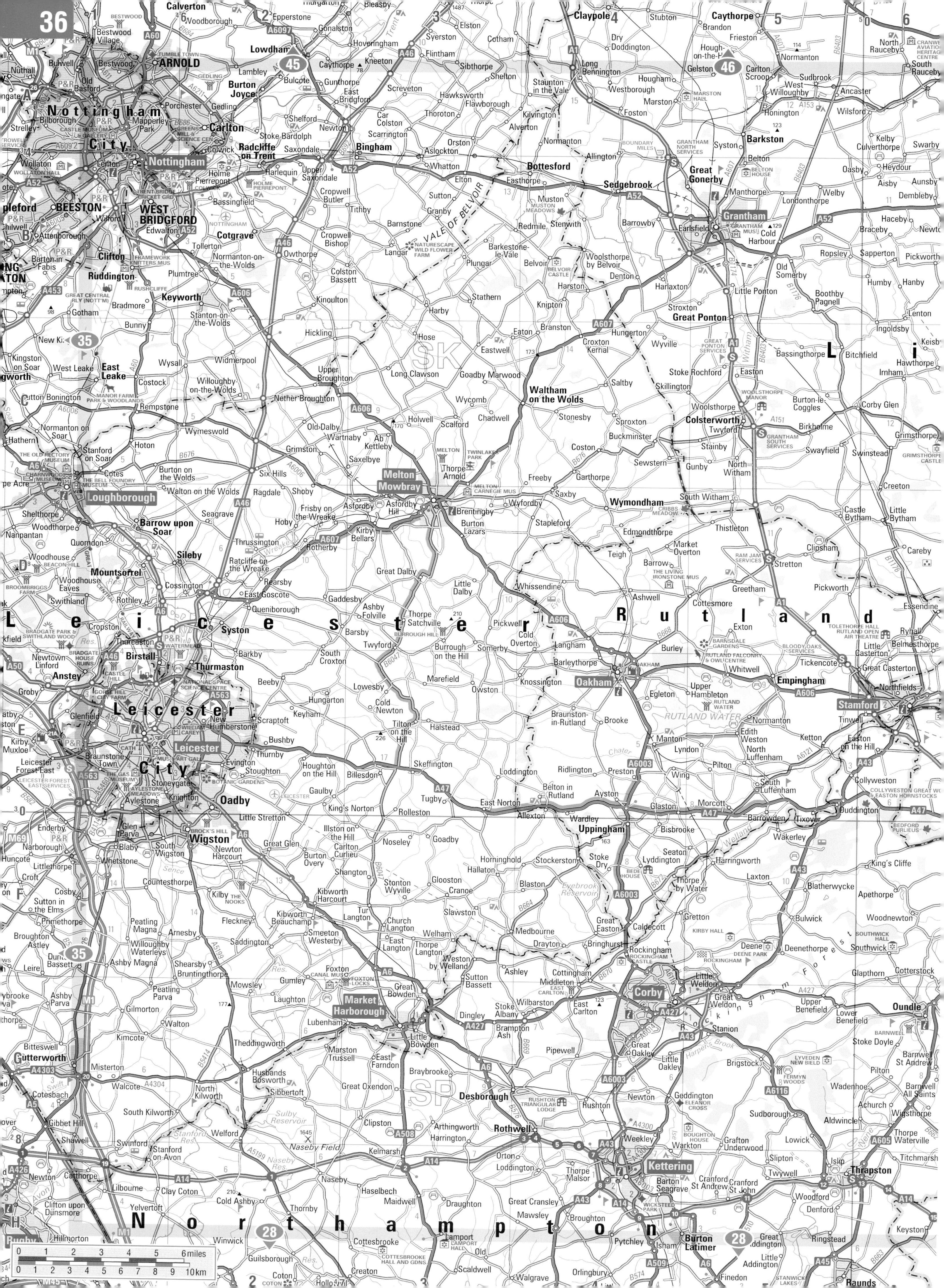
Calverton
Woodborough
Epperstone
Bleasby
Claypole
Stubton
Caythorpe
Bestwood Village
Lowdham
Gonalston
Hoveringham
Syerston
Elston
Cotham
Dry Doddington
Brandon
Frieston
North Rauceby
South Rauceby
Bulwell
Bestwood
ARNOLD
Caythorpe
Kneeton
Flintham
Sibthorpe
Long Bennington
Hough-on-the-Hill
Normanton
Nuthall
Old Basford
Lambley
Burton Joyce
Gunthorpe
East Bridgford
Screveton
Shelton
Staunton in the Vale
Hougham
Westborough
Gelston
Carlton Scroop
Sudbrook
West Willoughby
Ancaster
Nottingham
Mapperley Park
Gedling
Porchester
Hawksworth
Flawborough
Marston
Foston
Honington
Wilsford
Strelley
Bilborough
Carlton
Shelford
Car Colston
Thoroton
Kilvington
Alverton
Syston
Barkston
Kelby
Culverthorpe
Swarby
City
Stoke Bardolph
Newton
Scarrington
Orston
Normanton
Wollaton
Radcliffe on Trent
Saxondale
Bingham
Aslockton
Allington
Belton
Oasby
Heydour
Lenton
Holme Pierrepont
Harlequin
Upper Saxondale
Whatton
Elton
Bottesford
Great Gonerby
Aisby
Aunsby
Nottingham
Easthorpe
Sedgebrook
Manthorpe
Welby
Dembleby
Stapleford
BEESTON
WEST BRIDGFORD
Bassingfield
Cropwell Butler
Tithby
Sutton
Granby
Muston
Londonthorpe
Wilford
Edwalton
Barrowby
Grantham
Chilwell
Attenborough
Cotgrave
Cropwell Bishop
Barnstone
Redmile
Stenwith
Earlsfield
Cold Harbour
Haceby
Braceby
Newton
Tollerton
VALE OF BELVOIR
Langar
Barkestone-le-Vale
Sapperton
Ropsley
Pickworth
Clifton
Normanton-on-the-Wolds
Owthorpe
Plungar
Belvoir
Woolsthorpe by Belvoir
Barton in Fabis
Ruddington
Plumtree
Colston Bassett
Denton
Old Somerby
Harlaxton
Humby
Hanby
Harston
Keyworth
Bradmore
Kinoulton
Stathern
Knipton
Little Ponton
Boothby Pagnell
Gotham
Stanton-on-the-Wolds
Harby
Stroxton
Great Ponton
Lenton
Bunny
Branston
Hungerton
Ingoldsby
Hickling
Hose
Eaton
New Kingston
Kingston on Soar
West Leake
East Leake
Wysall
Widmerpool
Upper Broughton
Eastwell
Croxton Kerrial
Wyville
Bassingthorpe
Bitchfield
Keisby
Hawthorpe
Long Clawson
Goadby Marwood
Stoke Rochford
Easton
Irnham
Costock
Willoughby-on-the-Wolds
Waltham on the Wolds
Saltby
Skillington
Sutton Bonington
Rempstone
Nether Broughton
Wycomb
Woolsthorpe
Burton-le-Coggles
Corby Glen
Normanton on Soar
Wymeswold
Old Dalby
Holwell
Scalford
Chadwell
Stonesby
Sproxton
Colsterworth
Twyford
Birkholme
Grimsthorpe
Hathern
Hoton
Wartnaby
Ab Kettleby
Buckminster
Stanford on Soar
Grimston
Coston
Stainby
Swayfield
Swinstead
Burton on the Wolds
Saxelbye
Sewstern
Gunby
North Witham
Cotes
Six Hills
Melton Mowbray
Thorpe Arnold
Freeby
Garthorpe
Creeton
Loughborough
Walton on the Wolds
Ragdale
Shoby
Saxby
South Witham
Shelthorpe
Frisby on the Wreake
Asfordby
Asfordby Hill
Brentingby
Wyfordby
Wymondham
Castle Bytham
Little Bytham
Woodthorpe
Seagrave
Barrow upon Soar
Hoby
Stapleford
Burton Lazars
Thistleton
Nanpantan
Kirby Bellars
Edmondthorpe
Quorndon
Thrussington
Rotherby
Market Overton
Clipsham
Sileby
Teigh
Careby
Woodhouse
Ratcliffe on the Wreake
Great Dalby
Barrow
Stretton
Mountsorrel
Woodhouse Eaves
Cossington
Rearsby
Little Dalby
Whissendine
Greetham
Pickworth
Swithland
East Goscote
Gaddesby
Ashwell
Cottesmore
Rothley
Queniborough
Ashby Folville
Thorpe Satchville
Essendine
Leicester
Rutland
Cropston
Syston
Barsby
Pickwell
Exton
Ryhall
Thurcaston
Twyford
Cold Overton
Langham
Burley
Belmesthorpe
Birstall
Barkby
South Croxton
Burrough on the Hill
Somerby
Little Casterton
Newtown Linford
Thurmaston
Barleythorpe
Whitwell
Tickencote
Great Casterton
Anstey
Beeby
Marefield
Oakham
Empingham
Groby
Lowesby
Owston
Knossington
Upper Hambleton
Egleton
Northfields
Hungarton
Stamford
Glenfield
Leicester
Keyham
Cold Newton
Braunston-in-Rutland
Brooke
RUTLAND WATER
Normanton
Tinwell
Scraptoft
New Humberstone
Tilton on the Hill
Halstead
Manton
Edith Weston
Ketton
Easton on the Hill
Kirby Muxloe
Bushby
Lyndon
North Luffenham
Leicester Forest East
Braunstone Town
Leicester
Thurnby
Evington
Stoughton
Houghton on the Hill
Skeffington
Loddington
Ridlington
Preston
Pilton
Wing
Collyweston
City
Stoneygate
Billesdon
South Luffenham
Knighton
Oadby
Gaulby
Tugby
East Norton
Belton in Rutland
Ayston
Glaston
Morcott
Duddington
Aylestone
King's Norton
Rolleston
Allexton
Wardley
Barrowden
Tixover
Enderby
Glen Parva
Little Stretton
Uppingham
Bisbrooke
Narborough
Wigston
Illston on the Hill
Noseley
Goadby
Seaton
Wakerley
Blaby
South Wigston
Great Glen
Carlton Curlieu
Horninghold
Stockerston
Stoke Dry
Lyddington
Huncote
Whetstone
Newton Harcourt
Burton Overy
Hallaton
Harringworth
King's Cliffe
Littlethorpe
Shangton
Thorpe by Water
Laxton
Croft
Countesthorpe
Glooston
Blaston
Eyebrook Reservoir
Cranoe
Stonton Wyville
Blatherwycke
Apethorpe
Cosby
Kilby
Kibworth Harcourt
Sutton in the Elms
Fleckney
Tur Langton
Slawston
Great Easton
Caldecott
Gretton
Bulwick
Woodnewton
Primethorpe
Peatling Magna
Arnesby
Kibworth Beauchamp
Church Langton
Welham
Medbourne
Broughton Astley
Willoughby Waterleys
Saddington
Smeeton Westerby
East Langton
Thorpe Langton
Drayton
Bringhurst
Rockingham
Deene
Deenethorpe
Southwick
Dunton Bassett
Shearsby
Ashby Magna
Bruntingthorpe
Weston by Welland
Sutton Bassett
Ashley
Cottingham
Middleton
Little Weldon
Glapthorn
Cotterstock
Leire
Foxton
Gumley
Peatling Parva
Mowsley
Great Bowden
East Carlton
Wilbarston
Stoke Albany
Corby
Great Weldon
Upper Benefield
Lower Benefield
Oundle
Ashby Parva
Laughton
Market Harborough
Dingley
Brampton Ash
Gilmorton
Lubenham
Little Bowden
Stanion
Walton
Kimcote
Theddingworth
Marston Trussell
East Farndon
Great Oakley
Little Oakley
Stoke Doyle
Bitteswell
Pipewell
Brigstock
Barnwell St Andrew
Lutterworth
Misterton
Husbands Bosworth
Braybrooke
Lyveden New Bield
Pilton
Walcote
Great Oxendon
Wadenhoe
Barnwell All Saints
Cotesbach
North Kilworth
Sibbertoft
Desborough
Newton
Achurch
South Kilworth
Sulby Reservoir
Clipston
Rushton
Geddington
Wigsthorpe
Gibbet Hill
Rothwell
Sudborough
Aldwincle
Shawell
Welford
Naseby Field
Arthingworth
Harrington
Weekley
Boughton House
Lowick
Thorpe Waterville
Stanford Res.
Swinford
Stanford on Avon
Kelmarsh
Orton
Warkton
Grafton Underwood
Islip
Titchmarsh
Newton
Catthorpe
Naseby
Loddington
Thorpe Malsor
Kettering
Slipton
Twywell
Thrapston
Lilbourne
Clay Coton
Haselbech
Maidwell
Barton Seagrave
Cranford St Andrew
Cranford St John
Woodford
Denford
Clifton upon Dunsmore
Yelvertoft
Cold Ashby
Thornby
Draughton
Great Cransley
Mawsley
Northampton
Broughton
Keyston
Rugby
Hillmorton
Winwick
Cottesbrooke
Lamport
Pytchley
Isham
Burton Latimer
Great Addington
Ringstead
Little Addington
Guilsborough
Old
Scaldwell
Walgrave
Orlingbury
Finedon
Raunds
Creaton
Coton
SK
SP
0 1 2 3 4 5 6 miles
0 1 2 3 4 5 6 7 8 9 10 km

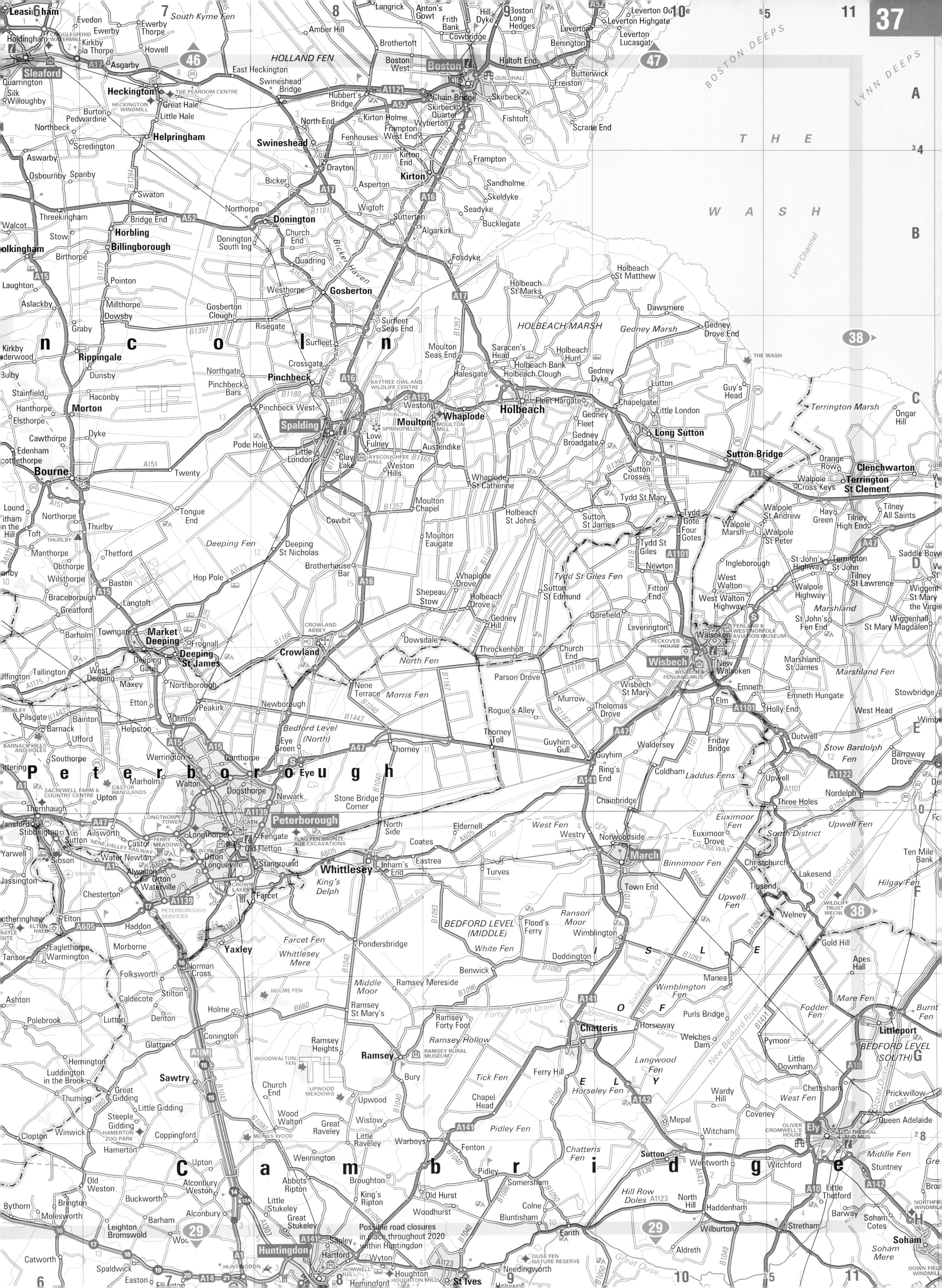

Sleaford
Holdingham
Quarrington
Silk Willoughby
Evedon
Ewerby
Ewerby Thorpe
Kirkby la Thorpe
Asgarby
Howell
South Kyme Fen
Heckington
Great Hale
Little Hale
Burton Pedwardine
Northbeck
Helpringham
Scredington
Aswarby
Osbournby
Spanby
Swaton
Threekingham
Walcot
Stow
Bridge End
Horbling
Billingborough
Birthorpe
Pointon
Laughton
Aslackby
Millthorpe
Dowsby
Graby
Rippingale
Dunsby
Stainfield
Haconby
Hanthorpe
Morton
Elsthorpe
Edenham
Cawthorpe
Dyke
Bourne
Northorpe
Thurlby
Toft
Manthorpe
Obthorpe
Wilsthorpe
Baston
Thetford
Braceborough
Greatford
Langtoft
Barholm
Towngate
Market Deeping
Deeping St James
Frognall
Deeping Gate
West Deeping
Tallington
Maxey
Northborough
Etton
Glinton
Peakirk
Pilsgate
Bainton
Barnack
Ufford
Helpston
Southorpe
Werrington
Gunthorpe
Marholm
Walton
Dogsthorpe
Newark
Upton
Thornhaugh
Wansford
Stibbington
Sutton
Ailsworth
Castor
Longthorpe
Water Newton
Sibson
Yarwell
Alwalton
Orton Longueville
Orton Waterville
Chesterton
Elton
Haddon
Stanground
Fengate
Old Fletton
Farcet
Yaxley
Morborne
Eaglethorpe
Warmington
Tansor
Folksworth
Norman Cross
Caldecote
Stilton
Ashton
Polebrook
Lutton
Denton
Holme
Conington
Glatton
Hemington
Luddington in the Brook
Sawtry
Thurning
Great Gidding
Little Gidding
Steeple Gidding
Winwick
Clopton
Coppingford
Hamerton
Upton
Old Weston
Alconbury Weston
Alconbury
Buckworth
Brington
Molesworth
Bythorn
Leighton Bromswold
Barham
Catworth
Spaldwick
Easton
Little Stukeley
Great Stukeley
Huntingdon
Sapley
Hartford
Wyton
Houghton
Hemingford
St Ives
Needingworth
Holland Fen
East Heckington
Swineshead Bridge
Swineshead
Brothertoft
Amber Hill
Langrick
Anton's Gowt
Frith Bank
Cowbridge
Hill Dyke
Boston Long Hedges
Boston West
Boston
Hubbert's Bridge
Kirton Holme
North End
Frampton West End
Fenhouses
Kirton End
Kirton
Drayton
Bicker
Asperton
Wigtoft
Sutterton
Algarkirk
Northorpe
Donington
Church End
Donington South Ing
Quadring
Bicker Haven
Westhorpe
Gosberton
Gosberton Clough
Risegate
Surfleet
Surfleet Seas End
Crossgate
Northgate
Pinchbeck
Pinchbeck Bars
Pinchbeck West
Spalding
Pode Hole
Little London
Twenty
Tongue End
Deeping Fen
Deeping St Nicholas
Hop Pole
Brotherhouse Bar
Cowbit
Crowland
Dowsdale
North Fen
Newborough
Bedford Level (North)
Eye Green
Eye
Thorney
Nene Terrace
Morris Fen
Stone Bridge Corner
North Side
Peterborough
Coates
Eastrea
Whittlesey
Inham's End
King's Delph
Eldernell
Turves
Farcet Fen
Whittlesey Mere
Pondersbridge
Middle Moor
Ramsey Mereside
Ramsey St Mary's
Ramsey Forty Foot
Ramsey Hollow
Ramsey Heights
Ramsey
Bury
Church End
Upwood
Wood Walton
Great Raveley
Little Raveley
Wistow
Warboys
Wennington
Abbots Ripton
Broughton
King's Ripton
Old Hurst
Woodhurst
Fenton
Pidley
Somersham
Colne
Bluntisham
Earith
Possible road closures in place throughout 2020 within Huntingdon
Leverton Outgate
Leverton Highgate
Leverton Lucasgate
Leverton
Benington
Haltoft End
Butterwick
Freiston
Skirbeck
Skirbeck Quarter
Wyberton
Fishtoft
Scrane End
Frampton
Sandholme
Skeldyke
Seadyke
Bucklegate
Fosdyke
Boston Deeps
Lynn Deeps
The Wash
Lynn Channel
Holbeach St Matthew
Holbeach St Marks
Dawsmere
Holbeach Marsh
Gedney Marsh
Gedney Drove End
Moulton Seas End
Saracen's Head
Holbeach Hurn
Holbeach Bank
Holbeach Clough
Gedney Dyke
Halesgate
Weston
Moulton
Whaplode
Holbeach
Fleet Hargate
Gedney
Fleet
Chapelgate
Lutton
Little London
Long Sutton
Guy's Head
Gedney Broadgate
Low Fulney
Austendike
Clay Lake
Weston Hills
Whaplode St Catherine
Moulton Chapel
Moulton Eaugate
Holbeach St Johns
Sutton Crosses
Tydd St Mary
Sutton St James
Sutton Bridge
Terrington Marsh
Ongar Hill
Orange Row
Clenchwarton
Walpole Cross Keys
Terrington St Clement
Tilney All Saints
Walpole St Andrew
Hay Green
Tilney High End
Walpole Marsh
Walpole St Peter
Tydd Gote
Four Gotes
Tydd St Giles
Newton
Tydd St Giles Fen
Sutton St Edmund
Whaplode Drove
Holbeach Drove
Shepeau Stow
Gedney Hill
Fitton End
Ingleborough
West Walton
West Walton Highway
Terrington St John
Tilney St Lawrence
St John's Highway
Walpole Highway
Marshland
St John's Fen End
Wiggenhall St Mary Magdalen
Gorefield
Leverington
Throckenholt
Church End
Parson Drove
Walsoken
Wisbech
New Walsoken
Marshland St James
Marshland Fen
Murrow
Wisbech St Mary
Emneth
Emneth Hungate
Elm
Tholomas Drove
Rogue's Alley
Thorney Toll
Guyhirn Gull
Guyhirn
Ring's End
Waldersey
Friday Bridge
Holly End
Outwell
West Head
Stowbridge
Stow Bardolph Fen
Barroway Drove
Coldham
Laddus Fens
Upwell
Nordelph
Chainbridge
Three Holes
West Fen
Westry
Norwoodside
March
Euximoor Fen
Euximoor Drove
Upwell Fen
South District
Ten Mile Bank
Binnimoor Fen
Christchurch
Lakesend
Town End
Tipsend
Hilgay Fen
Upwell Fen
Welney
Bedford Level (Middle)
White Fen
Flood's Ferry
Ransom Moor
Wimblington
Doddington
Benwick
Gold Hill
Apes Hall
Manea
Wimblington Fen
Purls Bridge
Fodder Fen
Mare Fen
Burnt Fen
Chatteris
Horseway
Welches Dam
Pymoor
Littleport
Bedford Level (South)
Langwood Fen
Little Downham
Tick Fen
Ferry Hill
Horseley Fen
Chettisham
Prickwillow
Chapel Head
Wardy Hill
West Fen
Coveney
Queen Adelaide
Pidley Fen
Mepal
Witcham
Ely
Chatteris Fen
Sutton
Wentworth
Witchford
Middle Fen
Stuntney
Hill Row Doles
North Hill
Haddenham
Little Thetford
Barway
Soham Cotes
Wilburton
Stretham
Soham
Aldreth
Soham Mere
Great Ouse
New Bedford River
Old Bedford River
Forty Foot Drain or Vermuden's Drain
Sixteen Foot Drain
Twenty Foot River
Nene
Isle of Ely
Lincoln
Peterborough
Cambridge
TF
TL
46
47
38
29

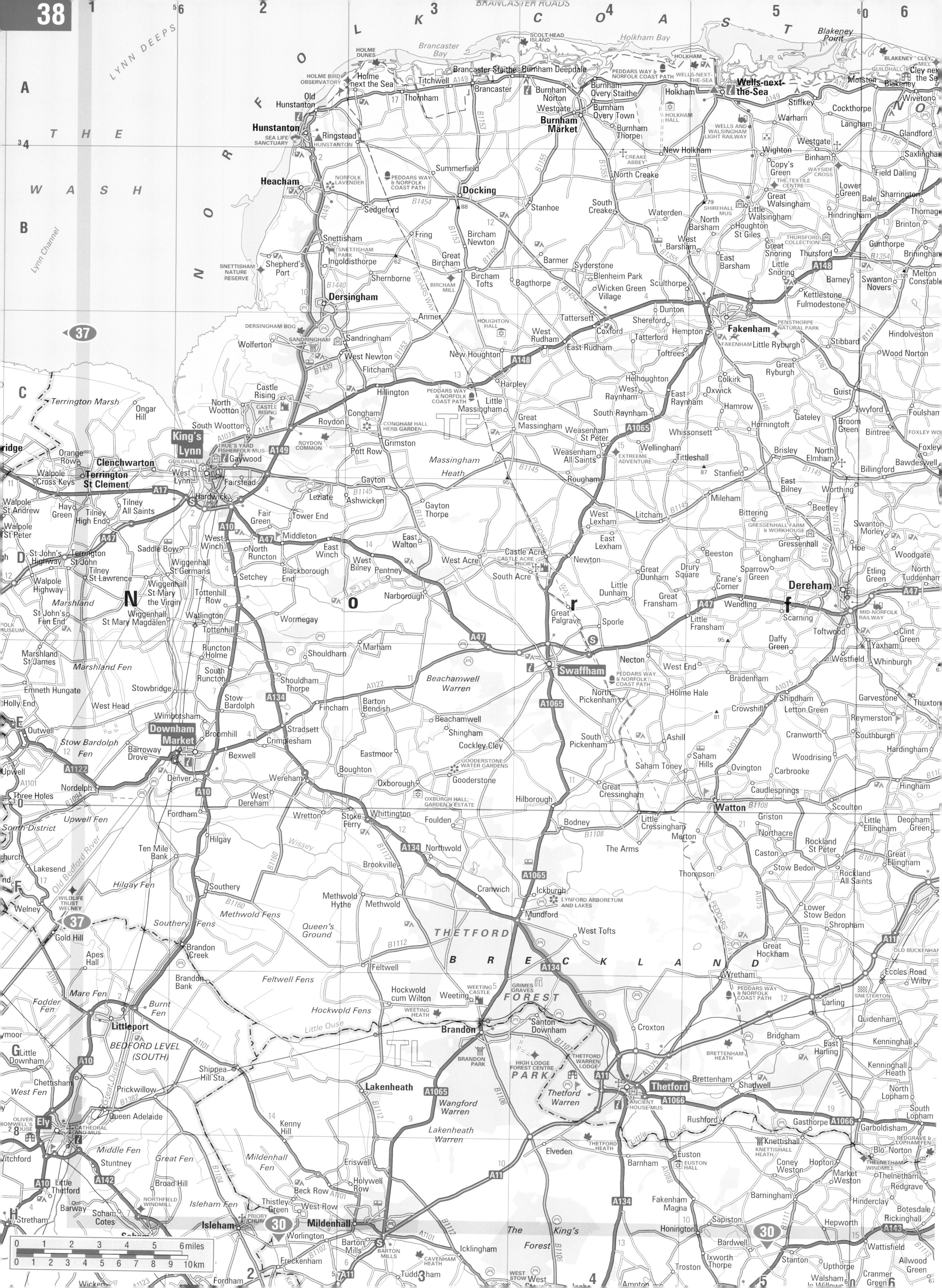
BRANCASTER ROADS
NORFOLK COAST
LYNN DEEPS
THE WASH
Lynn Channel
Brancaster Bay
Holkham Bay
Blakeney Point
SCOLT HEAD ISLAND
HOLME DUNES
HOLME BIRD OBSERVATORY
Holme next the Sea
Titchwell
Brancaster Staithe
Burnham Deepdale
Brancaster
Burnham Norton
Burnham Overy Staithe
Holkham
Wells-next-the-Sea
Morston
Blakeney
Cley next the Sea
Old Hunstanton
Hunstanton
Thornham
Westgate
Burnham Market
Burnham Overy Town
Burnham Thorpe
HOLKHAM HALL
WELLS AND WALSINGHAM LIGHT RAILWAY
Stiffkey
Warham
Cockthorpe
Langham
Wiveton
Glandford
SEA LIFE SANCTUARY
Ringstead
CREAKE ABBEY
New Holkham
Wighton
Binham
Saxlingham
Copy's Green
Field Dalling
WAYSIDE CROSS
THE TEXTILE CENTRE
Heacham
NORFOLK LAVENDER
PEDDARS WAY & NORFOLK COAST PATH
Summerfield
Docking
North Creake
South Creake
Stanhoe
Sedgeford
Waterden
North Barsham
SHIREHALL MUS
Little Walsingham
Great Walsingham
Lower Green
Bale
Sharrington
Hindringham
Thornage
Brinton
Snettisham
SNETTISHAM PARK
Fring
Bircham Newton
Great Bircham
Barmer
West Barsham
Houghton St Giles
THURSFORD COLLECTION
Great Snoring
Thursford
Gunthorpe
Briningham
Ingoldisthorpe
SNETTISHAM NATURE RESERVE
Shepherd's Port
Shernborne
BIRCHAM MILL
Bircham Tofts
Bagthorpe
Syderstone
Blenheim Park
Wicken Green Village
East Barsham
Little Snoring
Sculthorpe
Barney
Swanton Novers
Melton Constable
Kettlestone
Fulmodestone
Dersingham
Anmer
HOUGHTON HALL
West Rudham
Tattersett
Coxford
Dunton
Shereford
Tatterford
Hempton
Fakenham
PENSTHORPE NATURAL PARK
Hindolveston
DERSINGHAM BOG
SANDRINGHAM
Sandringham
Wolferton
West Newton
New Houghton
East Rudham
Toftrees
Little Ryburgh
Stibbard
Wood Norton
Flitcham
Hillington
Harpley
Helhoughton
Great Ryburgh
Colkirk
Guist
Castle Rising
CASTLE RISING
North Wootton
Terrington Marsh
Ongar Hill
Little Massingham
Great Massingham
West Raynham
East Raynham
Oxwick
Hamrow
Twyford
Foulsham
South Wootton
Congham
CONGHAM HALL HERB GARDEN
Roydon
Grimston
South Raynham
Weasenham St Peter
Whissonsett
Horningtoft
Gateley
Broom Green
Bintree
FOXLEY WOOD
King's Lynn
TRUE'S YARD FISHERFOLK MUS
GUILDHALL
Gaywood
ROYDON COMMON
Pott Row
Massingham Heath
Weasenham All Saints
Wellingham
EXTREME ADVENTURE
Tittleshall
Brisley
North Elmham
Foxley
Bawdeswell
Orange Row
Clenchwarton
Walpole Cross Keys
Terrington St Clement
West Lynn
Fairstead
Gayton
Rougham
Stanfield
Billingford
East Bilney
Worthing
Hardwick
Leziate
Ashwicken
Mileham
Walpole St Andrew
Hay Green
Tilney High End
Tilney All Saints
Fair Green
Tower End
Gayton Thorpe
West Lexham
Litcham
Bittering
GRESSENHALL FARM & WORKHOUSE
Beetley
Swanton Morley
Walpole St Peter
West Winch
Middleton
East Walton
East Lexham
Gressenhall
Hoe
St John's Highway
Terrington St John
Saddle Bow
North Runcton
East Winch
West Acre
Castle Acre
CASTLE ACRE PRIORY
Newton
Beeston
Longham
Woodgate
Tilney St Lawrence
Wiggenhall St Germans
Setchey
Blackborough End
West Bilney
Pentney
South Acre
Great Dunham
Drury Square
Crane's Corner
Sparrow Green
Etling Green
North Tuddenham
Walpole Highway
Wiggenhall St Mary the Virgin
Tottenhill Row
Little Dunham
Great Fransham
Dereham
Marshland
Wiggenhall St Mary Magdalen
Watlington
Narborough
Wendling
MID-NORFOLK RAILWAY
St John's Fen End
Wormegay
Great Palgrave
Sporle
Little Fransham
Scarning
Toftwood
Clint Green
Tottenhill
Daffy Green
Yaxham
Marshland St James
Runcton Holme
Shouldham
Marham
Westfield
Whinburgh
Marshland Fen
South Runcton
Necton
West End
Beachamwell Warren
Swaffham
Bradenham
Emneth Hungate
Stowbridge
Shouldham Thorpe
North Pickenham
Holme Hale
Shipdham
Garvestone
Thuxton
Holly End
West Head
Stow Bardolph
Fincham
Barton Bendish
Crowshill
Letton Green
Reymerston
Wimbotsham
Downham Market
Stradsett
Beachamwell
Shingham
Outwell
Broomhill
Crimplesham
Cockley Cley
South Pickenham
Ashill
Cranworth
Southburgh
Stow Bardolph Fen
Barroway Drove
Bexwell
Eastmoor
Saham Hills
Hardingham
Woodrising
Upwell
Denver
GOODERSTONE WATER GARDENS
Saham Toney
Ovington
Carbrooke
Boughton
Wereham
Gooderstone
Oxborough
Great Cressingham
Caudlesprings
Hingham
Nordelph
Three Holes
West Dereham
OXBURGH HALL, GARDEN & ESTATE
Hilborough
Watton
Scoulton
South District
Upwell Fen
Fordham
Wretton
Stoke Ferry
Whittington
Foulden
Bodney
Little Cressingham
Griston
Little Ellingham
Deopham Green
Merton
Northacre
Rockland St Peter
Hilgay
Ten Mile Bank
Wissey
Northwold
The Arms
Caston
Great Ellingham
Lakesend
Old Bedford River
Brookville
Stow Bedon
Thompson
Rockland All Saints
Hilgay Fen
Southery
Cranwich
Ickburgh
LYNFORD ARBORETUM AND LAKES
WILDLIFE TRUST WELNEY
Welney
Methwold Hythe
Methwold
Methwold Fens
Mundford
Lower Stow Bedon
Shropham
Southery Fens
Queen's Ground
THETFORD BRECKLAND
West Tofts
Gold Hill
Apes Hall
Brandon Creek
Great Hockham
OLD BUCKENHAM
Feltwell
Eccles Road
Wilby
Brandon Bank
Feltwell Fens
WEETING CASTLE
GRIMES GRAVES
FOREST
Wretham
SNETTERTON
Fodder Fen
Mare Fen
Burnt Fen
Hockwold cum Wilton
Weeting
Larling
Littleport
Hockwold Fens
WEETING HEATH
Little Ouse
Brandon
Santon Downham
Croxton
Quidenham
Bridgham
Kenninghall
BEDFORD LEVEL (SOUTH)
BRANDON PARK
HIGH LODGE FOREST CENTRE
THETFORD WARREN LODGE
BRETTENHAM HEATH
East Harling
Little Downham
Shippea Hill Sta.
PARK
Thetford Warren
Thetford
Brettenham
Shadwell
Kenninghall Heath
Chettisham
Prickwillow
Lakenheath
Wangford Warren
ANCIENT HOUSE MUS
North Lopham
West Fen
Great Ouse
Queen Adelaide
Rushford
Gasthorpe
Garboldisham
South Lopham
Ely
CATHEDRAL AND MUS
OLIVER CROMWELL'S HOUSE
Kenny Hill
Lakenheath Warren
THETFORD HEATH
Knettishall
KNETTISHALL HEATH
REDGRAVE & LOPHAM FEN
Blo' Norton
Middle Fen
Elveden
Witchford
Stuntney
Great Fen
Mildenhall Fen
Eriswell
Barnham
Euston
EUSTON HALL
Coney Weston
Hopton
Market Weston
THELNETHAM WINDMILL
Thelnetham
Little Thetford
Broad Hill
Holywell Row
Redgrave
NORTHFIELD WINDMILL
Beck Row
Fakenham Magna
Barningham
Hinderclay
Botesdale
Barway
Soham Cotes
Isleham Fen
Thistley Green
West Row
Rickinghall
Stretham
Isleham
PRIORY CHURCH
Mildenhall
The King's Forest
Sapiston
Hepworth
Honington
Worlington
Barton Mills
BARTON MILLS
Icklingham
Bardwell
Wattisfield
Ixworth Thorpe
Stanton
Allwood Green
Freckenham
CAVENHAM HEATH
Troston
Upthorpe
Cranmer Green
Fordham
Tuddenham
WEST STOW
West Stow
Walsham
Ampton
Wicken
miles
km

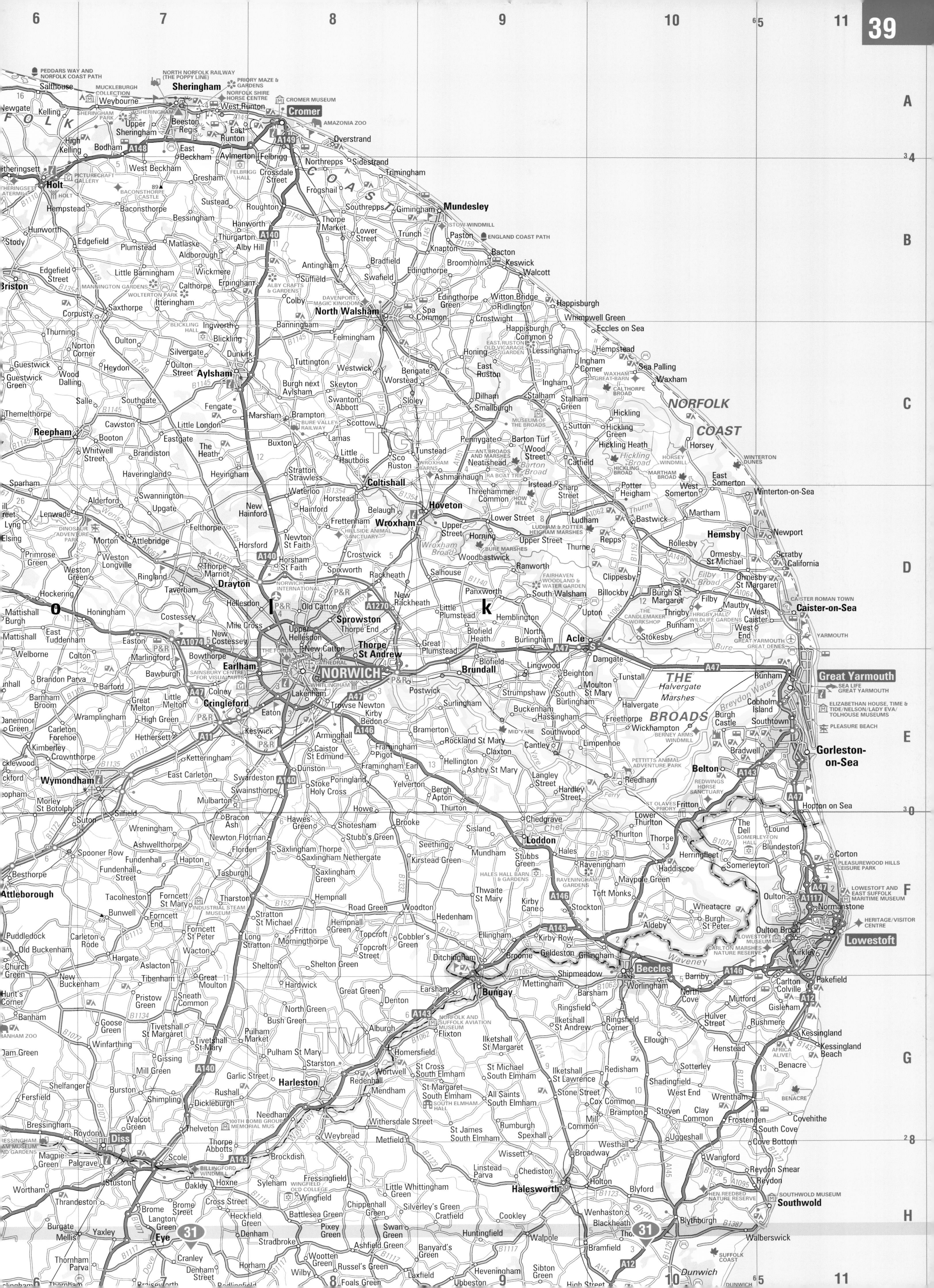

6
7
8
9
10
11
A
B
C
D
E
F
G
H
NORTH NORFOLK RAILWAY (THE POPPY LINE)
PEDDARS WAY AND NORFOLK COAST PATH
Sheringham
Salthouse
Weybourne
MUCKLEBURGH COLLECTION
PRIORY MAZE & GARDENS
NORFOLK SHIRE HORSE CENTRE
CROMER MUSEUM
West Runton
Cromer
AMAZONIA ZOO
Kelling
Upper Sheringham
Beeston Regis
East Runton
Overstrand
High Kelling
Bodham
East Beckham
Aylmerton
Felbrigg
Holt
West Beckham
Northrepps
Sidestrand
Trimingham
PICTURECRAFT GALLERY
FELBRIGG HALL
Gresham
Crossdale Street
BACONSTHORPE CASTLE
Frogshail
Hempstead
Baconsthorpe
Sustead
Roughton
Southrepps
Gimingham
Mundesley
Bessingham
Hanworth
Thorpe Market
STOW WINDMILL
Hunworth
Thurgarton
Lower Street
Trunch
Paston
ENGLAND COAST PATH
Stody
Edgefield
Plumstead
Matlaske
Alby Hill
Knapton
Bacton
Aldborough
Bradfield
Broomholm
Keswick
Edgefield Street
Little Barningham
Wickmere
Antingham
Swafield
Edingthorpe
Walcott
Briston
Calthorpe
Erpingham
Suffield
ALBY CRAFTS & GARDENS
MANNINGTON GARDENS
WOLTERTON PARK
Colby
Edingthorpe Green
Witton Bridge
Ridlington
Happisburgh
Corpusty
Saxthorpe
Itteringham
DAVENPORTS MAGIC KINGDOM
North Walsham
Spa Common
Crostwight
Whimpwell Green
Thurning
BLICKLING HALL
Ingworth
Banningham
Happisburgh Common
Eccles on Sea
Norton Corner
Oulton
Blickling
Felmingham
EAST RUSTON OLD VICARAGE GARDEN
Lessingham
Hempstead
Guestwick
Heydon
Silvergate
Dunkirk
Tuttington
Honing
Ingham Corner
Sea Palling
Guestwick Green
Wood Dalling
Oulton Street
Aylsham
Westwick
Bengate
East Ruston
WAXHAM GREAT BARN
Waxham
Burgh next Aylsham
Skeyton
Worstead
Ingham
CALTHORPE BROAD
Salle
Southgate
Swanton Abbott
Dilham
Stalham
Stalham Green
Themelthorpe
Fengate
Brampton
Sloley
Smallburgh
NORFOLK
BURE VALLEY RAILWAY
MUSEUM OF THE BROADS
COAST
Reepham
Cawston
Little London
Marsham
Scottow
Sutton
Hickling
Hickling Green
Booton
Eastgate
Lamas
Pennygate
Barton Turf
Horsey
Whitwell Street
Brandiston
The Heath
Buxton
Little Hautbois
Sco Ruston
Tunstead
Wood Street
Hickling Heath
ANT BROADS AND MARSHES
Barton Broad
Catfield
Hickling Broad
HORSEY WINDMILL
WINTERTON DUNES
Haveringland
Hevingham
Stratton Strawless
WROXHAM BARNS
Neatishead
MARTHAM BROAD
HICKLING BROAD
East Somerton
Sparham
Coltishall
Ashmanhaugh
Irstead
West Somerton
Winterton-on-Sea
Swannington
Waterloo
Horstead
Threehammer Common
Sharp Street
Potter Heigham
Alderford
Upgate
New Hainford
Hainford
Belaugh
Hoveton
Lower Street
Ludham
Bastwick
Martham
Lenwade
Felthorpe
Frettenham
Wroxham
Upper Street
LUDHAM & POTTER HEIGHAM MARSHES
Hemsby
Newport
DINOSAUR ADVENTURE PARK
Morton
Attlebridge
Horsford
Newton St Faith
HILLSIDE ANIMAL SANCTUARY
Horning
Wroxham Broad
Upper Street
Thurne
Repps
Rollesby
Elsing
Crostwick
BURE MARSHES
Scratby
Primrose Green
Weston Longville
Thorpe Marriot
Horsham St Faith
Spixworth
Rackheath
Salhouse
Woodbastwick
Ranworth
Ormesby St Michael
California
Weston Green
Ringland
Drayton
NORWICH INTERNATIONAL
Clippesby
Filby Broad
Ormesby St Margaret
Hockering
Taverham
New Rackheath
FAIRHAVEN WOODLAND & WATER GARDEN
Panxworth
South Walsham
Billockby
Burgh St Margaret
Filby
Mattishall
Honingham
Costessey
Hellesdon
Old Catton
Sprowston
Little Plumstead
Hemblington
Upton
THE CANDLEMAKER WORKSHOP
Thrigby
Mautby
THRIGBY HALL WILDLIFE GARDENS
West Caister
CAISTER ROMAN TOWN
Caister-on-Sea
Mattishall Burgh
Mile Cross
Upper Hellesdon
Thorpe End
Blofield Heath
North Burlingham
Runham
West End
East Tuddenham
Easton
New Costessey
New Catton
Thorpe St Andrew
Great Plumstead
Acle
Stokesby
GREAT YARMOUTH GREAT DENES
YARMOUTH
Welborne
Colton
Marlingford
Bowthorpe
THE FORUM
CATHEDRAL
Blofield
Lingwood
Damgate
Earlham
NORWICH
Brundall
Beighton
Moulton St Mary
Tunstall
THE
Runham
Great Yarmouth
SAINSBURY CENTRE FOR VISUAL ARTS
Halvergate Marshes
Breydon Water
SEA LIFE GREAT YARMOUTH
Brandon Parva
Barford
Bawburgh
Colney
WHITLINGHAM
Postwick
Strumpshaw
South Burlingham
Cobholm Island
Barnham Broom
Little Melton
Lakenham
Trowse Newton
Halvergate
ELIZABETHAN HOUSE, TIME & TIDE/NELSON/LADY EVA/ TOLHOUSE MUSEUMS
Great Melton
Cringleford
Eaton
Kirby Bedon
Surlingham
Buckenham
BROADS
Burgh Castle
Wramplingham
High Green
Hassingham
Freethorpe
Wickhampton
Southtown
Danemoor Green
Carleton Forehoe
Keswick
Arminghall
Bramerton
MID YARE
Southwood
BERNEY ARMS WINDMILL
PLEASURE BEACH
Hethersett
Caistor St Edmund
Framingham Pigot
Rockland St Mary
Cantley
Limpenhoe
Gorleston-on-Sea
Kimberley
Crownthorpe
Ketteringham
Claxton
Bradwell
Framingham Earl
Hellington
PETTITTS ANIMAL ADVENTURE PARK
Wymondham
East Carleton
Swardeston
Dunston
Ashby St Mary
Langley Street
Belton
Reedham
Stoke Holy Cross
Poringland
Yelverton
Bergh Apton
Hardley Street
REDWINGS HORSE SANCTUARY
Swainsthorpe
Morley St Botolph
Mulbarton
Thurton
ST OLAVES PRIORY
Fritton
Hopton on Sea
Suton
Silfield
Bracon Ash
Howe
Chedgrave
Lower Thurlton
Wreningham
Hawes' Green
Shotesham
Brooke
Sisland
Loddon
Thurlton
Thorpe
The Dell
Lound
Newton Flotman
Stubb's Green
SOMERLEYTON HALL
Ashwellthorpe
Florden
Seething
Mundham
Stubbs Green
Hales
Spooner Row
Fundenhall
Hapton
Saxlingham Thorpe
Saxlingham Nethergate
Kirstead Green
Herringfleet
Blundeston
Corton
Besthorpe
Fundenhall Street
Tasburgh
Saxlingham Green
HALES HALL BARN & GARDENS
Raveningham
RAVENINGHAM GARDENS
Haddiscoe
Maypole Green
Somerleyton
PLEASUREWOOD HILLS LEISURE PARK
Attleborough
Tacolneston
Forncett St Mary
Tharston
Hempnall
Thwaite St Mary
Toft Monks
Oulton
LOWESTOFT AND EAST SUFFOLK MARITIME MUSEUM
INDUSTRIAL STEAM MUSEUM
Kirby Cane
Stockton
Bunwell
Forncett End
Stratton St Michael
Road Green
Woodton
Hedenham
Wheatacre
Normanstone
HERITAGE/VISITOR CENTRE
Puddledock
Carleton Rode
Forncett St Peter
Long Stratton
Fritton
Hempnall Green
Topcroft
Cobbler's Green
Ellingham
Kirby Row
Burgh St Peter
Aldeby
Oulton Broad
Lowestoft
Old Buckenham
Morningthorpe
Topcroft Street
LOWESTOFT MUSEUM
Kirkley
Hargate
Wacton
Geldeston
Gillingham
CARLTON MARSHES NATURE RESERVE
Church Green
Aslacton
Shelton
Shelton Green
Ditchingham
Broome
Beccles
Waveney
Tibenham
Great Moulton
Shipmeadow
Barnby
Pakefield
New Buckenham
Hardwick
Mettingham
Worlingham
Carlton Colville
Hunt's Corner
Pristow Green
Sneath Common
Great Green
Earsham
Bungay
Barsham
North Cove
Mutford
Denton
Ringsfield
Gisleham
Banham
North Green
NORFOLK AND SUFFOLK AVIATION MUSEUM
Ilketshall St Andrew
Ringsfield Corner
Hulver Street
Rushmere
Goose Green
Tivetshall St Margaret
Bush Green
Alburgh
Flixton
Kessingland
BANHAM ZOO
Winfarthing
Tivetshall St Mary
Pulham Market
Ilketshall St Margaret
Ellough
Kessingland Beach
Pulham St Mary
Henstead
AFRICA ALIVE!
Dam Green
Gissing
Homersfield
Benacre
Starston
St Cross South Elmham
St Michael South Elmham
Ilketshall St Lawrence
Redisham
Mill Green
Garlic Street
Wortwell
Sotterley
Shelfanger
Burston
Harleston
Redenhall
St Margaret South Elmham
Stone Street
Shadingfield
Rushall
Mendham
SOUTH ELMHAM HALL
All Saints South Elmham
West End
Wrentham
Fersfield
Shimpling
Dickleburgh
Cox Common
BENACRE
Needham
Brampton
Stoven
Clay Common
Walcot Green
100TH BOMB GROUP MEMORIAL MUS
Mill Common
Covehithe
Bressingham
Thelveton
Withersdale Street
St James South Elmham
Rumburgh
Frostenden
Roydon
Diss
Weybread
Spexhall
South Cove
BRESSINGHAM STEAM MUSEUM AND GARDENS
Thorpe Abbotts
Metfield
Westhall
Uggeshall
Cove Bottom
Magpie Green
Palgrave
Scole
Brockdish
Wissett
Broadway
Wangford
BILLINGFORD WINDMILL
Linstead Parva
Chediston
Reydon Smear
Fressingfield
Holton
Reydon
Wortham
Stuston
Oakley
Hoxne
Syleham
WINGFIELD OLD COLLEGE
Little Whittingham Green
Halesworth
Blyford
SOUTHWOLD MUSEUM
Thrandeston
Brome
Brome Street
Cross Street
Wingfield
Chippenhall Green
Silverley's Green
HEN REEDBED NATURE RESERVE
Southwold
Burgate
Langton Green
Heckfield Green
Battlesea Green
Pixey Green
Cratfield
Cookley
Wenhaston
Blackheath
Blythburgh
Mellis
Yaxley
Eye
Denham
Swan Green
Huntingfield
Walpole
Walberswick
Stradbroke
Ashfield Green
Banyard's Green
Bramfield
Thornham Parva
Cranley
Wootten Green
Russel's Green
SUFFOLK COAST
Denham Street
Horham
Wilby
Laxfield
Heveningham
Sibton Green
Dunwich
Foals Green
Ubbeston
High Street
DUNWICH
TG
TM

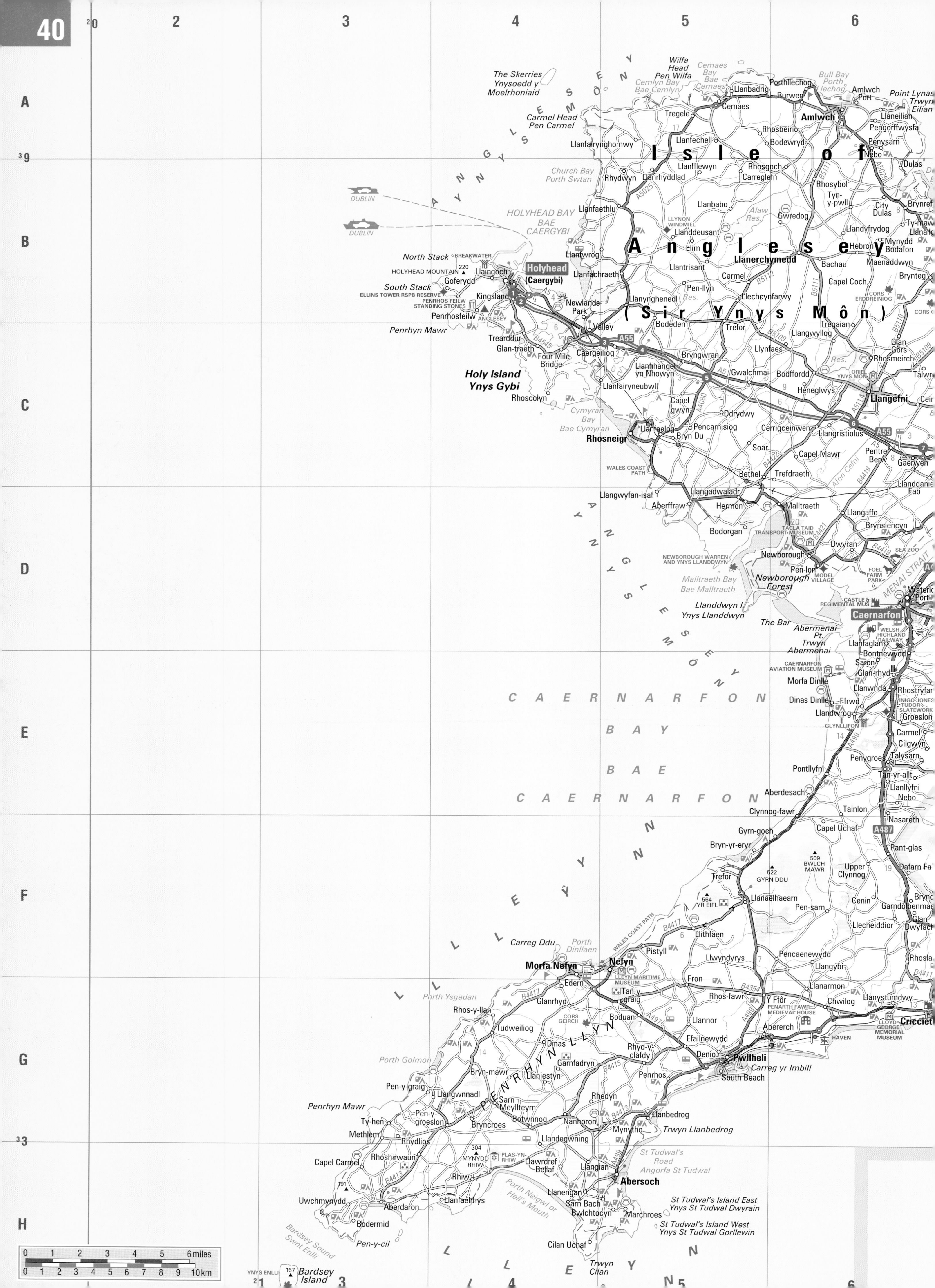

Isle of Anglesey
(Sir Ynys Môn)
Holy Island
Ynys Gybi
The Skerries
Ynysoedd y Moelrhoniaid
Carmel Head
Pen Carmel
Wilfa Head
Pen Wilfa
Cemaes Bay
Bae Cemaes
Cemlyn Bay
Bae Cemlyn
Bull Bay
Porth Llechog
Point Lynas
Porthllechog
Llanbadrig
Cemaes
Burwen
Amlwch Port
Amlwch
Tregele
Llanfechell
Rhosbeirio
Bodewryd
Llaneilian
Pengorffwysfa
Penysarn
Nebo
Dulas
Llanfairynghornwy
Llanfflewyn
Rhosgoch
Church Bay
Porth Swtan
Rhydwyn
Llanrhyddlad
Carreglefn
Rhosybol
Tyn-y-pwll
City Dulas
Llanfaethlu
Llanbabo
Alaw Res.
Gwredog
Llynon Windmill
Llanddeusant
Llandyfrydog
Mynydd Bodafon
Hebron
Holyhead Bay
Bae Caergybi
Dublin
Llanfwrog
Elim
Llanerchymedd
Maenaddwyn
North Stack
Breakwater
Holyhead Mountain
220
Holyhead
(Caergybi)
Llaingoch
Llantrisant
Bachau
Llanfachraeth
Carmel
Capel Coch
Brynteg
South Stack
Goferydd
Ellins Tower RSPB Reserve
Penrhos Feilw Standing Stones
Kingsland
Pen-llyn
Llechcynfarwy
Cors Erddreiniog
Newlands Park
Llanynghenedl
Penrhosfeilw
Anglesey
Valley
Bodedern
Trefor
Tregaian
Penrhyn Mawr
Trearddur
Glan-traeth
Four Mile Bridge
Caergeiliog
A55
Bryngwran
Llynfaes
Llangwyllog
Glan Gors
Rhosmeirch
Llanfihangel yn Nhowyn
Gwalchmai
Bodffordd
Oriel Ynys Môn
Rhoscolyn
Llanfairyneubwll
Heneglwys
Llangefni
Capel-gwyn
Cymyran Bay
Bae Cymyran
Ddrydwy
Llanfaelog
Pencarnisiog
Cerrigceinwen
Llangristiolus
Rhosneigr
Bryn Du
Soar
Capel Mawr
Pentre Berw
Gaerwen
Wales Coast Path
Bethel
Trefdraeth
Llanddaniel Fab
Llangwyfan-isaf
Llangadwaladr
Aberffraw
Hermon
Malltraeth
Llangaffo
Bodorgan
Tacla Taid Transport Museum
Brynsiencyn
Newborough Warren and Ynys Llanddwyn
Newborough
Dwyran
Sea Zoo
Pen-lon
Model Village
Foel Farm Park
Malltraeth Bay
Bae Malltraeth
Newborough Forest
Menai Strait
Llanddwyn I.
Ynys Llanddwyn
Castle & Regimental Mus
Caernarfon
The Bar
Abermenai Pt.
Trwyn Abermenai
Welsh Highland Railway
Llanfaglan
Bontnewydd
Saron
Caernarfon Aviation Museum
Glan-rhyd
Morfa Dinlle
Llanwnda
Rhostryfan
Dinas Dinlle
Ffrwd
Llandwrog
Inigo Jones Tudor Slatework
Glynllifon
Groeslon
Carmel
Cilgwyn
Caernarfon Bay
Bae Caernarfon
Penygroes
Talysarn
Pontllyfni
Tan-yr-allt
Llanllyfni
Nebo
Aberdesach
Clynnog-fawr
Tainlon
Nasareth
Capel Uchaf
A487
Gyrn-goch
Bryn-yr-eryr
Pant-glas
509 Bwlch Mawr
522 Gyrn Ddu
Upper Clynnog
Dafarn Fa
Trefor
564 Yr Eifl
Llanaelhaearn
Cenin
Garndolbenmaen
Pen-sarn
Llecheiddior
Wales Coast Path
Llithfaen
Carreg Ddu
Porth Dinllaen
Pistyll
Pencaenewydd
Morfa Nefyn
Nefyn
Llwyndyrys
Llangybi
Lleyn Maritime Museum
Edern
Fron
Llanarmon
Tan-y-graig
Porth Ysgadan
Glanrhyd
Rhos-fawr
Y Ffôr
Chwilog
Llanystumdwy
Rhos-y-llan
Penarth Fawr Medieval House
Cors Geirch
Boduan
Llannor
Lloyd George Memorial Museum
Criccieth
Tudweiliog
Aberech
Haven
Dinas
Efailnewydd
Rhyd-y-clafdy
Porth Golmon
Garnfadryn
Denio
Pwllheli
Carreg yr Imbill
Bryn-mawr
Llaniestyn
Penrhos
South Beach
Pen-y-graig
Llangwnnadl
Rhedyn
Penrhyn Mawr
Sarn Meyllteyrn
Penrhyn Llŷn
Pen-y-groeslon
Llanbedrog
Ty-hen
Bryncroes
Botwnnog
Nanhoron
Mynytho
Trwyn Llanbedrog
Methlem
Rhydlios
Llandegwning
St Tudwal's Road
Angorfa St Tudwal
304 Mynydd Rhiw
Plas-yn-Rhiw
Capel Carmel
Rhoshirwaun
Llawrdref Bellaf
Llangian
Rhiw
Abersoch
191
Porth Neigwl or Hell's Mouth
Uwchmynydd
Aberdaron
Llanfaelrhys
Llanengan
St Tudwal's Island East
Ynys St Tudwal Dwyrain
Sarn Bach
Bwlchtocyn
Marchroes
St Tudwal's Island West
Ynys St Tudwal Gorllewin
Bodermid
Bardsey Sound
Swnt Enlli
Pen-y-cil
Cilan Uchaf
Trwyn Cilan
Ynys Enlli
167
Bardsey Island
Anglesey
Ynys Môn
Llŷn
0 1 2 3 4 5 6 miles
0 1 2 3 4 5 6 7 8 9 10 km
A
B
C
D
E
F
G
H
2
3
4
5
6

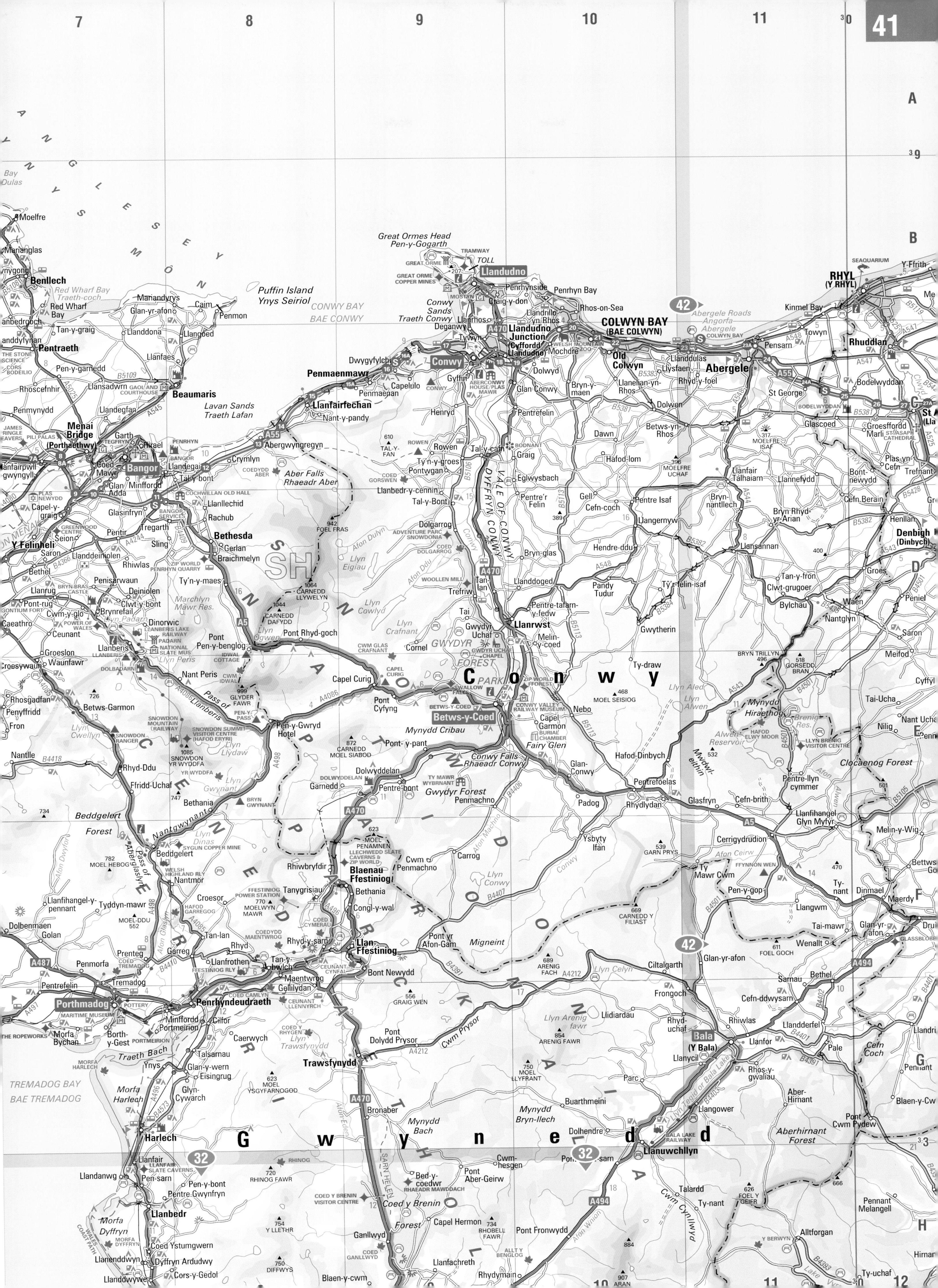
7
8
9
10
11
A
B
D
E
F
G
H
ANGLESEY
YNYS MÔN
Bay Dulas
Moelfre
Marianglas
Benllech
Red Wharf Bay
Traeth-coch
Red Wharf Bay
Pentraeth
Tan-y-graig
Llanddona
Llangoed
Penmon
Caim
Glan-yr-afon
Mariandyrys
Llanfaes
Pen-y-garnedd
Beaumaris
Rhoscefnhir
Llansadwrn
Penmynydd
Llandegfan
Menai Bridge
(Porthaethwy)
Garth
Hirael
Bangor
Llandegai
Tal-y-bont
Glan Adda
Minffordd
Coed Mawr
Capel-y-graig
Glasinfryn
Llanllechid
Rachub
Bethesda
Tregarth
Pentir
Seion
Y Felinheli
Saron
Llanddeiniolen
Rhiwlas
Gerlan
Braichmelyn
Sling
Bethel
Penisarwaun
Deiniolen
Ty'n-y-maes
Llanrug
Pont-rug
Cwm-y-glo
Brynrefail
Clwt-y-bont
Dinorwic
Caeathro
Ceunant
Llanberis
Groeslon
Waunfawr
Nant Peris
Pont Pen-y-benglog
Pont Rhyd-goch
Capel Curig
Pass of Llanberis
Rhosgadfan
Betws-Garmon
Penyffridd
Fron
Nantlle
Rhyd-Ddu
Ffridd-Uchaf
Beddgelert Forest
Beddgelert
Nantgwynant
Bethania
Pass of Aberglaslyn
Nantmor
Croesor
Llanfihangel-y-pennant
Tyddyn-mawr
Dolbenmaen
Golan
Tan-lan
Garreg
Rhyd
Prenteg
Penmorfa
Tremadog
Pentrefelin
Porthmadog
Llanfrothen
Penrhyndeudraeth
Minffordd
Portmeirion
Cilfor
Morfa Bychan
Borth-y-Gest
Traeth Bach
Ynys
Talsarnau
Caerwych
Llan-y-wern
Eisingrug
Glyn-Cywarch
TREMADOG BAY
BAE TREMADOG
Morfa Harlech
Harlech
Llanfair
Llandanwg
Pen-sarn
Pen-y-bont
Pentre Gwynfryn
Llanbedr
Morfa Dyffryn
Coed Ystumgwern
Llanenddwyn
Dyffryn Ardudwy
Llanddwywe
Cors-y-Gedol
Great Ormes Head
Pen-y-Gogarth
Llandudno
Puffin Island
Ynys Seiriol
CONWY BAY
BAE CONWY
Conwy Sands
Traeth Conwy
Penrhynside
Penrhyn Bay
Craig-y-don
Rhos-on-Sea
Llandrillo-yn-Rhos
Deganwy
Llanrhos
Tywyn
Llandudno Junction
(Cyffordd Llandudno)
Mochdre
COLWYN BAY
(BAE COLWYN)
Old Colwyn
Llanddulas
Llysfaen
Abergele
Abergele Roads
Angorfa
Abergele
Kinmel Bay
Towyn
Pensarn
RHYL
(Y RHYL)
Rhuddlan
Bodelwyddan
St George
Dwygyfylchi
Penmaenmawr
Penmaenan
Capelulo
Conwy
Gyffin
Llanfairfechan
Nant-y-pandy
Abergwyngregyn
Crymlyn
Lavan Sands
Traeth Lafan
Aber Falls
Rhaeadr Aber
Henryd
Rowen
Ty'n-y-groes
Pontwgan
Llanbedr-y-cennin
Tal-y-Bont
Tal-y-cafn
Graig
Eglwysbach
Dolgarrog
VALE OF CONWY
DYFFRYN CONWY
Dolwyd
Glan Conwy
Bryn-y-maen
Llanelian-yn-Rhos
Rhyd-y-foel
Dolwen
Betws-yn-Rhos
Pentrefelin
Dawn
Hafod-lom
Glascoed
Groesffordd Marli
Llanfair Talhaiarn
Llannefydd
Bont-newydd
Trefnant
Plas-yn-Cefn
Cefn Berain
Henllan
Denbigh
(Dinbych)
Gell
Cefn-coch
Pentre Isaf
Pentre'r Felin
Llangernyw
Bryn-nantllech
Bryn Rhyd-yr-Arian
Llansannan
Hendre-ddu
Bryn-glas
Tan-lan
Trefriw
Llanddoged
Pandy Tudur
Ty'n-y-felin-isaf
Tan-y-fron
Clwt-grugoer
Bylchau
Waen
Nantglyn
Groes
Peniel
Saron
Meifod
Pentre-tafarn-y-fedw
Llanrwst
Melin-y-coed
Gwytherin
Gwydyr Uchaf
Tai
Llyn Crafnant
Llyn Cowlyd
Llyn Eigiau
Cornel
GWYDYR FOREST PARK
Conwy
Betws-y-Coed
Ty-draw
Llyn Aled
Llyn Alwen
Mynydd Hiraethog
Alwen Reservoir
Brenig Res.
Nebo
Capel Garmon
Fairy Glen
Pont Cyfyng
Pen-y-Gwryd Hotel
Mynydd Cribau
Pont-y-pant
Conwy Falls
Rhaeadr Conwy
Glan-Conwy
Hafod-Dinbych
Pentrefoelas
Padog
Rhydlydan
Glasfryn
Cefn-brith
Pentre-llyn cymmer
Llanfihangel Glyn Myfyr
Clocaenog Forest
Tai-Ucha
Nilig
Dolwyddelan
Pentre-bont
Garnedd
Gwydyr Forest
Penmachno
Ysbyty Ifan
Cerrigydrudion
Melin-y-Wig
Cwm Penmachno
Carrog
Blaenau Ffestiniog
Rhiwbryfdir
Tanygrisiau
Bethania
Congl-y-wal
Llyn Conwy
Ty Mawr Cwm
Pen-y-gop
Llangwm
Tŷ-nant
Dinmael
Maerdy
Rhyd-y-sarn
Llan Ffestiniog
Pont yr Afon-Gam
Migneint
Tai-mawr
Glan-yr-afon
Wenallt
Tan-y-bwlch
Maentwrog
Gellilydan
Bont Newydd
Llyn Celyn
Ciltalgarth
Glan-yr-afon
Frongoch
Sarnau
Bethel
Cefn-ddwysarn
Llidiardau
Llyn Arenig fawr
Rhyd-uchaf
Rhiwlas
Llandderfel
Bala
(Y Bala)
Llanfor
Llanycil
Pale
Cefn Coch
Pont Dolydd Prysor
Cwm Prysor
Trawsfynydd
Llyn Trawsfynydd
Rhos-y-gwaliau
Parc
Aber-Hirnant
Bronaber
Mynydd Bach
Buarthmeini
Mynydd Bryn-llech
Llangower
Dolhendre
Llanuwchllyn
Pont Cwm Pydew
Aberhirnant Forest
Cwm-hesgen
Bed-y-coedwr
Pont Aber-Geirw
Coed y Brenin Forest
Capel Hermon
Pont Fronwydd
Talardd
Tŷ-nant
Cwm Cynllwyd
Pennant Melangell
Ganllwyd
Llanfachreth
Rhydymain
Alltforgan
Blaen-y-cwm
Ty-uchaf
SNOWDONIA NATIONAL PARK
Conwy
Gwynedd
SH
42
32
A55
A5
A470
A487
A494
A4086
A498
A4212
B4391
B4407
B5113

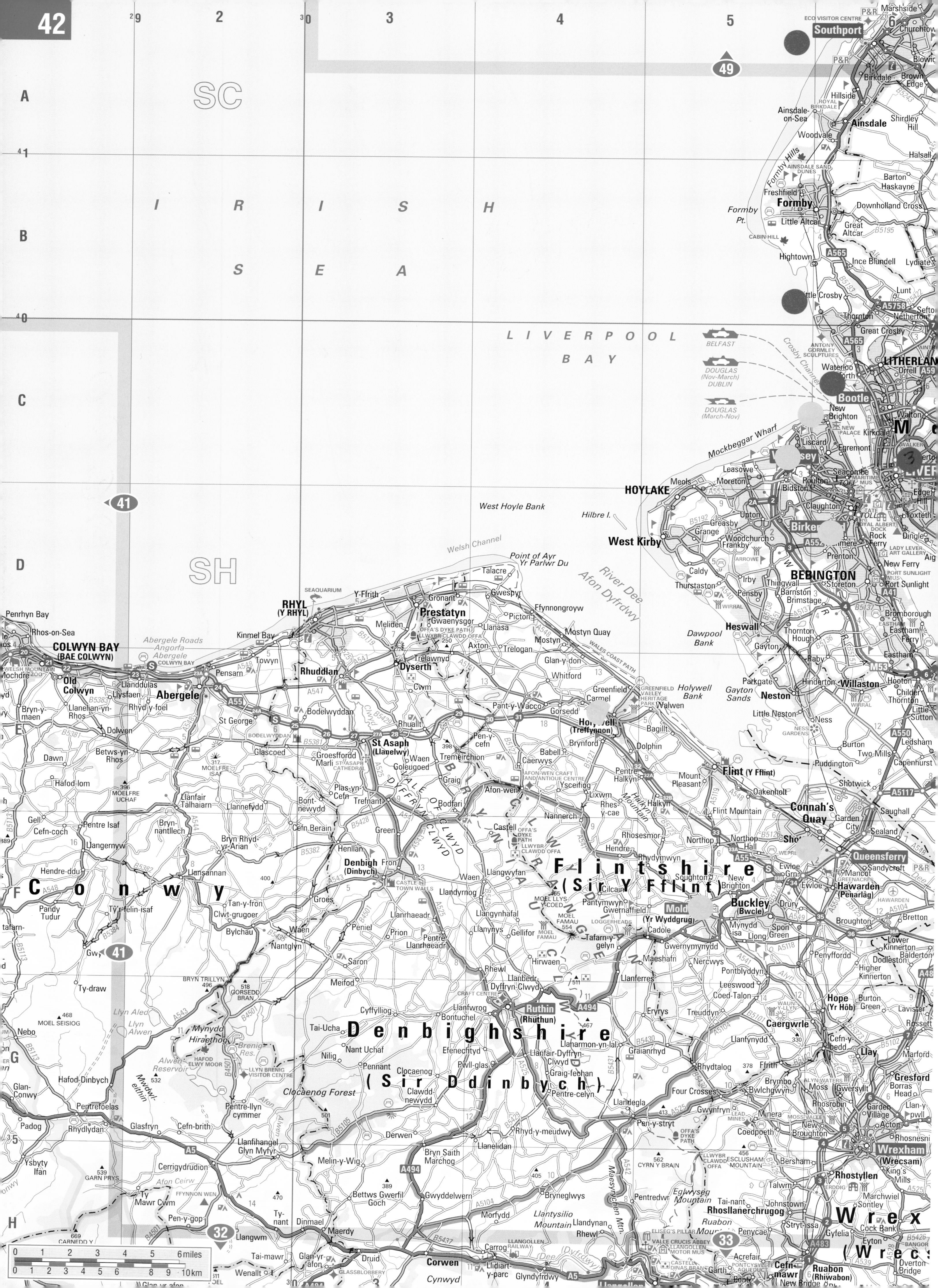
SC
IRISH SEA
LIVERPOOL BAY
SH
49
41
32
33
Southport
Birkdale
Hillside
Ainsdale-on-Sea
Ainsdale
Woodvale
Formby Hills
Freshfield
Formby
Formby Pt.
Little Altcar
Great Altcar
Hightown
Ince Blundell
Little Crosby
Thornton
Great Crosby
Waterloo
LITHERLAND
Bootle
New Brighton
Liscard
Egremont
Wallasey
Leasowe
Moreton
Meols
HOYLAKE
Bidston
Poulton
Seacombe
Birkenhead
Claughton
Upton
Greasby
Grange
Woodchurch
Frankby
West Kirby
Hilbre I.
West Hoyle Bank
Welsh Channel
Point of Ayr
Yr Parlwr Du
River Dee
Afon Dyfrdwy
Caldy
Thurstaston
Irby
Pensby
Thingwall
Barnston
Brimstage
BEBINGTON
Storeton
Heswall
Dawpool Bank
Gayton
Thornton Hough
Raby
Willaston
Parkgate
Gayton Sands
Neston
Little Neston
Ness
Burton
Puddington
Shotwick
Connah's Quay
Queensferry
Sandycroft
Mancot
Hawarden (Penarlâg)
Ewloe
Buckley (Bwcle)
Mold (Yr Wyddgrug)
Flint (Y Fflint)
Flintshire (Sir Y Fflint)
Holywell (Treffynnon)
Greenfield
Carmel
Gorsedd
Whitford
Mostyn
Mostyn Quay
Ffynnongroyw
Picton
Gwespyr
Talacre
Llanasa
Prestatyn
Gronant
Meliden
Dyserth
Trelawnyd
Rhuddlan
RHYL (Y RHYL)
Kinmel Bay
Towyn
Pensarn
Abergele
Abergele Roads
Llanddulas
Old Colwyn
COLWYN BAY (BAE COLWYN)
Rhos-on-Sea
Penrhyn Bay
Mochdre
St George
Bodelwyddan
St Asaph (Llanelwy)
Trefnant
Denbigh (Dinbych)
Henllan
Llansannan
Conwy
Denbighshire (Sir Ddinbych)
Ruthin (Rhuthun)
Llanferres
Caergwrle
Hope (Yr Hôb)
Llay
Gresford
Rhosllanerchrugog
Wrexham (Wrecsam)
Rhostyllen
Ruabon (Rhiwabon)
Cefn-mawr
Corwen
Cerrigydrudion
Clocaenog Forest
Cyffylliog
Derwen
Gwyddelwern
Llangwm
Pentrefoelas
Nebo
Glan-Conwy
Llyn Alwen
Alwen Reservoir
Llyn Brenig
Moel Famau
Llantysilio Mountain
Eglwyseg Mountain
Ruabon Mountain
Llangollen
0 1 2 3 4 5 6 miles
0 1 2 3 4 5 6 7 8 9 10 km

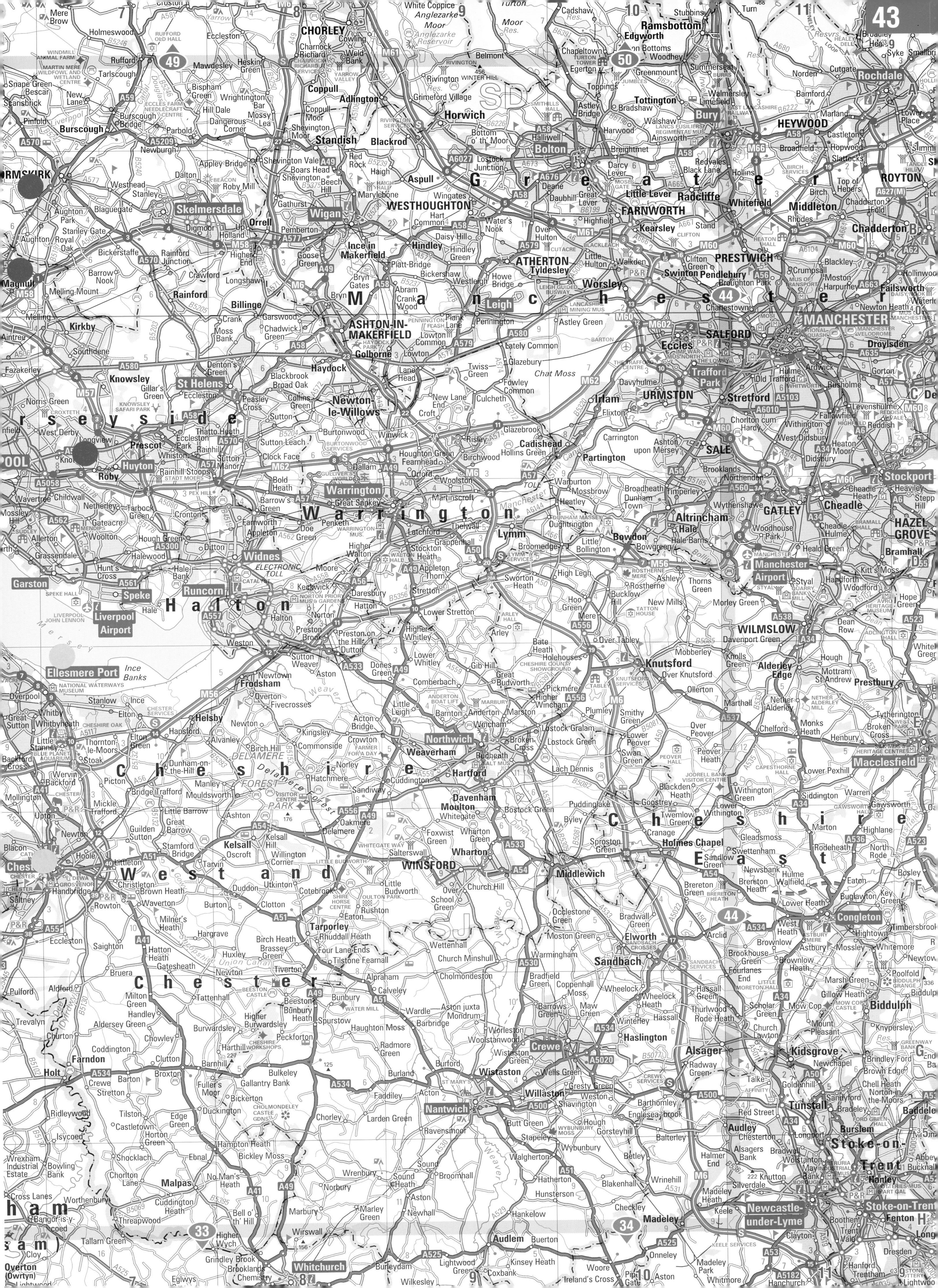
Greater Manchester
Merseyside
Warrington
Halton
Cheshire
Cheshire East
Cheshire West and Chester
SD
SJ
CHORLEY
Bolton
Bury
Rochdale
HEYWOOD
ROYTON
Wigan
Skelmersdale
ORMSKIRK
St Helens
Leigh
MANCHESTER
SALFORD
Trafford Park
Eccles
URMSTON
Stretford
SALE
Stockport
Cheadle
GATLEY
HAZEL GROVE
Altrincham
Manchester Airport
WILMSLOW
Macclesfield
Congleton
Biddulph
Kidsgrove
Stoke-on-Trent
Newcastle-under-Lyme
Crewe
Nantwich
Sandbach
Alsager
Middlewich
WINSFORD
Northwich
Knutsford
Lymm
Widnes
Runcorn
Liverpool Airport
Speke
Garston
Huyton
Prescot
Kirkby
Knowsley
Ellesmere Port
Frodsham
Helsby
Chester
Tarporley
Malpas
Farndon
Holt
Whitchurch
Audlem
Madeley
FARNWORTH
Radcliffe
PRESTWICH
Middleton
Chadderton
Failsworth
ATHERTON
Tyldesley
Worsley
WESTHOUGHTON
Horwich
Standish
ASHTON-IN-MAKERFIELD
Golborne
Haydock
Newton-le-Willows
Irlam
Partington
Cadishead
Chat Moss
Delamere Forest
Ince Banks
Mersey
Weaver
49
50
44
33
34
M6
M56
M62
M60
M61
M58
M57
M53
A49
A50
A51
A34
A556
A534

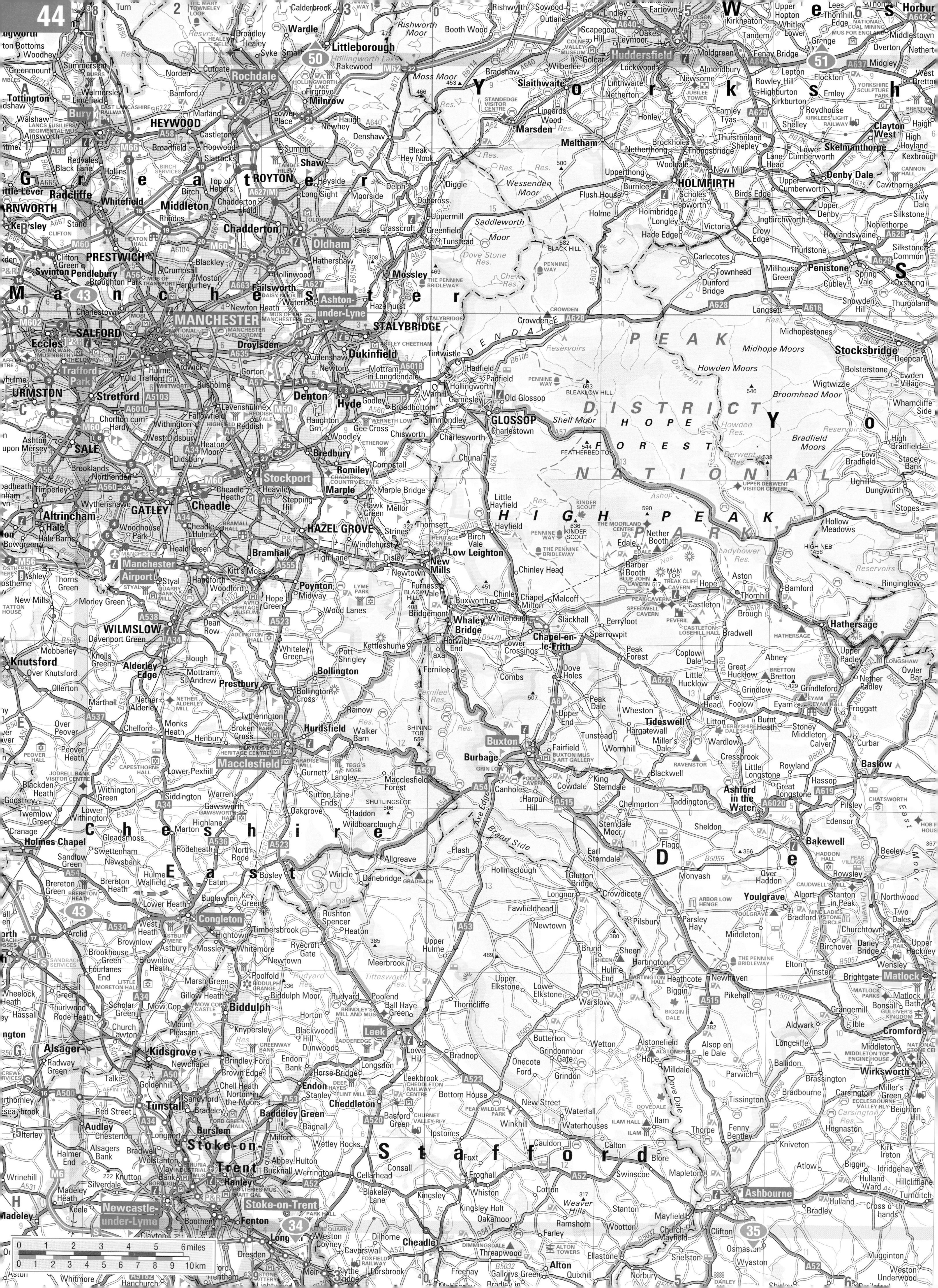

Turn
Calderbrook
Rishworth
Sowood
Lindley
Fartown
W
e
s
Horbury
Wardle
Littleborough
Rishworth Moor
Booth Wood
Outlane
Scapegoat Hill
Oakes
Upper Hopton
Kirkheaton
Lees
Thornhill Edge
Whitley Lower
Tandem
Grange
Middlestown
Overton
Netherton
Broadley
Healey
Syke
Small
50
Hollingworth Lake
Rakewood
Moss Moor
Huddersfield
Moldgreen
Fenay Bridge
51
Midgley
Tottington
Greenmount
Summerseat
Norden
Cutgate
Rochdale
Bradshaw
Slaithwaite
Wilberlee
Golcar
Lockwood
Almondbury
Lepton
Flockton
West Bretton
Walmersley
Bamford
Firgrove
Milnrow
Y
Linthwaite
Netherton
Newsome
Rowley Hill
Highburton
Kirkburton
Emley
o
r
k
s
h
Bury
HEYWOOD
Marland
Lower Place
Haugh
Newhey
Standedge Visitor Centre
Marsden
Lingards Wood
Honley
Farnley Tyas
Roydhouse
Walshaw
Ainsworth
Castleton
Denshaw
Meltham
Brockholes
Thurstonland
Shelley
Clayton West
High Haigh
Redvales
Black Lane
Broadfield
Hopwood
Slattocks
Summit
Bleak Hey Nook
Netherthong
Thongsbridge
Shepley
Lane Head
Lower Cumberworth
Skelmanthorpe
High Hoyland
Kexbrough
Hollins
Shaw
Wooldale
New Mill
Denby Dale
G
r
e
a
t
e
r
Top of Hebers
ROYTON
Heyside
Delph
Diggle
Wessenden Moor
Upperthong
Burnlee
HOLMFIRTH
Upper Cumberworth
Cawthorne
Little Lever
Radcliffe
Whitefield
Middleton
Chadderton Fold
Long Sight
Moorside
Dobcross
Flush House
Scholes
Birds Edge
Tivy Dale
FARNWORTH
Rhodes
Uppermill
Holme
Hepworth
Upper Denby
Silkstone
Kearsley
Stand
Chadderton
Oldham
Lees
Grasscroft
Greenfield
Saddleworth Moor
Holmbridge
Longley
Victoria
Ingbirchworth
Noblethorpe
Clifton
PRESTWICH
Tunstead
Black Hill
Hade Edge
Crow Edge
Hoylandswaine
Swinton
Pendlebury
Blackley
Crumpsall
Hathershaw
Dove Stone Res.
Carlecotes
Thurlstone
Silkstone Common
Broughton Park
Moston
Harpurhey
Hollinwood
Failsworth
Mossley
Millhouse Green
Townhead
Penistone
Spring Vale
Oxspring
M
a
n
c
h
e
s
t
e
r
43
Newton Heath
Ashton-under-Lyne
Hazelhurst
Dunford Bridge
Cubley
Snowden Hill
Thurgoland
Charlestown
Waterloo
Crowden
Langsett
Eccles
SALFORD
MANCHESTER
Droylsden
STALYBRIDGE
Midhopestones
Stocksbridge
P
E
A
K
Midhope Moors
Deepcar
Audenshaw
Dukinfield
Tintwistle
Howden Moors
Bolsterstone
Ewden Village
Trafford Park
Hulme
Ardwick
Gorton
Newton
Mottram in Longdendale
Hadfield
Padfield
Bleaklow Hill
Wigtwizzle
URMSTON
Stretford
Old Trafford
Rusholme
Denton
Hyde
Hollingworth
Broomhead Moor
Levenshulme
Fallowfield
Godley
Broadbottom
Gamesley
Old Glossop
Wharncliffe Side
D
I
S
T
R
I
C
T
Y
O
Chorlton cum Hardy
Withington
Reddish
Haughton Grn.
Gee Cross
Simmondley
GLOSSOP
Charlestown
Shelf Moor
H
O
P
E
Ashton upon Mersey
SALE
West Didsbury
Heaton Moor
Woodley
Chisworth
Charlesworth
F
O
R
E
S
T
High Bradfield
Bradfield Moors
Didsbury
Bredbury
Chunal
Featherbed Top
Low Bradfield
Stacey Bank
Brooklands
Northenden
Stockport
Romiley
Compstall
N
A
T
I
O
N
A
L
Timperley
Heaviley
Marple
Marple Bridge
Upper Derwent Visitor Centre
Ughill
Dungworth
Wythenshawe
Cheadle Heath
Stepping Hill
Hawk Green
Mellor
Little Hayfield
Ashop
Stopes
Altrincham
GATLEY
Cheadle
H
I
G
H
P
E
A
K
Hale
Hale Barns
Cheadle Hulme
Woodhouse Park
HAZEL GROVE
Strines
Thornsett
Birch Vale
Hayfield
Kinder Scout
Hollow Meadows
Bowgreen
Heald Green
Bramhall
Windlehurst
Disley
Low Leighton
Edale
Nether Booth
Ladybower Res.
High Neb
Manchester Airport
Kitt's Moss
High Lane
Newtown
New Mills
Chinley Head
Barber Booth
Mam Tor
Reservoirs
Mobberley
Ashley
Thorns Green
Styal
Handforth
Woodford
Poynton
Midway
Furness Vale
Chinley
Chapel Milton
Malcoff
Hope
Aston
Bamford
Ringinglow
New Mills
Morley Green
Hope Green
Wood Lanes
Bridgemont
Buxworth
Whaley Bridge
Whitehough
Slackhall
Perryfoot
Castleton
Thornhill
Brough
WILMSLOW
Dean Row
Sparrowpit
Bradwell
Hathersage
Davenport Green
Kettleshume
Horwich End
Lower Crossings
Chapel-en-le-Frith
Peak Forest
Upper Padley
Owler Bar
Knutsford
Knolls Green
Alderley Edge
Hough
Mottram St Andrew
Whiteley Green
Pott Shrigley
Bollington
Taxal
Fernilee
Combs
Dove Holes
Coplow Dale
Abney
Over Knutsford
Prestbury
Bollington Cross
Great Hucklow
Little Hucklow
Bretton
Grindleford
Nether Padley
Ollerton
Nether Alderley
Rainow
Grindlow
Eyam
Froggatt
Marthall
Tytherington
Peak Dale
Lane Head
Foolow
Over Peover
Chelford
Monks Heath
Broken Cross
Hurdsfield
Walker Barn
Shining Tor
Buxton
Upper End
Wheston
Tideswell
Litton
Burnt Heath
Stoney Middleton
Calver
Peover Heath
Henbury
Macclesfield
Burbage
Fairfield
Tunstead
Hargatewall
Wormhill
Miller's Dale
Wardlow
Curbar
Baslow
Lower Pexhill
Gurnett
Langley
Macclesfield Forest
Cressbrook
Little Longstone
Rowland
Blackden Heath
Withington Green
Siddington
Warren
Sutton Lane Ends
Shutlingsloe
Canholes
King Sterndale
Cowdale
Great Longstone
Hassop
Goostrey
Gawsworth
Haddon
Ashford in the Water
Pilsley
Lower Withington
Twemlow Green
Oakgrove
Wildboarclough
Harpur Hill
Chelmorton
Taddington
Edensor
Cranage
Holmes Chapel
C
h
e
s
h
i
r
e
Highlane
Marton
Sterndale Moor
Sheldon
Bakewell
Beeley
Gleadsmoss
Rodeheath
North Rode
Flash
Axe Edge
Brand Side
Flagg
Swettenham
Newsbank
Sandlow Green
E
a
s
t
Bosley
Allgreave
Earl Sterndale
D
e
Rowsley
Hulme Walfield
Eaton
Wincle
Danebridge
Hollinsclough
Monyash
Over Haddon
Brereton Green
Brereton Heath
Buglawton
Key Green
Glutton Bridge
Crowdicote
Youlgrave
Alport
Stanton in Peak
Northwood
Lower Heath
Rushton Spencer
Longnor
Fawfieldhead
Pilsbury
Parsley Hay
Bradford
Two Dales
43
Congleton
West Heath
Timbersbrook
Heaton
Newtown
Arbor Low Henge
Middleton
Churchtown
Arclid
Brownlow
Hightown
Astbury
Mossley
Whitemore
Ryecroft Gate
Upper Hulme
Brund
Sheen
Hartington
Darley Bridge
Birchover
Upper Hackney
Brookhouse Green
Brownlow Heath
Newtown
Meerbrook
Hulme End
Heathcote
Newhaven
Elton
Winster
Wensley
Fourlanes End
Poolfold
Tittesworth Res.
Upper Elkstone
Lower Elkstone
Biggin
Pikehall
Brightgate
Matlock
Hassall Green
Marsh Green
Gillow Heath
Biddulph Moor
Rudyard
Poolend
Thorncliffe
Warslow
Wheelock Heath
Thurlwood
Rode Heath
Scholar Green
Mow Cop
Biddulph
Horton
Ball Haye Green
Grangemill
Bonsall
Matlock Bath
Hassall
Church Lawton
Mount Pleasant
Knypersley
Blackwood Hill
Dunwood
Leek
Lowe Hill
Butterton
Grindonmoor Gate
Wetton
Alstonefield
Aldwark
Ible
Cromford
Alsager
Kidsgrove
Newchapel
Brindley Ford
Endon Bank
Bradnop
Onecote
Ford
Hope
Milldale
Alsop en le Dale
Longcliffe
Middleton
Radway Green
Talke
Brown Edge
Horse Bridge
Longsdon
Grindon
Parwich
Ballidon
Bolehill
Wirksworth
Goldenhill
Chell Heath
Norton-in-the-Moors
Endon
Stanley
Cheddleton
Leekbrook
Bottom House
New Street
Brassington
Carsington
Miller's Green
Barrow Green
Tunstall
Sandyford
Bradeley
Red Street
Audley
Burslem
Baddeley Green
Bagnall
Basford Green
Winkhill
Waterfall
Waterhouses
Ilam
Tissington
Bradbourne
Carsington Res.
Beighton Hill
Chesterton
Longport
Milton
Wetley Rocks
Ipstones
Thorpe
Fenny Bentley
Hognaston
Alsagers Bank
Bradwell
Wolstanton
Stoke-on-Trent
Abbey Hulton
Bucknall
Werrington
Cauldon
Calton
Kniveton
Kirk Ireton
S
t
a
f
f
o
r
d
Halmer End
Foxt
Blore
Wrinehill
Knutton
May Bank
Hanley
Cellarhead
Consall
Froghall
Swinscoe
Mapleton
Atlow
Biggin
Idridgehay
Madeley Heath
Silverdale
Blakeley Lane
Whiston
Cotton
Weaver Hills
Hulland Ward
Hillcliffane
Turnditch
Keele
Newcastle-under-Lyme
Stoke-on-Trent
Kingsley
Kingsley Holt
Ashbourne
Hulland
Cross o' th' hands
Madeley
Boothen
Fenton
34
Oakamoor
Ramshorn
Stanton
Mayfield
Bradley
Clayton
Longton
Weston Coyney
Dilhorne
Cheadle
Farley
Wootton
Church Mayfield
Clifton
35
Dresden
Caverswall
Threapwood
Alton Towers
Ellastone
Osmaston
Mugginton
Meir
Blythe Bridge
Forsbrook
Freehay
Alton
Quixhill
Norbury
Snelston
Wyaston
Weston Underwood
Hanchurch
Whitmore
Bradley in the Moors
Gallows Green
0
1
2
3
4
5
6 miles
0
1
2
3
4
5
6
7
8
9
10 km

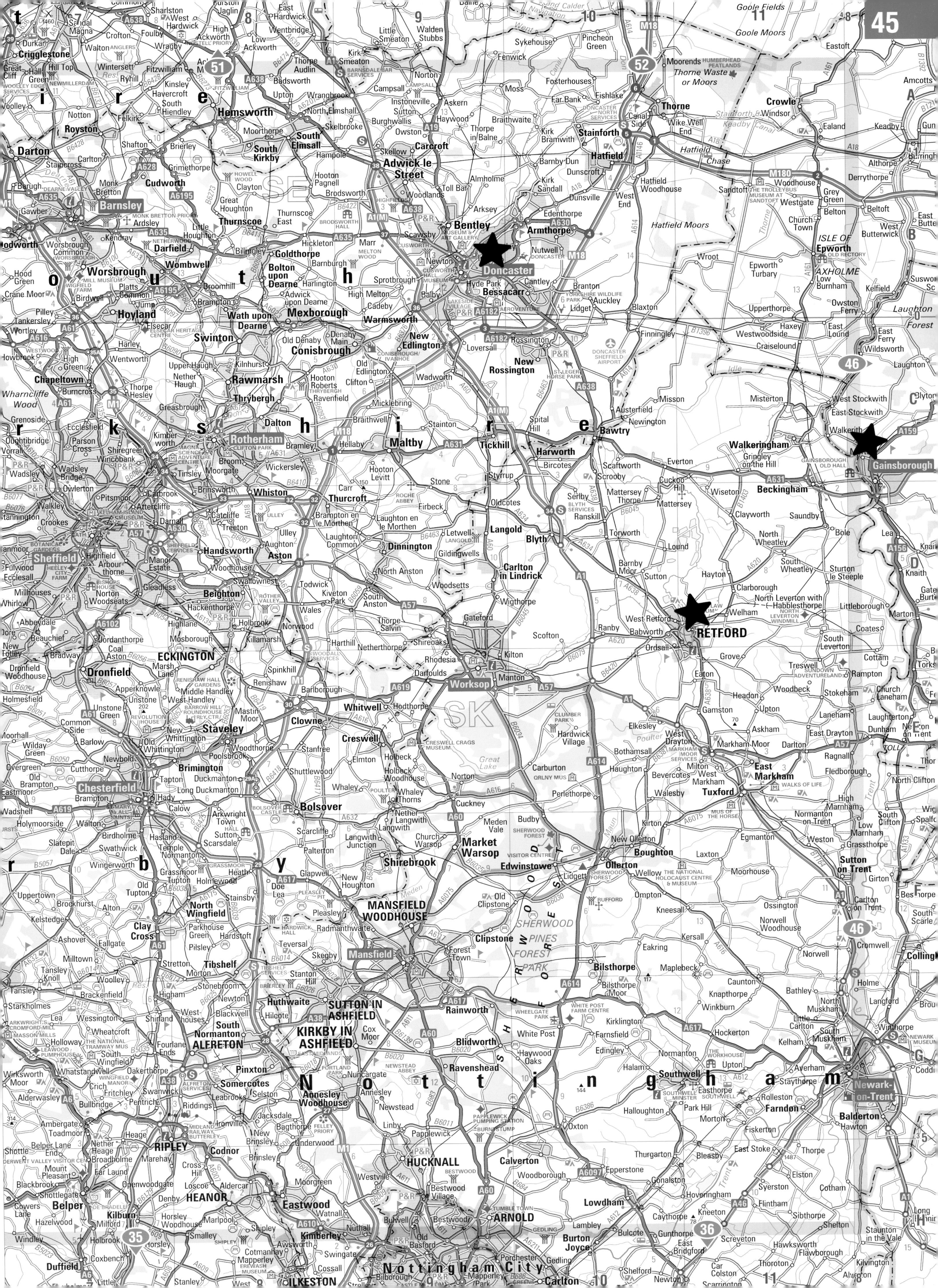

Goole Fields
Goole Moors
Eastoft
Amcotts
Sharlston
West Hardwick
East Hardwick
Wentbridge
Little Smeaton
Walden Stubbs
Sykehouse
Pincheon Green
Fenwick
Moorends
Thorne Waste or Moors
Crofton
Foulby
High Ackworth
Low Ackworth
Kirk Smeaton
Thorpe Audlin
Norton
Fosterhouses
Fishlake
Thorne
Crowle
Windsor
Cricklestone
Walton
Wragby
Winterset
Ryhill
Fitzwilliam
Badsworth
Campsall
Moss
Far Bank
Hemsworth
Upton
Wrangbrook
North Elmsall
Instoneville
Askern
Haywood
Braithwaite
Wike Well End
Stainforth
Ealand
Keadby
Notton
Royston
Felkirk
Havercroft
South Hiendley
Kinsley
Moorthorpe
South Elmsall
Skelbrooke
Burghwallis
Owston
Thorpe in Balne
Kirk Bramwith
Hatfield
Hatfield Chase
Darton
Shafton
Brierley
South Kirkby
Hampole
Skellow
Carcroft
Adwick le Street
Barnby Dun
Dunscroft
Althorpe
Cudworth
Grimethorpe
Hooton Pagnell
Brodsworth
Woodlands
Toll Bar
Almholme
Kirk Sandall
Dunsville
West End
Hatfield Woodhouse
Sandtoft
Woodhouse
Derrythorpe
Grey Green
Barnsley
Monk Bretton
Clayton
Great Houghton
Thurnscoe
Thurnscoe East
Arksey
Bentley
Edenthorpe
Armthorpe
Westgate
Belton
Beltoft
Church Town
Ardsley
Little Houghton
Hickleton
Marr
Scawsby
Nutwell
Hatfield Moors
Isle of Axholme
Epworth
Worsbrough
Darfield
Billingley
Goldthorpe
Bolton upon Dearne
Barnburgh
Doncaster
Wroot
Epworth Turbary
Wombwell
Harlington
Sprotbrough
Hyde Park
Cantley
Branton
Auckley
Low Burnham
Worsbrough
Platts Common
Broomhill
Adwick upon Dearne
High Melton
Bessacarr
Lidget
Blaxton
Owston Ferry
Hoyland
Brampton
Wath upon Dearne
Mexborough
Cadeby
Balby
Warmsworth
Haxey
Westwoodside
East Lound
Elsecar
Swinton
Old Denaby
Denaby Main
Conisbrough
New Edlington
Loversall
Rossington
Finningley
Craiselound
Wildsworth
Harley
Wentworth
Chapeltown
Upper Haugh
Nether Haugh
Kilnhurst
Rawmarsh
Old Edlington
Clifton
Hooton Roberts
Wadworth
New Rossington
Laughton
Burncross
Thorpe Hesley
Thrybergh
Ravenfield
Micklebring
Misson
Austerfield
Misterton
West Stockwith
East Stockwith
Greasbrough
Dalton
Braithwell
Stainton
Spital Hill
Bawtry
Newington
Walkeringham
Walkerith
Ecclesfield
Kimberworth
Rotherham
Hellaby
Bramley
Maltby
Tickhill
Harworth
Bircotes
Scaftworth
Scrooby
Everton
Gringley on the Hill
Gainsborough
Wincobank
Shiregreen
Tinsley
Brinsworth
Moorgate
Wickersley
Hooton Levitt
Stone
Styrrup
Beckingham
Whiston
Thurcroft
Carr
Firbeck
Oldcotes
Serlby
Mattersey Thorpe
Mattersey
Wiseton
Saundby
Catcliffe
Treeton
Ulley
Brampton en le Morthen
Laughton en le Morthen
Letwell
Langold
Blyth
Ranskill
Torworth
Clayworth
North Wheatley
Bole
Sheffield
Handsworth
Aughton
Aston
Laughton Common
Dinnington
Gildingwells
Lound
South Wheatley
Sturton le Steeple
Woodhouse
North Anston
Carlton in Lindrick
Barnby Moor
Sutton
Hayton
Clarborough
Todwick
Kiveton Park
South Anston
Woodsetts
Wigthorpe
Beighton
Swallownest
Norton
Woodseats
Gleadless
Hackenthorpe
Wales
Thorpe Salvin
Gateford
West Retford
Retford
Welham
North Leverton with Habblesthorpe
Littleborough
Norwood
Holbrook
Highlane
Killamarsh
Harthill
Netherthorpe
Shireoaks
Scofton
Ranby
Babworth
Ordsall
South Leverton
Coates
Coal Aston
Mosbrough
Eckington
Spinkhill
Rhodesia
Kilton
Worksop
Manton
Darfoulds
Grove
Treswell
Cottam
Rampton
Dronfield
Marsh Lane
Renishaw
Apperknowle
Middle Handley
West Handley
Unstone
Barlborough
Eaton
Headon
Woodbeck
Stokeham
Church Laneham
Unstone Green
Staveley
Mastin Moor
Whitwell
Hodthorpe
Clowne
Clumber Park
Elkesley
Gamston
Upton
Laneham
Dunham
Common Side
Barlow
Old Whittington
New Whittington
Woodthorpe
Creswell
Hardwick Village
West Drayton
Askham
East Drayton
Wilday Green
Newbold
Poolsbrook
Stanfree
Holbeck
Great Lake
Bothamsall
Markham Moor
Darlton
Ragnall
Overgreen
Cutthorpe
Brimington
Tapton
Duckmanton
Long Duckmanton
Shuttlewood
Elmton
Holbeck Woodhouse
Whaley
Whaley Thorns
Norton
Carburton
Haughton
Milton
West Markham
East Markham
Fledborough
Old Brampton
Chesterfield
Brampton
Hady
Calow
Bolsover
Cuckney
Perlethorpe
Walesby
Tuxford
North Clifton
Holymoorside
Walton
Arkwright Town
Sutton Scarsdale
Nether Langwith
Langwith
Meden Vale
Budby
High Marnham
Normanton on Trent
Low Marnham
South Clifton
Birdholme
Hasland
Temple Normanton
Scarcliffe
Palterton
Langwith Junction
Church Warsop
Market Warsop
Kirton
New Ollerton
Egmanton
Grassthorpe
Slatepit Dale
Swathwick
Wingerworth
Grassmoor
Heath
Glapwell
Shirebrook
Edwinstowe
Boughton
Ollerton
Laxton
Moorhouse
Sutton on Trent
Old Tupton
Tupton
Holmewood
Doe Lea
New Houghton
Wellow
Girton
Upper Town
Brockhurst
Alton
North Wingfield
Stainsby
Pleasley Hill
Old Clipstone
Rufford
Ompton
Ossington
Carlton on Trent
Kelstedge
Clay Cross
Parkhouse Green
Hardstoft
Pleasley
Mansfield Woodhouse
Radmanthwaite
Sherwood Pines Forest Park
Kneesall
Norwell Woodhouse
Ashover
Fallgate
Pilsley
Teversal
Clipstone
Kersall
Cromwell
Milltown
Tansley Knoll
Woolley
Stretton
Tibshelf
Skegby
Mansfield
Forest Town
Eakring
Norwell
Bilsthorpe
Maplebeck
Tansley
Brackenfield
Morton
Stanton Hill
Bilsthorpe Moor
Caunton
Holme
Higham
Stonebroom
Newton
Huthwaite
Sutton in Ashfield
Rainworth
Knapthorpe
Bathley
Langford
Starkholmes
Lea
Shirland
West-houses
Blackwell
Hilcote
Winkburn
North Muskham
Wessington
Wheatcroft
South Normanton
Kirkby in Ashfield
Cox Moor
Kirklington
Little Carlton
Winthorpe
Holloway
Crich
Fourlane Ends
Alfreton
Blidworth
White Post
Farnsfield
Hockerton
South Muskham
Kelham
South Wingfield
Haywood Oaks
Edingley
Normanton
Upton
Averham
Wirksworth Moor
Whatstandwell
Oakerthorpe
Pinxton
Ravenshead
Halam
Southwell
Staythorpe
Newark-on-Trent
Nottingham
Somercotes
Fritchley
Swanwick
Selston
Annesley
Annesley Woodhouse
Newstead
Easthorpe
Rolleston
Farndon
Alderwasley
Bullbridge
Pentrich
Leabrooks
Riddings
Halloughton
Park Hill
Morton
Balderton
Hawton
Ambergate
Toadmoor
Ironville
Jacksdale
Bagthorpe
Linby
Papplewick
Oxton
Fiskerton
Heage
Nether Heage
Ripley
Codnor
New Brinsley
Underwood
Belper Lane End
Shottle
Broadholme
Marehay
Brinsley
Hucknall
Calverton
Thurgarton
Bleasby
East Stoke
Thorpe
Mount Pleasant
Far Laund
Cross Hill
Loscoe
Aldercar
Woodborough
Epperstone
Elston
Syerston
Cotham
Blackbrook
Shottlegate
Belper
Openwoodgate
Denby
Heanor
Moorgreen
Eastwood
Westville
Bestwood Village
Gonalston
Hoveringham
Flintham
Cowers Lane
Hazelwood
Kilburn
Milford
Horsley Woodhouse
Marlpool
Watnall
Bulwell
Bestwood
Arnold
Lowdham
Caythorpe
Kneeton
Sibthorpe
Long Bennington
Windley
Holbrook
Horsley
Smalley
Shipley
Kimberley
Nuthall
Old Basford
Lambley
Burton Joyce
Bulcote
Gunthorpe
East Bridgford
Screveton
Shelton
Staunton in the Vale
Duffield
Coxbench
Little Eaton
Stanley
Cotmanhay
Mapperley
West Hallam
Ilkeston
Awsworth
Swingate
Cossall
Bilborough
Nottingham City
Mapperley Park
Porchester
Gedling
Carlton
Shelford
Newton
Car Colston
Scarrington
Hawksworth
Flawborough
Thoroton
Kilvington
Alverton

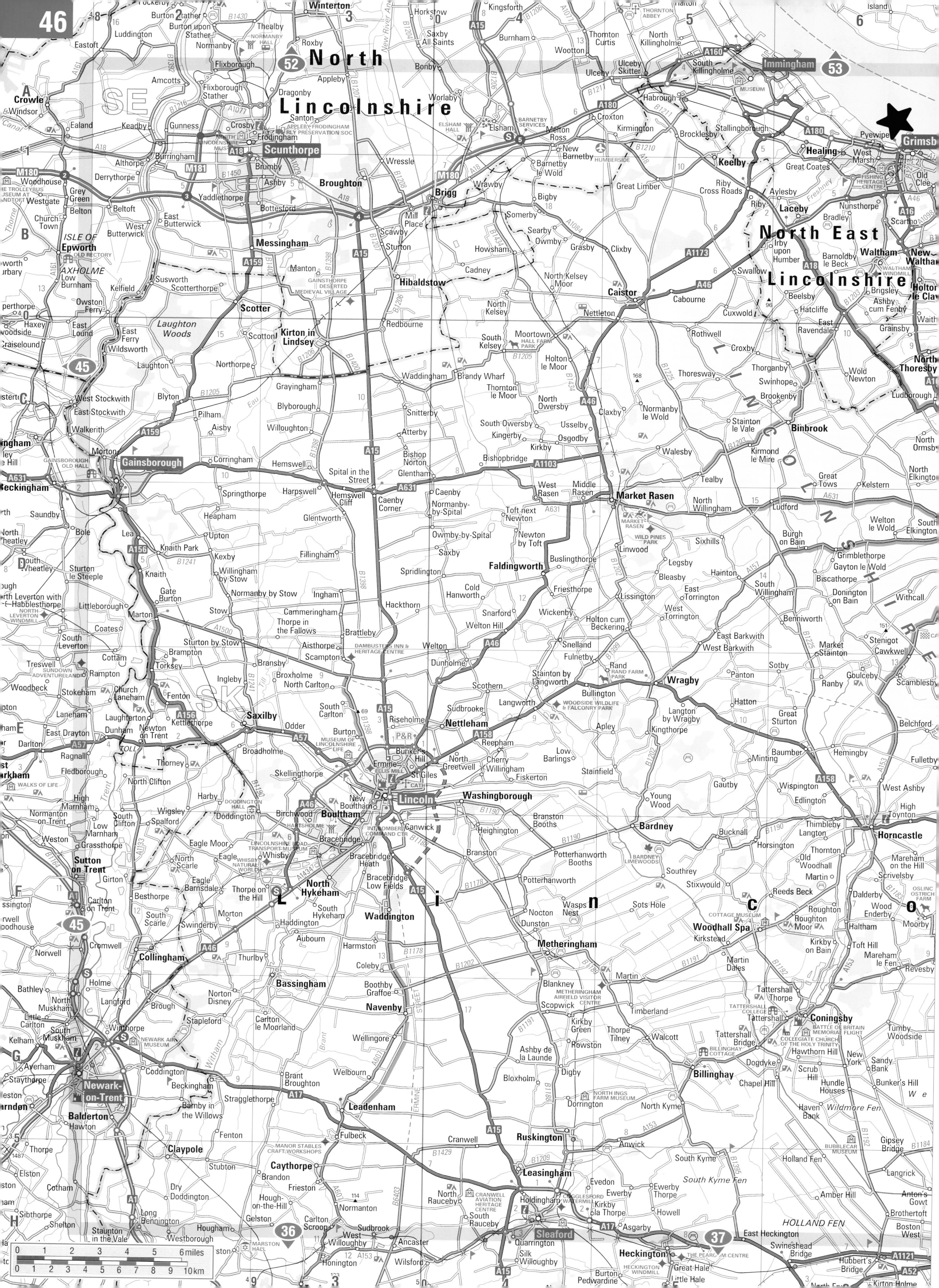
North
Lincolnshire
North East
Lincolnshire
Lincoln
Scunthorpe
Gainsborough
Brigg
Immingham
Grimsb
Market Rasen
Caistor
Horncastle
Sleaford
Newark-on-Trent
Woodhall Spa
Coningsby
Saxilby
Epworth
Crowle
Winterton
Broughton
Messingham
Kirton in Lindsey
Hibaldstow
Scotter
Laceby
Healing
Keelby
Binbrook
Wragby
Nettleham
Washingborough
Bardney
Metheringham
Waddington
North Hykeham
Bassingham
Navenby
Leadenham
Ruskington
Leasingham
Heckington
Billinghay
Collingham
Claypole
Caythorpe
Faldingworth
Tealby
Humberside
Laughton Woods
Isle of Axholme
Wildmore Fen
South Kyme Fen
Holland Fen
Sutton on Trent
Balderton
Boultham
Bracebridge Heath
Welton
Dunholme
Walesby
Thoresway
Ludford
Kelstern
Bucknall
Tattershall
Tattershall Bridge
Dogdyke
Asgarby
Ancaster
Wilsford
Honington
Quarrington
Silk Willoughby
Dorrington
Digby
Scopwick
Blankney
Martin
Timberland
Walcott
Cranwell
Anwick
North Kyme
South Kyme
Welbourn
Wellingore
Fulbeck
Brant Broughton
Stragglethorpe
Coddington
Beckingham
Barnby in the Willows
Fenton
Stubton
Dry Doddington
Long Bennington
Hougham
Westborough
Staunton in the Vale
Shelton
Sibthorpe
Cotham
Elston
Thorpe
Hawton
Farndon
Winthorpe
South Muskham
North Muskham
Holme
Langford
Brough
Norton Disney
Stapleford
Carlton le Moorland
Thurlby
Aubourn
Harmston
Coleby
Boothby Graffoe
Haddington
South Hykeham
Skellingthorpe
Doddington
Eagle
Whisby
Birchwood
Canwick
Branston
Heighington
Potterhanworth
Nocton
Dunston
Stixwould
Southrey
Thimbleby
Langton
Horsington
Edlington
Wispington
Baumber
Minting
Gautby
Hemingby
West Ashby
Belchford
Fulletby
Great Sturton
Hatton
Panton
Sotby
Ranby
Market Stainton
Benniworth
East Barkwith
West Barkwith
Langton by Wragby
Kingthorpe
Apley
Stainfield
Fiskerton
Cherry Willingham
Reepham
Sudbrooke
Langworth
Scothern
Bullington
Fulnetby
Rand
Snelland
Holton cum Beckering
Wickenby
Lissington
Friesthorpe
Snarford
Cold Hanworth
Hackthorn
Spridlington
Saxby
Owmby-by-Spital
Normanby-by-Spital
Caenby
Caenby Corner
Glentham
Bishop Norton
Atterby
Snitterby
Waddingham
Brandy Wharf
Redbourne
Cadney
Howsham
Searby
Owmby
Grasby
Clixby
Somerby
Bigby
Barnetby le Wold
New Barnetby
Melton Ross
Elsham
Wrawby
Kirmington
Croxton
Ulceby
Habrough
Stallingborough
Brocklesby
Great Limber
Riby
Aylesby
Irby upon Humber
Swallow
Cabourne
Nettleton
Rothwell
Cuxwold
Croxby
Thorganby
Swinhope
Brookenby
Stainton le Vale
Normanby le Wold
Claxby
Usselby
Osgodby
Kirkby
Kingerby
North Owersby
South Owersby
Thornton le Moor
Holton le Moor
Moortown
South Kelsey
North Kelsey
Bishopbridge
West Rasen
Middle Rasen
Toft next Newton
Newton by Toft
Buslingthorpe
Linwood
Legsby
Bleasby
Sixhills
North Willingham
East Torrington
West Torrington
Hainton
South Willingham
Burgh on Bain
Gayton le Wold
Biscathorpe
Donington on Bain
Withcall
Stenigot
Cawkwell
Scamblesby
Gulceby
Hemswell
Hemswell Cliff
Harpswell
Spital in the Street
Glentworth
Fillingham
Ingham
Cammeringham
Brattleby
Thorpe in the Fallows
Aisthorpe
Scampton
Broxholme
North Carlton
South Carlton
Burton
Riseholme
Odder
Ingleby
Bransby
Sturton by Stow
Stow
Normanby by Stow
Willingham by Stow
Kexby
Upton
Heapham
Springthorpe
Corringham
Blyton
Pilham
Aisby
Willoughton
Blyborough
Grayingham
Northorpe
Laughton
Scotton
East Ferry
Wildsworth
Susworth
Scotterthorpe
Kelfield
Owston Ferry
East Lound
Haxey
Graiseley
Low Burnham
Belton
Beltoft
Westgate
Woodhouse
Grey Green
Church Town
Derrythorpe
Althorpe
Keadby
Gunness
Burringham
Crosby
Frodingham
Brumby
Ashby
Bottesford
Yaddlethorpe
East Butterwick
West Butterwick
Eastoft
Luddington
Amcotts
Flixborough
Flixborough Stather
Burton upon Stather
Normanby
Thealby
Roxby
Appleby
Dragonby
Santon
Wressle
Scawby
Sturton
Mill Place
Bonby
Worlaby
Saxby All Saints
Horkstow
Kingsforth
Burnham
Thornton Curtis
Wootton
North Killingholme
South Killingholme
Ulceby Skitter
Pyewipe
West Marsh
Great Coates
Nunsthorpe
Scartho
Bradley
Waltham
New Waltham
Barnoldby le Beck
Brigsley
Ashby cum Fenby
Beelsby
Hatcliffe
East Ravendale
Grainsby
Wold Newton
North Thoresby
Ludborough
North Ormsby
North Elkington
South Elkington
Welton le Wold
Gayton le Wold
Grimblethorpe
Morton
Walkerith
East Stockwith
West Stockwith
Lea
Knaith Park
Knaith
Gate Burton
Marton
Littleborough
Sturton le Steeple
Saundby
Bole
South Wheatley
North Wheatley
North Leverton with Habblesthorpe
South Leverton
Coates
Cottam
Treswell
Rampton
Brampton
Torksey
Woodbeck
Stokeham
Church Laneham
Laneham
Fenton
Kettlethorpe
Laughterton
Newton on Trent
Dunham
East Drayton
Darlton
Ragnall
Thorney
Broadholme
Harby
Fledborough
North Clifton
South Clifton
Spalford
Wigsley
High Marnham
Low Marnham
Normanton on Trent
Weston
Grassthorpe
Girton
Carlton on Trent
Besthorpe
South Scarle
North Scarle
Swinderby
Morton
Eagle Moor
Thorpe on the Hill
Norwell
Cromwell
Bathley
Little Carlton
Kelham
Averham
Staythorpe
Newark Air Museum
Lincolnshire Road Transport Museum
Museum of Lincolnshire Life
Gainsborough Old Hall
Doddington Hall
Woodside Wildlife & Falconry Park
Dambusters Inn & Heritage Centre
Metheringham Airfield Visitor Centre
Battle of Britain Memorial Flight
Cranwell Aviation Heritage Centre
Cogglesford Watermill
Heckington Windmill
The Pearoom Centre
Bubblecar Museum
North Ings Farm Museum
Manor Stables Craft Workshops
Cottage Museum
Bardney Limewoods
Wild Pines Park
Hall Farm Park
Rand Farm Park
Humberside
Elsham Hall
Barnetby Services
Appleby-Frodingham Rly Preservation Soc
Gainsthorpe Deserted Medieval Village
Sundown Adventureland
Walks of Life
Thornton Abbey
Normanby Hall
Old Rectory
Fishing Heritage Centre
Waltham Windmill
Osgodby
Coningsby
Tumby Woodside
New York
Sandy Bank
Bunker's Hill
Haven Bank
Scrub Hill
Hundle Houses
Chapel Hill
Gipsey Bridge
Langrick
Amber Hill
Anton's Gowt
Brothertoft
Boston West
Hubbert's Bridge
Swineshead Bridge
East Heckington
Great Hale
Little Hale
Burton Pedwardine
Howell
Ewerby
Ewerby Thorpe
Evedon
Kirkby la Thorpe
Holdingham
North Rauceby
South Rauceby
Normanton
Sudbrook
West Willoughby
Carlton Scroop
Gelston
Hough-on-the-Hill
Frieston
Brandon
Ashby de la Launde
Kirkby Green
Rowston
Thorpe Tilney
Bloxholm
Kirkstead
Martin Dales
Tattershall Thorpe
Kirkby on Bain
Haltham
Roughton
Roughton Moor
Reeds Beck
Dalderby
Wood Enderby
Moorby
Toft Hill
Mareham le Fen
Revesby
Mareham on the Hill
Scrivelsby
High Toynton
Young Wood
Branston Booths
Potterhanworth Booths
Wasps Nest
Sots Hole
Low Barlings
Greetwell
Bunker's Hill
St Giles
Ermine
New Boultham
Bracebridge
Bracebridge Low Fields
Toll
Trent
Witham
Ermine Street
Scale 0 1 2 3 4 5 6 miles
0 1 2 3 4 5 6 7 8 9 10 km

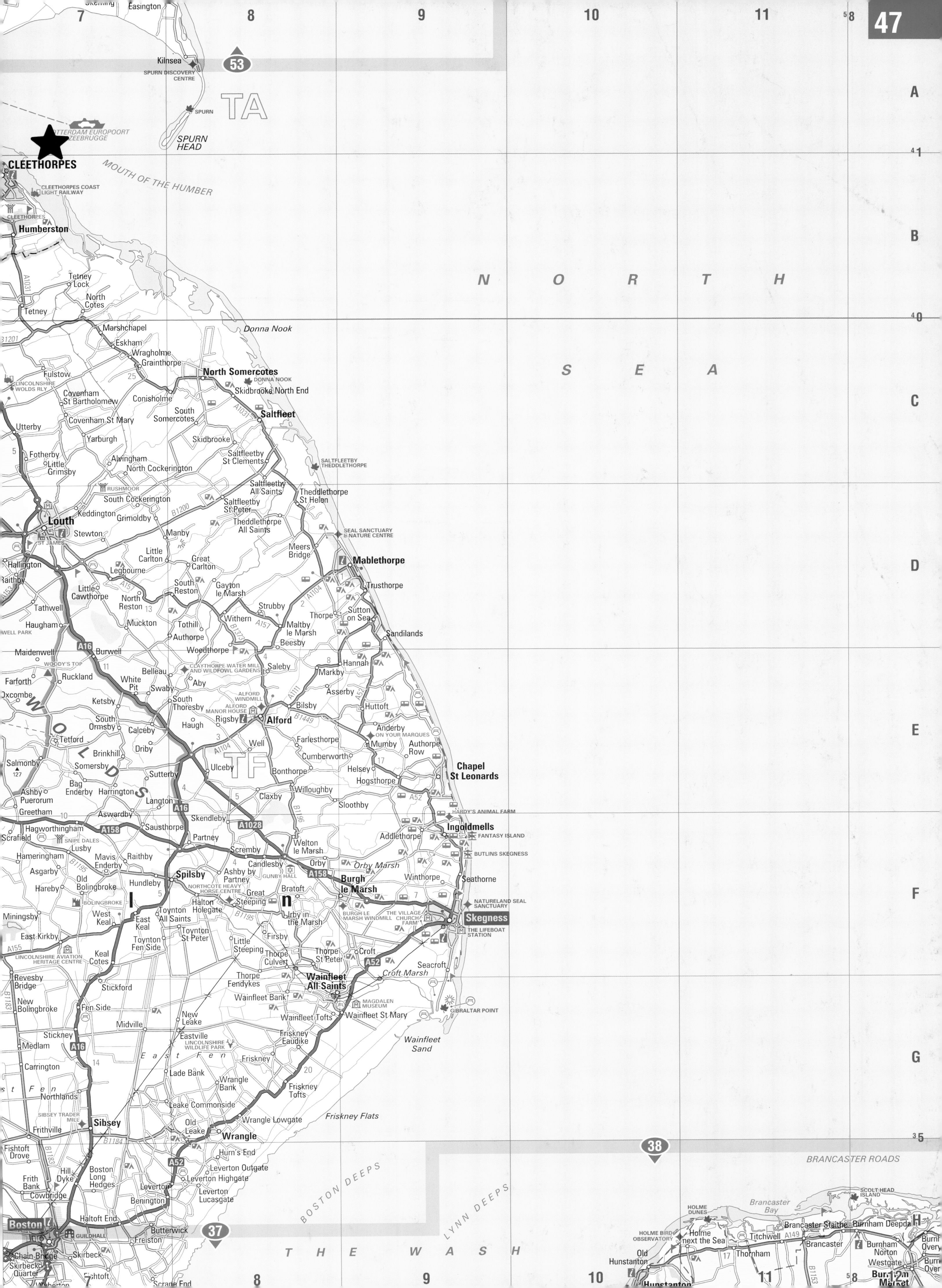

7   8   9   10   11

A
B
C
D
E
F
G
H

Skerning   Easington

Kilnsea
53
SPURN DISCOVERY CENTRE
SPURN
SPURN HEAD
TA

ROTTERDAM EUROPOORT ZEEBRUGGE
CLEETHORPES
MOUTH OF THE HUMBER
CLEETHORPES COAST LIGHT RAILWAY
CLEETHORPES
Humberston

N O R T H

S E A

Tetney Lock
North Cotes
Tetney
Marshchapel
Donna Nook
Eskham
Wragholme
Grainthorpe
Fulstow
LINCOLNSHIRE WOLDS RLY
North Somercotes
DONNA NOOK
Covenham St Bartholomew
Conisholme
Skidbrooke North End
South Somercotes
Saltfleet
Utterby
Covenham St Mary
Yarburgh
Skidbrooke
Fotherby
Little Grimsby
Alvingham
North Cockerington
Saltfleetby St Clements
SALTFLEETBY THEDDLETHORPE
RUSHMOOR
South Cockerington
Saltfleetby All Saints
Theddlethorpe St Helen
Hallington
Raithby
Louth
St JAMES
Keddington
Grimoldby
Saltfleetby St Peter
Theddlethorpe All Saints
SEAL SANCTUARY & NATURE CENTRE
Stewton
Manby
Meers Bridge
Mablethorpe
Legbourne
Little Carlton
Great Carlton
Trusthorpe
Little Cawthorpe
South Reston
Gayton le Marsh
Strubby
Thorpe
Sutton on Sea
Tathwell
Haugham
North Reston
Muckton
Tothill
Authorpe
Maltby le Marsh
Beesby
Sandilands
Maidenwell
Burwell
WOODY'S TOP
Woodthorpe
Saleby
Hannah
Markby
Asserby
Huttoft
Farforth
Oxcombe
Ruckland
White Pit
Belleau
Swaby
CLAYTHORPE WATER MILL AND WILDFOWL GARDENS
Aby
Anderby ON YOUR MARQUES
Ketsby
South Thoresby
ALFORD WINDMILL
Bilsby
Mumby
Authorpe Row
Tetford
South Ormsby
Calceby
Driby
Rigsby
ALFORD MANOR HOUSE
Alford
Farlesthorpe
Cumberworth
Salmonby
Somersby
Well
Ulceby
Bonthorpe
Helsey
Hogsthorpe
Chapel St Leonards
Ashby Puerorum
Brinkhill
WOLDS
TF
Claxby
Willoughby
Sloothby
Greetham
Bag Enderby
Harrington
Langton
Skendleby
Partney
HARDY'S ANIMAL FARM
Hagworthingham
Aswardby
Sausthorpe
Welton le Marsh
Addlethorpe
Ingoldmells
FANTASY ISLAND
Scrafield
SNIPE DALES
Lusby
Mavis Enderby
Raithby
Scremby
Orby
Orby Marsh
BUTLINS SKEGNESS
Hameringham
Asgarby
Old Bolingbroke
Hundleby
Ashby by Partney
GUNBY HALL
Candlesby
Winthorpe
Seathorne
Hareby
Miningsby
West Keal
East Keal
Spilsby
NORTHCOTE HEAVY HORSE CENTRE
Great Steeping
Bratoft
Irby in the Marsh
Burgh le Marsh
BURGH LE MARSH WINDMILL
THE VILLAGE CHURCH FARM
NATURELAND SEAL SANCTUARY
East Kirkby
LINCOLNSHIRE AVIATION HERITAGE CENTRE
Toynton All Saints
Halton Holegate
Toynton St Peter
Firsby
Skegness
THE LIFEBOAT STATION
Keal Cotes
Toynton Fen Side
Little Steeping
Thorpe St Peter
Thorpe Culvert
Croft
Seacroft
Revesby Bridge
Stickford
Thorpe Fendykes
Wainfleet All Saints
Croft Marsh
New Bolingbroke
Fen Side
Wainfleet Bank
MAGDALEN MUSEUM
Wainfleet St Mary
GIBRALTAR POINT
Stickney
Midville
New Leake
LINCOLNSHIRE WILDLIFE PARK
Wainfleet Tofts
Medlam
Carrington
East Fen
Eastville
Wrangle Bank
Friskney Eaudike
Wainfleet Sand
Northlands
Lade Bank
Wrangle Tofts
Friskney Tofts
Stickney
Leake Commonside
SIBSEY TRADER MILL
Friskney Flats
Frithville
Sibsey
Old Leake
Wrangle
Wrangle Lowgate
Fishtoft Drove
Frith Bank
Hill Dyke
Boston Long Hedges
Hurn's End
38
BRANCASTER ROADS
Cowbridge
Leverton Outgate
BOSTON DEEPS
Leverton Highgate
Leverton Lucasgate
HOLME DUNES
Brancaster Bay
SCOLT HEAD ISLAND
Boston
GUILDHALL
Benington
HOLME BIRD OBSERVATORY
Holme next the Sea
Brancaster Staithe
Burnham Deepdale
Chain Bridge
Skirbeck
Skirbeck Quarter
Haltoft End
Freiston
37
Butterwick
Old Hunstanton
Thornham
Titchwell
Brancaster
Burnham Norton Westgate
Fishtoft
Scrane End
THE WASH
LYNN DEEPS
Hunstanton
Bur
A158
A16
A1028
A52
A157
B1200
A1031
A1104
A1111
A1028
A1195
A1183
A1184
A1183

8   9   10   11

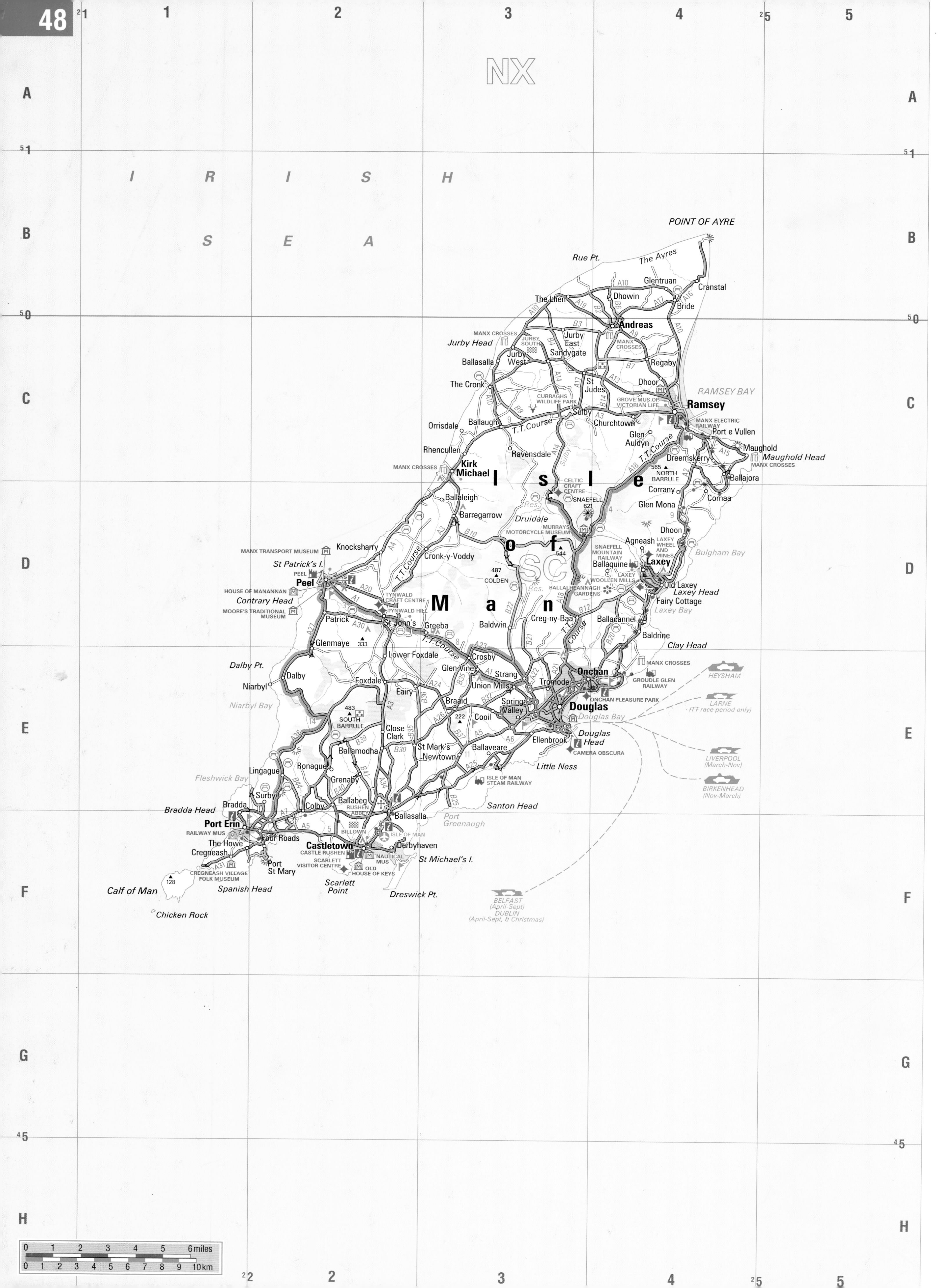
NX
IRISH SEA
Isle of Man
SC
POINT OF AYRE
Rue Pt.
The Ayres
Glentruan
Cranstal
Dhowin
Bride
The Lhen
Andreas
Jurby Head
Jurby East
Jurby West
Sandygate
Ballasalla
Regaby
The Cronk
St Judes
Dhoor
RAMSEY BAY
Ramsey
CURRAGHS WILDLIFE PARK
GROVE MUS OF VICTORIAN LIFE
Orrisdale
Ballaugh
Sulby
Churchtown
T.T. Course
Port e Vullen
Glen Auldyn
Maughold
Maughold Head
Rhencullen
Ravensdale
Dreemskerry
Kirk Michael
MANX CROSSES
MANX ELECTRIC RAILWAY
CELTIC CRAFT CENTRE
NORTH BARRULE
Ballajora
Corrany
Cornaa
Ballaleigh
SNAEFELL 621
Glen Mona
Barregarrow
Druidale
MURRAYS MOTORCYCLE MUSEUM
Dhoon
Agneash
LAXEY WHEEL AND MINES
Bulgham Bay
MANX TRANSPORT MUSEUM
Knocksharry
SNAEFELL MOUNTAIN RAILWAY
Cronk-y-Voddy
St Patrick's I.
Ballaquine
Laxey
PEEL
Peel
COLDEN
LAXEY WOOLLEN MILLS
Old Laxey
Laxey Head
HOUSE OF MANANNAN
TYNWALD CRAFT CENTRE
BALLALHEANNAGH GARDENS
Fairy Cottage
Contrary Head
TYNWALD HILL
Laxey Bay
MOORE'S TRADITIONAL MUSEUM
Patrick
St John's
Creg-ny-Baa
Ballacannel
Greeba
Baldwin
Glenmaye
Baldrine
Clay Head
Lower Foxdale
Crosby
Dalby Pt.
Glen Vine
Strang
Onchan
Dalby
Union Mills
Tromode
GROUDLE GLEN RAILWAY
HEYSHAM
Niarbyl
Foxdale
Eairy
Braaid
Spring Valley
ONCHAN PLEASURE PARK
LARNE
(TT race period only)
Niarbyl Bay
SOUTH BARRULE
Cooil
Douglas
Douglas Bay
Close Clark
Douglas Head
Ellenbrook
St Mark's
Ballaveare
CAMERA OBSCURA
LIVERPOOL
(March-Nov)
Ballamodha
Newtown
Little Ness
Ronague
Lingague
Grenaby
ISLE OF MAN STEAM RAILWAY
BIRKENHEAD
(Nov-March)
Fleshwick Bay
Surby
Bradda
Ballabeg
Bradda Head
Colby
RUSHEN ABBEY
Ballasalla
Santon Head
Port Erin
Port Greenaugh
RAILWAY MUS
Four Roads
BILLOWN
ISLE OF MAN
The Howe
Castletown
Derbyhaven
Cregneash
CASTLE RUSHEN
NAUTICAL MUS
St Michael's I.
SCARLETT VISITOR CENTRE
Port St Mary
OLD HOUSE OF KEYS
CREGNEASH VILLAGE FOLK MUSEUM
Scarlett Point
Calf of Man
Spanish Head
Dreswick Pt.
BELFAST (April-Sept)
DUBLIN (April-Sept, & Christmas)
Chicken Rock
0 1 2 3 4 5 6 miles
0 1 2 3 4 5 6 7 8 9 10 km

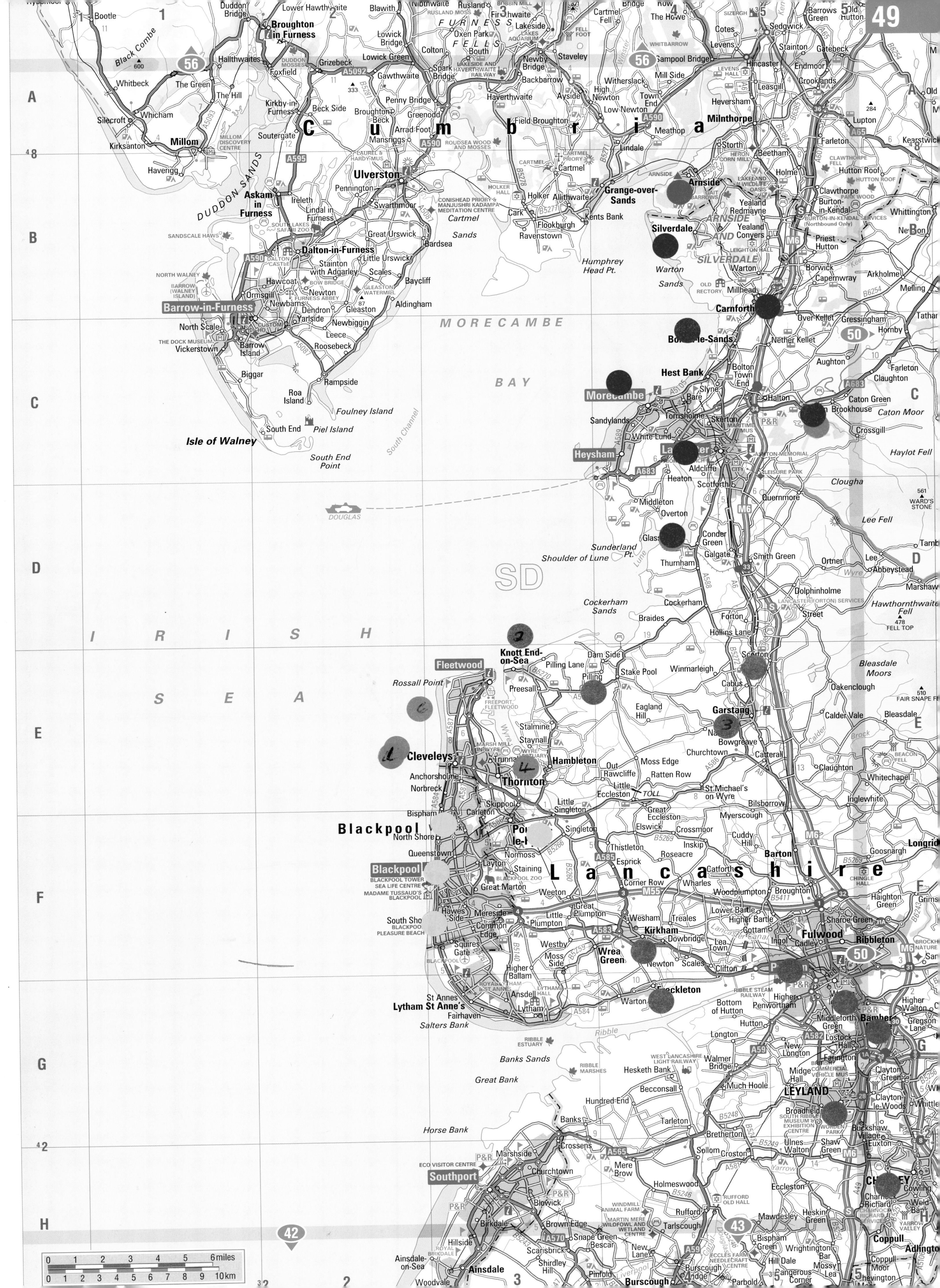
Cumbria
Lancashire
MORECAMBE
BAY
IRISH
SEA
SD
Broughton in Furness
Millom
Ulverston
Askam in Furness
Dalton-in-Furness
Barrow-in-Furness
Isle of Walney
DUDDON SANDS
Cartmel Sands
Grange-over-Sands
Arnside
Silverdale
Milnthorpe
Carnforth
Bolton-le-Sands
Hest Bank
Morecambe
Heysham
Lancaster
Glasson
Cockerham Sands
Knott End-on-Sea
Fleetwood
Cleveleys
Thornton
Hambleton
Garstang
Blackpool
Lytham St Anne's
Kirkham
Wrea Green
Freckleton
Preston
Fulwood
LEYLAND
Chorley
Southport
Ormskirk
Banks Sands
Horse Bank
Great Bank
0 1 2 3 4 5 6 miles
0 1 2 3 4 5 6 7 8 9 10 km

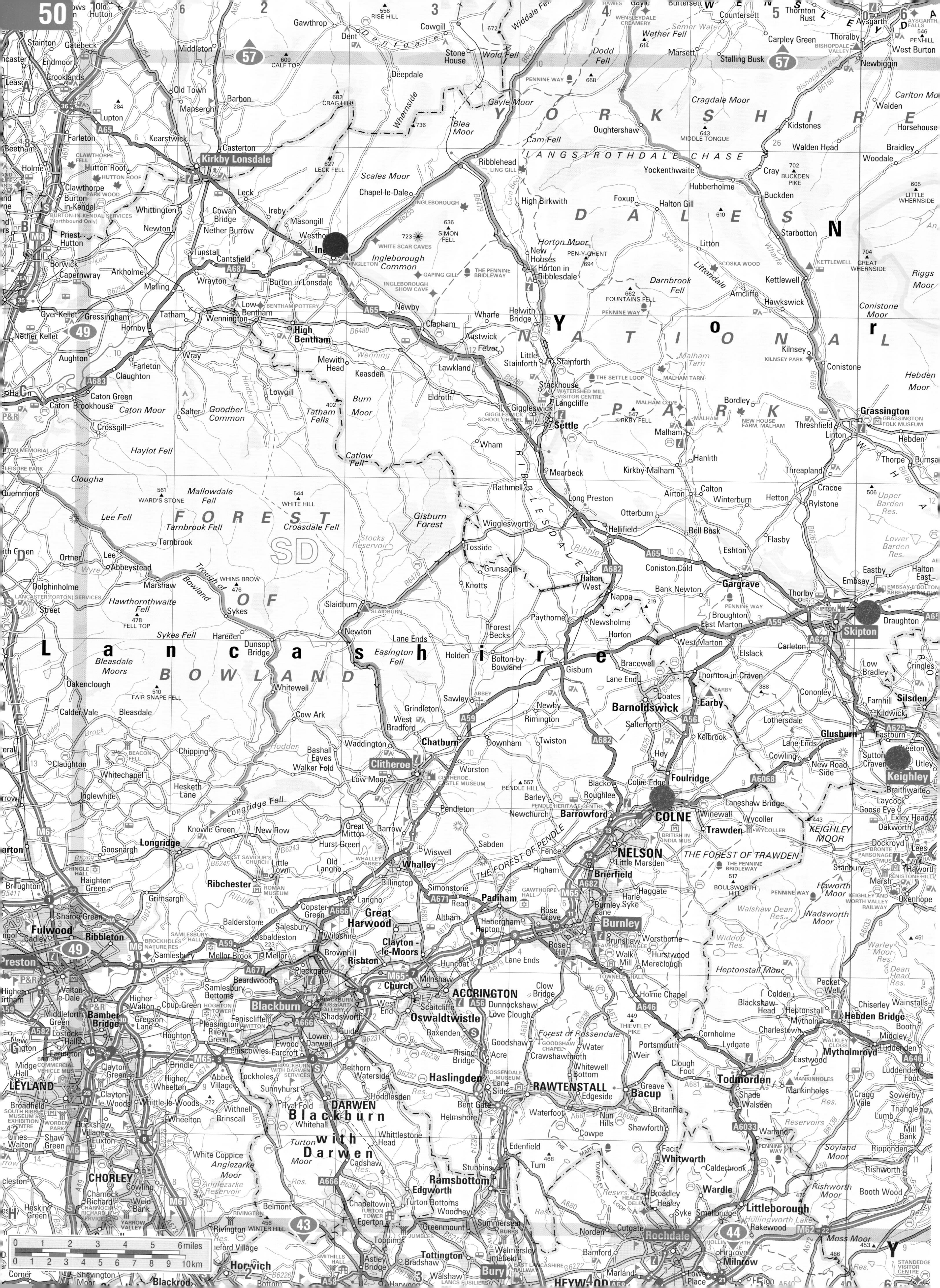

Y O R K S H I R E
D A L E S
N A T I O N A L
P A R K
FOREST OF BOWLAND
Lancashire
SD
LANGSTROTHDALE CHASE
Kirkby Lonsdale
Ingleton
Settle
Clitheroe
Skipton
Keighley
COLNE
NELSON
Burnley
ACCRINGTON
Blackburn
Preston
Rochdale
Bury
LEYLAND
CHORLEY
DARWEN
Blackburn with Darwen
RAWTENSTALL
Haslingden
Bacup
Todmorden
Hebden Bridge
Littleborough
Whitworth
Ramsbottom
Edgworth
Horwich
Tottington
Oswaldtwistle
Clayton-le-Moors
Great Harwood
Padiham
Whalley
Longridge
Ribchester
Fulwood
Barnoldswick
Earby
Gisburn
Slaidburn
Dunsop Bridge
Grassington
Kettlewell
Malham
Horton in Ribblesdale
Clapham
High Bentham
Low Bentham
Burton in Lonsdale
Dent
Hawes
Gargrave
Hellifield
Long Preston
Barrowford
Brierfield
Trawden
Haworth
Oxenhope
Silsden
Glusburn
Sutton-in-Craven
Cowling
Foulridge
Chatburn
Waddington
Chipping
Whitewell
Hornby
Caton
Wray
Halton West
Bolton-by-Bowland
Stainforth
Giggleswick
Langcliffe
Airton
Hetton
Rylstone
Cracoe
Embsay
Thorlby
Draughton
Carleton
Cononley
Lothersdale
Kildwick
Thornton-in-Craven
Salterforth
Kelbrook
Higham
Fence
Sabden
Read
Simonstone
Billington
Langho
Wilpshire
Mellor
Samlesbury
Walton-le-Dale
Bamber Bridge
Lostock Hall
Whittle-le-Woods
Withnell
Brinscall
Belmont
Egerton
Turton Bottoms
Helmshore
Edenfield
Stubbins
Summerseat
Waterfoot
Shawforth
Britannia
Walsden
Cornholme
Wardle
Smallbridge
Milnrow
Norden
Cutgate
Bamford
Heywood
Ribble
Hodder
Wenning
Lune
Wharfe
Ribblesdale
Littondale
Dentdale
Trough of Bowland
Catlow Fell
Tatham Fells
Burn Moor
Scales Moor
Blea Moor
Gayle Moor
Cam Fell
Wold Fell
Dodd Fell
Wether Fell
Cragdale Moor
Darnbrook Fell
Fountains Fell
Ingleborough
Ingleborough Common
Pen-y-ghent
Simon Fell
Whernside
Gisburn Forest
Stocks Reservoir
Pendle Hill
THE FOREST OF PENDLE
THE FOREST OF TRAWDEN
KEIGHLEY MOOR
Forest of Rossendale
Anglezarke Moor
Heptonstall Moor
Soyland Moor
Rishworth Moor
Haworth Moor
White Scar Caves
Ingleborough Show Cave
Gaping Gill
Pennine Way
The Pennine Bridleway
Burton-in-Kendal Services
Lancaster (Forton) Services
Samlesbury Hall
Clitheroe Castle Museum
Pendle Heritage Centre
Towneley Hall
Gawthorpe Hall
Malham Tarn
Malham Cove
Kirkby Malham
A65
A59
A56
A629
A646
A682
A683
A687
A666
A6068
A58
B6478
B6480
B6479
B6255
B6160
B6265
M6
M65
M61
M62
57
49
43
44
0 1 2 3 4 5 6 miles
0 1 2 3 4 5 6 7 8 9 10 km

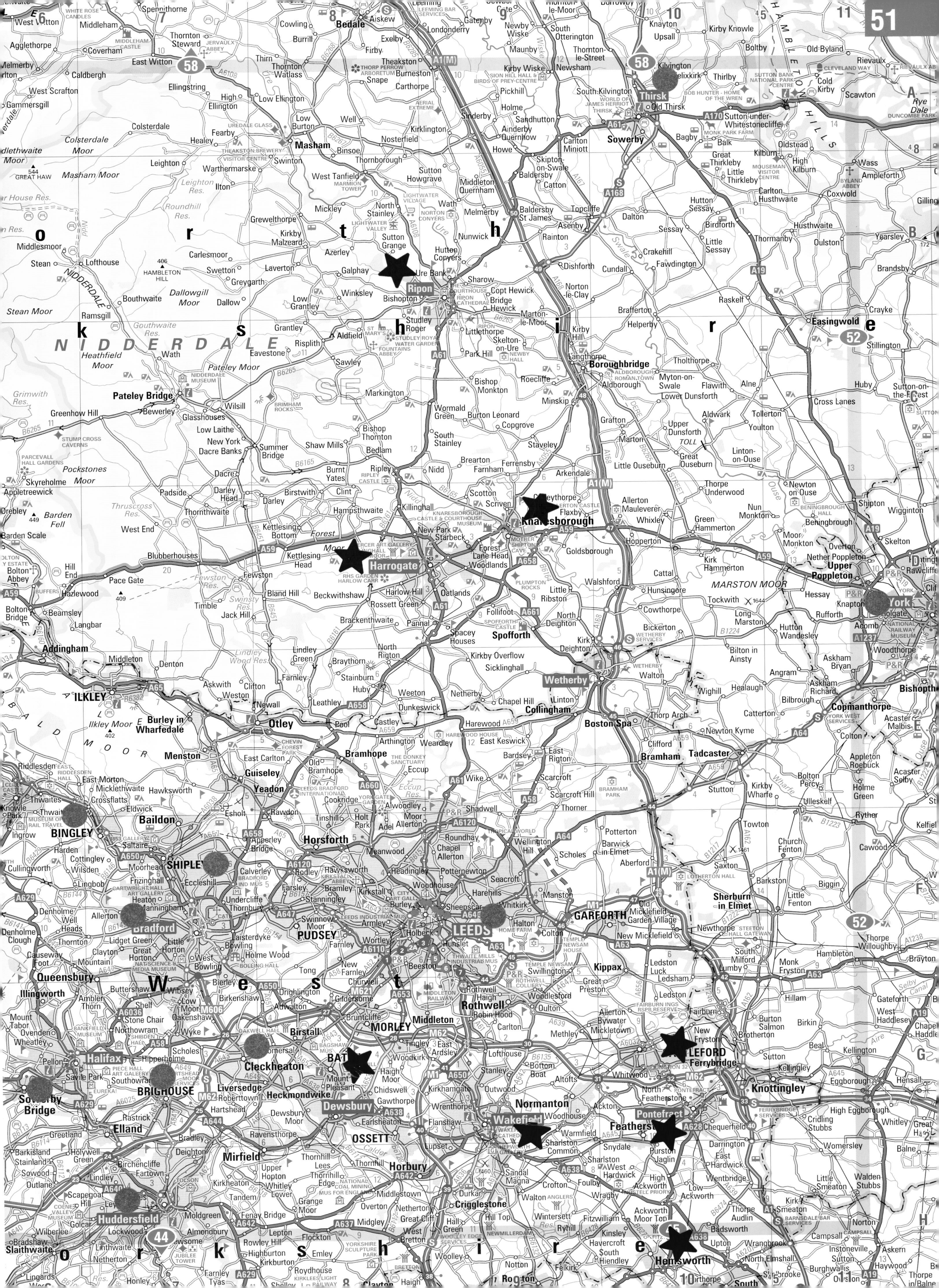

Bedale
Masham
Thirsk
Sowerby
Ripon
Pateley Bridge
NIDDERDALE
Harrogate
Knaresborough
Boroughbridge
Easingwold
York
Wetherby
Spofforth
Otley
ILKLEY
Burley in Wharfedale
Guiseley
Yeadon
Baildon
BINGLEY
SHIPLEY
Bradford
Horsforth
PUDSEY
LEEDS
GARFORTH
Tadcaster
Boston Spa
Collingham
MORLEY
Rothwell
Middleton
Halifax
BRIGHOUSE
Cleckheaton
Heckmondwike
Dewsbury
OSSETT
Mirfield
Elland
Sowerby Bridge
Huddersfield
Wakefield
Normanton
Pontefract
Ferrybridge
Knottingley
Hemsworth
Horbury
Crigglestone
Sherburn in Elmet
Selby
North Yorkshire
West Yorkshire
MARSTON MOOR
HAMBLETON HILLS

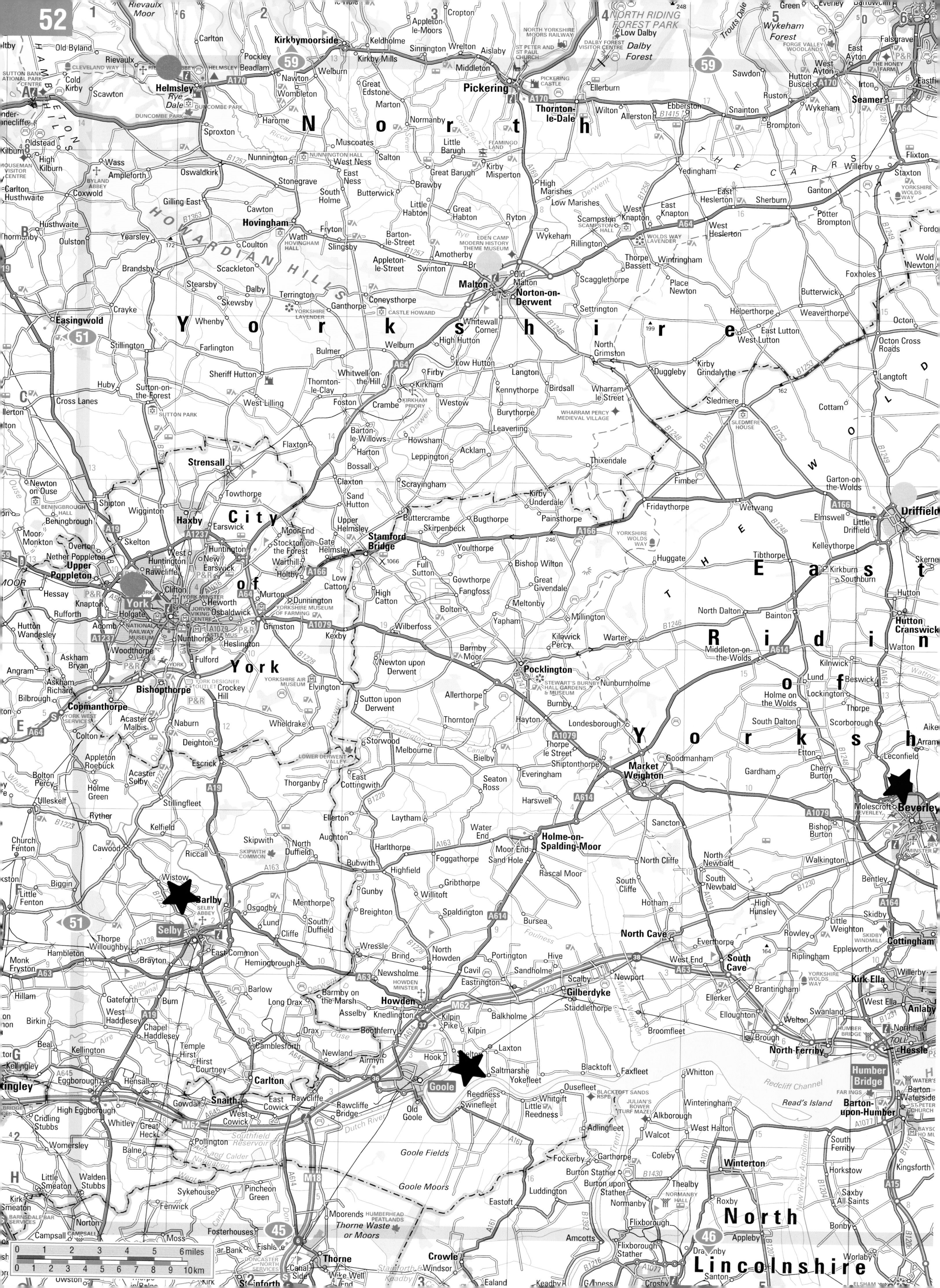

North Yorkshire
City of York
The East Riding of Yorkshire
North Lincolnshire
HOWARDIAN HILLS
HAMBLETON HILLS
THE CARRS
THE WOLDS
NORTH RIDING FOREST PARK
Dalby Forest
Wykeham Forest
Rievaulx Moor
Helmsley
Rievaulx
Old Byland
Cold Kirby
Scawton
Carlton
Pockley
Beadlam
Kirkbymoorside
Kirkby Mills
Keldholme
Nawton
Wombleton
Welburn
Appleton-le-Moors
Cropton
Sinnington
Wrelton
Aislaby
Middleton
Pickering
Thornton-le-Dale
Ellerburn
Wilton
Allerston
Ebberston
Snainton
Brompton
Sawdon
Hutton Buscel
West Ayton
East Ayton
Falsgrave
Irton
Seamer
Ruston
Wykeham
Flixton
Staxton
Willerby
Ganton
Sherburn
Yedingham
East Heslerton
West Heslerton
Potter Brompton
Harome
Sproxton
Great Edstone
Marton
Normanby
Muscoates
Salton
Little Barugh
Great Barugh
Kirby Misperton
West Ness
East Ness
Nunnington
Oswaldkirk
Ampleforth
Wass
Oldstead
High Kilburn
Kilburn
Coxwold
Husthwaite
Stonegrave
South Holme
Butterwick
Brawby
Little Habton
Great Habton
Ryton
High Marishes
Low Marishes
Scampston
West Knapton
East Knapton
Rillington
Wykeham
Gilling East
Cawton
Hovingham
Wath
Fryton
Slingsby
Barton-le-Street
Appleton-le-Street
Amotherby
Swinton
Malton
Old Malton
Norton-on-Derwent
Thorpe Bassett
Wintringham
Place Newton
Scagglethorpe
Settrington
Yearsley
Oulston
Coulton
Brandsby
Scackleton
Stearsby
Skewsby
Dalby
Terrington
Coneysthorpe
Ganthorpe
Castle Howard
Crayke
Easingwold
Whenby
Stillington
Farlington
Bulmer
Welburn
Whitewell Corner
High Hutton
Low Hutton
North Grimston
Duggleby
Kirby Grindalythe
Helperthorpe
Weaverthorpe
Butterwick
Foxholes
East Lutton
West Lutton
Octon
Octon Cross Roads
Langtoft
Cottam
Sledmere
Huby
Sutton-on-the-Forest
Sheriff Hutton
Thornton-le-Clay
Whitwell-on-the-Hill
Firby
Kirkham
Langton
Kennythorpe
Birdsall
Wharram le Street
Wharram Percy Medieval Village
Cross Lanes
West Lilling
Foston
Crambe
Westow
Burythorpe
Leavening
Barton-le-Willows
Howsham
Harton
Flaxton
Leppington
Acklam
Thixendale
Fimber
Garton-on-the-Wolds
Driffield
Little Driffield
Elmswell
Strensall
Newton on Ouse
Bossall
Claxton
Scrayingham
Kirby Underdale
Sand Hutton
Fridaythorpe
Wetwang
Kelleythorpe
Shipton
Beningbrough
Wigginton
Haxby
Towthorpe
Earswick
Upper Helmsley
Buttercrambe
Bugthorpe
Skirpenbeck
Painsthorpe
Moor Monkton
Skelton
Overton
Nether Poppleton
Upper Poppleton
Huntington
New Earswick
Stockton on the Forest
Gate Helmsley
Stamford Bridge
Youlthorpe
Huggate
Tibthorpe
Kirkburn
Southburn
Hessay
Rawcliffe
Clifton
Warthill
Holtby
Low Catton
High Catton
Full Sutton
Bishop Wilton
Great Givendale
Gowthorpe
Fangfoss
Knapton
York
Heworth
Osbaldwick
Murton
Dunnington
Meltonby
Millington
North Dalton
Bainton
Hutton
Rufforth
Acomb
Holgate
Heslington
Grimston
Bolton
Yapham
Kilnwick Percy
Warter
Hutton Cranswick
Hutton Wandesley
Woodthorpe
Nunthorpe
Fulford
Kexby
Wilberfoss
Barmby Moor
Pocklington
Nunburnholme
Middleton-on-the-Wolds
Watton
Askham Bryan
Askham Richard
Angram
Bishopthorpe
Crockey Hill
Elvington
Newton upon Derwent
Kilnwick
Lund
Beswick
Lockington
Holme on the Wolds
Bilbrough
Copmanthorpe
Acaster Malbis
Naburn
Wheldrake
Sutton upon Derwent
Allerthorpe
Thornton
Burnby
Hayton
Londesborough
South Dalton
Scorborough
Thorpe
Colton
Deighton
Escrick
Storwood
Melbourne
Bielby
Thorpe le Street
Shiptonthorpe
Goodmanham
Market Weighton
Etton
Gardham
Cherry Burton
Leconfield
Appleton Roebuck
Acaster Selby
Bolton Percy
Holme Green
Stillingfleet
Thorganby
East Cottingwith
Seaton Ross
Everingham
Harswell
Ulleskelf
Ryther
Kelfield
Ellerton
Laytham
Water End
Holme-on-Spalding-Moor
Sancton
Molescroft
Beverley
Bishop Burton
Church Fenton
Cawood
Riccall
Skipwith
North Duffield
Aughton
Harlthorpe
Foggathorpe
Moor End
Sand Hole
North Cliffe
North Newbald
South Newbald
Walkington
Wistow
Barlby
Biggin
Little Fenton
Osgodby
Menthorpe
Bubwith
Highfield
Gunby
Breighton
Willitoft
Gribthorpe
Spaldington
Rascal Moor
South Cliffe
Hotham
High Hunsley
Bentley
Skidby
Selby
Thorpe Willoughby
Lund
South Duffield
Cliffe
Bursea
North Cave
Everthorpe
Rowley
Little Weighton
Cottingham
Hambleton
Monk Fryston
East Common
Brayton
Hemingbrough
Wressle
Brind
North Howden
Portington
Hive
Sandholme
South Cave
Riplingham
Eppleworth
Hillam
Gateforth
Burn
Barlow
Long Drax
Barmby on the Marsh
Newsholme
Cavil
Eastrington
Scalby
Gilberdyke
Newport
West End
Ellerker
Brantingham
Kirk Ella
West Ella
Anlaby
Birkin
West Haddlesey
Chapel Haddlesey
Asselby
Howden
Knedlington
Kilpin Pike
Kilpin
Balkholme
Staddlethorpe
Elloughton
Swanland
Welton
Brough
North Ferriby
Hessle
Beal
Kellington
Temple Hirst
Hirst Courtney
Drax
Camblesforth
Newland
Airmyn
Boothferry
Hook
Laxton
Saltmarshe
Yokefleet
Blacktoft
Faxfleet
Broomfleet
Whitton
Humber Bridge
Redcliff Channel
Read's Island
Barton-upon-Humber
Barton Waterside
Kellingley
Eggborough
Hensall
Carlton
Snaith
Gowdall
Rawcliffe
Rawcliffe Bridge
East Cowick
West Cowick
Goole
Old Goole
Reedness
Swinefleet
Ousefleet
Whitgift
Little Reedness
Adlingfleet
Alkborough
Winteringham
West Halton
Walcot
Coleby
Winterton
South Ferriby
High Eggborough
Cridling Stubbs
Whitley
Great Heck
Pollington
Balne
Womersley
Goole Fields
Goole Moors
Fockerby
Garthorpe
Burton Stather
Burton upon Stather
Thealby
Normanby
Horkstow
Kingsforth
Saxby All Saints
Little Smeaton
Walden Stubbs
Sykehouse
Pincheon Green
Fenwick
Kirk Smeaton
Norton
Campsall
Moss
Eastoft
Luddington
Flixborough
Roxby
Bonby
Moorends
Thorne Waste or Moors
Fosterhouses
Fishlake
Thorne
Crowle
Amcotts
Flixborough Stather
Appleby
Worlaby
Stainforth
Wike Well
Canal Side
Eastoft
Ealand
Keadby
Crosby
Santon
Dragonby
Stainforth & Keadby Canal
Dutch River
Southfield Reservoir
Aire and Calder Navigation
Selby Canal
Pocklington Canal
Foulness
Derwent
Ouse
Rye
Wharfe
Trent
New River Ancholme
Market Weighton Canal
A170
A64
A19
A1079
A166
A614
A63
A163
A1237
A645
A1041
A161
A15
A1077
A164
A169
M62
M18
B1257
B1363
B1248
B1251
B1252
B1253
B1249
B1246
B1228
B1230
B1222
B1223
B1392
B1430
B1216
B1204
B1258
B1415
59
51
45
46
0 1 2 3 4 5 6 miles
0 1 2 3 4 5 6 7 8 9 10 km

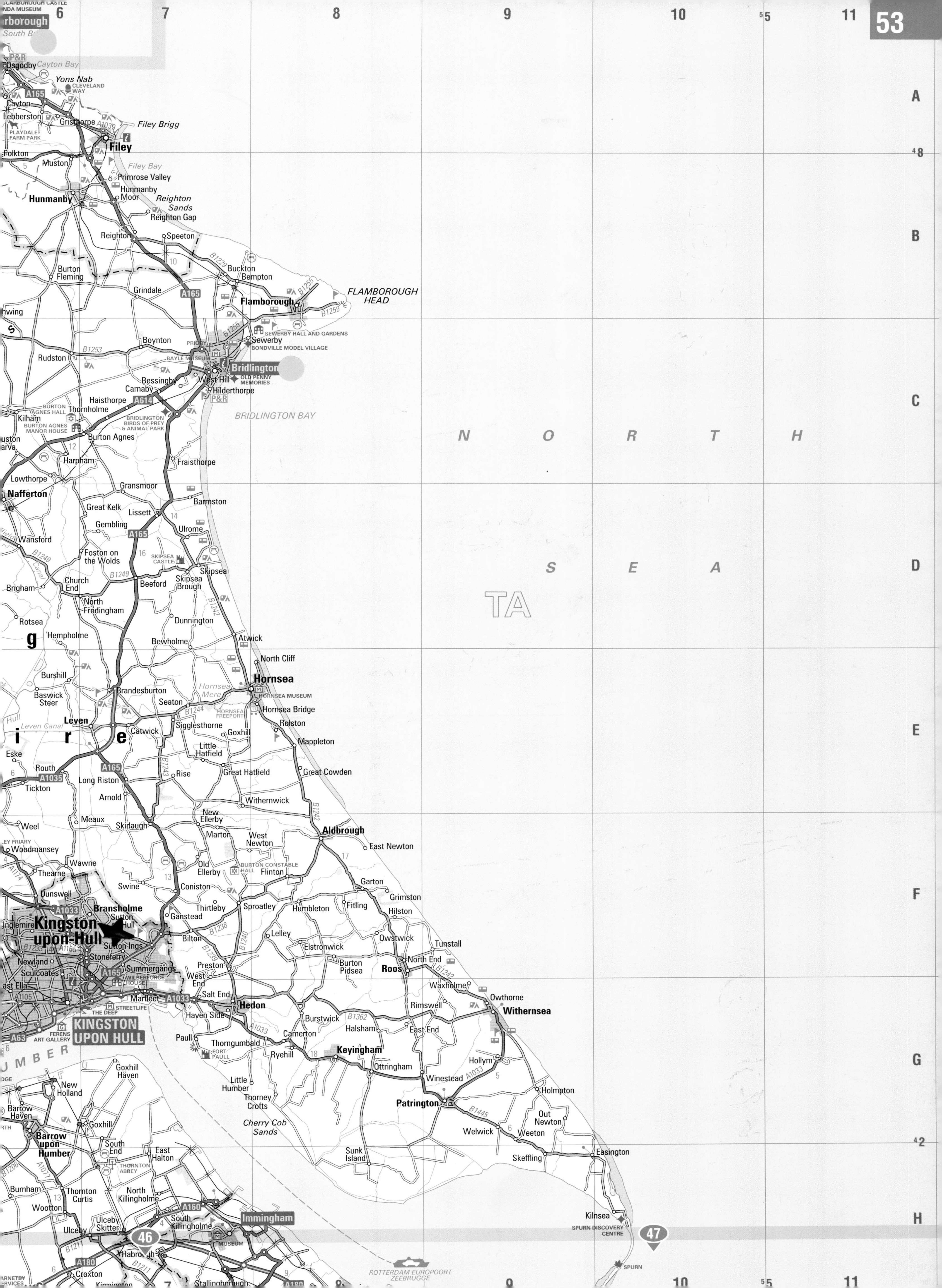
6
7
8
9
10
11
A
B
C
D
E
F
G
H
Osgodby
Cayton Bay
Yons Nab
CLEVELAND WAY
Cayton
Lebberston
Gristhorpe
Filey Brigg
PLAYDALE FARM PARK
Filey
Folkton
Muston
Filey Bay
Primrose Valley
Hunmanby
Hunmanby Moor
Reighton Sands
Reighton Gap
Reighton
Speeton
Buckton
Bempton
Burton Fleming
Grindale
Flamborough
FLAMBOROUGH HEAD
SEWERBY HALL AND GARDENS
Sewerby
BONDVILLE MODEL VILLAGE
Boynton
PRIORY
BAYLE MUSEUM
Rudston
Bridlington
Bessingby
West Hill
OLD PENNY MEMORIES
Carnaby
Hilderthorpe
Haisthorpe
BURTON AGNES HALL
Thornholme
BRIDLINGTON BAY
BRIDLINGTON BIRDS OF PREY & ANIMAL PARK
Kilham
BURTON AGNES MANOR HOUSE
Burton Agnes
N O R T H
Harpham
Fraisthorpe
Lowthorpe
Nafferton
Gransmoor
Barmston
Great Kelk
Lissett
Gembling
Ulrome
Wansford
Foston on the Wolds
SKIPSEA CASTLE
Skipsea
Church End
Beeford
Skipsea Brough
Brigham
S E A
North Frodingham
TA
Rotsea
Dunnington
Hempholme
Atwick
Bewholme
North Cliff
Burshill
Hornsea
Brandesburton
Hornsea Mere
HORNSEA MUSEUM
Baswick Steer
Seaton
Hornsea Bridge
HORNSEA FREEPORT
Leven
Leven Canal
Sigglesthorne
Rolston
Catwick
Goxhill
Mappleton
Little Hatfield
Eske
Routh
Long Riston
Rise
Great Hatfield
Great Cowden
Tickton
Arnold
Withernwick
New Ellerby
Weel
Meaux
Skirlaugh
Aldbrough
Marton
West Newton
East Newton
Woodmansey
Wawne
Old Ellerby
BURTON CONSTABLE HALL
Flinton
Thearne
Swine
Coniston
Garton
Dunswell
Grimston
Bransholme
Thirtleby
Sproatley
Humbleton
Fitling
Hilston
Sutton on Hull
Ganstead
Kingston upon Hull
Lelley
Owstwick
Tunstall
Bilton
Elstronwick
Sutton Ings
North End
Stoneferry
Burton Pidsea
Roos
Newland
Preston
Sculcoates
Summergangs
West End
Waxholme
WILBERFORCE HOUSE
Owthorne
Marfleet
Salt End
Withernsea
Hedon
Rimswell
STREETLIFE
THE DEEP
Haven Side
Burstwick
KINGSTON UPON HULL
Halsham
FERENS ART GALLERY
East End
Camerton
Paull
Thorngumbald
Keyingham
FORT PAULL
Ryehill
Hollym
Goxhill Haven
Ottringham
New Holland
Winestead
Little Humber
Holmpton
Thorney Crofts
Patrington
Barrow Haven
Goxhill
Out Newton
Cherry Cob Sands
Welwick
Weeton
Barrow upon Humber
South End
East Halton
Skeffling
Easington
Sunk Island
THORNTON ABBEY
Burnham
Thornton Curtis
North Killingholme
Wootton
Kilnsea
Immingham
SPURN DISCOVERY CENTRE
Ulceby
Ulceby Skitter
South Killingholme
46
47
MUSEUM
Habrough
Croxton
SPURN
ROTTERDAM EUROPOORT ZEEBRUGGE
Stallingborough
A165
A1039
A614
A1035
A1033
A1165
A63
A1105
A1077
A160
A180
B1229
B1255
B1259
B1253
B1249
B1242
B1244
B1243
B1238
B1239
B1240
B1362
B1445
B1206
B1211

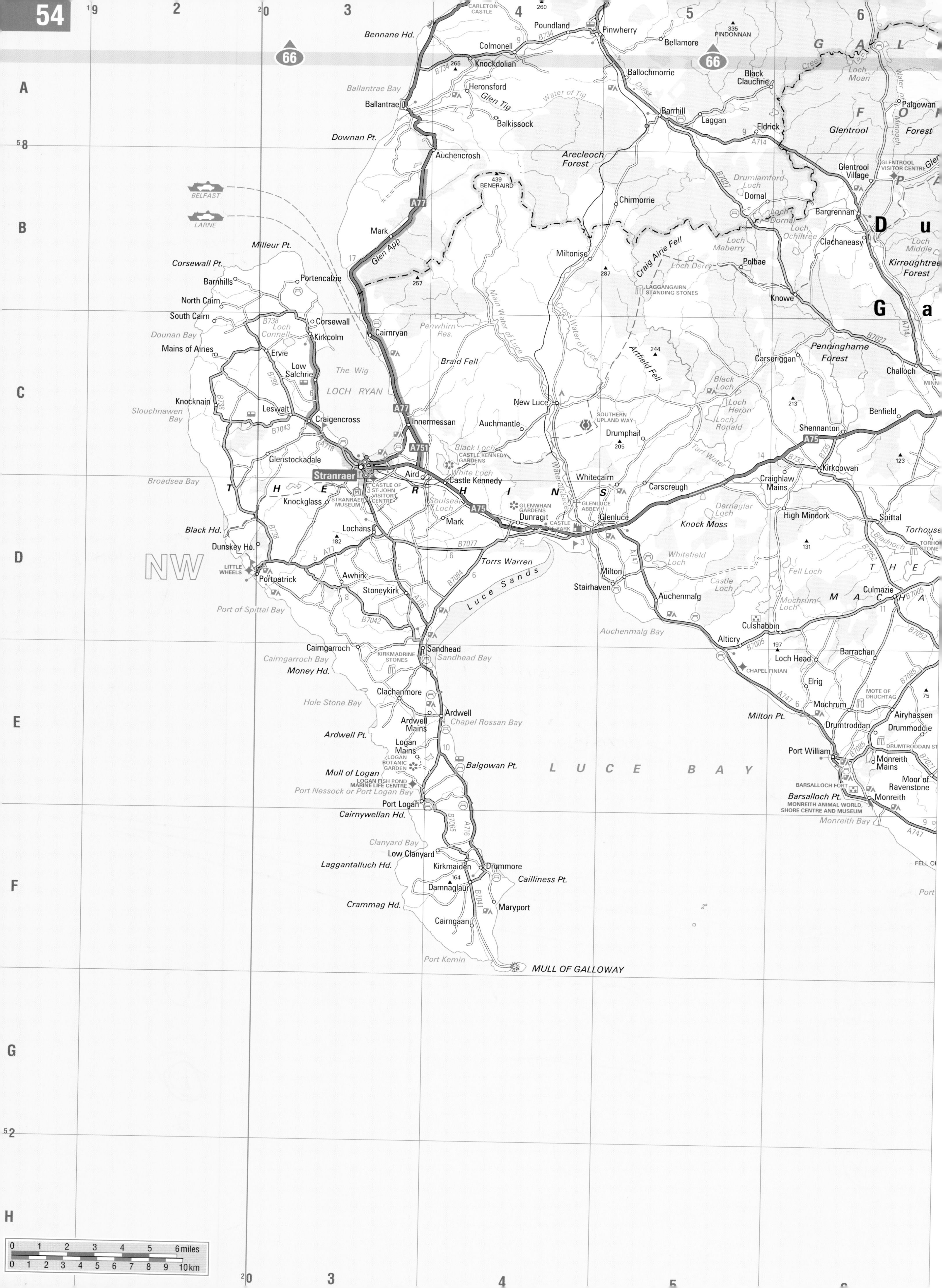

Bennane Hd.
Carleton Castle
Poundland
Pinwherry
Bellamore
335 Pindonnan
Colmonell
Knockdolian
Ballochmorrie
Black Clauchrie
Ballantrae Bay
Heronsford
Glen Tig
Water of Tig
Ballantrae
Barrhill
Laggan
Eldrick
Glentrool
Forest
Palgowan
Balkissock
Downan Pt.
Auchencrosh
Arecleoch Forest
Glentrool Village
Glentrool Visitor Centre
439 Benerairl
Drumlamford Loch
Dornal
Belfast
Larne
A77
Chirmorrie
Bargrennan
Loch Dornal
Loch Ochiltree
Mark
Loch Maberry
Clachaneasy
Loch Middle
Kirroughtree Forest
Milleur Pt.
Glen App
Miltonise
Craig Airie Fell
Loch Derry
Polbae
Corsewall Pt.
Barnhills
Portencalzie
Laggangairn Standing Stones
Knowe
North Cairn
South Cairn
Corsewall
Loch Connell
Kirkcolm
Cairnryan
Penwhirn Res.
Dounan Bay
Mains of Airies
Ervie
Main Water of Luce
Cross Water of Luce
Artfield Fell
Penninghame Forest
Carseriggan
Challoch
Low Salchrie
The Wig
Braid Fell
LOCH RYAN
Black Loch
Loch Heron
Loch Ronald
Knocknain
New Luce
Slouchnawen Bay
Leswalt
Craigencross
Innermessan
Auchmantle
Southern Upland Way
Drumphail
Benfield
Shennanton
A75
A751
Glenstockadale
Castle Kennedy Gardens
White Loch
Tarf Water
Craighlaw Mains
Kirkcowan
Stranraer
Aird
Castle Kennedy
Broadsea Bay
Castle of St John Visitor Centre
Stranraer Museum
Whitecairn
Carscreugh
THE RHINS
Knockglass
Soulseat Loch
Glenwhan Gardens
Glenluce Abbey
Glenluce
Dernaglar Loch
High Mindork
Spittal
Torhouse
Lochans
Mark
Dunragit
Castle of Park
Knock Moss
Black Hd.
Dunskey Ho.
B7077
Whitefield Loch
NW
Little Wheels
Torrs Warren
Fell Loch
Portpatrick
Awhirk
Milton
Stairhaven
Luce Sands
Stoneykirk
Castle Loch
Culmazie
THE MACHARS
Auchenmalg
Mochrum Loch
Port of Spittal Bay
Culshabbin
Auchenmalg Bay
Alticry
Cairngarroch
Sandhead
Cairngarroch Bay
Kirkmadrine Stones
Sandhead Bay
Loch Head
Barrachan
Money Hd.
Chapel Finian
Elrig
Hole Stone Bay
Clachanmore
Mote of Druchtag
Mochrum
Airyhassen
Ardwell
Ardwell Mains
Chapel Rossan Bay
Milton Pt.
Drumtroddan
Drummoddie
Ardwell Pt.
Logan Mains
Drumtroddan Stones
Logan Botanic Garden
Port William
Balgowan Pt.
LUCE BAY
Monreith Mains
Mull of Logan
Logan Fish Pond Marine Life Centre
Moor of Ravenstone
Port Nessock or Port Logan Bay
Barsalloch Fort
Port Logan
Barsalloch Pt.
Monreith
Monreith Animal World, Shore Centre and Museum
Cairnywellan Hd.
Monreith Bay
Clanyard Bay
Low Clanyard
Laggantalluch Hd.
Kirkmaiden
Drummore
Cailliness Pt.
Damnaglaur
Crammag Hd.
Maryport
Cairngaan
Port Kemin
MULL OF GALLOWAY
0 1 2 3 4 5 6 miles
0 1 2 3 4 5 6 7 8 9 10 km

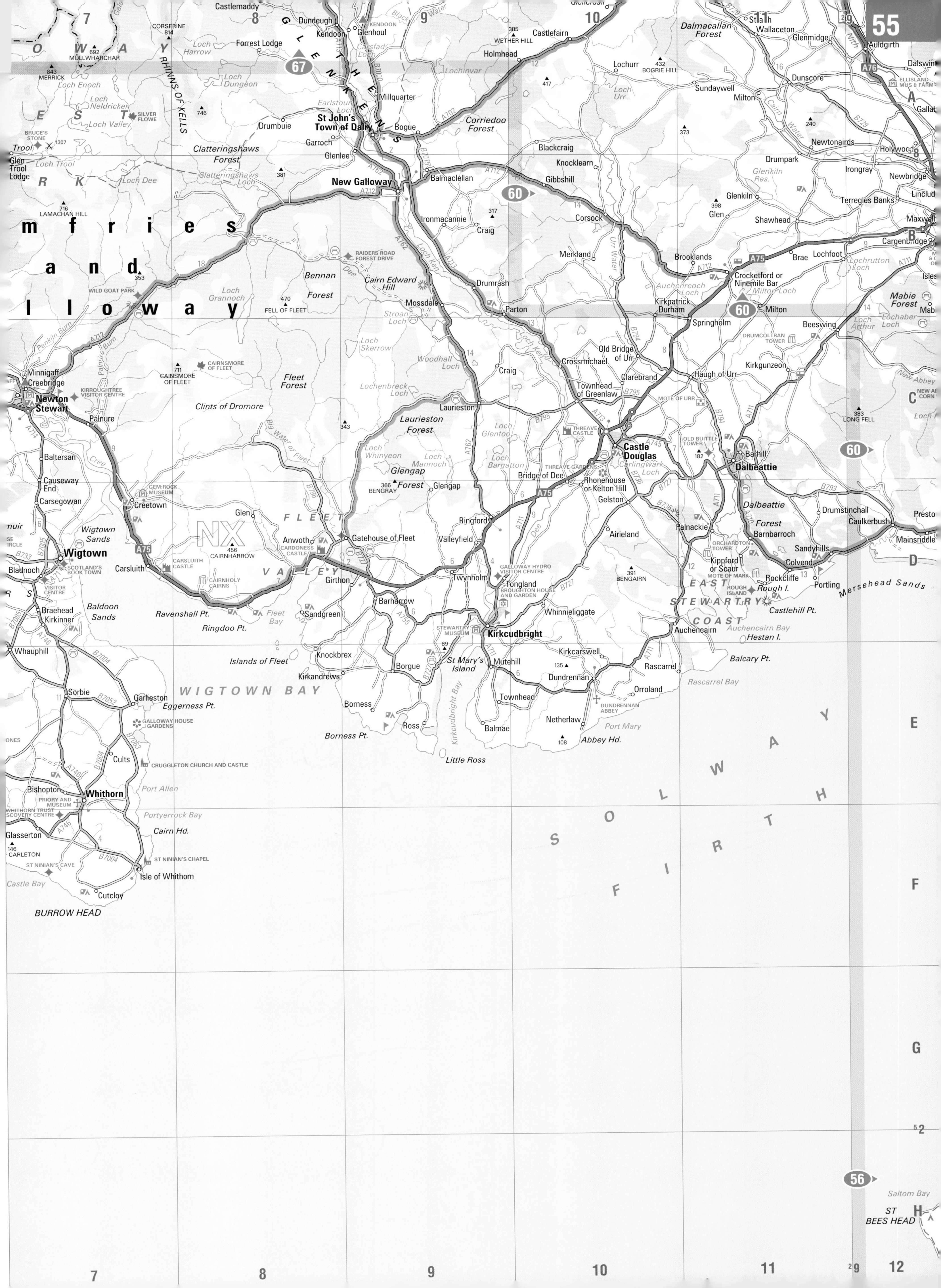

Castlemaddy
Dundeugh
Kendoon
Glenhoul
Castlefairn
Holmhead
Forrest Lodge
Loch Harrow
Loch Dungeon
Loch Enoch
Loch Neldricken
Loch Valley
Loch Trool
Glen Trool Lodge
Loch Dee
Lamachan Hill
Mullwharchar
Merrick
Corserine
Rhinns of Kells
Glenkens
Lochinvar
Millquarter
St John's Town of Dalry
Bogue
Corriedoo Forest
Drumbuie
Garroch
Glenlee
Clatteringshaws Forest
Clatteringshaws Loch
New Galloway
Balmaclellan
Blackcraig
Knocklearn
Gibbshill
Ironmacannie
Craig
Corsock
Dumfries and Galloway
Raiders Road Forest Drive
Bennan
Forest
Cairn Edward Hill
Mossdale
Loch Grannoch
Fell of Fleet
Wild Goat Park
Drumrash
Parton
Stroan Loch
Loch Skerrow
Woodhall Loch
Crossmichael
Old Bridge of Urr
Clarebrand
Townhead of Greenlaw
Laurieston
Laurieston Forest
Cairnsmore of Fleet
Fleet Forest
Clints of Dromore
Minnigaff
Creebridge
Newton Stewart
Kirroughtree Visitor Centre
Palnure
Baltersan
Causeway End
Carsegowan
Creetown
Gem Rock Museum
Wigtown Sands
Wigtown
Bladnoch
Scotland's Book Town
Carsluith
Carsluith Castle
Cairnharrow
Glen
Fleet Valley
Anwoth
Gatehouse of Fleet
Cardoness Castle
Loch Whinyeon
Loch Mannoch
Glengap Forest
Bengray
Glengap
Ringford
Valleyfield
Threave Castle
Castle Douglas
Carlingwark Loch
Bridge of Dee
Threave Gardens
Rhonehouse or Kelton Hill
Gelston
Loch Glentoo
Loch Bargatton
Airieland
Girthon
Twynholm
Tongland
Galloway Hydro Visitor Centre
Broughton House and Garden
Barharrow
Sandgreen
Kirkcudbright
Stewartry Museum
Whinnieligate
Ravenshall Pt.
Ringdoo Pt.
Fleet Bay
Baldoon Sands
Braehead
Kirkinner
Whauphill
Islands of Fleet
Knockbrex
Kirkandrews
Borgue
St Mary's Isle
Mutehill
Kirkcarswell
Rascarrel
Dundrennan
Dundrennan Abbey
Orroland
Townhead
Balmae
Ross
Borness
Borness Pt.
Little Ross
Kirkcudbright Bay
Netherlaw
Port Mary
Abbey Hd.
Wigtown Bay
Sorbie
Garlieston
Eggerness Pt.
Galloway House Gardens
Cults
Cruggleton Church and Castle
Bishopton
Whithorn
Priory and Museum
Whithorn Trust Discovery Centre
Port Allen
Portyerrock Bay
Cairn Hd.
Glasserton
Carleton
St Ninian's Cave
St Ninian's Chapel
Isle of Whithorn
Castle Bay
Cutcloy
Burrow Head
Solway Firth
Dalmacallan Forest
Stroth
Wallaceton
Glenmidge
Auldgirth
Dalswinton
Ellisland Mus & Farm
Lochurr
Bogrie Hill
Loch Urr
Dunscore
Sundaywell
Milton
Cairn Water
Newtonairds
Holywood
Drumpark
Irongray
Newbridge
Glenkiln Res.
Glenkiln
Terregles Banks
Lincluden
Glen
Shawhead
Maxwelltown
Cargenbridge
Brooklands
Brae
Lochfoot
Lochrutton Loch
Auchenreoch Loch
Crocketford or Ninemile Bar
Milton Loch
Milton
Kirkpatrick Durham
Springholm
Mabie Forest
Lochaber Loch
Loch Arthur
Beeswing
Drumcoltran Tower
Kirkgunzeon
Haugh of Urr
Mote of Urr
New Abbey
Long Fell
Old Buittle Tower
Barhill
Dalbeattie
Dalbeattie Forest
Barnbarroch
Drumstinchall
Caulkerbush
Mainsriddle
Sandyhills
Colvend
Palnackie
Orchardton Tower
Kippford or Scaur
Mote of Mark
Rockcliffe
Rough Island
Rough I.
Portling
Mersehead Sands
Castlehill Pt.
East Stewartry Coast
Auchencairn
Auchencairn Bay
Hestan I.
Balcary Pt.
Rascarrel Bay
Merkland
Urr Water
Loch Ken
Saltom Bay
St Bees Head
NX

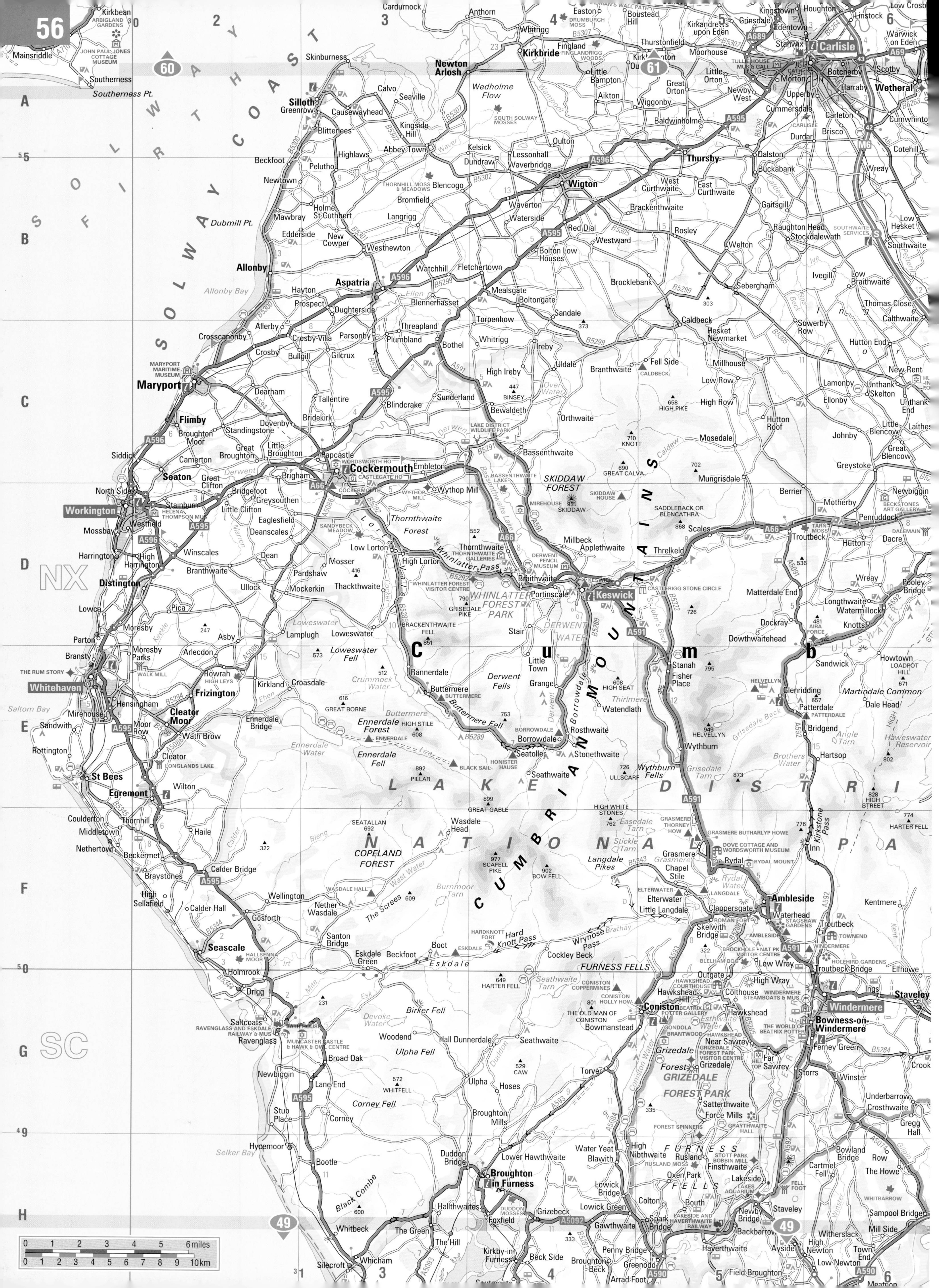

60
61
49
SOLWAY FIRTH
SOLWAY COAST
Southerness Pt.
Dubmill Pt.
Allonby Bay
Saltom Bay
Selker Bay
NX
SC
Cumbria
CUMBRIAN MOUNTAINS
LAKE DISTRICT NATIONAL PARK
Kirkbean
ARBIGLAND GARDENS
JOHN PAUL JONES COTTAGE MUSEUM
Mainsriddle
Southerness
Cardurnock
Anthorn
Easton
Boustead Hill
Kirkandrews upon Eden
Grinsdale
Kingstown
Houghton
Low Crosby
Linstock
Edentown
Stanwix
Carlisle
Warwick on Eden
Whitrigg
Drumburgh Moss
Finglands
Kirkbride
Thurstonfield
Moorhouse
Skinburness
Newton Arlosh
Wedholme Flow
Little Bampton
Great Orton
Little Orton
Morton
Botcherby
Scotby
Harraby
Wetheral
Upperby
Silloth
Greenrow
Calvo
Seaville
Causewayhead
Kingside Hill
South Solway Mosses
Aikton
Wiggonby
Newby West
Cummersdale
Carleton
Cumwhinton
Baldwinholme
Blitterlees
Durdar
Brisco
Highlaws
Abbey Town
Kelsick
Dundraw
Lessonhall
Waverbridge
Oulton
Thursby
Dalston
Cotehill
Beckfoot
Pelutho
Newtown
Thornhill Moss & Meadows
Blencogo
Wigton
West Curthwaite
East Curthwaite
Buckabank
Wreay
Holme St Cuthbert
Bromfield
Waverton
Waterside
Brackenthwaite
Gaitsgill
Mawbray
Langrigg
Red Dial
Rosley
Raughton Head
Stockdalewath
Low Hesket
Edderside
New Cowper
Westnewton
Westward
Bolton Low Houses
Welton
Southwaite
Allonby
Watchhill
Fletchertown
Ivegill
Low Braithwaite
Aspatria
Brocklebank
Sebergham
Hayton
Prospect
Oughterside
Blennerhasset
Mealsgate
Boltongate
Thomas Close
Calthwaite
Crosscanonby
Allerby
Crosby Villa
Parsonby
Threapland
Plumbland
Torpenhow
Sandale
Caldbeck
Hesket Newmarket
Sowerby Row
Crosby
Bullgill
Gilcrux
Bothel
Whitrigg
Ireby
Hutton End
Maryport Maritime Museum
Maryport
High Ireby
Uldale
Fell Side
Branthwaite
Millhouse
New Rent
Dearham
Tallentire
Sunderland
Binsey
Over Water
Low Row
Lamonby
Unthank
Skelton
Flimby
Blindcrake
Bewaldeth
High Pike
High Row
Ellonby
Broughton Moor
Dovenby
Bridekirk
Orthwaite
Hutton Roof
Standingstone
Lake District Wildlife Park
Little Blencow
Laithes
Siddick
Great Broughton
Little Broughton
Papcastle
Knott
Mosedale
Johnby
Great Blencow
Camerton
Wordsworth Ho
Bassenthwaite
Seaton
Great Clifton
Brigham
Cockermouth
Castlegate Ho
Embleton
Great Calva
Mungrisdale
Greystoke
North Side
Bridgefoot
Wythop Mill
Bassenthwaite Lake
Skiddaw Forest
Berrier
Newbiggin
Workington
Stainburn
Greysouthen
Helena Thompson Mus
Little Clifton
Mirehouse
Skiddaw House
Skiddaw
Saddleback or Blencathra
Motherby
Beckstones Art Gallery
Westfield
Eaglesfield
Sandybeck Meadow
Thornthwaite Forest
Penruddock
Mossbay
Deanscales
Scales
Tarn Moss
Troutbeck
Dacre
Dalemain
Harrington
High Harrington
Winscales
Dean
Low Lorton
Thornthwaite
Thornthwaite Galleries
Millbeck
Applethwaite
Threlkeld
Hutton
Mosser
High Lorton
Whinlatter Pass
Derwent Pencil Museum
Distington
Branthwaite
Pardshaw
Whinlatter Forest Visitor Centre
Braithwaite
Keswick
Castlerigg Stone Circle
Wreay
Pooley Bridge
Lowca
Ullock
Mockerkin
Thackthwaite
Whinlatter Forest Park
Grisedale Pike
Portinscale
Matterdale End
Pica
Longthwaite
Watermillock
Moresby
Asby
Loweswater
Brackenthwaite Fell
Lamplugh
Stair
Derwent Water
Dockray
Aira Force
Knotts
Parton
Arlecdon
Dowthwaitehead
Ullswater
Bransty
Moresby Parks
Loweswater Fell
Little Town
Stanah
Fisher Place
Sandwick
Howtown
Loadpot Hill
The Rum Story
Whitehaven
Walk Mill
Rowrah
High Leys
Kirkland
Croasdale
Crummock Water
Rannerdale
Derwent Fells
Grange
High Seat
Helvellyn
Glenridding
Martindale Common
Frizington
Buttermere
Thirlmere
Watendlath
Patterdale
Dale Head
Hensingham
Cleator Moor
Great Borne
Buttermere Fell
Rosthwaite
Grisedale Beck
Mirehouse
Ennerdale Bridge
Ennerdale Forest
High Stile
Borrowdale
Bridgend
Sandwith
Moor Row
Wath Brow
Ennerdale
Seatoller
Stonethwaite
Wythburn
Angle Tarn
Haweswater Reservoir
Honister Hause
Black Sail
Rottington
Cleator
Ennerdale Water
Ennerdale Fell
Seathwaite
Ullscarf
Wythburn Fells
Hartsop
Brothers Water
Longlands Lake
Pillar
Grisedale Tarn
St Bees
Egremont
Wilton
Great Gable
High Street
Harter Fell
Kirkstone Pass
High White Stones
Easedale Tarn
Grasmere Thorney How
Grasmere Butharlyp Howe
Couldertons
Thornhill
Seatallan
Wasdale Head
Middletown
Haile
Stickle Tarn
Inn
Nethertown
Copeland Forest
Dove Cottage and Wordsworth Museum
Grasmere
Beckermet
Scafell Pike
Bow Fell
Langdale Pikes
Chapel Stile
Rydal
Rydal Mount
Rydal Water
Braystones
Calder Bridge
Wasdale Hall
Wast Water
Burnmoor Tarn
Elterwater
Langdale
Ambleside
Kentmere
High Sellafield
Wellington
Calder Hall
Nether Wasdale
The Screes
Little Langdale
Clappersgate
Roman Fort
Waterhead
Stagshaw Gardens
Troutbeck
Gosforth
Skelwith Bridge
Townend
Santon Bridge
Hardknott Fort
Hard Knott Pass
Wrynose Pass
Brockhole Nat Pk Visitor Centre
Windermere
Seascale
Hallsenna Moor
Eskdale Green
Beckfoot
Boot
Eskdale
Cockley Beck
Blelham Bog
Low Wray
Holehird Gardens
Troutbeck Bridge
Elfhowe
Holmrook
Furness Fells
Outgate
High Wray
Ings
Staveley
Harter Fell
Seathwaite Tarn
Coniston Coppermines
Hawkshead Courthouse
Hawkshead Hill
Colthouse
Windermere Steamboats & Mus.
Drigg
Coniston Holly How
Coniston
Beatrix Potter Gallery
Hawkshead
Bowness-on-Windermere
Saltcoats
Ravenglass and Eskdale Railway & Mus
Ravenglass
Muncaster Castle & Hawk & Owl Centre
Birker Fell
Devoke Water
Woodend
Hall Dunnerdale
The Old Man of Coniston
Bowmanstead
Esthwaite Water
Gondola
Brantwood
The World of Beatrix Potter
Ferney Green
Seathwaite
Ulpha Fell
Grizedale
Grizedale Forest Park Visitor Centre
Near Sawrey
Far Sawrey
Hill Top
Broad Oak
Caw
Grizedale Forest
Storrs
Crook
Newbiggin
Lane End
Whitfell
Ulpha
Hoses
Torver
Winster
Underbarrow
Crosthwaite
Corney Fell
Satterthwaite
Force Mills
Stub Place
Corney
Broughton Mills
Forest Spinners
Graythwaite Hall
Gregg Hall
Hycemoor
Water Yeat
Blawith
High Nibthwaite
Furness Fells
Rusland
Stott Park Bobbin Mill
Finsthwaite
Rusland Moss
Bootle
Duddon Bridge
Lower Hawthwaite
Broughton in Furness
Oxen Park
Lakeside
Lakeside Aquarium
Fell Foot
Bowland Bridge
Row
Cartmel Fell
The Howe
Black Combe
Lowick Bridge
Colton
Whitbarrow
Hallthwaites
Foxfield
Duddon Mosses
Grizebeck
Lowick Green
Bouth
Newby Bridge
Staveley
Sampool Bridge
Whitbeck
The Green
Gawthwaite
Spark Bridge
Lakeside and Haverthwaite Railway
Backbarrow
Witherslack
Mill Side
The Hill
Haverthwaite
Ayside
High Newton
Town End
Kirkby-in-Furness
Beck Side
Penny Bridge
Broughton Beck
Greenodd
Low Newton
Silecroft
Whicham
Arrad Foot
Field Broughton
Meathop
0 1 2 3 4 5 6 miles
0 1 2 3 4 5 6 7 8 9 10 km

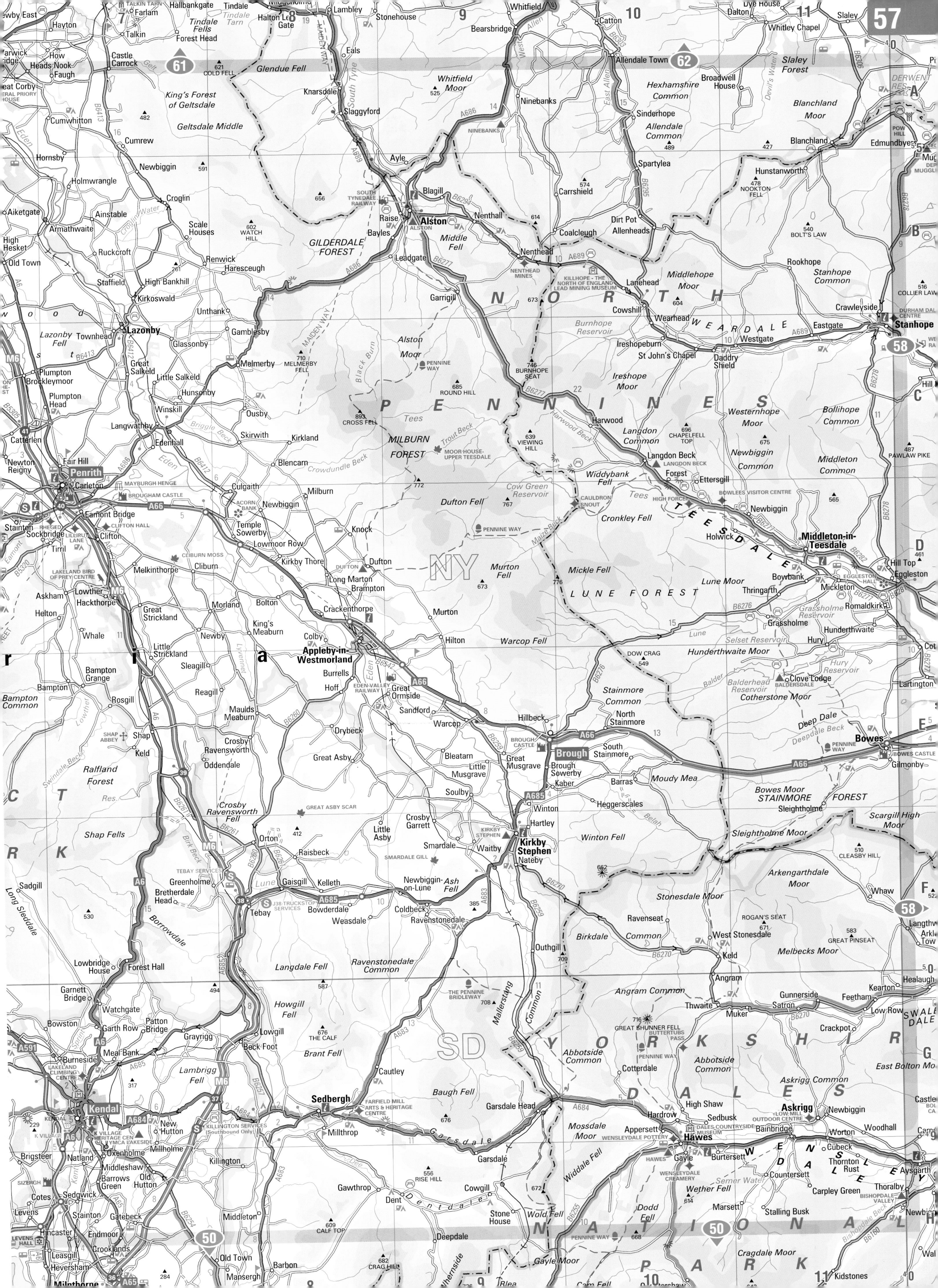

Hayton
Farlam
Hallbankgate
Tindale
Tindale Fells
Tindale Tarn
Halton Lea Gate
Lambley
Stonehouse
Whitfield
Catton
Dalton
Dye House
Slaley
Whitley Chapel
Talkin
Forest Head
Bearsbridge
Allendale Town
Slaley Forest
How
Heads Nook
Faugh
Castle Carrock
Gelt
621 COLD FELL
Glendue Fell
Eals
MAIDEN WAY
Whitfield Moor
Hexhamshire Common
Broadwell House
Devil's Water
Blanchland Moor
King's Forest of Geltsdale
Knarsdale
South Tyne
East Allen
West Allen
Ninebanks
Sinderhope
Allendale Common
Cumwhitton
Slaggyford
A686
NINEBANKS
Cumrew
Geltsdale Middle
Blanchland
Edmundbyers
Hornsby
Ayle
Spartylea
Newbiggin
Hunstanworth
Holmwrangle
Croglin
SOUTH TYNEDALE RAILWAY
Blagill
Carrshield
478 NOOKTON FELL
Aiketgate
Ainstable
Croglin Water
Raise
Alston
Nenthall
Dirt Pot
Allenheads
Armathwaite
Scale Houses
602 WATCH HILL
Bayles
Middle Fell
Coalcleugh
540 BOLT'S LAW
High Hesket
Ruckcroft
GILDERDALE FOREST
Nenthead
Old Town
Renwick
Haresceugh
Leadgate
NENTHEAD MINES
KILLHOPE - THE NORTH OF ENGLAND LEAD MINING MUSEUM
Rookhope
Stanhope Common
Staffield
High Bankhill
Lanehead
Middlehope Moor
Kirkoswald
Garrigill
N O R T H
Cowshill
Crawleyside
Unthank
Wearhead
W E A R D A L E
Eastgate
Stanhope
Lazonby
Lazonby Fell
Townhead
Gamblesby
Glassonby
Burnhope Reservoir
Ireshopeburn
Westgate
Alston Moor
Black Burn
St John's Chapel
Daddry Shield
Great Salkeld
Melmerby
710 MELMERBY FELL
PENNINE WAY
Plumpton
Brockleymoor
Little Salkeld
685 ROUND HILL
746 BURNHOPE SEAT
Ireshope Moor
Plumpton Head
Hunsonby
P E N N I N E S
Westernhope Moor
Bollihope Common
Winskill
Ousby
893 CROSS FELL
Tees
Harwood
Harwood Beck
Langwathby
Langdon Common
696 CHAPELFELL TOP
Catterlen
Edenhall
Skirwith
Kirkland
MILBURN FOREST
Trout Beck
639 VIEWING HILL
Newbiggin Common
Middleton Common
487 PAWLAW PIKE
Fair Hill
Newton Reigny
Penrith
Blencarn
Crowdundle Beck
MOOR HOUSE-UPPER TEESDALE
Langdon Beck
Widdybank Fell
Forest
Ettersgill
Carleton
MAYBURGH HENGE
Culgaith
Milburn
Cow Green Reservoir
BOWLEES VISITOR CENTRE
BROUGHAM CASTLE
Dufton Fell
CAULDRON SNOUT
HIGH FORCE
Newbiggin
Eamont Bridge
ACORN BANK
Cronkley Fell
Stainton
Sockbridge
CLIFTON HALL
Clifton
Temple Sowerby
Knock
PENNINE WAY
T E E S D A L E
Holwick
Middleton-in-Teesdale
Tirril
Lowmoor Row
Maize Beck
CLIBURN MOSS
Kirkby Thore
Melkinthorpe
Cliburn
DUFTON
Dufton
NY
Murton Fell
Mickle Fell
Hill Top
Eggleston
LAKELAND BIRD OF PREY CENTRE
Long Marton
Lune Moor
Bowbank
Askham
Lowther
Hackthorpe
Brampton
L U N E   F O R E S T
Thringarth
Mickleton
Romaldkirk
Helton
Great Strickland
Morland
Bolton
Crackenthorpe
Murton
Grassholme Reservoir
Grassholme
Whale
King's Meaburn
Newby
Colby
Hilton
Lune
Selset Reservoir
Hunderthwaite
Little Strickland
Appleby-in-Westmorland
Warcop Fell
DOW CRAG 549
Hunderthwaite Moor
Hury
Bampton Grange
Sleagill
Burrells
Hury Reservoir
Balder
Balderhead Reservoir
Clove Lodge
BALDERSDALE
Lartington
Bampton
Hoff
EDEN VALLEY RAILWAY
Great Ormside
Stainmore Common
Cotherstone Moor
Bampton Common
Reagill
Rosgill
Mauld's Meaburn
Sandford
North Stainmore
Hillbeck
Deep Dale
Deepdale Beck
SHAP ABBEY
Shap
Drybeck
Warcop
BROUGH CASTLE
Brough
South Stainmore
Bowes
BOWES CASTLE
Keld
Crosby Ravensworth
Great Asby
Bleatarn
Great Musgrave
Little Musgrave
Brough Sowerby
Kaber
Barras
Moudy Mea
Gilmonby
Ralfland Forest
Oddendale
Soulby
Bowes Moor
STAINMORE
FOREST
Winton
Heggerscales
Sleightholme
GREAT ASBY SCAR
Scargill High Moor
Crosby Ravensworth Fell
Crosby Garrett
Hartley
Belah
Shap Fells
Little Asby
KIRKBY STEPHEN
Kirkby Stephen
Winton Fell
Sleightholme Moor
Orton
Smardale
Waitby
510 CLEASBY HILL
Raisbeck
SMARDALE GILL
Nateby
Arkengarthdale Moor
TEBAY SERVICES
Greenholme
Gaisgill
Kelleth
Newbiggin-on-Lune
Ash Fell
Whaw
Sadgill
Bretherdale Head
Tebay
J38 TRUCKSTOP SERVICES
Bowderdale
Coldbeck
Stonesdale Moor
Long Sleddale
Borrowdale
Weasdale
Ravenstonedale
Ravenseat
ROGAN'S SEAT
671
Birkdale
Common
West Stonesdale
GREAT PINSEAT
Outhgill
Melbecks Moor
Keld
Lowbridge House
Forest Hall
Langdale Fell
Ravenstonedale Common
Angram
Healaugh
Garnett Bridge
THE PENNINE BRIDLEWAY
Mallerstang
Common
Angram Common
Kearton
Feetham
Gunnerside
Satron
Watchgate
Howgill Fell
Thwaite
Muker
Low Row
SWALEDALE
Bowston
Patton Bridge
Garth Row
676 THE CALF
GREAT SHUNNER FELL
BUTTERTUBS PASS
Crackpot
Lowgill
Grayrigg
SD
Y O R K S H I R E
Meal Bank
Beck Foot
Brant Fell
Abbotside Common
PENNINE WAY
Burneside
LAKELAND CLIMBING CENTRE
Lambrigg Fell
Cautley
Cotterdale
East Bolton Moor
Askrigg Common
Kendal
Sedbergh
FARFIELD MILL ARTS & HERITAGE CENTRE
Baugh Fell
Garsdale Head
D A L E S
High Shaw
Hardrow
Askrigg
Newbiggin
New Hutton
KILLINGTON SERVICES (Southbound Only)
Millthrop
Mossdale Moor
Sedbusk
DALES COUNTRYSIDE MUSEUM
Bainbridge
Woodhall
K VILLAGE HERITAGE CEN
Garsdale
Appersett
WENSLEYDALE POTTERY
Hawes
Worton
Brigsteer
Natland
Oxenholme
Millholme
Widdale Fell
Gayle
Burtersett
Cubeck
Thornton Rust
Killington
W E N S L E Y D A L E
Middleshaw
Old Hutton
Dee
WENSLEYDALE CREAMERY
Countersett
Aysgarth
SIZERGH
Barrows Green
556 RISE HILL
Semer Water
Thoralby
Gawthrop
Cowgill
Wether Fell
Carpley Green
Cotes
Sedgwick
Dent
D e n t d a l e
BISHOPDALE VALLEY
Levens
Stainton
Gatebeck
Stone House
Wold Fell
Dodd Fell
Marsett
Stalling Busk
Bishopdale Beck
Middleton
Hincaster
Endmoor
609 CALF TOP
Deepdale
PENNINE WAY
N A T I O N A L
LEVENS HALL
Crooklands
Leasgill
Old Town
Heversham
CRAG HILL
Barbon
Gayle Moor
Cragdale Moor
P A R K
Milnthorpe
Mansergh
Kidstones
Tindale Tarn

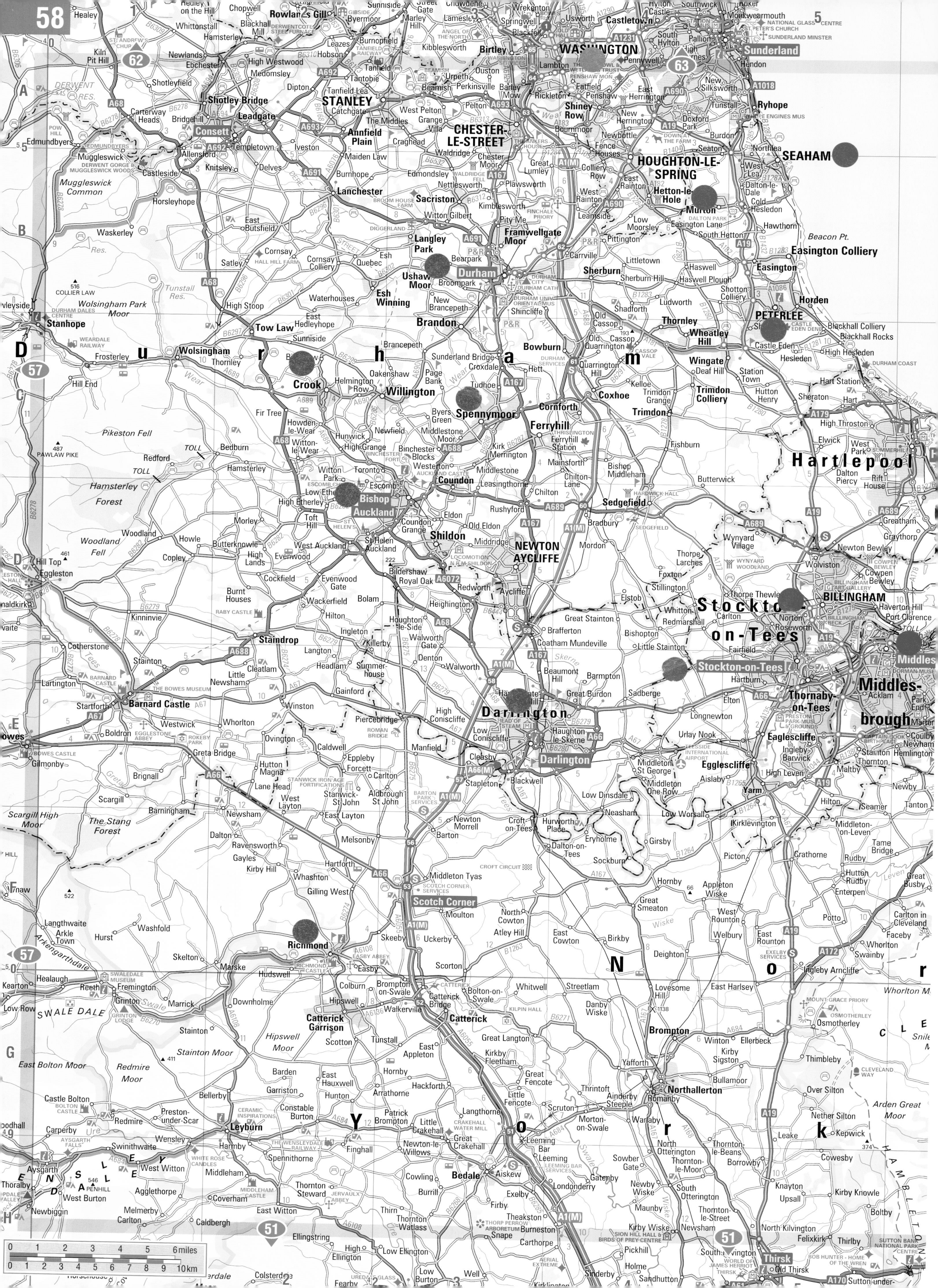
Durham
North Yorkshire
Washington
Sunderland
Seaham
Houghton-le-Spring
Hetton-le-Hole
Chester-le-Street
Stanley
Consett
Shotley Bridge
Lanchester
Sacriston
Durham
Peterlee
Easington Colliery
Horden
Stanhope
Wolsingham
Tow Law
Crook
Willington
Spennymoor
Ferryhill
Bishop Auckland
Shildon
Newton Aycliffe
Sedgefield
Hartlepool
Billingham
Stockton-on-Tees
Middlesbrough
Thornaby-on-Tees
Eaglescliffe
Yarm
Darlington
Barnard Castle
Staindrop
Scotch Corner
Richmond
Catterick Garrison
Catterick
Northallerton
Bedale
Leyburn
Thirsk
Hamsterley Forest
Swale Dale
Wensleydale
Scale

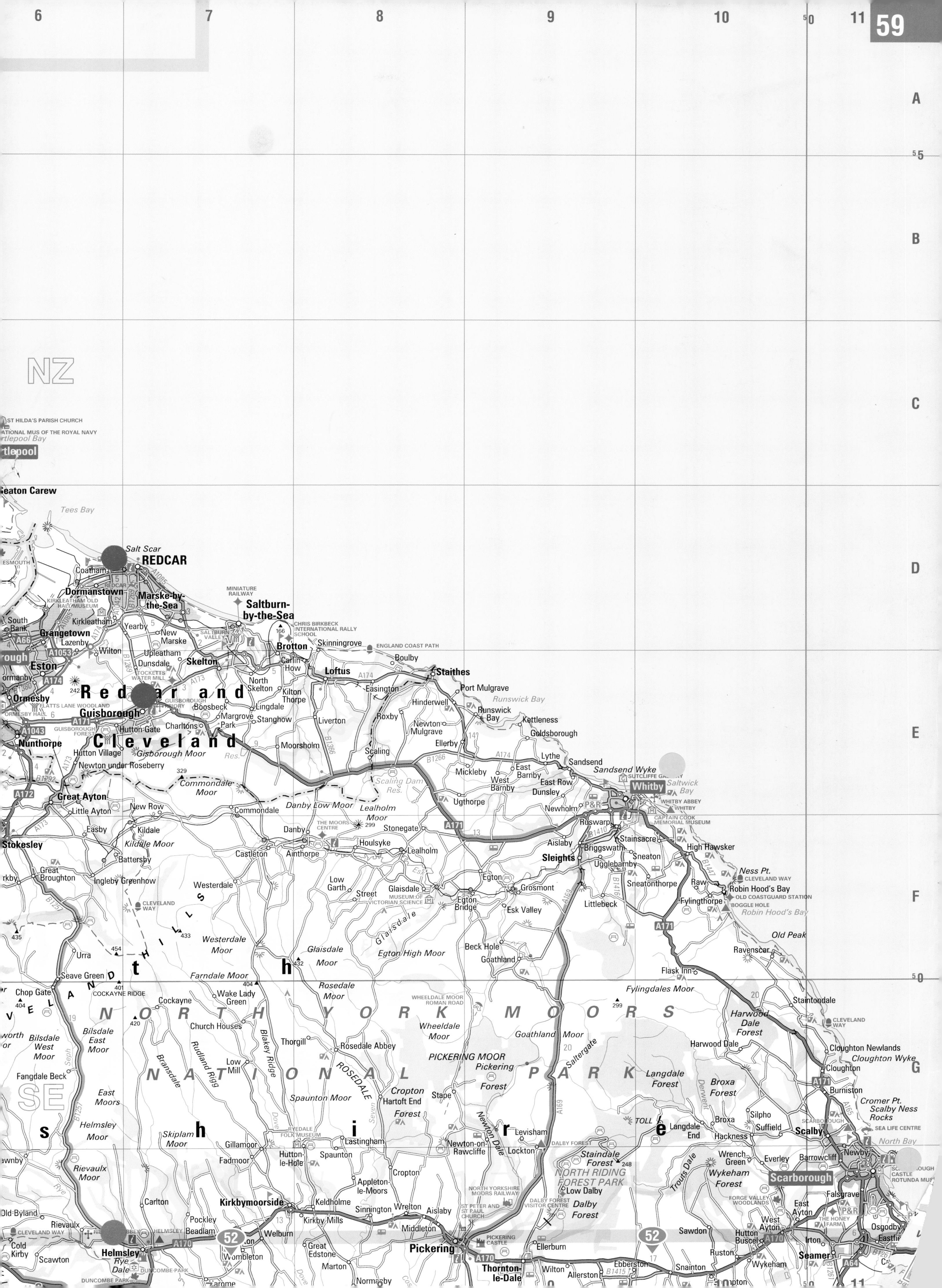

6   7   8   9   10   11

A

B

C

D

E

F

G

NZ

SE

ST HILDA'S PARISH CHURCH
NATIONAL MUS OF THE ROYAL NAVY
rtlepool Bay
tlepool

eaton Carew

Tees Bay

Salt Scar
REDCAR
Coatham
Dormanstown
Kirkleatham Old
Hall Museum
Marske-by-the-Sea
Kirkleatham
Yearby
New Marske
Upleatham
Wilton
Lazenby
Dunsdale
Skelton
North Skelton
Kilton Thorpe
Brotton
Carlin How
Skinningrove
MINIATURE RAILWAY
Saltburn-by-the-Sea
CHRIS BIRKBECK INTERNATIONAL RALLY SCHOOL
TOCKETTS WATER MILL
Loftus
Easington
Boulby
ENGLAND COAST PATH
Staithes
Port Mulgrave
Runswick Bay
Hinderwell
Runswick Bay
Kettleness
Newton Mulgrave
Goldsborough
Ellerby
Mickleby
Lythe
Sandsend
Sandsend Wyke
SUTCLIFFE GALLERY
East Barnby
West Barnby
East Row
Dunsley
Whitby
Saltwick Bay
WHITBY ABBEY
WHITBY
P&R
Newholm
CAPTAIN COOK MEMORIAL MUSEUM
Ruswarp
Aislaby
Briggswath
Stainsacre
Sneaton
High Hawsker
Sleights
Ugglebarnby
Raw
Ness Pt.
CLEVELAND WAY
Robin Hood's Bay
OLD COASTGUARD STATION
Sneatonthorpe
Fylingthorpe
BOGGLE HOLE
Robin Hood's Bay
Old Peak
Ravenscar
Flask Inn

South Bank
Grangetown
Eston
Ormesby
ORMESBY HALL
Nunthorpe
Guisborough
GUISBOROUGH FOREST
Hutton Village
Hutton-Gate
GUISBOROUGH PRIORY
Charltons
Boosbeck
Lingdale
Margrove Park
Stanghow
Liverton
Roxby
Moorsholm
Scaling
Scaling Dam Res.
R e d c a r   a n d
C l e v e l a n d
Newton under Roseberry
Gisborough Moor
Commondale Moor
Great Ayton
Little Ayton
New Row
Easby
Kildale
Battersby
Commondale
Danby Low Moor
Lealholm Moor
Stonegate
THE MOORS CENTRE
Castleton
Ainthorpe
Danby
Houlsyke
Lealholm
Egton
Egton Bridge
Stokesley
Great Broughton
Ingleby Greenhow
Kildale Moor
Westerdale
Low Garth
Street
Glaisdale
MUSEUM OF VICTORIAN SCIENCE
Grosmont
Esk Valley
Littlebeck
CLEVELAND WAY
Urra
Westerdale Moor
Glaisdale Moor
Egton High Moor
Beck Hole
Goathland
Seave Green
Farndale Moor
Rosedale Moor
Fylingdales Moor
Staintondale
Chop Gate
COCKAYNE RIDGE
Cockayne
Wake Lady Green
Church Houses
WHEELDALE MOOR ROMAN ROAD
Wheeldale Moor
Goathland Moor
Harwood Dale Forest
CLEVELAND WAY
Bilsdale West Moor
Bilsdale East Moor
Thorgill
Low Mill
Rosedale Abbey
PICKERING MOOR
Saltergate
Harwood Dale
Cloughton Newlands
Cloughton Wyke
Fangdale Beck
East Moors
Blakey Ridge
Rudland Rigg
Bransdale
ROSEDALE
N O R T H   Y O R K   M O O R S
N A T I O N A L   P A R K
Langdale Forest
Broxa Forest
Cloughton
Burniston
Cromer Pt.
Scalby Ness Rocks
SEA LIFE CENTRE
Helmsley Moor
Skiplam Moor
Spaunton Moor
Cropton
Hartoft End Forest
Stape
Pickering Forest
Newton Dale
Levisham
Langdale End
Broxa
Silpho
Suffield
Hackness
Scalby
Ryevaulx Moor
Gillamoor
RYEDALE FOLK MUSEUM
Lastingham
Spaunton
Hutton-le-Hole
Newton-on-Rawcliffe
Lockton
TOLL
Wrench Green
Everley
Barrowcliff
North Bay
THE HONEY FARM
Fadmoor
Cropton
NORTH YORKSHIRE MOORS RAILWAY
DALBY FOREST
Staindale Forest
NORTH RIDING FOREST PARK
Wykeham Forest
Troutsdale
FORGE VALLEY WOODLANDS
West Ayton
East Ayton
P&R
SC CASTLE ROTUNDA MUS
Cold Kirby
Rievaulx
Old Byland
Helmsley
Rye Dale
DUNCOMBE PARK
Scawton
Pockley
Beadlam
Kirkbymoorside
Keldholme
Kirkby Mills
Sinnington
Wrelton
Aislaby
Middleton
Low Dalby
DALBY FOREST VISITOR CENTRE
ST PETER AND ST PAUL CHURCH
PICKERING CASTLE
Pickering
Ellerburn
Sawdon
Hutton Buscel
Ruston
Wykeham
Seamer
Osgodby
Eastfie
Welburn
Great Edstone
Marton
Middleton
Ebberston
Snainton
Scarborough
Thornton-le-Dale
Wilton
Allerston
Wombleton
Normanby
arome

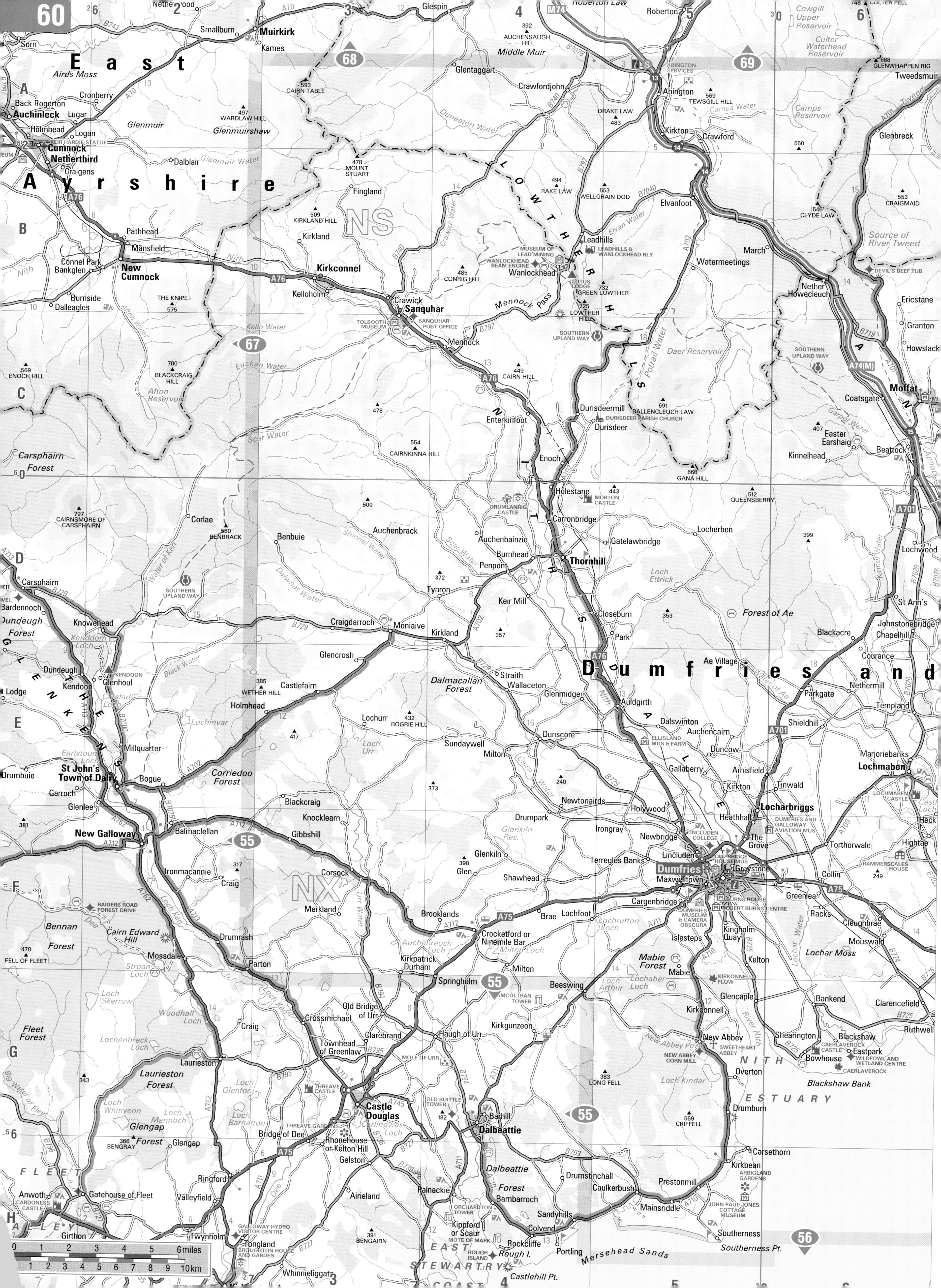
East Ayrshire
Dumfries and
Muirkirk
Kames
Smallburn
Glespin
Roberton
Cowgill Upper Reservoir
Culter Waterhead Reservoir
Glenwhappen Rig
Tweedsmuir
Airds Moss
Cronberry
Back Rogerton
Auchinleck
Lugar
Holmhead
Logan
Cumnock
Netherthird
Craigens
Glenmuir
Glenmuirshaw
Wardlaw Hill
Cairn Table
Auchensaugh Hill
Middle Muir
Glentaggart
Crawfordjohn
Abington
Abington Services
Tewsgill Hill
Camps Water
Camps Reservoir
Drake Law
Duneaton Water
Kirkton
Crawford
Glenbreck
Dalblair
Glenmuir Water
Mount Stuart
Fingland
Lowther Hills
Rake Law
Wellgrain Dod
Elvanfoot
Craigmaid
Clyde Law
Source of River Tweed
Kirkland Hill
Kirkland
Pathhead
Mansfield
Connel Park
Bankglen
New Cumnock
Kirkconnel
Kelloholm
Burnside
Dalleagles
The Knipe
Conrig Hill
Leadhills
Museum of Lead Mining
Leadhills & Wanlockhead Rly
Wanlockhead Beam Engine
Wanlockhead
Lotus Lodge
Green Lowther
Lowther Hill
Mennock Pass
Elvan Water
Watermeetings
March
Devil's Beef Tub
Nether Howecleuch
Ericstane
Granton
Howslack
Crawick
Sanquhar
Tolbooth Museum
Sanquhar Post Office
Mennock
Kello Water
Southern Upland Way
Daer Reservoir
Potrail Water
Enoch Hill
Blackcraig Hill
Afton Water
Afton Reservoir
Euchan Water
Cairn Hill
Moffat
Coatsgate
Ballencleuch Law
Durisdeermill
Durisdeer
Durisdeer Parish Church
Enterkinfoot
Easter Earshaig
Garpel Water
Beattock
Kinnelhead
Scar Water
Cairnkinna Hill
Enoch
Gana Hill
Carsphairn Forest
Cairnsmore of Carsphairn
Corlae
Benbrack
Holestane
Morton Castle
Queensberry
Drumlanrig Castle
Carronbridge
Locherben
Auchenbrack
Benbuie
Shinnel Water
Auchenbainzie
Burnhead
Gatelawbridge
Thornhill
Lochwood
Loch Ettrick
Carsphairn
Bardennoch
Dundeugh Forest
Water of Ken
Dalwhat Water
Penpont
Tynron
Keir Mill
Closeburn
Forest of Ae
St Ann's
Johnstonebridge
Chapelhill
Knowehead
Kendoon Loch
Craigdarroch
Moniaive
Kirkland
Park
Blackacre
Courance
Glenkens
Dundeugh
Kendoon
Glenhoul
Glencrosh
Black Water
Straith
Wallaceton
Dalmacallan Forest
Ae Village
Nethermill
Parkgate
Templand
Lodge
Wether Hill
Castlefairn
Holmhead
Glenmidge
Auldgirth
Nithsdale
Lochinvar
Lochurr
Bogrie Hill
Dalswinton
Auchencairn
Shieldhill
Earlstoun Loch
Millquarter
Loch Urr
Sundaywell
Dunscore
Ellisland Mus & Farm
Duncow
Marjoriebanks
Lochmaben
Drumbuie
St John's Town of Dalry
Garroch
Bogue
Corriedoo Forest
Milton
Cairn Water
Gallaberry
Amisfield
Tinwald
Lochmaben Castle
Glenlee
Blackcraig
Kirkton
Locharbriggs
Newtonairds
Holywood
Heathhall
Knocklearn
Drumpark
Glenkiln Res.
Irongray
Newbridge
Lincluden College
Dumfries and Galloway Aviation Mus
The Grove
Torthorwald
Heck
Hightae
New Galloway
Balmaclellan
Gibbshill
Glenkiln
Terregles Banks
Lincluden
Old Bridge House Mus
Dumfries
Maxwelltown
Greystone
Collin
Rammerscales House
Ironmacannie
Craig
Glen
Shawhead
Corsock
Raiders Road Forest Drive
Bennan Forest
Cairn Edward Hill
Merkland
Urr Water
Brooklands
Brae
Lochfoot
Lochrutton Loch
Cargenbridge
Burns House
Robert Burns Centre
Dumfries Museum & Camera Obscura
Greenlea
Racks
Cleughbrae
Mouswald
Lochar Moss
Lochar Water
Fell of Fleet
Mossdale
Drumrash
Stroan Loch
Loch Ken
Parton
Auchenreoch Loch
Crocketford or Ninemile Bar
Milton Loch
Milton
Kirkpatrick Durham
Isle steps
Kingholm Quay
Kelton
Mabie Forest
Mabie
Kirkconnell Flow
Lochaber Loch
Loch Arthur
Beeswing
Springholm
Colltran Tower
Loch Skerrow
Woodhall Loch
Fleet Forest
Craig
Crossmichael
Old Bridge of Urr
Glencaple
Kirkconnell
Bankend
Clarencefield
Ruthwell
Lochenbreck Loch
Townhead of Greenlaw
Clarebrand
Haugh of Urr
Kirkgunzeon
Mote of Urr
New Abbey
Sweetheart Abbey
New Abbey Corn Mill
New Abbey Pow
River Nith
Shearington
Blackshaw
Caerlaverock Castle
Eastpark
Bowhouse
Caerlaverock Wildfowl and Wetland Centre
Laurieston
Laurieston Forest
Loch Glentoo
Threave Castle
Old Buittle Tower
Long Fell
Loch Kindar
Overton
Nith Estuary
Blackshaw Bank
Loch Whinyeon
Loch Mannoch
Loch Bargatton
Threave Gardens
Castle Douglas
Carlingwark Loch
Barhill
Dalbeattie
Criffell
Drumburn
Glengap Forest
Bengray
Glengap
Bridge of Dee
Rhonehouse or Kelton Hill
Gelston
Carsethorn
Kirkbean
Arbigland Gardens
Fleet
Ringford
Dalbeattie Forest
Drumstinchall
Caulkerbush
Prestonmill
Anworth
Cardoness Castle
Gatehouse of Fleet
Valleyfield
Airieland
Palnackie
Barnbarroch
Mainsriddle
John Paul Jones Cottage Museum
Orchardton Tower
Sandyhills
Colvend
Girthon
Twynholm
Galloway Hydro Visitor Centre
Tongland
Broughton House and Garden
Kippford or Scaur
Mote of Mark
Bengairn
Rockcliffe
Rough Island
Rough I.
Portling
Southerness
Southerness Pt.
Mersehead Sands
Whinnieliggate
East Stewartry Coast
Castlehill Pt.
NS
NX
6 miles
10 km

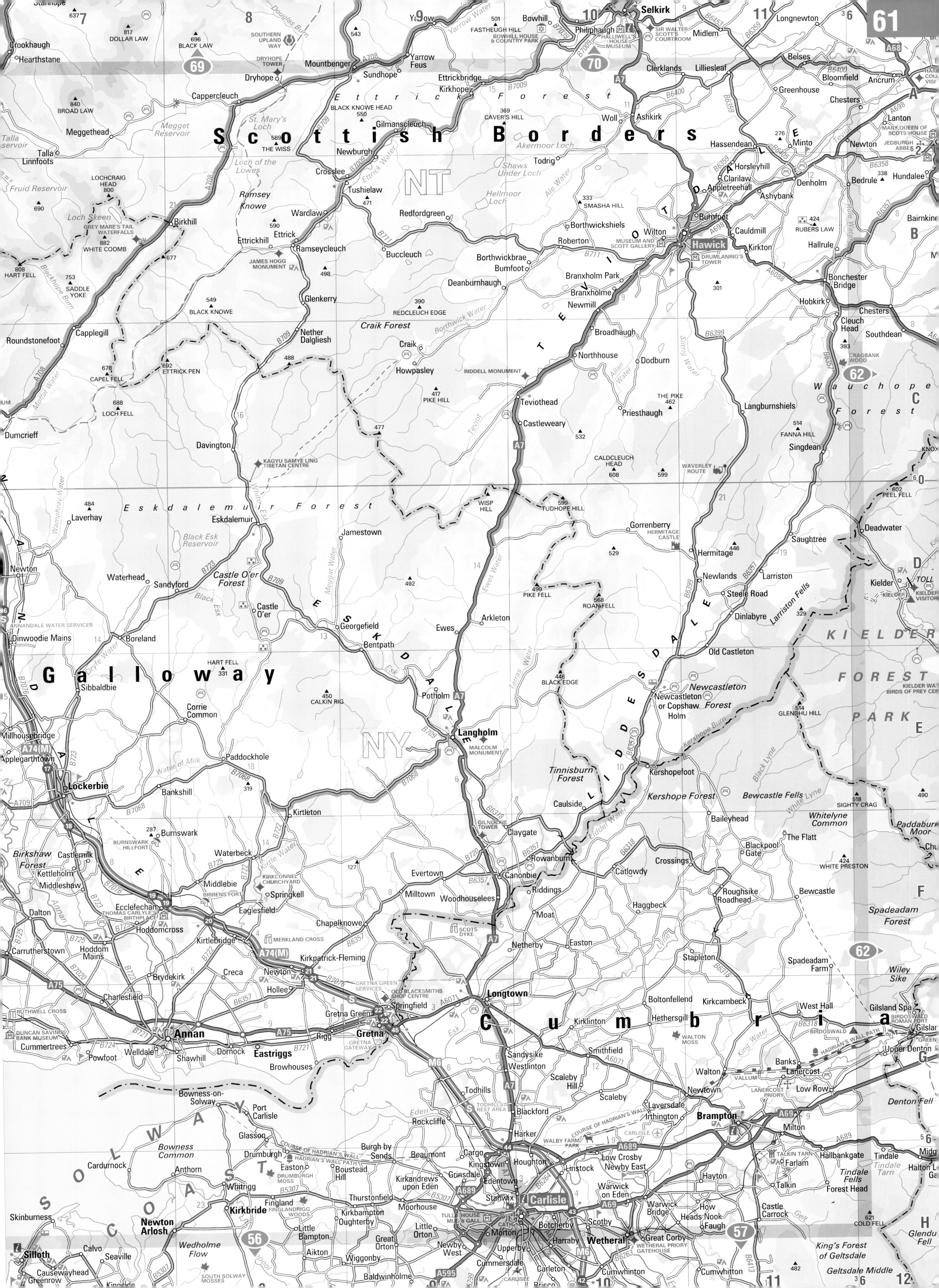
Scottish Borders
Galloway
Cumbria
Solway Coast
NT
NY
Ettrick Forest
Eskdalemuir Forest
Craik Forest
Wauchope Forest
Kielder Forest Park
Teviotdale
Eskdale
Liddesdale
Annandale
Selkirk
Hawick
Langholm
Lockerbie
Annan
Gretna
Longtown
Carlisle
Brampton
Newcastleton or Copshaw Holm
Eastriggs
Wetheral
Silloth
Kirkbride
Newton Arlosh
Ashkirk
Wilton
Denholm
Bonchester Bridge
Chesters
Southdean
Teviothead
Castleweary
Branxholme
Newmill
Broadhaugh
Northhouse
Roberton
Buccleuch
Ettrick
Ettrickbridge
Yarrow
Mountbenger
Tushielaw
Cappercleuch
Birkhill
Capplegill
Eskdalemuir
Bentpath
Ewes
Canonbie
Kershopefoot
Saughtree
Kielder
Gilsland
Lanercost
Walton
Kirklinton
Smithfield
Westlinton
Rockcliffe
Burgh by Sands
Drumburgh
Bowness-on-Solway
Port Carlisle
Ecclefechan
Hoddomcross
Kirtlebridge
Kirkpatrick-Fleming
Springfield
Boreland
Sibbaldbie
Middlebie
Waterbeck
Dalton
Cummertrees
Powfoot
Moffat Water
Megget Reservoir
St. Mary's Loch
Black Esk Reservoir
Hadrian's Wall
Waverley Route
Hermitage Castle
Scots Dyke
Malcolm Monument
Gilnockie Tower
Tinnisburn Forest
Kershope Forest
Bewcastle Fells
Spadeadam Forest
62
69
70
56
57

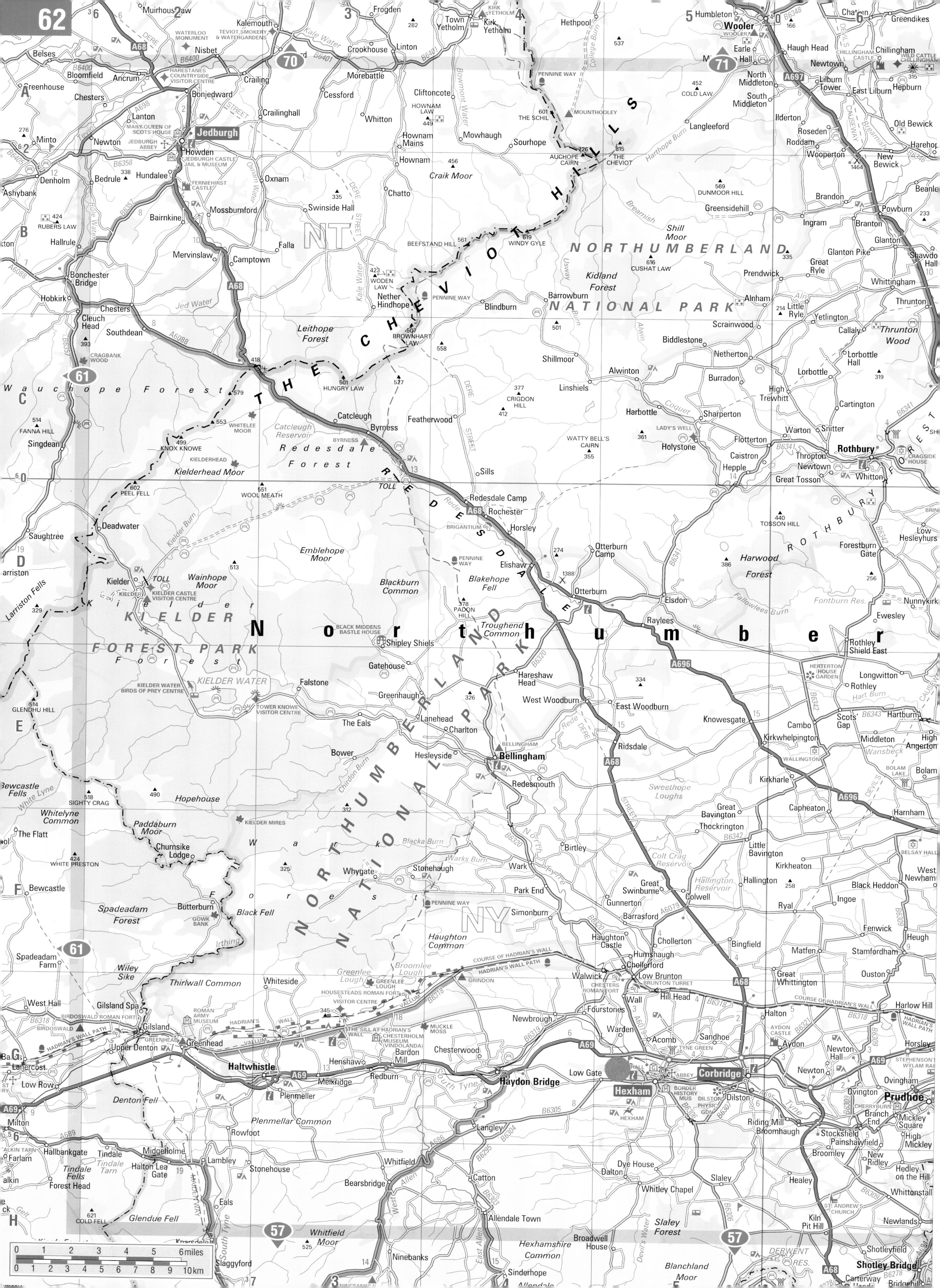
THE CHEVIOT HILLS
NORTHUMBERLAND NATIONAL PARK
Northumber
KIELDER FOREST PARK
Kielder Forest
Redesdale Forest
Wark Forest
REDESDALE
NORTHUMBERLAND NATIONAL PARK
ROTHBURY FOREST
NT
NY
Wooler
Jedburgh
Rothbury
Otterburn
Bellingham
Haltwhistle
Haydon Bridge
Hexham
Corbridge
Prudhoe
Kielder
Kielder Water
Kidland Forest
Harwood Forest
Spadeadam Forest
Thrunton Wood
Leithope Forest
Slaley Forest
Allendale Town
Gilsland
Greenhead
Chollerford
Alwinton
Harbottle
Elsdon
Kirkwhelpington
Byrness
Catcleugh
Rochester
Simonburn
Wark
The Cheviot
Windy Gyle
Craik Moor
Emblehope Moor
Blackburn Common
Kielderhead Moor
Wainhope Moor
Hopehouse
Haughton Common
Thirlwall Common
Denton Fell
Plenmellar Common
Hexhamshire Common
Glendue Fell
Black Fell
Wauchope Forest
A68
A69
A696
A697
A6088
A698
B6320
B6318
B6341
B6342
Hadrian's Wall Path
Course of Hadrian's Wall
Pennine Way
Dere Street
Dere Street
70
71
61
61
57
57
0 1 2 3 4 5 6 miles
0 1 2 3 4 5 6 7 8 9 10 km

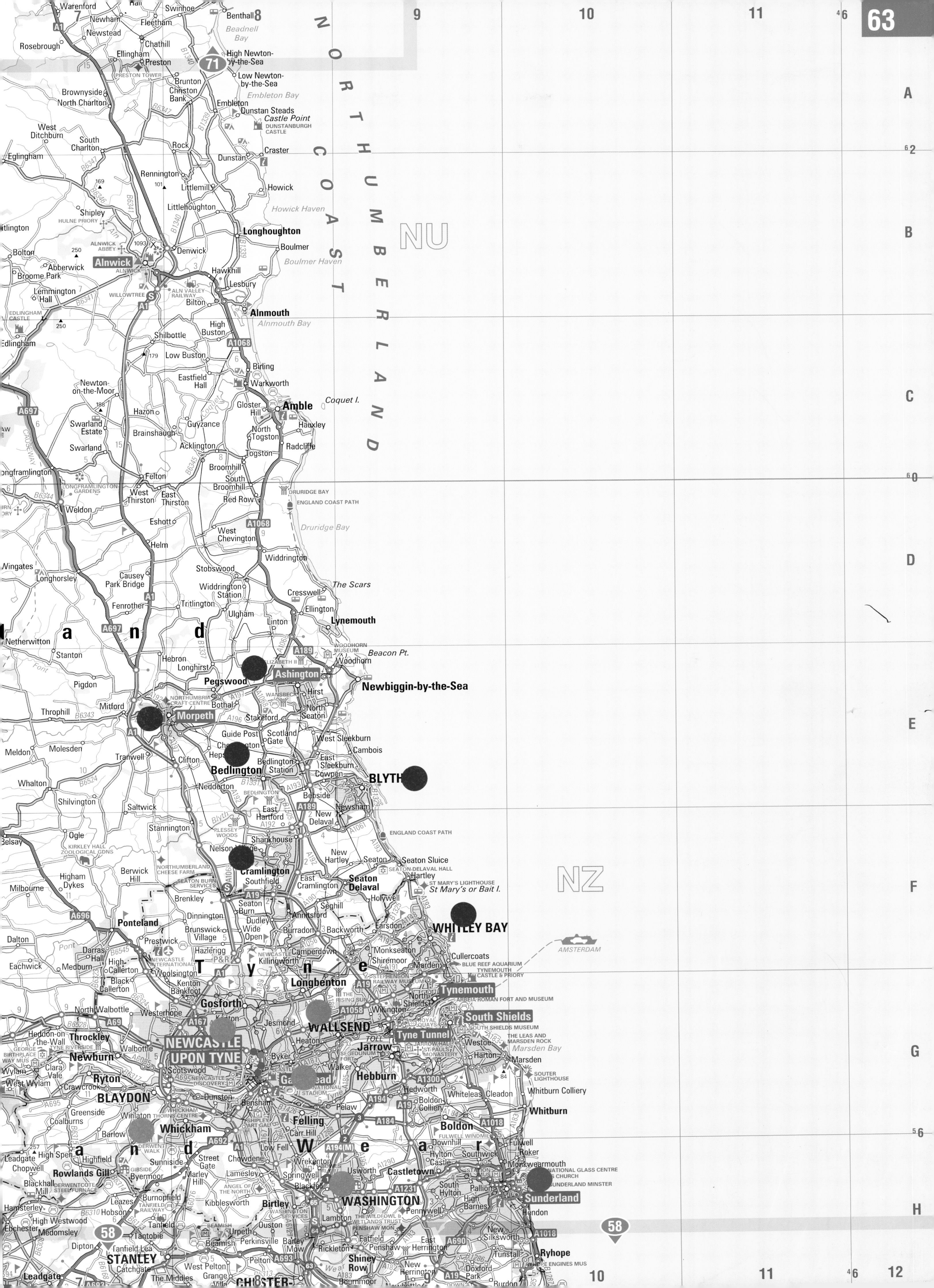

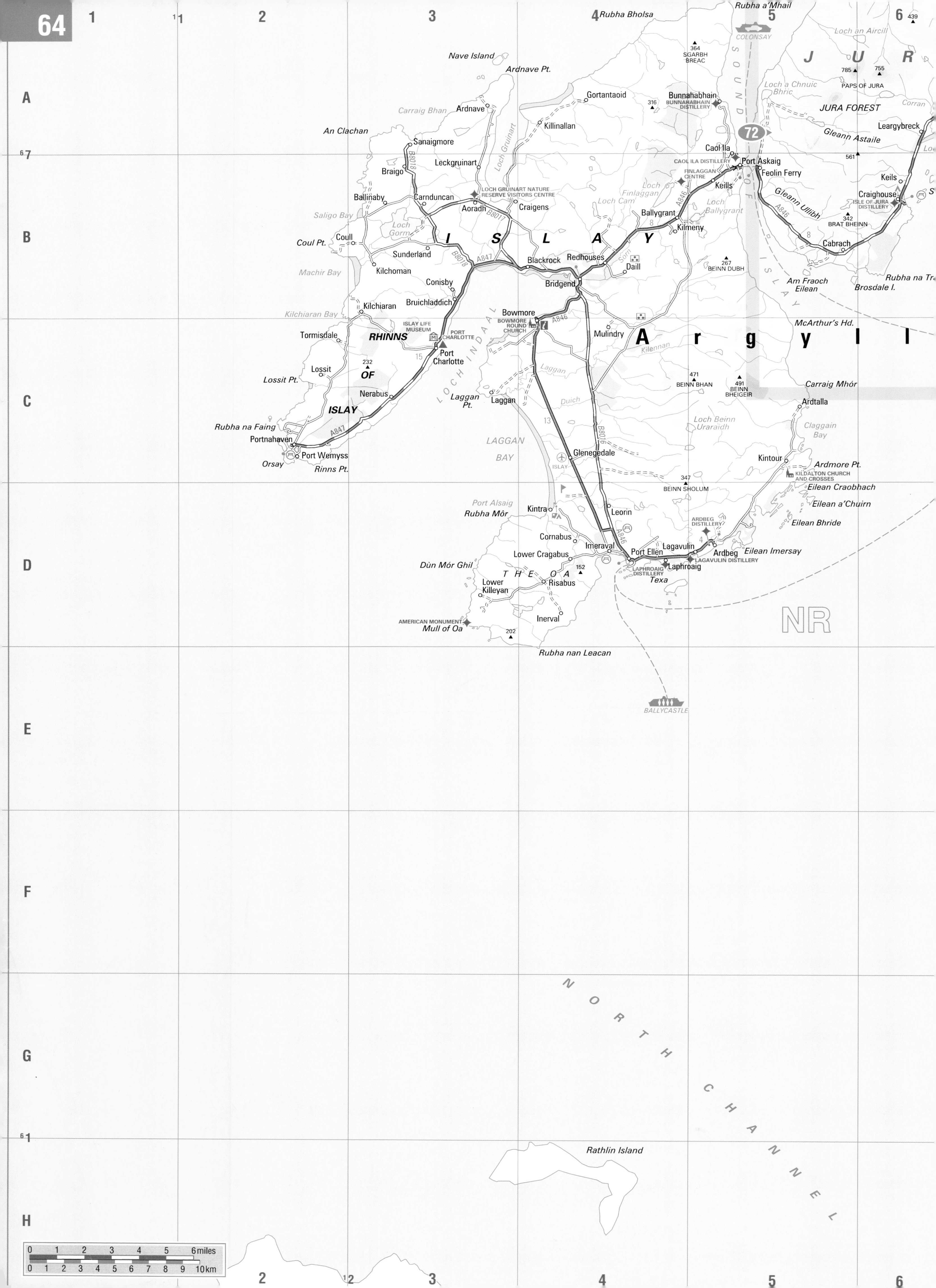

1 ¹1 2 3 4 *Rubha Bholsa* *Rubha a'Mhail* 5 6 ⁴39

COLONSAY
Loch an Aircill

J U R A

785 ▲ 755 ▲
PAPS OF JURA

Nave Island
Ardnave Pt.

Loch a Chnuic
Bhric

JURA FOREST

Corran

A
Gortantaoid **Bunnahabhain**
BUNNAHABHAIN
DISTILLERY

Carraig Bhan Ardnave
Killinallan
316 ▲

Leargybreck
Gleann Astaile

An Clachan Sanaigmore
⁶7
Caol Ila
Port Askaig
CAOL ILA DISTILLERY
561 ▲
Keils

Leckgruinart

Braigo
Port Askaig
Feolin Ferry

Craighouse
ISLE OF JURA
DISTILLERY

Ballinaby Carnduncan
LOCH GRUINART NATURE
RESERVE VISITORS CENTRE
FINLAGGAN
CENTRE
Keills

Gleann Ullibh

342 ▲
BRAT BHEINN

B
Aoradh B8017 Craigens
Loch Finlaggan
Ballygrant
Loch
Ballygrant

I S L A Y
Kilmeny

Cabrach

Saligo Bay
Loch
Gorm

Coul Pt. Coull
Sunderland
Blackrock Redhouses
Sorn Daill
Am Fraoch
Eilean
Rubha na Tr
Brosdale I.

Machir Bay Kilchoman
Bridgend
267 ▲
BEINN DUBH

Conisby
McArthur's Hd.

Kilchiaran Bay Kilchiaran
Bruichladdich
Bowmore
BOWMORE
ROUND
CHURCH
A846
Mulindry
A r g y l l

Tormisdale
ISLAY LIFE
MUSEUM
Port
Charlotte
Kilennan

RHINNS
15
Port
Charlotte
471 ▲
BEINN BHAN
491 ▲
BEINN
BHEIGEIR
Carraig Mhór

C
Lossit Pt. Lossit 232 ▲
OF
Loch Beinn
Uraraidh
Ardtalla

Nerabus
Laggan
Pt. Laggan
Duich
Claggain
Bay

ISLAY
13
B8016

Rubha na Faing
Portnahaven
LAGGAN
BAY
A847
ISLAY
Glenegedale
347 ▲
Kintour
Ardmore Pt.

Port Wemyss
Eilean Craobhach

Orsay *Rinns Pt.*
BEINN SHOLUM
Eilean a'Chuirn

Port Alsaig
Rubha Mór
Kintra
Leorin
ARDBEG
DISTILLERY
Eilean Bhride

D
Dùn Mór Ghil
Cornabus Imeraval
A846
Lagavulin
Ardbeg
Eilean Imersay

Lower Cragabus
Port Ellen
LAGAVULIN DISTILLERY

THE OA
Risabus
152 ▲
LAPHROAIG
DISTILLERY
Laphroaig
Texa

Lower
Killeyan

Inerval
NR

AMERICAN MONUMENT
Mull of Oa 202 ▲

Rubha nan Leacan

E
BALLYCASTLE

F

G
N O R T H

H
C H A N N E L

⁶1
Rathlin Island

0 1 2 3 4 5 6miles
0 1 2 3 4 5 6 7 8 9 10km

1 ¹2 2 3 4 5 6

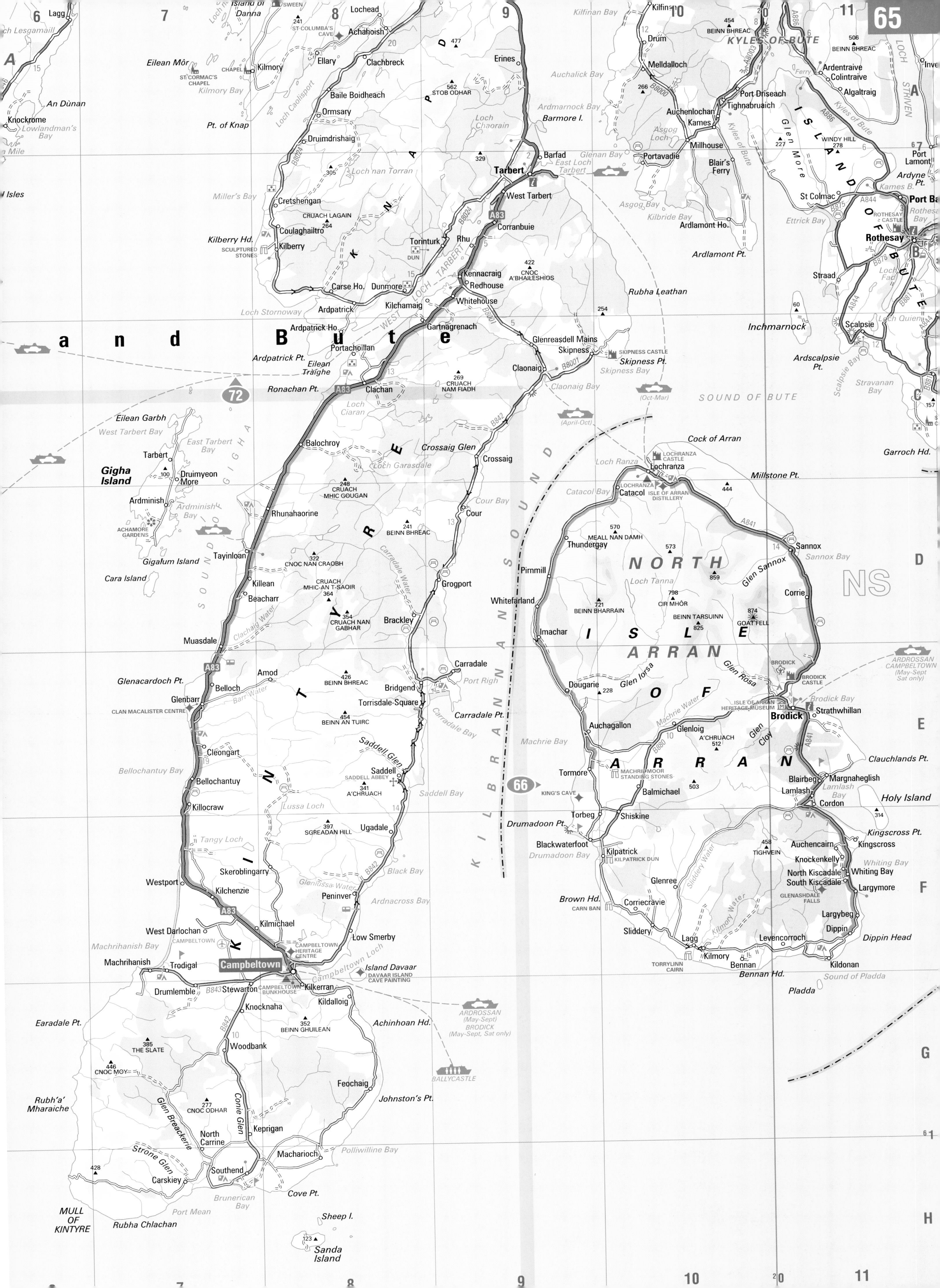
Lagg
Loch Lesgamaill
Eilean Mòr
St Cormac's Chapel
Kilmory Bay
An Dùnan
Knockrome
Lowlandman's Bay
Pt. of Knap
Isles
Lochead
St Columba's Cave
Achahoish
Ellary
Clachbreck
Kilmory
Baile Boidheach
Ormsary
Loch Caolisport
Druimdrishaig
Loch nan Torran
Miller's Bay
Cretshengan
Cruach Lagain
Coulaghailtro
Kilberry
Kilberry Hd.
Sculptured Stones
Torinturk
Dun
Carse Ho.
Dunmore
Loch Stornoway
Ardpatrick
Ardpatrick Ho.
Portachoillan
Ardpatrick Pt.
Eilean Traighe
Ronachan Pt.
Clachan
Loch Ciaran
a n d B u t e
K N A P D A L E
Stob Odhar
Erines
Loch Chaorain
Barfad
Tarbert
East Loch Tarbert
West Tarbert
Corranbuie
Rhu
West Loch Tarbert
Kennacraig
Redhouse
Whitehouse
Kilchamaig
Gartnagrenach
Cnoc a'Bhaileshios
Kilfinan Bay
Auchalick Bay
Ardmarnock Bay
Barmore I.
Glenan Bay
Asgog Bay
Asgog Loch
Kilbride Bay
Ardlamont Ho.
Ardlamont Pt.
Rubha Leathan
Kilfinan
Drum
Melldalloch
Beinn Bhreac
Kyles of Bute
Auchenlochan
Kames
Tighnabruaich
Port Driseach
Millhouse
Portavadie
Blair's Ferry
Kyles of Bute
Ardentraive
Colintraive
Algaltraig
Loch Striven
Island of Bute
Glen More
Windy Hill
Port Lamont
Ardyne Pt.
Kames B.
St Colmac
Port Ba
Rothesay Castle
Rothesay Bay
Ettrick Bay
Rothesay
Straad
Loch Fad
Loch Quien
Inchmarnock
Scalpsie
Scalpsie Bay
Ardscalpsie Pt.
Stravanan Bay
Garroch Hd.
Glenreasdell Mains
Skipness
Skipness Castle
Skipness Pt.
Skipness Bay
Claonaig
Claonaig Bay
Sound of Bute
(Oct-Mar)
(April-Oct)
Cruach nam Fiadh
Eilean Garbh
West Tarbert Bay
East Tarbert Bay
Tarbert
Gigha Island
Druimyeon More
Ardminish
Ardminish Bay
Achamore Gardens
Sound of Gigha
Gigalum Island
Cara Island
Balochroy
Loch Garasdale
Cruach Mhic Gougan
Crossaig Glen
Crossaig
Rhunahaorine
Tayinloan
Cnoc nan Craobh
Beinn Bhreac
Cour Bay
Cour
Carradale Water
Killean
Beacharr
Cruach Mhic-an t-Saoir
Cruach nan Gabhar
Grogport
Brackley
Clachaig Water
Muasdale
Carradale
Port Righ
Amod
Belloch
Barr Water
Glenacardoch Pt.
Glenbarr
Clan Macalister Centre
Bridgend
Torrisdale-Square
Carradale Pt.
Carradale Bay
Beinn an Tuirc
Cleongart
Saddell Glen
Bellochantuy Bay
Bellochantuy
Saddell
Saddell Abbey
A'Chruach
Saddell Bay
Killocraw
Lussa Loch
Sgreadan Hill
Ugadale
Tangy Loch
Westport
Skeroblingarry
Black Bay
Glenlussa Water
Kilchenzie
Peninver
Ardnacross Bay
K I N T Y R E
West Darlochan
Kilmichael
Low Smerby
Machrihanish Bay
Campbeltown
Campbeltown Heritage Centre
Campbeltown Loch
Machrihanish
Trodigal
Campbeltown
Island Davaar
Davaar Island Cave Painting
Drumlemble
Stewarton
Campbeltown Bunkhouse
Kilkerran
Kildalloig
Knocknaha
Beinn Ghuilean
Achinhoan Hd.
Ardrossan (May-Sept)
Brodick (May-Sept, Sat only)
Earadale Pt.
The Slate
Woodbank
Cnoc Moy
Ballycastle
Feochaig
Johnston's Pt.
Rubh'a' Mharaiche
Glen Breackerie
Cnoc Odhar
Conie Glen
North Carrine
Keprigan
Strone Glen
Machrioch
Polliwilline Bay
Southend
Carskiey
Cove Pt.
Brunerican Bay
Mull of Kintyre
Port Mean
Rubha Chlachan
Sheep I.
Sanda Island
Kilbrannan Sound
Cock of Arran
Lochranza Castle
Loch Ranza
Lochranza
Millstone Pt.
Catacol Bay
Catacol
Isle of Arran Distillery
Meall nan Damh
Thundergay
North
Loch Tanna
Glen Sannox
Sannox
Sannox Bay
Pirnmill
Cir Mhòr
Beinn Bharrain
Beinn Tarsuinn
Goat Fell
Corrie
Whitefarland
Imachar
Isle of Arran
Glen Iorsa
Glen Rosa
Brodick Castle
Brodick Bay
Ardrossan Campbeltown (May-Sept Sat only)
Dougarie
Isle of Arran Heritage Museum
Brodick
Strathwhillan
Machrie Water
Glenloig
Auchagallon
A'Chruach
Glen Cloy
Machrie Bay
Clauchlands Pt.
Tormore
Machrie Moor Standing Stones
Balmichael
Blairbeg
Margnaheglish
Lamlash
Lamlash Bay
Holy Island
King's Cave
Cordon
Torbeg
Shiskine
Drumadoon Pt.
Kingscross Pt.
Blackwaterfoot
Drumadoon Bay
Tighvein
Auchencairn
Kingscross
Kilpatrick
Kilpatrick Dun
Knockenkelly
Whiting Bay
North Kiscadale
South Kiscadale
Sliddery Water
Glenree
Largymore
Brown Hd.
Carn Ban
Corriecravie
Glenashdale Falls
Kilmory Water
Largybeg
Sliddery
Dippin
Dippin Head
Lagg
Levencorroch
Kilmory
Bennan
Kildonan
Torrylinn Cairn
Bennan Hd.
Sound of Pladda
Pladda
NS

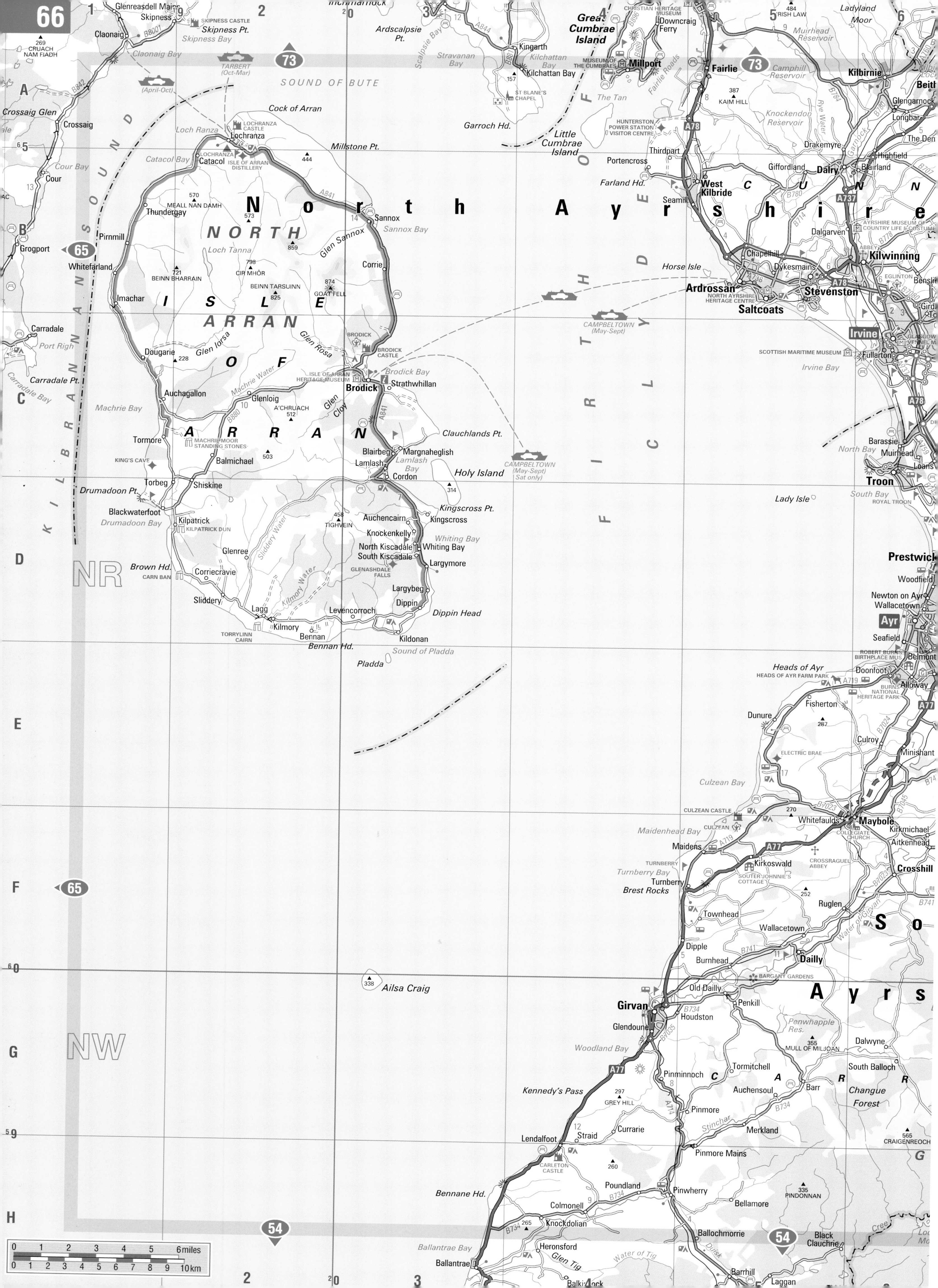
North Ayrshire
NORTH ISLE OF ARRAN
ARRAN
KILBRANNAN SOUND
SOUND OF BUTE
FIRTH OF CLYDE
CUNNINGHAME
South Ayrshire
CARRICK
Glenreasdell Mains
Skipness
Skipness Castle
Skipness Pt.
Skipness Bay
Claonaig
Claonaig Bay
Cruach nam Fiadh
Crossaig Glen
Crossaig
Cour Bay
Cour
Grogport
Carradale
Port Righ
Carradale Pt.
Carradale Bay
Tarbert (Oct-Mar)
(April-Oct)
Cock of Arran
Loch Ranza
Lochranza
Lochranza Castle
Isle of Arran Distillery
Catacol Bay
Catacol
Millstone Pt.
Meall nan Damh
Thundergay
Pirnmill
Whitefarland
Imachar
Loch Tanna
Beinn Bharrain
Cir Mhòr
Beinn Tarsuinn
Goat Fell
Glen Sannox
Sannox
Sannox Bay
Corrie
Brodick
Brodick Castle
Brodick Bay
Isle of Arran Heritage Museum
Strathwhillan
Glen Iorsa
Glen Rosa
Dougarie
Machrie Water
Auchagallon
Glenloig
A'Chruach
Glen Cloy
Machrie Bay
Tormore
Machrie Moor Standing Stones
King's Cave
Balmichael
Clauchlands Pt.
Blairbeg
Margnaheglish
Lamlash
Lamlash Bay
Cordon
Holy Island
Campbeltown (May-Sept) Sat only
Torbeg
Shiskine
Drumadoon Pt.
Blackwaterfoot
Drumadoon Bay
Kilpatrick
Kilpatrick Dun
Kingscross Pt.
Kingscross
Auchencairn
Tighvein
Knockenkelly
Whiting Bay
North Kiscadale
South Kiscadale
Glenashdale Falls
Largymore
Sliddery Water
Glenree
Brown Hd.
Carn Ban
Corriecravie
Kilmory Water
Largybeg
Dippin
Dippin Head
Sliddery
Lagg
Levencorroch
Torrylinn Cairn
Kilmory
Bennan
Bennan Hd.
Kildonan
Sound of Pladda
Pladda
Ailsa Craig
NR
NW
Inchmarnock
Ardscalpsie Pt.
Scalpsie Bay
Stravanan Bay
Kingarth
Kilchattan Bay
St Blane's Chapel
Garroch Hd.
Great Cumbrae Island
Christian Heritage Museum
Downcraig Ferry
Millport
Museum of the Cumbraes
The Tan
Little Cumbrae Island
Hunterston Power Station Visitor Centre
Portencross
Farland Hd.
Fairlie
Fairlie Roads
Kaim Hill
Hill of Stake
Muirhead Reservoir
Camphill Reservoir
Knockendon Reservoir
Rye Water
Ladyland Moor
Misty Law
Kilbirnie
Beith
Glengarnock
Longbar
The Den
Drakemyre
Highfield
Blairland
Giffordland
Dalry
Thirdpart
West Kilbride
Seamill
Ayrshire Museum of Country Life & Costume
Dalgarven
Chapelhill
Dykesmains
Kilwinning
Eglinton
Horse Isle
Ardrossan
North Ayrshire Heritage Centre
Saltcoats
Stevenston
Campbeltown (May-Sept)
Irvine
Scottish Maritime Museum
Fullarton
Irvine Bay
Barassie
Muirhead
North Bay
Troon
Loans
South Bay
Royal Troon
Lady Isle
Prestwick
Woodfield
Newton on Ayr
Wallacetown
Ayr
Seafield
Robert Burns Birthplace Mus.
Belmont
Heads of Ayr
Heads of Ayr Farm Park
Doonfoot
Burns National Heritage Park
Alloway
Dunure
Fisherton
Culroy
Electric Brae
Minishant
Culzean Bay
Culzean Castle
Culzean
Whitefaulds
Maybole
Collegiate Church
Kirkmichael
Maidenhead Bay
Maidens
Aitkenhead
Turnberry
Turnberry Bay
Brest Rocks
Kirkoswald
Souter Johnnie's Cottage
Crossraguel Abbey
Crosshill
Townhead
Ruglen
Wallacetown
Water of Girvan
Dipple
Burnhead
Dailly
Bargany Gardens
Old Dailly
Penkill
Girvan
Glendoune
Houdston
Penwhapple Res.
Woodland Bay
Mull of Miljoan
Dalwyne
South Balloch
Pinminnoch
Tormitchell
Auchensoul
Barr
Changue Forest
Kennedy's Pass
Grey Hill
Pinmore
Stinchar
Merkland
Craigenreoch
Lendalfoot
Straid
Currarie
Pinmore Mains
Carleton Castle
Bennane Hd.
Poundland
Pinwherry
Pindonnan
Colmonell
Bellamore
Knockdolian
Ballochmorrie
Black Clauchrie
Ballantrae Bay
Heronsford
Glen Tig
Water of Tig
Duisk
Ballantrae
Barrhill
Laggan
Balkissock
A78
A737
A77
A841
A719
A714
B734
B741
B7023
B880
B842
73
65
54
0 1 2 3 4 5 6 miles
0 1 2 3 4 5 6 7 8 9 10 km

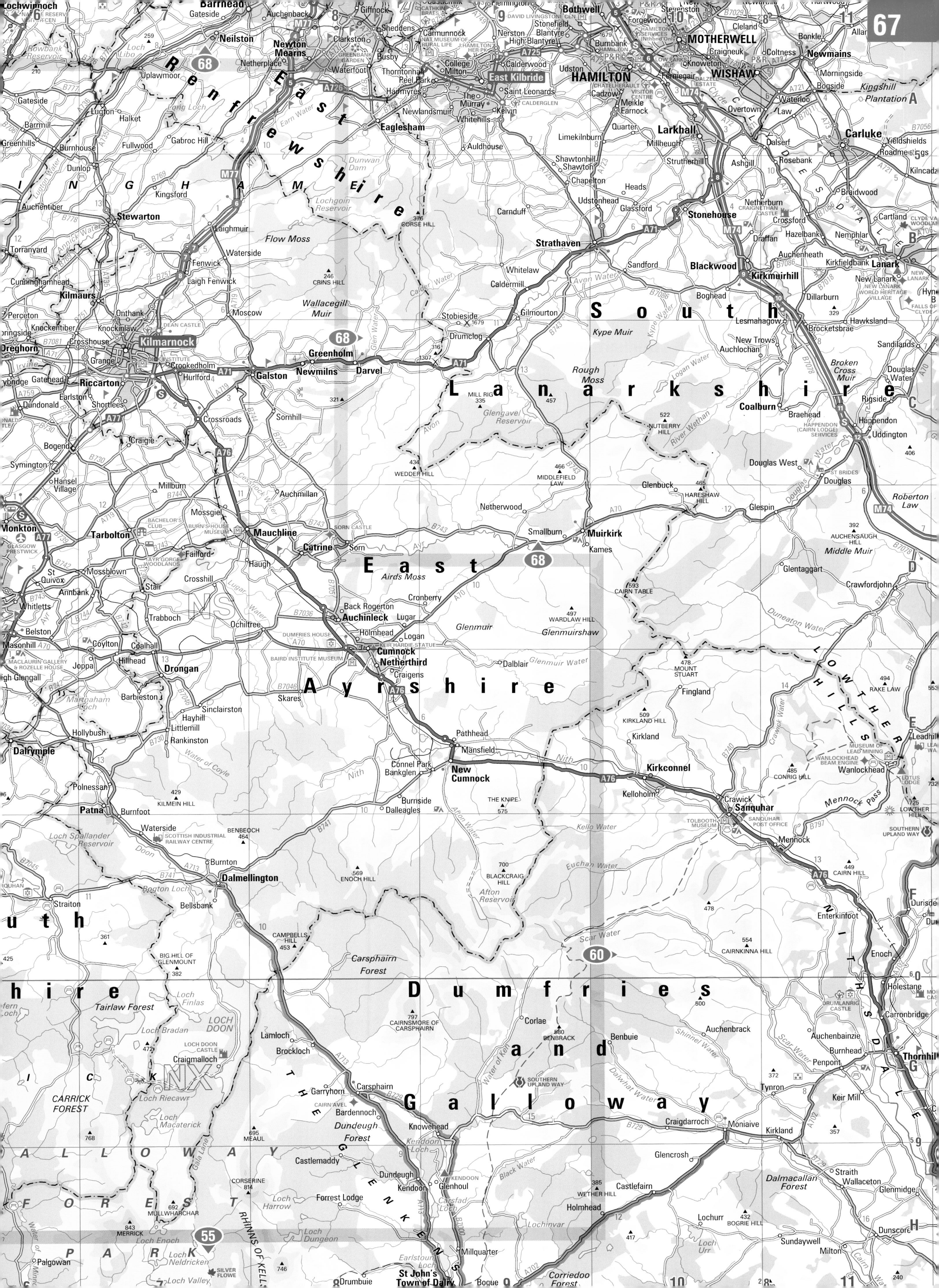
Lochwinnoch
Barrhead
Gateside
Auchenback
Giffnock
Bothwell
Stevenston
Neilston
Newton Mearns
Sheddens
Clarkston
Carmunnock
Nerston
High Blantyre
Stonefield
Blantyre
Forgewood
Cleland
MOTHERWELL
Bonkle
Newmains
Netherplace
Busby
Waterfoot
Thorntonhall
Peel Park
College Milton
East Kilbride
Calderwood
Udston
HAMILTON
Burnbank
Knoweton
Craigneuk
WISHAW
Coltness
Morningside
Uplawmoor
Renfrewshire
East Renfrewshire
Hairmyres
Saint Leonards
The Murray
Kelvin
Whitehills
Newlandsmuir
Cadzow
Meikle Earnock
Fernieg̃ait
Bogside
Kingshill Plantation
Waterloo
Overtown
Law
Gateside
Lugton
Halket
Long Loch
Earn Water
Eaglesham
Quarter
Larkhall
Millheugh
Dalserf
Carluke
Yieldshields
Roadmeetings
Barmill
Fullwood
Gabroc Hill
Auldhouse
Limekilnburn
Kilncadzow
Greenhills
Burnhouse
Dunwan Dam
Shawtonhill
Shawton
Strutherhill
Ashgill
Rosebank
Dunlop
Chapelton
Braidwood
Kingsford
Lochgoin Reservoir
Heads
Udstonhead
Glassford
Netherburn
Craignethan Castle
Crossford
Cartland
Auchentiber
Stewarton
Carnduff
Stonehouse
Hazelbank
Nemphlar
Laighmuir
CORSE HILL
Flow Moss
Strathaven
Torranyard
Waterside
Fenwick
Laigh Fenwick
CRINS HILL
Whitelaw
Caldermill
Sandford
Blackwood
Kirkmuirhill
Auchenheath
Kirkfieldbank
Lanark
New Lanark
Cunninghamhead
Kilmaurs
Wallacegill Muir
Calder Water
Avon Water
Boghead
Dillarburn
Perceton
Onthank
Moscow
Stobieside
Gilmourton
South
Hawksland
Knockentiber
Knockinlaw
Dean Castle
Drumclog
Kype Muir
Lesmahagow
Brocketsbrae
Kilmarnock
Crosshouse
Dreghorn
Grange
Greenholm
Glen Water
New Trows
Auchlochan
Sandilands
Crookedholm
Hurlford
Galston
Newmilns
Darvel
Rough Moss
Logan Water
Broken Cross Muir
Douglas Water
Riccarton
Gatehead
Earlston
Shortlees
Lanarkshire
MILL RIG
Glengavel Reservoir
Coalburn
Braehead
Rigside
Dundonald
Crossroads
Sornhill
Avon
NUTBERRY HILL
River Wethan
Happendon
Uddington
Craigie
Bogend
Symington
WEDDER HILL
MIDDLEFIELD LAW
Douglas West
Douglas
Glenbuck
HARESHAW HILL
Roberton Law
Hansel Village
Millburn
Auchmillan
Netherwood
Glespin
Monkton
Mossgiel
Bachelor's Club
Burns House Museum
Mauchline
Sorn Castle
Tarbolton
Catrine
Sorn
Smallburn
Muirkirk
Kames
AUCHENSAUGH HILL
Middle Muir
Failford
Glasgow Prestwick
Ayr Gorge Woodlands
Haugh
East
Airds Moss
Glentaggart
St Quivox
Mossblown
Stair
Crosshill
CAIRN TABLE
Crawfordjohn
Annbank
Whitletts
NS
Back Rogerton
Cronberry
Auchinleck
Lugar
WARDLAW HILL
Glenmuirshaw
Duneaton Water
Trabboch
Ochiltree
Lugar Water
Belston
Dumfries House
Holmhead
Logan
Glenmuir
Masonhill
Coylton
Coalhall
Keir Hardie Statue
Cumnock
Netherthird
Baird Institute Museum
Dalblair
Glenmuir Water
Maclaurin Gallery & Rozelle House
Joppa
Hillhead
Drongan
Craigens
MOUNT STUART
Lowther Hills
High Glengall
Ayrshire
Skares
Fingland
RAKE LAW
Barbieston
Sinclairston
Hayhill
Littlemill
KIRKLAND HILL
Kirkland
Hollybush
Rankinston
Pathhead
Mansfield
Dalrymple
Water of Coyle
Connel Park
Bankglen
New Cumnock
Nith
Kirkconnel
Museum of Lead Mining
Wanlockhead Beam Engine
Wanlockhead
CONRIG HILL
Leadhills
Polnessan
KILMEIN HILL
Kelloholm
Lotus Lodge
Patna
Burnfoot
Burnside
Dalleagles
THE KNIPE
Crawick
Sanquhar
Mennock Pass
LOWTHER HILL
Waterside
Scottish Industrial Railway Centre
BENBEOCH
Tolbooth Museum
Sanquhar Post Office
Kello Water
Southern Upland Way
Loch Spallander Reservoir
Doon
Afton Water
Mennock
Burnton
Dalmellington
ENOCH HILL
BLACKCRAIG HILL
Euchan Water
CAIRN HILL
Straiton
Bogton Loch
Bellsbank
Afton Reservoir
Durisdeer
Enterkinfoot
South
CAMPBELLS HILL
Scar Water
CAIRNKINNA HILL
BIG HILL OF GLENMOUNT
Enoch
Carsphairn Forest
Holestane
Ayrshire
Tairlaw Forest
Loch Finlas
LOCH DOON
Dumfries
CAIRNSMORE OF CARSPHAIRN
Corlae
Drumlanrig Castle
Carronbridge
Auchenbrack
Loch Bradan
Lamloch
Brockloch
BENBRACK
Benbuie
Shinnel Water
Auchenbainzie
LOCH DOON CASTLE
Craigmalloch
and
Burnhead
Thornhill
Penpont
Water of Ken
Southern Upland Way
Scar Water
NX
CARRICK FOREST
Loch Riecawr
The Glenkens
Garryhorn
Carsphairn
Tynron
Keir Mill
Cairn'avel
Bardennoch
Galloway
Dalwhat Water
Nithsdale
Loch Macaterick
Dundeugh Forest
Knowehead
Craigdarroch
Moniaive
Kirkland
MEAUL
Kendoon Loch
Castlemaddy
Glencrosh
Galloway
Straith
Wallaceton
Dundeugh
Kendoon
Glenhoul
Black Water
Dalmacallan Forest
Glenmidge
CORSERINE
Forrest Lodge
Loch Harrow
Carsfad Loch
WETHER HILL
Castlefairn
Forest
MULLWHARCHAR
Holmhead
Lochurr
BOGRIE HILL
Dunscore
MERRICK
Loch Enoch
Loch Dungeon
Lochinvar
Park
Loch Neldricken
Rhinns of Kells
Millquarter
Sundaywell
Loch Urr
Milton
Palgowan
Silver Flowe
Earlstoun Loch
Loch Valley
Drumbuie
St John's Town of Dalry
Bogue
Corriedoo Forest
Cairn

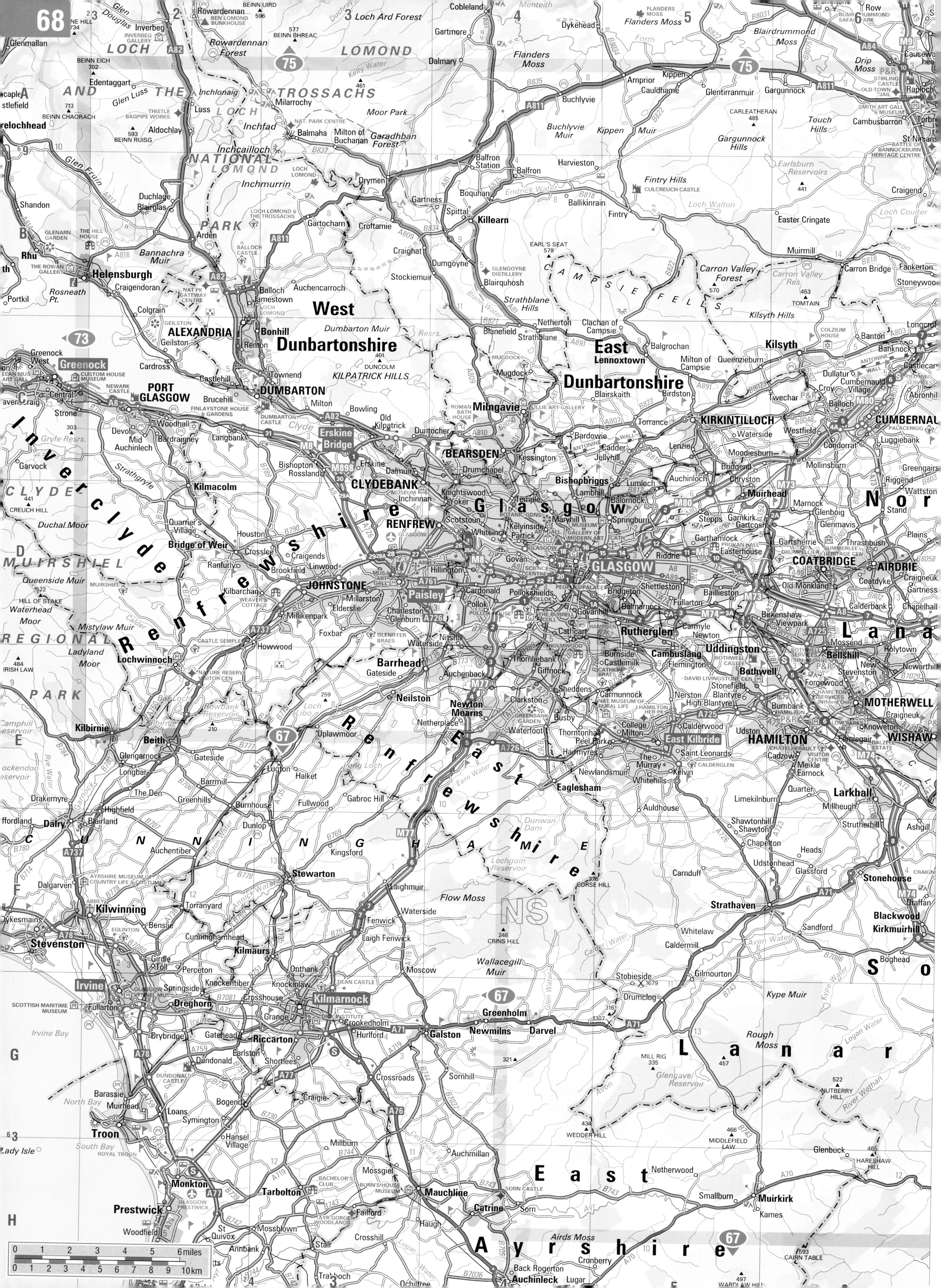
LOCH LOMOND AND THE TROSSACHS NATIONAL PARK
Loch Ard Forest
Flanders Moss
Blairdrummond Moss
West Dunbartonshire
Dumbarton Muir
KILPATRICK HILLS
East Dunbartonshire
CAMPSIE FELLS
Kilsyth Hills
Carron Valley Forest
Gargunnock Hills
Touch Hills
Fintry Hills
Inverclyde
Renfrewshire
East Renfrewshire
Glasgow
GLASGOW
CLYDE MUIRSHIEL REGIONAL PARK
CUNNINGHAME
North Lanarkshire
South Lanarkshire
East Ayrshire
Helensburgh
Rhu
Greenock
PORT GLASGOW
ALEXANDRIA
DUMBARTON
Balloch
Bonhill
Renton
Milngavie
BEARSDEN
CLYDEBANK
RENFREW
Paisley
JOHNSTONE
Kilmacolm
Bridge of Weir
Lochwinnoch
Kilbirnie
Beith
Dalry
Kilwinning
Stevenston
Irvine
Troon
Prestwick
Monkton
Kilmarnock
Stewarton
Kilmaurs
Galston
Newmilns
Darvel
Mauchline
Catrine
Sorn
Muirkirk
Strathaven
Eaglesham
East Kilbride
HAMILTON
MOTHERWELL
WISHAW
Larkhall
Stonehouse
COATBRIDGE
AIRDRIE
CUMBERNAULD
KIRKINTILLOCH
Kilsyth
Lennoxtown
Bishopbriggs
Rutherglen
Cambuslang
Uddingston
Bellshill
Barrhead
Neilston
Newton Mearns
Killearn
Drymen
Balfron
Buchlyvie
Kippen
Fintry
Luss
Balmaha
Gartocharn
Strathblane
Blanefield
Auchinleck
Riccarton
Hurlford
Tarbolton
Irvine Bay
North Bay
South Bay
Lady Isle
Rosneath Pt.
Flow Moss
Wallacegill Muir
Kype Muir
Rough Moss
Airds Moss
NS
0 1 2 3 4 5 6 miles
0 1 2 3 4 5 6 7 8 9 10 km

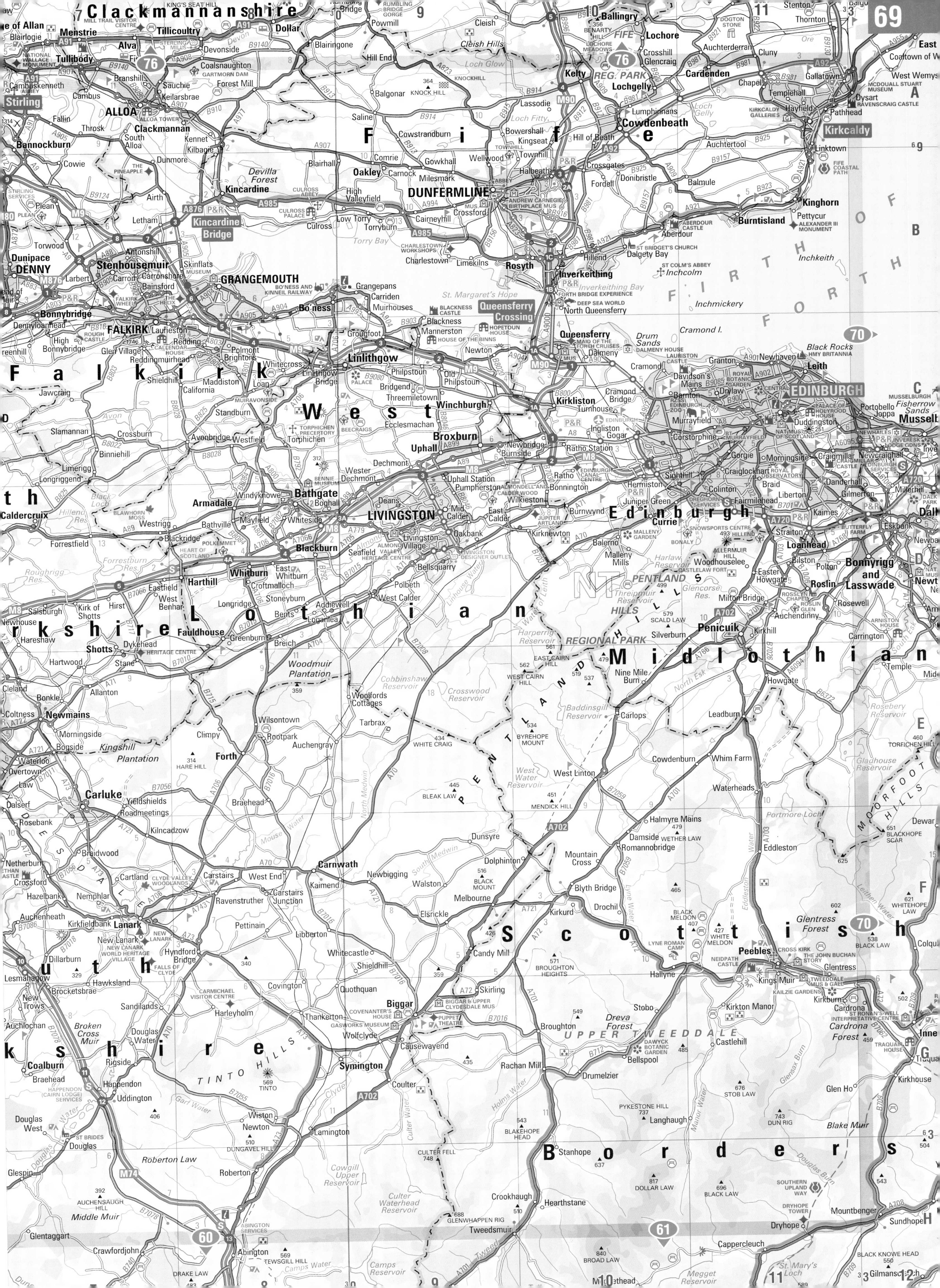
Clackmannanshire
Menstrie
Tillicoultry
Dollar
Alva
Tullibody
Stirling
ALLOA
Clackmannan
Kincardine
Kincardine Bridge
Stenhousemuir
DENNY
GRANGEMOUTH
FALKIRK
Bonnybridge
Bo'ness
Linlithgow
Falkirk
Fife
Saline
Oakley
DUNFERMLINE
Rosyth
Inverkeithing
Queensferry Crossing
Queensferry
Kelty
Lochgelly
Cowdenbeath
Cardenden
Kirkcaldy
Kinghorn
Burntisland
Aberdour
FIRTH OF FORTH
Inchkeith
Leith
EDINBURGH
Musselburgh
West Lothian
Winchburgh
Broxburn
Uphall
Kirkliston
Bathgate
Armadale
LIVINGSTON
Blackburn
Whitburn
Harthill
Shotts
Fauldhouse
Edinburgh
Currie
Dalkeith
Loanhead
Bonnyrigg and Lasswade
Penicuik
Roslin
Midlothian
PENTLAND HILLS REGIONAL PARK
Carluke
Forth
Lanark
Carnwath
Biggar
West Linton
Peebles
Scottish Borders
Lanarkshire
TINTO HILLS
UPPER TWEEDDALE
Abington
Tweedsmuir
Douglas
Coalburn
Lesmahagow
MOORFOOT HILLS
Glentress Forest
Cardrona Forest
60
61
70
76

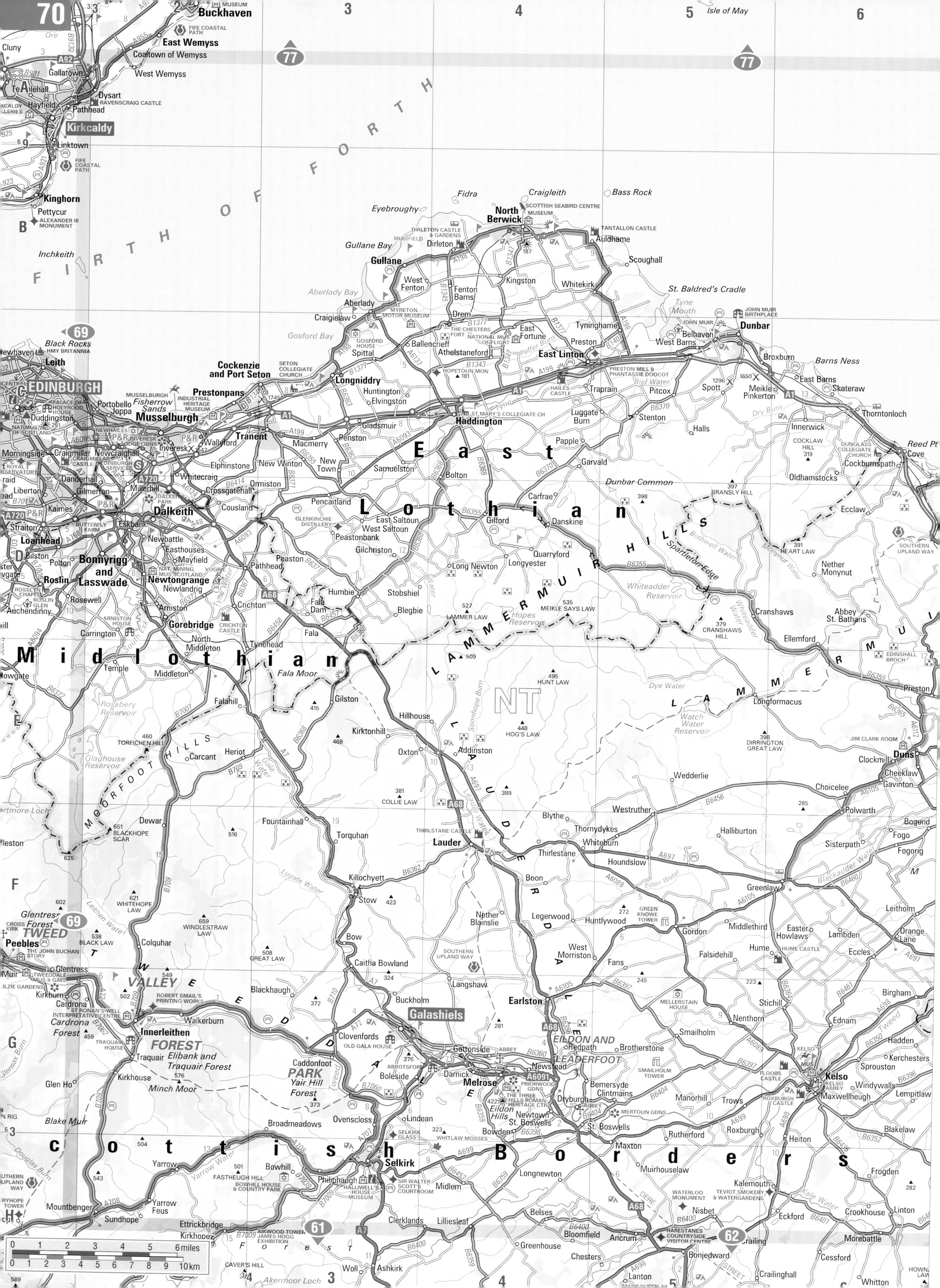

70
Buckhaven
Museum
Fife Coastal Path
East Wemyss
Coaltown of Wemyss
West Wemyss
Isle of May
77
Cluny
Gallatown
Dysart
Ravenscraig Castle
Hayfield
Pathhead
Kirkcaldy
Linktown
Kinghorn
Pettycur
Alexander III Monument
Inchkeith
Firth of Forth
Fidra
Craigleith
Bass Rock
Eyebroughy
North Berwick
Scottish Seabird Centre
Tantallon Castle
Auldhame
Dirleton Castle & Gardens
Dirleton
Gullane Bay
Gullane
Scoughall
West Fenton
Fenton Barns
Kingston
Whitekirk
St. Baldred's Cradle
Aberlady Bay
Aberlady
Craigielaw
Myreton Motor Museum
Drem
Tyninghame
Tyne Mouth
John Muir Birthplace
Dunbar
Belhaven
West Barns
Gosford Bay
Gosford House
Ballencrieff
The Chesters Fort
National Mus of Flight
East Fortune
Preston
East Linton
Spittal
Athelstaneford
Hopetoun Mon
69
Black Rocks
HMY Britannia
Leith
Edinburgh
Cockenzie and Port Seton
Seton Collegiate Church
Longniddry
Preston Mill & Phantassie Doocot
Broxburn
Barns Ness
East Barns
Skateraw
Hailes Castle
Traprain
Pitcox
Spott
Meikle Pinkerton
Musselburgh
Industrial Heritage Museum
Prestonpans
Huntington
Elvington
Portobello
Joppa
Fisherrow Sands
Duddingston
Palace of Holyroodhouse
National Mus of Scotland
Haddington
St Mary's Collegiate Ch
Luggate Burn
Stenton
Halls
Dry Burn
Thorntonloch
Innerwick
Tranent
Gladsmuir
Penston
Macmerry
Wallyford
Inveresk
Craigmillar Castle
Newcraighall
Morningside
Elphinstone
New Winton
New Town
Samuelston
East
Papple
Garvald
Cocklaw Hill
Dunglass Collegiate Church
Reed Pt
Cove
Cockburnspath
Oldhamstocks
Bolton
Whitecraig
Danderhall
Liberton
Gilmerton
Millerhill
Crossgatehall
Ormiston
Dunbar Common
Bransly Hill
Kaimes
Dalkeith Park
Dalkeith
Cousland
Pencaitland
Carfrae
Lothian
Glenkinchie Distillery
East Saltoun
West Saltoun
Gifford
Danskine
Ecclaw
Straiton
Butterfly Farm
Eskbank
Loanhead
Newbattle
Peastonbank
Bilston
Easthouses
Mayfield
Gilchriston
Quarryford
Longyester
Hills
Bothwell Water
Spartleton Edge
Heart Law
Southern Upland Way
Bonnyrigg and Lasswade
Polton
Nat. Mining Mus Scotland
Vogrie
Newtongrange
Pathhead
Peaston
Long Newton
Lammermuir
Nether Monynut
Monynut Water
Roslin
Rosslyn Chapel
Roslin Glen
Newlandrig
Crichton
Humbie
Stobshiel
Whiteadder Reservoir
Rosewell
Auchendinny
Arniston House
Arniston
Gorebridge
Crichton Castle
Fala Dam
Blegbie
Lammer Law
Hopes Reservoir
Meikle Says Law
Cranshaws
Cranshaws Hill
Abbey St. Bathans
Carrington
North Middleton
Fala
Ellemford
Edinshall Broch
Midlothian
Temple
Tynehead
Middleton
Fala Moor
Hunt Law
Dye Water
Lammermuir
Preston
Rosebery Reservoir
Falahill
Gilston
NT
Longformacus
Watch Water Reservoir
Hillhouse
Torfichen Hill
Heriot
Carcant
Kirktonhill
Hog's Law
Dirrington Great Law
Jim Clark Room
Gladhouse Reservoir
Oxton
Addinston
Clockmill
Duns
Moorfoot Hills
Lauder
Wedderlie
Cheeklaw
Gavinton
Choicelee
Collie Law
Westruther
Polwarth
Bogend
Dewar
Fountainhall
Blythe
Thornydykes
Whiteburn
Halliburton
Fogo
Blackhope Scar
Torquhan
Thirlestane Castle
Sisterpath
Fogorig
Thirlestane
Houndslow
Killochyett
Boon
Eden Water
Greenlaw
Blackadder Water
Stow
Whitehope Law
Nether Blainslie
Legerwood
Huntlywood
Green Knowe Tower
Leitholm
Glentress Forest
Tweed
Windlestraw Law
Bow
Gordon
Middlethird
Easter Howlaws
Lambden
Orange Lane
Peebles
Black Law
The John Buchan Story
Colquhar
Great Law
West Morriston
Falsidehill
Hume
Hume Castle
Eccles
Glentress
Southern Upland Way
Caitha Bowland
Fans
Tweed Valley
Tweeddale Museum & Gallery
Kirkburn
Cardrona
Robert Smail's Printing Works
Langshaw
Blackhaugh
Buckholm
Earlston
Mellerstain House
Stichill
Birgham
St Ronan's Well Interpretative Centre
Cardrona Forest
Walkerburn
Galashiels
Nenthorn
Ednam
Innerleithen
Traquair House
Clovenfords
Old Gala House
Smailholm
Eildon and Leaderfoot
Redpath
Brotherstone
Hadden
Forest
Traquair
Elibank and Traquair Forest
Caddonfoot
Park
Gattonside
Abbey
Kelso Mus
Kerchesters
Sprouston
Glen Ho
Kirkhouse
Yair Hill Forest
Abbotsford
Boleside
Darnick
Newstead
Smailholm Tower
Floors Castle
Kelso
Kelso Abbey
Windywalls
Melrose
Priorwood Gdns
Bemersyde
Clintmains
Maxwellheugh
Lempitlaw
Minch Moor
The Three Hills Roman Heritage Ctre
Dryburgh Abbey
Manorhill
Trows
Roxburgh Castle
Eildon Hills
Newtown St. Boswells
Mertoun Gdns
Lindean
St. Boswells
Blake Muir
Broadmeadows
Ovenscloss
Selkirk Glass
Whitlaw Mosses
Bowden
Rutherford
Roxburgh
Heiton
Blakelaw
Scottish
Yarrow
Selkirk
Maxton
Borders
Fastheugh Hill
Bowhill House & Country Park
Bowhill
Philiphaugh
Halliwell's House Museum
Sir Walter Scott's Courtroom
Midlem
Longnewton
Muirhouselaw
Frogden
Mountbenger
Yarrow Feus
Waterloo Monument
Teviot Smokery & Watergardens
Kalemouth
Nisbet
Crookhouse
Linton
Sundhope
Ettrickbridge
Aikwood Tower James Hogg Exhibition
Clerklands
Lilliesleaf
Belses
Eckford
Kirkhope
61
Forest
Bloomfield
Ancrum
Harestanes Countryside Visitor Centre
62
Crailing
Morebattle
Greenhouse
Chesters
Bonjedward
Cessford
Caver's Hill
Akermoor Loch
Woll
Ashkirk
Lanton
Crailinghall
Whitton
0 1 2 3 4 5 6 miles
0 1 2 3 4 5 6 7 8 9 10 km

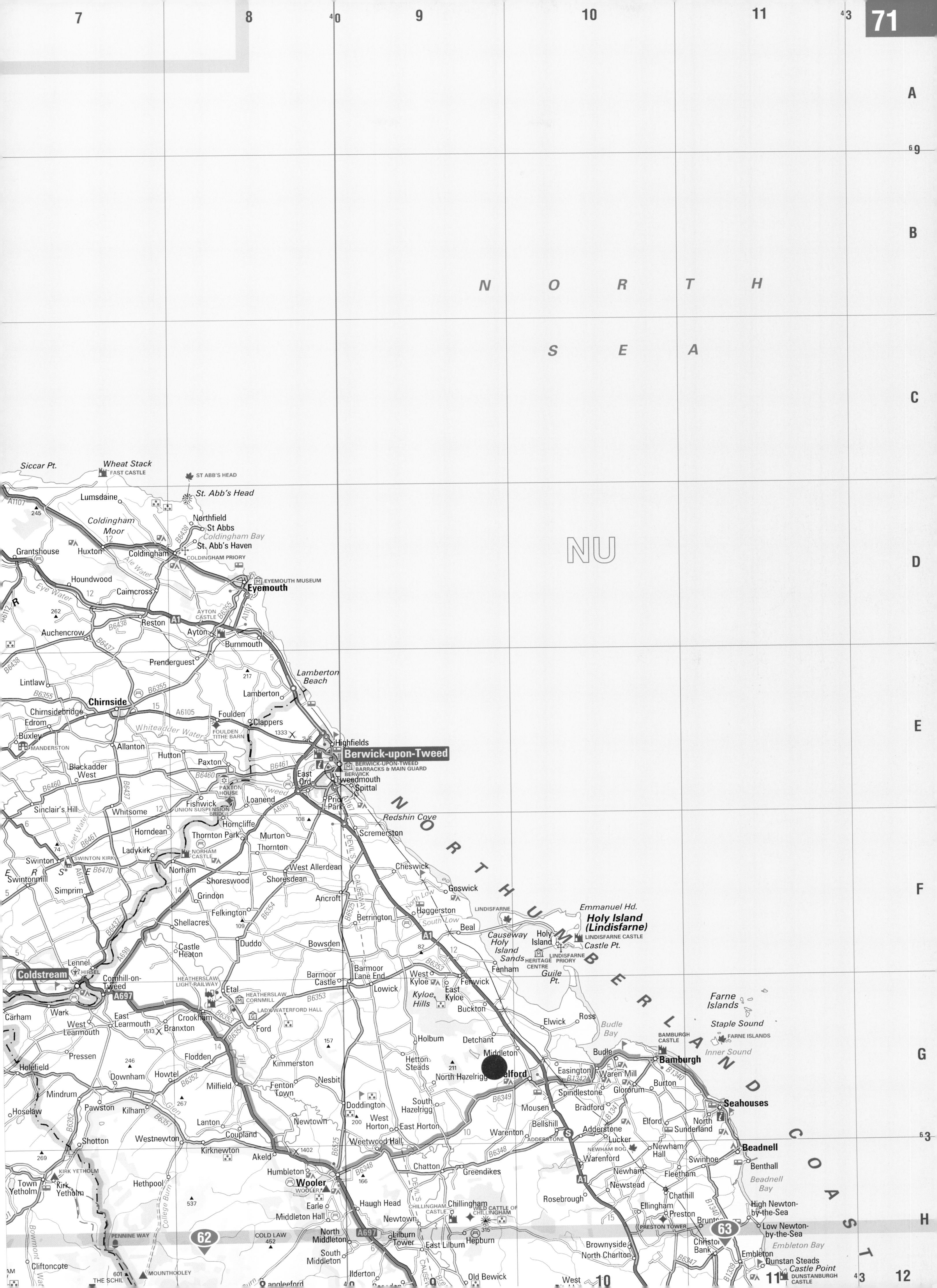

NORTH SEA
NU
NORTHUMBERLAND COAST
Siccar Pt.
Wheat Stack
FAST CASTLE
ST ABB'S HEAD
St. Abb's Head
Lumsdaine
Coldingham Moor
Northfield
St Abbs
Coldingham Bay
St. Abb's Haven
Grantshouse
Huxton
Coldingham
COLDINGHAM PRIORY
Houndwood
Cairncross
Eye Water
EYEMOUTH MUSEUM
Eyemouth
AYTON CASTLE
Reston
Ayton
Auchencrow
Burnmouth
Prendergues
Lamberton Beach
Lintlaw
Lamberton
Chirnside
Chirnsidebridge
Edrom
Foulden
Clappers
Whiteadder Water
FOULDEN TITHE BARN
Buxley
MANDERSTON
Allanton
Hutton
Highfields
Berwick-upon-Tweed
BERWICK-UPON-TWEED BARRACKS & MAIN GUARD
BERWICK
Paxton
Blackadder West
East Ord
Tweedmouth
Spittal
PAXTON HOUSE
Tweed
Sinclair's Hill
Whitsome
Fishwick
UNION SUSPENSION BRIDGE
Loanend
Prior Park
Redshin Cove
Horncliffe
Scremerston
Horndean
Thornton Park
Murton
Thornton
Ladykirk
NORHAM CASTLE
SWINTON KIRK
Swinton
Swintonmill
Norham
West Allerdean
Cheswick
Simprim
Shoreswood
Shoresdean
Goswick
Grindon
Ancroft
North Low
Haggerston
LINDISFARNE
Emmanuel Hd.
Holy Island (Lindisfarne)
LINDISFARNE CASTLE
Castle Pt.
Felkington
Berrington
South Low
Beal
Causeway
Holy Island Sands
Holy Island
HERITAGE CENTRE
LINDISFARNE PRIORY
Shellacres
Duddo
Bowsden
Castle Heaton
Fenham
Guile Pt.
Lennel
HIRSEL
Coldstream
Cornhill-on-Tweed
HEATHERSLAW LIGHT RAILWAY
Barmoor Lane End
Barmoor Castle
West Kyloe
Fenwick
Etal
HEATHERSLAW CORNMILL
Lowick
Kyloe Hills
East Kyloe
LADY WATERFORD HALL
Buckton
Farne Islands
Carham
Wark
East Learmouth
Crookham
West Learmouth
Branxton
Ford
Elwick
Ross
Budle Bay
Staple Sound
BAMBURGH CASTLE
FARNE ISLANDS
Holburn
Detchant
Pressen
Flodden
Kimmerston
Middleton
Budle
Bamburgh
Inner Sound
Holefield
Downham
Howtel
Hetton Steads
North Hazelrigg
Belford
Easington
Waren Mill
Burton
Mindrum
Milfield
Nesbit
Fenton Town
Spindlestone
Glororum
Seahouses
Hoselaw
Pawston
Kilham
Glen
Doddington
South Hazelrigg
Mousen
Bradford
Lanton
Newtown
West Horton
East Horton
Bellshill
Elford
North Sunderland
Shotton
Westnewton
Coupland
Weetwood Hall
Warenton
ADDERSTONE
Adderstone
Lucker
NEWHAM BOG
Warenford
Newham Hall
Swinhoe
Beadnell
Kirknewton
Akeld
KIRK YETHOLM
Town Yetholm
Kirk Yetholm
Hethpool
Humbleton
Wooler
WOOLER
Chatton
Greendikes
Newham
Fleetham
Benthall
Newstead
Beadnell Bay
College Burn
Earle
Haugh Head
CHILLINGHAM CASTLE
Chillingham
WILD CATTLE OF CHILLINGHAM
Rosebrough
Chathill
Ellingham
High Newton-by-the-Sea
Middleton Hall
Newtown
Preston
Brunton
Low Newton-by-the-Sea
PENNINE WAY
COLD LAW
North Middleton
Lilburn Tower
Hepburn
PRESTON TOWER
Christon Bank
Embleton Bay
South Middleton
East Lilburn
Brownyside
North Charlton
Embleton
Dunstan Steads
Castle Point
DUNSTANBURGH CASTLE
Clifton
MOUNTHOOLEY
THE SCHIL
Ilderton
Old Bewick
West
DEVIL'S CAUSEWAY
A1
A1107
A6112
A6105
A698
A697
A1167
B6438
B6437
B6355
B6460
B6461
B6470
B6354
B6525
B6353
B6349
B6348
B6352
B6351
B1342
B1341
B1340
B6347
B1339
62
63

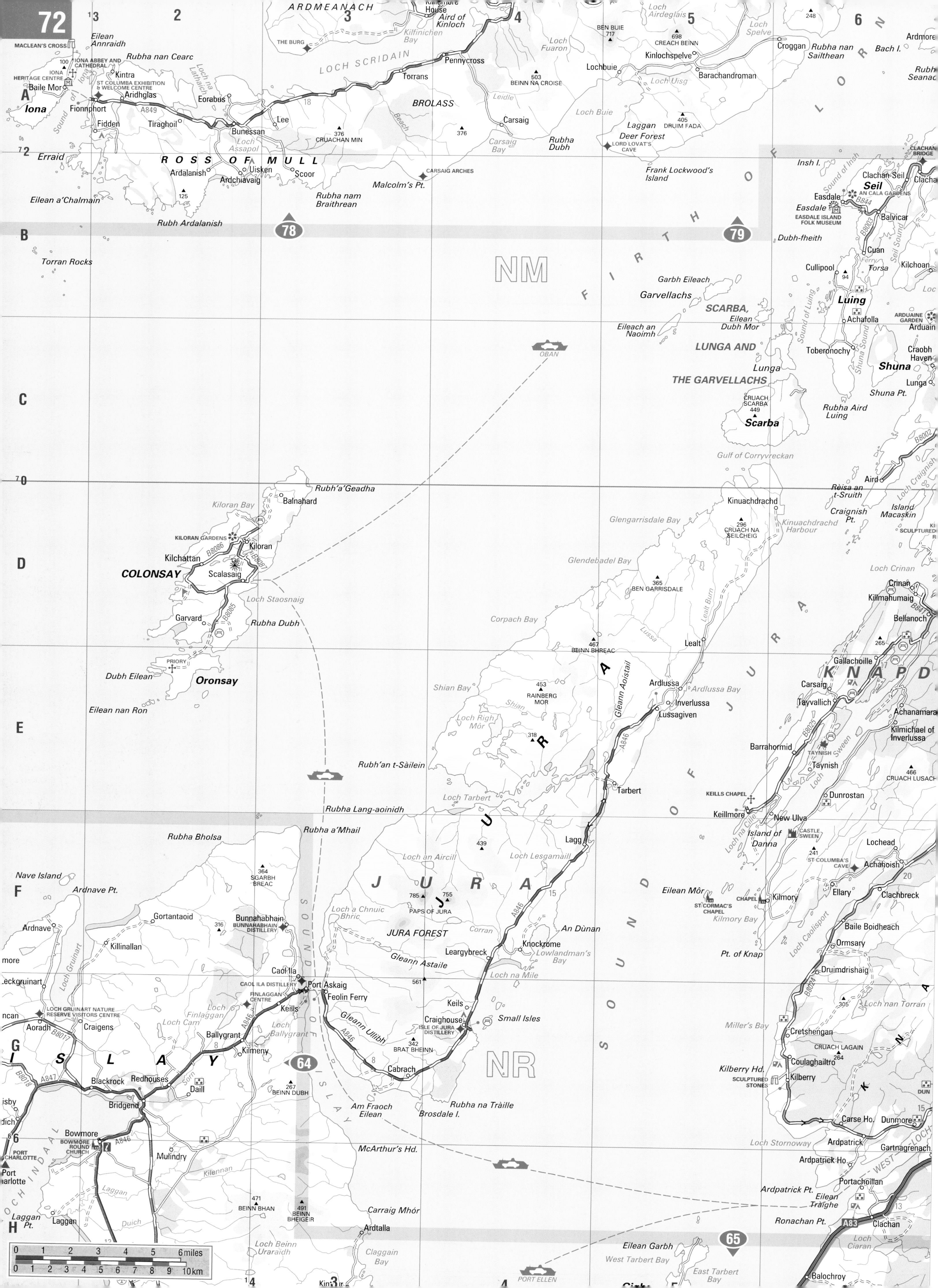
ARDMEANACH
THE BURG
Aird of Kinloch
LOCH SCRIDAIN
Pennycross
Torrans
BEN BUIE 717
CREACH BEINN
Kinlochspelve
Lochbuie
Barachandroman
Croggan
Rubha nan Sailthean
Bach I.
Ardmore
Iona
Baile Mor
Fionnphort
Fidden
Aridhglas
Kintra
IONA ABBEY AND CATHEDRAL
IONA HERITAGE CENTRE
MACLEAN'S CROSS
Rubha nan Cearc
Eilean Annraidh
ST COLUMBA EXHIBITION & WELCOME CENTRE
Eorabus
Tiraghoil
Bunessan
Lee
CRUACHAN MIN
BEINN NA CROISE
BROLASS
Carsaig
Carsaig Bay
Rubha Dubh
Loch Buie
Laggan Deer Forest
LORD LOVAT'S CAVE
DRUIM FADA
Erraid
ROSS OF MULL
Ardalanish
Uisken
Ardchiavaig
Scoor
CARSAIG ARCHES
Malcolm's Pt.
Rubha nam Braithrean
Eilean a'Chalmain
Rubh Ardalanish
Frank Lockwood's Island
Insh I.
Seil
Clachan-Seil
Easdale
AN CALA GARDENS
EASDALE ISLAND FOLK MUSEUM
Balvicar
Dubh-fheith
Cuan
Torran Rocks
NM
FIRTH OF LORN
Garbh Eileach
Garvellachs
SCARBA, LUNGA AND THE GARVELLACHS
Eileach an Naoimh
Eilean Dubh Mor
Lunga
Cullipool
Luing
Achafolla
Toberonochy
ARDUAINE GARDEN
Arduain
Craobh Haven
Shuna
Shuna Pt.
Rubha Aird Luing
OBAN
CRUACH SCARBA 449
Scarba
Gulf of Corryvreckan
Aird
Rèisa an t-Sruith
Craignish Pt.
Island Macaskin
Rubh'a'Geadha
Balnahard
Kiloran Bay
KILORAN GARDENS
Kiloran
Kilchattan
COLONSAY
Scalasaig
Loch Staosnaig
Garvard
Rubha Dubh
PRIORY
Dubh Eilean
Oronsay
Eilean nan Ron
Kinuachdrachd
Kinuachdrachd Harbour
Glengarrisdale Bay
CRUACH NA SEILCHEIG
Glendebadel Bay
BEN GARRISDALE
Corpach Bay
BEINN BHREAC
Lealt
Loch Crinan
Crinan
Kilmahumaig
Bellanoch
Gallachoille
KNAPDALE
Carsaig
Tayvallich
Achanamara
Kilmichael of Inverlussa
Barrahormid
TAYNISH
Taynish
CRUACH LUSACH
Shian Bay
RAINBERG MOR
Loch Righ Mòr
Ardlussa
Ardlussa Bay
Inverlussa
Lussagiven
Gleann Aoistail
JURA
SOUND OF JURA
Rubh'an t-Sàilein
Tarbert
Loch Tarbert
KEILLS CHAPEL
Keillmore
Dunrostan
New Ulva
CASTLE SWEEN
Island of Danna
Lochead
ST COLUMBA'S CAVE
Achahoish
Rubha Lang-aoinidh
Rubha a'Mhail
Rubha Bholsa
Lagg
Loch an Aircill
Loch Lesgamaill
SGARBH BREAC
Nave Island
Ardnave Pt.
Ardnave
Gortantaoid
Bunnahabhain
BUNNAHABHAIN DISTILLERY
Killinallan
PAPS OF JURA
Loch a Chnuic Bhric
JURA FOREST
Corran
An Dùnan
Knockrome
Lowlandman's Bay
Leargybreck
Gleann Astaile
Loch na Mile
Eilean Môr
ST CORMAC'S CHAPEL
Kilmory
Kilmory Bay
Ellary
Clachbreck
Baile Boidheach
Ormsary
Pt. of Knap
Druimdrishaig
Loch Caolisport
Caol Ila
CAOL ILA DISTILLERY
Port Askaig
FINLAGGAN CENTRE
Feolin Ferry
Keills
Loch Finlaggan
Loch Gruinart
LOCH GRUINART NATURE RESERVE VISITORS CENTRE
Aoradh
Craigens
Loch Cam
Ballygrant
Loch Ballygrant
Kilmeny
Gleann Ullibh
Craighouse
ISLE OF JURA DISTILLERY
Small Isles
BRAT BHEINN
Cabrach
Miller's Bay
Cretshengan
CRUACH LAGAIN
Coulaghailtro
Loch nan Torran
ISLAY
Blackrock
Redhouses
Daill
BEINN DUBH
Bridgend
Sound of Islay
Am Fraoch Eilean
Rubha na Tràille
Brosdale I.
NR
Kilberry Hd.
SCULPTURED STONES
Kilberry
Carse Ho.
Dunmore
Bowmore
BOWMORE ROUND CHURCH
PORT CHARLOTTE
Port Charlotte
Mulindry
McArthur's Hd.
Loch Stornoway
Ardpatrick
Gartnagrenach
Ardpatrick Ho.
Portachoillan
Ardpatrick Pt.
Eilean Traighe
Ronachan Pt.
Clachan
Loch Indaal
Laggan Pt.
Laggan
BEINN BHAN
BEINN BHEIGEIR
Carraig Mhór
Ardtalla
Loch Beinn Uraraidh
Claggain Bay
Eilean Garbh
West Tarbert Bay
East Tarbert Bay
PORT ELLEN
Loch Ciaran
Balochroy
78
79
64
65
0 1 2 3 4 5 6 miles
0 1 2 3 4 5 6 7 8 9 10 km

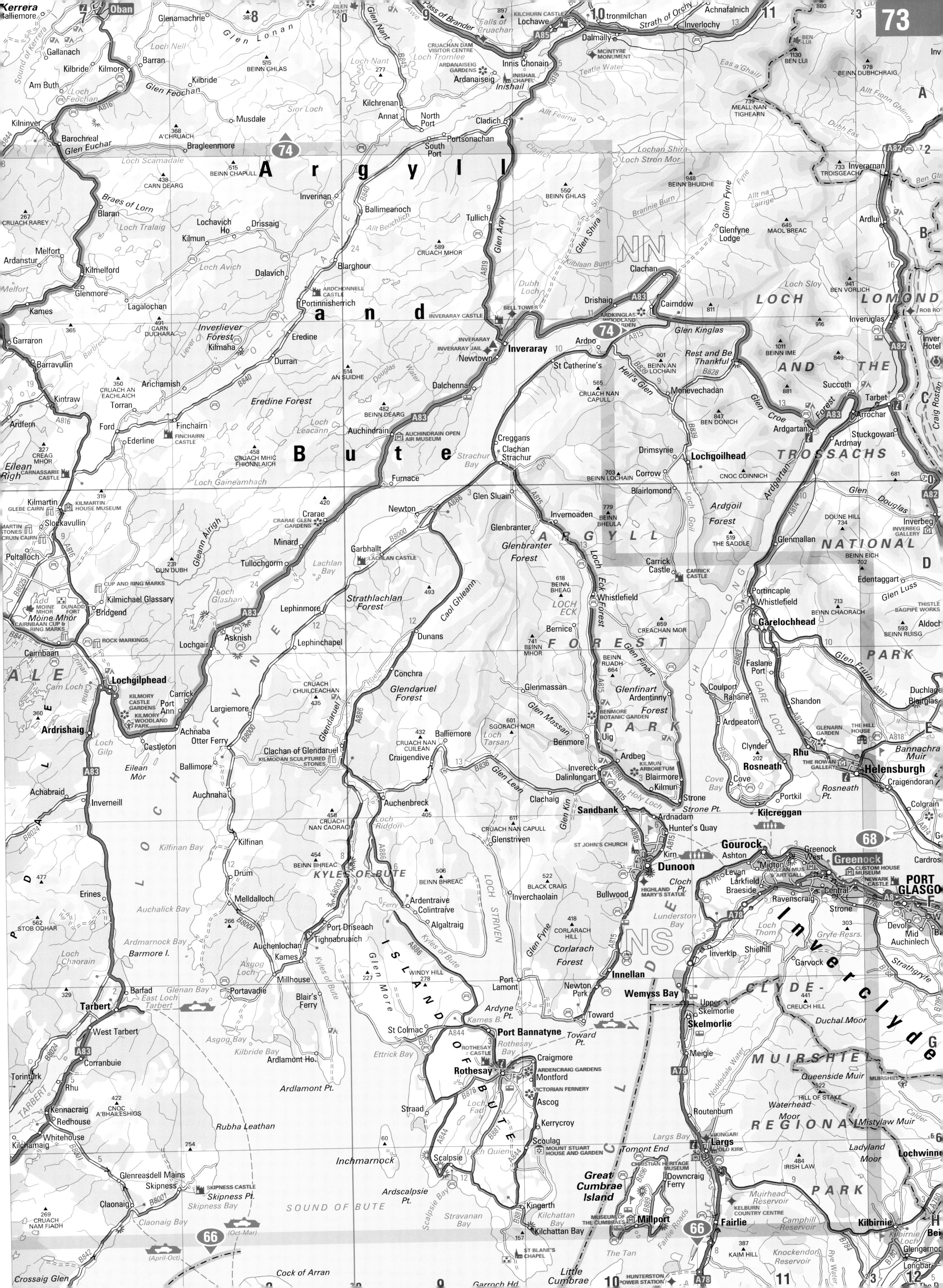
Kerrera
Oban
Glenamachrie
Glen Lonan
Loch Nell
Gallanach
Barran
Kilbride
Kilmore
Am Buth
Loch Feochan
Glen Feochan
515 BEINN GHLAS
Kilninver
Musdale
368 A'CHRUACH
Barochreal
Glen Euchar
Bragleenmore
Loch Scamadale
438 CARN DEARG
515 BEINN CHAPULL
Argyll
and
Bute
Braes of Lorn
Blaran
267 CRUACH RAREY
Loch Tralaig
Lochavich Ho
Drissaig
Kilmun
Loch Avich
Melfort
Ardanstur
Kilmelford
Glenmore
Lagalochan
Kames
365
491 CARN DUCHARA
Inverliever Forest
Kilmaha
Garraron
Barravullin
350 CRUACH AN EACHLAICH
Torran
Arichamish
Kintraw
Ardfern
Ford
Ederline
Finchairn
FINCHAIRN CASTLE
227 CREAG MHOR
Eilean Righ
CARNASSARIE CASTLE
458 CRUACH MHIC FHIONNLAICH
Loch Gaineamhach
Kilmartin
KILMARTIN HOUSE MUSEUM
GLEBE CAIRN
Slockavullin
319
Poltalloch
231 DUN DUBH
Gleann Airigh
CUP AND RING MARKS
Kilmichael Glassary
Bridgend
Moine Mhor
DUNADD FORT
ROCK MARKINGS
Cairnbaan
Crinan Canal
Lochgilphead
Cam Loch
KILMORY CASTLE GARDENS
KILMORY WOODLAND PARK
Carrick
Port Ann
Ardrishaig
360
Achnaba
Castleton
Loch Gilp
Eilean Mòr
Achabraid
Inverneill
477
Erines
562 STOB ODHAR
Loch Chaorain
Barmore I.
Barfad
East Loch Tarbert
Tarbert
West Tarbert
Corranbuie
Torinturk
Rhu
422 CNOC A'BHAILESHIOS
Kennacraig
Redhouse
Whitehouse
Kilchamaig
Glenreasdell Mains
Skipness
SKIPNESS CASTLE
Skipness Pt.
Skipness Bay
Claonaig
Claonaig Bay
269 CRUACH NAM FIADH
Crossaig Glen
Cock of Arran
Glen Nant
Pass of Brander
Falls of Cruachan
897
KILCHURN CASTLE
Lochawe
Dalmally
Tyndrum
Strath of Orchy
Achnafalnich
Inverlochy
CRUACHAN DAM VISITOR CENTRE
Loch Tromlee
Loch Nant
277
ARDANAISEIG GARDENS
Ardanaiseig
Innis Chonain
INISHAIL CHAPEL
Inishail
MCINTYRE MONUMENT
Teatle Water
Sior Loch
Kilchrenan
Annat
North Port
Cladich
Portsonachan
South Port
Inverinan
Ballimeanoch
Allt Beochlich
Tullich
Glen Aray
589 CRUACH MHOR
Blarghour
Dalavich
ARDCHONNELL CASTLE
Portinnisherrich
Eredine
Durran
514 AN SUIDHE
Douglas Water
Eredine Forest
482 BEINN DEARG
Loch Leacann
Auchindrain
AUCHINDRAIN OPEN AIR MUSEUM
Dalchenna
INVERARAY CASTLE
BELL TOWER
INVERARAY JAIL
Inveraray
Newtown
Dubh Loch
Furnace
Strachur Bay
420
Crarae
CRARAE GLEN GARDENS
Minard
Tullochgorm
Lachlan Bay
Garbhallt
LACHLAN CASTLE
Strathlachlan Forest
493
Caol Ghleann
Lephinmore
Asknish
Lochgair
Lephinchapel
Dunans
Conchra
Glendaruel Forest
CRUACH CHUILCEACHAN
Largiemore
Otter Ferry
Clachan of Glendaruel
KILMODAN SCULPTURED STONES
432 CRUACH NAN CUILEAN
Balliemore
Craigendive
Ballimore
Auchnaha
Auchenbreck
458 CRUACH NAN CAORACH
Loch Riddon
Kilfinan
Kilfinan Bay
Drum
454 BEINN BHREAC
KYLES OF BUTE
506 BEINN BHREAC
Melldalloch
Auchalick Bay
Ardentraive
Colintraive
Port Driseach
Tighnabruaich
Algaltraig
Ardmarnock Bay
Auchenlochan
Kames
Asgog Loch
Millhouse
Portavadie
Glenan Bay
Blair's Ferry
WINDY HILL
ISLAND OF BUTE
Glen More
Asgog Bay
Kilbride Bay
Ardlamont Ho.
Ardlamont Pt.
St Colmac
Ettrick Bay
Kames B.
Ardyne Pt.
Port Bannatyne
ROTHESAY CASTLE
Rothesay Bay
Rothesay
Craigmore
ARDENCRAIG GARDENS
Montford
VICTORIAN FERNERY
Ascog
Straad
Loch Fad
Kerrycroy
Scoulag
MOUNT STUART HOUSE AND GARDEN
Loch Quien
Scalpsie
Rubha Leathan
Inchmarnock
Ardscalpsie Pt.
Scalpsie Bay
SOUND OF BUTE
Stravanan Bay
Kingarth
Kilchattan Bay
ST BLANE'S CHAPEL
Garroch Hd
948 BEINN BHUIDHE
Lochan Shira
Loch Stron Mor
Glen Fyne
Brannie Burn
550 BEINN GHLAS
Glen Shira
Kilblaan Burn
Glenfyne Lodge
Clachan
Drishaig
ARDKINGLAS WOODLAND GARDEN
Cairndow
Ardno
Glen Kinglas
St Catherine's
901 BEINN AN LOCHAIN
Rest and Be Thankful
Hell's Glen
565 CRUACH NAN CAPULL
Monevechadan
Glen Croe
847 BEN DONICH
Creggans
Clachan Strachur
Drimsynie
Lochgoilhead
703 BEINN LOCHAIN
Corrow
Blairlomond
Glen Sluain
Newton
Invernoaden
779 BEINN BHEULA
Glenbranter
Glenbranter Forest
Ardgoil Forest
519 THE SADDLE
Carrick Castle
CARRICK CASTLE
618 BEINN BHEAG
Loch Eck
Whistlefield
Bernice
741 BEINN MHOR
FOREST
BEINN RUADH 664
Glen Finart
Glenmassan
Glenfinart
Ardentinny
BENMORE BOTANIC GARDEN
601 SGORACH MOR
Glen Massan
Loch Tarsan
Benmore
Uig
PARK
Ardbeg
KILMUN ARBORETUM
Blairmore
Kilmun
Inverecket
Dalinlongart
Glen Lean
Clachaig
Glen Kin
Sandbank
Holy Loch
Strone
Strone Pt.
Ardnadam
Hunter's Quay
611 CRUACH NAN CAPULL
Glenstriven
ST JOHN'S CHURCH
Kirn
Dunoon
Cloch Pt.
HIGHLAND MARY'S STATUE
522 BLACK CRAIG
Loch Striven
Inverchaolain
Bullwood
418 CORLARACH HILL
Corlarach Forest
Glen Fyne
Lunderston Bay
Innellan
Port Lamont
Newton Park
Wemyss Bay
Toward
Toward Pt.
Great Cumbrae Island
Tomont End
CHRISTIAN HERITAGE MUSEUM
Downcraig Ferry
MUSEUM OF THE CUMBRAES
Millport
Fairlie Roads
Little Cumbrae
HUNTERSTON POWER STATION
The Tan
880
BEN LUI
1130 BEN LUI
978 BEINN DUBHCHRAIG
Eas a'Ghaill
739 MEALL NAN TIGHEARN
Allt Fionn Ghlinne
Dubh Eas
733 TROISGEACH
Inverarnan
Ben Glas
Allt na Lairige
645 MAOL BREAC
Ardlui
Loch Sloy
941 BEN VORLICH
LOCH LOMOND
ROB ROY
916
Inveruglas
1011 BEINN IME
849
Inver Hotel
AND THE
881
Succoth
Tarbet
Arrochar
Ardgartan
Forest
Craig Rostan
Stuckgowan
Ardmay
TROSSACHS
CNOC COINNICH
681
Glen Douglas
DOUNE HILL 734
INVERBEG GALLERY
Inverbeg
Glenmallan
NATIONAL
BEINN EICH 702
Edentaggart
Glen Luss
Portincaple
Whistlefield
713 BEINN CHAORACH
THISTLE BAGPIPE WORKS
Aldochlay
Garelochhead
593 BEINN RUISG
Glen Fruin
PARK
Faslane Port
Gare Loch
Shandon
Coulport
Rahane
Duchlage
Blairglas
Ardpeaton
GLENARN GARDEN
THE HILL HOUSE
Clynder
202
Rosneath
Rhu
THE ROWAN GALLERY
Bannachra Muir
Helensburgh
Cove Bay
Cove
Portkil
Craigendoran
Rosneath Pt.
Kilcreggan
Colgrain
Gourock
Ashton
Greenock West
Greenock
McLEAN MUS & ART GALL
CUSTOM HOUSE MUSEUM
NEWARK CASTLE
PORT GLASGOW
Cardross
Levan
Larkfield
Braeside
Central
Ravenscraig
Strone
Inverclyde
Loch Thom
Gryfe Resrs.
303
Devol
Mid Auchinlech
Inverkip
Shielhill
Garvock
Strathgryfe
CLYDE-
441 CREUCH HILL
Upper Skelmorlie
Skelmorlie
Dunrod Moor
Meigle
MUIRSHIEL
Queenside Muir
522 HILL OF STAKE
Noddsdale Water
Waterhead Moor
Routenburn
REGIONAL
Mistylaw Muir
Largs Bay
VIKINGAR!
Largs
OLD KIRK
Ladyland Moor
Lochwinnoch
484 IRISH LAW
PARK
Muirhead Reservoir
KELBURN COUNTRY CENTRE
Camphill Reservoir
Fairlie
Kilbirnie
387 KAIM HILL
Knockendon Reservoir
Rye Water
Glengarnock
Longbar
Kilbirnie Loch

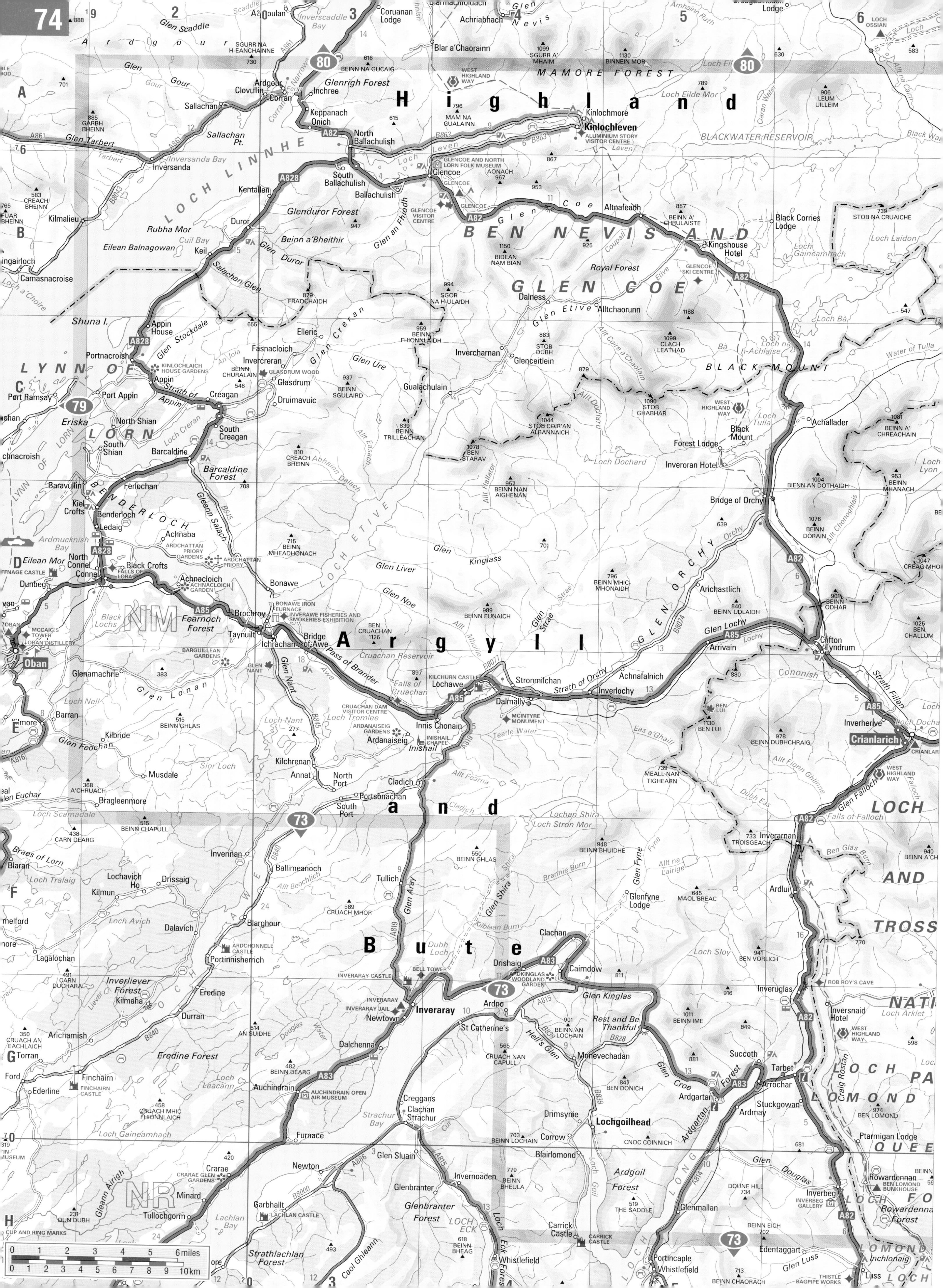

Highland
Argyll and Bute
BEN NEVIS AND GLEN COE
MAMORE FOREST
LOCH LINNHE
LYNN OF LORN
LORN
BENDERLOCH
LOCH ETIVE
BLACK MOUNT
GLEN ORCHY
LOCH LOMOND AND THE TROSSACHS NATIONAL PARK
Ardgour
Glen Scaddle
Inverscaddle Bay
Coruanan Lodge
Achriabhach
Glen Nevis
Blar a'Chaorainn
Kinlochmore
Kinlochleven
ALUMINIUM STORY VISITOR CENTRE
BLACKWATER RESERVOIR
Clovullin
Corran
Inchree
Glenrigh Forest
Keppanach
Onich
North Ballachulish
South Ballachulish
Ballachulish
Glencoe
GLENCOE AND NORTH LORN FOLK MUSEUM
GLENCOE VISITOR CENTRE
Glen Tarbert
Sallachan
Sallachan Pt.
Inversanda Bay
Inversanda
Kentallen
Glenduror Forest
Glen Duror
Duror
Kilmalieu
Rubha Mor
Cuil Bay
Keil
Eilean Balnagowan
Camasnacroise
Salachan Glen
Shuna I.
Appin House
Glen Stockdale
Portnacroish
KINLOCHLAICH HOUSE GARDENS
Appin
Port Appin
Port Ramsay
Eriska
Strath of Appin
Creagan
North Shian
South Shian
South Creagan
Loch Creran
Barcaldine
Barcaldine Forest
Ferlochan
Baravullin
Kiel Crofts
Benderloch
Ledaig
Ardmucknish Bay
Achnaba
ARDCHATTAN PRIORY GARDENS
ARDCHATTAN PRIORY
Eilean Mor
North Connel
Connel
Black Crofts
FALLS OF LORA
Dunbeg
Achnacloich
ACHNACLOICH GARDEN
Bonawe
BONAWE IRON FURNACE
INVERAWE FISHERIES AND SMOKERIES EXHIBITION
Brochroy
Fearnoch Forest
Taynuilt
Ichrachan
Bridge of Awe
Pass of Brander
Cruachan Reservoir
Falls of Cruachan
KILCHURN CASTLE
Lochawe
Dalmally
Stronmilchan
Strath of Orchy
Inverlochy
Achnafalnich
MCINTYRE MONUMENT
Teatle Water
Oban
OBAN DISTILLERY
MCCAIG'S TOWER
Glenamachrie
BARGUILLEAN GARDENS
GLEN NANT
Glen Nant
Glen Lonan
Loch Nell
Barran
Kilbride
Glen Feochan
CRUACHAN DAM VISITOR CENTRE
Loch Tromlee
ARDANAISEIG GARDENS
Ardanaiseig
Innis Chonain
Inishail
INISHAIL CHAPEL
Loch Nant
Kilchrenan
Annat
North Port
Cladich
Portsonachan
South Port
Sior Loch
Musdale
Bragleenmore
Loch Scamadale
BEINN CHAPULL
CARN DEARG
Braes of Lorn
Loch Tralaig
Lochavich Ho
Drissaig
Kilmun
Inverinan
Ballimeanoch
Tullich
Glen Aray
Glen Shira
Loch Avich
Dalavich
Blarghour
CRUACH MHOR
Lagalochan
ARDCHONNELL CASTLE
Portinnisherrich
Inverliever Forest
Kilmaha
Eredine
Durran
Arichamish
Eredine Forest
Torran
Ford
Finchairn
FINCHAIRN CASTLE
Ederline
Loch Leacann
Auchindrain
AUCHINDRAIN OPEN AIR MUSEUM
Loch Gaineamhach
Furnace
Crarae
CRARAE GLEN GARDENS
Minard
Tullochgorm
Gleann Airigh
CUP AND RING MARKS
Dubh Loch
INVERARAY CASTLE
BELL TOWER
INVERARAY JAIL
Inveraray
Newtown
Dalchenna
Creggans
Clachan Strachur
Strachur Bay
Glen Sluain
Newton
Invernoaden
Glenbranter
Glenbranter Forest
Garbhallt
LACHLAN CASTLE
Lachlan Bay
Strathlachlan Forest
Caol Ghleann
LOCH ECK
Whistlefield
Clachan
Drishaig
ARDKINGLAS WOODLAND GARDEN
Cairndow
Ardno
St Catherine's
Glen Kinglas
Rest and Be Thankful
Hell's Glen
Monevechadan
Glen Croe
Ardgartan
Ardgartan Forest
Arrochar
Tarbet
Succoth
Stuckgowan
Ardmay
Drimsynie
Lochgoilhead
Corrow
Blairlomond
Loch Goil
Ardgoil Forest
CNOC COINNICH
THE SADDLE
Glenmallan
Carrick Castle
CARRICK CASTLE
Loch Long
Portincaple
Whistlefield
Glen Douglas
DOUNE HILL
Inverbeg
INVERBEG GALLERY
Edentaggart
Glen Luss
Luss
Inchlonaig
Rowardennan
BEN LOMOND BUNKHOUSE
Rowardennan Forest
Ptarmigan Lodge
BEN LOMOND
Craig Rostan
Inversnaid Hotel
Loch Arklet
ROB ROY'S CAVE
Inveruglas
Loch Sloy
BEN VORLICH
Ardlui
Inverarnan
Ben Glas Burn
Falls of Falloch
Glen Falloch
Crianlarich
WEST HIGHLAND WAY
Inverherive
Strath Fillan
Tyndrum
Clifton
Cononish
BEN LUI
BEINN DUBHCHRAIG
MEALL NAN TIGHEARN
TROISGEACH
Eas a' Ghaill
Glen Fyne
Glenfyne Lodge
MAOL BREAC
Lochan Shira
Loch Stron Mor
BEINN BHUIDHE
Brannie Burn
Kilblaan Burn
BEINN IME
Glen Lochy
Arrivain
Arichastlich
BEINN UDLAIDH
BEINN ODHAR
BEN CHALLUM
Bridge of Orchy
BEINN DORAIN
BIENN AN DOTHAIDH
BEINN MHANACH
Achallader
Loch Tulla
Black Mount
Forest Lodge
Inveroran Hotel
Loch Dochard
STOB GHABHAR
STOB COIR'AN ALBANNAICH
BEN STARAV
BEINN NAN AIGHENAN
Glen Kinglass
Glen Liver
Glen Noe
BEINN EUNAICH
Glen Strae
BEN CRUACHAN
BEINN MHIC MHONAIDH
Glen Etive
Inverchaman
Glenceitlein
Gualachulain
Dalness
Alltchaorunn
STOB DUBH
CLACH LEATHAD
Royal Forest
GLENCOE SKI CENTRE
Kingshouse Hotel
Black Corries Lodge
Altnafeadh
BEINN A' CHRULAISTE
BIDEAN NAM BIAN
SGOR NA H-ULAIDH
BEINN FHIONNLAIDH
Glen Creran
Glen Ure
Elleric
Fasnacloich
Invercreran
BEINN CHURALAIN
GLASDRUM WOOD
Glasdrum
Druimavuic
BEINN SGULAIRD
BEINN TRILLEACHAN
CREACH BHEINN
BEINN MHEADHONACH
Glen an Fhiodh
Beinn a'Bheithir
FRAOCHAIDH
AONACH
MAM NA GUALAINN
BINNEIN MOR
SGURR A' MHAIM
SGURR NA H-EANCHAINNE
BEINN NA GUCAIG
Loch Eilde Mor
LEUM UILLEIM
LOCH OSSIAN
STOB NA CRUAICHE
Loch Laidon
Loch Gaineamhach
Loch Bà
Water of Tulla
BEINN A' CHREACHAIN
CREAG MHOR
GARBH BHEINN
CREACH BHEINN
AN SUIDHE
CRUACH AN EACHLAICH
BEINN DEARG
CRUACH MHIC FHIONNLAIDH
BEINN LOCHAIN
BEINN BHEULA
BEINN BHEAG
BEINN EICH
BEINN CHAORACH
BEN DONICH
CRUACH NAN CAPULL
BEINN AN LOCHAIN
BEINN GHLAS
A'CHRUACH
BEINN CHAPULL
CARN DUCHARA
DUN DUBH
80
79
73
NM
NR
0 1 2 3 4 5 6 miles
0 1 2 3 4 5 6 7 8 9 10 km

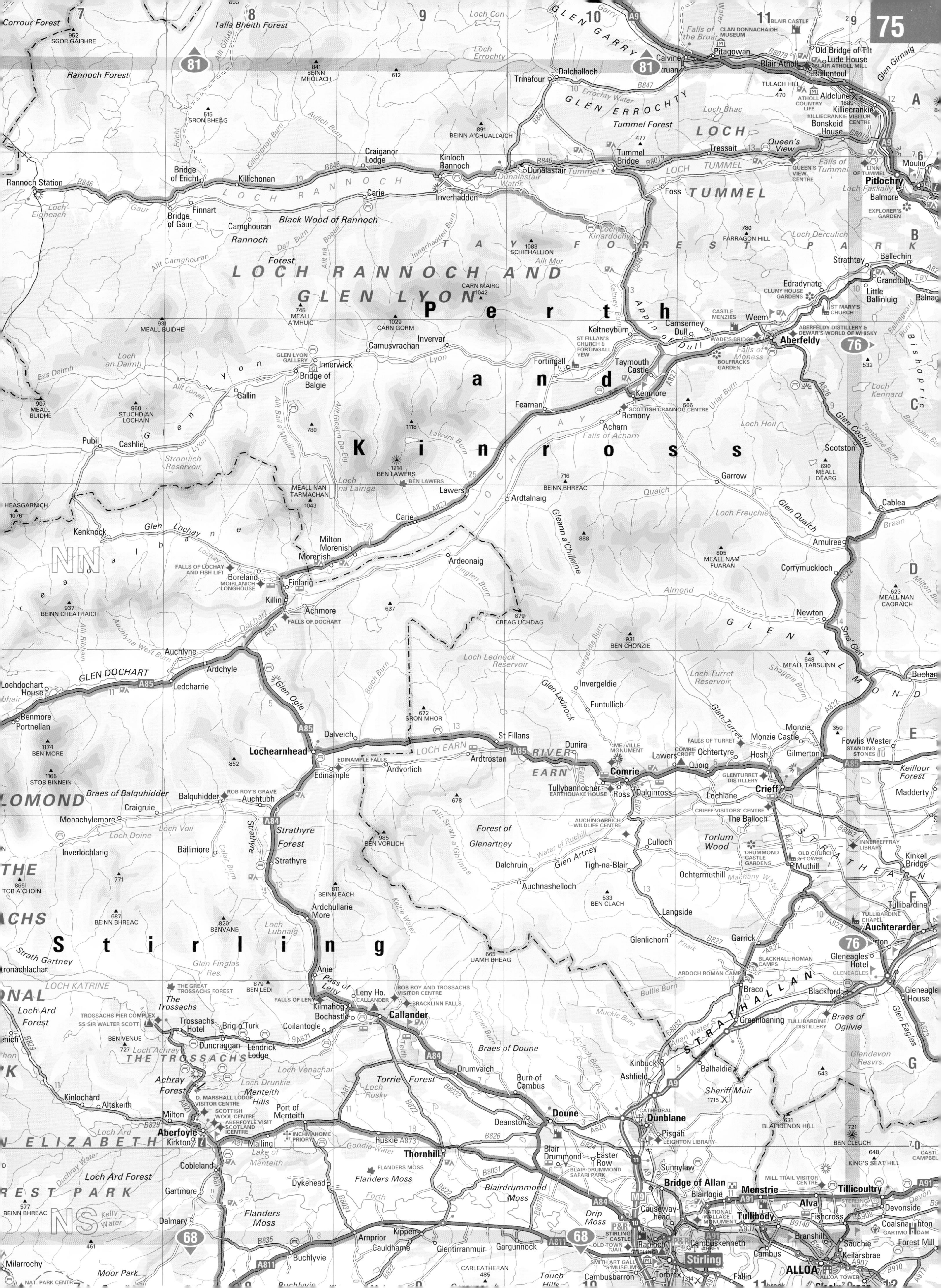

Corrour Forest
952 SGOR GAIBHRE
Talla Bheith Forest
Loch Con
GLEN GARRY
Falls of the Bruar
CLAN DONNACHAIDH MUSEUM
BLAIR CASTLE
Old Bridge of Tilt
Lude House
Rannoch Forest
841 BEINN MHOLACH
612
Loch Errochty
Calvine
Pitagowan
Blair Atholl
BLAIR ATHOLL MILL
Ballentoul
Glen Girnaig
Trinafour
Dalchalloch
Errochty Water
GLEN ERROCHTY
Struan
TULACH HILL 470
ATHOLL COUNTRY LIFE
Aldclune
Killiecrankie
KILLIECRANKIE VISITOR CENTRE
Bonskeid House
515 SRON BHEAG
Aulich Burn
891 BEINN A'CHUALLAICH
Tummel Forest
Loch Bhac
LOCH
477
Queen's View
Tressait
Craiganor Lodge
Kinloch Rannoch
Tummel Bridge
Dunalastair
Dunalastair Water
QUEEN'S VIEW CENTRE
Falls of Tummel
LINN OF TUMMEL
Moulin
Pitlochry
Rannoch Station
Bridge of Ericht
Killichonan
LOCH RANNOCH
LOCH TUMMEL
Foss
TUMMEL
Loch Faskally
Balmore
EXPLORER'S GARDEN
Loch Eigheach
Gaur
Bridge of Gaur
Finnart
Carie
Inverhadden
Camghouran
Black Wood of Rannoch
Rannoch
Forest
Loch Kinardochy
780 FARRAGON HILL
Loch Derculich
TAY FOREST PARK
1083 SCHIEHALLION
Allt Mor
Strathtay
Ballechin
Grandtully
Edradynate
CLUNY HOUSE GARDENS
Little Ballinluig
Balnag
ST MARY'S CHURCH
LOCH RANNOCH AND GLEN LYON
CARN MAIRG 1042
745 MEALL A'MHUIC
1029 CARN GORM
931 MEALL BUIDHE
Perth and Kinross
CASTLE MENZIES
Camserney
Dull
Weem
Keltneyburn
Appin of Dull
WADE'S BRIDGE
ABERFELDY DISTILLERY & DEWAR'S WORLD OF WHISKY
Aberfeldy
Falls of Moness
BOLFRACKS GARDEN
Bishopric
532
Camusvrachan
Invervar
ST FILLAN'S CHURCH & FORTINGALL YEW
Fortingall
Taymouth Castle
GLEN LYON GALLERY
Innerwick
Bridge of Balgie
Loch an Daimh
Eas Daimh
907 MEALL BUIDHE
960 STUCHD AN LOCHAIN
Gallin
Kenmore
Fearnan
SCOTTISH CRANNOG CENTRE
566
Remony
Acharn
Falls of Acharn
Loch Kennard
Glen Cochill
Loch Hoil
780
1118
Lawers Burn
Pubil
Cashlie
Stronuich Reservoir
1214 BEN LAWERS
Scotston
Garrow
690 MEALL DEARG
716 BEINN BHREAC
Quaich
HEASGARNICH 1076
MEALL NAN TARMACHAN 1043
Loch na Lairige
Lawers
Ardtalnaig
LOCH TAY
Cablea
Glen Quaich
Loch Freuchie
Braan
Kenknock
Glen Lochay
Carie
888
Gleann a' Chilleine
Milton Morenish
Morenish
Amulree
805 MEALL NAM FUARAN
Corrymuckloch
NN
FALLS OF LOCHAY AND FISH LIFT
Boreland
MOIRLANICH LONGHOUSE
Finlarig
Killin
Ardeonaig
Finglen Burn
Almond
623 MEALL NAN CAORAICH
937 BEINN CHEATHAICH
Achmore
637
879 CREAG UCHDAG
FALLS OF DOCHART
Newton
Sma' Glen
GLEN ALMOND
Auchlyne
931 BEN CHONZIE
Loch Lednock Reservoir
648 MEALL TARSUINN
Lochdochart House
GLEN DOCHART
Ardchyle
Ledcharrie
Glen Ogle
Invergeldie
Loch Turret Reservoir
Buchan
Benmore
Portnellan
Funtullich
Glen Lednock
672 SRON MHOR
1174 BEN MORE
Dalveich
St Fillans
Dunira
MELVILLE MONUMENT
FALLS OF TURRET
Monzie Castle
Monzie
Fowlis Wester
STANDING STONES
Lochearnhead
LOCH EARN
RIVER EARN
Ardtrostan
COMRIE CROFT
Lawers
Ochtertyre
Quoig
Hosh
Gilmerton
Keillour Forest
1165 STOB BINNEIN
EDINAMPLE FALLS
Edinample
Ardvorlich
Comrie
GLENTURRET DISTILLERY
Crieff
Madderty
Braes of Balquhidder
ROB ROY'S GRAVE
Balquhidder
Auchtubh
Tullybannocher
EARTHQUAKE HOUSE
Ross
Dalginross
Lochlane
852
678
LOMOND
Craigruie
CRIEFF VISITORS' CENTRE
The Balloch
Monachylemore
Loch Voil
AUCHINGARRICH WILDLIFE CENTRE
Forest of Glenartney
Loch Doine
Strathyre Forest
985 BEN VORLICH
Torlum Wood
INNERPEFFRAY LIBRARY
Inverlochlarig
Ballimore
Strathyre
Water of Ruchill
Culloch
DRUMMOND CASTLE GARDENS
OLD CHURCH & TOWER
Muthill
Kinkell Bridge
771
Glen Artney
Dalchruin
Tigh-na-Blair
Ochtermuthill
Machany Water
STRATHEARN
865 TOB A'CHOIN
811 BEINN EACH
Auchnashelloch
533 BEN CLACH
Tullibardine
687 BEINN BHREAC
Ardchullarie More
Langside
TULLIBARDINE CHAPEL
Auchterarder
820 BENVANE
Loch Lubnaig
Keltie Water
Glenlichorn
Garrick
Stirling
Strath Gartney
Tronachlachar
665 UAMH BHEAG
Knaik
Gleneagles Hotel
BLACKHALL ROMAN CAMPS
GLENEAGLES
Glen Finglas Res.
ARDOCH ROMAN CAMP
LOCH KATRINE
THE GREAT TROSSACHS FOREST
879 BEN LEDI
Anie
Pass of Leny
Braco
STRATHALLAN
Gleneagle House
Loch Ard Forest
The Trossachs
FALLS OF LENY
Leny Ho.
CALLANDER
ROB ROY AND TROSSACHS VISITOR CENTRE
BRACKLINN FALLS
Bullie Burn
Blackford
TROSSACHS PIER COMPLEX
SS SIR WALTER SCOTT
Trossachs Hotel
Brig o'Turk
Kilmahog
Bochastle
Callander
Mucklie Burn
Greenloaning
TULLIBARDINE DISTILLERY
Braes of Ogilvie
BEN VENUE 727
Loch Achray
Duncraggan
Lendrick Lodge
Coilantogle
Braes of Doune
Allan Water
Glen Eagles
THE TROSSACHS
Loch Venachar
Drumvaich
Burn of Cambus
Kinbuck
Balhaldie
Glendevon Resvrs.
Achray Forest
Loch Drunkie
Torrie Forest
Loch Rusky
Ashfield
543
Menteith Hills
Sheriff Muir
1715
Kinlochard
Altskeith
D. MARSHALL LODGE VISITOR CENTRE
SCOTTISH WOOL CENTRE
ABERFOYLE VISIT SCOTLAND iCENTRE
Port of Menteith
Milton
Aberfoyle
Loch Ard
Doune
CATHEDRAL
Dunblane
Deanston
631 BLAIRDENON HILL
Kirkton
ELIZABETH
INCHMAHOME PRIORY
Malling
Lake of Menteith
Goodie Water
Ruskie
Pisgah
LEIGHTON LIBRARY
721 BEN CLEUCH
Thornhill
Blair Drummond
Easter Row
BLAIR DRUMMOND SAFARI PARK
648 KING'S SEAT HILL
CASTLE CAMPBELL
Cobleland
Duchray Water
FLANDERS MOSS
Flanders Moss
Sunnylaw
Loch Ard Forest
FOREST PARK
Dykehead
Bridge of Allan
Blairlogie
MILL TRAIL VISITOR CENTRE
Menstrie
Tillicoultry
Blairdrummond Moss
Forth
Gartmore
Drip Moss
Causewayhead
NATIONAL WALLACE MONUMENT
Alva
Tullibody
Devonside
Fishcross
577 BEINN BHREAC
NS
Kelty Water
Flanders Moss
Dalmary
STIRLING CASTLE
OLD TOWN JAIL
Raploch
Cambuskenneth
Stirling
Cambus
Coalsnaughton
Sauchie
Forest Mill
Branshill
Keilarsbrae
461
Kippen
Arnprior
Cauldhame
Glentirranmuir
Gargunnock
Buchlyvie
Milarrochy
Moor Park
CARLEATHERAN 485
SMITH ART GALLERY & MUSEUM
Touch Hills
Torbrex
Cambusbarron
Fallin
ALLOA
ALLOA TOWER
NAT. PARK CENTRE

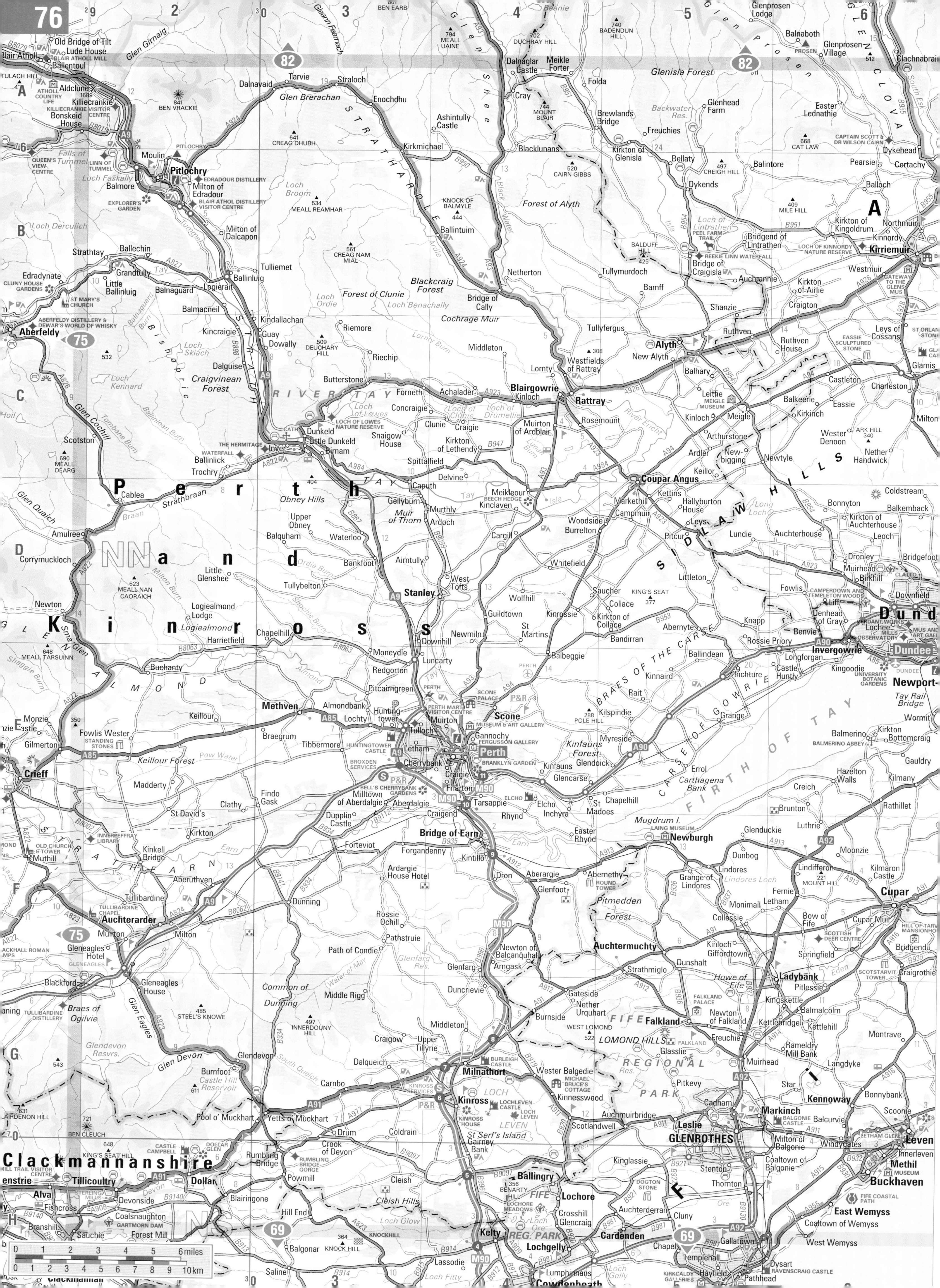

76
Old Bridge of Tilt
Lude House
Blair Atholl
Ballentoul
Aldclune
Killiecrankie
Bonskeid House
Pitlochry
Moulin
Balmore
Milton of Edradour
Milton of Dalcapon
Ben Vrackie
Creag Dhubh
Dalnavaid
Tarvie
Straloch
Glen Brerachan
Enochdhu
Kirkmichael
Ashintully Castle
Loch Broom
Meall Reamhar
Strathardle
Glen Shee
Dalnaglar Castle
Meikle Forter
Folda
Cray
Mount Blair
Blacklunans
Brewlands Bridge
Kirkton of Glenisla
Glenisla Forest
Glenhead Farm
Freuchies
Bellaty
Creigh Hill
Balintore
Dykehead
Cortachy
Pearsie
Balloch
Glen Prosen
Glenprosen Lodge
Balnaboth
Glenprosen Village
Clachnabrain
Glen Clova
Easter Lednathie
Cat Law
Captain Scott & Dr Wilson Cairn
Cairn Gibbs
Forest of Alyth
Knock of Balmyle
Ballintuim
Dykends
Mile Hill
Kirkton of Kingoldrum
Northmuir
Kinnordy
Kirriemuir
Loch of Lintrathen
Peel Farm Trail
Bridgend of Lintrathen
Loch of Kinnordy Nature Reserve
Baldouff Hill
Reekie Linn Waterfall
Bridge of Craigisla
Auchrannie
Westmuir
Kirkton of Airlie
Craigton
Netherton
Tullymurdoch
Bamff
Shanzie
Ruthven
Ruthven House
Leys of Cossans
Glamis
Eassie Sculptured Stone
Strathtay
Ballechin
Grandtully
Edradynate
Cluny House Gardens
Little Ballinluig
St Mary's Church
Ballinluig
Balnaguard
Logierait
Tulliemet
Creag nam Mial
Loch Ordie
Forest of Clunie
Blackcraig Forest
Loch Benachally
Bridge of Cally
Cochrage Muir
Balmacneil
Aberfeldy Distillery & Dewar's World of Whisky
Aberfeldy
Kindallachan
Kincraigie
Guay
Dowally
Deuchary Hill
Riemore
Riechip
Middleton
Tullyfergus
Alyth
New Alyth
Westfields of Rattray
Lornty
Loch Skiach
Dalguise
Loch Kennard
Craigvinean Forest
Butterstone
Forneth
Achalader
Blairgowrie
Kinloch
Rattray
Balhary
Castleton
Charleston
Glen Cochill
River Tay
Loch of Lowes Nature Reserve
Concraigie
Clunie
Craigie
Loch of Clunie
Loch of Drumellie
Muirton of Ardblair
Rosemount
Leitfie
Meigle Museum
Meigle
Kinloch
Balkeerie
Eassie
Kirkinch
Scotston
Dunkeld
Little Dunkeld
Birnam
Snaigow House
Kirkton of Lethendy
The Hermitage
Inver
Ballinlick
Trochry
Meall Dearg
Spittalfield
Delvine
Caputh
Arthurstone
Ardler
Newbigging
Newtyle
Wester Denoon
Ark Hill
Nether Handwick
Coupar Angus
Keillor
Perth
Cablea
Strathbraan
Obney Hills
Gellyburn
Murthly
Muir of Thorn
Ardoch
Meikleour
Kinclaven
Markethill
Kettins
Hallyburton House
Sidlaw Hills
Coldstream
Bonnyton
Balkemback
Glen Quaich
Amulree
Braan
Upper Obney
Balquharn
Waterloo
Cargill
Woodside
Burrelton
Campmuir
Leys
Pitcur
Lundie
Auchterhouse
Kirkton of Auchterhouse
Leoch
Corrymuckloch
and
Little Glenshee
Bankfoot
Airntully
West Tofts
Whitefield
Littleton
Dronley
Muirhead
Birkhill
Bridgefoot
Meall nan Caoraich
Tullybelton
Stanley
Wolfhill
Saucher
Collace
King's Seat
Fowlis
Camperdown and Templeton Woods
Downfield
Newton
Logiealmond Lodge
Logiealmond
Guildtown
Kinrossie
Kirkton of Collace
Knapp
Denhead of Gray
Dundee
Kinross
Chapelhill
Harrietfield
Newmiln
St Martins
Bandirran
Abernyte
Benvie
Meall Tarsuinn
Downhill
Moneydie
Luncarty
Balbeggie
Ballindean
Rossie Priory
Invergowrie
Longforgan
Kingoodie
Buchanty
Glen Almond
Redgorton
Braes of the Carse
Kinnaird
Inchture
Castle Huntly
University Botanic Gardens
Newport-on-Tay
Tay Rail Bridge
Rait
Pitcairngreen
Methven
Almondbank
Lochty
Huntingtower
Scone Palace
Scone
Kilspindie
Pole Hill
Carse of Gowrie
Grange
Firth of Tay
Wormit
Monzie Castle
Fowlis Wester
Keillour
Standing Stones
Braegrum
Tibbermore
Tulloch
Muirton
Museum & Art Gallery
Fergusson Gallery
Gannochy
Myreside
Kinfauns Forest
Balmerino
Balmerino Abbey
Kirkton
Bottomcraig
Gilmerton
Keillour Forest
Pow Water
Huntingtower Castle
Letham
Cherrybank
Branklyn Garden
Kinfauns
Glendoick
Errol
Carthagena Bank
Gauldry
Crieff
Madderty
Findo Gask
Broxden Services
Bell's Cherrybank Gardens
Craigie
Friarton
Glencarse
Hazelton Walls
Kilmany
Clathy
Milltown of Aberdalgie
Aberdalgie
Tarsappie
Elcho
Echo
Inchyra
St Madoes
Chapelhill
Creich
St David's
Dupplin Castle
Craigend
Rhynd
Brunton
Rathillet
Kirkton
Bridge of Earn
Easter Rhynd
Mugdrum I.
Laing Museum
Newburgh
Glenduckie
Luthrie
Innerpeffray Library
Old Church & Tower
Muthill
Kinkell Bridge
Strathearn
Forteviot
Forgandenny
Kintillo
Dunbog
Moonzie
Ardargie House Hotel
Dron
Aberargie
Abernethy
Round Tower
Lindores
Grange of Lindores
Lindifferon
Mount Hill
Kilmaron Castle
Aberuthven
Glenfoot
Lindores Loch
Fernie
Tullibardine
Tullibardine Chapel
Dunning
Pitmedden Forest
Monimail
Letham
Cupar
Auchterarder
Milton
Rossie Ochill
Collessie
Bow of Fife
Cupar Muir
Murton
Pathstruie
Kinloch
Scottish Deer Centre
Hill of Tarvit Mansionhouse
Gleneagles Hotel
Path of Condie
Newton of Balcanquhal
Auchtermuchty
Giffordtown
Springfield
Bridgend
Blackford
Glenfarg
Arngask
Dunshalt
Ladybank
Scotstarvit Tower
Craigrothie
Gleneagles House
Common of Dunning
Middle Rigg
Duncrievie
Strathmiglo
Howe of Fife
Pitlessie
Kingskettle
Tullibardine Distillery
Braes of Ogilvie
Glen Eagles
Steel's Knowe
Innerdouny Hill
Burnside
Gateside
Nether Urquhart
Falkland Palace
Newton of Falkland
Balmalcolm
Kettlebridge
Kettlehill
Fife
Falkland
West Lomond
Lomond Hills
Regional Park
Freuchie
Montrave
Middleton
Craigow
Upper Tillyrie
Glassie
Rameldry Mill Bank
Glendevon Resvrs.
Glen Devon
Glendevon
Dalqueich
Burleigh Castle
Milnathort
Muirhead
Langdyke
Burnfoot
Castle Hill Reservoir
Wester Balgedie
Michael Bruce's Cottage
Kinnesswood
Pitkevy
Star
Kennoway
Bonnybank
Carnbo
Kinross Services
Kinross
Loch Leven
Lochleven Castle
Kinross House
Cadham
Markinch
Balgonie Castle
Balcurvie
Scoonie
Pool o' Muckhart
Yetts o' Muckhart
Auchmuirbridge
Scotlandwell
Leslie
Glenrothes
Milton of Balgonie
Windygates
Leven
Ben Cleuch
Drum
Coldrain
Crook of Devon
St Serf's Island
Gairney Bank
Innerleven
Clackmannanshire
King's Seat Hill
Castle Campbell
Dollar Glen
Rumbling Bridge
Rumbling Bridge Gorge
Powmill
Kinglassie
Stenton
Coaltown of Balgonie
Methil
Tillicoultry
Dollar
Cleish
Ballingry
Benarty Hill
Lochore Meadows
Lochore
Dogton Stone
Thornton
Buckhaven
Alva
Fishcross
Devonside
Blairingone
Cleish Hills
Crosshill
Glencraig
Auchterderran
Cluny
Fife Coastal Path
East Wemyss
Coaltown of Wemyss
Branshill
Sauchie
Coalsnaughton
Gartmorn Dam
Forest Mill
Hill End
Loch Glow
Kelty
Reg. Park
Cardenden
Gallatown
West Wemyss
Balgonar
Knock Hill
Knockhill
Lochgelly
Chapel
Templehall
Dysart
Ravenscraig Castle
Saline
Lassodie
Loch Fitty
Lumphinnans
Loch Gelly
Kirkcaldy Galleries
Hayfield
Pathhead
Cowdenbeath
0 1 2 3 4 5 6 miles
0 1 2 3 4 5 6 7 8 9 10 km

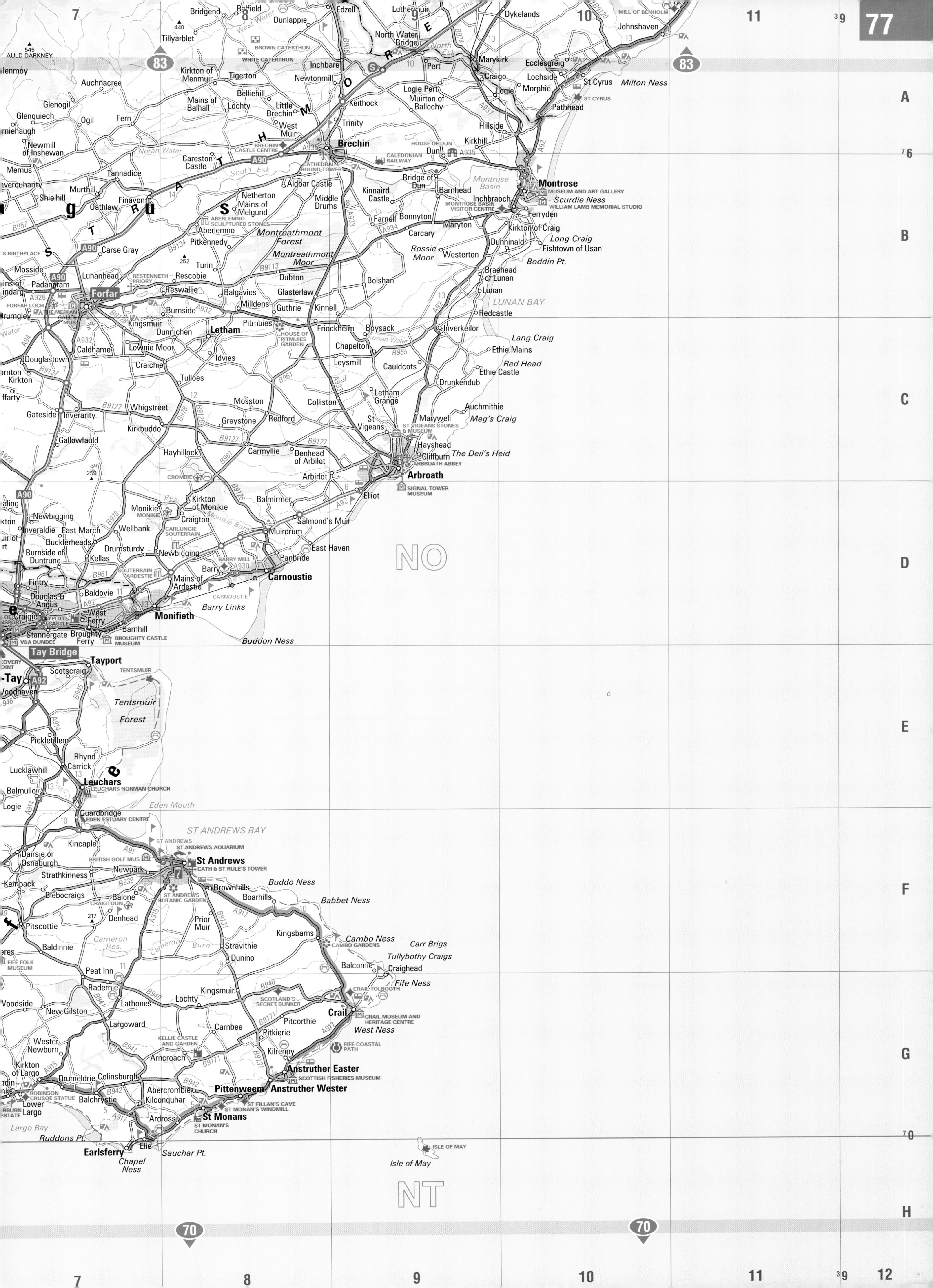

83
Montrose
Brechin
Forfar
Letham
Arbroath
Carnoustie
Monifieth
Tayport
Tay Bridge
Leuchars
St Andrews
Crail
Anstruther Easter
Anstruther Wester
Pittenweem
St Monans
Earlsferry
Elie
NO
NT
Edzell
Dunlappie
Tillyarblet
Bridgend
North Water Bridge
Luthermuir
Dykelands
Johnshaven
Marykirk
Pert
Inchbare
Newtonmill
Kirkton of Menmuir
Tigerton
Auchnacree
Glenogil
Glenquiech
Ogil
Fern
Bellichill
Mains of Balhall
Lochty
Little Brechin
West Muir
Keithock
Trinity
Logie Pert
Muirton of Ballochy
Craigo
Logie
Ecclesgreig
Lochside
Morphie
St Cyrus
Milton Ness
Pathhead
Hillside
Kirkhill
Dun
Newmill of Inshewan
Memus
Careston Castle
Tannadice
Murthill
Oathlaw
Finavon
Shielhill
Netherton
Mains of Melgund
Aldbar Castle
Middle Drums
Kinnaird Castle
Bridge of Dun
Barnhead
Montrose Basin
Inchbraoch
Scurdie Ness
Ferryden
Aberlemno
Pitkennedy
Montreathmont Forest
Montreathmont Moor
Farnell
Bonnyton
Carcary
Maryton
Kirkton of Craig
Long Craig
Fishtown of Usan
Rossie Moor
Westerton
Dunninald
Boddin Pt.
Carse Gray
Turin
Rescobie
Mosside
Padanaram
Lunanhead
Reswallie
Dubton
Bolshan
Braehead of Lunan
Lunan
Lunan Bay
Redcastle
Balgavies
Glasterlaw
Milldens
Guthrie
Kinnell
Burnside
Kingsmuir
Dunnichen
Pitmuies
Friockheim
Boysack
Inverkeilor
Lang Craig
Ethie Mains
Red Head
Ethie Castle
Caldhame
Lownie Moor
Idvies
Chapelton
Leysmill
Cauldcots
Drunkendub
Douglastown
Craichie
Tulloes
Letham Grange
Auchmithie
Meg's Craig
Colliston
Mosston
Whigstreet
Gateside
Inverarity
Kirkbuddo
Greystone
Redford
Marywell
St Vigeans
Gallowfauld
Hayshead
Cliffburn
The Deil's Heid
Hayhillock
Carmyllie
Denhead of Arbilot
Arbirlot
Elliot
Balmirmer
Monikie
Kirkton of Monikie
Craigton
Salmond's Muir
Newbigging
Inveraldie
East March
Wellbank
Muirdrum
Buckierheads
Drumsturdy
East Haven
Burnside of Duntrune
Kellas
Panbride
Barry
Mains of Ardestie
Fintry
Baldovie
Douglas & Angus
Craigie
West Ferry
Stannergate
Broughty Ferry
Barnhill
Barry Links
Buddon Ness
Scotscraig
Tentsmuir Forest
Pickletillem
Rhynd
Carrick
Lucklawhill
Balmullo
Logie
Eden Mouth
Guardbridge
St Andrews Bay
Kincaple
Dairsie or Osnaburgh
Newpark
Strathkinness
Kemback
Brownhills
Buddo Ness
Boarhills
Babbet Ness
Blebocraigs
Balone
Denhead
Prior Muir
Pitscottie
Kingsbarns
Cambo Ness
Carr Brigs
Stravithie
Dunino
Baldinnie
Balcomie
Tullybothy Craigs
Craighead
Fife Ness
Peat Inn
Radernie
Lathones
Lochty
Kingsmuir
Woodside
New Gilston
Largoward
Carnbee
Pitcorthie
Pitkierie
West Ness
Wester Newburn
Kilrenny
Arncroach
Kirkton of Largo
Drumeldrie
Colinsburgh
Abercrombie
Kilconquhar
Balchrystie
Lower Largo
Largo Bay
Ardross
Ruddons Pt.
Chapel Ness
Sauchar Pt.
Isle of May
70

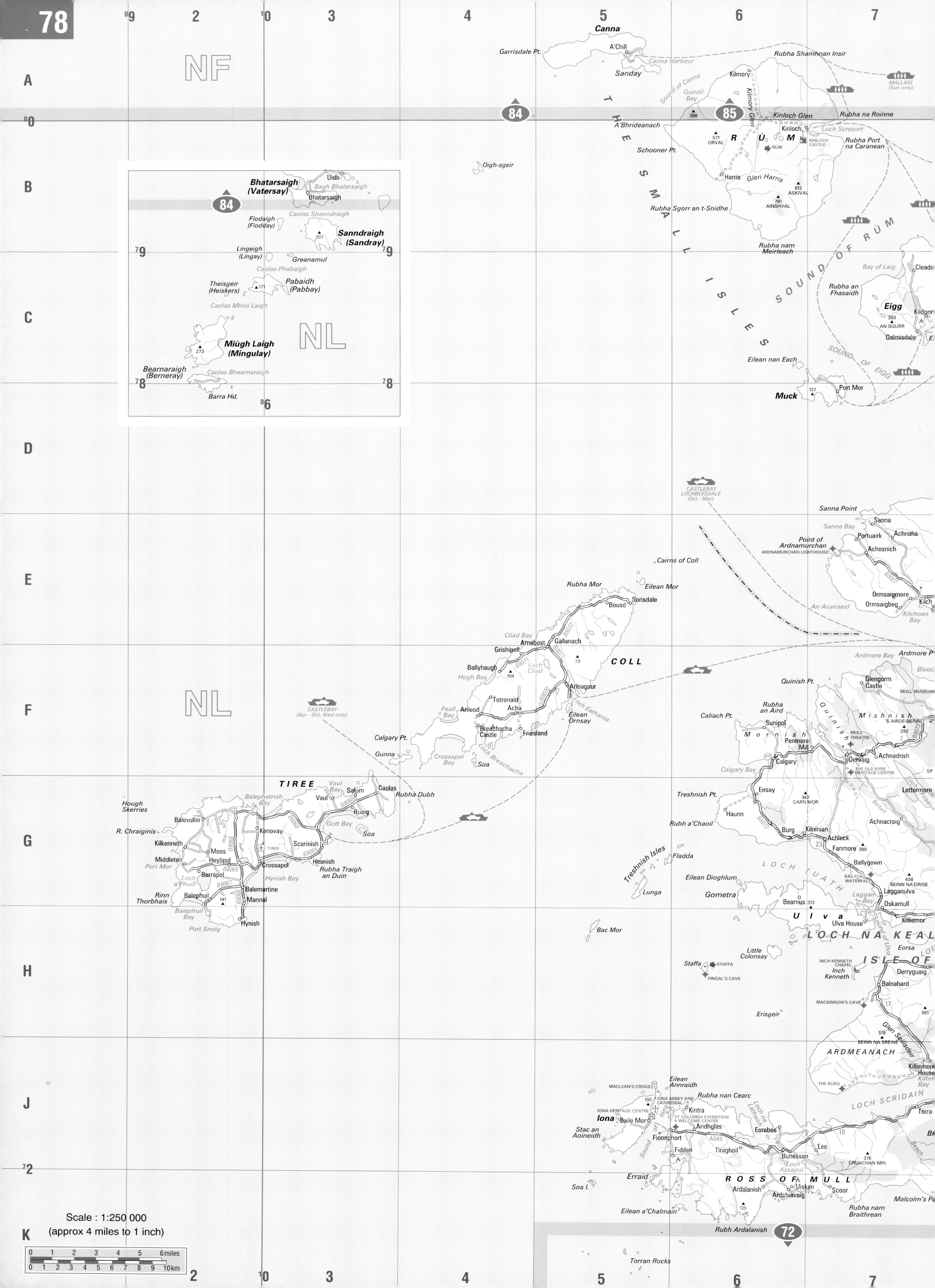
NF
NL
Canna
A'Chill
Garrisdale Pt.
Canna Harbour
Sanday
Rubha Shamhnan Insir
Kilmory
MALLAIG (Sun only)
Sound of Canna
Guirdil Bay
Kilmory Glen
Kinloch Glen
Rubha na Roinne
A'Bhrideanach
Kinloch
Loch Scresort
KINLOCH CASTLE
Rubha Port na Caranean
571 ORVAL
R U M
RÙM
Schooner Pt.
Oigh-sgeir
Harris
Glen Harris
812 ASKIVAL
781 AINSHVAL
Rubha Sgorr an t-Snidhe
Rubha nam Meirleach
THE SMALL ISLES
SOUND OF RÙM
Bay of Laig
Cleadale
Rubha an Fhasaidh
Eigg
393 AN SGURR
Kildonnan
Galmisdale
SOUND OF EIGG
Eilean nan Each
Muck
137
Port Mor
Bhatarsaigh (Vatersay)
Uidh
Bagh Bhatarsaigh
Bhatarsaigh
Caolas Shanndraigh
Flodaigh (Flodday)
Sanndraigh (Sandray)
207
Lingeigh (Lingay)
Greanamul
Caolas Phabaigh
Theisgeir (Heiskers)
171
Pabaidh (Pabbay)
Caolas Mhiui Laigh
Miùgh Laigh (Mingulay)
273
Bearnaraigh (Berneray)
Caolas Bhearnaraigh
Barra Hd.
84
85
CASTLEBAY LOCHBOISDALE (Oct - Mar)
Sanna Point
Sanna Bay
Sanna
Portuairk
Achnaha
Point of Ardnamurchan
ARDNAMURCHAN LIGHTHOUSE
Achosnich
Cairns of Coll
Rubha Mor
Eilean Mor
Sorisdale
Bousd
Ormsaigmore
Ormsaigbeg
Kilchoan Bay
An Acairseid
Cliad Bay
Arnabost
Gallanach
Grishipoll
Loch Cliad
73
COLL
Ballyhaugh
104
Hogh Bay
Arinagour
Totronald
Feall Bay
Arileod
Acha
Loch Eatharna
Eilean Ornsay
Breachacha Castle
Friesland
CASTLEBAY (Apr - Oct, Wed only)
Calgary Pt.
Gunna
Crossapol Bay
Soa
Loch Breachacha
Ardmore Bay
Ardmore Pt
Quinish Pt.
Glengorm Castle
MULL MUSEUM
Rubha an Aird
Caliach Pt.
Sunipol
Mishnish
S AIRDE-BEINN 292
Mornish
Penmore Mill
Quinish
MULL THEATRE
Calgary
Dervaig
Achnadrish
THE OLD BYRE HERITAGE CENTRE
Calgary Bay
TIREE
Vaul Bay
Salum
Caolas
Balephetrish Bay
Vaul
Rubha Dubh
Ruaig
Hough Skerries
Balevullin
Kenovay
Gott Bay
Soa
R. Chraiginis
Kilkenneth
Scarinish
Moss
TIREE
Middleton
Port Mor
Heylipol
Crossapol
Heanish
Rubha Traigh an Duin
Loch a'Phuill
Barrapol
Hynish Bay
Balemartine
Rinn Thorbhais
Balephuil
141
Mannal
Balephuil Bay
Port Snoig
Hynish
Ensay
Treshnish Pt.
342 CARN MOR
Lettermore
Haunn
Achnacraig
Rubh a'Chaoil
Burg
Kilninian
Achleck
Fanmore 390
Treshnish Isles
Fladda
LOCH TUATH
Ballygown
Eilean Dioghlum
EAS FORS WATERFALL
424 BEINN NA DRISE
Lunga
Gometra
Laggan Bay
Lagganulva
Oskamull
Ulva
Ulva House
Killiemor
LOCH NA KEAL
Eorsa
ISLE OF
Bac Mor
Little Colonsay
Staffa
STAFFA
FINGAL'S CAVE
INCH KENNETH CHAPEL
Inch Kenneth
Derryguaig
Balnahard
MACKINNON'S CAVE
561
Erisgeir
519
BEINN NA SREINE
Glen Seilisdeir
ARDMEANACH
Killiemore House
THE BURG
Kilfinichen Bay
Eilean Annraidh
MACLEAN'S CROSS
100
IONA ABBEY AND CATHEDRAL
Rubha nan Cearc
IONA HERITAGE CENTRE
Kintra
ST COLUMBA EXHIBITION & WELCOME CENTRE
LOCH SCRIDAIN
Torranuisg
Iona
Baile Mor
Aridhglas
Loch na Lathaich
Stac an Aoineidh
Sound of Iona
Eorabus
Fionnphort
A849
Fidden
Tiraghoil
Bunessan
Lee
376 CRUACHAN MIN
Loch Assapol
Erraid
Soa I.
ROSS OF MULL
Ardalanish
Uisken
Scoor
Ardchiavaig
Malcolm's Point
125
Eilean a'Chalmain
Rubha nam Braithrean
Rubh Ardalanish
72
Torran Rocks
Scale : 1:250 000
(approx 4 miles to 1 inch)
0 1 2 3 4 5 6 miles
0 1 2 3 4 5 6 7 8 9 10km

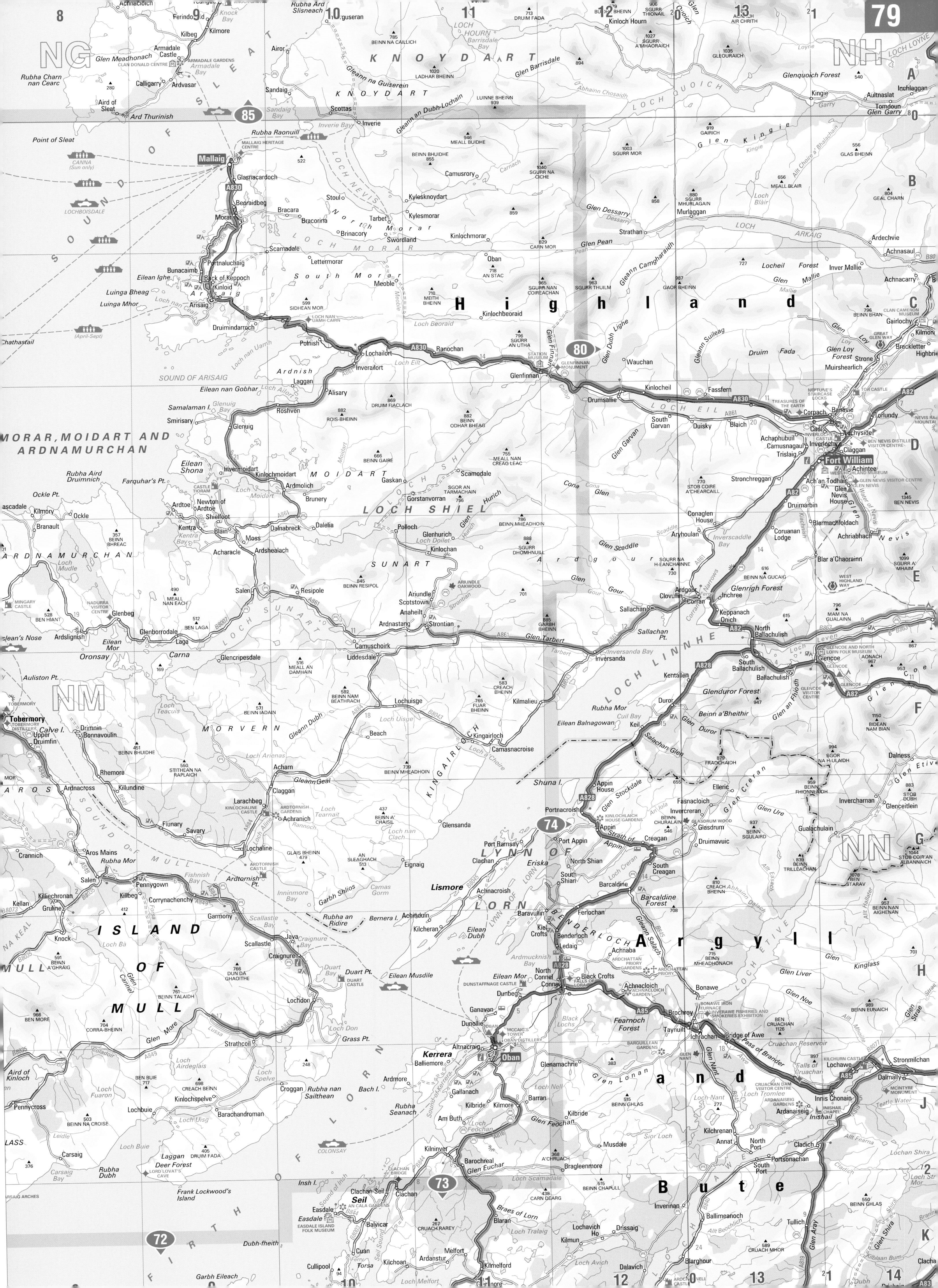
NG
NH
NM
NN
Highland
Argyll and Bute
KNOYDART
SOUND OF SLEAT
Mallaig
Glen Meadhonach
Armadale Castle
Armadale Gardens
Clan Donald Centre
Rubha Charn nan Cearc
Calligarry
Ardvasar
Aird of Sleat
Ard Thurinish
Point of Sleat
Sandaig
Scottas
Inverie
Airor
Loch Hourn
Ladhar Bheinn
Glen Barrisdale
Kinloch Hourn
Loch Quoich
Glenquoich Forest
Loch Loyne
Kingie
Aultnaslat
Inchlaggan
Tomdoun
Glen Garry
Glen Kingie
Loch Nevis
Meall Buidhe
Camusrory
Sgurr na Ciche
Glasnacardoch
Beoraidbeg
Morar
Stoul
Kylesknoydart
Kylesmorar
Tarbet
Bracara
Bracorina
Brinacory
Swordland
North Morar
Loch Morar
Kinlochmorar
Glen Dessarry
Murlaggan
Strathan
Loch Arkaig
Glen Pean
Ardechvie
Achnasaul
Scamadale
Lettermorar
South Morar
Meoble
Oban
Bunacaimb
Portnaluchaig
Back of Keppoch
Kinloid
Arisaig
Eilean Ighe
Luinga Bheag
Luinga Mhor
Loch nan Ceall
Druimindarroch
Loch nan Uamh
Polnish
Lochailort
Inversilort
Ranochan
Loch Eilt
Loch Beoraid
Kinlochbeoraid
Glenfinnan
Glenfinnan Monument
Glen Finnan
Glen Dubh Lighe
Wauchan
Kinlocheil
Fassfern
Loch Eil
Drumsallie
South Garvan
Duisky
Blaich
Corpach
Banavie
Caol
Inverlochy Castle
Lochyside
Fort William
Claggan
Achintee
Glen Nevis
Ben Nevis
Locheil Forest
Glen Mallie
Inver Mallie
Achnacarry
Gairlochy
Glen Loy
Brackletter
Strone
Muirshearlich
Torlundy
Sound of Arisaig
Ardnish
Laggan
Alisary
Eilean nan Gobhar
Loch Ailort
Roshven
Samalaman I.
Smirisary
Glenuig
Morar, Moidart and Ardnamurchan
Eilean Shona
Inversanda
Kinlochmoidart
Moidart
Ardmolich
Brunery
Loch Shiel
Gaskan
Scamodale
Glen Garvan
Stronchreggan
Trislaig
Camusnagaul
Achaphubuil
Rubha Aird Druimnich
Farquhar's Pt.
Castle Tioram
Ockle Pt.
Ardtoe
Newton of Ardtoe
Shielfoot
Kilmory
Ockle
Branault
Kentra
Blain
Moss
Dalnabreck
Dalelia
Polloch
Glenhurich
Glen Hurich
Kinlochan
Conaglen House
Aryhoulan
Inverscaddle Bay
Glen Scaddle
Ardgour
Corran
Clovullin
Onich
Inchree
Keppanach
Glenrigh Forest
North Ballachulish
South Ballachulish
Ballachulish
Glencoe
Loch Leven
Ardnamurchan
Loch Mudle
Mingary Castle
Nadurra Visitor Centre
Ben Hiant
Acharacle
Ardshealach
Salen
Resipole
Ben Resipol
Sunart
Ariundle
Scotstown
Anaheilt
Strontian
Ardnastang
Loch Sunart
Glenbeg
Glenborrodale
Laga
Ben Laga
Ardslignish
Maclean's Nose
Eilean Mor
Oronsay
Carna
Glencripesdale
Camuschoirk
Liddesdale
Glen Tarbert
Sallachan
Sallachan Pt.
Inversanda Bay
Loch Linnhe
Kentallen
Glenduror Forest
Glen Duror
Duror
Beinn a'Bheithir
Rubha Mor
Cuil Bay
Keil
Salachan Glen
Eilean Balnagowan
Shuna I.
Appin House
Glen Stockdale
Fasnacloich
Glen Creran
Elleric
Invercreran
Glasdrum
Glen Ure
Gualachulain
Glen Etive
Dalness
Inverchanan
Glenceitlein
Auliston Pt.
Tobermory
Calve I.
Drimnin
Bonnavoulin
Morvern
Gleann Dubh
Lochuisge
Loch Uisge
Beach
Kingairloch
Camasnacroise
Kilmalieu
Loch a' Choire
Kingairloch
Rhemore
Ardnacross
Killundine
Acharn
Gleann Geal
Claggan
Larachbeg
Kinlochaline Castle
Achranich
Ardtornish Gardens
Loch Arienas
Glensanda
Fiunary
Savary
Sound of Mull
Lochaline
Ardtornish Castle
Ardtornish Pt.
Aros Mains
Rubha Mor
Cranich
Salen
Pennygown
Killbeg
Corrynachenchy
Fishnish Bay
Kellan
Killiechronan
Gruline
Garmony
Scallastle Bay
Island of Mull
Knock
Loch Ba
Glen Cannel
Scallastle
Java
Craignure
Duart Pt.
Duart Castle
Lochdon
Grass Pt.
Glen More
Strathcoil
Ben More
Airds of Kinloch
Loch Airdeglais
Loch Spelve
Pennycross
Lochbuie
Loch Uisg
Kinlochspelve
Barachandroman
Croggan
Loch Buie
Carsaig
Laggan
Deer Forest
Lord Lovat's Cave
Rubha Dubh
Frank Lockwood's Island
Firth of Lorn
Port Ramsay
Lynn of Lorn
Eriska
Clachan
Lismore
Achnacroish
Port Appin
North Shian
South Shian
Creagan
South Creagan
Barcaldine
Barcaldine Forest
Strath of Appin
Loch Creran
Bernera I.
Rubha an Ridire
Achinduin
Kilcheran
Eilean Dubh
Baravullin
Kiel Crofts
Benderloch
Ledaig
Ardmucknish Bay
Ferlochan
Achnaba
Ardchattan Priory
Bonawe
Glen Salach
Eilean Musdile
Eilean Mor
Dunstaffnage Castle
North Connel
Connel
Black Crofts
Falls of Lora
Achnacloich
Dunbeg
Ganavan
Dunollie
Oban
Kerrera
Ballimore
Altnacraig
McCaig's Tower
Oban Distillery
Gallanach
Kilbride
Kilmore
Barran
Glenamachrie
Glen Lonan
Glen Feochan
Loch Feochan
Am Buth
Rubha Seanach
Ardmore
Bach I.
Rubha nan Sailthean
Brochroy
Taynuilt
Ichrachan
Bridge of Awe
Pass of Brander
Cruachan Reservoir
Ben Cruachan
Glen Nant
Loch Awe
Glen Noe
Glen Liver
Kinglass
Falls of Cruachan
Kilchurn Castle
Lochawe
Stronmilchan
Dalmally
Innis Chonain
Ardanaiseig
Inishail
Loch Nant
Kilchrenan
Annat
North Port
Portsonachan
Cladich
South Port
Musdale
Sior Loch
Kilninver
Barochreal
Glen Euchar
Bragleenmore
Loch Scamadale
Insh I.
Clachan-Seil
Clachan Bridge
Seil
An Cala Gardens
Easdale
Easdale Island Folk Museum
Balvicar
Cuan
Torsa
Kilchoan
Melfort
Ardanstur
Loch Melfort
Kilmelford
Braes of Lorn
Blaran
Loch Tralaig
Inverinan
Lochavich Ho
Drissaig
Kilmun
Loch Avich
Dalavich
Ballimeanoch
Tullich
Blarghour
Glen Aray
Glen Shira
Lochan Shira
Dubh-fheith
Garbh Eileach
Cullipool

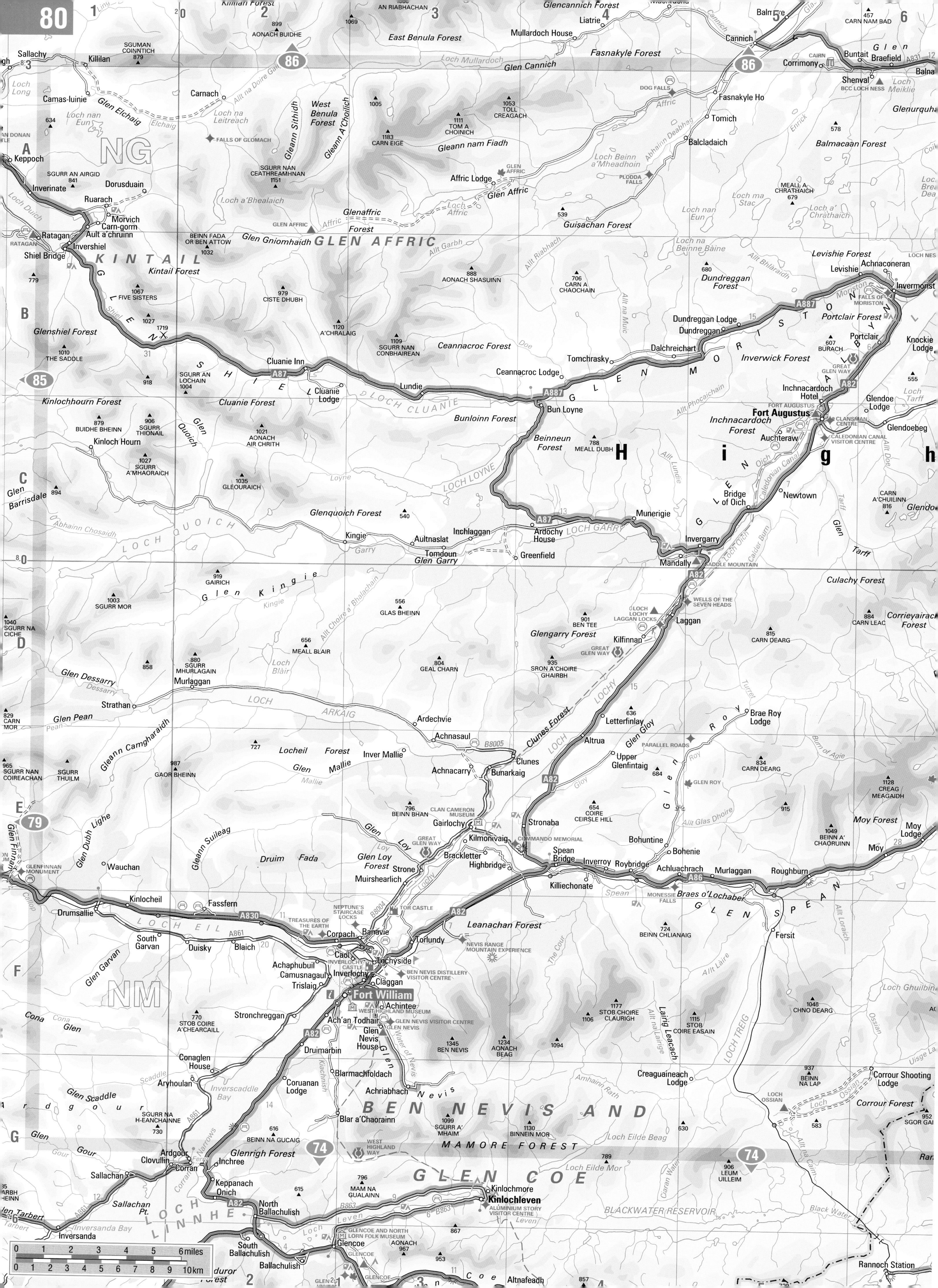
Glencannich Forest
Liatrie
Cannich
Mullardoch House
East Benula Forest
Fasnakyle Forest
Glen Cannich
Loch Mullardoch
AN RIABHACHAN
AONACH BUIDHE
SGUMAN COINNTICH
Sallachy
Killilan
86
Buntait
Glen
Braefield
Corrimony
Balna
Shenval
Loch Meiklie
Glenurquha
Carnach
Camas-luinie
Glen Elchaig
Loch nan Eun
Loch na Leitreach
FALLS OF GLOMACH
West Benula Forest
Gleann Sithidh
Gleann A'Choilich
TOM A CHOINICH
TOLL CREAGACH
CARN EIGE
Gleann nam Fiadh
DOG FALLS
Fasnakyle Ho
Tomich
Balcladaich
Balmacaan Forest
Keppoch
NG
SGURR AN AIRGID
Inverinate
Dorusduain
SGURR NAN CEATHREAMHNAN
Loch Beinn a'Mheadhoin
PLODDA FALLS
Affric Lodge
GLEN AFFRIC
Glen Affric
Loch Affric
Loch a'Bhealaich
Loch Duich
Ruarach
Morvich
Carn-gorm
Ault a'chruinn
Ratagan
RATAGAN
Invershiel
Shiel Bridge
Glenaffric Forest
GLEN AFFRIC
Glen Gniomhaidh
BEINN FADA OR BEN ATTOW
Guisachan Forest
Loch nan Eun
Loch ma Stac
MEALL A CHRATHAICH
Loch a' Chrathaich
Loch na Beinne Bàine
Levishie Forest
Levishie
Achnaconeran
Invermorist
KINTAIL
Kintail Forest
FIVE SISTERS
CISTE DHUBH
AONACH SHASUINN
CARN A CHAOCHAIN
Dundreggan Forest
FALLS OF MORISTON
Portclair Forest
Glenshiel Forest
GLEN SHIEL
THE SADDLE
A'CHRALAIG
SGURR NAN CONBHAIREAN
Ceannacroc Forest
Dundreggan Lodge
Dundreggan
Dalchreichart
Tomchrasky
BURACH
Portclair
Knockie Lodge
Inverwick Forest
GLEN MORISTON
GREAT GLEN WAY
85
Cluanie Inn
A87
SGURR AN LOCHAIN
Lundie
Ceannacroc Lodge
A887
Inchnacardoch Hotel
Glendoe Lodge
Loch Tarff
Kinlochhourn Forest
Cluanie Forest
Cluanie Lodge
LOCH CLUANIE
Bun Loyne
Bunloinn Forest
FORT AUGUSTUS
Fort Augustus
CLANSMAN CENTRE
Inchnacardoch Forest
Auchteraw
CALEDONIAN CANAL VISITOR CENTRE
Glendoebeg
BUIDHE BHEINN
SGURR THIONAIL
AONACH AIR CHRITH
Kinloch Hourn
Glen Quoich
Beinneun Forest
MEALL DUBH
Highland
SGURR A'MHAORAICH
GLEOURAICH
LOCH LOYNE
Glen Barrisdale
Glenquoich Forest
GLEN GARRY
Bridge of Oich
Caledonian Canal
Newtown
CARN A'CHUILINN
Glen Tarff
Abhainn Chosaidh
LOCH QUOICH
Kingie
Aultnaslat
Inchlaggan
Ardochy House
LOCH GARRY
Munerigie
Invergarry
Tomdoun
Glen Garry
Greenfield
Mandally
SADDLE MOUNTAIN
A82
GAIRICH
Glen Kingie
SGURR MOR
GLAS BHEINN
Culachy Forest
WELLS OF THE SEVEN HEADS
LOCH LOCHY LAGGAN LOCKS
SGURR NA CICHE
BEN TEE
Laggan
CARN LEAC
Corrieyairack Forest
MEALL BLAIR
Glengarry Forest
Kilfinnan
CARN DEARG
Glen Dessarry
SGURR MHURLAGAIN
Murlaggan
GEAL CHARN
Loch Blàir
SRON A'CHOIRE GHAIRBH
Strathan
LOCH ARKAIG
Ardechvie
LOCH LOCHY
Letterfinlay
Brae Roy Lodge
Glen Pean
CARN MOR
Gleann Camgharaidh
Achnasaul
B8005
Clunes Forest
Altrua
Glen Gloy
Glen Roy
PARALLEL ROADS
Locheil Forest
Glen Mallie
Inver Mallie
Clunes
Upper Glenfintaig
CARN DEARG
SGURR NAN COIREACHAN
SGURR THUILM
GAOR BHEINN
Achnacarry
Bunarkaig
GLEN ROY
CREAG MEAGAIDH
79
BEINN BHAN
CLAN CAMERON MUSEUM
COIRE CEIRSLE HILL
Moy Forest
Moy Lodge
Glen Dubh Lighe
Gleann Suileag
Gairlochy
Stronaba
Glen Loy
GREAT GLEN WAY
Kilmonivaig
COMMANDO MEMORIAL
Bohuntine
Glen Glas Dhoire
BEINN A' CHAORUINN
Moy
GLENFINNAN MONUMENT
Wauchan
Druim Fada
Brackletter
Glen Loy Forest
Highbridge
Spean Bridge
Inverroy
Roybridge
Bohenie
Strone
Achluachrach
Murlaggan
Roughburn
Muirshearlich
Killiechonate
MONESSIE FALLS
Braes o'Lochaber
A86
GLEN SPEAN
Kinlocheil
Fassfern
Drumsallie
LOCH EIL
A830
NEPTUNE'S STAIRCASE LOCKS
TOR CASTLE
TREASURES OF THE EARTH
Corpach
Banavie
Leanachan Forest
BEINN CHLIANAIG
Fersit
South Garvan
Duisky
A861
Blaich
Caol
Lochyside
Torlundy
NEVIS RANGE MOUNTAIN EXPERIENCE
The Cour
INVERLOCHY CASTLE
Achaphubuil
Camusnagaul
Inverlochy
Claggan
BEN NEVIS DISTILLERY VISITOR CENTRE
Trislaig
Glen Garvan
NM
Fort William
Achintee
WEST HIGHLAND MUSEUM
Loch Ghuilbinn
Cona Glen
STOB COIRE A'CHEARCAILL
Stronchreggan
Ach'an Todhair
GLEN NEVIS VISITOR CENTRE
Glen Nevis House
STOB CHOIRE CLAURIGH
STOB COIRE EASAIN
CHNO DEARG
Druimarbin
BEN NEVIS
AONACH BEAG
Larig Leacach
LOCH TREIG
Conaglen House
Blarmachfoldach
Creaguaineach Lodge
BEINN NA LAP
Corrour Shooting Lodge
Glen Scaddle
Aryhoulan
Inverscaddle Bay
Coruanan Lodge
Achriabhach
Ardgour
LOCH OSSIAN
Corrour Forest
SGURR NA H-EANCHAINNE
Blar a'Chaorainn
BEN NEVIS AND MAMORE FOREST
SGURR A' MHAIM
BINNEIN MOR
Glen Gour
Clovullin
Corran
BEINN NA GUCAIG
74
WEST HIGHLAND WAY
Loch Eilde Beag
SGOR GAI
Glenrigh Forest
Inchree
Loch Eilde Mor
LEUM UILLEIM
Sallachan
Keppanach
Onich
MAM NA GUALAINN
GLEN COE
Kinlochmore
Kinlochleven
ALUMINIUM STORY VISITOR CENTRE
Sallachan Pt.
LOCH LINNHE
North Ballachulish
B863
BLACKWATER RESERVOIR
Black Water
Glen Tarbert
Inversanda
Inversanda Bay
GLENCOE AND NORTH LORN FOLK MUSEUM
Glencoe
AONACH
South Ballachulish
Ballachulish
Altnafeadh
Rannoch Station
0 1 2 3 4 5 6 miles
0 1 2 3 4 5 6 7 8 9 10 km

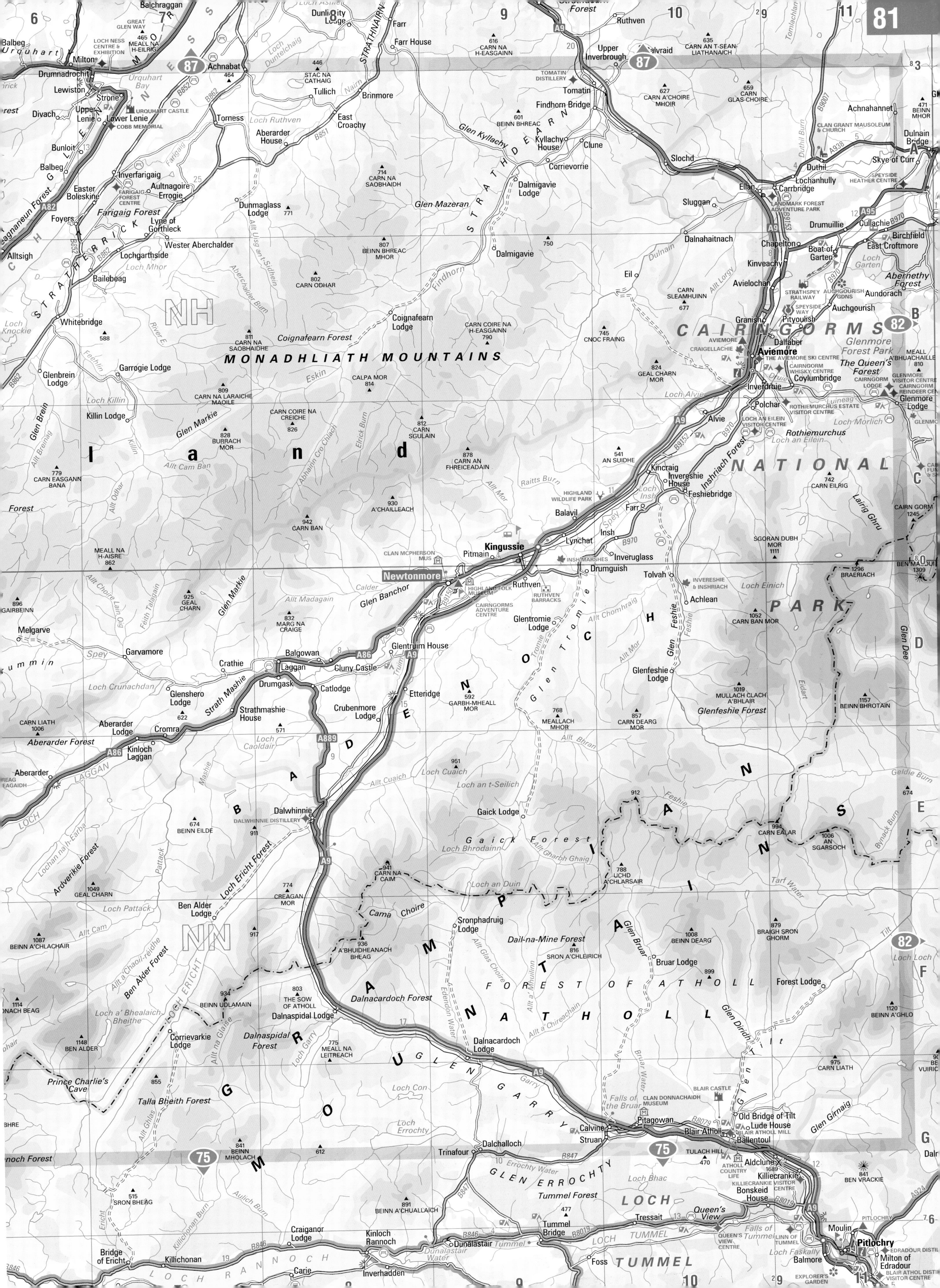

MONADHLIATH MOUNTAINS
CAIRNGORMS
NATIONAL
PARK
GRAMPIAN MOUNTAINS
BADENOCH
FOREST OF ATHOLL
LOCH NESS
GLEN MORE
STRATHERRICK
STRATHDEARN
STRATHNAIRN
Upland
NH
NN
87
82
75
A9
A86
A889
A82
A95
A938
B862
B852
B851
B9152
B970
B847
B846
B8019
B8079
B9153
B9007
Balchraggan
Balbeg
Urquhart
Milton
LOCH NESS CENTRE & EXHIBITION
GREAT GLEN WAY
465 MEALL NA H-EILRIG
Drumnadrochit
Lewiston
Strone
URQUHART CASTLE
Urquhart Bay
Divach
Upper Lenie
Lower Lenie
COBB MEMORIAL
Bunloit
Achnabat
Torness
Loch Ruthven
Aberarder House
Dunlichity Lodge
Farr
Farr House
Loch Duntelchaig
446 STAC NA CATHAIG
Tullich
Brinmore
East Croachy
616 CARN NA H-EASGAINN
Ruthven
Upper Inverbrough
Alvraid
635 CARN AN T-SEAN-LIATHANAICH
TOMATIN DISTILLERY
Tomatin
Findhorn Bridge
627 CARN A'CHOIRE MHOIR
659 CARN GLAS-CHOIRE
601 BEINN BHREAC
Glen Kyllachy
Kyllachy House
Clune
Corrievorrie
Slochd
Achnahannet
CLAN GRANT MAUSOLEUM & CHURCH
Dulnain Bridge
Skye of Curr
Duthil
Lochanhully
Carrbridge
SPEYSIDE HEATHER CENTRE
LANDMARK FOREST ADVENTURE PARK
Ellan
Sluggan
Inverfarigaig
Aultnagoire
Errogie
Easter Boleskine
FARIGAIG FOREST CENTRE
Farigaig Forest
Foyers
Lyne of Gorthleck
Wester Aberchalder
Alltsigh
Lochgarthside
Loch Mhor
Bailebeag
714 CARN NA SAOBHAIDH
Dunmaglass Lodge
771
Dalmigavie Lodge
Glen Mazeran
Dalmigavie
807 BEINN BHREAC MHOR
750
Drumuillie
Cullachie
Dalnahaitnach
Chapelton
Boat of Garten
Birchfield
East Croftmore
Loch Garten
Abernethy Forest
Kinveachy
Avielochan
STRATHSPEY RAILWAY
AUCHGOURISH GDNS
Aundorach
Auchgourish
SPEYSIDE WAY
Pityoulish
Granish
Eil
CARN SLEAMHUINN 677
802 CARN ODHAR
Whitebridge
588
Coignafearn Lodge
Coignafearn Forest
CARN COIRE NA H-EASGAINN 790
811 CARN NA SAOBHAIDHE
745 CNOC FRAING
AVIEMORE
CRAIGELLACHIE
Aviemore
Dalfaber
THE AVIEMORE SKI CENTRE
CAIRNGORM WHISKY CENTRE
Glenmore Forest Park
The Queen's Forest
Coylumbridge
MEALL A'BHUACHAILLE 810
GLENMORE VISITOR CENTRE
CAIRNGORM REINDEER CENTRE
CAIRNGORM LODGE
Glenmore Lodge
Inverdruie
Polchar
ROTHIEMURCHUS ESTATE VISITOR CENTRE
Loch Morlich
LOCH AN EILEIN VISITOR CENTRE
Rothiemurchus
Loch an Eilein
Loch Alvie
Alvie
Glenbrein Lodge
Garrogie Lodge
Loch Killin
Killin Lodge
809 CARN NA LARAICHE MAOILE
CALPA MOR 814
824 GEAL CHARN MOR
Glen Brein
Glen Markie
828 BURRACH MOR
CARN COIRE NA CREICHE 826
812 CARN SGULAIN
878 CARN AN FHREICEADAIN
541 AN SUIDHE
Kincraig
Inshriach Forest
Inveresbie House
Feshiebridge
742 CARN EILRIG
779 CARN EASGANN BANA
Allt Cam Ban
HIGHLAND WILDLIFE PARK
Loch Insh
Raitts Burn
930 A'CHAILLEACH
Balavil
Farr
942 CARN BAN
Lynchat
Insh
Lairig Ghru
CAIRN GORM 1245
SGORAN DUBH MOR 1111
Forest
MEALL NA H-AISRE 862
CLAN MCPHERSON MUS
Pitmain
Kingussie
INSH MARSHES
Inveruglass
Drumguish
Tolvah
1296 BRAERIACH
BEN MACDUI 1309
Newtonmore
HIGHLAND FOLK MUSEUM
Ruthven
RUTHVEN BARRACKS
INVERESHIE & INSHRIACH
Achlean
Loch Einich
896 GAIRBEINN
925 GEAL CHARN
Glen Banchor
Allt Madagain
CAIRNGORMS ADVENTURE CENTRE
Glentromie Lodge
Glen Tromie
Allt Chomhraig
1052 CARN BAN MOR
Melgarve
832 MARG NA CRAIGE
Glen Feshie
Glen Dee
Garvamore
Spey
Balgowan
Glentruim House
Crathie
Laggan
Cluny Castle
Loch Crunachdan
Drumgask
Catlodge
Etteridge
Glenshero Lodge
Strath Mashie
592 GARBH-MHEALL MOR
Glenfeshie Lodge
1019 MULLACH CLACH A'BHLAIR
Glenfeshie Forest
1157 BEINN BHROTAIN
Eidart
CARN LIATH 1006
622
Strathmashie House
Crubenmore Lodge
768 MEALLACH MHOR
857 CARN DEARG MOR
Aberarder Lodge
Cromra
571
Aberarder Forest
Kinloch Laggan
Loch Caoldair
Allt Bhran
Aberarder
LAGGAN
951
Loch Cuaich
Allt Cuaich
Loch an t-Seilich
Geldie Burn
674
Dalwhinnie
DALWHINNIE DISTILLERY
674 BEINN EILDE
911
Gaick Lodge
912
Feshie
994 CARN EALAR
1006 AN SGARSOCH
Bynack Burn
Gaick Forest
Loch Bhrodainn
Ardverikie Forest
Loch Ericht Forest
941 CARN NA CAIM
788 UCHD A'CHLARSAIR
Tarf Water
1049 GEAL CHARN
774 CREAGAN MOR
Loch an Duin
Loch Pattack
Ben Alder Lodge
Cama' Choire
Sronphadruig Lodge
879 BRAIGH SRON GHORM
1087 BEINN A'CHLACHAIR
917
936 A'BHUIDHEANACH BHEAG
Dail-na-Mine Forest
816 SRON A'CHLEIRICH
1008 BEINN DEARG
Glen Bruar
Bruar Lodge
899
Forest Lodge
Tilt
Loch Loch
Ben Alder Forest
LOCH ERICHT
934 BEINN UDLAMAIN
803 THE SOW OF ATHOLL
Dalnaspidal Lodge
Dalnacardoch Forest
Edendon Water
Allt Glas Choire
Glen Diridh
1120 BEINN A'GHLO
1114 CARN DEARG
Loch a' Bhealaich Bheithe
1148 BEN ALDER
Corrievarkie Lodge
Dalnaspidal Forest
775 MEALL NA LEITREACH
Dalnacardoch Lodge
GLEN GARRY
975 CARN LIATH
Prince Charlie's Cave
855
Talla Bheith Forest
Loch Con
Falls of the Bruar
CLAN DONNACHAIDH MUSEUM
BLAIR CASTLE
Glen Girnaig
Loch Errochty
Calvine
Pitagowan
Blair Atholl
Old Bridge of Tilt
Lude House
BLAIR ATHOLL MILL
Bailentoul
Struan
841 BEINN MHOLACH
612
Trinafour
Dalchalloch
GLEN ERROCHTY
Errochty Water
TULACH HILL 470
ATHOLL COUNTRY LIFE
Aldclune
Killiecrankie
KILLIECRANKIE VISITOR CENTRE
841 BEN VRACKIE
Bonskeid House
Rannoch Forest
515 SRON BHEAG
891 BEINN A'CHUALLAICH
Tummel Forest
477
Loch Bhac
LOCH TUMMEL
Tressait
Queen's View
QUEEN'S VIEW CENTRE
Falls of Tummel
Tummel Bridge
Moulin
PITLOCHRY
Pitlochry
EDRADOUR DISTILLERY
Milton of Edradour
BLAIR ATHOL DISTILLERY VISITOR CENTRE
LINN OF TUMMEL
Loch Faskally
Balmore
Craiganor Lodge
Kinloch Rannoch
Dunalastair
Dunalastair Water
Bridge of Ericht
Killichonan
Carie
Inverhadden
Foss
LOCH RANNOCH
EXPLORER'S GARDEN
Aulich Burn
Killichonan Burn
6
7
8
9
10
11
A
B
C
D
E
F
G

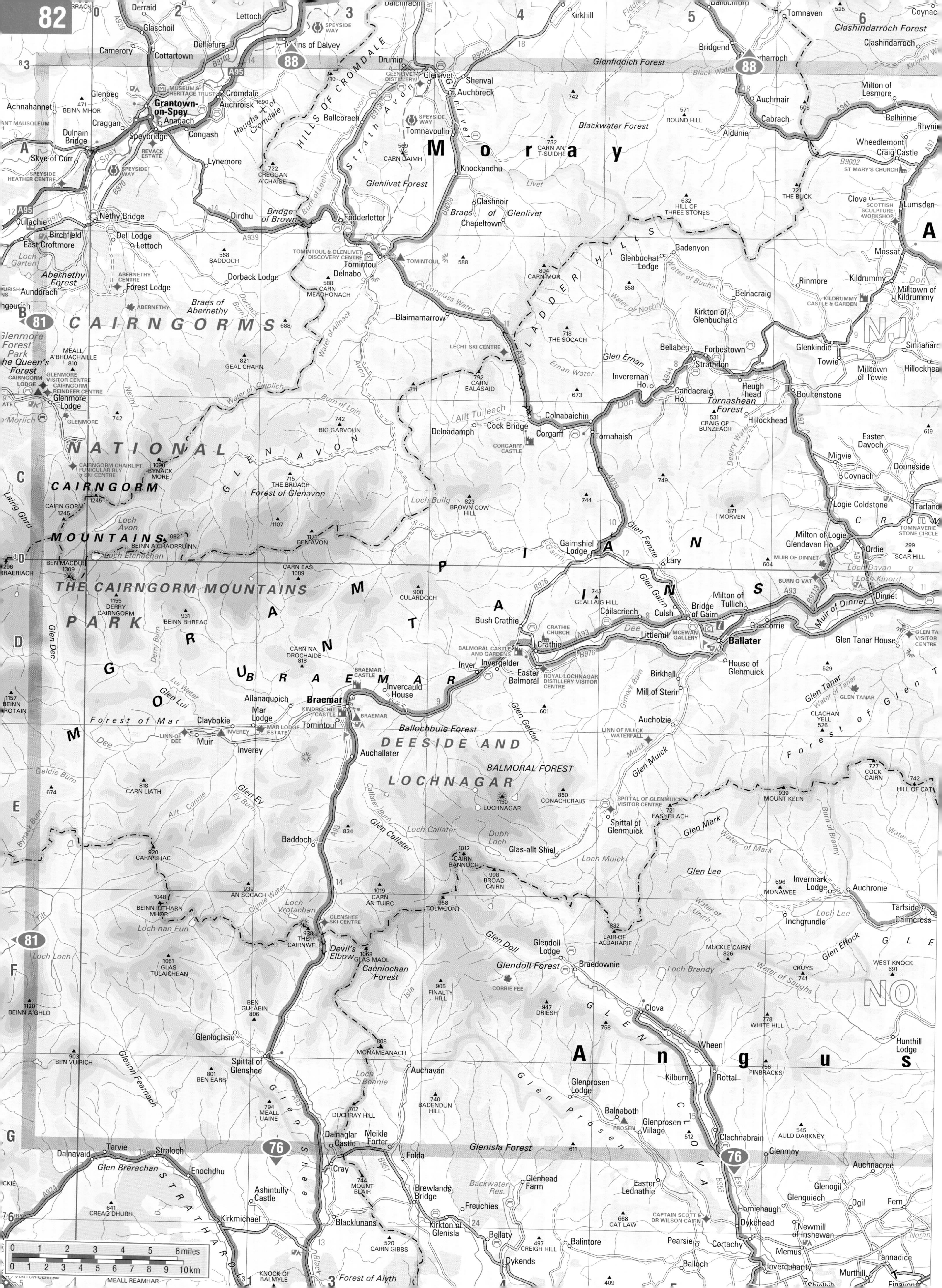
Derraid
Glaschoil
Lettoch
Dalchirach
Ballochford
Tomnaven
Coynach
Clashindarroch Forest
Clashindarroch
Camerory
Dellefure
Mains of Dalvey
SPEYSIDE WAY
Cottartown
88
HILLS OF CROMDALE
Drumin
Glenlivet
Shenval
Auchbreck
Bridgend
Corharrach
Glenfiddich Forest
Black Water
Kirkhill
Milton of Lesmore
Glenbeg
471 BEINN MHOR
Achnahannet
Grantown-on-Spey
MUSEUM & HERITAGE TRUST
Cromdale
Auchroisk
Haughs of Cromdale
Anagach
Craggan
Ballcorach
Strath Avon
Tomnavoulin
GLENLIVET DISTILLERY
742
Blackwater Forest
571 ROUND HILL
Auchmair
Cabrach
Aldunie
Belhinnie
Rhynie
Dulnain Bridge
Speybridge
Congash
Skye of Curr
REVACK ESTATE
Lynemore
722 CREGGAN A'CHAISE
569 CARN DAIMH
732 CARN AN T-SUIDHE
Moray
Knockandhu
Livet
Glenlivet Forest
Wheedlemont
Craig Castle
ST MARY'S CHURCH
SPEYSIDE HEATHER CENTRE
Cullachie
Nethy Bridge
Dirdhu
Bridge of Brown
Burn of Lochy
Fodderletter
Clashnoir
Braes of Glenlivet
Chapeltown
632 HILL OF THREE STONES
721 THE BUCK
Clova
SCOTTISH SCULPTURE WORKSHOP
Lumsden
Birchfield
East Croftmore
Dell Lodge
Lettoch
Loch Garten
568 BADDOCH
TOMINTOUL & GLENLIVET DISCOVERY CENTRE
Tomintoul
TOMINTOUL
588
LADDER HILLS
Badenyon
Glenbuchat Lodge
Mossat
Abernethy Forest
ABERNETHY CENTRE
Forest Lodge
Aundorach
Dorback Lodge
Delnabo
588 CARN MEADHONACH
804 CARN MOR
Water of Buchat
658
Rinmore
Kildrummy
Milltown of Kildrummy
KILDRUMMY CASTLE & GARDEN
Braes of Abernethy
ABERNETHY
CAIRNGORMS
688
Water of Ailnack
Blairnamarrow
Conglass Water
Water of Nochty
Belnacraig
Kirkton of Glenbuchat
81
Glenmore Forest Park
Queen's Forest
MEALL A'BHUACHAILLE 810
GLENMORE VISITOR CENTRE
CAIRNGORM LODGE
CAIRNGORM REINDEER CENTRE
Glenmore Lodge
821 GEAL CHARN
LECHT SKI CENTRE
718 THE SOCACH
Bellabeg
Forbestown
Strathdon
Glenkindie
Towie
Milltown of Towie
Sinnahard
Hillockhead
792 CARN EALASAID
Glen Ernan
Ernan Water
Inverernan Ho.
Candacraig Ho.
Heugh-head
Boultenstone
673
GLENMORE
742
Water of Caiplich
Burn of Loin
711
742 BIG GARVOUN
Allt Tuileach
Delnadamph
Cock Bridge
CORGARFF CASTLE
Corgarff
Colnabaichin
Tornahaish
Don
Tornashean Forest
531 CRAIG OF BUNZEACH
Hillockhead
Easter Davoch
619
NATIONAL
GLEN AVON
CAIRNGORM CHAIRLIFT, FUNICULAR RLY & SKI CENTRE
1090 BYNACK MORE
CAIRNGORM
715 THE BRUACH
Forest of Glenavon
Deskry Water
749
Migvie
Coynach
Douneside
Logie Coldstone
Tarland
CAIRN GORM 1245
1245
Loch Avon
1107
Loch Builg
823 BROWN COW HILL
744
871 MORVEN
CROMAR
TOMNAVERIE STONE CIRCLE
Lairig Ghru
MOUNTAINS
1082
BEINN A'CHAORRUINN
1171 BEN AVON
Loch Etchachan
Gairnshiel Lodge
Glen Fenzie
GRAMPIAN MOUNTAINS
Milton of Logie
Glendavan Ho.
MUIR OF DINNET
Ordie
299 SCAR HILL
Loch Davan
BEN MACDUI 1309
BRAERIACH 1296
THE CAIRNGORM MOUNTAINS
CARN EAS 1089
Gairn
Lary
604
BURN O VAT
Loch Kinord
900 CULARDOCH
B976
743 GEALLAIG HILL
Glen Gairn
Milton of Tullich
Dinnet
PARK
1155 DERRY CAIRNGORM
931 BEINN BHREAC
Bush Crathie
Coilacriech
Culsh
Bridge of Gairn
Muir of Dinnet
Glascorrie
Glen Tanar House
GLEN TANAR VISITOR CENTRE
Glen Dee
Derry Burn
CARN NA DROCHAIDE 818
CRATHIE CHURCH
Crathie
Littlemill
MCEWAN GALLERY
Ballater
BALMORAL CASTLE AND GARDENS
Inver
Invergelder
Easter Balmoral
ROYAL LOCHNAGAR DISTILLERY VISITOR CENTRE
Birkhall
House of Glenmuick
529
BRAEMAR CASTLE
Invercauld House
Girnock Burn
Mill of Sterin
Glen Tanar
Water of Tanar
GLEN TANAR
1157 BEINN BHROTAIN
Lui Water
Glen Lui
Allanaquoich
Braemar
KINDROCHIT CASTLE
BRAEMAR
Mar Lodge
Claybokie
Forest of Mar
Tomintoul
601
Glen Gelder
Aucholzie
CLACHAN YELL 526
Forest of Glen Tanar
INVEREY
MAR LODGE ESTATE
LINN OF DEE
Muir
Inverey
Dee
Ballochbuie Forest
DEESIDE AND LOCHNAGAR
LINN OF MUICK WATERFALL
Muick
Glen Muick
Auchallater
BALMORAL FOREST
727 COCK CAIRN
742 HILL OF CAT
Geldie Burn
674
818 CARN LIATH
Glen Ey
Ey Burn
Allt Connie
Callater Burn
1150 LOCHNAGAR
850 CONACHCRAIG
SPITTAL OF GLENMUICK VISITOR CENTRE
721 FASHEILACH
939 MOUNT KEEN
Burn of Branny
Water of Tarf
Bynack Burn
834
Glen Callater
Loch Callater
Dubh Loch
Spittal of Glenmuick
Glen Mark
Water of Mark
Baddoch
920 CARN BHAC
1012 CAIRN BANNOCH
Glas-allt Shiel
Loch Muick
Glen Lee
998 BROAD CAIRN
696 MONAWEE
Invermark Lodge
Auchronie
939 AN SOCACH
Clunie Water
1019 CARN AN TUIRC
958 TOLMOUNT
Water of Unich
Loch Lee
Tarfside
Cairncross
1048 BEINN IUTHARN MHOR
Loch Vrotachan
GLENSHEE SKI CENTRE
Loch nan Eun
933 THE CAIRNWELL
832 LAIR OF ALDARARIE
Inchgrundle
Glen Effock
Tilt
Glen Doll
Glendoll Lodge
Braedownie
MUCKLE CAIRN 826
Loch Loch
Devil's Elbow
1068 GLAS MAOL
Caenlochan Forest
Glendoll Forest
Loch Brandy
Water of Saughs
CRUYS 741
WEST KNOCK 691
1051 GLAS TULAICHEAN
905 FINALTY HILL
CORRIE FEE
Isla
947 DRIESH
GLEN CLOVA
NO
1120 BEINN A'GHLO
BEN GULABIN 806
Clova
758
778 WHITE HILL
Hunthill Lodge
Glenlochsie
808 MONAMEANACH
903 BEN VUIRICH
Wheen
Angus
Gleann Fearnach
801 BEN EARB
Spittal of Glenshee
Auchavan
Glen Prosen
Kilburn
Rottal
756 FINBRACKS
Loch Beanie
740 BADENDUN HILL
Glenprosen Lodge
794 MEALL UAINE
Glen Shee
702 DUCHRAY HILL
Balnaboth
PROSEN
Glenprosen Village
512
545 AULD DARKNEY
Tarvie
Straloch
Dalnaglar Castle
Meikle Forter
Glenisla Forest
611
Clachnabrain
76
Glenmoy
Dalnavaid
Enochdhu
Cray
Folda
Glen Brerachan
STRATHARDLE
744 MOUNT BLAIR
Glenhead Farm
Easter Lednathie
Auchnacree
Glenogil
641 CREAG DHUBH
Ashintully Castle
Brewlands Bridge
Backwater Res.
Glenquiech
Ogil
Fern
Kirkmichael
Blacklunans
Freuchies
668 CAT LAW
CAPTAIN SCOTT & DR WILSON CAIRN
Hornieshaugh
Dykehead
Newmill of Inshewan
Kirkton of Glenisla
Bellaty
Balintore
Pearsie
Cortachy
Memus
Noran
520 CAIRN GIBBS
497 CREIGH HILL
Dykends
Balloch
Tannadice
Inverquharity
Murthill
KNOCK OF BALMYLE
MEALL REAMHAR
Forest of Alyth
409
Black
Finavon
0 1 2 3 4 5 6 miles
0 1 2 3 4 5 6 7 8 9 10 km

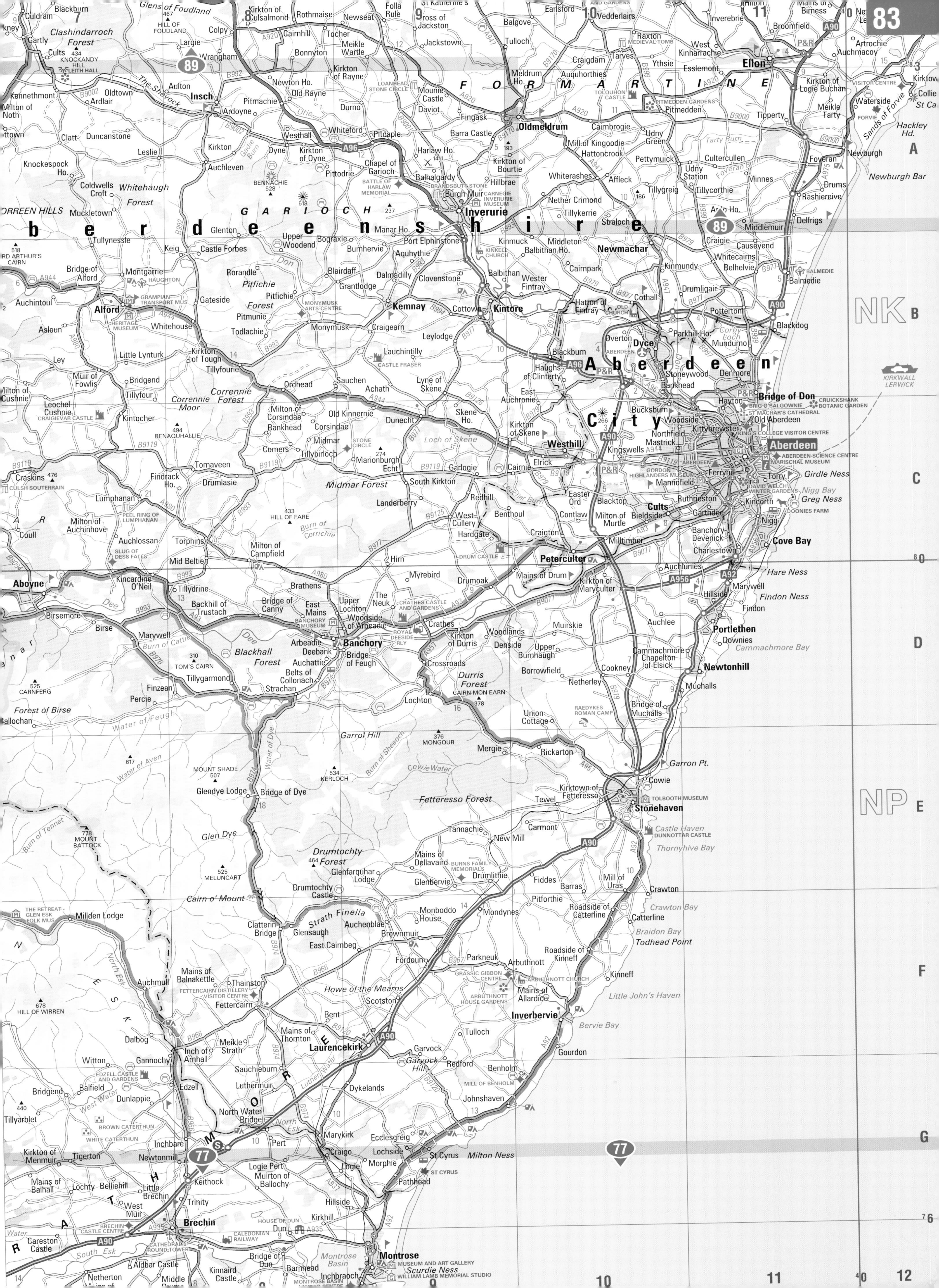
Aberdeenshire
Aberdeen City
GARIOCH
FORMARTINE
Aberdeen
Inverurie
Oldmeldrum
Ellon
Insch
Kintore
Kemnay
Alford
Westhill
Dyce
Newmachar
Bridge of Don
Cults
Peterculter
Banchory
Aboyne
Stonehaven
Newtonhill
Portlethen
Cove Bay
Inverbervie
Laurencekirk
Montrose
Brechin
Edzell
Fettercairn
St Cyrus
Balmedie
Newburgh
Monymusk
Echt
Kincardine O'Neil
Torphins
Drumoak
Crathes
Potterton
Blackdog
Kingswells
Bucksburn
Hazlehead
Mannofield
Ferryhill
Torry
Nigg
Kincorth
Garthdee
Bieldside
Milltimber
Muchalls
Findon
Hillside
Marywell
Crawton
Catterline
Kinneff
Gourdon
Johnshaven
Marykirk
Craigo
Logie Pert
North Water Bridge
Luthermuir
Auchenblae
Drumlithie
Glenbervie
Fordoun
Arbuthnott
Bervie Bay
Todhead Point
Garron Pt.
Girdle Ness
Greg Ness
Hare Ness
Findon Ness
Milton Ness
Scurdie Ness
Montrose Basin
Fetteresso Forest
Durris Forest
Midmar Forest
Blackhall Forest
Forest of Birse
Drumtochty Forest
Pitfichie Forest
Whitehaugh Forest
Correnie Forest
Clashindarroch Forest
Howe of the Mearns
Strath Finella
Glen Dye
Cairn o' Mount
Bridge of Dye
Clatterin Bridge
Water of Feugh
Water of Dye
North Esk
South Esk
Dee
Don
Sands of Forvie
Newburgh Bar
Castle Fraser
Crathes Castle and Gardens
Drum Castle
Dunnottar Castle
Craigievar Castle
Fasque
Pitmedden Gardens
Tolquhon Castle
Haddo
Leith Hall
Grampian Transport Mus.
Aberdeen Science Centre
Marischal Museum
St Machar's Cathedral
Tolbooth Museum
Lewis Grassic Gibbon Centre
Arbuthnott Church
House of Dun
Caledonian Railway
Brechin Castle Centre
Museum and Art Gallery
William Lamb Memorial Studio
A90
A96
A93
A92
A944
A947
A956
A957
A980
A937
A935
B9077
B979
B974
B966
B993
89
77
NK
NP
Kirkwall
Lerwick

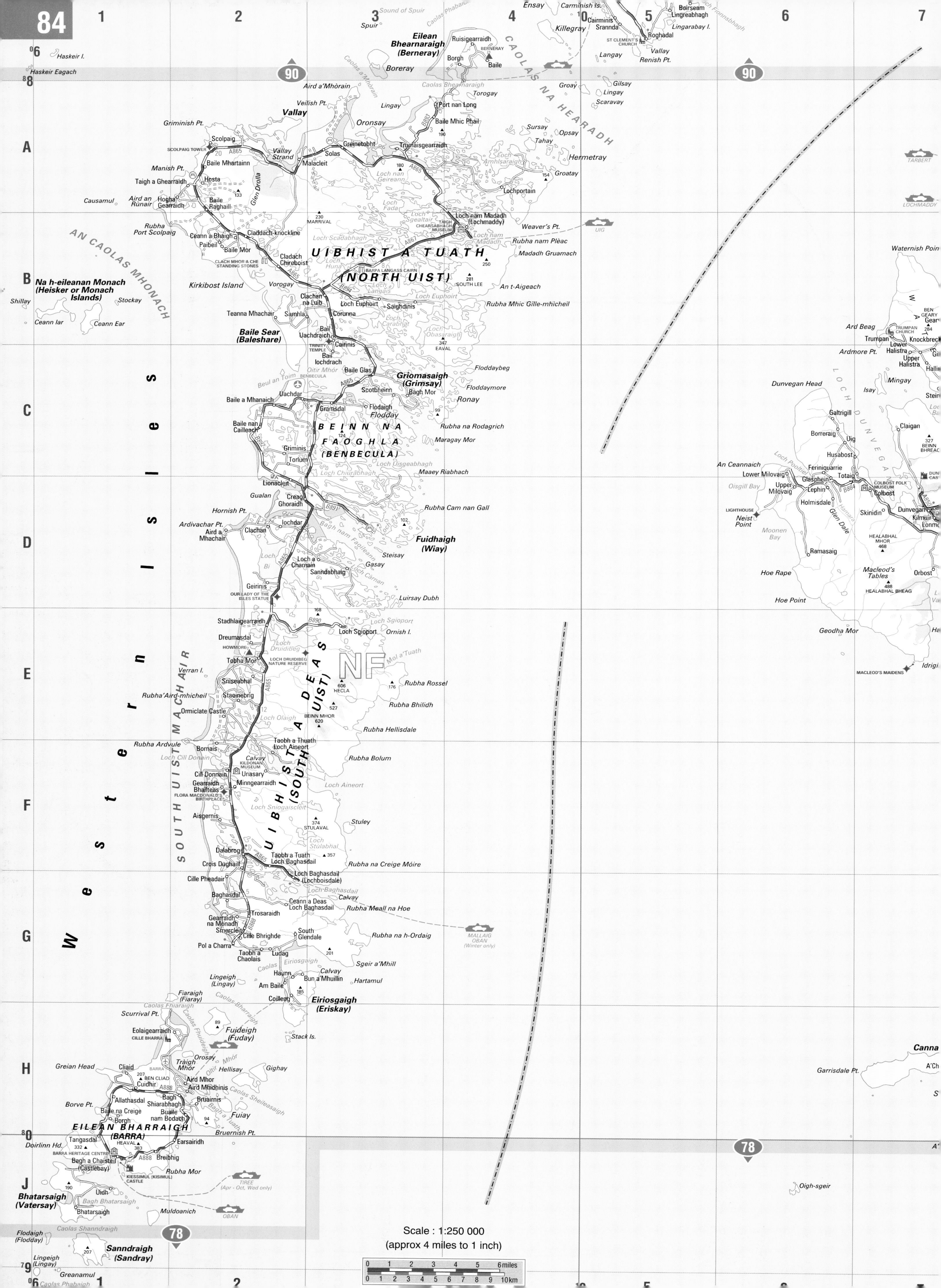
Eilean Bhearnaraigh (Berneray)
Boreray
Vallay
Oronsay
Scolpaig
Sollas
Lochmaddy
Loch nam Madadh (Lochmaddy)
CAOLAS NA HEARADH
AN CAOLAS MHONACH
Na h-eileanan Monach (Heisker or Monach Islands)
Shillay
Ceann Iar
Ceann Ear
Stockay
Kirkibost Island
UIBHIST A TUATH (NORTH UIST)
Baile Sear (Baleshare)
Griomasaigh (Grimsay)
Ronay
BEINN NA FAOGHLA (BENBECULA)
Fuidhaigh (Wiay)
Western Isles
SOUTH UIST MACHAIR
UIBHIST A DEAS (SOUTH UIST)
NF
Loch Baghasdail (Lochboisdale)
Eiriosgaigh (Eriskay)
Fuideigh (Fuday)
EILEAN BHARRAIGH (BARRA)
Bhatarsaigh (Vatersay)
Sanndraigh (Sandray)
Fiaraigh (Fiaray)
Lingeigh (Lingay)
Flodaigh (Flodday)
Canna
Dunvegan Head
LOCH DUNVEGAN
Dunvegan
Neist Point
Macleod's Tables
Hoe Point
Idrigill
Waternish Point
90
78
Scale : 1:250 000
(approx 4 miles to 1 inch)
0 1 2 3 4 5 6 miles
0 1 2 3 4 5 6 7 8 9 10 km

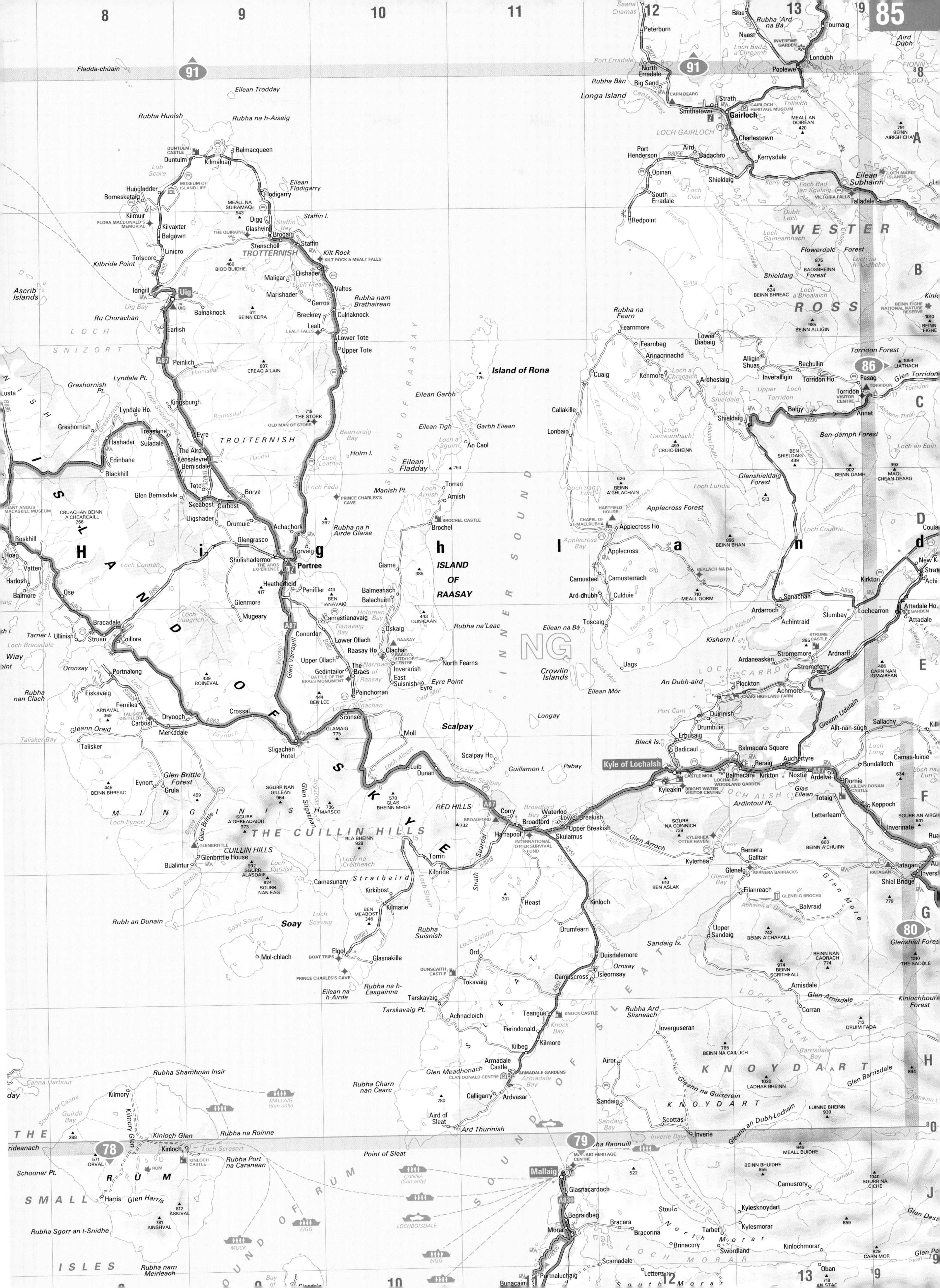
8
9
10
11
12
13
91
Fladda-chùain
Eilean Trodday
Rubha Hunish
Rubha na h-Aiseig
Duntulm Castle
Duntulm
Balmacqueen
Kilmaluag
Lub Score
Hungladder
Borneskeitaig
Museum of Island Life
Eilean Flodigarry
Flodigarry
Kilmuir
Flora Macdonald's Memorial
Kilvaxter
Balgown
Meall na Suiramach
543
Digg
Staffin I.
Glashvin
Brogaig
The Quiraing
Stenscholl
Staffin
TROTTERNISH
Linicro
Totscore
Kilbride Point
Kilt Rock
Kilt Rock & Mealt Falls
466
Biod Buidhe
Elishader
Maligar
Valtos
Marishader
Garros
Rubha nam Brathairean
Ascrib Islands
Idrigill
Uig
Uig Bay
Balnaknock
611
Beinn Edra
Culnaknock
Breckrey
Lealt
Lealt Falls
Ru Chorachan
Earlish
Lower Tote
Upper Tote
LOCH
SNIZORT
Peinlich
Hinnisdal
607
Creag a' Lain
Gresborish Pt.
Lyndale Pt.
Kingsburgh
719
The Storr
Old Man of Storr
Lyndale Ho.
Greshornish
Treaslane
Suladale
Flashader
Edinbane
Blackhill
Eyre
TROTTERNISH
The Aird
Kensaleyre
Bernisdale
Glen Bernisdale
Tote
Borve
Skeabost
Carbost
Uigshader
Drumuie
Cruachan Beinn a' Chearcaill
266
Giant Angus Macaskill Museum
Achachork
Prince Charles's Cave
392
Rubha na h Airde Glaise
Roskhill
Glengrasco
Torvaig
Shulishadermor
The Aros Experience
Portree
Roag
Vatten
Loch Connan
Heatherfield
417
Harlosh
Balmore
Ose
Penifiler
413
Ben Tianavaig
Glenmore
Mugeary
Bracadale
Tarner I.
Ullinish
Struan
Coillore
Camastianavaig
Conordan
Lower Ollach
Raasay Ho.
Upper Ollach
Gedintailor
The Braes
Battle of the Braes Monument
Peinchorran
444
Ben Lee
Oronsay
Portnalong
439
Roineval
Rubha nan Clach
Fiskavaig
Fernilea
Arnaval
369
Talisker Distillery
Carbost
Drynoch
Crossal
Gleann Oraid
Merkadale
Talisker Bay
Talisker
Sconser
Glamaig
775
Sligachan Hotel
Moll
Glen Brittle Forest
445
Beinn Bhreac
Eynort
Grula
459
Sgurr nan Gillean
964
Glen Sligachan
736
Marsco
Loch Eynort
Sgurr a' Ghreadaidh
973
THE CUILLIN HILLS
Bla Bheinn
928
Glenbrittle
CUILLIN HILLS
Glenbrittle House
Bualintur
992
Sgurr Alasdair
924
Sgurr nan Eag
Loch Coruisk
Camasunary
Strathaird
Kirkibost
Ben Meabost
346
Kilmarie
Rubh an Dunain
Soay
Soay Sound
Mol-chlach
Elgol
Boat Trips
Glasnakille
Prince Charles's Cave
Rubha Suisnish
Eilean na h-Airde
Rubha na h-Easgainne
SKYE
ISLE OF SKYE
Eilean Garbh
Eilean Tigh
Garbh Eilean
An Caol
Holm I.
Eilean Fladday
254
Torran
Arnish
Manish Pt.
Brochel Castle
Brochel
Island of Rona
125
SOUND OF RAASAY
ISLAND OF RAASAY
Glame
385
Balmeanach
Balachuirn
443
Dun Caan
Oskaig
Raasay
Clachan
Raasay Outdoor Centre
Inverarish
East Suisnish
North Fearns
Eyre
Eyre Point
Rubha na' Leac
Scalpay
Scalpay Ho.
Luib
Dunan
Loch Ainort
570
Glas Bheinn Mhor
RED HILLS
Corry
Broadford
732
Harrapool
Torrin
Kilbride
Strath Suardal
Waterloo
Lower Breakish
Upper Breakish
Skulamus
International Otter Survival Fund
Glen Arroch
Heast
301
Kinloch
Drumfearn
Ord
Dunscaith Castle
Tokavaig
Duisdalemore
Ornsay
Camuscross
Isleornsay
Tarskavaig
Tarskavaig Pt.
Achnacloich
Teangue
Knock Castle
Ferindonald
Kilbeg
Kilmore
SLEAT
SOUND OF SLEAT
Glen Meadhonach
Armadale Castle
Clan Donald Centre
Armadale Gardens
Armadale Bay
Rubha Charn nan Cearc
280
Calligarry
Ardvasar
Aird of Sleat
Ard Thurinish
Point of Sleat
INNER SOUND
NG
Crowlin Islands
Eilean Mór
Eilean na Bà
Longay
Guillamon I.
Pabay
Kyle of Lochalsh
Kyleakin
Bright Water Visitor Centre
Castle Moil
Rubha Bàn
Longa Island
Port Erradale
North Erradale
Big Sand
Carn Dearg
Smithstown
Strath
Gairloch
Gairloch Heritage Museum
LOCH GAIRLOCH
Charlestown
Port Henderson
Aird
Badachro
Opinan
South Erradale
Shieldaig
Kerrysdale
Redpoint
Peterburn
Brae
Naast
Rubha 'Ard na Bà
Inverewe Garden
Tournaig
Londubh
Poolewe
Aird Dubh
Meall an Doirean
420
791
Beinn Airigh Cha'
Eilean Subhainn
Loch Maree Islands
Talladale
Loch Bad an Sgalaig
Victoria Falls
WESTER ROSS
Flowerdale Forest
875
Baosbheinn Forest
Shieldaig
624
Beinn Bhreac
Beinn Eighe National Nature Reserve
1010
Beinn Eighe
985
Beinn Alligin
Rubha na Fearn
Fearnmore
Fearnbeg
Arinacrinachd
Kenmore
Lower Diabaig
Alligin Shuas
Inveralligin
Rechullin
Torridon Ho.
Torridon Forest
1054
Liathach
86
Fasag
Glen Torridon
Torridon
Torridon Visitor Centre
Annat
Cuaig
Ardheslaig
Shieldaig
Balgy
Callakille
Lonbain
493
Croic-Bheinn
Ben Shieldaig
439
Ben-damph Forest
902
Beinn Damh
993
Maol Chean-dearg
626
Beinn a' Chlachain
Glenshieldaig Forest
513
Hartfield House
Chapel of St Maelrubha
Applecross Forest
Applecross Ho.
Applecross
Loch Coultrie
896
Beinn Bhan
Bealach na Ba
Camusteel
Camusterrach
Culduie
Ard-dhubh
710
Meall Gorm
Kirkton
Sanachan
Ardarroch
Achintraid
Slumbay
Lochcarron
Attadale Ho.
Attadale
Toscaig
Uags
Kishorn I.
Strome Castle
395
Ardaneaskan
Stromemore
Ardnarff
Stromeferry
486
Carn nan Iomairean
An Dubh-aird
Plockton
Craig Highland Farm
Achmore
Duirinish
Drumbuie
Gleann Udalain
Sallachy
Allt-nan-sùgh
Erbusaig
Black Is.
Badicaul
Balmacara Square
Reraig
Auchertyre
Balmacara
Kirkton
Nostie
Ardelve
Dornie
Eilean Donan Castle
Bundalloch
Camas-luinie
634
Lochalsh Woodland Garden
LOCH ALSH
Glas Eilean
Ardintoul Pt.
Totaig
Letterfearn
Keppoch
Sgurr an Airgid
841
Invérinate
Sgurr na Coinnich
739
Kylerhea Otter Haven
Kylerhea
Bernera
Galltair
Glenelg
Bernera Barracks
603
Beinn a' Chuirn
Ratagan
Shiel Bridge
610
Ben Aslak
Eilanreach
Glenelg Brochs
Balvraid
Glen More
779
Upper Sandaig
742
Beinn a' Chapaill
80
Glenshiel Forest
1010
The Saddle
Sandaig Is.
974
Beinn Sgritheall
Beinn nan Caorach
774
Arnisdale
Glen Arnisdale
Corran
Rubha Ard Slisneach
Kinlochhourn Forest
LOCH HOURN
713
Druim Fada
Inverguseran
785
Beinn na Caillich
Airor
KNOYDART
1020
Ladhar Bheinn
Glen Barrisdale
894
Gleann na Guiserein
Sandaig
Scottas
939
Luinne Bheinn
Inverie
Inverie Bay
Gleann an Dubh-Lochain
946
Meall Buidhe
Rubha Shamhnan Insir
Canna Harbour
Kilmory
Mallaig (Sun only)
Guirdil Bay
388
THE
Kinloch Glen
Rubha na Roinne
78
Kinloch
Kinloch Castle
Loch Scresort
Rubha Port na Caranean
571
Orval
Rùm
Schooner Pt.
RÙM
SMALL
ISLES
Harris
Glen Harris
812
Askival
781
Ainshval
Rubha Sgorr an t-Snidhe
Rubha nam Meirleach
SOUND OF RÙM
Canna (Sun only)
Lochboisdale
Eigg
Muck
79
Mallaig Heritage Centre
Mallaig
522
Glasnacardoch
A830
Beoraidbeg
Morar
Bracara
Bracorina
Stoul
LOCH NEVIS
Tarbet
Kylesknoydart
Kylesmorar
North Morar
Brinacory
Swordland
Kinlochmorar
LOCH MORAR
Scamadale
Portnaluchaig
Letterm...
South Morar
Bunacaimb
Oban
718
An Stac
829
Carn Mor
Beinn Bhuidhe
855
Camusrory
1040
Sgurr na Ciche
859
A87
A855
A850
A863
B885
B8083
A851
B8056
A896
A890
A832
B8021
A830
Glen Varragill
Sligachan
Caolas Scalpay
Raasay Narrows

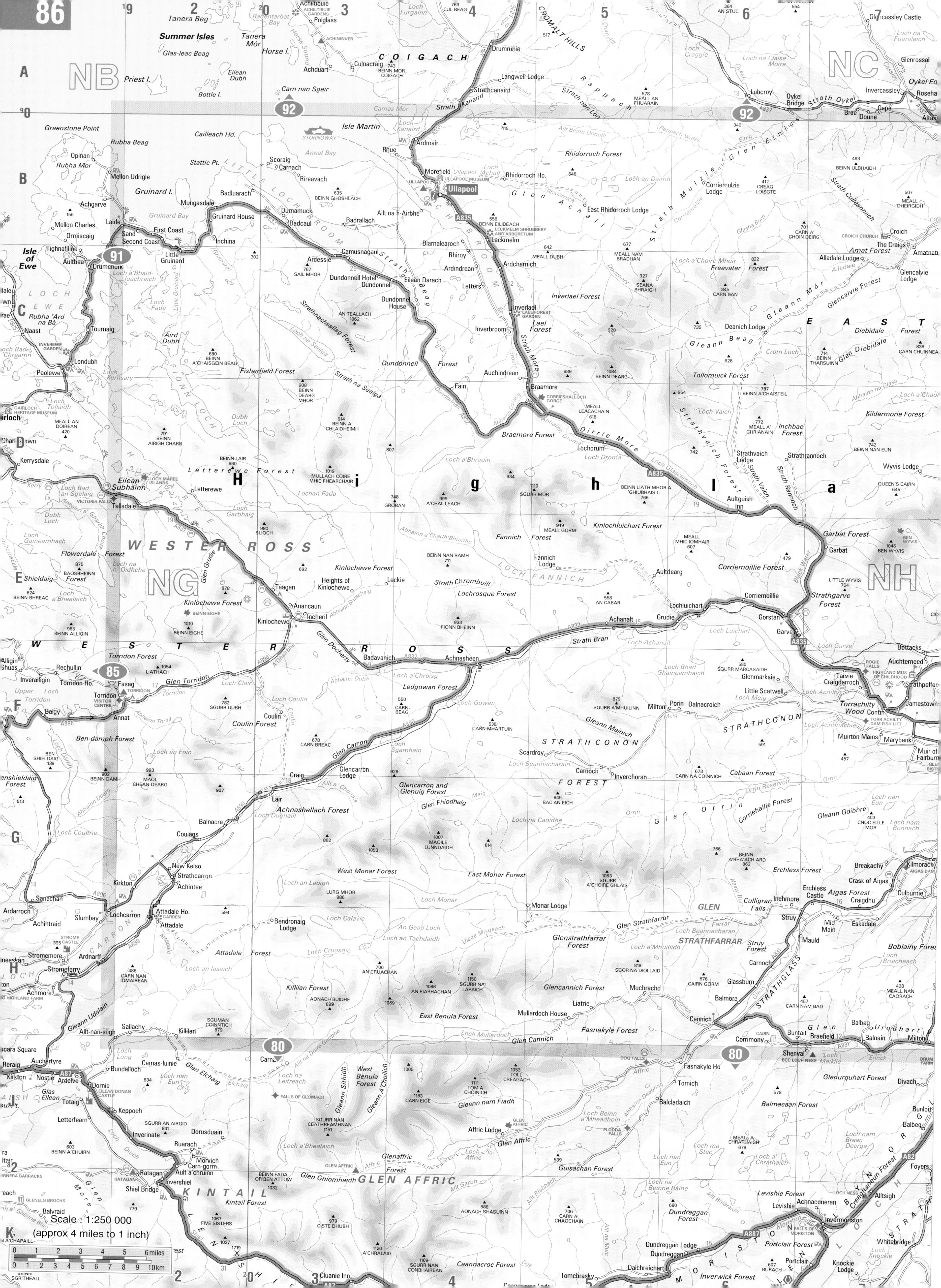
NB
NC
NG
NH
Summer Isles
Tanera Beg
Tanera Mór
Horse I.
Glas-leac Beag
Priest I.
Eilean Dubh
Bottle I.
Achiltibuie
Polglass
Achduart
Culnacraig
COIGACH
Carn nan Sgeir
Isle Martin
Drumrunie
Langwell Lodge
Strathcanaird
Strath Kanaird
CROMALT HILLS
Rappach
Strath nan Lon
Lubcroy
Oykel Bridge
Strath Oykel
Invercassley
Rosehall
Glencassley Castle
Greenstone Point
Rubha Beag
Cailleach Hd.
Stattic Pt.
Opinan
Rubha Mor
Mellon Udrigle
Gruinard I.
Gruinard Bay
Scoraig
Carnach
Rireavach
Annat Bay
LITTLE LOCH BROOM
Ardmair
Rhue
Morefield
Ullapool
Rhidorroch Forest
Rhidorroch Ho.
Glen Achall
East Rhidorroch Lodge
Strath Mulzie
Corriemulzie Lodge
Strath Cuileannach
Croick
Amat Forest
Alladale Lodge
Glencalvie Lodge
Glencalvie Forest
Mungasdale
Badluarach
Achgarve
Mellon Charles
Ormiscaig
Laide
Sand
First Coast
Second Coast
Gruinard House
Inchina
Little Gruinard
Dundonnell
Badcaul
Durnamuck
Badrallach
Allt na h-Airbhe
LOCH BROOM
Leckmelm
Blarnalearoch
Rhiroy
Ardindrean
Ardcharnich
Letters
Inverlael
Inverlael Forest
Isle of Ewe
Tighnafiline
Aultbea
Drumchork
Loch Ewe
Rubha 'Ard na Bà
Naast
Tournaig
Inverewe Garden
Londubh
Poolewe
Ardessie
Camusnagaul
Strath Beag
Dundonnell Hotel
Eilean Darach
Dundonnell House
Strathnasheallag Forest
An Teallach
Aird Dubh
Fisherfield Forest
Strath na Sealga
Dundonnell Forest
Inverbroom
Lael Forest
Strath More
Auchindrean
Fain
Braemore
Corrieshalloch Gorge
Deanich Lodge
Gleann Mór
Gleann Beag
Diebidale
EAST
Tollomuick Forest
Kildermorie Forest
Gairloch
Charlestown
Kerrysdale
Fionn Loch
Dubh Loch
Letterewe Forest
Letterewe
Eilean Subhainn
Loch Maree
Talladale
Braemore Forest
Dirrie More
Lochdrum
Loch Droma
Loch Glascarnoch
Strathvaich Forest
Strathvaich Lodge
Strath Vaich
Strath Rannoch
Inchbae Forest
Wyvis Lodge
Highland
Aultguish Inn
Kinlochluichart Forest
Fannich Forest
Fannich Lodge
Loch Fannich
Garbat Forest
Garbat
Ben Wyvis
Corriemoillie Forest
WESTER ROSS
Flowerdale Forest
Shieldaig Forest
Glen Grudie
Kinlochewe Forest
Heights of Kinlochewe
Kinlochewe
Taagan
Anancaun
Incheril
Leckie
Strath Chrombuill
Lochrosque Forest
Aultdearg
Lochluichart
Corriemoillie
Strathgarve Forest
Gorstan
Garve
Grudie
Achanalt
Strath Bran
Glen Docherty
Torridon Forest
Rechullin
Inveralligin
Torridon Ho.
Fasag
Torridon
Glen Torridon
Badavanich
Achnasheen
Ledgowan Forest
Annat
Coulin Forest
Coulin
Glenmarksie
Little Scatwell
Milton
Porin
Dalnacroich
STRATHCONON
Torrachilty Wood
Contin
Strathpeffer
Jamestown
Auchterneed
Tarvie
Craigdarroch
Muirton Mains
Marybank
Muir of Fairburn
Ben-damph Forest
Glen Carron
Glencarron Lodge
Craig
Lair
Scardroy
Carnoch
Inverchoran
Cabaan Forest
STRATHCONON FOREST
Glencarron and Glenuig Forest
Glen Fhiodhaig
Achnashellach Forest
Glen Orrin
Corriehallie Forest
Gleann Goibhre
Balnacra
Coulags
West Monar Forest
East Monar Forest
Erchless Forest
Breakachy
Crask of Aigas
Kilmorack
New Kelso
Strathcarron
Achintee
Kirkton
Lochcarron
Sanachan
Ardarroch
Achintraid
Slumbay
Attadale Ho.
Attadale
Attadale Forest
Bendronaig Lodge
Loch Monar
Monar Lodge
Glen Strathfarrar
Glenstrathfarrar Forest
STRATHFARRAR
Struy Forest
Culligran Falls
Inchmore
Erchless Castle
Aigas Forest
Craigdhu
Culburnie
Struy
Eskadale
Mauld
Boblainy Forest
Stromemore
Ardnarff
Stromeferry
Achmore
Killilan Forest
Glencannich Forest
Muchrachd
Carnoch
Glassburn
Balmore
STRATHGLASS
East Benula Forest
Mullardoch House
Liatrie
Cannich
Sallachy
Allt-nan-sugh
Killilan
Gleann Udalain
Loch Mullardoch
Glen Cannich
Fasnakyle Forest
Corrimony
Buntait
Glen Urquhart
Balbeg
Balnain
Milton
Shenval
Auchertyre
Reraig
Kirkton
Nostie
Ardelve
Dornie
Eilean Donan Castle
Glas Eilean
Totaig
Bundalloch
Camas-luinie
Glen Elchaig
Carnach
Falls of Glomach
West Benula Forest
Gleann Sithidh
Gleann A'Choilich
Gleann nam Fiadh
Fasnakyle Ho
Tomich
Balcladaich
Glenurquhart Forest
Divach
Balmacaan Forest
Bunloit
Keppoch
Letterfearn
Inverinate
Dorusduain
Ruarach
Morvich
Carn-gorm
Ault a'chruinn
Ratagan
Inverhiel
Shiel Bridge
Affric Lodge
Glen Affric
Plodda Falls
Glenaffric Forest
GLEN AFFRIC
Glen Gniomhaidh
Guisachan Forest
KINTAIL
Kintail Forest
Glen Shiel
Glenelg
Balvraid
Glen More
Levishie Forest
Levishie
Achnaconeran
Dundreggan Forest
Invermoriston
Alltsigh
Foyers
Creag nan Forest
Dundreggan Lodge
Dundreggan
Portclair Forest
Portclair
GLEN MORISTON
Whitebridge
Knockie Lodge
Ceannacroc Forest
Tomchrasky
Dalchreichart
Inverwick Forest
Cluanie Inn
Five Sisters
Scale : 1:250 000
(approx 4 miles to 1 inch)
6 miles
10km

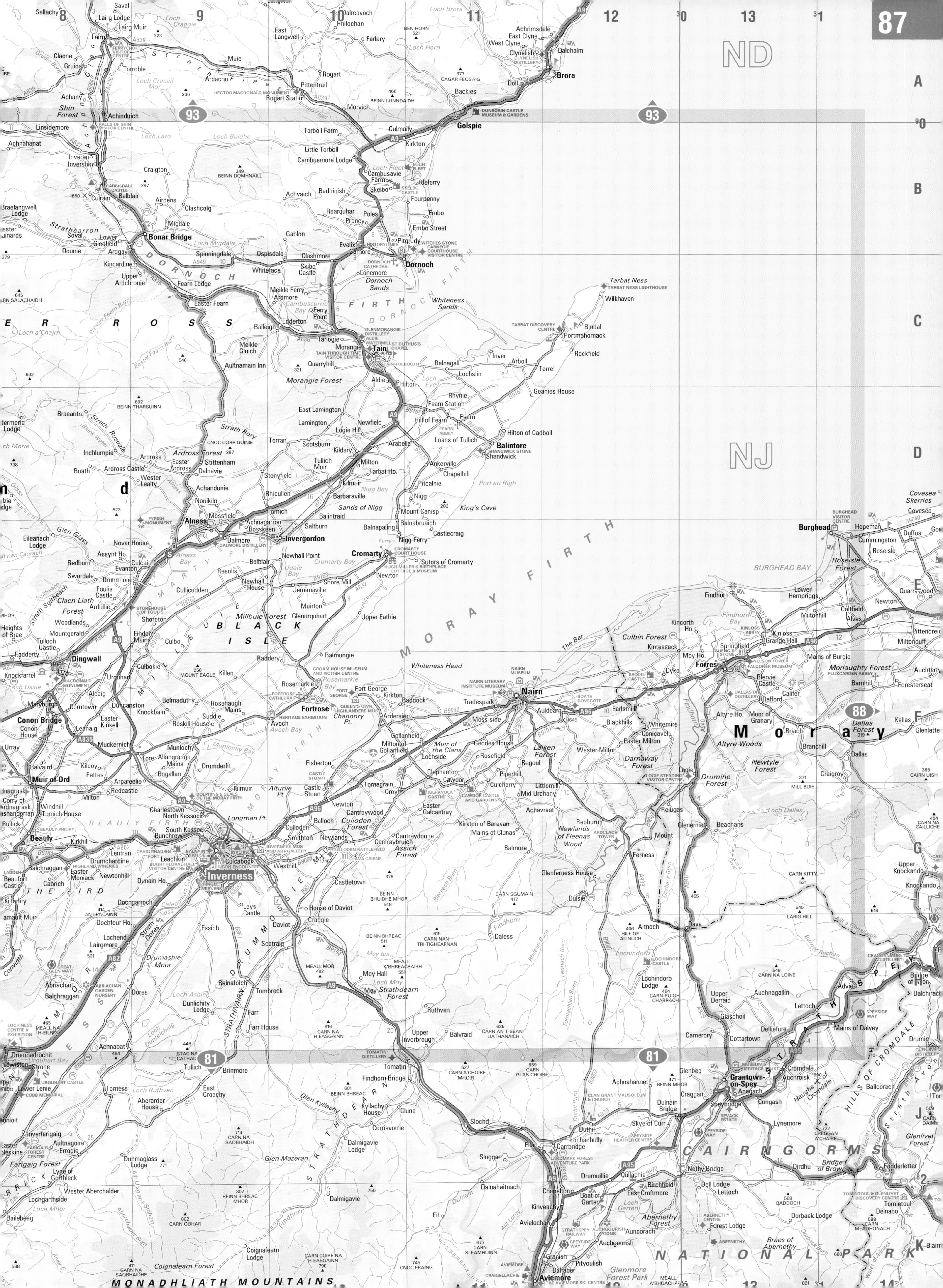
ND
NJ
93
81
88
A
B
C
D
E
F
G
H
J
K
8
9
10
11
12
13
Lairg
Brora
Golspie
Dornoch
Bonar Bridge
Tain
Balintore
Alness
Invergordon
Cromarty
Dingwall
Conon Bridge
Muir of Ord
Beauly
Inverness
Fortrose
Nairn
Forres
Burghead
Grantown-on-Spey
Aviemore
Moray
MORAY FIRTH
DORNOCH FIRTH
BLACK ISLE
BEAULY FIRTH
CAIRNGORMS NATIONAL PARK
MONADHLIATH MOUNTAINS
HILLS OF CROMDALE
STRATHSPEY
STRATHDEARN
STRATHNAIRN
DRUMMOSSIE MUIR
ROSS
Tarbat Ness
Portmahomack
Rockfield
Wilkhaven
Whiteness Head
Burghead Bay
Culbin Forest
Findhorn
Kinloss
Dalcross
Cawdor
Croy
Ardersier
Fort George
Rosemarkie
Avoch
Munlochy
Evanton
Strathpeffer
Drumnadrochit
Tomatin
Carrbridge
Boat of Garten
Nethy Bridge
Dulnain Bridge
Lochindorb
Dava
Ferness
Auldearn
Glen Mazeran
Glen Kyllachy
Loch Ness
Urquhart Castle
Dores
Farr
Tomintoul
Dallas
Cromdale

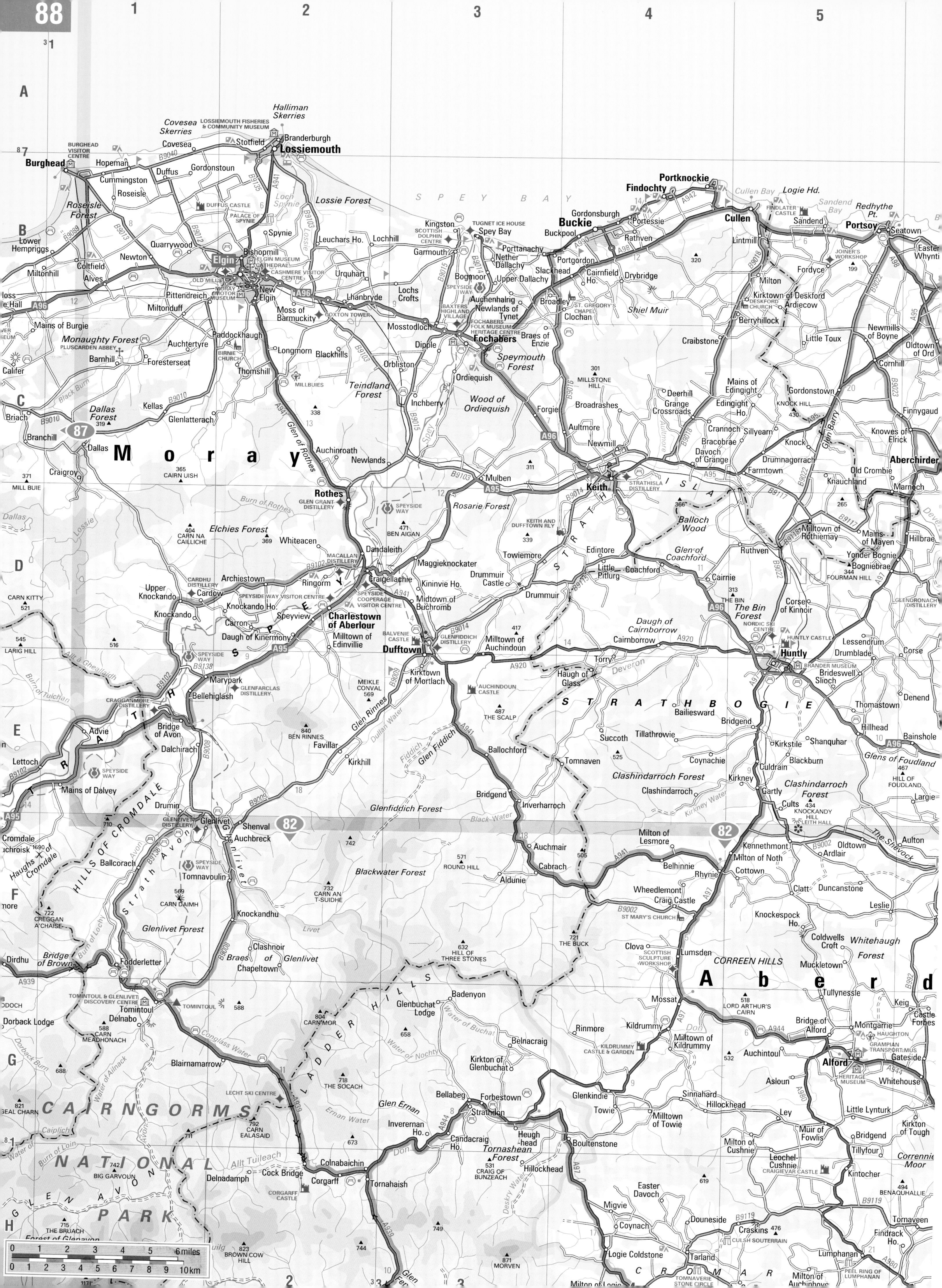

88
Halliman Skerries
Covesea Skerries
LOSSIEMOUTH FISHERIES & COMMUNITY MUSEUM
Branderburgh
Lossiemouth
Stotfield
Covesea
BURGHEAD VISITOR CENTRE
Burghead
Hopeman
Duffus
Gordonstoun
Cummingston
Roseisle
Roseisle Forest
Loch Spynie
Lossie Forest
DUFFUS CASTLE
PALACE OF SPYNIE
Spynie
Lower Hempriggs
Quarrywood
Bishopmill
Elgin
ELGIN MUSEUM
CATHEDRAL
CASHMERE VISITOR CENTRE
OLD MILLS
MORAY MOTOR MUSEUM
New Elgin
Newton
Coltfield
Miltonhill
Alves
Pittendreich
Miltonduff
Mains of Burgie
Monaughty Forest
PLUSCARDEN ABBEY
Barnhill
Foresterseat
Califer
Auchtertyre
Paddockhaugh
BIRNIE CHURCH
Thornshill
Longmorn
Blackhills
MILLBUIES
Moss of Barmuckity
COXTON TOWER
Lhanbryde
Urquhart
Lochs Crofts
Leuchars Ho.
Lochhill
Garmouth
Kingston
SCOTTISH DOLPHIN CENTRE
TUGNET ICE HOUSE
Spey Bay
SPEY BAY
Porttanachy
Nether Dallachy
Upper Dallachy
Bogmoor
SPEYSIDE WAY
Auchenhalrig
Newlands of Tynet
BAXTERS HIGHLAND VILLAGE
FOCHABERS FOLK MUSEUM HERITAGE CENTRE
Mosstodloch
Fochabers
Dipple
Braes of Enzie
Speymouth Forest
Orbliston
Ordiequish
Wood of Ordiequish
Teindland Forest
Inchberry
Spey
Kellas
Glenlatterach
Dallas Forest
Briach
Branchill
Dallas
Moray
Glen of Rothes
Auchinroath
Newlands
Craigroy
MILL BUIE
CAIRN UISH
Rothes
GLEN GRANT DISTILLERY
SPEYSIDE WAY
BEN AIGAN
Burn of Rothes
Elchies Forest
CARN NA CAILLICHE
Whiteacen
MACALLAN DISTILLERY
Dandaleith
Maggieknockater
Archiestown
CARDHU DISTILLERY
Upper Knockando
Cardow
Ringorm
Craigellachie
SPEYSIDE WAY VISITOR CENTRE
SPEYSIDE COOPERAGE VISITOR CENTRE
Kininvie Ho.
Drummuir Castle
Knockando Ho.
Knockando
Carron
Speyview
Charlestown of Aberlour
Midtown of Buchromb
Daugh of Kinermony
Milltown of Edinvillie
BALVENIE CASTLE
GLENFIDDICH DISTILLERY
Dufftown
Milltown of Auchindoun
CARN KITTY
LARIG HILL
Burn of Tulchan
Marypark
GLENFARCLAS DISTILLERY
Bellehiglash
CRAGGANMORE DISTILLERY
Advie
Bridge of Avon
Lettoch
Dalchirach
SPEYSIDE WAY
Mains of Dalvey
HILLS OF CROMDALE
Drumin
GLENLIVET DISTILLERY
Glenlivet
Shenval
Auchbreck
Cromdale
Haughs of Cromdale
Ballcorach
Tomnavoulin
CARN DAIMH
Strath Avon
CREGGAN A'CHAISE
Knockandhu
Glenlivet Forest
Clashnoir
Braes of Glenlivet
Chapeltown
Bridge of Brown
Dirdhu
Fodderletter
TOMINTOUL & GLENLIVET DISCOVERY CENTRE
Tomintoul
Delnabo
Dorback Lodge
CARN MEADHONACH
Conglass Water
Blairnamarrow
LECHT SKI CENTRE
CAIRNGORMS
NATIONAL PARK
SEAL CHARN
CARN EALASAID
BIG GARVOUN
Delnadamph
Cock Bridge
Corgarff
CORGARFF CASTLE
Tornahaish
THE BRUACH
BROWN COW HILL
Forest of Glenavon
GLEN AVON
Allt Tuileach
LADDER HILLS
CARN MOR
Glenbuchat Lodge
Badenyon
THE SOCACH
Glen Ernan
Ernan Water
Inverernan Ho.
Candacraig Ho.
Bellabeg
Forbestown
Strathdon
Heugh-head
Tornashean Forest
CRAIG OF BUNZEACH
Hillockhead
MORVEN
Kirkton of Glenbuchat
Belnacraig
Kirkton of Mortlach
MEIKLE CONVAL
Glen Rinnes
BEN RINNES
Favillar
Kirkhill
Dullan Water
Glen Fiddich
AUCHINDOUN CASTLE
THE SCALP
Ballochford
Bridgend
Glenfiddich Forest
Inverharroch
Black Water
Auchmair
Cabrach
Aldunie
ROUND HILL
Blackwater Forest
CARN AN T-SUIDHE
HILL OF THREE STONES
Livet
Buckie
Buckpool
Gordonsburgh
Portessie
Rathven
Findochty
Portknockie
Cullen Bay
Logie Hd.
Cullen
FINDLATER CASTLE
Sandend
Sandend Bay
Redhythe Pt.
Portsoy
Seatown
Portgordon
Slackhead
Cairnfield Ho.
Drybridge
Broadley
ST. GREGORY'S CHAPEL
Clochan
Shiel Muir
MILLSTONE HILL
Forgie
Broadrashes
Aultmore
Newmill
Keith
STRATHISLA DISTILLERY
Mulben
Rosarie Forest
KEITH AND DUFFTOWN RLY
Towiemore
Drummuir
Edintore
Little Pitlurg
Coachford
STRATH ISLA
Balloch Wood
Glen of Coachford
Deerhill
Grange Crossroads
Edingight Ho.
Mains of Edingight
Crannoch
Sillyearn
Bracobrae
Davoch of Grange
Lintmill
Milton
Kirktown of Deskford
DESKFORD CHURCH
Berryhillock
Craibstone
Ardiecow
Fordyce
JOINER'S WORKSHOP
Newmills of Boyne
Little Toux
Oldtown of Ord
Cornhill
Gordonstown
KNOCK HILL
Knock
Glen Barry
Knowes of Elrick
Finnygaud
Aberchirder
Drumnagorrach
Farmtown
Old Crombie
Knauchland
Marnoch
Milltown of Rothiemay
Mains of Mayen
Yonder Bognie
Bogniebrae
FOURMAN HILL
Hillbrae
Ruthven
Cairnie
THE BIN
The Bin Forest
Corse of Kinnoir
NORDIC SKI CENTRE
HUNTLY CASTLE
Huntly
BRANDER MUSEUM
Daugh of Cairnborrow
Cairnborrow
Torry
Haugh of Glass
Deveron
STRATHBOGIE
Bailiesward
Bridgend
Tillathrowie
Succoth
Tomnaven
Coynachie
Clashindarroch Forest
Clashindarroch
Kirkney
Kirkney Water
Gartly
Clashindarroch Forest
Cults
KNOCKANDY HILL
LEITH HALL
Kirkstile
Shanquhar
Culdrain
Blackburn
Glens of Foudland
HILL OF FOUDLAND
Largie
Lessendrum
Drumblade
Brideswell
Slioch
Corse
Denend
Thomastown
Hillhead
Bainshole
Milton of Lesmore
Kennethmont
Milton of Noth
Oldtown
Ardlair
The Shevock
Aulton
Belhinnie
Rhynie
Cottown
Clatt
Duncanstone
Wheedlemont
Craig Castle
ST MARY'S CHURCH
Leslie
Knockespock Ho.
Coldwells Croft
Whitehaugh Forest
THE BUCK
Clova
SCOTTISH SCULPTURE WORKSHOP
Lumsden
CORREEN HILLS
Muckletown
Aberd
Tullynessle
Mossat
LORD ARTHUR'S CAIRN
Keig
Castle Forbes
Bridge of Alford
Montgarrie
HAUGHTON
GRAMPIAN TRANSPORT MUS
Alford
HERITAGE MUSEUM
Gateside
Whitehouse
Rinmore
Kildrummy
Milltown of Kildrummy
KILDRUMMY CASTLE & GARDEN
Auchintoul
Asloun
Glenkindie
Towie
Sinnahard
Hillockhead
Milltown of Towie
Ley
Little Lynturk
Muir of Fowlis
Bridgend
Kirkton of Tough
Boultenstone
Milton of Cushnie
Leochel-Cushnie
CRAIGIEVAR CASTLE
Tillyfour
Corrennie Moor
Kintocher
BENAQUHALLIE
Easter Davoch
Migvie
Coynach
Douneside
Craskins
CULSH SOUTERRAIN
Tornaveen
Findrack Ho.
Logie Coldstone
Tarland
CROMAR
TOMNAVERIE STONE CIRCLE
Lumphanan
PEEL RING OF LUMPHANAN
Milton of Auchinhove
Deskry Water
Water of Buchat
Water of Nochty
Don
0 1 2 3 4 5 6 miles
0 1 2 3 4 5 6 7 8 9 10km

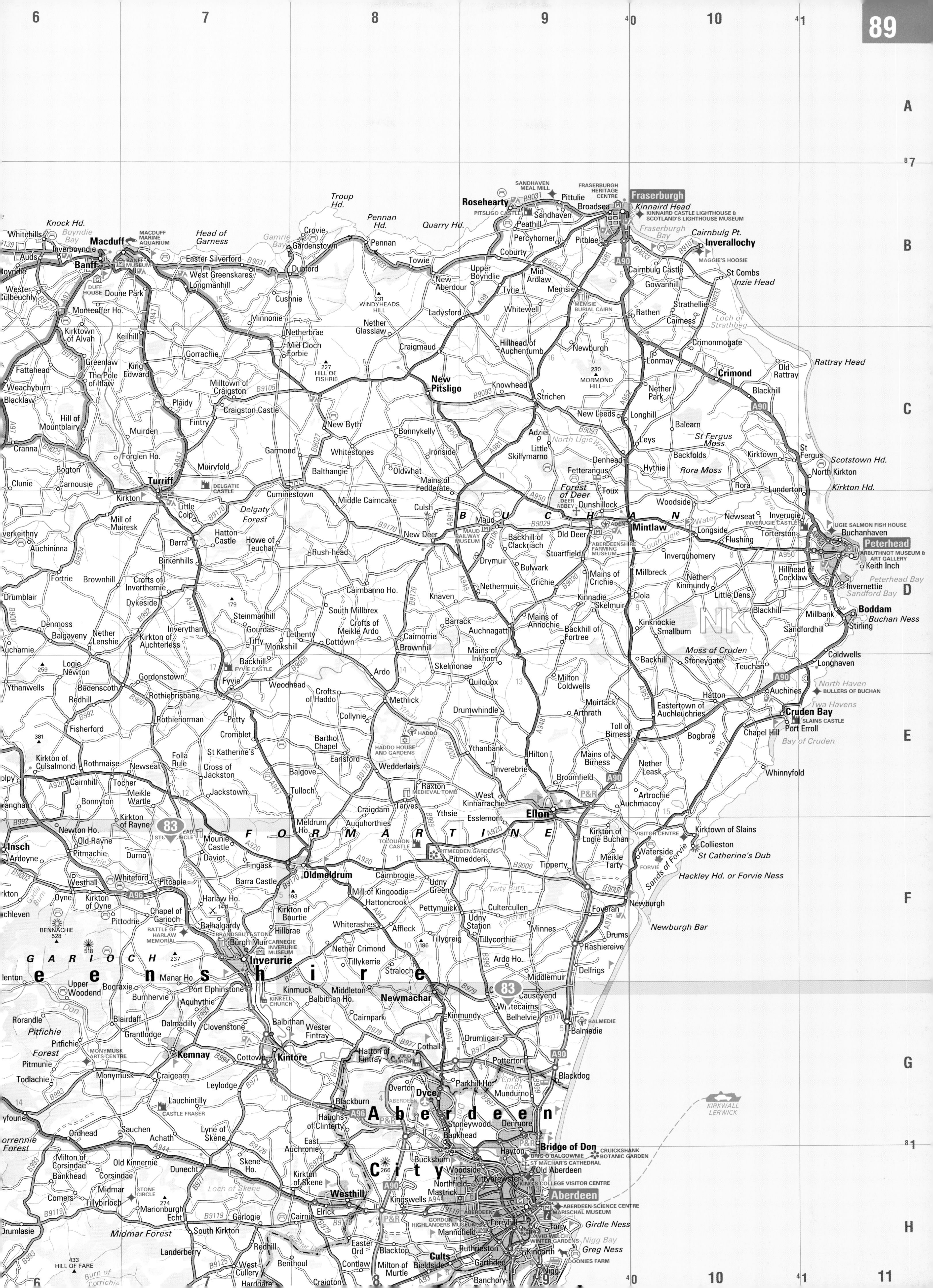

Fraserburgh
Kinnaird Head
KINNAIRD CASTLE LIGHTHOUSE & SCOTLAND'S LIGHTHOUSE MUSEUM
FRASERBURGH HERITAGE CENTRE
SANDHAVEN MEAL MILL
Rosehearty
Pittulie
Broadsea
Sandhaven
PITSLIGO CASTLE
Peathill
Percyhorner
Pitblae
Fraserburgh Bay
Cairnbulg Pt.
Inverallochy
Cairnbulg Castle
MAGGIE'S HOOSIE
St Combs
Inzie Head
Gowanhill
Strathellie
Loch of Strathbeg
Rathen
Cairness
Crimonmogate
Troup Hd.
Pennan Hd.
Quarry Hd.
Knock Hd.
Boyndie Bay
Whitehills
Macduff
MACDUFF MARINE AQUARIUM
Head of Garness
Gamrie Bay
Crovie
Gardenstown
Pennan
Auds
Inverboyndie
Banff
BANFF MUSEUM
Easter Silverford
Dubford
Towie
New Aberdour
Upper Boyndie
Coburty
Mid Ardlaw
Memsie
MEMSIE BURIAL CAIRN
Tyrie
Whitewell
Western Culbeuchly
DUFF HOUSE
Doune Park
West Greenskares
Longmanhill
Cushnie
231 WINDYHEADS HILL
Ladysford
Montcoffer Ho.
Minnonie
Netherbrae
Nether Glasslaw
Kirktown of Alvah
Keilhill
Mid Cloch Forbie
Craigmaud
Hillhead of Auchentumb
Newburgh
Lonmay
Crimond
Old Rattray
Rattray Head
Fattahead
Greenlaw
King Edward
Gorrachie
227 HILL OF FISHRIE
230 MORMOND HILL
The Pole of Itlaw
New Pitsligo
Knowhead
Strichen
Nether Park
Blackhill
Weachyburn
Milltown of Craigston
Blacklaw
Plaidy
Craigston Castle
New Byth
New Leeds
Longhill
Hill of Mountblairy
Fintry
Muirden
Bonnykelly
Adziel
North Ugie Water
Leys
Balearn
St Fergus Moss
St Fergus
Scotstown Hd.
Cranna
Garmond
Whitestones
Ironside
Little Skillymarno
Backfolds
Kirktown
North Kirkton
Forglen Ho.
Bogton
Muiryfold
Oldwhat
Denhead
Hythie
Rora Moss
Kirkton Hd.
Balthangie
Mains of Fedderate
Fetterangus
Rora
Lunderton
Clunie
Carnousie
Turriff
DELGATIE CASTLE
Forest of Deer
DEER ABBEY
Toux
Dunshillock
Woodside
Cuminestown
Middle Cairncake
Culsh
Kirkton
Little Colp
Delgaty Forest
Maud
MAUD RAILWAY MUSEUM
B U C H A N
Mintlaw
ADEN
ABERDEENSHIRE FARMING MUSEUM
Newseat
Inverugie
INVERUGIE CASTLE
UGIE SALMON FISH HOUSE
Buchanhaven
Peterhead
ARBUTHNOT MUSEUM & ART GALLERY
Mill of Muiresk
Hatton Castle
New Deer
Backhill of Clackriach
Old Deer
Longside
Flushing
Torterston
Keith Inch
Auchininna
Darra
Howe of Teuchar
Rush-head
Stuartfield
South Ugie Water
Inverquhomery
Hillhead of Cocklaw
Peterhead Bay
Birkenhills
Drymuir
Bulwark
Mains of Crichie
Millbreck
Nether Kinmundy
Invernettie
Sandford Bay
Fortrie
Brownhill
Crofts of Inverthernie
Nethermuir
Crichie
Drumblair
Dykeside
179
Cairnbanno Ho.
Knaven
Kinnadie
Skelmuir
Clola
Little Dens
Boddam
Buchan Ness
Steinmanhill
South Millbrex
Barrack
Mains of Annochie
Blackhill
Millbank
Stirling
Denmoss
Balgaveny
Nether Lenshie
Kirkton of Auchterless
Inverythan
Gourdas
Tifty
Lethenty
Monkshill
Crofts of Meikle Ardo
Cottown
Cairnorrie
Brownhill
Auchnagatt
Backhill of Fortree
Kinknockie
Smallburn
NK
Sandfordhill
Auchairnie
Logie Newton
259
Backhill
FYVIE CASTLE
Mains of Inkhorn
Skelmonae
Moss of Cruden
Backhill
Stoneygate
Teuchan
Coldwells
Longhaven
Ythanwells
Badenscoth
Gordonstown
Ardo
Quilquox
Milton Coldwells
Fyvie
Rothiebrisbane
Woodhead
Crofts of Haddo
Methlick
North Haven
Auchiries
BULLERS OF BUCHAN
Redhill
Muirtack
Arthrath
Hatton
Eastertown of Auchleuchries
Cruden Bay
SLAINS CASTLE
Twa Havens
Rothienorman
Petty
Collynie
Drumwhindle
Fisherford
Cromblet
Toll of Birness
Chapel Hill
Port Erroll
381
HADDO
Barthol Chapel
Bogbrae
Bay of Cruden
Kirkton of Culsalmond
Rothmaise
Folla Rule
St Katherine's
HADDO HOUSE AND GARDENS
Earlsford
Ythanbank
Hilton
Mains of Birness
Nether Leask
Newseat
Cross of Jackston
Wedderlairs
Inverebrie
Broomfield
Whinnyfold
Cairnhill
Tocher
Balgove
Raxton
MEDIEVAL TOMB
Meikle Wartle
Jackstown
Tulloch
West Kinharrachie
Artrochie
Auchmacoy
Bonnyton
Craigdam
Tarves
Ythsie
Esslemont
Ellon
Kirktown of Slains
Kirkton of Rayne
Newton Ho.
Old Rayne
Meldrum Ho.
Auquhorthies
F O R M A R T I N E
Kirkton of Logie Buchan
VISITOR CENTRE
Collieston
Insch
Ardoyne
Pitmachie
Mounie Castle
Durno
Daviot
TOLQUHON CASTLE
PITMEDDEN GARDENS
Pitmedden
Tipperty
Meikle Tarty
Waterside
FORVIE
St Catherine's Dub
Fingask
Oldmeldrum
Cairnbrogie
Udny Green
Hackley Hd. or Forvie Ness
Sands of Forvie
Westhall
Whiteford
Pitcaple
Barra Castle
Mill of Kingoodie
Hattoncrook
Tarty Burn
Oyne
Kirkton of Oyne
Harlaw Ho.
193
Pettymuick
Culterculen
Foveran
Newburgh
Pittodrie
Chapel of Garioch
1411
Kirkton of Bourtie
Udny Station
Foveran Burn
Drums
Newburgh Bar
BENNACHIE 528
BATTLE OF HARLAW MEMORIAL
Balhalgardy
BRANDSBUTT STONE
Hillbrae
Whiterashes
Affleck
Tillygreig
Tillycorthie
Minnes
Rashierieve
518
Burgh Muir
CARNEGIE INVERURIE MUSEUM
Nether Crimond
186
237
Tillykerrie
Ardo Ho.
Delfrigs
G A R I O C H
Inverurie
Straloch
Middlemuir
e e n s h i r e
Manar Ho.
Upper Woodend
Bograxie
Port Elphinstone
Kinmuck
Middleton
Balbithan Ho.
Newmachar
83
Causeyend
Whitecairns
Burnhervie
Aquhythie
KINKELL CHURCH
Belhelvie
Rorandle
Pitfichie Forest
Blairdaff
Dalmadilly
Clovenstone
Balbithan
Wester Fintray
Cairnpark
Kinmundy
Balmedie
BALMEDIE
Grantlodge
Pitfichie
MONYMUSK ARTS CENTRE
Pitmunie
Kemnay
Cottown
Kintore
Hatton of Fintray
OLD CHURCH
Cothall
Drumligair
Potterton
Todlachie
Monymusk
Craigearn
Leylodge
Parkhill Ho.
Blackdog
Overton
Dyce
Corby Loch
Mundurno
Lauchintilly
CASTLE FRASER
Blackburn
Aberdeen City
Haughs of Clinterty
P&R
Stoneywood
Denmore
KIRKWALL LERWICK
Sauchen
Achath
Lyne of Skene
Bankhead
Ordhead
East Auchronie
Bridge of Don
Hayton
BRIG O'BALGOWNIE
CRUICKSHANK BOTANIC GARDEN
ST MACHAR'S CATHEDRAL
Old Aberdeen
Milton of Corsindae
Old Kinnernie
Skene Ho.
Bucksburn
Woodside
Bankhead
Corsindae
Dunecht
266
Kirkton of Skene
Kittybrewster
KING'S COLLEGE VISITOR CENTRE
Midmar
STONE CIRCLE
Loch of Skene
Westhill
Northfield
Mastrick
Aberdeen
ABERDEEN SCIENCE CENTRE
Comers
Tillybirloch
274
Marionburgh
Echt
Garlogie
Cairnie
Elrick
Kingswells
MARISCHAL MUSEUM
GORDON HIGHLANDERS MUSEUM
ABERDEEN
Ferryhill
Girdle Ness
Drumlasie
Midmar Forest
South Kirkton
Mannofield
Torry
DAVID WELCH WINTER GARDENS
Nigg Bay
Landerberry
Redhill
Easter Ord
Blacktop
Cults
Ruthrieston
Kincorth
Greg Ness
433 HILL OF FARE
Burn of Corrichie
West Cullery
Hardgate
Benthoul
Craigton
Contlaw
Milton of Murtle
Bieldside
Garthdee
Banchory-Devenick
Nigg
DOONIES FARM
A90
A96
A98
A947
A948
A950
A952
A975
A981
A920
A944
A93
B9031
B9032
B9033
B9093
B9105
B9170
B9029
B9030
B9005
B9000
B9001
B992
B993
B979
B977
B994
B999
B9119
B9125
B9126
B9027
B9025
B9024
B9139
B9121
B9107
6
7
8
9
10
11
A
B
C
D
E
F
G
H

1 2 3 4 10 5 6 7

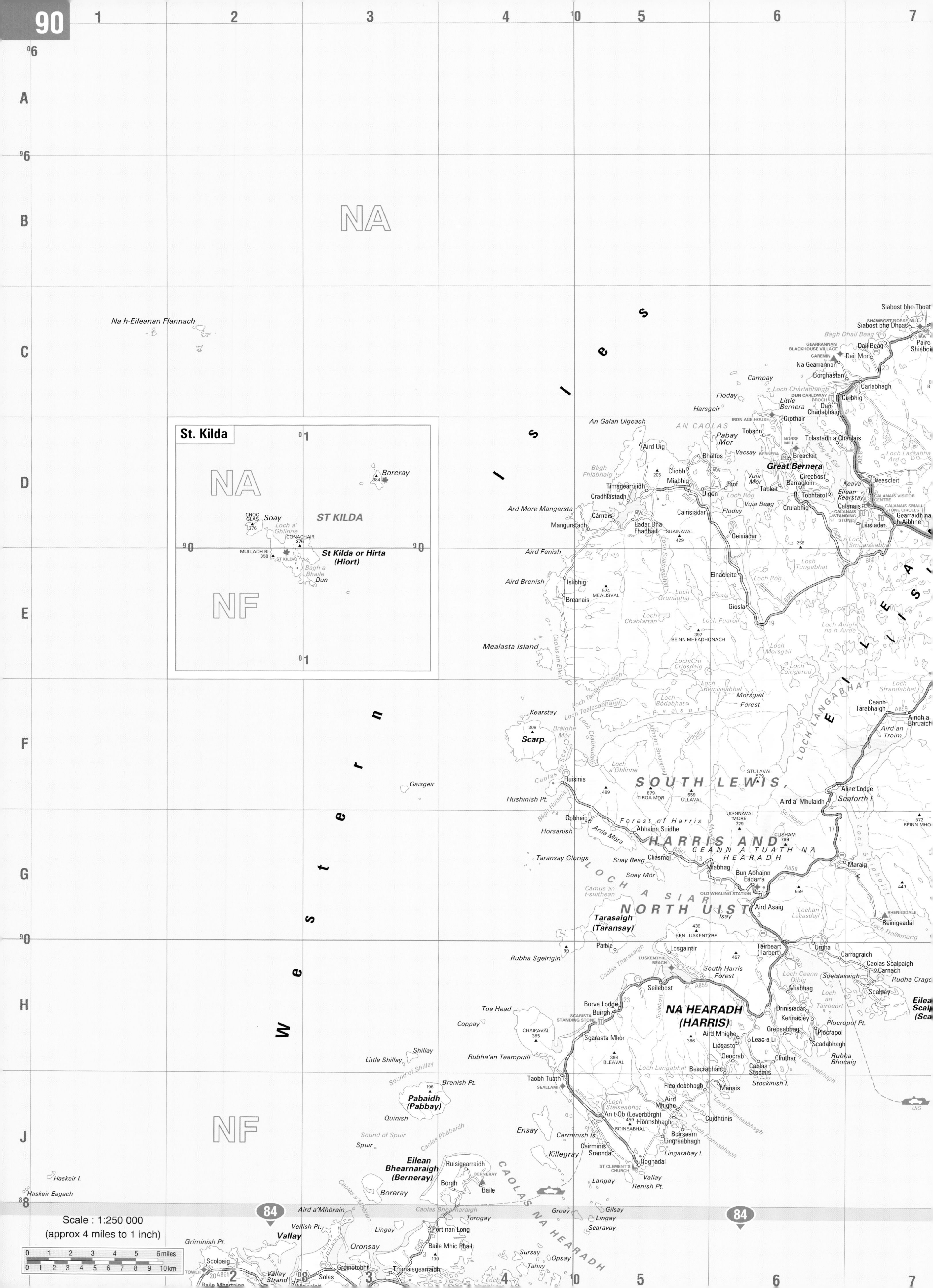

A

B

NA

C

Na h-Eileanan Flannach

Siabost bho Thuat
SHAWBOST/NORSE MILL
Siabost bho Dheas
Bàgh Dhail Beag
Pairc
Shiabo
GEARRANNAN
BLACKHOUSE VILLAGE Dail Beag
GARENIN Dail Mòr
Na Gearrannan
Borghastan
Campay Carlabhagh
Loch Chàrlabhaigh
Floday Little Cirbhig
Bernera Dun
DUN CARLOWAY BROCH Chàrlabhaigh
Harsgeir IRON AGE HOUSE Crothair
An Galan Uigeach Pabay Great Bernera Keava
Tobson Mòr Circebost Eilean
Aird Uig Breacleit Barraglom Kearstay
Bàgh Bhaltos Vacsay Vuia CALANAIS VISITOR CENTRE
Fhiabhaig Cliobh Mòr Tacleit Calanais
Timsgearraidh Miabhig Uigen Crulabhig CALANAIS SMALL
Cradhlastadh Riof Vuia Beag STONE CIRCLES
205 Floday Linsiadar
Cnrnais Cairisiadar Gearraidh na h-Aibhne
Ard More Mangersta Eadar Dha Geisiadar
Mangurstadh Fhadhail SUAINAVAL 256
429 B8011
Aird Fenish Loch
Tungabhat
Einacleite Loch Ròg B8011
Islibhig 574 Loch
Aird Brenish MEALISVAL Grunabhat Giosla
Breanais Giosla Loch Fuaroll 19
Loch 397
Chaolartan BEINN MHEADHONACH
Mealasta Island Loch Loch
Morsgail Coirigerod
Loch Cro
Criosdaig Loch
Strandabhat
D

St. Kilda   0   1

NA

Boreray
384
CNOC GLAS Soay ST KILDA
376 Loch a'
Ghlinne
CONACHAIR
376
MULLACH BI ST KILDA St Kilda or Hirta
358 (Hiort)
Bàgh a'
Bhaile Dun

NF

0   1

E

F

Ceann
Tarabhaigh Airidh a
Bhruaich
Aird an
Troim
Loch Morsgail 572
Bodabhat Forest BEINN MHO
Kearstay Loch Beinisabhal
308 Loch Tealasabhaigh
Bràighe Loch Crabhadail
Scarp Mòr
SOUTH LEWIS,
489 679 659 Aline Lodge
Huisinis TIRGA MÒR ULLAVAL Aird a' Mhulaidh Seaforth I.
Hushinish Pt. STULAVAL 17
Loch 579
a'Ghlinne UISGNAVAL
MORE
Gobhaig Forest of Harris 729 HARRIS AND
Horsanish Abhainn Suidhe CLISHAM CEANN A TUATH NA
Arda Mòra 799 HEARADH
Taransay Glorigs Soay Beag Cliasmol 13
Soay Mòr Miabhag 449
Camus an Bun Abhainn 559
t-suidhean 559 Eadarra
OLD WHALING STATION Aird Asaig Reinigeadal
Tarasaigh Isay NORTH UIST
(Taransay) 436
BEN LUSKENTYRE
Paible 467 Tàirbeart
Rubha Sgeirigin Losgaintir (Tarbert) Urgha
99 Carragraich
LUSKENTYRE Caolas Scalpaigh
BEACH South Harris Carnach
Seilebost Forest Rudha Cragc
A859 Loch Ceann
Miabhag Dibig
Borve Lodge 23 Sgeotasaigh
Toe Head Buirgh Loch Scalpay
Coppay NA HEARADH an Eilea
SCARISTA (HARRIS) Tàirbeart Scal
STANDING STONE Drinisiadar (Sca
CHAIPAVAL Sgarasta Mhor Kennacley
365 386 Aird Mhighe Plocropol Pt.
Shillay Liceasto Greosabhagh
Little Shillay 398 Geocrab Plocrapol
Sound of Shillay BLEAVAL Leac a Li Scadabhagh
Rubha'an Teampuill Cluthar Rubha
Taobh Tuath Beacrabhaic Bhocaig
Brenish Pt. SEALLAM Flepideabhagh Caolas
196 Loch Manais Stocinis
Pabaidh Quinish An t-Ob Steiseabhat Aird Stockinish I.
(Pabbay) (Leverburgh) Mhighe Loch Finnsbhagh
Fionnsbhagh Cuidhtinis
Boirseam Lingreabhagh
Ensay Carminish Is. Lingarabay I. UIG
ROINEVAL Cairminis
Eilean Spuir Killegray Srannda
Bhearnaraigh Sound of Spuir Roghadal
(Berneray) ST CLEMENT'S
Haskeir I. Boreray Ruisigearraidh CHURCH Valley
BERNERAY Renish Pt.
Haskeir Eagach Borgh Baile Langay

NF

G

H

J

8

84

84

Scale : 1:250 000
(approx 4 miles to 1 inch)

0 1 2 3 4 5 6 miles
0 1 2 3 4 5 6 7 8 9 10km

Aird a'Mhòrain Gilsay
Veilish Pt. Groay Lingay
Valley Port nan Long Scaravay
Griminish Pt. Lingay Sursay
Oronsay Toragay Opsay
TOWER Solas Baile Mhic Phail Tahay
20 A865 Greinetobht 190
Baile Mhartainn Valley Strand Trumaisgearraidh

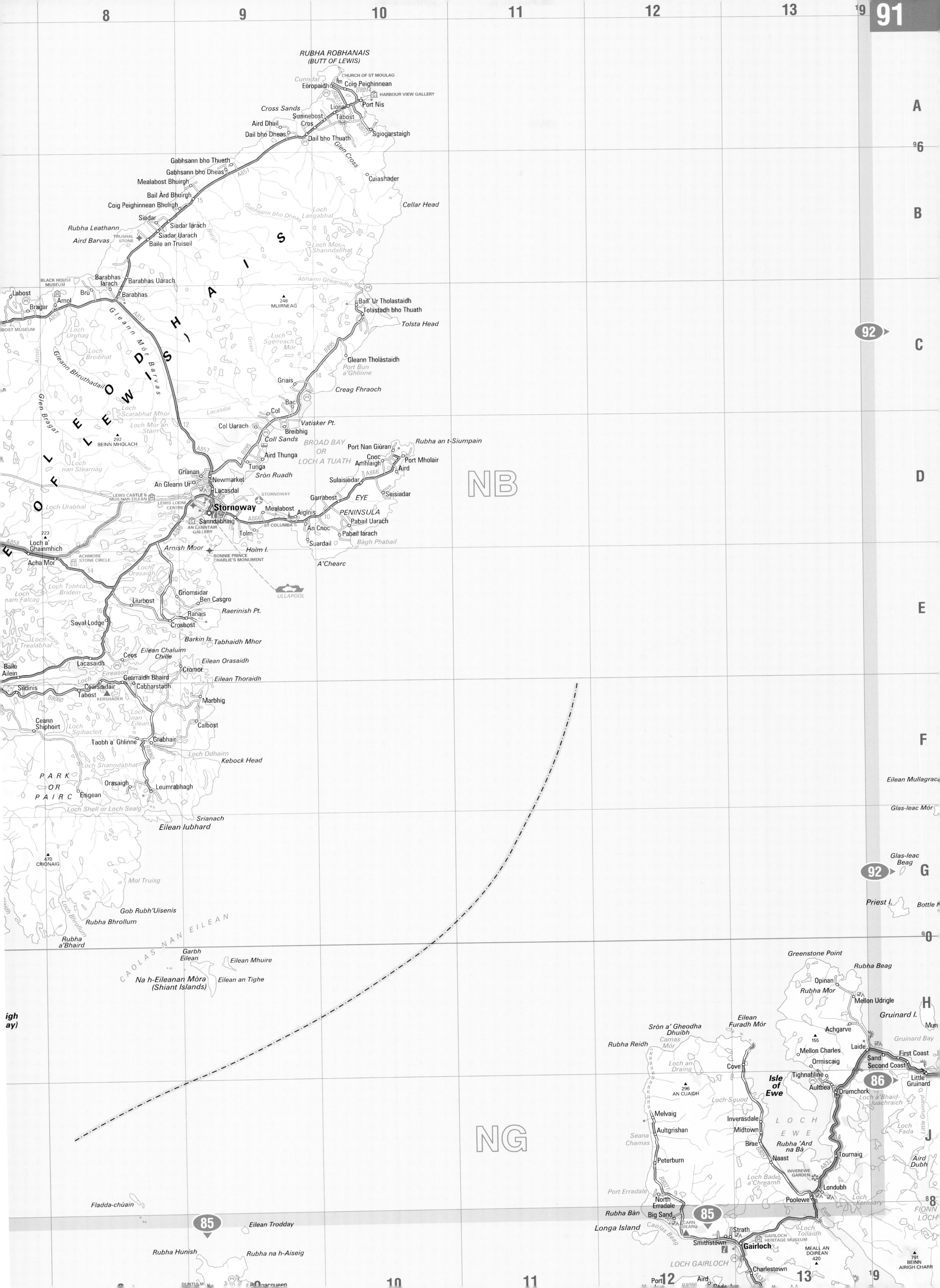

RUBHA ROBHANAIS
(BUTT OF LEWIS)
CHURCH OF ST MOULAG
Cunndal
Eòropaidh
Coig Peighinnean
B8014
HARBOUR VIEW GALLERY
Port Nis
Cross Sands
Lional
Suaineabost
Cros
Tàbost
Aird Dhail
Sgiogarstaigh
Dail bho Dheas
Dail bho Thuath
Glen Cross
Gabhsann bho Thuath
Gabhsann bho Dheas
Mealabost Bhuirgh
Cuiashader
Bail Ard Bhuirgh
Coig Peighinnean Bhuirgh
Cellar Head
A857
Rubha Leathann
Siadar
Siadar Iarach
Loch
Langabhat
TRUSHAL
STONE
Aird Barvas
Siadar Uarach
Baile an Truiseil
Loch Mòr
Shanndabhat
BLACK HOUSE
MUSEUM
Barabhas
Iarach
Barabhas Uarach
Abhainn Ghlearadha
Bail' Ur Tholastaidh
Labost
Arnol
Brù
Barabhas
248
MUIRNEAG
Tolastadh bho Thuath
Bragar
A858
Loch
Urghag
Loch
Breibhat
Tolsta Head
Loch
Sgeireach
Mor
BOST MUSEUM
Gleann Mòr Barvas
Gleann Tholàstaidh
Port Bun
a'Ghlinne
Gleann Bhruthadail
Griais
Griais
Creag Fhraoch
Loch
nan Stearnag
292
BEINN MHOLACH
Loch
Scarabhat Mhòr
Loch Mòr an
Stàrrir
12
Lacasdal
Bac
Col
Col Uarach
Breibhig
Vatisker Pt.
A857
Coll Sands
NB
A858
Loch
nam Falcag
A857
B895
Aird Thunga
Tunga
Sròn Ruadh
Port Nan Giùran
Rubha an t-Siumpain
Grianan
An Gleann Ur
Newmarket
Lacasdal
STORNOWAY
Cnoc
Amhlaigh
Port Mholair
Aird
LEWS CASTLE &
MUS NAN EILEAN
Sulaisiadar
A866
EYE
Seisiadar
Loch
Urabhal
LEWIS LODG
CENTRE
Stornoway
Garrabost
PENINSULA
223
Grioda
Stornoway
Mealabost
Aiginis
Pabail Uarach
Loch a'
Ghainmhich
AN LANNTAIR
GALLERY
Sanndabhaig
A866
Pabail Iarach
Acha Mor
Arnish Moor
Tolm
An Cnoc
ST COLUMBA
Suardail
Bàgh Phabail
ACHMORE
STONE CIRCLE
BONNIE PRINCE
CHARLIE'S MONUMENT
Holm I.
A'Chearc
Loch
Tobhta
Bridein
Loch
Orasaigh
ULLAPOOL
Griomsidar
Ben Casgro
Liurbost
Raerinish Pt.
Soval Lodge
Ranais
Crosbost
Loch
Trealabhal
Barkin Is.
Tabhaidh Mhòr
Ceos
Eilean Chaluim
Chille
Baile
Ailein
Lacasaidh
Eilean Orasaidh
Cromot
Gearraidh Bhaird
Eilean Thoraidh
Sildinis
Cearsiadair
Cabharstadh
Tabost
KERSHADER
Marbhig
13
Loch
nan
Eilean
Calbost
Ceann
Shiphoirt
Loch
Sgibacleit
Taobh a' Ghlinne
Grabhair
Loch Odhairn
Kebock Head
PARK
OR
PAIRC
Loch Shanndabhat
Orasaigh
Leumrabhagh
Eisgean
Loch Shell or Loch Sealg
Srianach
Eilean Iubhard
470
CRIONAIG
Mol Truisg
Gob Rubh'Uisenis
92
Rubha Bhrollum
Rubha
a'Bhaird
CAOLAS NAN EILEAN
Garbh
Eilean
Eilean Mhuire
Na h-Eileanan Mòra
(Shiant Islands)
Eilean an Tighe
igh
ay)
NG
Fladda-chùain
85
Eilean Troddav
Rubha Hunish
Rubha na h-Aiseig
10
11

Eilean Mullagrace
Glas-leac Mór
Glas-leac
Beag
92
Priest I.
Bottle
9
Greenstone Point
Rubha Beag
Rubha Mòr
Opinan
Mellon Udrigle
Sròn a' Gheodha
Dhuibh
Eilean
Furadh Mór
Gruinard I.
Achgarve
Mun
Camas
Mór
Gruinard Bay
Rubha Reidh
155
Mellon Charles
Laide
Sand
First Coast
Loch an
Draing
Cove
Second Coast
Ormiscaig
Isle
of
Ewe
Tighnafiline
86
Drumchork
Little
Gruinard
296
AN CUAIDH
Aultbea
Loch a'Bhaid-
luachraich
Melvaig
Inverasdale
Loch Sguod
Midtown
LOCH
EWE
Loch
Fada
Aultgrishan
Brae
Seana
Chamas
Rubha 'Ard
na Bà
Peterburn
Naast
Tournaig
INVEREWE
GARDEN
Loch Bad
a'Chreamh
Londubh
Loch Kernsary
Port Erradale
Poolewe
FIONN
LOCH
North
Erradale
Rubha Bàn
85
Aird
Dubh
Big Sand
CARN
DEARG
Strath
Loch
Tollaidh
Longa Island
Caolas Beag
GAIRLOCH
HERITAGE MUSEUM
8
Smithstown
Gairloch
LOCH GAIRLOCH
MEALL AN
DOIREAN
420
BEINN
AIRIGH CHARR
Charlestown
12
13
9

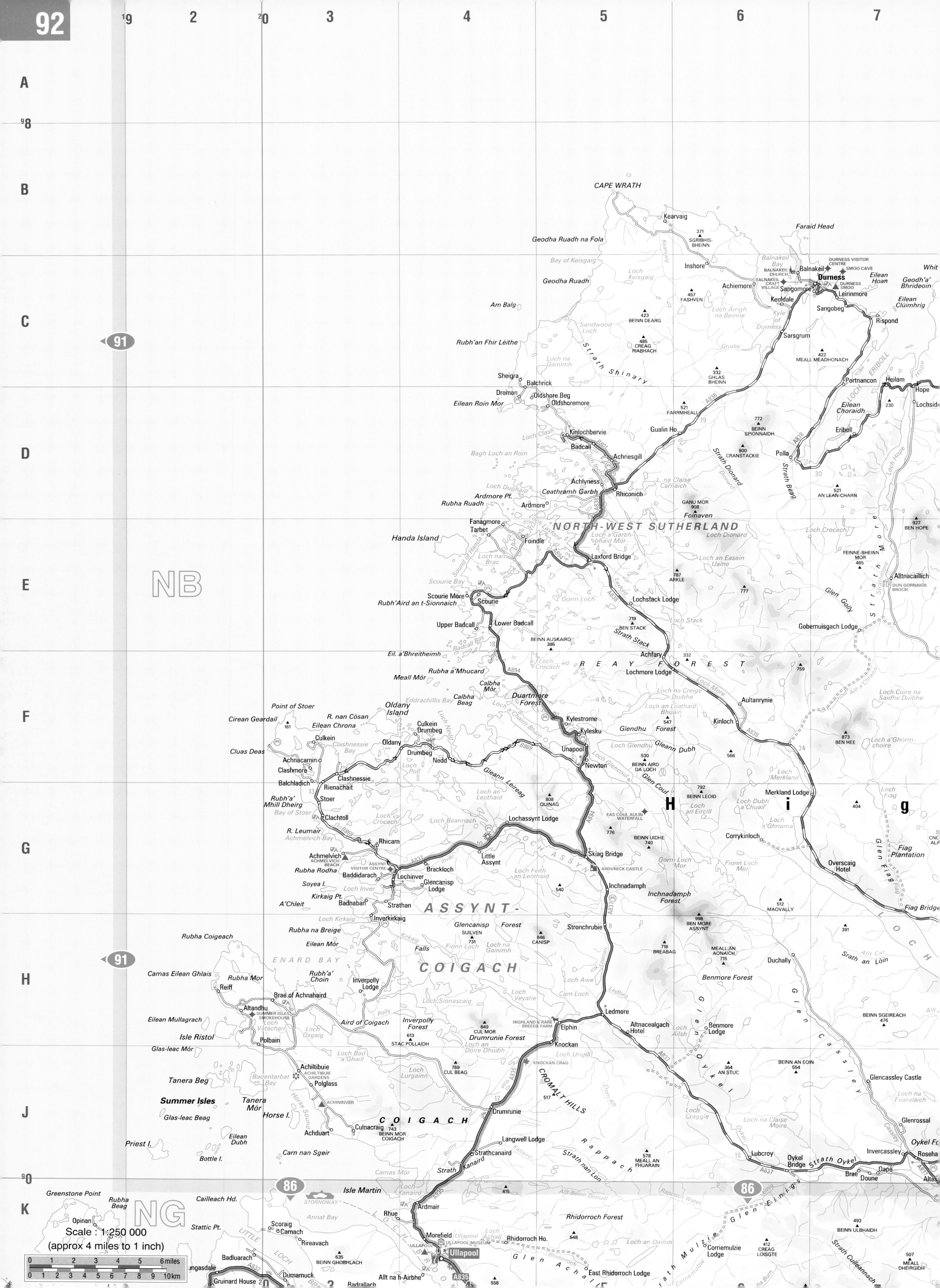

CAPE WRATH
Kearvaig
371 SGRIBHIS-BHEINN
Faraid Head
Geodha Ruadh na Fola
Bay of Keisgaig
Loch Keisgaig
Inshore
Balnakeil Bay
Balnakeil
BALNAKEIL CHURCH
BALNAKEIL CRAFT VILLAGE
DURNESS VISITOR CENTRE
SMOO CAVE
Durness
DURNESS SMOO
Eilean Hoan
Geodh'a' Bhrideoin
Geodha Ruadh
Achiemore
Sangomore
Leirinmore
457 FASHVEN
Keoldale
Loch Airigh na Beinne
Kyle of Durness
Sangobeg
Eilean Clùimhrig
Am Balg
423 BEINN DEARG
Sandwood Loch
Rispond
Sarsgrum
Rubh'an Fhir Léithe
485 CREAG RIABHACH
Grudie
422 MEALL MEADHONACH
Loch na Gainimh
Strath Shinary
332 GHLAS BHEINN
Sheigra
Balchrick
Portnancon
Heilam
Hope
LOCH ERIBOLL
Droman
Oldshore Beg
Oldshoremore
Eilean Roin Mor
521 FARRMHEALL
Eilean Choraidh
230
Lochside
772 BEINN SPIONNAIDH
Kinlochbervie
Gualin Ho
Eriboll
Loch Clash
Badcall
Bagh Loch an Roin
800 CRANSTACKIE
Polla
Achriesgill
Strath Dionard
Strath Beag
Loch Hope
L. na Claise Carnaich
Achlyness
Loch Dughaill
Ceathramh Garbh
Rhiconich
521 AN LEAN-CHARN
Ardmore Pt.
Rubha Ruadh
Ardmore
GANU MOR 908
Foinaven
927 BEN HOPE
Fanagmore
Tarbet
NORTH-WEST SUTHERLAND
Loch Dionard
Loch Crocach
Handa Island
Foindle
Loch a'Garbh-bhaid Mòr
Loch nam Brac
Laxford Bridge
Loch an Easain Uaine
FEINNE-BHEINN MOR 465
Sound of Handa
787 ARKLE
Alltnacaillich
DUN DORNAIGIL BROCH
NB
Scourie Bay
Scourie More
Scourie
Gorm Loch
Lochstack Lodge
777
Glen Golly
Strath More
Rubh'Aird an t-Sionnaich
719 BEN STACK
Loch Stack
Upper Badcall
Lower Badcall
Gobernuisgach Lodge
Badcall Bay
Strath Stack
BEINN AUSKAIRD 386
Eil. a'Bhreitheimh
Loch Crocach
REAY FOREST
Achfary
332
759
Rubha a'Mhucard
Lochmore Lodge
Loch More
Meall Mòr
Calbha Mòr
Duartmore Forest
Loch na Creige Duibhe
Loch Coire na Saidhe Duibhe
Calbha Beag
Eddrachillis Bay
Aultanrynie
Point of Stoer
Oldany Island
Loch a'Chàirn Bhàin
Kylestrome
Loch an Leathaid Bhuain
Kinloch
R. nan Còsan
Cirean Geardail 161
Eilean Chrona
Culkein Drumbeg
Kylesku
Glendhu
Forest
873 BEN HEE
Loch a'Ghorm-choire
Culkein
Oldany
Loch Nedd
Clashnessie Bay
Loch Glendhu
Gleann Dubh
Unapool
566
Cluas Deas
Achnacarnin
Drumbeg
Nedd
Clashmore
Loch Poll
530 BEINN AIRD DA LOCH
Newton
Loch Glencoul
Glen Coul
Clashnessie
Gleann Leireag
Loch Merkland
Balchladich
Rienachait
Loch an Leothaid
792 BEINN LEOID
Merkland Lodge
Loch Fiag
Rubh'a' Mhill Dheirg
Stoer
808 QUINAG
Loch an Eircill
Loch Dubh a'Chuail
404
H i g
Bay of Stoer
Clachtoll
Loch Crocach
Loch Beannach
Lochassynt Lodge
EAS COUL AULIN WATERFALL
Loch a'Ghriama
R. Leumair
Achmelvich Bay
LOCH ASSYNT
776
BEINN UIDHE 740
Corrykinloch
Glen Fiag
Fiag Plantation
Rhicarn
Achmelvich
ACHMELVICH BEACH
ASSYNT VISITOR CENTRE
Little Assynt
Skiag Bridge
Gorm Loch Mòr
Fionn Loch Mòr
Overscaig Hotel
Rubha Rodha
Baddidarach
Brackloch
River Inver
ARDVRECK CASTLE
Lochinver
Glencanisp Lodge
Loch Fèith an Leòthaid
Soyea I.
Loch Inver
Inchnadamph
540
Inchnadamph Forest
Kirkaig Pt.
Badnaban
Strathan
A'Chleit
ASSYNT-
512 MAOVALLY
Fiag Bridge
Loch Kirkaig
Inverkirkaig
998 BEN MORE ASSYNT
LOCH
391
Rubha Coigeach
Rubha na Breige
Glencanisp Forest
SUILVEN 731
Stronchrubie
846 CANISP
Eilean Mòr
Kirkaig
Falls
Fionn Loch
Loch na Gainimh
718 BREABAG
MEALL AN AONAICH 715
Strath an Lòin
ENARD BAY
Duchally
COIGACH
Camas Eilean Ghlais
Rubha Mor
Rubh'a' Choin
Loch Awe
Benmore Forest
Reiff
Inverpolly Lodge
Loch Veyatie
Cam Loch
Glen Oykel
Glen Cassley
Brae of Achnahaird
Loch Sionascaig
Ledbeg
Altandhu
SUMMER ISLES SMOKEHOUSE
Ledmore
Eilean Mullagrach
Polly
Loch Vatachan
Aird of Coigach
Inverpolly Forest
HIGHLAND & RARE BREEDS FARM
Elphin
Altnacealgach Hotel
Benmore Lodge
Loch Ailsh
BEINN SGEIREACH 476
Isle Ristol
Loch Osgaig
849 CUL MOR
Drumrunie Forest
Polbain
STAC POLLAIDH
Loch an Doire Dhuibh
Knockan
Glas-leac Mòr
Loch Bad a'Ghaill
Loch Urigill
KNOCKAN CRAG
769 CUL BEAG
BEINN AN EOIN 554
Achiltibuie
ACHILTIBUIE GARDENS
Tanera Beg
Badentarbat Bay
Loch Lurgainn
CROMALT HILLS
364 AN STUC
Glencassley Castle
Polglass
Loch na Fuaralaich
ACHININVER
517
Summer Isles
Tanera Mòr
Drumrunie
Loch Craggie
Horse Sound
Horse I.
COIGACH
Loch na Claise Moire
Glenrossal
Glas-leac Beag
Culnacraig
743 BEINN MOR COIGACH
Achduart
Oykel Forest
Priest I.
Eilean Dubh
Langwell Lodge
Rappach
578 MEALL AN FHUARAIN
Invercassley
Rosehall
Bottle I.
Carn nan Sgeir
Strathcanaird
Lubcroy
Oykel Bridge
Strath Oykel
Strath nan Lon
Strath Kanaird
Brae
Oape
Doune
Altass
Camas Mòr
Greenstone Point
Isle Martin
Loch Kanaird
415
Allt Beinn Donuill
Rappach Water
Rubha Beag
Cailleach Hd.
STORNOWAY
Glen Einig
NG
Ardmair
Annat Bay
Rhue
Rhidorroch Forest
493 BEINN ULBHAIDH
Opinan
Scoraig
Carnach
Stattic Pt.
Morefield
Ullapool
ULLAPOOL MUSEUM
Loch Achall
Rhidorroch Ho.
548
Loch an Daimh
Strath Mulzie
Corriemulzie Lodge
412 CREAG LOISGTE
LITTLE LOCH BROOM
Rireavach
LOCH BROOM
Glen Achall
Strath Cuileannach
Badluarach
635 BEINN GHOBHLACH
507 MEALL DHEIRGIDH
Durnamuck
East Rhidorroch Lodge
Gruinard House
Badrallach
Allt na h-Airbhe
558
91
86
Scale : 1:250 000
(approx 4 miles to 1 inch)
0 1 2 3 4 5 6 miles
0 1 2 3 4 5 6 7 8 9 10 km

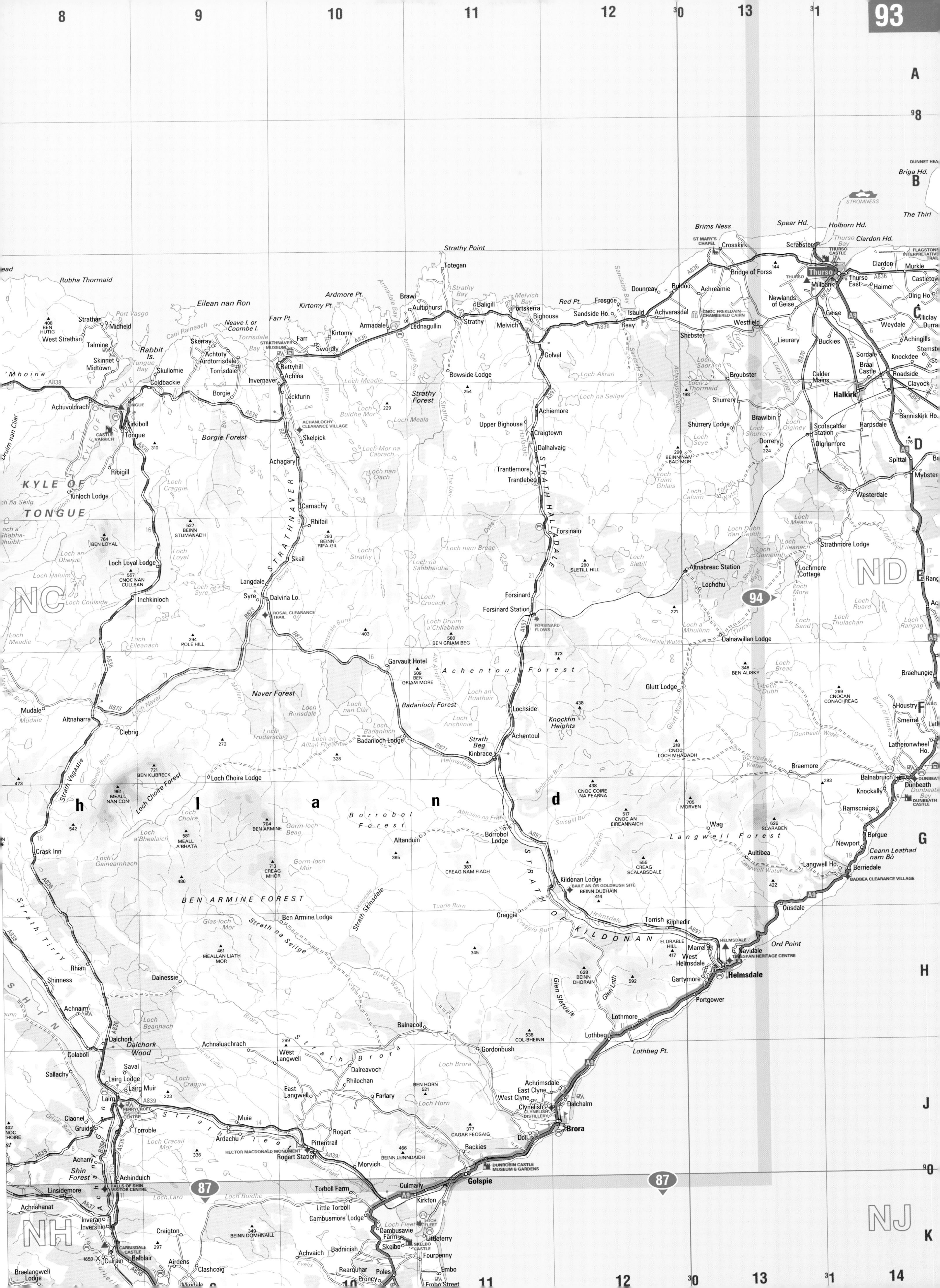
8
9
10
11
12
13
A
B
C
D
E
F
G
H
J
K
14
DUNNET HEAD
Briga Hd.
STROMNESS
The Thirl
Brims Ness
Spear Hd.
Holborn Hd.
Clardon Hd.
ST MARY'S CHAPEL
Crosskirk
Scrabster
Thurso Bay
THURSO CASTLE
FLAGSTONE INTERPRETATIVE TRAIL
Strathy Point
Totegan
Thurso
Thurso East
Clardon
Murkle
Castletown
Haimer
Olrig Ho.
Bridge of Forss
Millbank
Rubha Thormaid
Eilean nan Ron
Ardmore Pt.
Kirtomy Pt.
Brawl
Aultiphurst
Baligill
Melvich Bay
Portskerra
Bighouse
Red Pt.
Fresgoe
Sandside Bay
Dounreay
Buldoo
Achreamie
Newlands of Geise
Geise
Weydale
Achingills
Port Vasgo
Strathan
Midfield
West Strathan
Talmine
Skinnet
Midtown
Caol Raineach
Neave I. or Coombe I.
Farr Pt.
Rabbit Is.
Skerray
Achtoty
Airdtorrisdale
Torrisdale
Torrisdale Bay
Tongue Bay
Skullomie
Farr
Swordly
Kirtomy
Armadale
Armadale Bay
Lednagullin
Strathy
Melvich
Sandside Ho.
Isauld
Reay
Achvarasdal
CNOC FREKEDAIN CHAMBERED CAIRN
Westfield
Shebster
Lieurary
Buckies
Sordale
Braal Castle
Knockdee
Roadside
Clayock
STRATHNAVER MUSEUM
Bettyhill
Achina
Invernaver
Coldbackie
Borgie
Leckfurin
Golval
Loch Akran
Loch Meadie
Bowside Lodge
Strathy Forest
Loch na Seilge
Loch Saorach
Loch Thormaid
Broubster
Calder Mains
Halkirk
A'Mhoine
Achuvoldrach
Tongue
Kirkiboll
KYLE OF TONGUE
CASTLE VARRICH
Borgie Forest
ACHANLOCHY CLEARANCE VILLAGE
Skelpick
Loch Buidhe Mor
Loch Meala
Achiemore
Upper Bighouse
Craigtown
Dalhalvaig
Shurrery
Shurrery Lodge
Brawlbin
Scotscalder Station
Olgrinmore
Harpsdale
Banniskirk Ho.
Dorrery
Spittal
Mybster
Drium nan Cliar
Ribigill
Loch Craggie
Achagary
Loch Mor na Caorach
Loch nan Clach
Trantlemore
Trantlebeg
STRATH HALLADALE
BEINN NAM BAD MOR
Loch Tuim Ghlais
Loch Scye
Loch Caluim
Westerdale
KYLE OF TONGUE
Kinloch Lodge
Carnachy
Rhifail
BEINN STUMANADH
BEINN RIFA-GIL
STRATHNAVER
Forsinain
Loch Dubh nan Geodh
Loch Meadie
Strathmore Lodge
BEN LOYAL
Loch an Dherue
Loch Loyal
Loch Loyal Lodge
CNOC NAN CULLEAN
Skail
Loch Strathy
Loch nam Breac
Loch na Sabhaidhe
SLETILL HILL
Loch Sletill
Loch Gaineimh
Loch Eileanach
Altnabreac Station
Lochdhu
Lochmore Cottage
ND
Loch Halluim
NC
Loch Coulside
Inchkinloch
Loch Syre
Langdale
Syre
Dalvina Lo.
ROSAL CLEARANCE TRAIL
Loch Crocach
Forsinard
Forsinard Station
FORSINARD FLOWS
94
Loch More
Loch Ruard
Loch Thulachan
Loch Sand
Loch Rangag
Loch Meadie
Loch Eileanach
POLE HILL
Loch Druim a'Chliabhain
BEN GRIAM BEG
Loch a' Mhuilinn
Dalnawillan Lodge
Rumsdale Water
Garvault Hotel
BEN GRIAM MORE
Achentoul Forest
BEN ALISKY
Loch Breac
Loch Dubh
Braehungie
Glutt Lodge
CNOCAN CONACHREAG
Naver Forest
Loch Rimsdale
Loch nan Clàr
Loch an Ruathair
Badanloch Forest
Loch Arichlinie
Lochside
Knockfin Heights
Houstry
Smerral
Latheron
Mudale
Altnaharra
Clebrig
Loch Naver
Loch Truderscaig
Loch an Alltan Fhearna
Loch Badanloch
Badanloch Lodge
Strath Beg
Kinbrace
Achentoul
CNOC LOCH MHADADH
Dunbeath Water
Latheronwheel Ho.
Strath Vagastie
BEN KLIBRECK
Loch Choire Forest
Loch Choire Lodge
Helmsdale
Braemore
Berriedale Water
Balnabruich
Dunbeath
Knockally
DUNBEATH CASTLE
MEALL NAN CON
h
l
a
n
d
Borrobol Forest
CNOC COIRE NA PEARNA
MORVEN
SCARABEN
Ramscraigs
Loch Choire
Loch a' Bhealaich
MEALL A'BHATA
BEN ARMINE
Gorm-loch Beag
Altanduin
Borrobol Lodge
Abhainn na Frithe
CNOC AN EIREANNAICH
Wag
Langwell Forest
Borgue
Newport
Ceann Leathad nam Bò
Crask Inn
Loch Gaineamhach
CREAG MHOR
Gorm-loch Mor
CREAG NAM FIADH
STRATH
Kildonan Lodge
BAILE AN OR GOLDRUSH SITE
BEINN DUBHAIN
CREAG SCALABSDALE
Aultibea
Langwell Water
Langwell Ho.
Berriedale
BADBEA CLEARANCE VILLAGE
Strath Tirry
BEN ARMINE FOREST
Strath Skinsdale
Tuarie Burn
Craggie
OF KILDONAN
Torrish
Kilphedir
Ousdale
Glas-loch Mor
Ben Armine Lodge
Strath na Seilge
MEALLAN LIATH MOR
ELDRABLE HILL
Marrel
HELMSDALE
Navidale
Ord Point
TIMESPAN HERITAGE CENTRE
West Helmsdale
Helmsdale
Gartymore
Portgower
Rhian
Shinness
SHIN
Dalnessie
BEINN DHORAIN
Glen Loth
Glen Sletdale
Black Water
Achnairn
Loch Beannach
Brora
Balnacoil
COL-BHEINN
Lothmore
Lothbeg
Lothbeg Pt.
Dalchork
Dalchork Wood
Achnaluachrach
West Langwell
Strath Brora
Gordonbush
Colaboll
Loch Brora
Saval
Sallachy
Lairg Lodge
Loch Craggie
Dalreavoch
Rhilochan
BEN HORN
Achrimsdale
East Clyne
West Clyne
Clynelish
CLYNELISH DISTILLERY
Dalchalm
Lairg Muir
East Langwell
Farlary
Loch Horn
Lairg
FERRYCROFT VISITOR CENTRE
Claonel
Gruids
Muie
Strath Fleet
Torroble
Rogart
CAGAR FEOSAIG
Brora
Ardachu
Pittentrail
Backies
Doll
Loch Cracail Mor
HECTOR MACDONALD MONUMENT
Rogart Station
BEINN LUNNDAIDH
DUNROBIN CASTLE MUSEUM & GARDENS
Achany
Shin Forest
Morvich
Achinduich
Linsidemore
FALLS OF SHIN VISITOR CENTRE
87
Torboll Farm
Culmaily
Golspie
NJ
Achnahanat
Loch Laro
Loch Buidhe
Little Torboll
Kirkton
Inveran
Invershin
Cambusmore Lodge
Loch Fleet
NH
Craigton
BEINN DOMHNAILL
Cambusavie Farm
Littleferry
CARBISDALE CASTLE
Culrain
Balblair
Airdens
Achvaich
Badninish
Skelbo
SKELBO CASTLE
Fourpenny
Braelangwell Lodge
Clashcoig
Rearquhar
Poles
Embo
Migdale
Evelix
Proncy
Embo Street
A836
A838
A897
A9
B871
B873
B874
B870
A882
A839
A837
B864

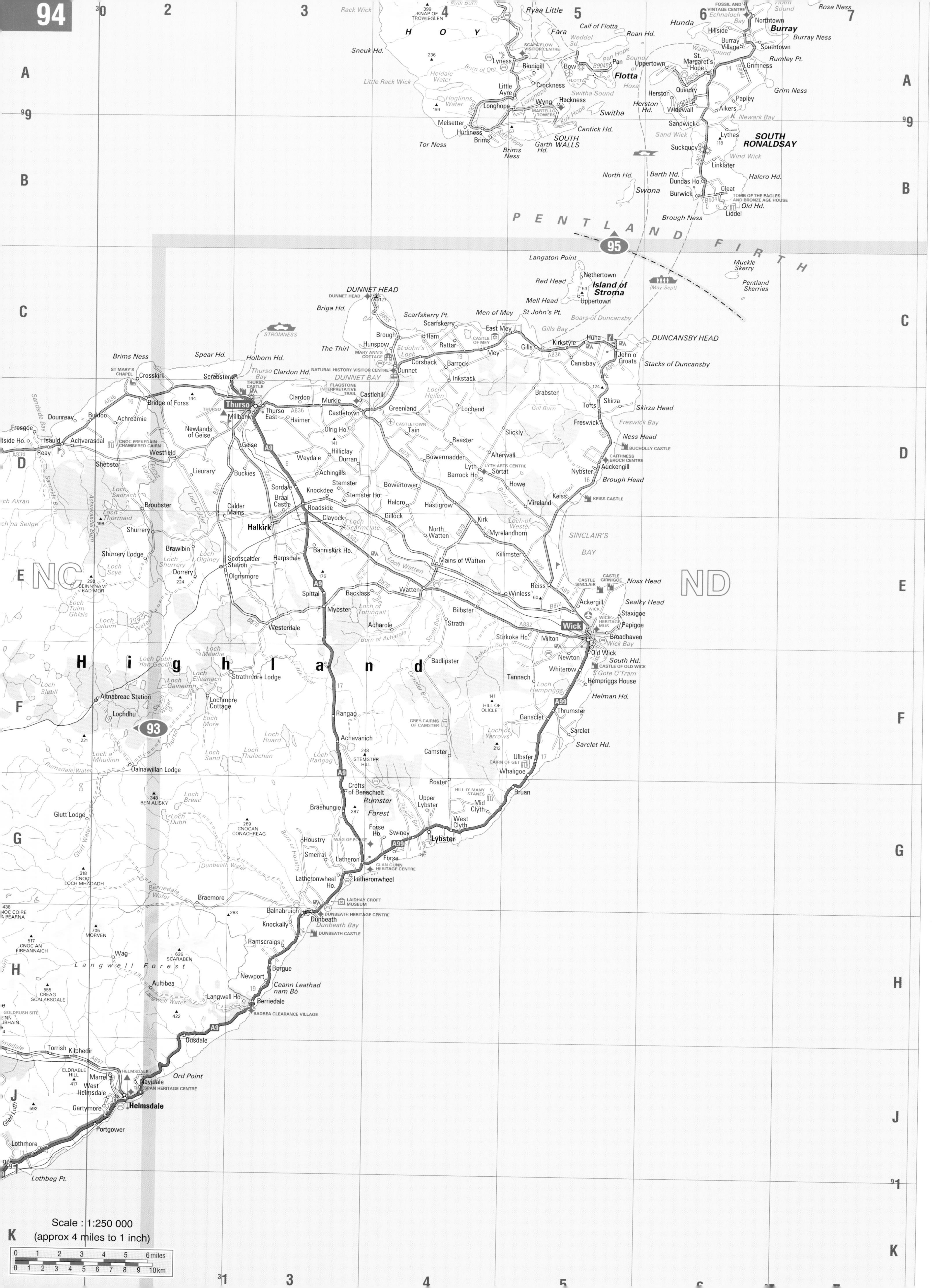
HOY
Flotta
Burray
SOUTH RONALDSAY
SOUTH WALLS
Swona
PENTLAND FIRTH
95
Island of Stroma
DUNNET HEAD
DUNCANSBY HEAD
John o' Groats
Thurso
Dunnet
Castletown
Halkirk
Wick
Lybster
Dunbeath
Berriedale
Helmsdale
Highland
NC
ND
93
Scale : 1:250 000
(approx 4 miles to 1 inch)
6 miles
10 km

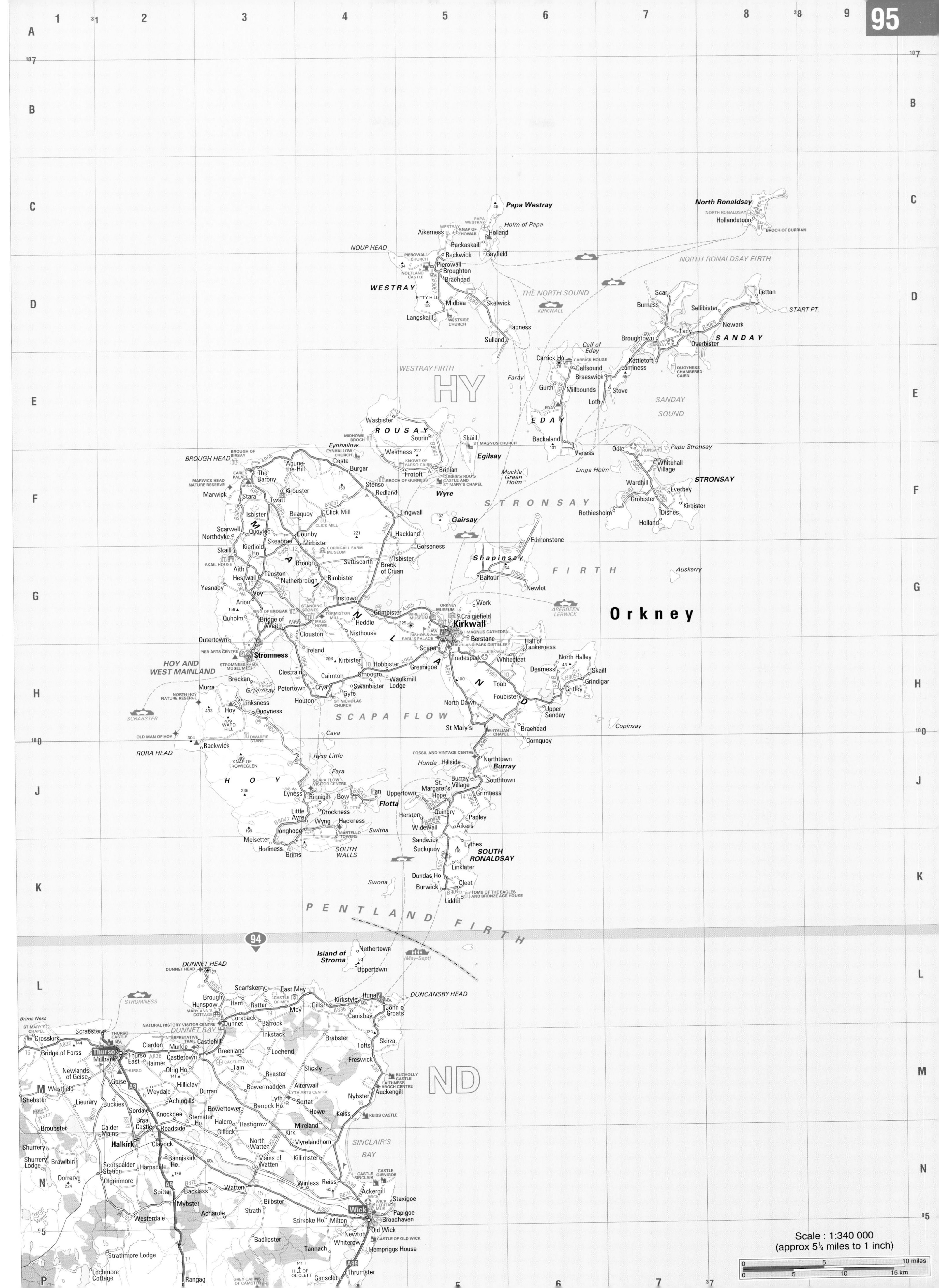
Orkney
HY
ND
Papa Westray
North Ronaldsay
Hollandstoun
Holm of Papa
Aikerness
Holland
Backaskaill
NOUP HEAD
Rackwick
Gayfield
Pierowall
Broughton
Braehead
NORTH RONALDSAY FIRTH
WESTRAY
THE NORTH SOUND
Midbea
Skelwick
Langskaill
Rapness
Sulland
Scar
Burness
Lettan
Sellibister
START PT.
Newark
Lady
Broughtown
Overbister
SANDAY
Calf of Eday
Carrick Ho.
Calfsound
Kettletoft
Braeswick
Laminess
WESTRAY FIRTH
Faray
Guith
Millbounds
Stove
Loth
SANDAY SOUND
EDAY
Backaland
Veness
Wasbister
ROUSAY
Sourin
Skaill
Egilsay
Eynhallow
Westness
Costa
Burgar
Papa Stronsay
Whitehall Village
Odie
BROUGH HEAD
Linga Holm
Muckle Green Holm
STRONSAY
Wardhill
Everbay
Grobister
Kirbister
Rothiesholm
Dishes
Holland
The Barony
Abune-the-Hill
Marwick
Stara
Twatt
Kirbuster
Stenso
Redland
Frotoft
Wyre
Gairsay
Tingwall
Beaquoy
Click Mill
Isbister
Scarwell
Northdyke
Quoyloo
Skeabrae
Dounby
Mirbister
Hackland
Gorseness
Skaill
Kierfiold Ho
Brough
Settiscarth
Isbister
Breck of Cruan
Shapinsay
Edmonstone
FIRTH
Auskerry
Balfour
Newlot
Aith
Hestwall
Tenston
Netherbrough
Bimbister
Yesnaby
Voy
Arion
Finstown
Work
Grimbister
Craigiefield
Quholm
Bridge of Waith
Heddle
Kirkwall
Outertown
Clouston
Nisthouse
Berstane
Hall of Tankerness
Stromness
Ireland
Scapa
Tradespark
Whitecleat
North Halley
Skaill
Grindigar
HOY AND WEST MAINLAND
Kirbister
Hobbister
Greenigoe
Deerness
Breckan
Clestrain
Cairnton
Smoogro
Waulkmill Lodge
Toab
Gritley
Murra
Graemsay
Petertown
Crya
Swanbister
Foubister
Gyre
Houton
North Dawn
Upper Sanday
Linksness
Hoy
Quoyness
SCAPA FLOW
St Mary's
Braehead
Copinsay
Cava
OLD MAN OF HOY
Rackwick
Cornquoy
RORA HEAD
Rysa Little
Hunda
Hillside
Northtown
Burray
Fara
Burray Village
Southtown
HOY
Lyness
Pan
Uppertown
St. Margaret's Hope
Grimness
Rinnigill
Bow
Flotta
Little Ayre
Crockness
Herston
Quindry
Papley
Wyng
Hackness
Widewall
Aikers
Longhope
Switha
Melsetter
Sandwick
Lythes
Hurliness
Brims
SOUTH WALLS
Suckquoy
SOUTH RONALDSAY
Linklater
Swona
Dundas Ho.
Cleat
Burwick
Liddel
PENTLAND FIRTH
94
Nethertown
Island of Stroma
Uppertown
DUNNET HEAD
Scarfskerry
East Mey
Brough
Hunspow
Ham
Rattar
Kirkstyle
Huna
DUNCANSBY HEAD
Mey
Gills
John o' Groats
Canisbay
Brims Ness
Corsback
Dunnet
Barrock
DUNNET BAY
Inkstack
Scrabster
Crosskirk
Castlehill
Brabster
Tofts
Skirza
Clardon
Murkle
Thurso
Bridge of Forss
Greenland
Lochend
Millbank
Thurso East
Haimer
Castletown
Freswick
Tain
Newlands of Geise
Olrig Ho.
Slickly
Reaster
Geise
Westfield
Weydale
Hilliclay
Bowermadden
Alterwall
Durran
Nybster
Auckengill
Lyth
Shebster
Lieurary
Buckies
Achingills
Sortat
Barrock Ho.
Bowertower
Howe
Sordale
Knockdee
Keiss
Broubster
Calder Mains
Braal Castle
Roadside
Stemster Ho.
Halcro
Hastigrow
Mireland
Halkirk
Gillock
Kirk
Shurrery
Clayock
North Watten
Myrelandhorn
SINCLAIR'S BAY
Shurrery Lodge
Brawlbin
Banniskirk Ho.
Mains of Watten
Killimster
Scotscalder Station
Harpsdale
Dorrery
Olgrinmore
Watten
Winless
Reiss
Ackergill
Spittal
Backlass
Staxigoe
Wick
Mybster
Bilbster
Papigoe
Westerdale
Acharole
Strath
Stirkoke Ho.
Milton
Broadhaven
Old Wick
Newton
Badlipster
Whiterow
Strathmore Lodge
Tannach
Hempriggs House
Lochmore Cottage
Thrumster
Rangag
Gansclet
Scale : 1:340 000
(approx 5¼ miles to 1 inch)
10 miles
15 km

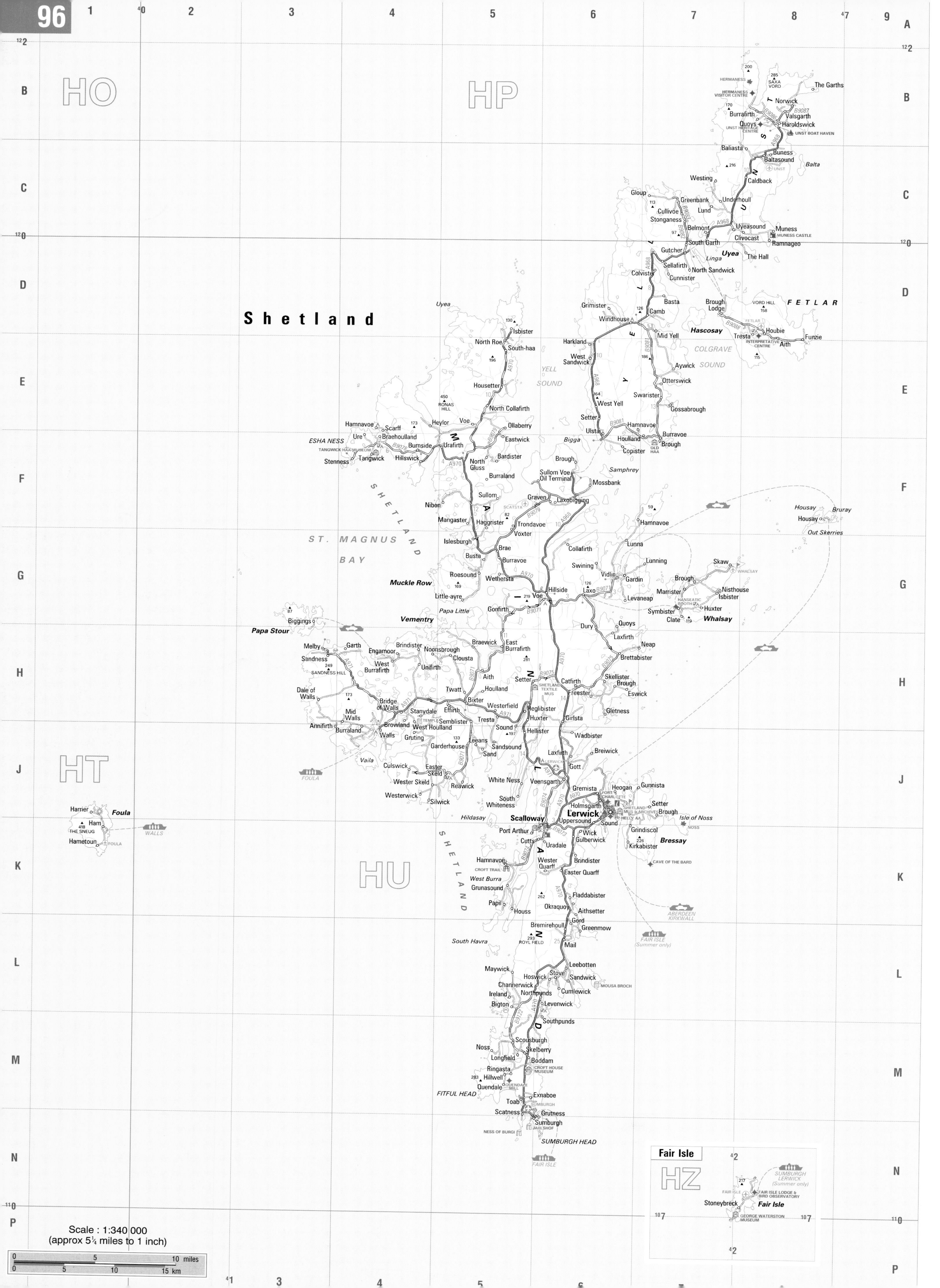

96
Shetland
HO
HP
HT
HU
HZ
Unst
Yell
Fetlar
Mainland
Hermaness
Saxa Vord
The Garths
Norwick
Burrafirth
Valsgarth
Haroldswick
Quoys
Unst Heritage Centre
Unst Boat Haven
Baliasta
Buness
Baltasound
Balta
Westing
Caldback
Gloup
Greenbank
Underhoull
Cullivoe
Lund
Stonganess
Uyeasound
Muness
Muness Castle
Belmont
Clivocast
Ramnageo
South Garth
Uyea
Linga
The Hall
Gutcher
Sellafirth
North Sandwick
Cunnister
Colvister
Basta
Brough Lodge
Vord Hill
Grimister
Camb
Windhouse
Hascosay
Houbie
Funzie
Mid Yell
Tresta
Fetlar Interpretative Centre
Aith
Harkland
West Sandwick
Colgrave Sound
Yell Sound
Aywick
Otterswick
Swarister
Gossabrough
West Yell
Setter
Hamnavoe
Ulsta
Burravoe
Houlland
Brough
Copister
Old Haa
Bigga
Samphrey
Uyea
Isbister
North Roe
South-haa
Housetter
Ronas Hill
North Collafirth
Hamnavoe
Scarff
Heylor
Voe
Ollaberry
Esha Ness
Ure
Braehoulland
Eastwick
Tangwick Haa Museum
Burnside
Urafirth
Stenness
Tangwick
Hillswick
North Gluss
Bardister
Burraland
Brough
Sullom Voe Oil Terminal
Mossbank
Shetland
St. Magnus Bay
Sullom
Nibon
Scatsta
Graven
Laxobigging
Housay
Bruray
Out Skerries
Mangaster
Haggrister
Trondavoe
Voxter
Hamnavoe
Islesburgh
Busta
Brae
Collafirth
Lunna
Burravoe
Swining
Lunning
Skaw
Whalsay
Roesound
Muckle Row
Wethersta
Vidlin
Gardin
Brough
Marrister
Nisthouse
Isbister
Hillside
Laxo
Levaneap
Hanseatic Booth
Little-ayre
Voe
Symbister
Huxter
Clate
Papa Little
Gonfirth
Vementry
Biggings
Papa Stour
Dury
Quoys
Laxfirth
Neap
Melby
Garth
Brindister
Braewick
East Burrafirth
Sandness
Engamoor
Noonsbrough
Clousta
Brettabister
Sandness Hill
West Burrafirth
Unifirth
Aith
Setter
Catfirth
Skellister
Brough
Eswick
Shetland Textile Mus
Dale of Walls
Twatt
Houlland
Freester
Bridge of Walls
Bixter
Mid Walls
Stanydale
Effirth
Westerfield
Heglibister
Gletness
Temple
Huxter
Annifirth
Burraland
Browland
Sembister
West Houlland
Tresta
Sound
Girlsta
Hellister
Walls
Gruting
Garderhouse
Sandsound
Wadbister
Sand
Leeans
Vaila
Foula
Culswick
Easter Skeld
Laxfirth
Breiwick
Gott
Lerwick
Westerwick
Wester Skeld
Reawick
White Ness
Veensgarth
Gremista
Heogan
Gunnista
Fort Charlotte
Setter
Silwick
South Whiteness
Holmsgarth
Brough
Harrier
Foula
Ham
The Sneug
Hametoun
Walls
Hildasay
Scalloway
Uppersound
Sound
Isle of Noss
Shetland Mus & Archives
Noss
Grindiscol
Port Arthur
Cutts
Wick
Gulberwick
Bressay
Kirkabister
Uradale
Hamnavoe
Croft Trail
Wester Quarff
Brindister
Cave of the Bard
West Burra
Easter Quarff
Grunasound
Fladdabister
Papil
Okraquoy
Aithsetter
Houss
Aberdeen Kirkwall
Gord
Greenmow
Bremirehoull
Fair Isle (Summer only)
South Havra
Royl Field
Mail
Leebotten
Maywick
Hoswick
Stove
Sandwick
Mousa Broch
Channerwick
Ireland
Northpunds
Cumlewick
Bigton
Levenwick
Southpunds
Scousburgh
Noss
Skelberry
Longfield
Boddam
Croft House Museum
Ringasta
Hillwell
Quendale
Quendale Mill
Fitful Head
Exnaboe
Toab
Sumburgh
Scatness
Grutness
Jarlshof
Ness of Burgi
Sumburgh Head
Fair Isle
Fair Isle
Sumburgh Lerwick (Summer only)
Fair Isle Lodge & Bird Observatory
Stoneybreck
Fair Isle
George Waterston Museum
A968
A970
A971
B9081
B9082
B9084
B9071
B9074
B9075
B9076
B9087
Scale : 1:340 000
(approx 5¼ miles to 1 inch)
0 5 10 miles
0 5 10 15 km

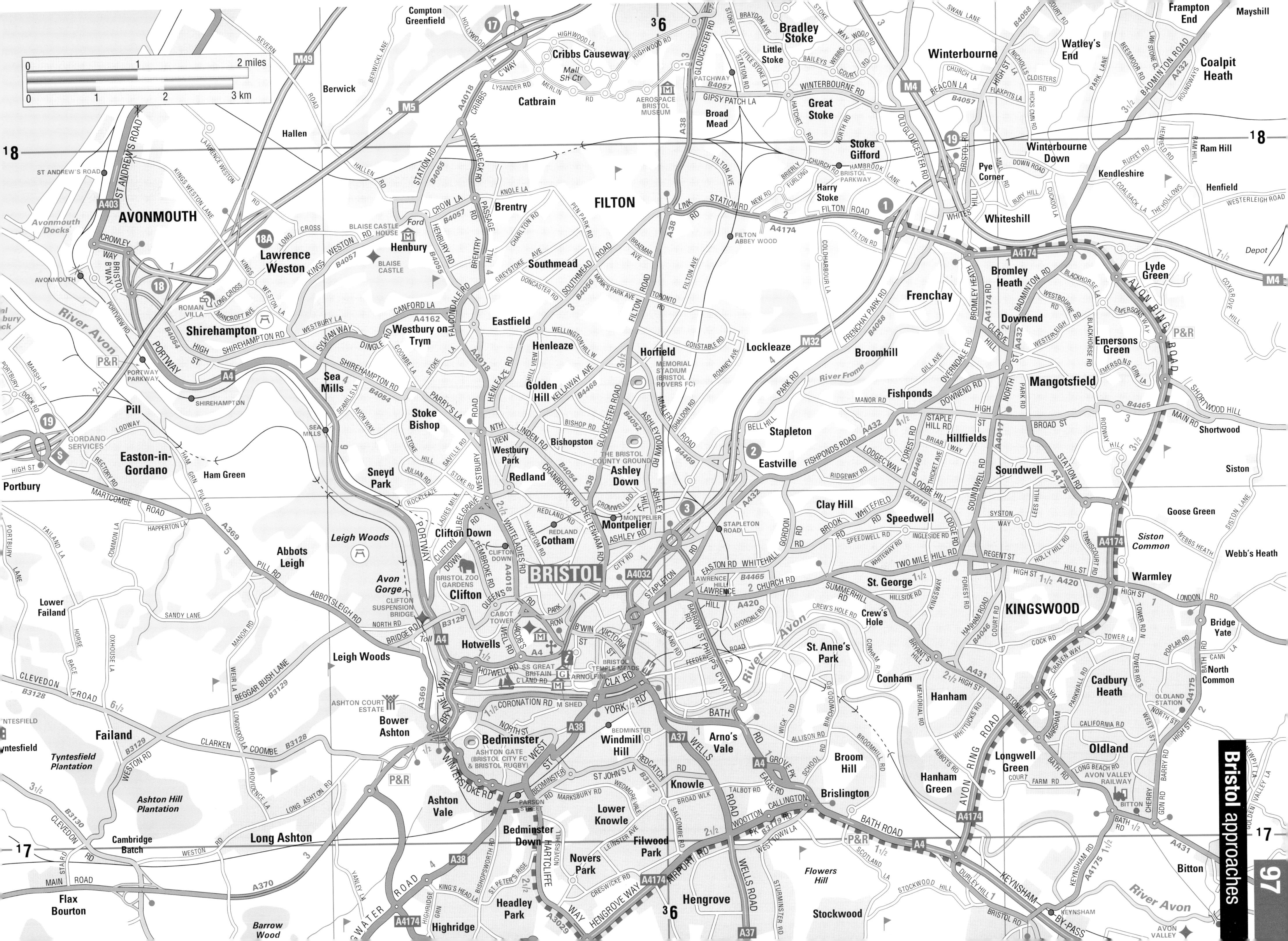
BRISTOL
AVONMOUTH
FILTON
KINGSWOOD
Mayshill
Frampton End
Coalpit Heath
Ram Hill
Henfield
Siston
Webb's Heath
Bridge Yate
North Common
Bitton
Lyde Green
Emersons Green
Mangotsfield
Goose Green
Siston Common
Warmley
Oldland
Cadbury Heath
Kendleshire
Watley's End
Winterbourne Down
Winterbourne
Whiteshill
Pye Corner
Bromley Heath
Downend
Soundwell
Longwell Green
Frenchay
Fishponds
Hillfields
Speedwell
St George
Hanham
Hanham Green
Conham
Crew's Hole
Stoke Gifford
Harry Stoke
Bradley Stoke
Little Stoke
Great Stoke
Broomhill
Clay Hill
Broom Hill
Brislington
Stockwood
Flowers Hill
St Anne's Park
Stapleton
Eastville
Lockleaze
Broad Mead
Arno's Vale
Hengrove
Knowle
Filwood Park
Horfield
Ashley Down
Montpelier
Windmill Hill
Lower Knowle
Novers Park
Cribbs Causeway
Catbrain
Southmead
Henleaze
Golden Hill
Bishopston
Cotham
Redland
Westbury Park
Eastfield
Brentry
Clifton Down
Clifton
Hotwells
Bedminster
Bedminster Down
Headley Park
Highridge
Ashton Vale
Compton Greenfield
Henbury
Westbury on Trym
Stoke Bishop
Sneyd Park
Leigh Woods
Avon Gorge
Bower Ashton
Berwick
Hallen
Sea Mills
Lawrence Weston
Abbots Leigh
Long Ashton
Barrow Wood
Shirehampton
Ham Green
Pill
Easton-in-Gordano
Failand
Ashton Hill Plantation
Cambridge Batch
Flax Bourton
Lower Failand
Tyntesfield Plantation
Portbury
Avonmouth Docks
River Avon
River Frome
AVON RING ROAD
BADMINTON ROAD
GLOUCESTER ROAD
FILTON ROAD
PORTWAY
ST ANDREW'S ROAD
WELLS ROAD
BATH ROAD
KEYNSHAM BY-PASS
HENGROVE WAY
HARTCLIFFE
WINTERSTOKE RD
BRUNEL WAY
M4
M5
M32
M49
A4174
A38
A4
A37
A432
A420
A431
A369
A403
A4018
A3029
A370
2 miles
3 km
18
17
36

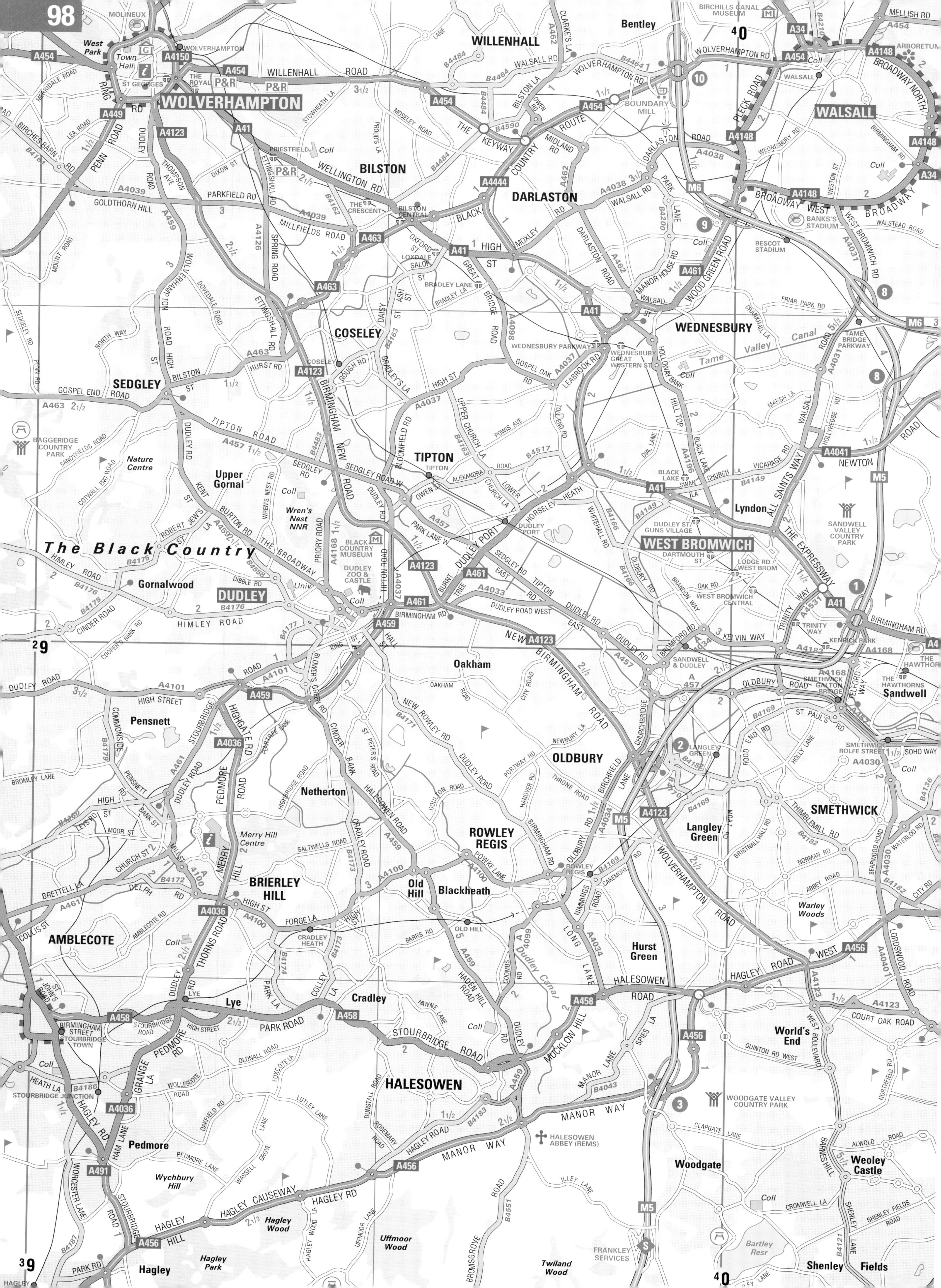
WOLVERHAMPTON
WILLENHALL
Bentley
WALSALL
BILSTON
DARLASTON
COSELEY
SEDGLEY
WEDNESBURY
TIPTON
Upper Gornal
The Black Country
Gornalwood
DUDLEY
WEST BROMWICH
Lyndon
Oakham
Pensnett
OLDBURY
Netherton
ROWLEY REGIS
SMETHWICK
Langley Green
BRIERLEY HILL
Old Hill
Blackheath
AMBLECOTE
Hurst Green
Lye
Cradley
World's End
HALESOWEN
Pedmore
Woodgate
Weoley Castle
Hagley
Shenley Fields
Sandwell
Wren's Nest NNR
Black Country Museum
Dudley Zoo & Castle
Merry Hill Centre
Baggeridge Country Park
Sandwell Valley Country Park
Woodgate Valley Country Park
Halesowen Abbey (rems)
Wychbury Hill
Hagley Wood
Hagley Park
Uffmoor Wood
Twiland Wood
Bartley Resr
Frankley Services
Warley Woods
Banks's Stadium
Bescot Stadium
Birchills Canal Museum
Arboretum
Molineux
The Hawthorns
Tame Valley Canal
Dudley Canal

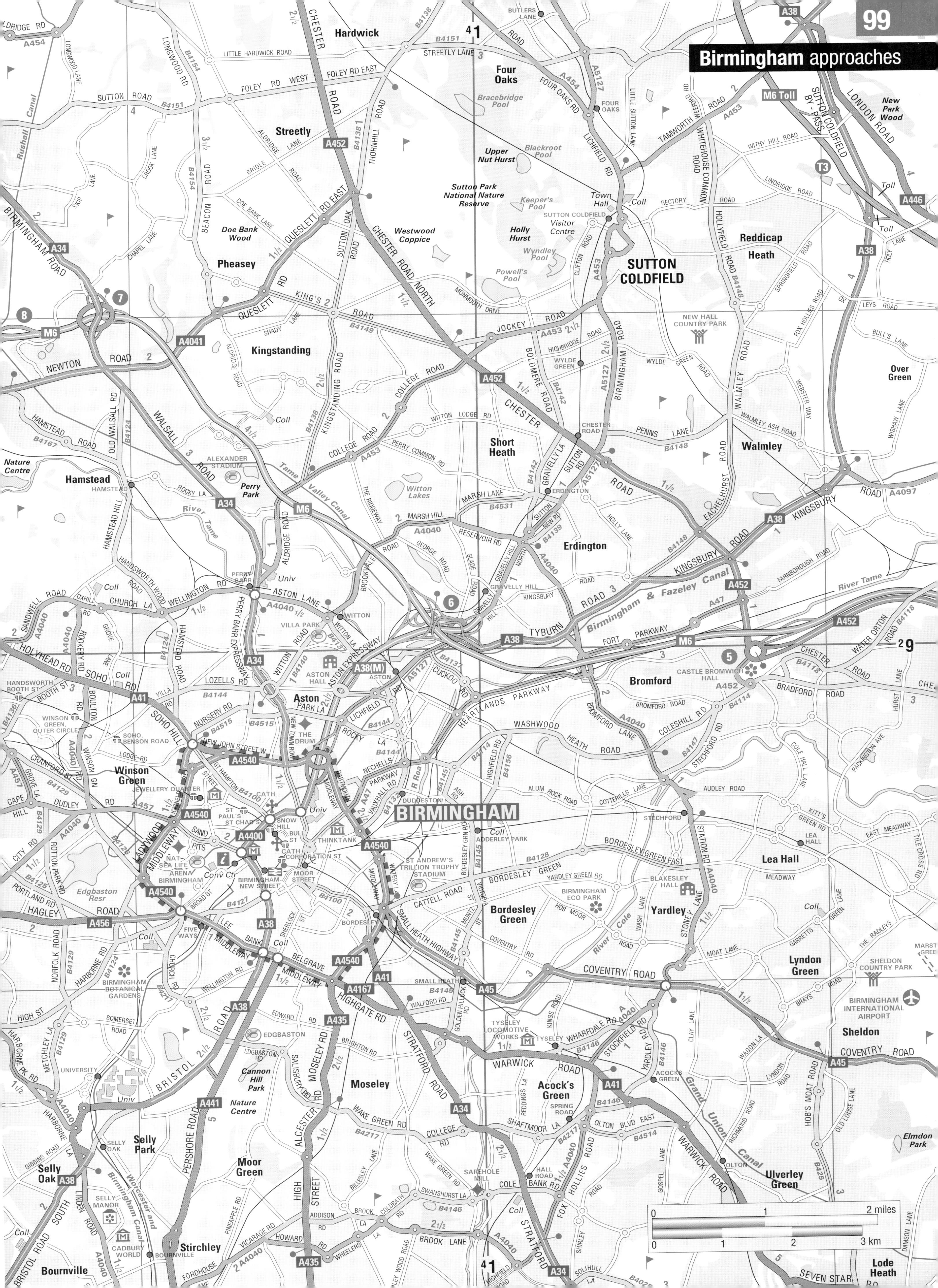
Hardwick
Four Oaks
Streetly
Upper Nut Hurst
Sutton Park National Nature Reserve
Westwood Coppice
Doe Bank Wood
Pheasey
Holly Hurst
SUTTON COLDFIELD
Reddicap Heath
New Park Wood
Kingstanding
NEW HALL COUNTRY PARK
Over Green
Short Heath
Walmley
Nature Centre
Hamstead
ALEXANDER STADIUM
Perry Park
Witton Lakes
Erdington
VILLA PARK
ASTON HALL
Aston
Bromford
CASTLE BROMWICH HALL
Winson Green
JEWELLERY QUARTER
BIRMINGHAM
THINKTANK
NAT SEA LIFE
ARENA BIRMINGHAM
Conv Ctr
BIRMINGHAM NEW STREET
ST ANDREW'S TRILLION TROPHY STADIUM
Lea Hall
Edgbaston Resr
BIRMINGHAM ECO PARK
Bordesley Green
Yardley
BIRMINGHAM BOTANICAL GARDENS
EDGBASTON
Lyndon Green
SHELDON COUNTRY PARK
BIRMINGHAM INTERNATIONAL AIRPORT
TYSELEY LOCOMOTIVE WORKS
Sheldon
Cannon Hill Park
Moseley
Acock's Green
Nature Centre
Selly Park
Selly Oak
Moor Green
SAREHOLE MILL
Elmdon Park
Ulverley Green
SELLY MANOR
CADBURY WORLD
Stirchley
Bournville
Lode Heath
0 1 2 miles
0 1 2 3 km

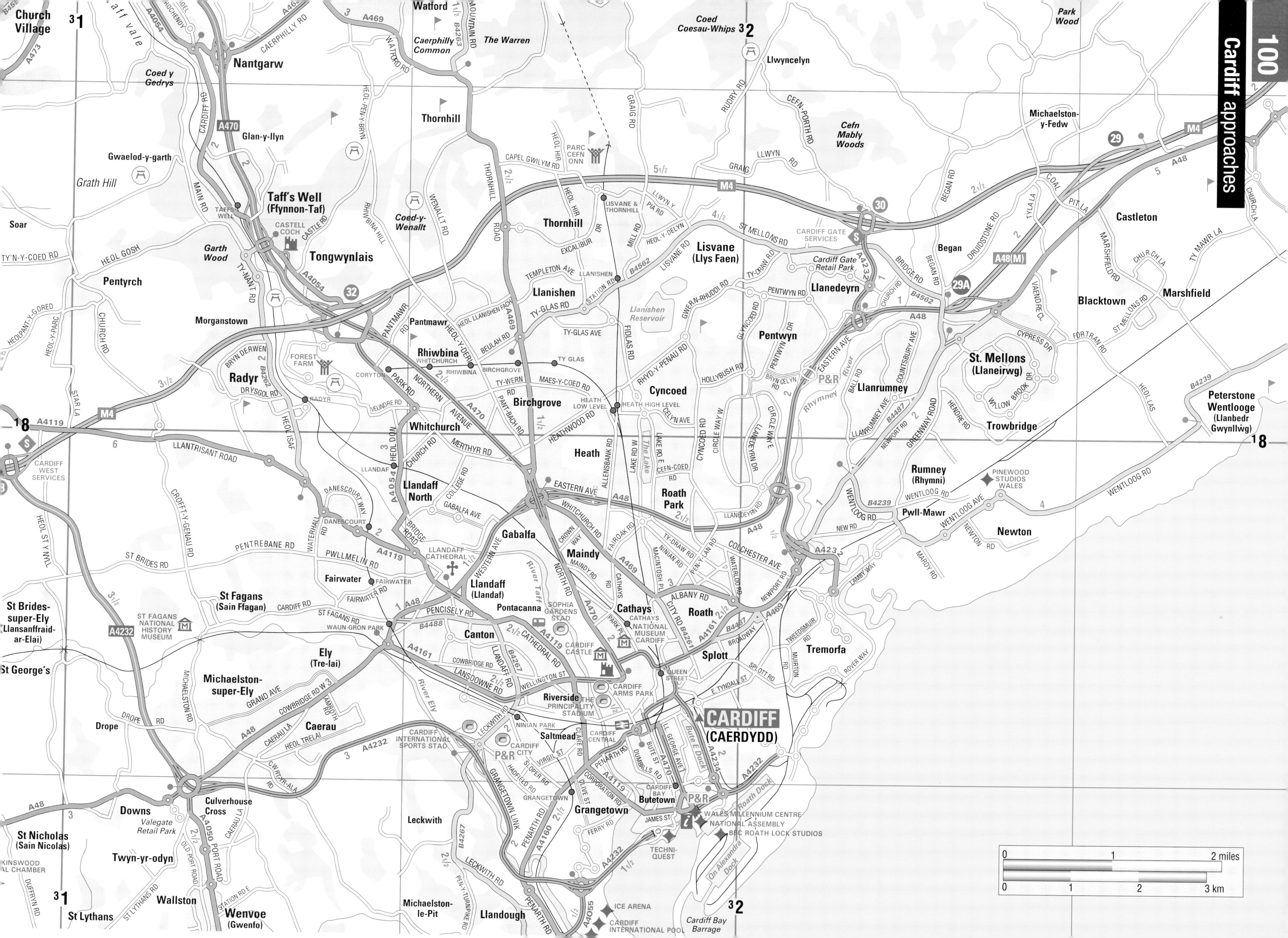
CARDIFF
(CAERDYDD)
Church Village
Watford
Caerphilly Common
The Warren
Coed Coesau-Whips
Llwyncelyn
Park Wood
Michaelston-y-Fedw
Cefn Mably Woods
Nantgarw
Coed y Gedrys
Glan-y-llyn
Gwaelod-y-garth
Grath Hill
Thornhill
Soar
Taff's Well
(Ffynnon-Taf)
Coed-y-Wenallt
Garth Wood
Tongwynlais
Pentyrch
Morganstown
Castleton
Began
Lisvane
(Llys Faen)
Llanedeyrn
Blacktown
Marshfield
Llanishen
Llanishen Reservoir
Pentwyn
St. Mellons
(Llaneirwg)
Pantmawr
Rhiwbina
Radyr
Cyncoed
Llanrumney
Birchgrove
Whitchurch
Trowbridge
Peterstone Wentlooge
(Llanbedr Gwynllŵg)
Heath
Rumney
(Rhymni)
Llandaff North
Roath Park
Pwll-Mawr
Newton
Gabalfa
Maindy
Fairwater
Llandaff
(Llandaf)
St Fagans
(Sain Ffagan)
Pontacanna
Cathays
Roath
St Brides-super-Ely
(Llansanffraid-ar-Elai)
Canton
Splott
Tremorfa
St George's
Ely
(Tre-lai)
Michaelston-super-Ely
Riverside
Drope
Caerau
Saltmead
Culverhouse Cross
Downs
Leckwith
Grangetown
Butetown
St Nicholas
(Sain Nicolas)
Twyn-yr-odyn
Wallston
St Lythans
Wenvoe
(Gwenfo)
Michaelston-le-Pit
Llandough
Valegate Retail Park
Cardiff Gate Retail Park
CARDIFF GATE SERVICES
CARDIFF WEST SERVICES
PINEWOOD STUDIOS WALES
ST FAGANS NATIONAL HISTORY MUSEUM
LLANDAFF CATHEDRAL
SOPHIA GARDENS STAD
CARDIFF CASTLE
CATHAYS NATIONAL MUSEUM CARDIFF
CARDIFF ARMS PARK
THE PRINCIPALITY STADIUM
CARDIFF INTERNATIONAL SPORTS STAD
CARDIFF CITY
WALES MILLENNIUM CENTRE
NATIONAL ASSEMBLY
BBC ROATH LOCK STUDIOS
TECHNIQUEST
ICE ARENA
CARDIFF INTERNATIONAL POOL
Cardiff Bay Barrage
River Taff
River Ely
Rhymney River
Bute E Dock
Roath Dock
On Alexandra Dock
M4
A48(M)
A48
A469
A470
A4232
A4119
A4160
A4161
A4054
A4055
A4050
29
29A
30
32
0
1
2 miles
0
1
2
3 km

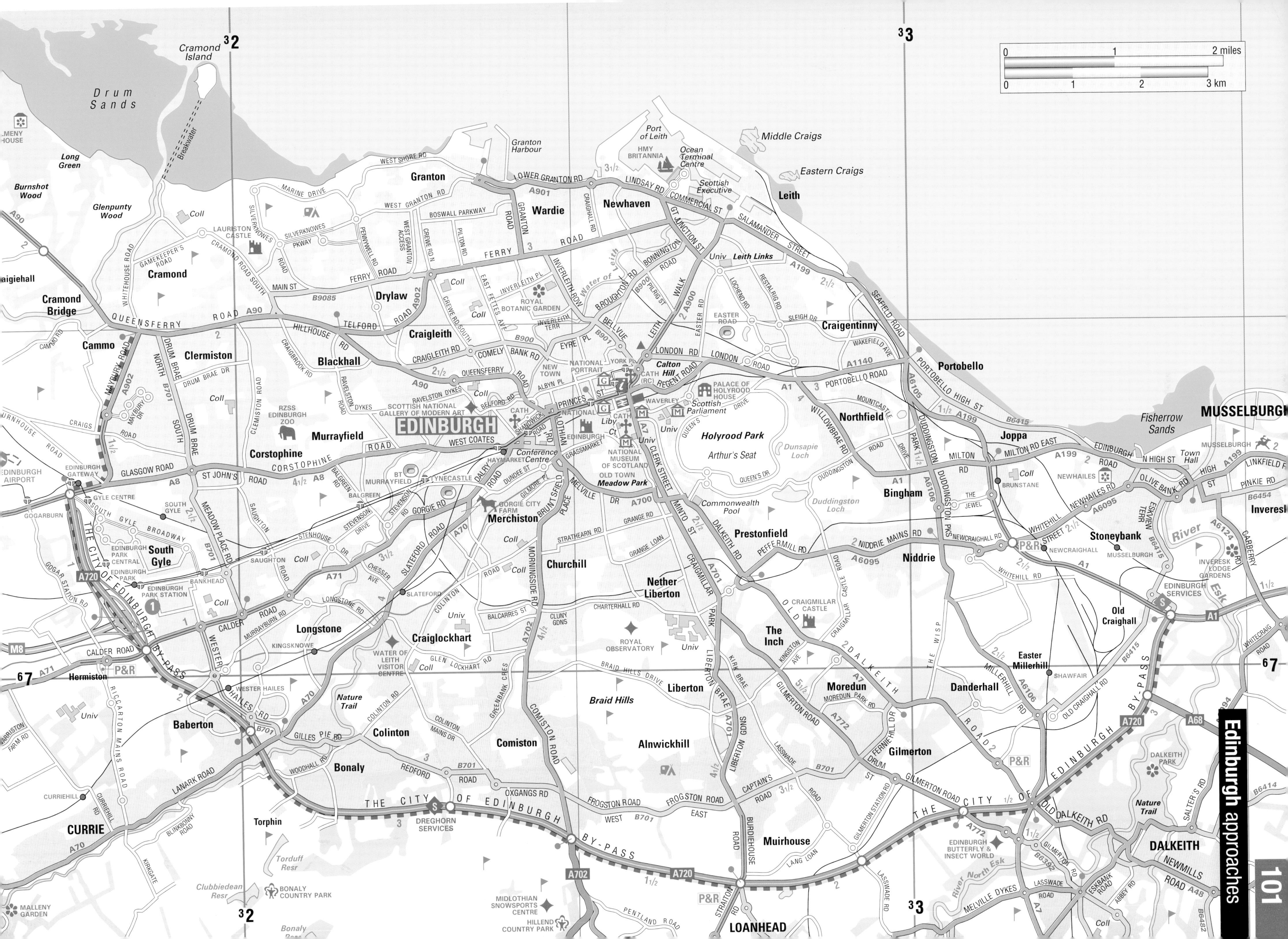
EDINBURGH
MUSSELBURGH
DALKEITH
LOANHEAD
CURRIE
Leith
Port of Leith
Newhaven
Granton
Granton Harbour
Wardie
Portobello
Joppa
Craigentinny
Northfield
Bingham
Niddrie
Stoneybank
Old Craighall
Easter Millerhill
Danderhall
Gilmerton
Moredun
The Inch
Prestonfield
Holyrood Park
Arthur's Seat
Nether Liberton
Liberton
Alnwickhill
Braid Hills
Muirhouse
Churchill
Merchiston
Comiston
Craiglockhart
Colinton
Bonaly
Longstone
Murrayfield
Corstophine
Blackhall
Craigleith
Drylaw
Clermiston
Cramond
Cramond Island
Cramond Bridge
Cammo
South Gyle
Baberton
Hermiston
Torphin
Drum Sands
Fisherrow Sands
Middle Craigs
Eastern Craigs
Calton Hill
Meadow Park
Duddingston Loch
Dunsapie Loch
Commonwealth Pool
Burnshot Wood
Glenpunty Wood
Long Green
Nature Trail
Torduff Resr
Clubbiedean Resr
Bonaly Country Park
Midlothian Snowsports Centre
Hillend Country Park
Dreghorn Services
Edinburgh Services
Edinburgh Airport
Royal Observatory
Royal Botanic Garden
RZSS Edinburgh Zoo
Scottish Parliament
Palace of Holyroodhouse
THE CITY OF EDINBURGH BY-PASS
A720
A1
A7
A8
A90
A70
A71
A702
M8
2 miles
3 km
32
33
67

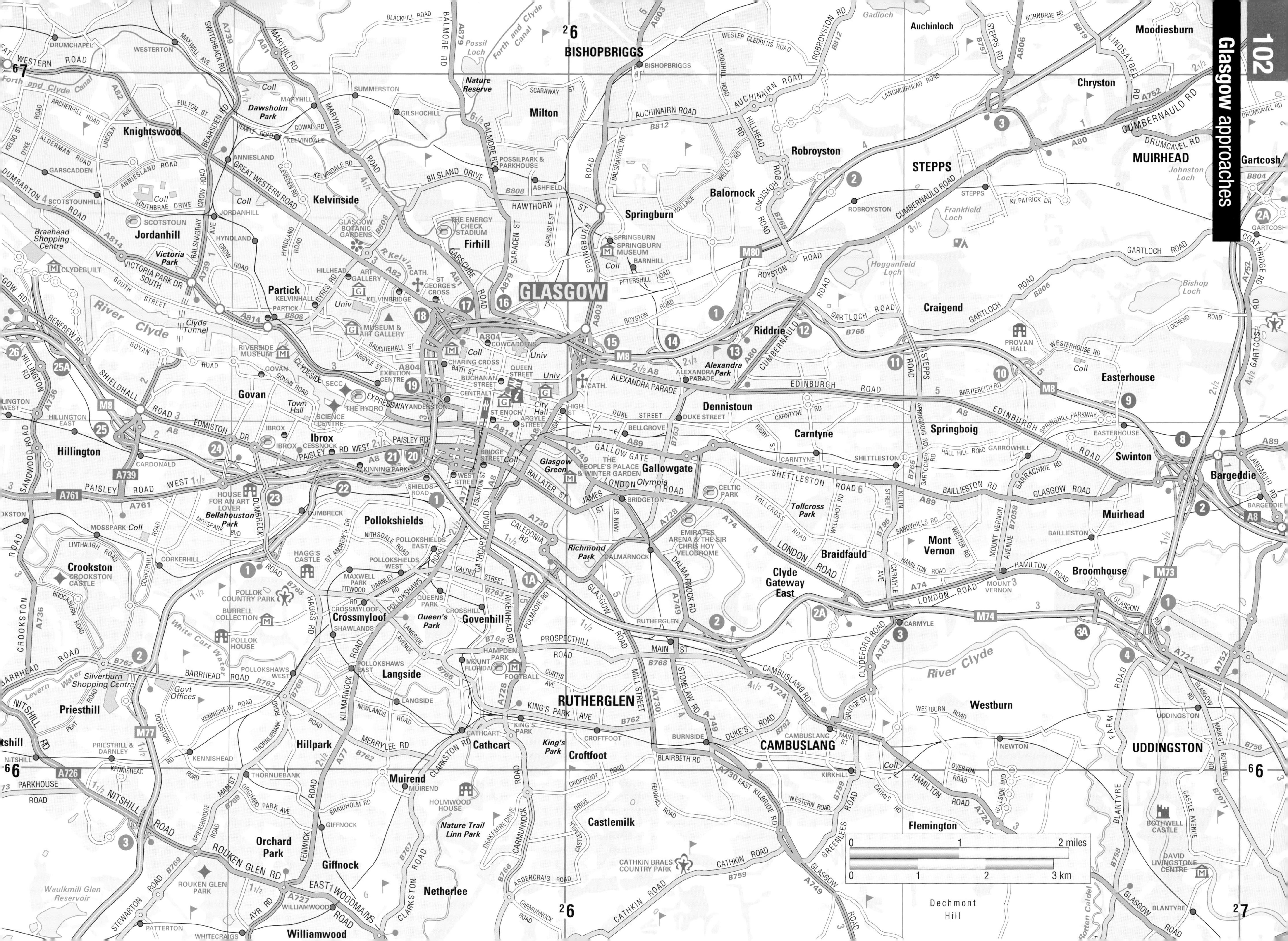
GLASGOW
BISHOPBRIGGS
Auchinloch
Moodiesburn
Chryston
MUIRHEAD
Gartcosh
Knightswood
Milton
Robroyston
STEPPS
Balornock
Springburn
Kelvinside
Firhill
Jordanhill
Partick
Craigend
Riddrie
Easterhouse
Govan
Dennistoun
Carntyne
Springboig
Swinton
Bargeddie
Hillington
Ibrox
Gallowgate
Muirhead
Pollokshields
Crookston
Mont Vernon
Braidfauld
Clyde Gateway East
Broomhouse
Crossmyloof
Govanhill
Langside
RUTHERGLEN
Westburn
Priesthill
Hillpark
Cathcart
Croftfoot
CAMBUSLANG
UDDINGSTON
Muirend
Castlemilk
Flemington
Orchard Park
Giffnock
Netherlee
Williamwood
Dechmont Hill
River Clyde
White Cart Water
Dawsholm Park
Victoria Park
Bellahouston Park
Queen's Park
Tollcross Park
King's Park
Richmond Park
Glasgow Green
Alexandra Park
Nature Trail Linn Park
Waulkmill Glen Reservoir
Cathkin Braes Country Park
Rouken Glen Park
Pollok Country Park
0
1
2 miles
0
1
2
3 km

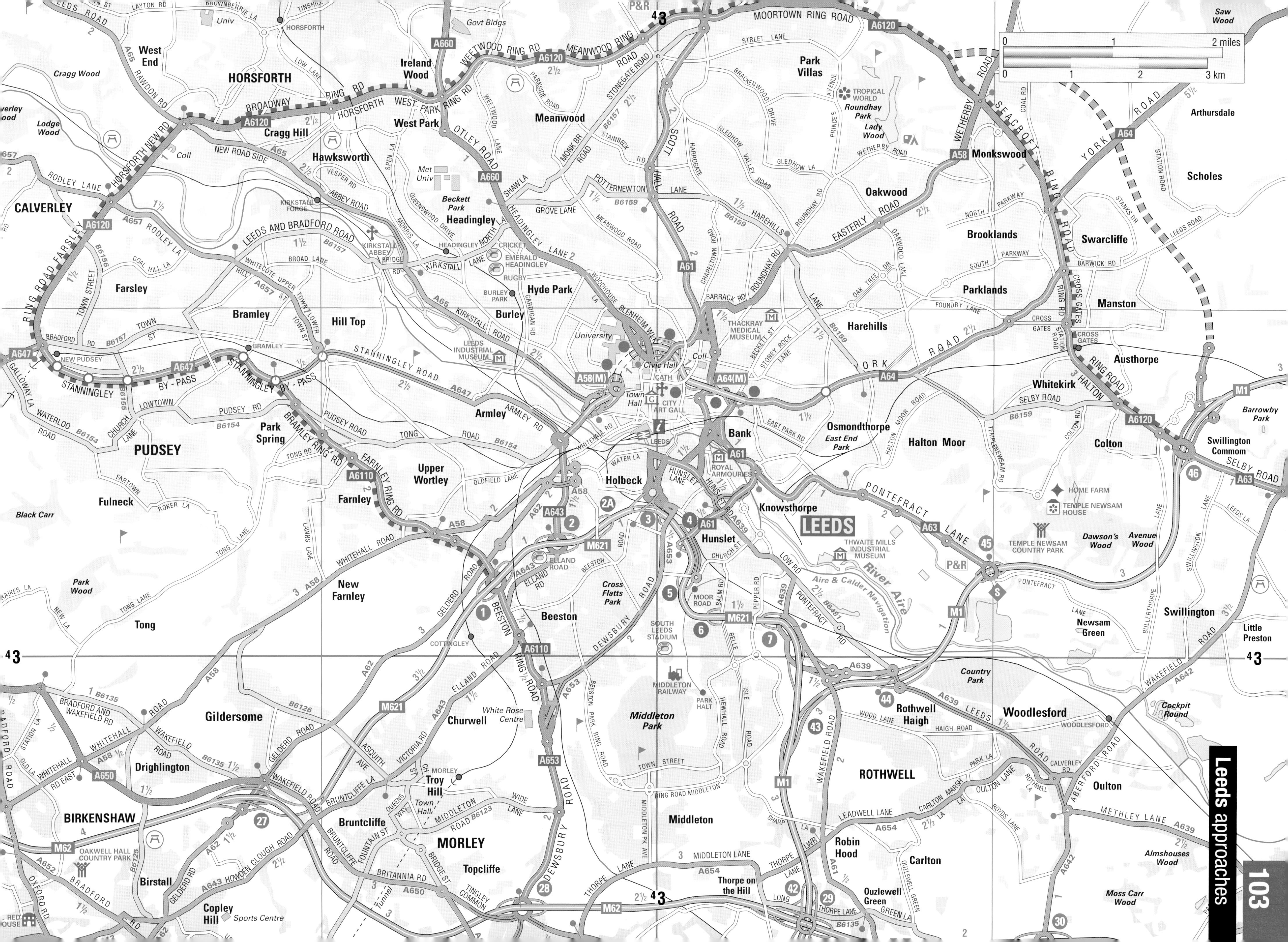

103
Leeds approaches
LEEDS
River Aire
Aire & Calder Navigation
Saw Wood
Arthursdale
Scholes
Swarcliffe
Manston
Austhorpe
Colton
Whitekirk
Swillington
Swillington Common
Barrowby Park
Little Preston
Newsam Green
Woodlesford
Oulton
Almshouses Wood
Moss Carr Wood
Avenue Wood
Dawson's Wood
Cockpit Round
Country Park
HOME FARM
TEMPLE NEWSAM HOUSE
TEMPLE NEWSAM COUNTRY PARK
Monkswood
Brooklands
Parklands
Halton Moor
Rothwell Haigh
ROTHWELL
Carlton
Ouzlewell Green
Robin Hood
Oakwood
Harehills
Osmondthorpe
East End Park
THWAITE MILLS INDUSTRIAL MUSEUM
Knowsthorpe
Bank
ROYAL ARMOURIES
Hunslet
TROPICAL WORLD
Roundhay Park
Lady Wood
Park Villas
THACKRAY MEDICAL MUSEUM
Civic Hall
CATH
CITY ART GALL
Town Hall
University
Holbeck
Cross Flatts Park
SOUTH LEEDS STADIUM
MIDDLETON RAILWAY
PARK HALT
Middleton Park
Middleton
Thorpe on the Hill
Beeston
ELLAND ROAD
White Rose Centre
Churwell
Troy Hill
Town Hall
MORLEY
Topcliffe
TINGLEY COMMON
Meanwood
Hyde Park
Burley
BURLEY PARK
CRICKET
EMERALD HEADINGLEY
RUGBY
Headingley
Beckett Park
Met Univ
Govt Bldgs
Ireland Wood
West Park
Armley
LEEDS INDUSTRIAL MUSEUM
Upper Wortley
Farnley
New Farnley
Hill Top
Hawksworth
KIRKSTALL ABBEY
KIRKSTALL FORGE
HORSFORTH
Cragg Hill
Bramley
Park Spring
PUDSEY
Gildersome
Bruntcliffe
Drighlington
Copley Hill
Sports Centre
Birstall
BIRKENSHAW
OAKWELL HALL COUNTRY PARK
West End
Farsley
Fulneck
Tong
Cragg Wood
Lodge Wood
CALVERLEY
Park Wood
Black Carr
NEW PUDSEY
STANNINGLEY
RING ROAD
MOORTOWN RING ROAD
SEACROFT RING ROAD
WETHERBY ROAD
YORK ROAD
SELBY ROAD
PONTEFRACT LANE
DEWSBURY ROAD
WAKEFIELD ROAD
ABERFORD ROAD
OTLEY ROAD
HEADINGLEY LANE
KIRKSTALL ROAD
STANNINGLEY ROAD
FARNLEY RING RD
BRAMLEY RING RD
STANNINGLEY BY-PASS
HORSFORTH NEW RD
RING ROAD FARSLEY
BEESTON RING ROAD
GELDERD ROAD
ELLAND ROAD
SCOTT HALL ROAD
EASTERLY ROAD
ROUNDHAY RD
M1
M62
M621
A64(M)
A58(M)
A61
A63
A64
A58
A62
A65
A6120
A639
A642
A643
A647
A650
A653
A654
A657
A660
A6110
43
2 miles
3 km

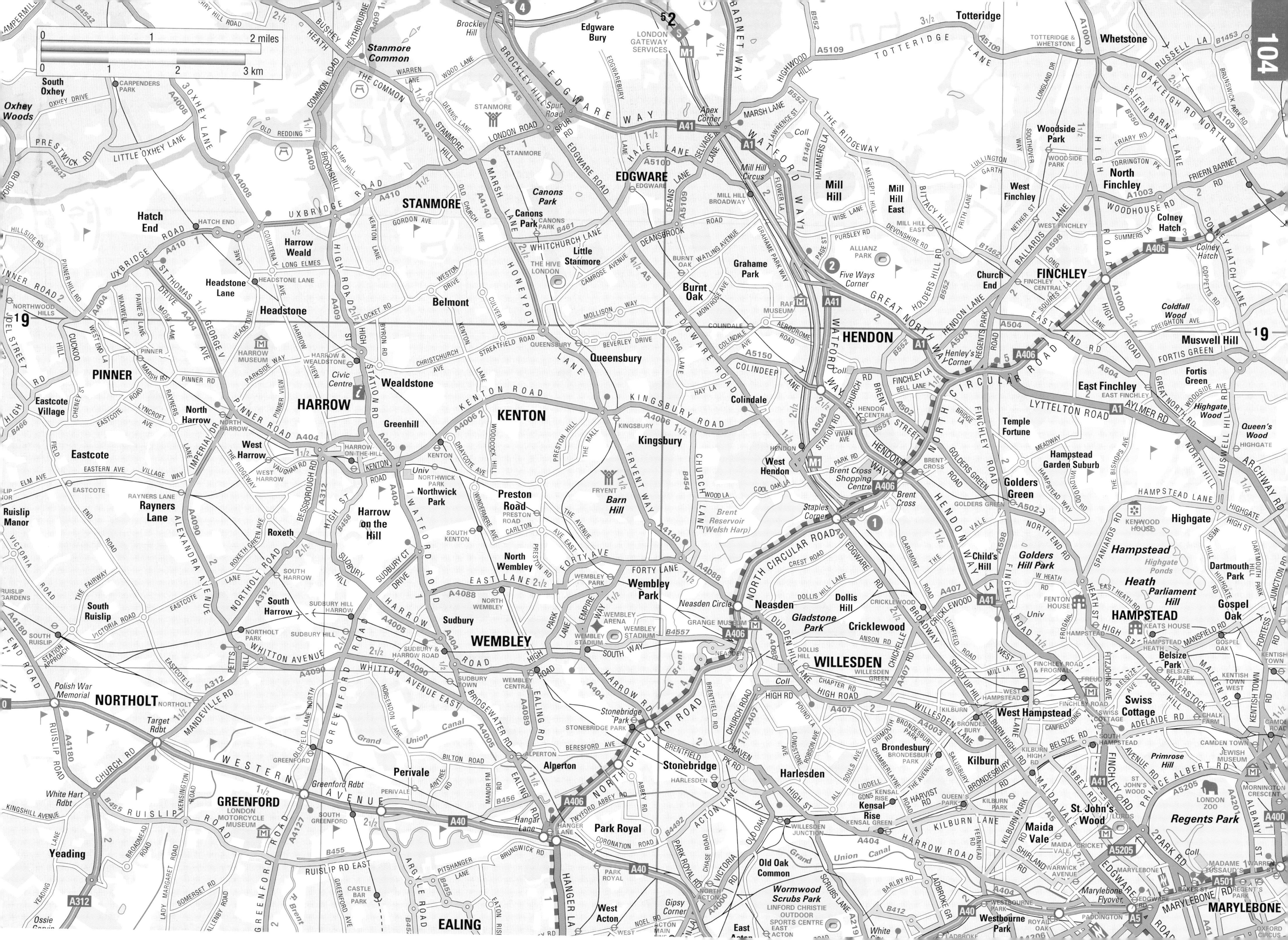
Totteridge
Whetstone
Edgware Bury
London Gateway Services
Stanmore Common
South Oxhey
Oxhey Woods
Woodside Park
North Finchley
West Finchley
Colney Hatch
Mill Hill
Mill Hill East
Hatch End
Harrow Weald
STANMORE
Canons Park
EDGWARE
Little Stanmore
Grahame Park
Burnt Oak
Five Ways Corner
Church End
FINCHLEY
Coldfall Wood
Headstone Lane
Headstone
Belmont
HENDON
Muswell Hill
Fortis Green
PINNER
Queensbury
Civic Centre
Wealdstone
HARROW
KENTON
Colindale
East Finchley
Highgate Wood
Queen's Wood
Eastcote Village
North Harrow
Greenhill
Kingsbury
Temple Fortune
West Harrow
Eastcote
West Hendon
Brent Cross Shopping Centre
Hampstead Garden Suburb
Northwick Park
Preston Road
Barn Hill
Brent Cross
Golders Green
Highgate
Ruislip Manor
Rayners Lane
Harrow on the Hill
Roxeth
Brent Reservoir (Welsh Harp)
Staples Corner
Hampstead
Child's Hill
Golders Hill Park
Dartmouth Park
North Wembley
Wembley Park
Heath
Parliament Hill
South Ruislip
South Harrow
Neasden
Dollis Hill
Gladstone Park
Cricklewood
Sudbury
HAMPSTEAD
Gospel Oak
WEMBLEY
WILLESDEN
Belsize Park
Polish War Memorial
NORTHOLT
West Hampstead
Swiss Cottage
Target Rdbt
Stonebridge Park
Brondesbury
Kilburn
Primrose Hill
Perivale
Alperton
Stonebridge
Harlesden
White Hart Rdbt
GREENFORD
Kensal Rise
St. John's Wood
Regents Park
Yeading
Park Royal
Maida Vale
Old Oak Common
Wormwood Scrubs Park
EALING
West Acton
Gipsy Corner
Westbourne Park
MARYLEBONE
Marylebone Flyover
2 miles
3 km

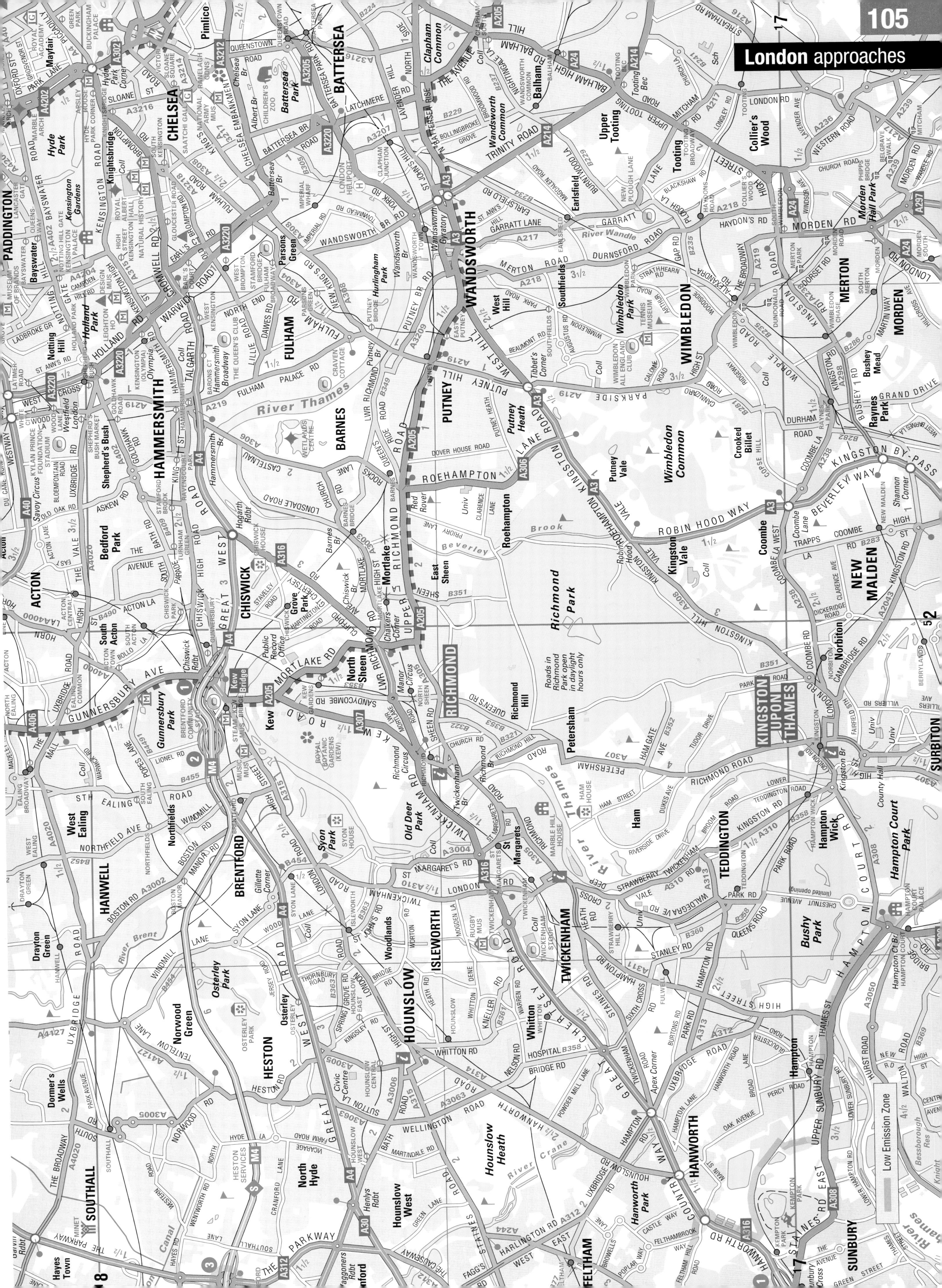
PADDINGTON
Bayswater
Kensington Gardens
Hyde Park
Knightsbridge
Mayfair
Pimlico
CHELSEA
BATTERSEA
Battersea Park
Clapham Common
Balham
Wandsworth Common
Upper Tooting
Tooting
Collier's Wood
Earlsfield
WANDSWORTH
Parsons Green
Holland Park
Notting Hill
FULHAM
HAMMERSMITH
Olympia
River Thames
BARNES
PUTNEY
Putney Heath
West Hill
Southfields
Wimbledon Park
WIMBLEDON
MERTON
Morden Hall Park
MORDEN
Wimbledon Common
Crooked Billet
Raynes Park
Putney Vale
Roehampton
East Sheen
Mortlake
Richmond Park
Kingston Vale
Coombe
NEW MALDEN
Norbiton
KINGSTON UPON THAMES
SURBITON
Petersham
Richmond Hill
RICHMOND
North Sheen
Kew
Royal Botanic Gardens (Kew)
CHISWICK
Grove Park
Bedford Park
Shepherd's Bush
ACTON
South Acton
Gunnersbury Park
BRENTFORD
Old Deer Park
Syon Park
St Margarets
Ham
TEDDINGTON
Hampton Wick
Hampton Court Park
Bushy Park
TWICKENHAM
ISLEWORTH
Woodlands
HOUNSLOW
Osterley Park
Northfields
West Ealing
HANWELL
Drayton Green
Norwood Green
HESTON
Whitton
Hounslow Heath
HANWORTH
Hanworth Park
Hampton
SUNBURY
FELTHAM
Hounslow West
North Hyde
SOUTHALL
Dormer's Wells
Hayes Town
Low Emission Zone

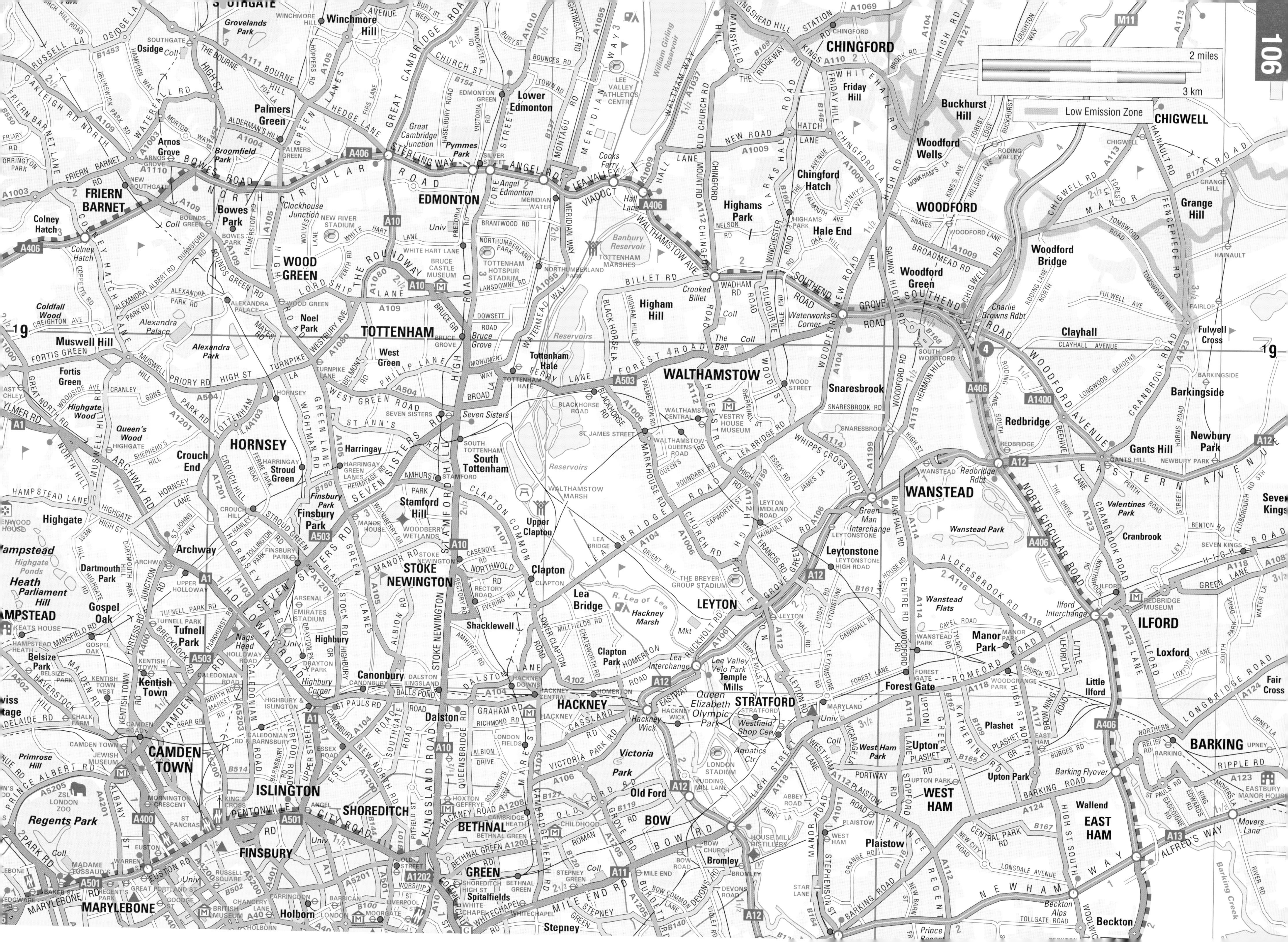
2 miles
3 km
Low Emission Zone
CHINGFORD
Friday Hill
Buckhurst Hill
CHIGWELL
Grange Hill
Woodford Wells
WOODFORD
Chingford Hatch
Highams Park
Hale End
Woodford Bridge
Woodford Green
Charlie Browns Rdbt
Clayhall
Fullwell Cross
Barkingside
Newbury Park
Gants Hill
Redbridge
Snaresbrook
WALTHAMSTOW
Higham Hill
Crooked Billet
Waterworks Corner
Winchmore Hill
Osidge
Lower Edmonton
Palmers Green
Great Cambridge Junction
Pymmes Park
Arnos Grove
Broomfield Park
EDMONTON
Angel Edmonton
FRIERN BARNET
Colney Hatch
Bowes Park
Clockhouse Junction
WOOD GREEN
Noel Park
TOTTENHAM
Bruce Grove
Tottenham Hale
West Green
Muswell Hill
Fortis Green
Alexandra Palace
Alexandra Park
Coldfall Wood
Highgate Wood
Queen's Wood
HORNSEY
Crouch End
Stroud Green
Harringay
Seven Sisters
South Tottenham
Stamford Hill
Finsbury Park
Upper Clapton
Highgate
Archway
Dartmouth Park
Parliament Hill
Gospel Oak
Tufnell Park
Kentish Town
CAMDEN TOWN
Primrose Hill
Regents Park
MARYLEBONE
Belsize Park
STOKE NEWINGTON
Clapton
Lea Bridge
Shacklewell
Highbury
Canonbury
Dalston
ISLINGTON
SHOREDITCH
FINSBURY
Holborn
BETHNAL GREEN
Spitalfields
Stepney
HACKNEY
Clapton Park
Victoria Park
Old Ford
BOW
Bromley
Hackney Wick
Lea Interchange
Temple Mills
Queen Elizabeth Olympic Park
STRATFORD
LEYTON
Leytonstone
WANSTEAD
Green Man Interchange
Wanstead Park
Wanstead Flats
Valentines Park
Cranbrook
Manor Park
Forest Gate
Ilford Interchange
ILFORD
Loxford
Little Ilford
Upton Park
Plashet
West Ham Park
WEST HAM
Plaistow
Wallend
EAST HAM
Barking Flyover
BARKING
Beckton
Beckton Alps
Movers Lane
Fair Cross
Seven Kings
Hackney Marsh
Walthamstow Marsh
Reservoirs
Banbury Reservoir
William Girling Reservoir
North Circular Road

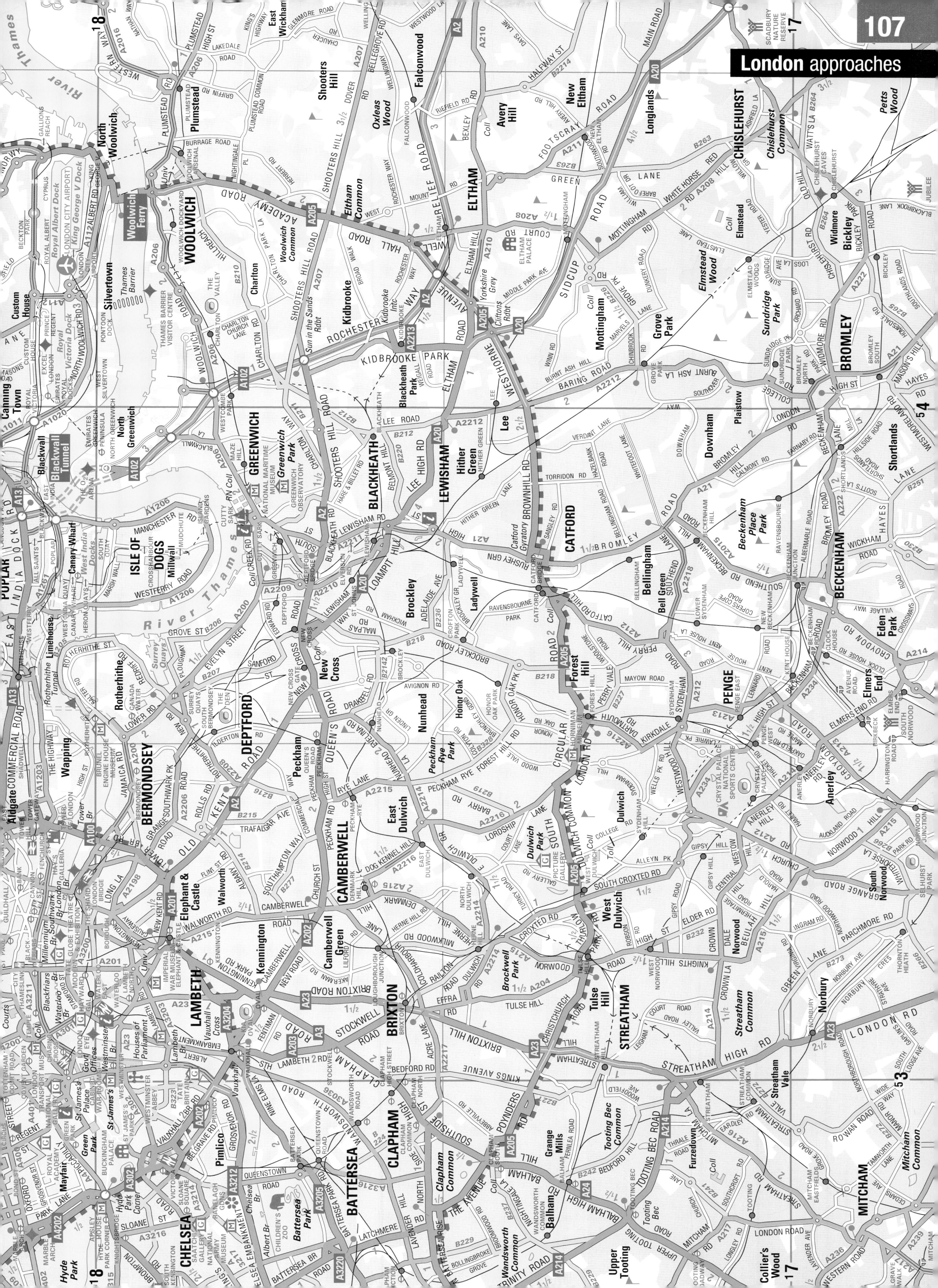
River Thames
Plumstead
North Woolwich
Woolwich
Woolwich Ferry
Shooters Hill
Falconwood
Oxleas Wood
Eltham Common
Eltham
Avery Hill
New Eltham
Longlands
Chislehurst
Chislehurst Common
Petts Wood
Custom House
Silvertown
Thames Barrier
Charlton
Kidbrooke
Woolwich Common
Sidcup
Mottingham
Grove Park
Elmstead Wood
Sundridge Park
Bromley
Widmore
Bickley
Canning Town
Blackwall
Blackwall Tunnel
North Greenwich
Greenwich
Greenwich Park
Blackheath
Blackheath Park
Lewisham
Hither Green
Lee
Plaistow
Downham
Shortlands
Poplar
Isle of Dogs
Millwall
Canary Wharf
Catford
Bellingham
Bell Green
Beckenham Place Park
Beckenham
Limehouse
Rotherhithe
Brockley
Ladywell
New Cross
Deptford
Forest Hill
Penge
Eden Park
Elmers End
Wapping
Bermondsey
Peckham
Nunhead
Honor Oak
Peckham Rye Park
Anerley
Aldgate
East Dulwich
Dulwich
Dulwich Park
Camberwell
Walworth
Elephant & Castle
South Norwood
West Dulwich
Kennington
Camberwell Green
Brockwell Park
Tulse Hill
Norwood
Norbury
Lambeth
Brixton
Streatham
Streatham Common
Streatham Vale
Clapham
Battersea
Pimlico
Chelsea
Mayfair
Green Park
Hyde Park
Clapham Common
Balham
Grange Mills
Tooting Bec Common
Tooting Bec
Furzedown
Mitcham
Mitcham Common
Wandsworth Common
Upper Tooting
Collier's Wood
Battersea Park

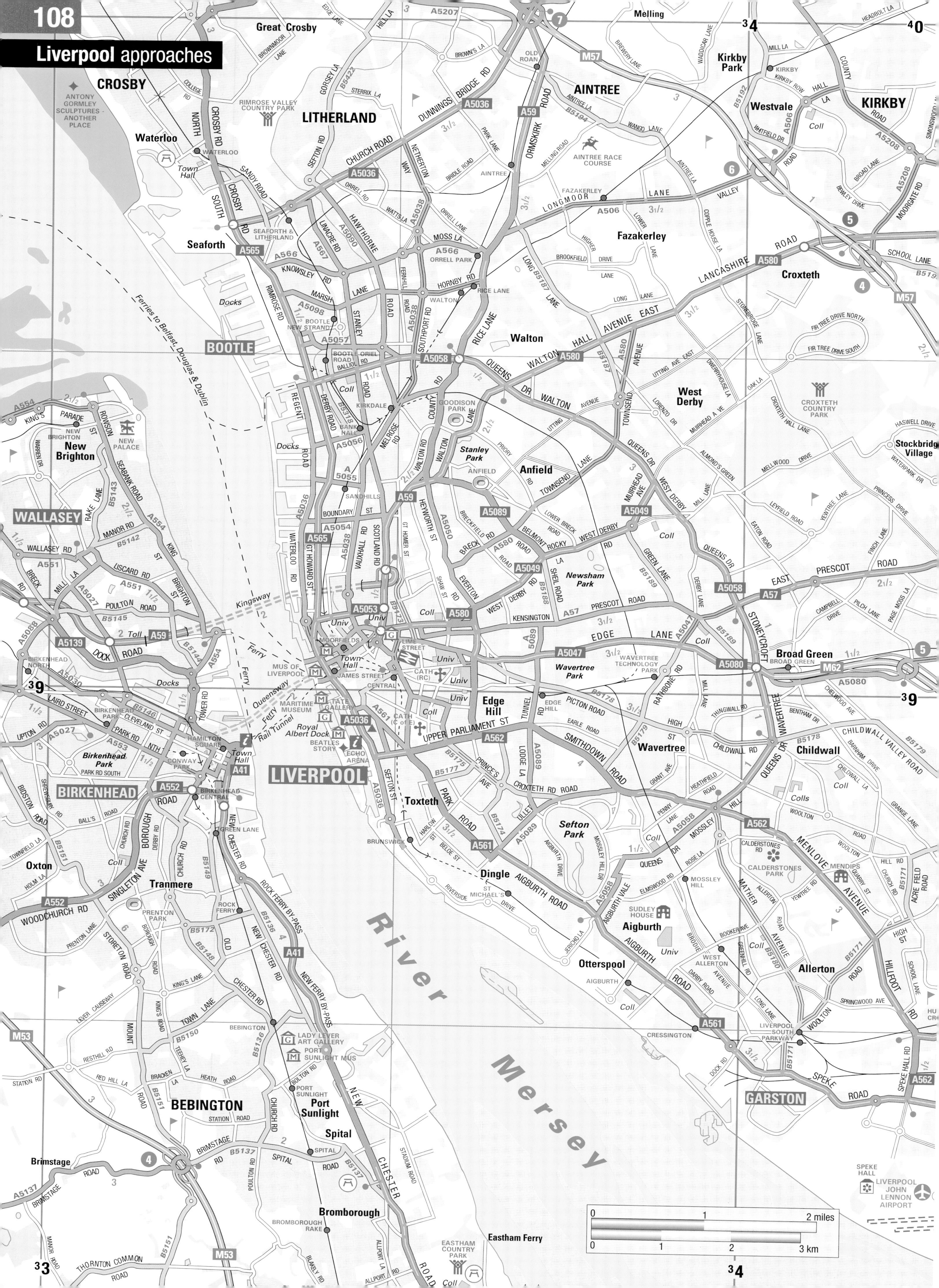
CROSBY
ANTONY GORMLEY SCULPTURES - ANOTHER PLACE
Waterloo
Great Crosby
Melling
LITHERLAND
RIMROSE VALLEY COUNTRY PARK
AINTREE
AINTREE RACE COURSE
Kirkby Park
Westvale
KIRKBY
Seaforth
Fazakerley
Croxteth
Docks
BOOTLE
Ferries to Belfast, Douglas & Dublin
Walton
West Derby
CROXTETH COUNTRY PARK
New Brighton
NEW PALACE
Stanley Park
Anfield
Stockbridge Village
WALLASEY
Newsham Park
Kingsway
Broad Green
Wavertree Park
WAVERTREE TECHNOLOGY PARK
MUS OF LIVERPOOL
MARITIME MUSEUM
TATE GALLERY
Royal Albert Dock
BEATLES STORY
ECHO ARENA
Queensway
Rail Tunnel
Birkenhead Park
HAMILTON SQUARE
BIRKENHEAD
LIVERPOOL
Edge Hill
Wavertree
Childwall
Toxteth
Sefton Park
Oxton
Tranmere
CALDERSTONES PARK
MENDIPS
Dingle
SUDLEY HOUSE
Aigburth
Allerton
Otterspool
River Mersey
LADY LEVER ART GALLERY
PORT SUNLIGHT MUS
Port Sunlight
GARSTON
BEBINGTON
Spital
Brimstage
Bromborough
Eastham Ferry
EASTHAM COUNTRY PARK
SPEKE HALL
LIVERPOOL JOHN LENNON AIRPORT
0 1 2 miles
0 1 2 3 km
M57
M62
M53
A5036
A59
A580
A565
A561
A562
A41
33
34
39
40

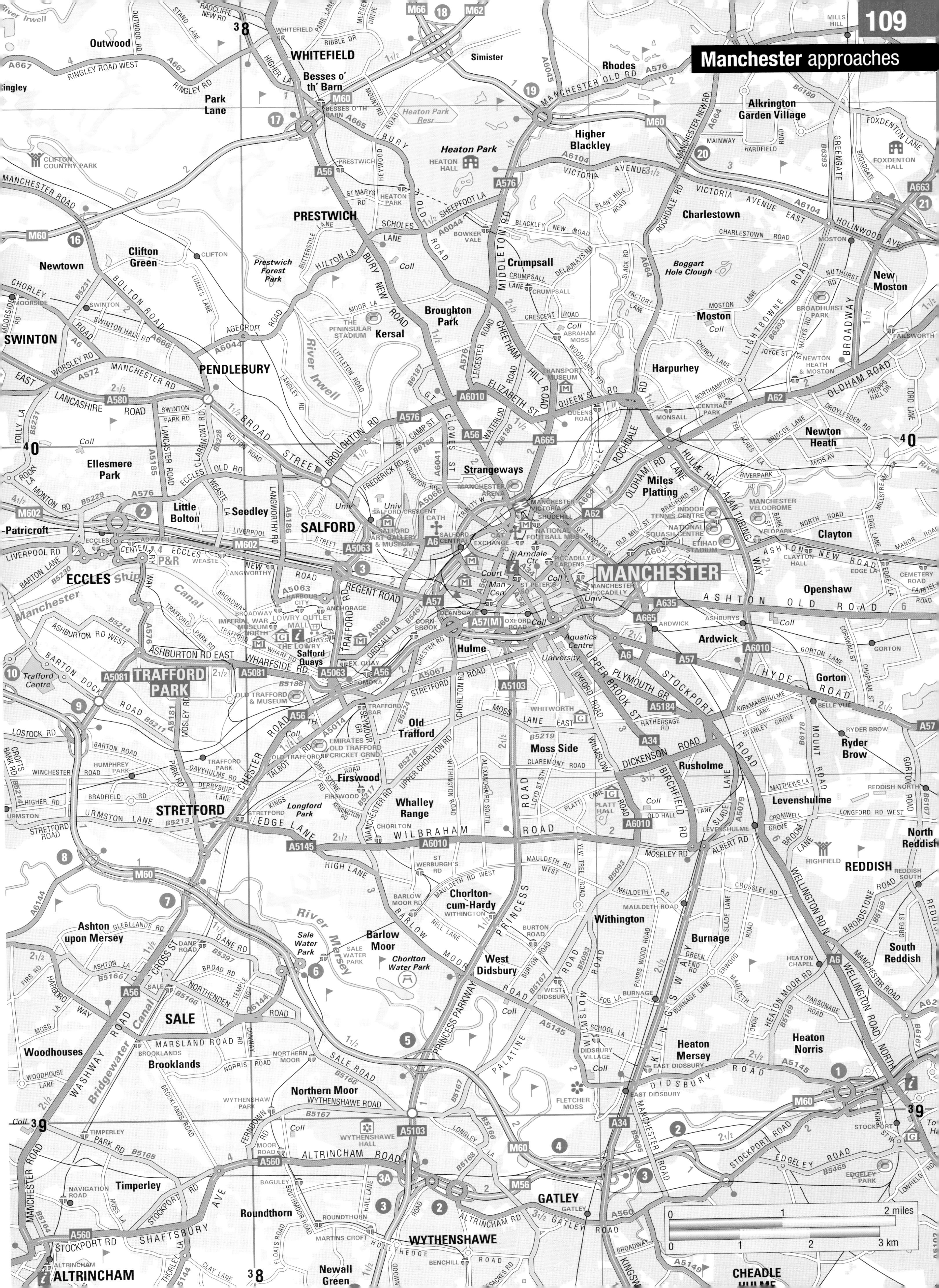
Outwood
WHITEFIELD
Besses o' th' Barn
Simister
Rhodes
Park Lane
Alkrington Garden Village
Higher Blackley
Heaton Park
Heaton Park Resr
CLIFTON COUNTRY PARK
FOXDENTON HALL
PRESTWICH
Charlestown
Clifton Green
Newtown
Prestwich Forest Park
Crumpsall
Boggart Hole Clough
New Moston
Moston
SWINTON
Kersal
Broughton Park
PENDLEBURY
Harpurhey
Ellesmere Park
Strangeways
Newton Heath
Miles Platting
Little Bolton
Seedley
SALFORD
Clayton
Patricroft
ECCLES
MANCHESTER
Openshaw
Ardwick
TRAFFORD PARK
Salford Quays
Hulme
Gorton
Trafford Centre
Old Trafford
Moss Side
Ryder Brow
Rusholme
Firswood
Whalley Range
STRETFORD
Longford Park
Levenshulme
North Reddish
REDDISH
Chorlton-cum-Hardy
Withington
Ashton upon Mersey
Sale Water Park
Barlow Moor
Chorlton Water Park
Burnage
South Reddish
West Didsbury
SALE
Woodhouses
Brooklands
Heaton Mersey
Heaton Norris
Northern Moor
FLETCHER MOSS
WYTHENSHAWE HALL
Timperley
GATLEY
Roundthorn
WYTHENSHAWE
ALTRINCHAM
Newall Green
CHEADLE
River Irwell
River Mersey
Manchester Ship Canal
Bridgewater Canal
M60
M62
M66
M602
M56
A56
A6
A57(M)
0 1 2 miles
0 1 2 3 km

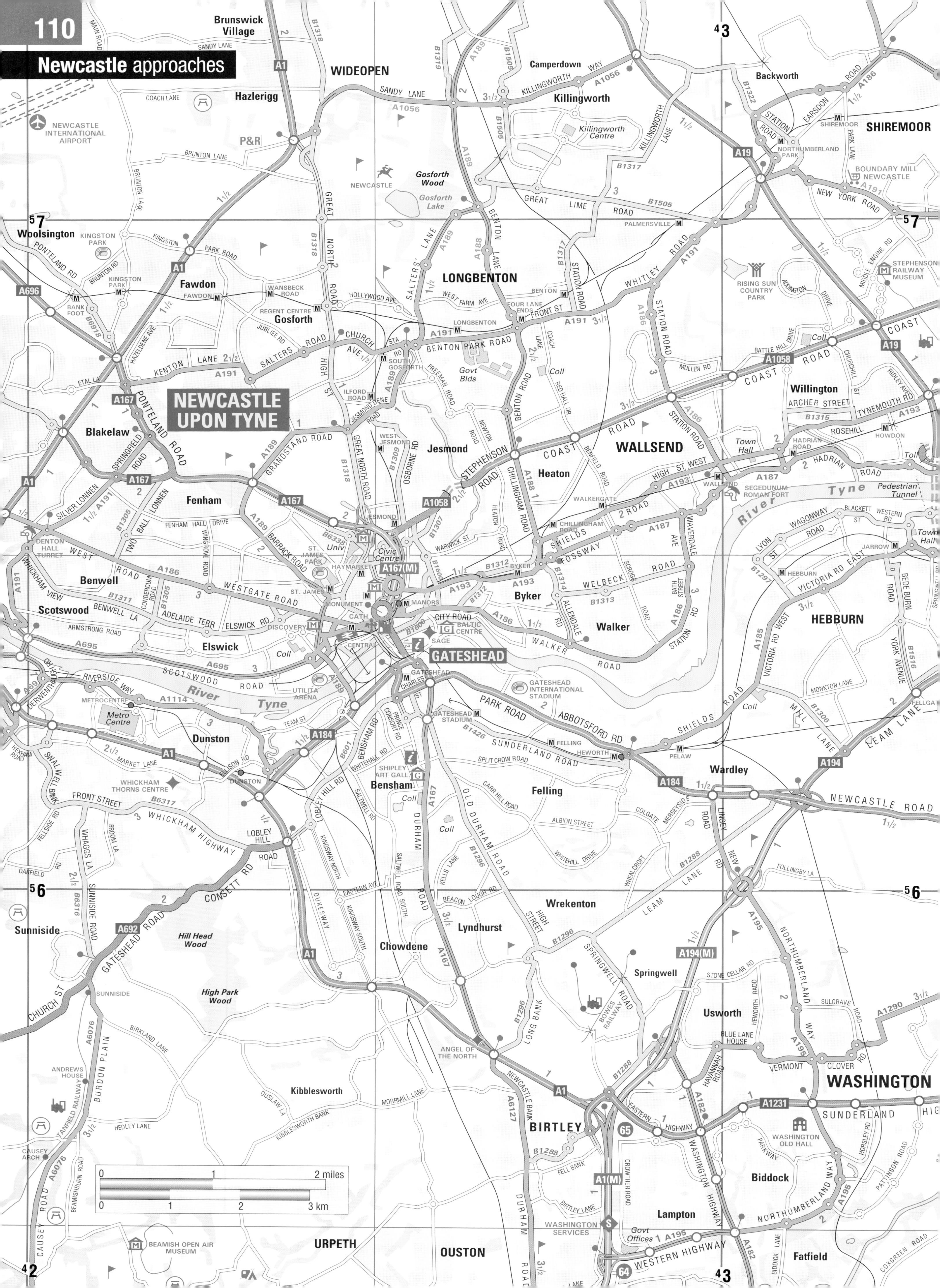
Brunswick Village
WIDEOPEN
Hazlerigg
NEWCASTLE INTERNATIONAL AIRPORT
Camperdown
Killingworth
Killingworth Centre
Backworth
SHIREMOOR
BOUNDARY MILL NEWCASTLE
Gosforth Wood
Gosforth Lake
NEWCASTLE
Woolsington
KINGSTON PARK
Fawdon
LONGBENTON
Gosforth
PALMERSVILLE
RISING SUN COUNTRY PARK
STEPHENSON RAILWAY MUSEUM
Govt Blds
Willington
NEWCASTLE UPON TYNE
Blakelaw
Jesmond
WALLSEND
Town Hall
HOWDON
Heaton
SEGEDUNUM ROMAN FORT
Pedestrian Tunnel
Fenham
River Tyne
Univ
Civic Centre
Benwell
Byker
HEBBURN
Scotswood
Walker
Elswick
DISCOVERY
BALTIC CENTRE
SAGE
GATESHEAD
GATESHEAD INTERNATIONAL STADIUM
METROCENTRE
Metro Centre
UTILITA ARENA
Dunston
GATESHEAD STADIUM
WHICKHAM THORNS CENTRE
SHIPLEY ART GALL.
Bensham
Wardley
Felling
LOBLEY HILL
Wrekenton
Sunniside
Hill Head Wood
Lyndhurst
Chowdene
Springwell
High Park Wood
Usworth
ANGEL OF THE NORTH
WASHINGTON
ANDREWS HOUSE
Kibblesworth
BIRTLEY
WASHINGTON OLD HALL
CAUSEY ARCH
Biddick
Lampton
WASHINGTON SERVICES
Govt Offices
BEAMISH OPEN AIR MUSEUM
URPETH
OUSTON
Fatfield
0 1 2 miles
0 1 2 3 km

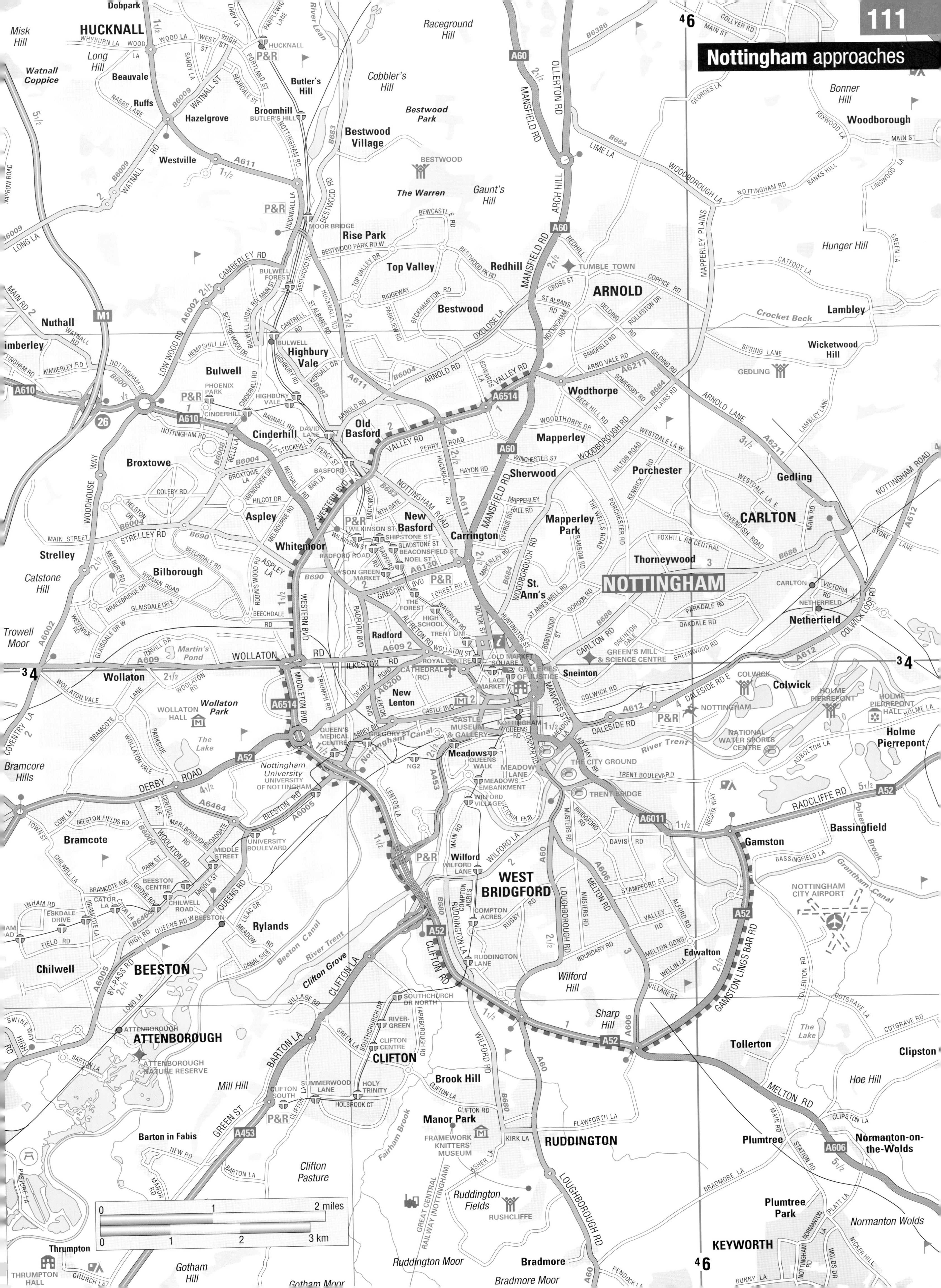
HUCKNALL
Dobpark
Misk Hill
Watnall Coppice
Long Hill
Beauvale
Ruffs
Hazelgrove
Westville
Broomhill
Butler's Hill
Raceground Hill
Cobbler's Hill
Bestwood Park
Bestwood Village
BESTWOOD
The Warren
Gaunt's Hill
Rise Park
Top Valley
Redhill
Bestwood
TUMBLE TOWN
ARNOLD
Bonner Hill
Woodborough
Hunger Hill
Crocket Beck
Lambley
Wicketwood Hill
GEDLING
Nuthall
Kimberley
Bulwell
BULWELL
Highbury Vale
BULWELL FOREST
PHOENIX PARK
CINDERHILL
Cinderhill
Old Basford
Wodthorpe
Mapperley
Porchester
Gedling
CARLTON
Broxtowe
Aspley
New Basford
Carrington
Sherwood
Mapperley Park
Whitemoor
Strelley
Bilborough
Catstone Hill
Trowell Moor
Thorneywood
NOTTINGHAM
St. Ann's
Netherfield
Radford
THE FOREST
HIGH SCHOOL
TRENT UNI
Martin's Pond
WOLLATON
Wollaton
OLD MARKET SQUARE
GALLERIES OF JUSTICE
LACE MARKET
CATHEDRAL (RC)
Sneinton
GREEN'S MILL & SCIENCE CENTRE
COLWICK
Colwick
HOLME PIERREPONT
HOLME PIERREPONT HALL
New Lenton
WOLLATON HALL
Wollaton Park
The Lake
QUEEN'S MEDICAL CENTRE
CASTLE MUSEUM & GALLERY
NOTTINGHAM
NATIONAL WATER SPORTS CENTRE
Holme Pierrepont
River Trent
Bramcore Hills
Nottingham University
UNIVERSITY OF NOTTINGHAM
Meadows
THE CITY GROUND
MEADOW LANE
TRENT BRIDGE
Bramcote
UNIVERSITY BOULEVARD
Wilford
Gamston
Bassingfield
WEST BRIDGFORD
COMPTON ACRES
NOTTINGHAM CITY AIRPORT
Grantham Canal
Chilwell
BEESTON
Rylands
Beeton Canal
Clifton Grove
Edwalton
Wilford Hill
Sharp Hill
ATTENBOROUGH
ATTENBOROUGH NATURE RESERVE
CLIFTON
Tollerton
The Lake
Clipston
Brook Hill
Mill Hill
Hoe Hill
Barton in Fabis
Manor Park
FRAMEWORK KNITTERS' MUSEUM
RUDDINGTON
Plumtree
Normanton-on-the-Wolds
Clifton Pasture
Ruddington Fields
RUSHCLIFFE
Plumtree Park
Normanton Wolds
KEYWORTH
Thrumpton
THRUMPTON HALL
Gotham Hill
Ruddington Moor
Bradmore
Gotham Moor
Bradmore Moor
Fairham Brook
M1
A60
A610
A611
A6514
A6211
A612
A52
A6011
A606
A453
A6005
A6464
A6002
A609
A6200
A6130
A6520
B6386
B684
B686
B6004
B690
B682
B683
B600
B6009
B6008
B6006
B680
0 1 2 miles
0 1 2 3 km

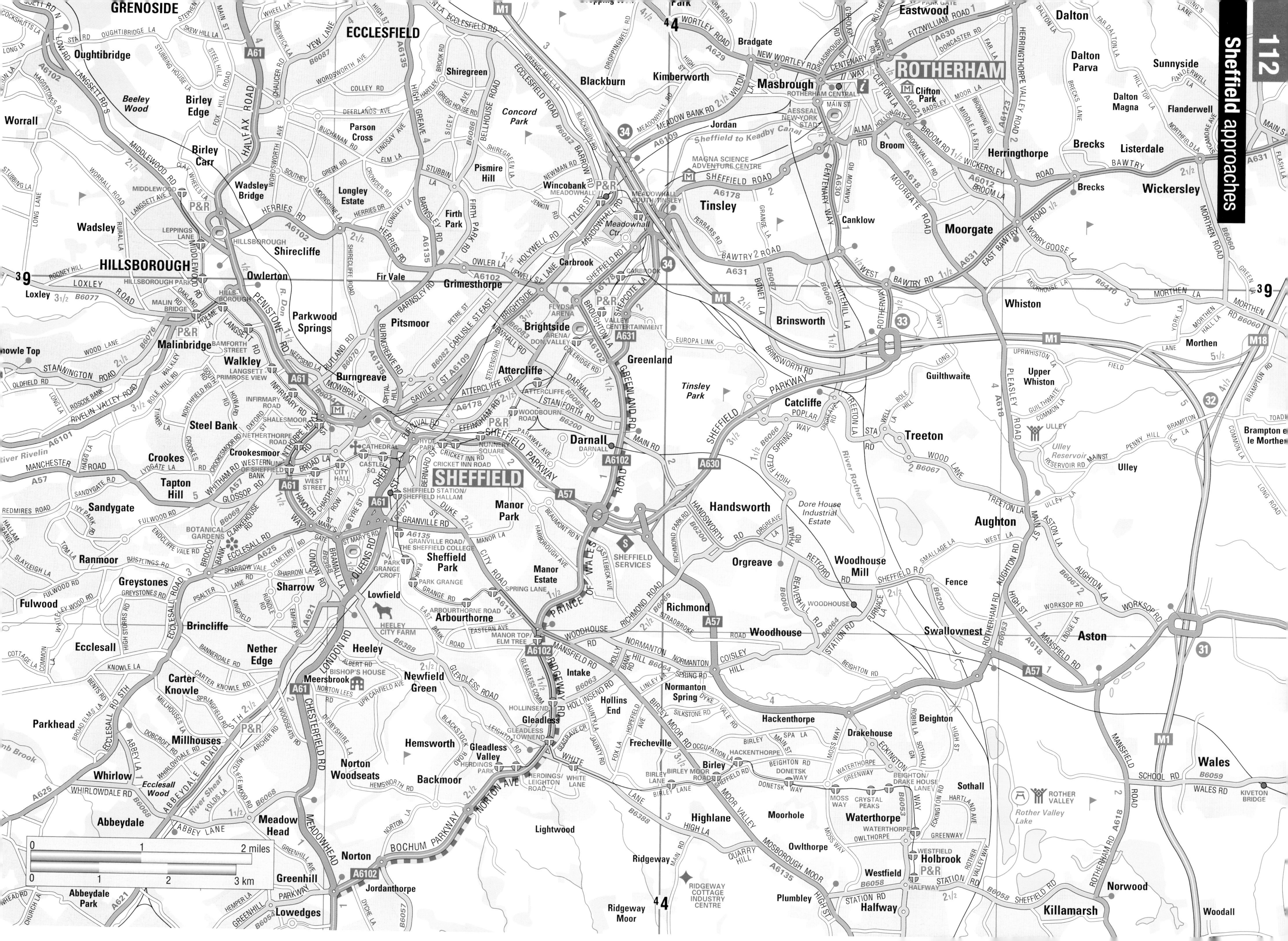
GRENOSIDE
ECCLESFIELD
HILLSBOROUGH
ROTHERHAM
SHEFFIELD
Oughtibridge
Worrall
Beeley Wood
Birley Edge
Birley Carr
Wadsley
Wadsley Bridge
Loxley
Owlerton
Shirecliffe
Parson Cross
Longley Estate
Shiregreen
Concord Park
Blackburn
Kimberworth
Bradgate
Masbrough
Eastwood
Clifton Park
Dalton
Dalton Parva
Dalton Magna
Sunnyside
Flanderwell
Brecks
Listerdale
Herringthorpe
Broom
Wickersley
Moorgate
Canklow
Jordan
Tinsley
Wincobank
Pismire Hill
Firth Park
Fir Vale
Grimesthorpe
Carbrook
Brightside
Pitsmoor
Parkwood Springs
Malinbridge
Walkley
Burngreave
Attercliffe
Darnall
Greenland
Tinsley Park
Brinsworth
Whiston
Morthen
Catcliffe
Treeton
Guilthwaite
Upper Whiston
Ulley
Aughton
Brampton en le Morthen
Steel Bank
Crookes
Crookesmoor
Tapton Hill
Sandygate
Ranmoor
Greystones
Fulwood
Ecclesall
Brincliffe
Sharrow
Nether Edge
Carter Knowle
Parkhead
Millhouses
Whirlow
Ecclesall Wood
Abbeydale
Abbeydale Park
Meadow Head
Norton
Greenhill
Lowedges
Jordanthorpe
Norton Woodseats
Meersbrook
Heeley
Lowfield
Sheffield Park
Manor Park
Manor Estate
Arbourthorne
Newfield Green
Hemsworth
Backmoor
Gleadless Valley
Gleadless
Intake
Hollins End
Frecheville
Lightwood
Handsworth
Orgreave
Woodhouse Mill
Richmond
Woodhouse
Normanton Spring
Hackenthorpe
Birley
Highlane
Ridgeway
Ridgeway Moor
Moorhole
Owlthorpe
Plumbley
Waterthorpe
Westfield
Halfway
Holbrook
Drakehouse
Beighton
Sothall
Swallownest
Fence
Aston
Wales
Norwood
Killamarsh
Woodall
Sheffield Services
Meadowhall
0 1 2 miles
0 1 2 3 km

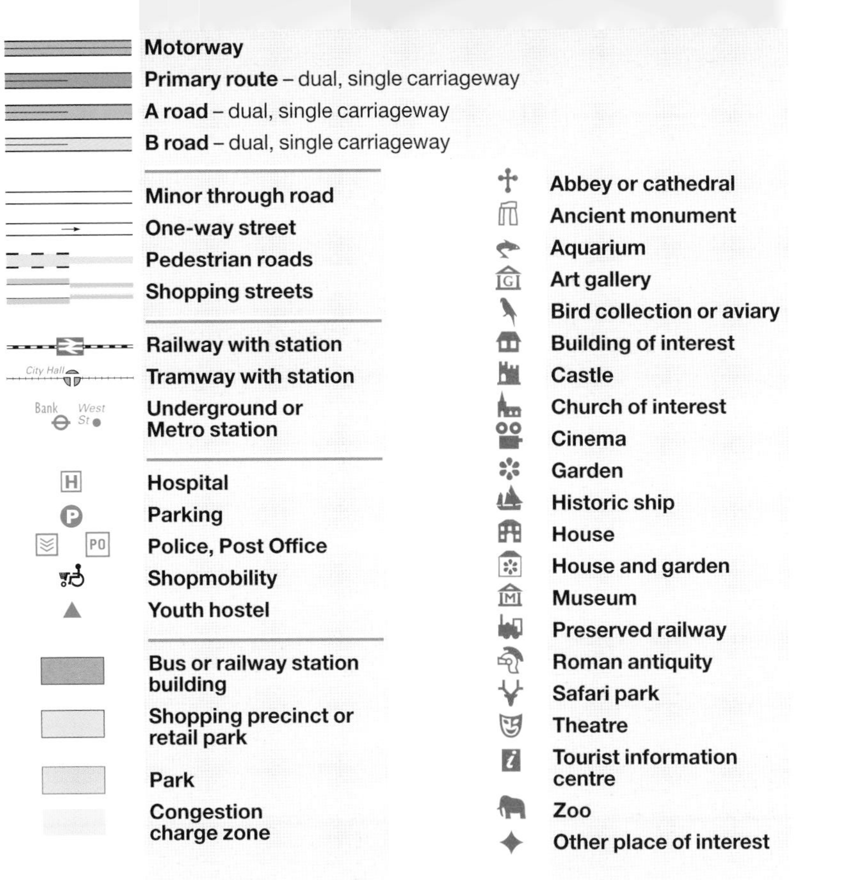

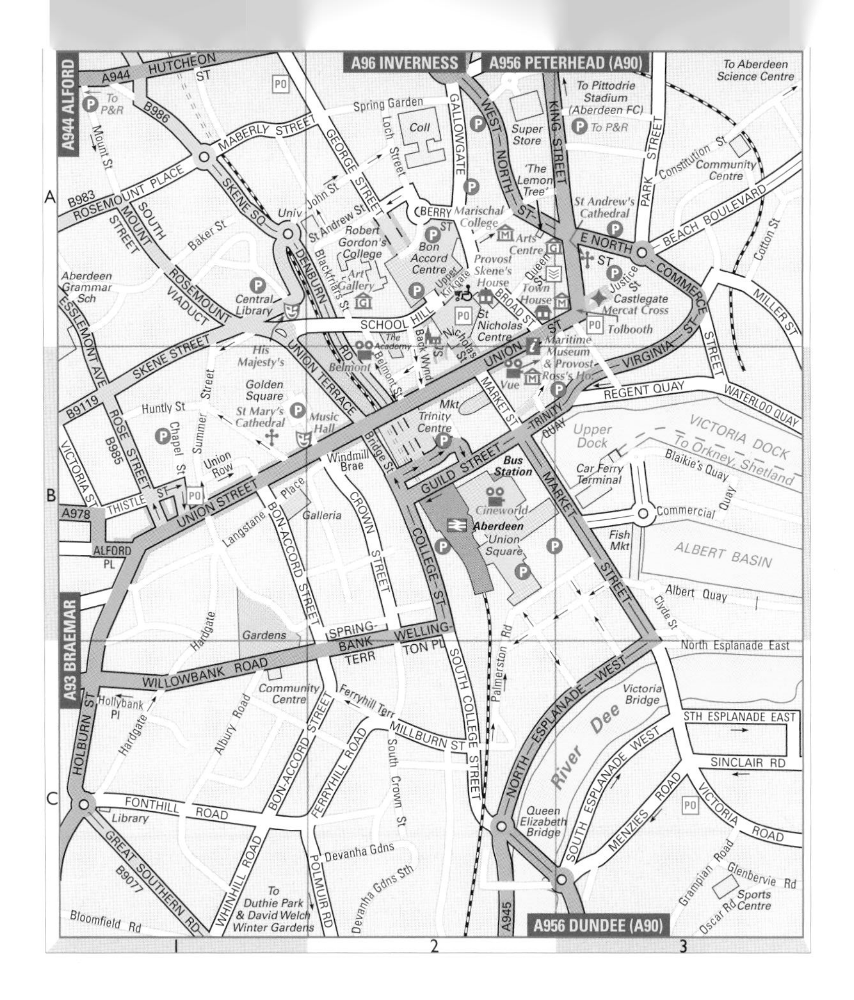

Blackpool

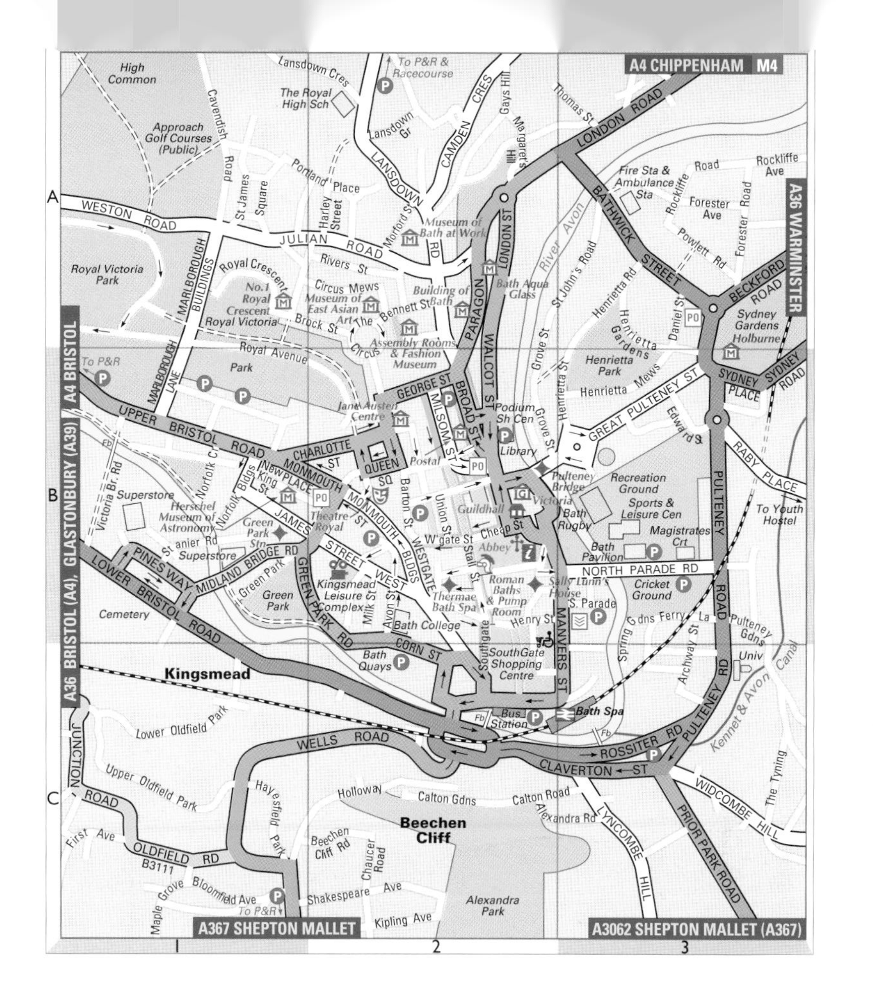

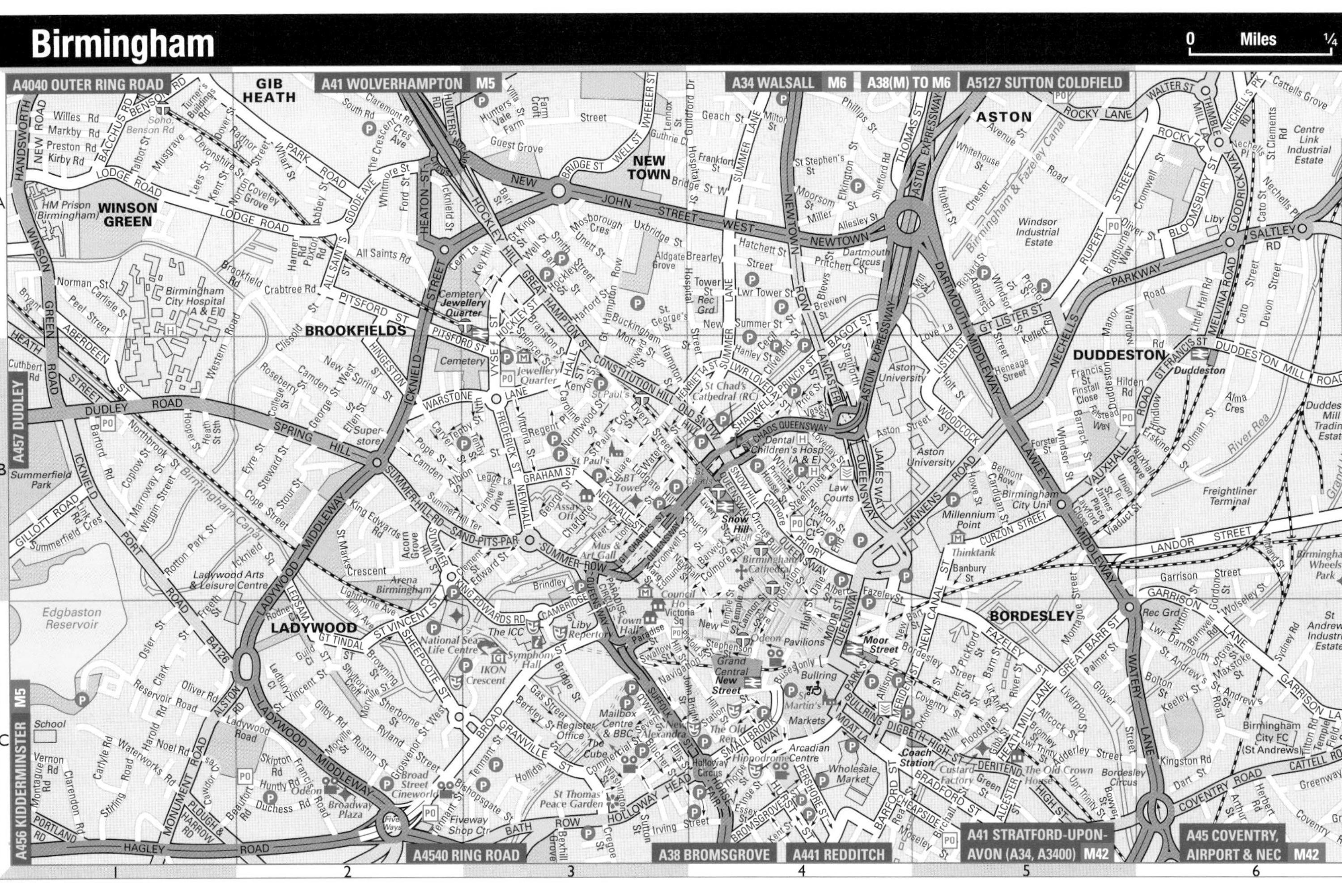

Legend:

- Motorway
- Primary route – dual, single carriageway
- A road – dual, single carriageway
- B road – dual, single carriageway
- Minor through road
- One-way street
- Pedestrian roads
- Shopping streets
- Railway with station
- Tramway with station
- Underground or Metro station
- Hospital
- Parking
- Police, Post Office
- Shopmobility
- Youth hostel
- Bus or railway station building
- Shopping precinct or retail park
- Park
- Congestion charge zone

- Abbey or cathedral
- Ancient monument
- Aquarium
- Art gallery
- Bird collection or aviary
- Building of interest
- Castle
- Church of interest
- Cinema
- Garden
- Historic ship
- House
- House and garden
- Museum
- Preserved railway
- Roman antiquity
- Safari park
- Theatre
- Tourist information centre
- Zoo
- Other place of interest

Birmingham

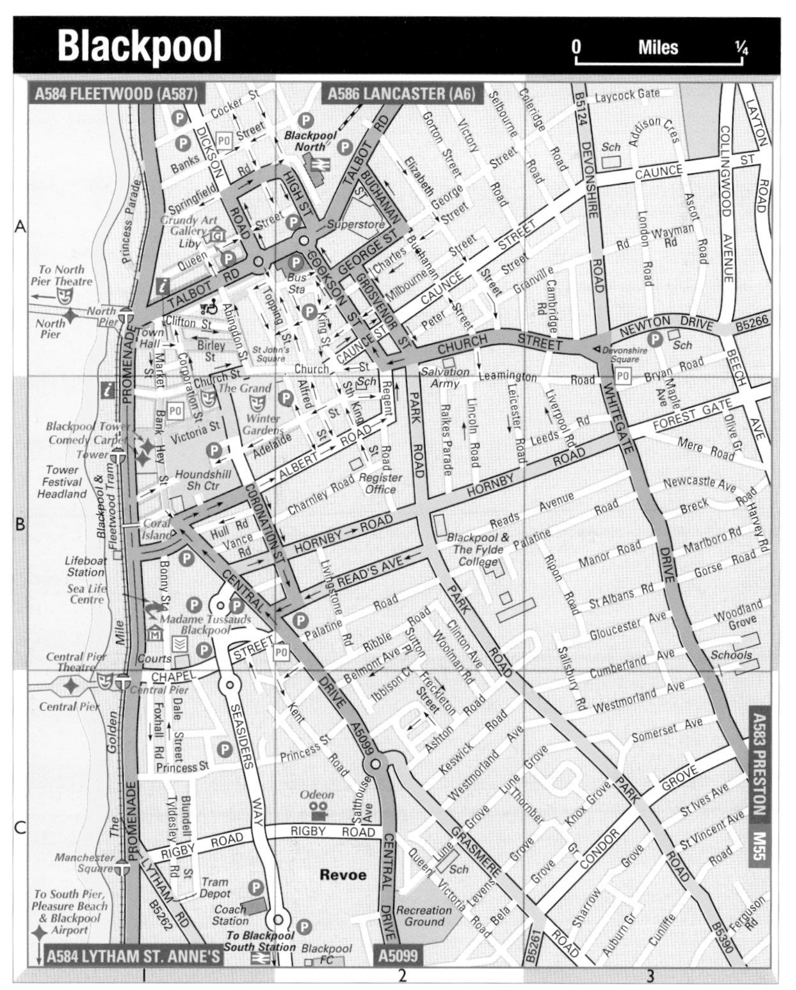

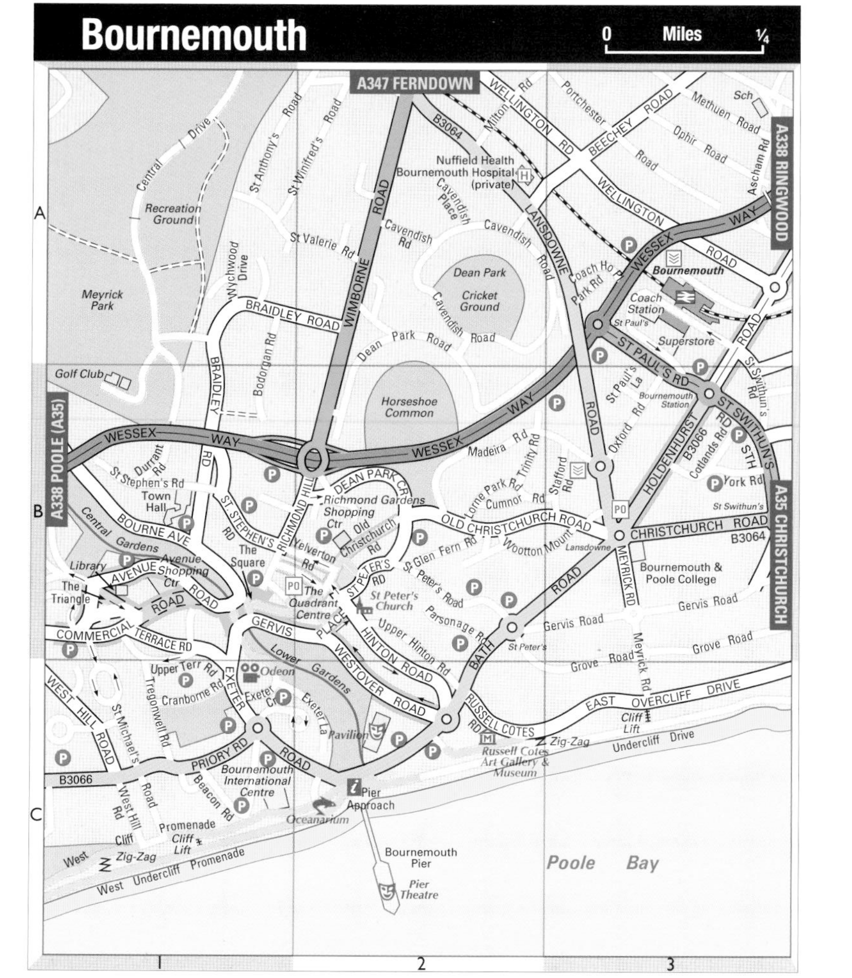
Bournemouth
0 Miles ¼
A347 FERNDOWN
A338 RINGWOOD
A35 CHRISTCHURCH
A338 POOLE (A35)
Poole Bay

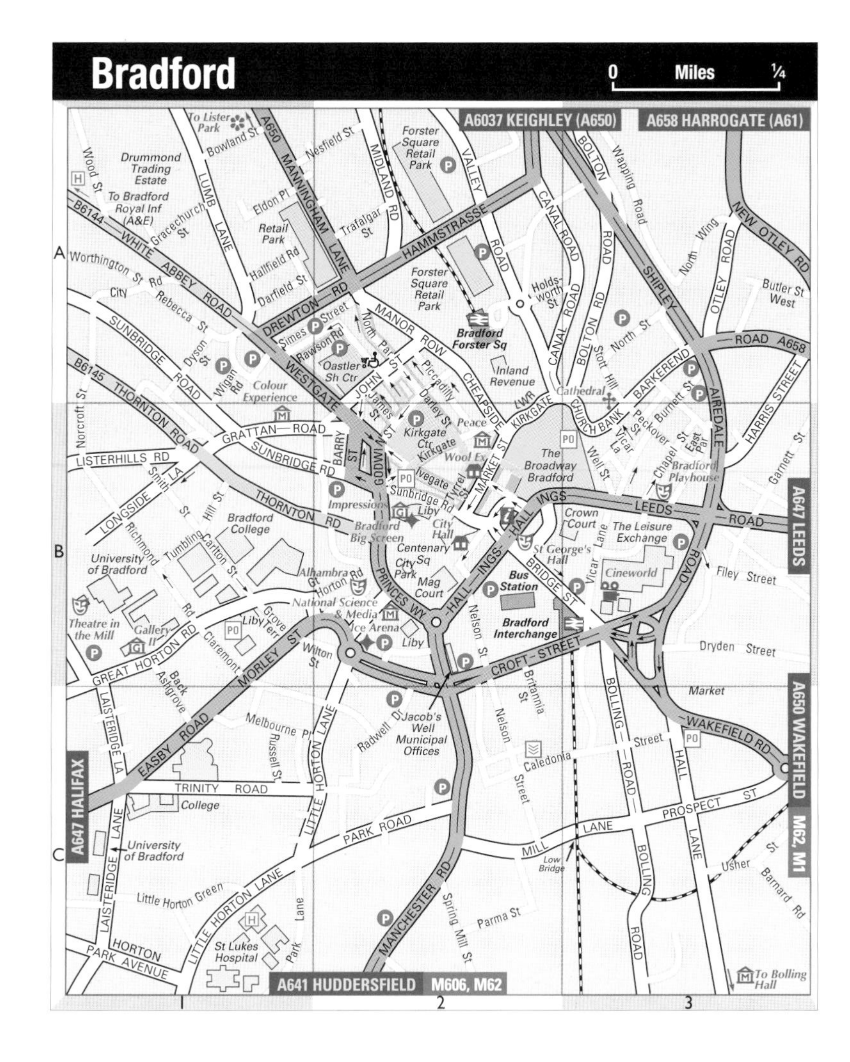
Bradford
0 Miles ¼
A6037 KEIGHLEY (A650)
A658 HARROGATE (A61)
A647 LEEDS
A650 WAKEFIELD M62, M1
A641 HUDDERSFIELD M606, M62
A647 HALIFAX

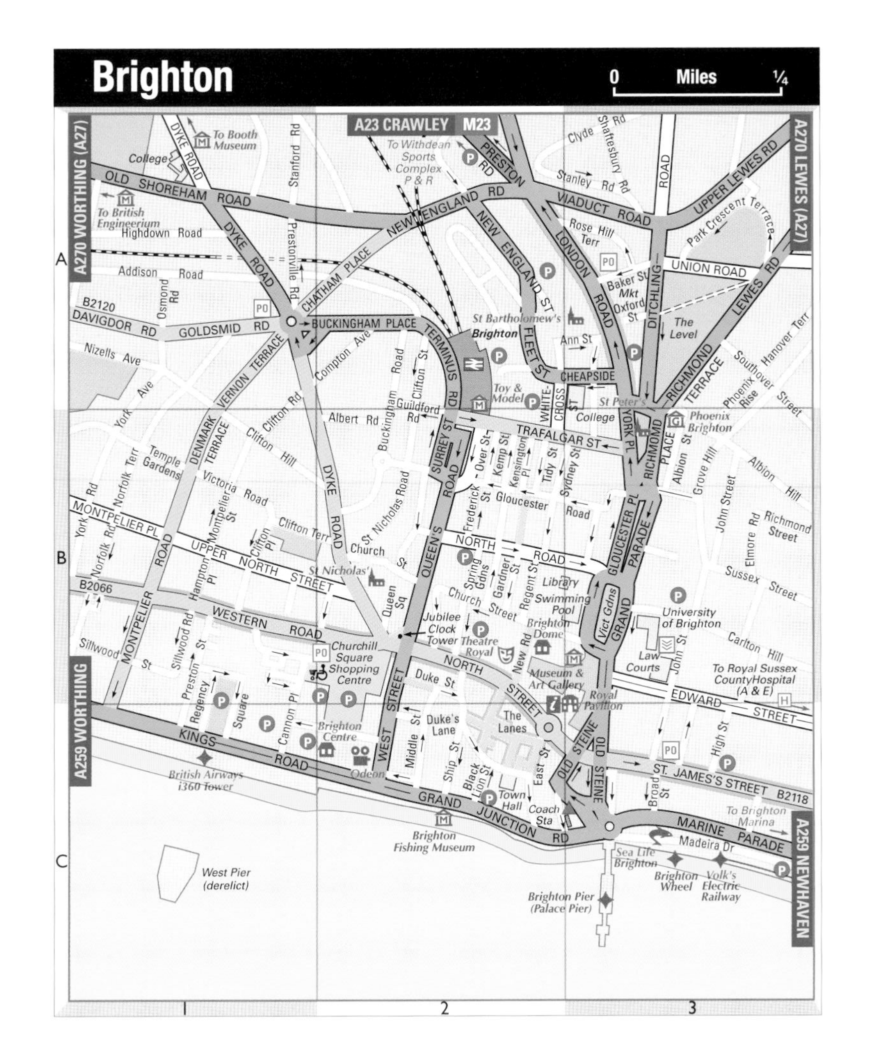
Brighton
0 Miles ¼
A23 CRAWLEY M23
A270 LEWES (A27)
A270 WORTHING (A27)
A259 WORTHING
A259 NEWHAVEN

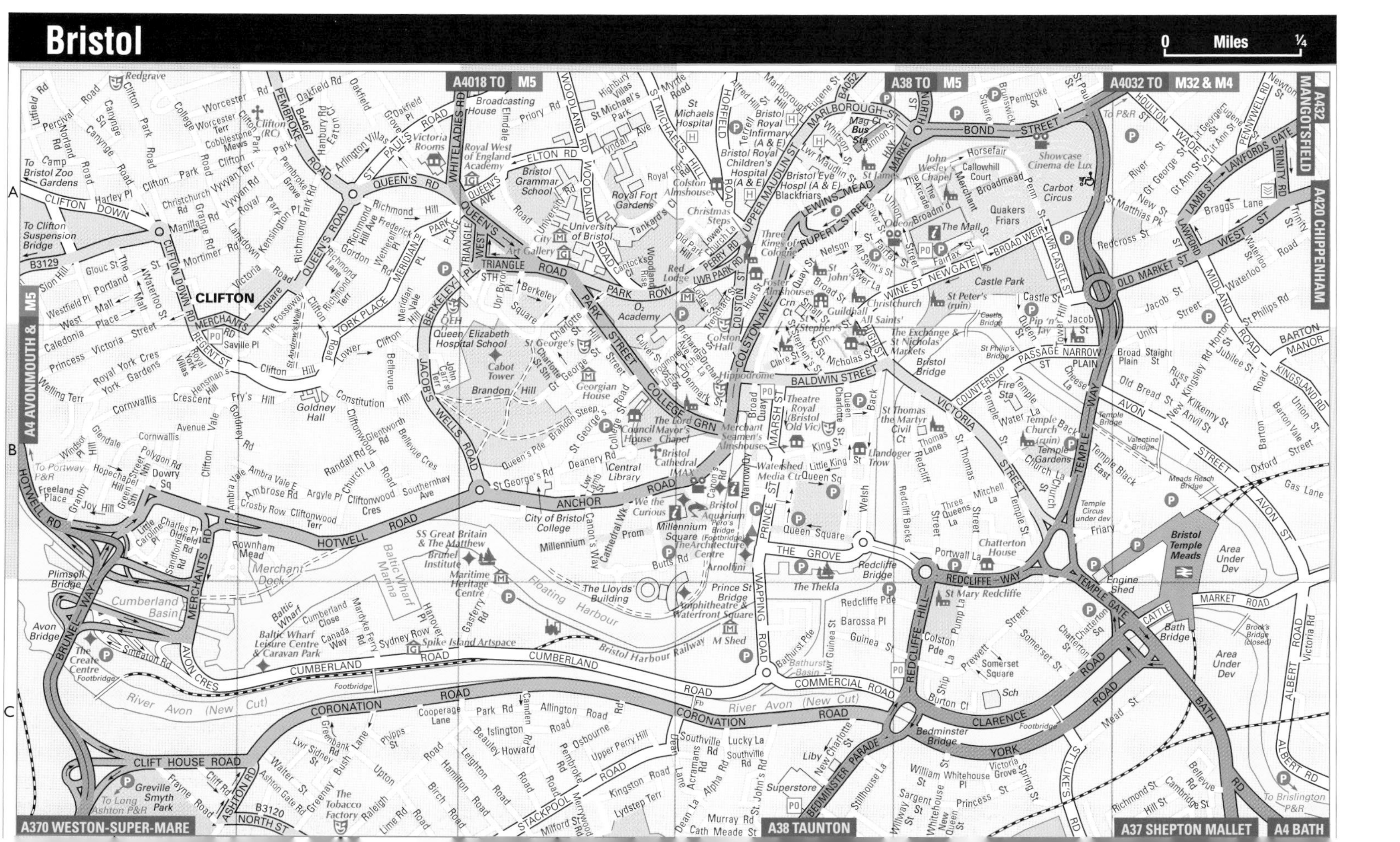
Bristol
0 Miles ¼
A4018 TO M5
A38 TO M5
A4032 TO M32 & M4
A432 MANGOTSFIELD
A420 CHIPPENHAM
A4 AVONMOUTH & M5
A370 WESTON-SUPER-MARE
A38 TAUNTON
A37 SHEPTON MALLET
A4 BATH
CLIFTON

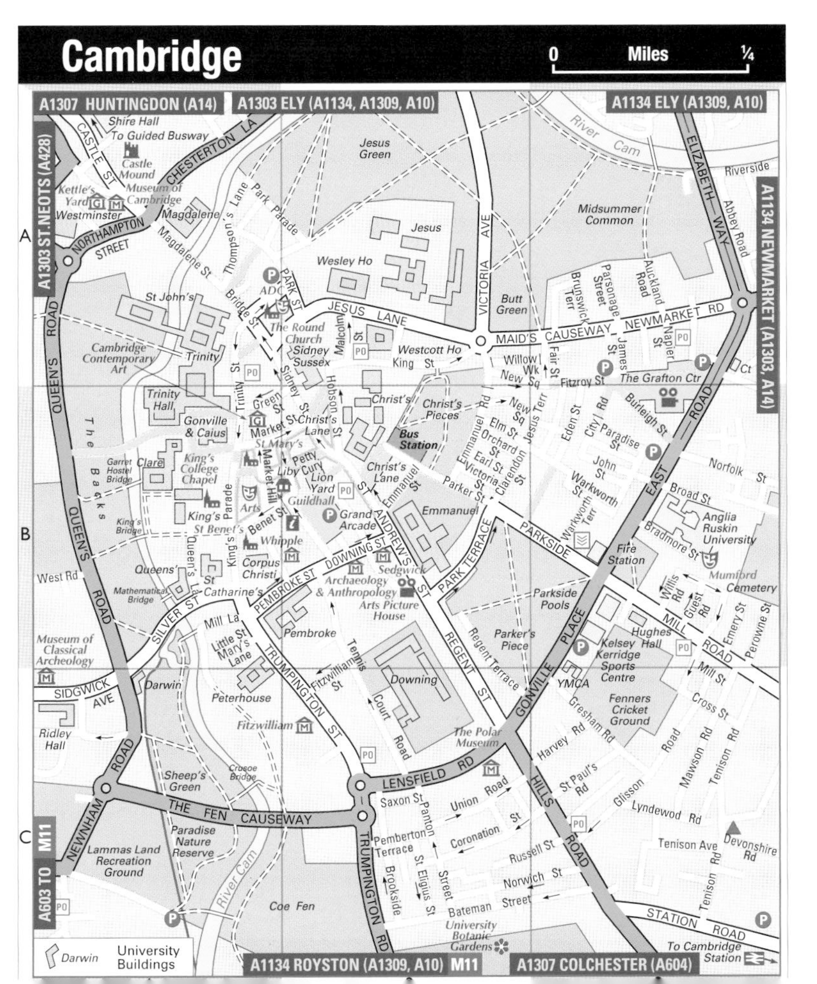
Cambridge
0 Miles ¼
A1307 HUNTINGDON (A14)
A1303 ELY (A1134, A1309, A10)
A1134 ELY (A1309, A10)
A1134 NEWMARKET (A1303, A14)
A1303 ST NEOTS (A428)
A603 TO M11
A1134 ROYSTON (A1309, A10) M11
A1307 COLCHESTER (A604)

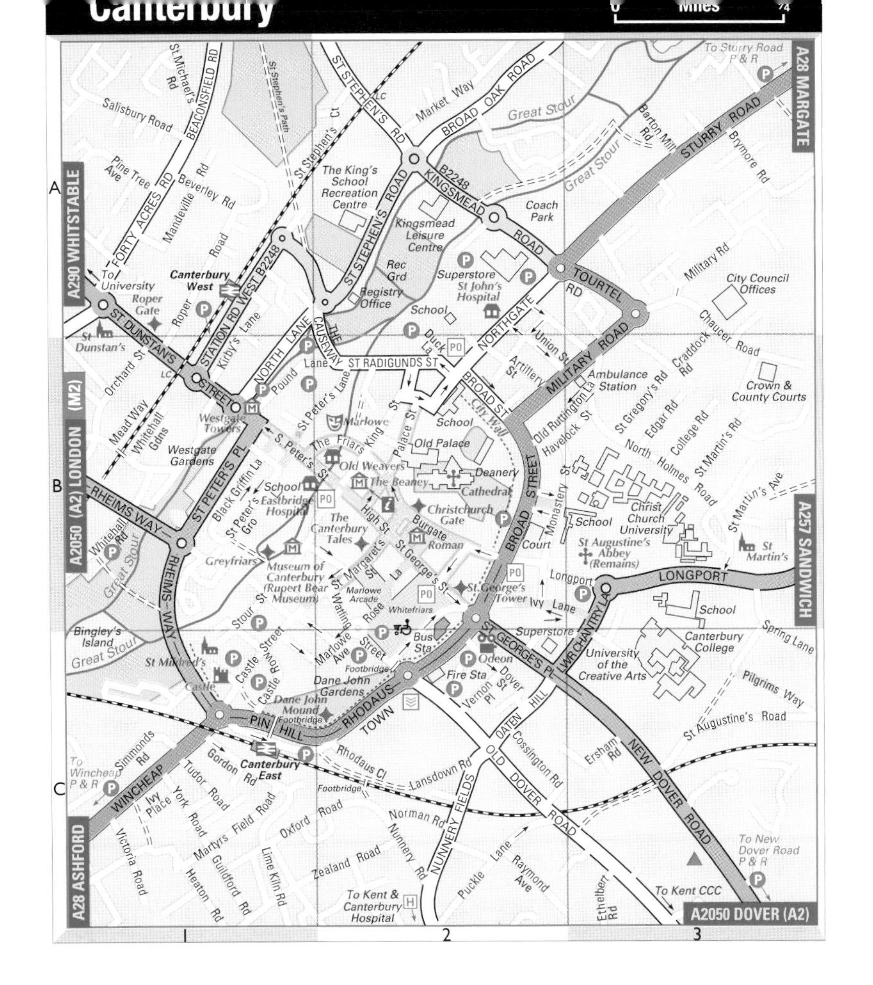
Canterbury
Miles
A28 MARGATE
A290 WHITSTABLE
A2050 (A2) LONDON (M2)
A257 SANDWICH
A28 ASHFORD
A2050 DOVER (A2)

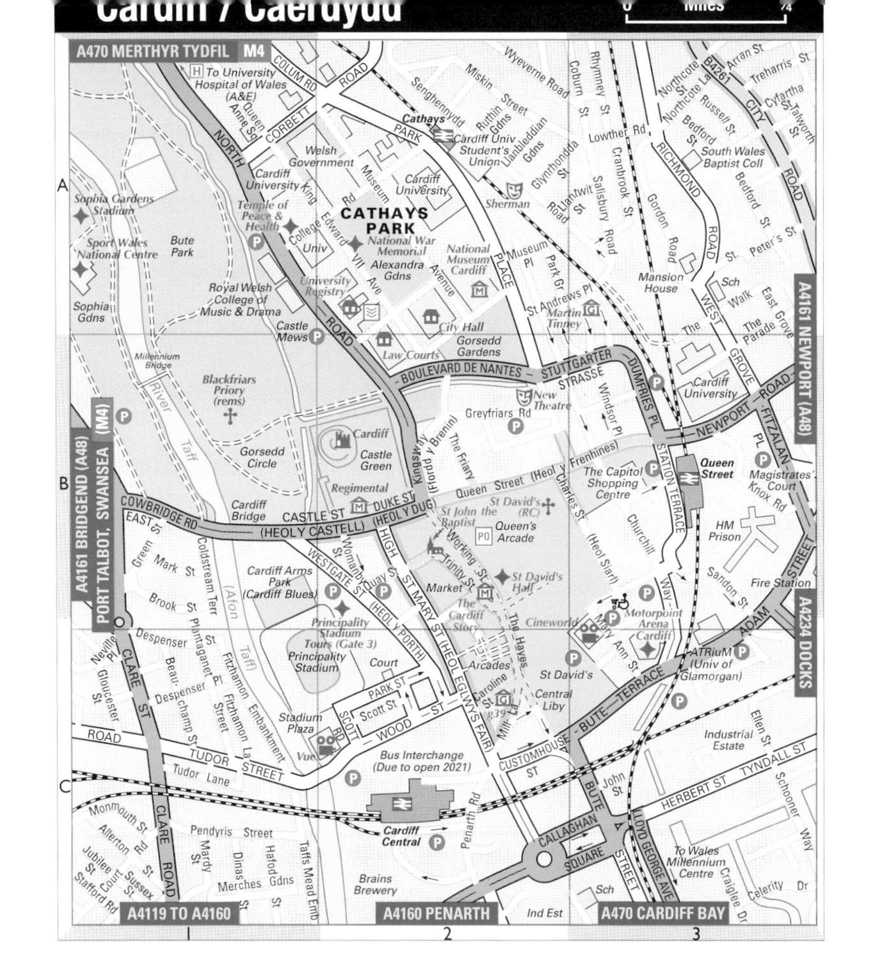
Cardiff / Caerdydd
Miles
A470 MERTHYR TYDFIL M4
A4161 NEWPORT (A48)
A4161 BRIDGEND (A48) PORT TALBOT, SWANSEA (M4)
A4234 DOCKS
A4119 TO A4160
A4160 PENARTH
A470 CARDIFF BAY

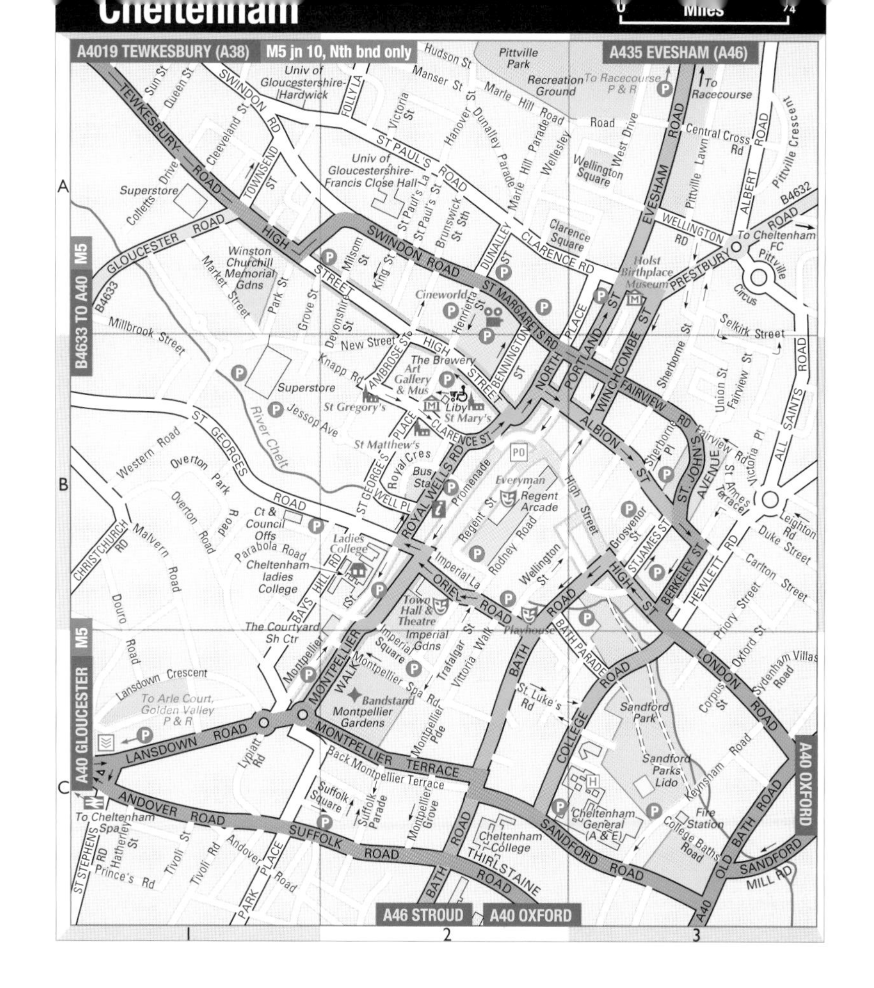
Cheltenham
Miles
A4019 TEWKESBURY (A38)
M5 jn 10, Nth bnd only
A435 EVESHAM (A46)
B4633 TO A40 M5
A40 GLOUCESTER M5
A40 OXFORD
A46 STROUD
A40 OXFORD

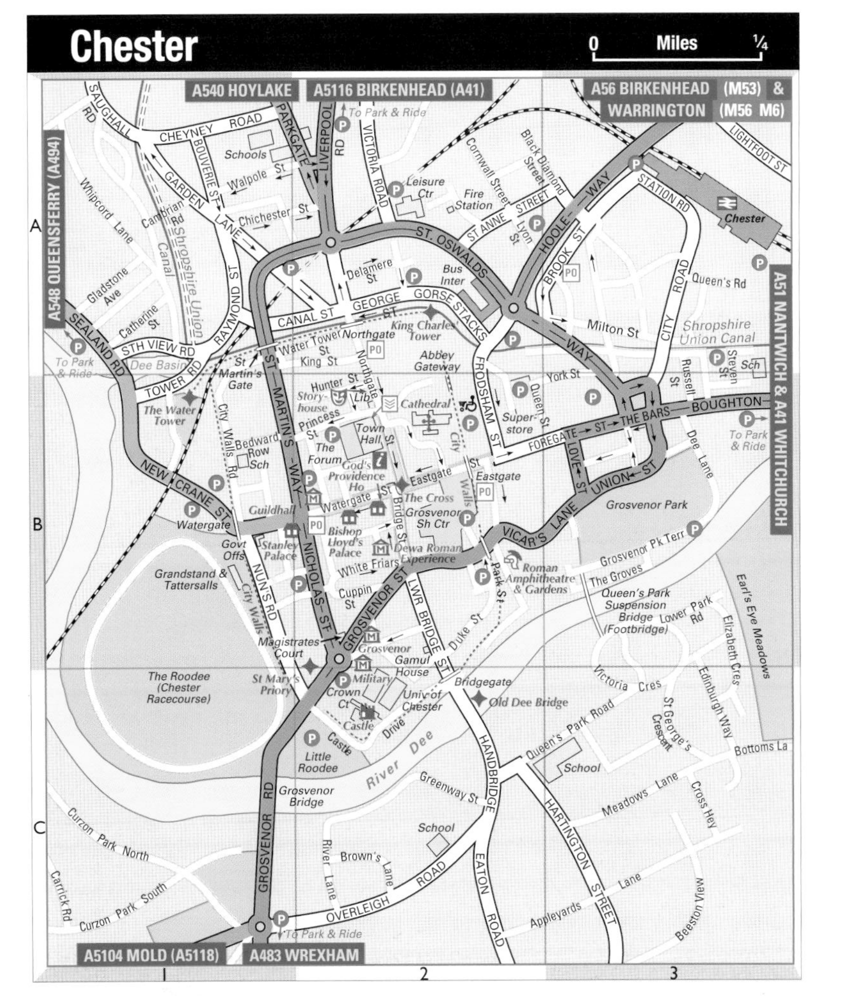
Chester
Miles
A540 HOYLAKE
A5116 BIRKENHEAD (A41)
A56 BIRKENHEAD (M53) & WARRINGTON (M56 M6)
A548 QUEENSFERRY (A494)
A51 NANTWICH & A41 WHITCHURCH
A5104 MOLD (A5118)
A483 WREXHAM

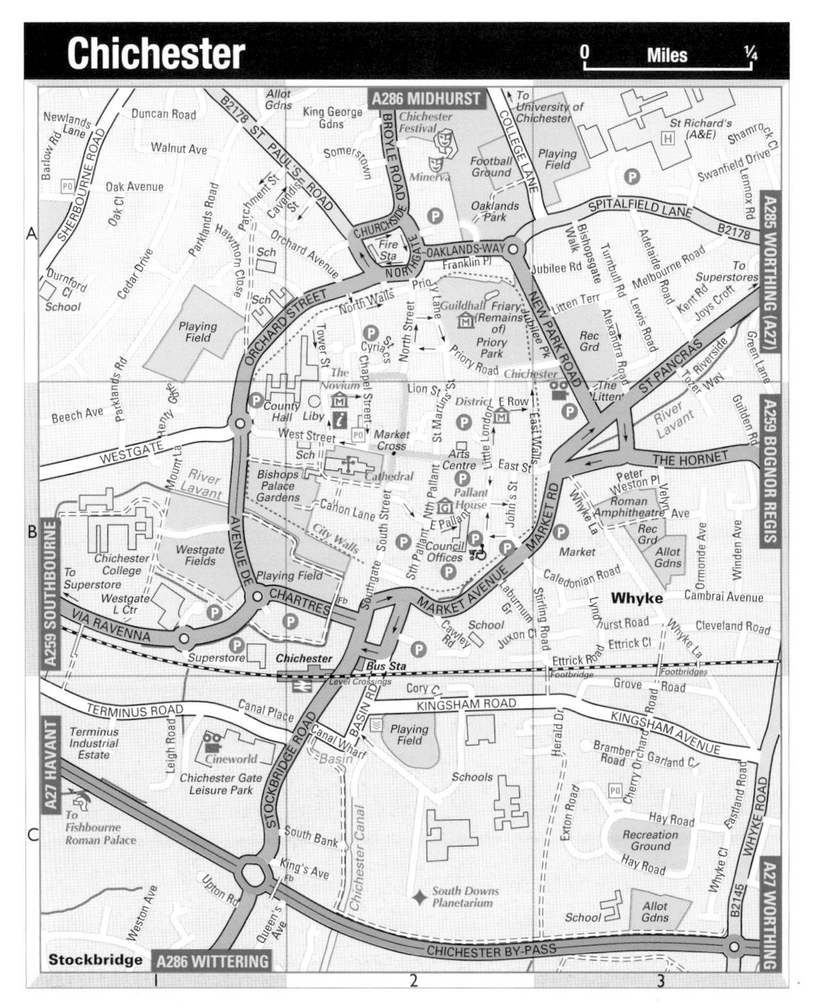
Chichester
Miles
A286 MIDHURST
A285 WORTHING (A27)
A259 BOGNOR REGIS
A259 SOUTHBOURNE
A27 HAVANT
A27 WORTHING
Stockbridge
A286 WITTERING

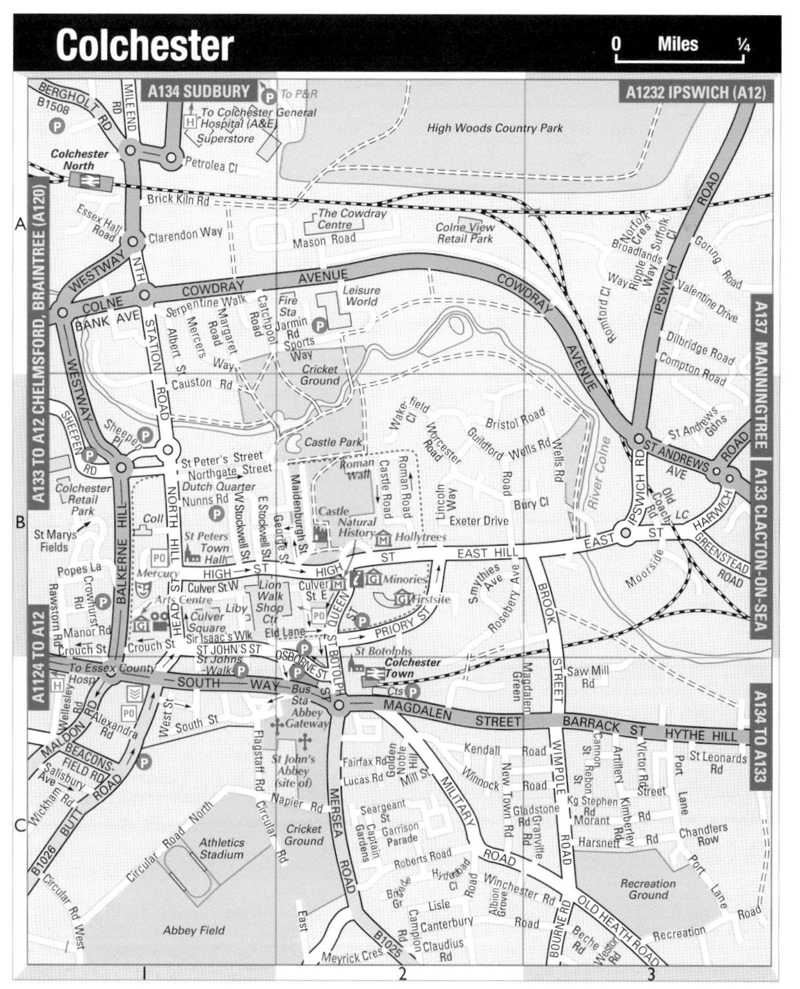
Colchester
Miles
A134 SUDBURY
A1232 IPSWICH (A12)
A133 TO A12 CHELMSFORD, BRAINTREE (A120)
A137 MANNINGTREE
A133 CLACTON-ON-SEA
A1124 TO A12
A134 TO A133

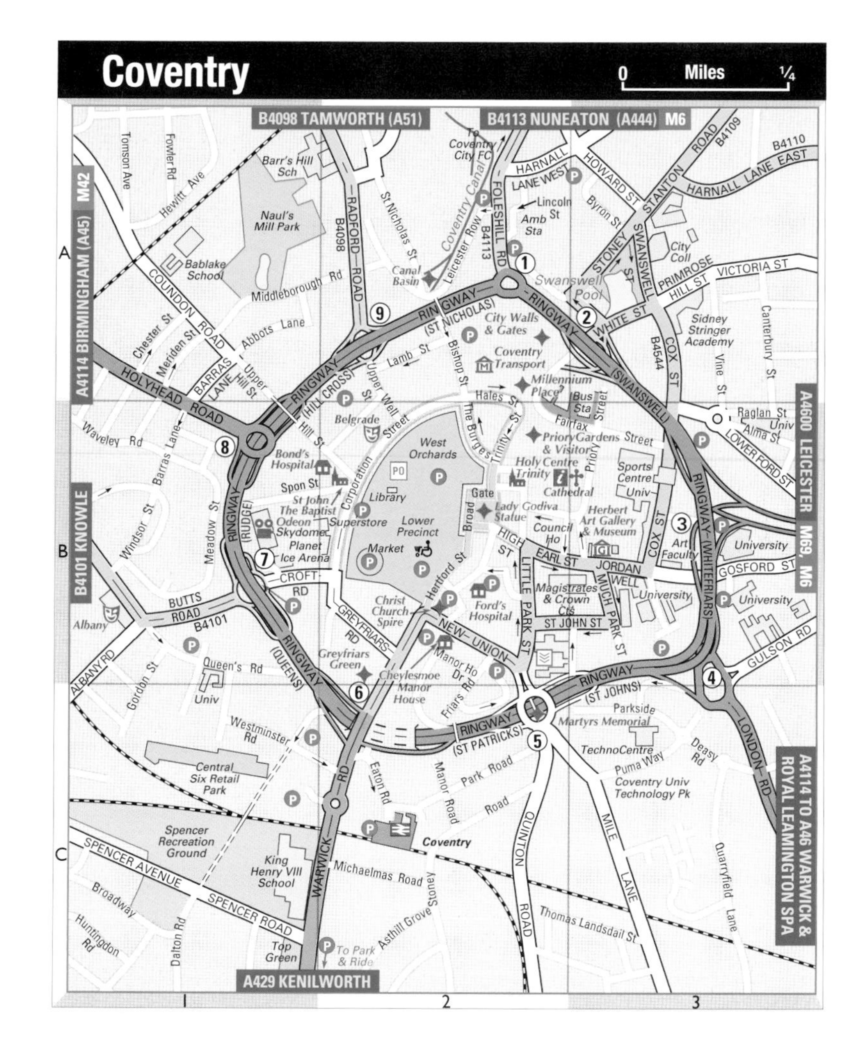
Coventry
Miles
B4098 TAMWORTH (A51)
B4113 NUNEATON (A444) M6
A4600 LEICESTER M69, M6
A4114 TO A46 WARWICK & ROYAL LEAMINGTON SPA
A429 KENILWORTH
B4101 KNOWLE
A4114 BIRMINGHAM (A45) M42

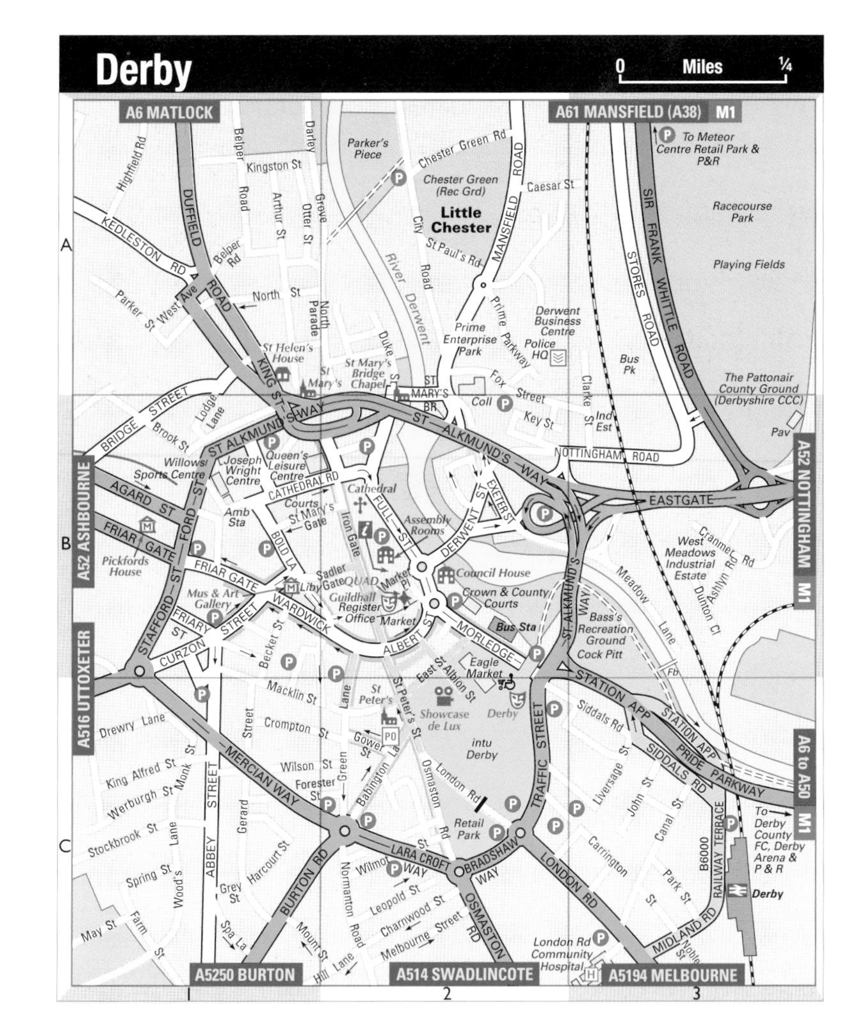
Derby
Miles
A6 MATLOCK
A61 MANSFIELD (A38) M1
A52 NOTTINGHAM M1
A6 to A50 M1
A5250 BURTON
A514 SWADLINCOTE
A5194 MELBOURNE
A516 UTTOXETER
A52 ASHBOURNE

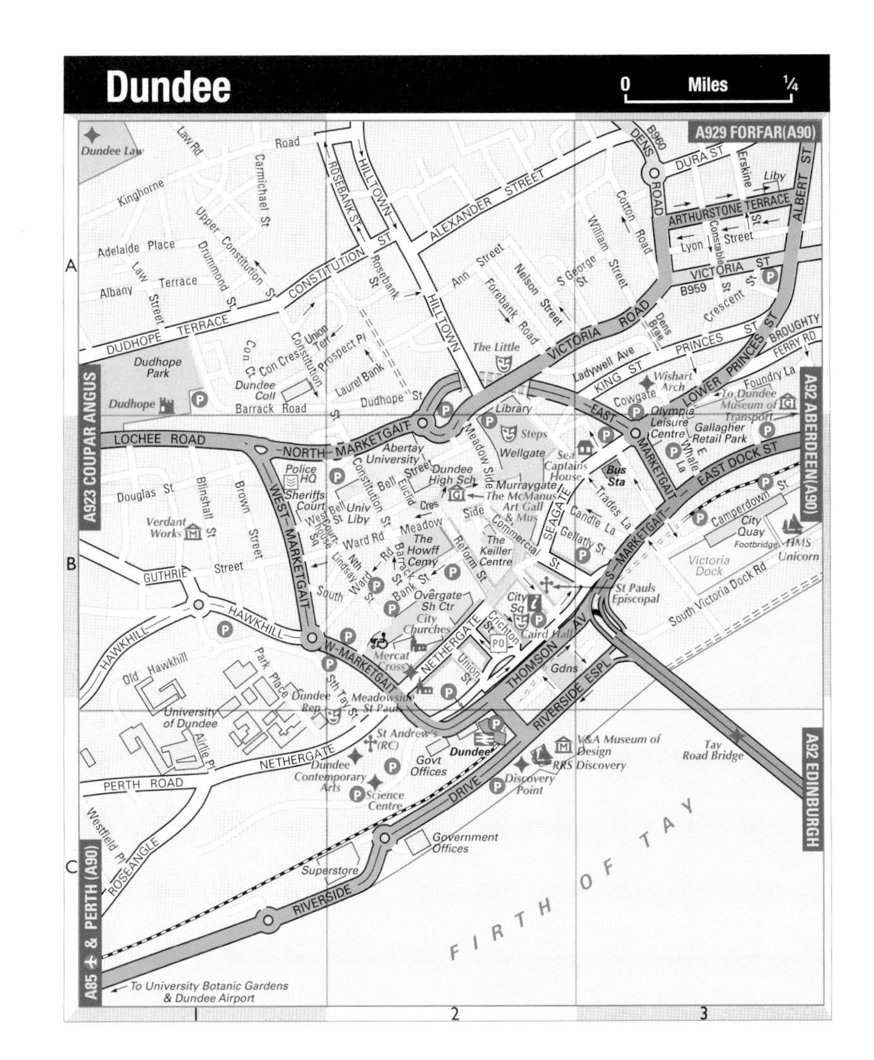
Dundee
Miles
A929 FORFAR(A90)
A92 ABERDEEN(A90)
A92 EDINBURGH
A85 & PERTH (A90)
A923 COUPAR ANGUS
FIRTH OF TAY

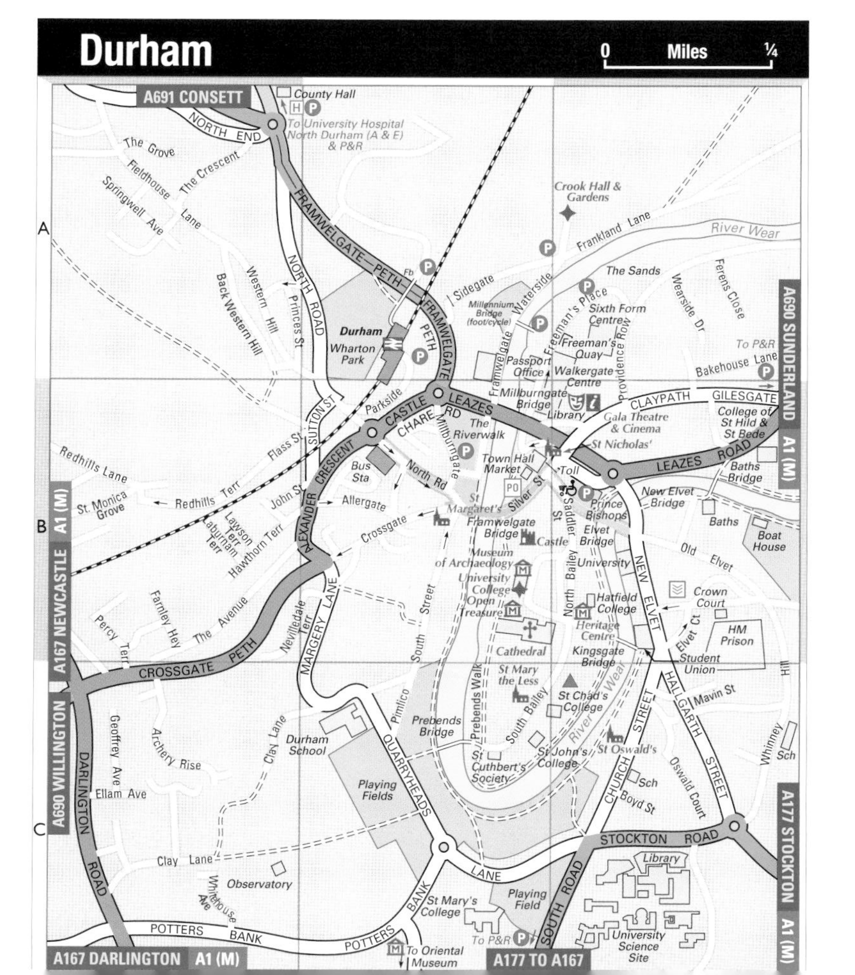
Durham
Miles
A691 CONSETT
A690 SUNDERLAND A1 (M)
A177 STOCKTON A1 (M)
A177 TO A167
A167 DARLINGTON A1 (M)
A690 WILLINGTON A167 NEWCASTLE A1 (M)

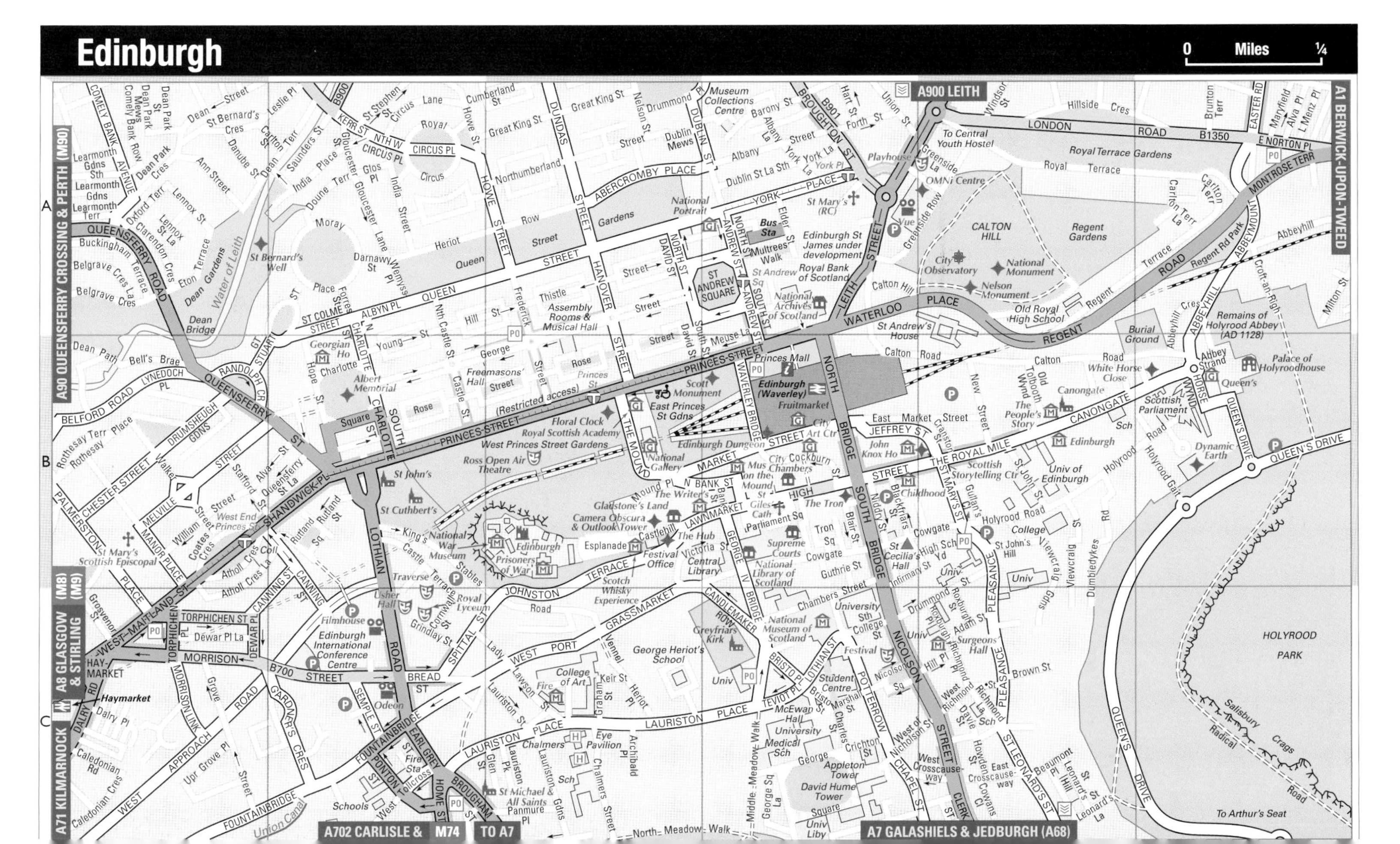
Edinburgh
Miles
A900 LEITH
A1 BERWICK-UPON-TWEED
A7 GALASHIELS & JEDBURGH (A68)
A702 CARLISLE & M74 TO A7
A71 KILMARNOCK
A8 GLASGOW (M8) & STIRLING (M9)
A90 QUEENSFERRY CROSSING & PERTH (M90)
HOLYROOD PARK

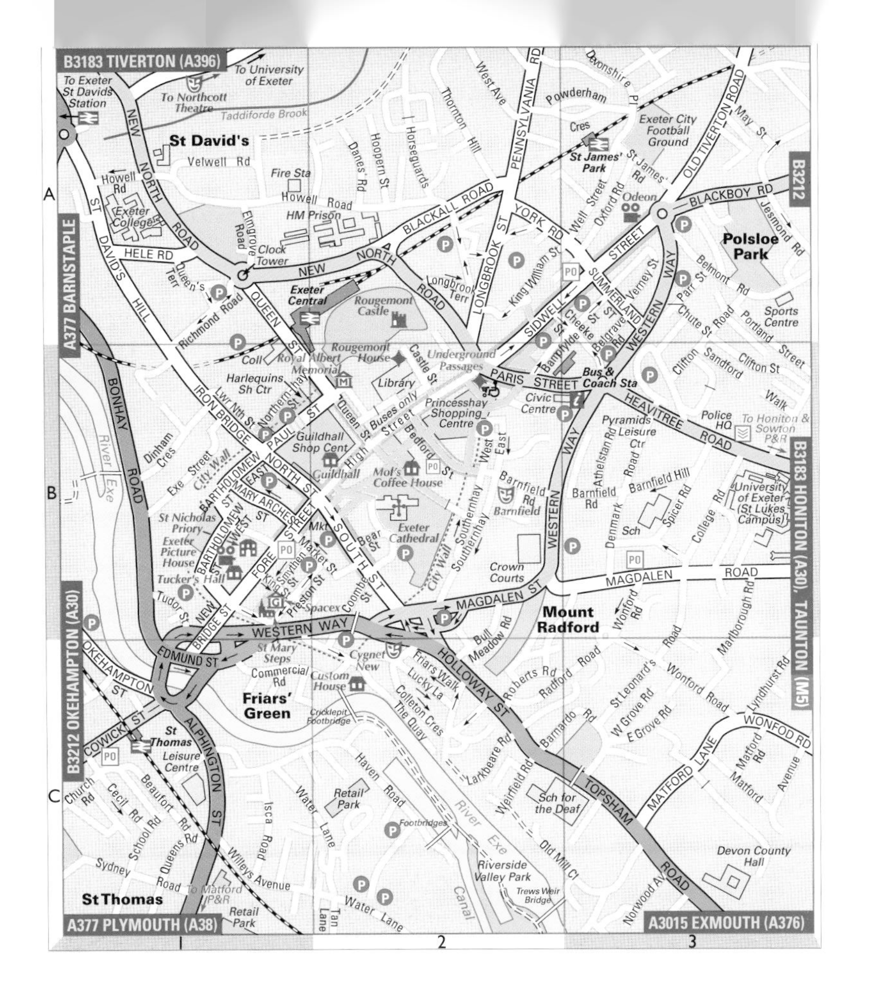
B3183 TIVERTON (A396)
B3212
B3183 HONITON (A30), TAUNTON (M5)
A3015 EXMOUTH (A376)
A377 PLYMOUTH (A38)
B3212 OKEHAMPTON (A30)
A377 BARNSTAPLE
St David's
Polsloe Park
Mount Radford
Friars' Green
St Thomas

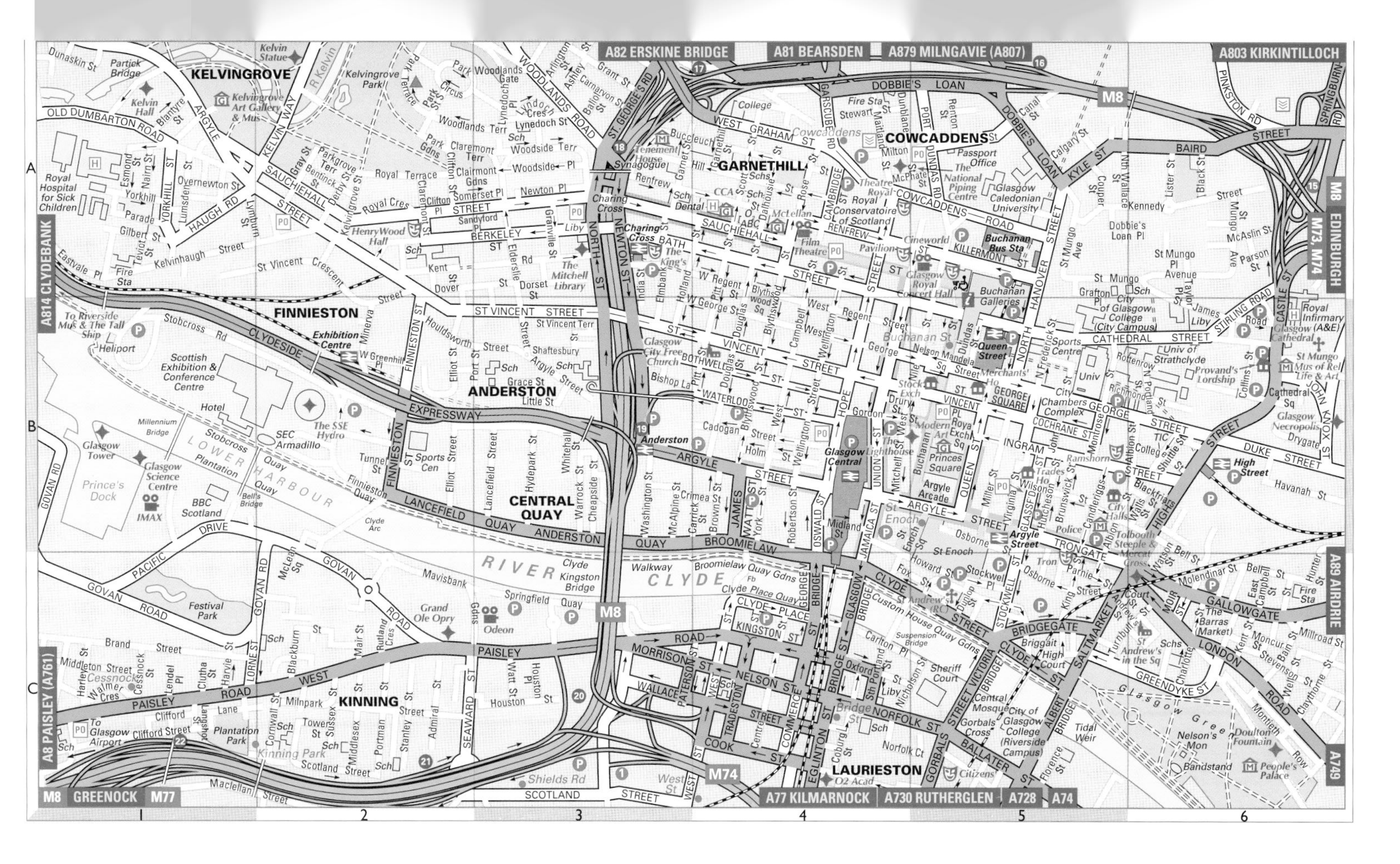
A82 ERSKINE BRIDGE
A81 BEARSDEN
A879 MILNGAVIE (A807)
A803 KIRKINTILLOCH
M8 EDINBURGH M73, M74
A89 AIRDRIE
A749
A77 KILMARNOCK
A730 RUTHERGLEN
A728
A74
M8 GREENOCK M77
A8 PAISLEY (A761)
A814 CLYDEBANK
KELVINGROVE
GARNETHILL
COWCADDENS
FINNIESTON
ANDERSTON
CENTRAL QUAY
KINNING
LAURIESTON

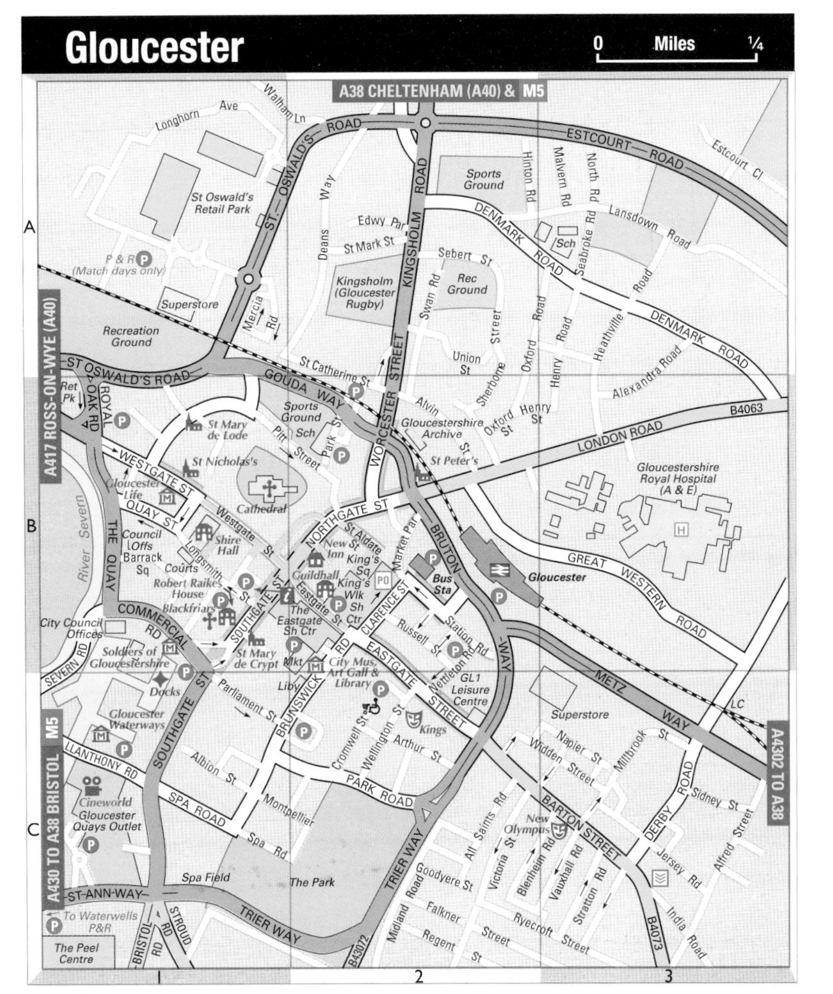
Gloucester
0 Miles ¼
A38 CHELTENHAM (A40) & M5
A4302 TO A38
A417 ROSS-ON-WYE (A40)
A430 TO A38 BRISTOL M5

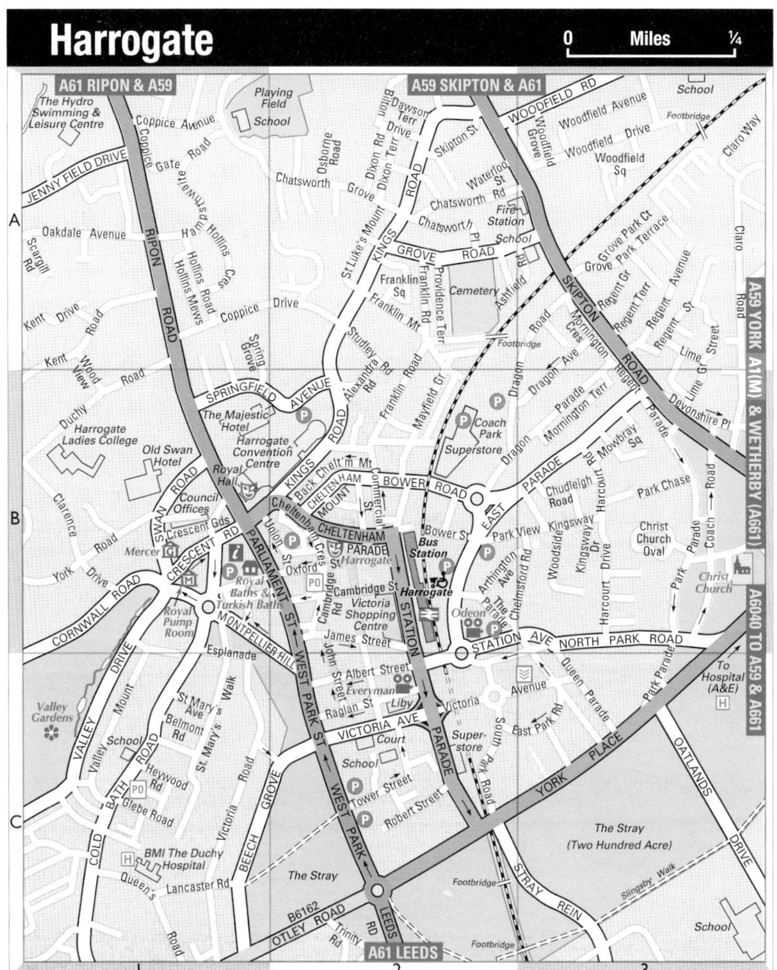
Harrogate
0 Miles ¼
A61 RIPON & A59
A59 SKIPTON & A61
A59 YORK A1(M) & WETHERBY (A661)
A6040 TO A59 & A661
A61 LEEDS

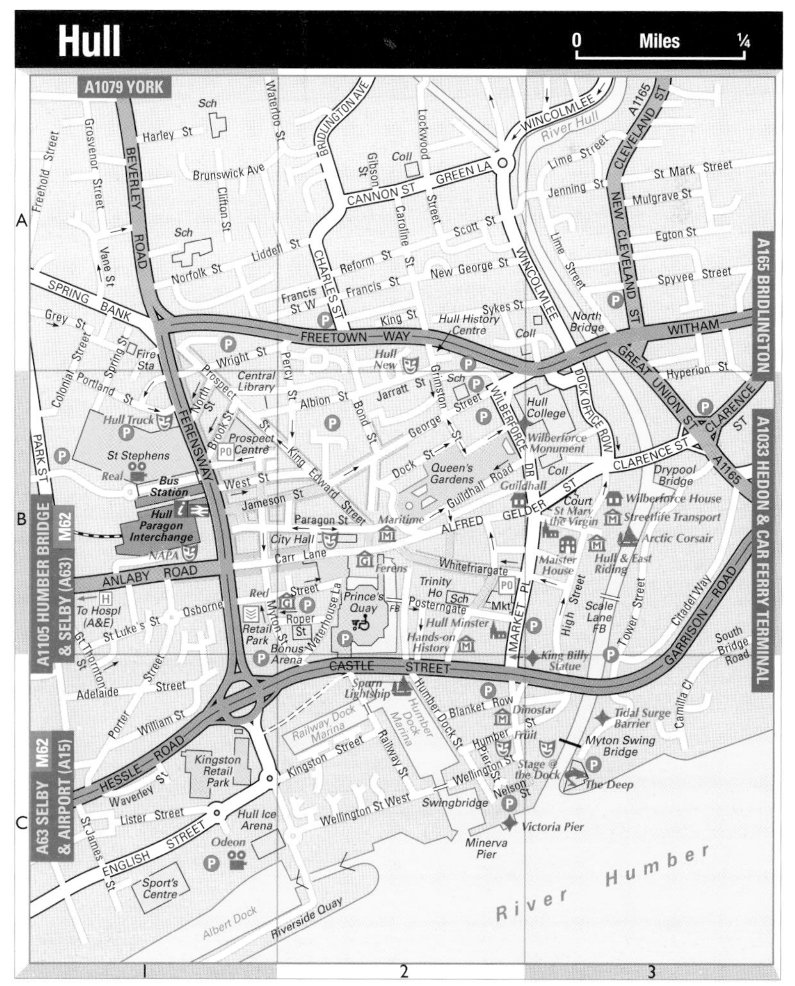
Hull
0 Miles ¼
A1079 YORK
A165 BRIDLINGTON
A1033 HEDON & CAR FERRY TERMINAL
A1105 HUMBER BRIDGE & SELBY (A63) M62
A63 SELBY M62 & AIRPORT (A15)
River Humber

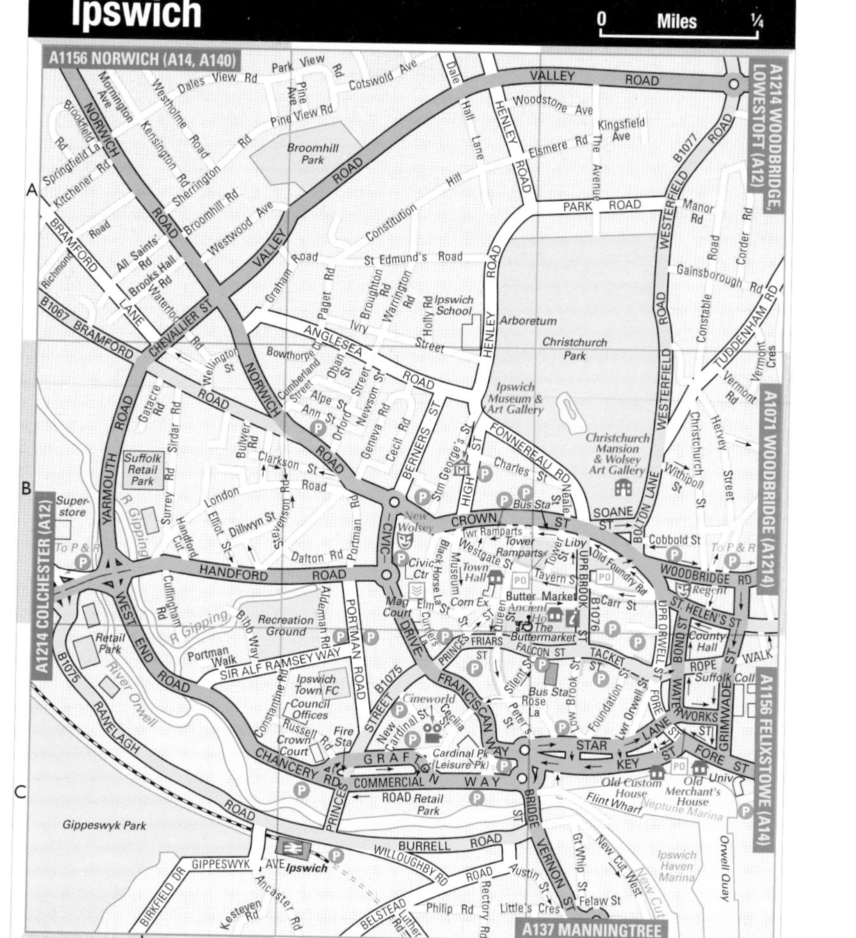
Ipswich
0 Miles ¼
A1156 NORWICH (A14, A140)
A1214 WOODBRIDGE, LOWESTOFT (A12)
A1071 WOODBRIDGE (A1214)
A1156 FELIXSTOWE (A14)
A137 MANNINGTREE
A1214 COLCHESTER (A12)

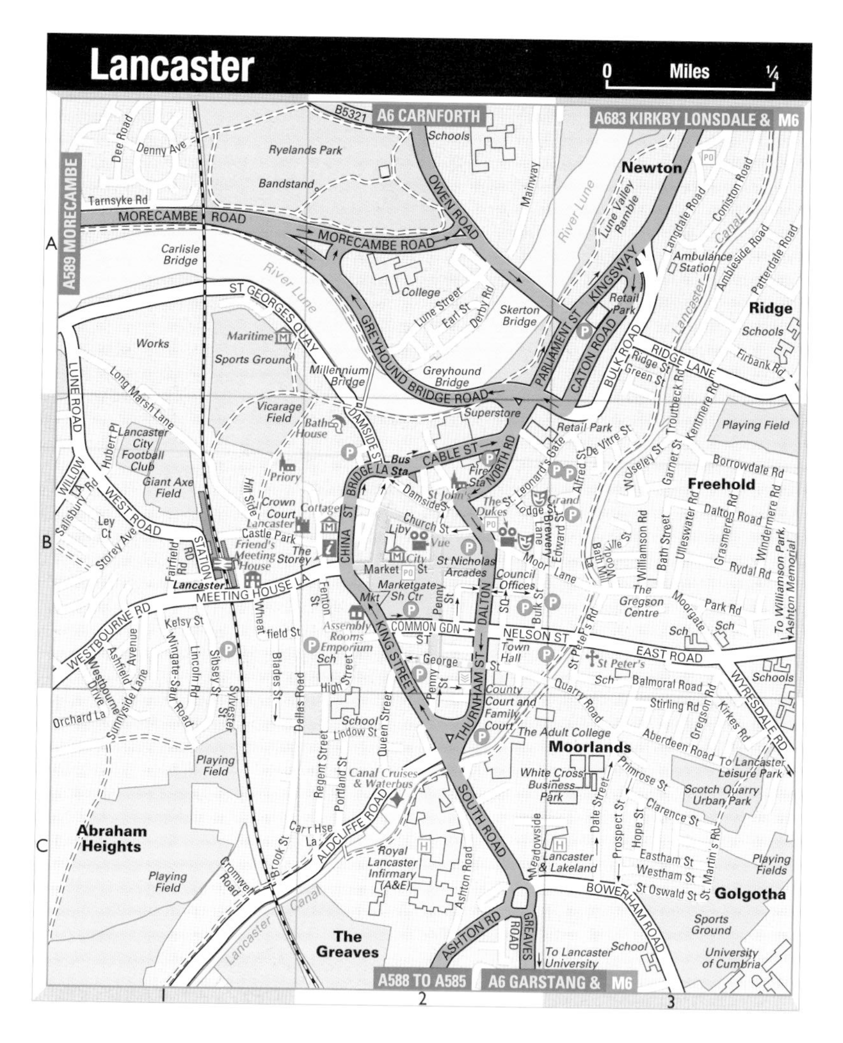
Lancaster
0 Miles ¼
A6 CARNFORTH
A683 KIRKBY LONSDALE & M6
A589 MORECAMBE
A588 TO A585
A6 GARSTANG & M6
Newton
Ridge
Freehold
Moorlands
Golgotha
Abraham Heights
The Greaves

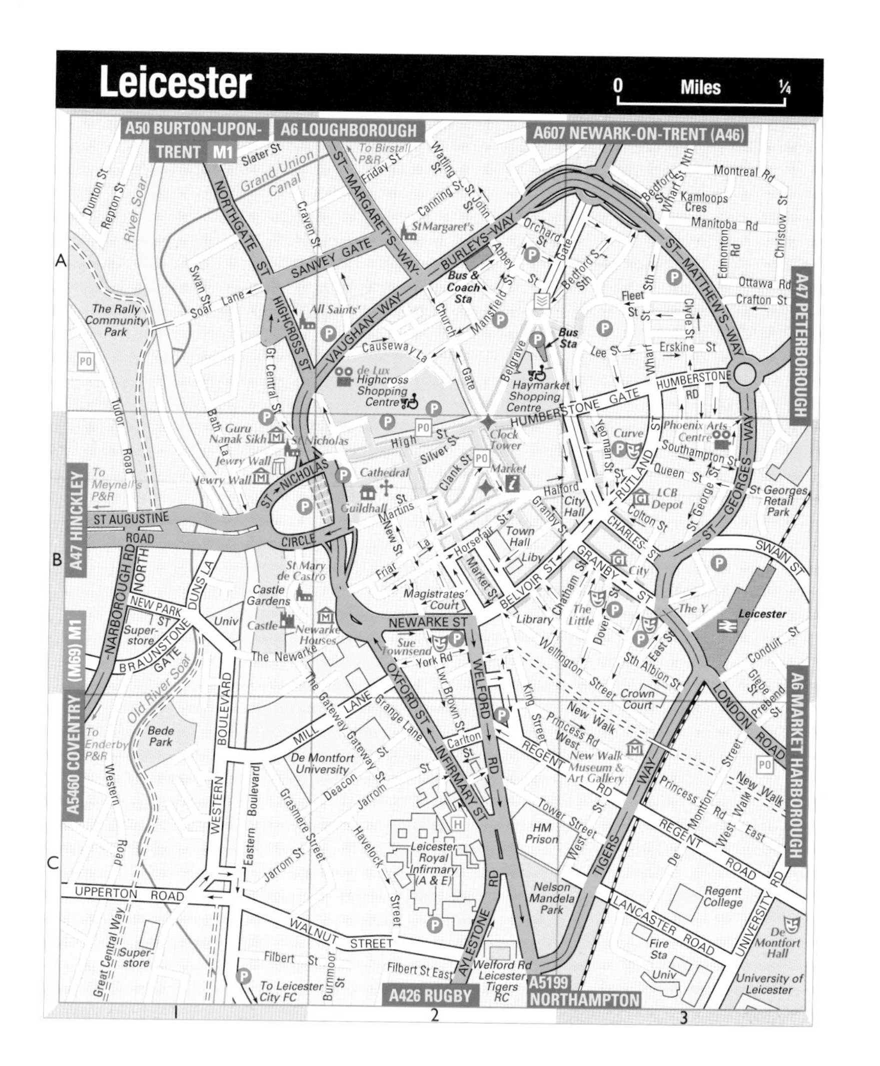
Leicester
0 Miles ¼
A50 BURTON-UPON-TRENT M1
A6 LOUGHBOROUGH
A607 NEWARK-ON-TRENT (A46)
A47 PETERBOROUGH
A47 HINCKLEY
A5460 COVENTRY (M69) M1
A6 MARKET HARBOROUGH
A426 RUGBY
A5199 NORTHAMPTON

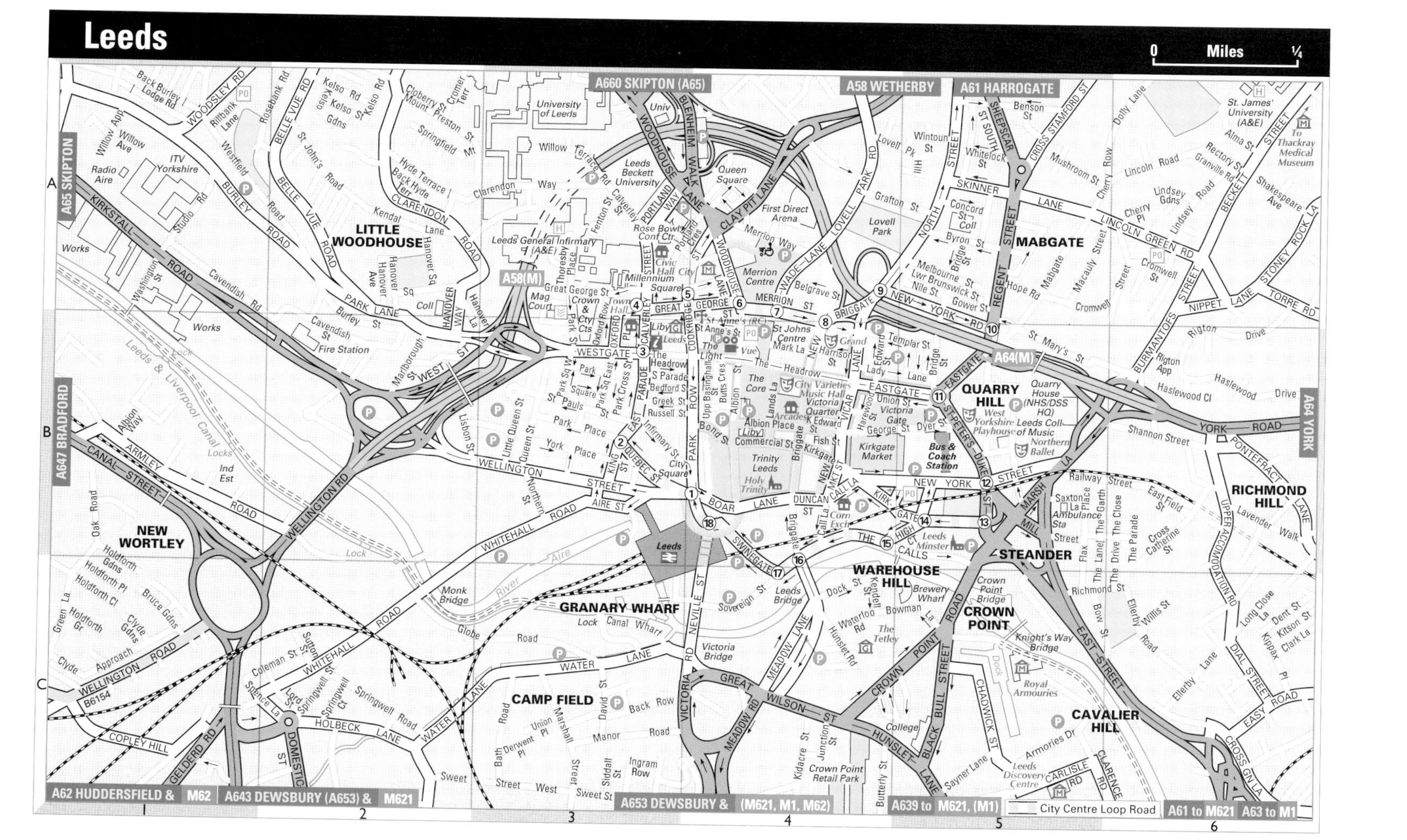
Leeds
0 Miles ¼
A660 SKIPTON (A65)
A58 WETHERBY
A61 HARROGATE
A65 SKIPTON
A647 BRADFORD
A64 YORK
A62 HUDDERSFIELD & M62
A643 DEWSBURY (A653) & M621
A653 DEWSBURY & (M621, M1, M62)
A639 to M621, (M1)
City Centre Loop Road
A61 to M621 A63 to M1
LITTLE WOODHOUSE
MABGATE
QUARRY HILL
RICHMOND HILL
NEW WORTLEY
GRANARY WHARF
WAREHOUSE HILL
STEANDER
CROWN POINT
CAMP FIELD
CAVALIER HILL

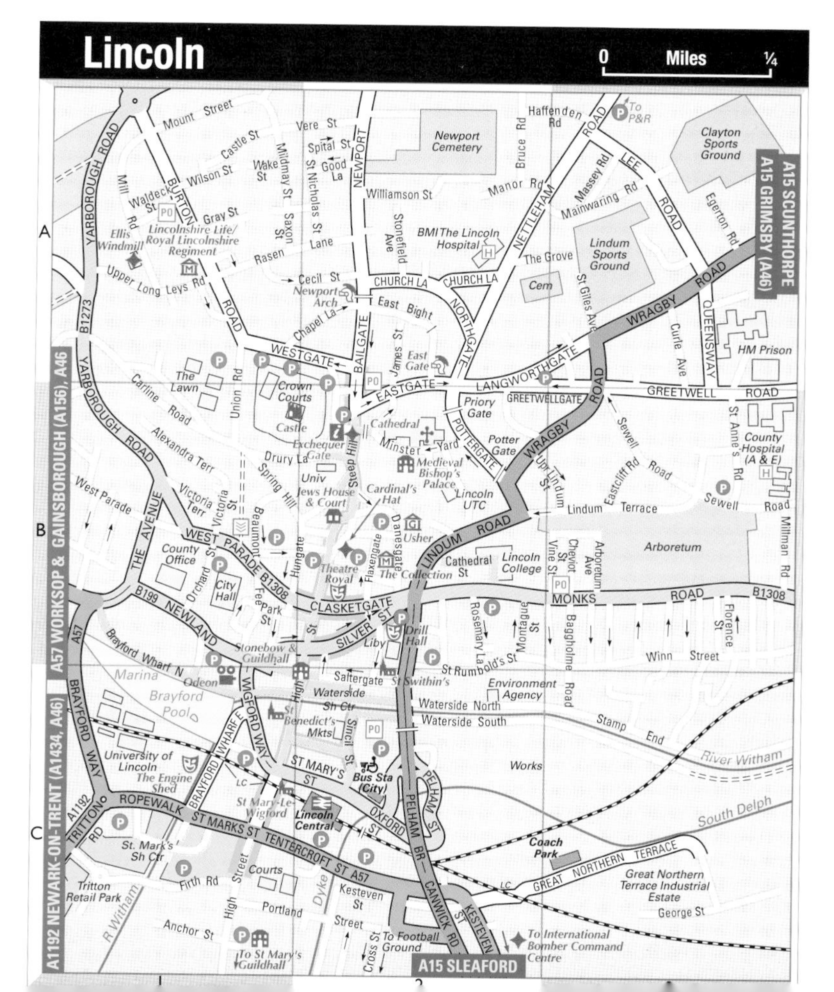
Lincoln
0 Miles ¼
A15 SCUNTHORPE
A15 GRIMSBY (A46)
A57 WORKSOP & GAINSBOROUGH (A156), A46
A1192 NEWARK-ON-TRENT (A1434, A46)
A15 SLEAFORD

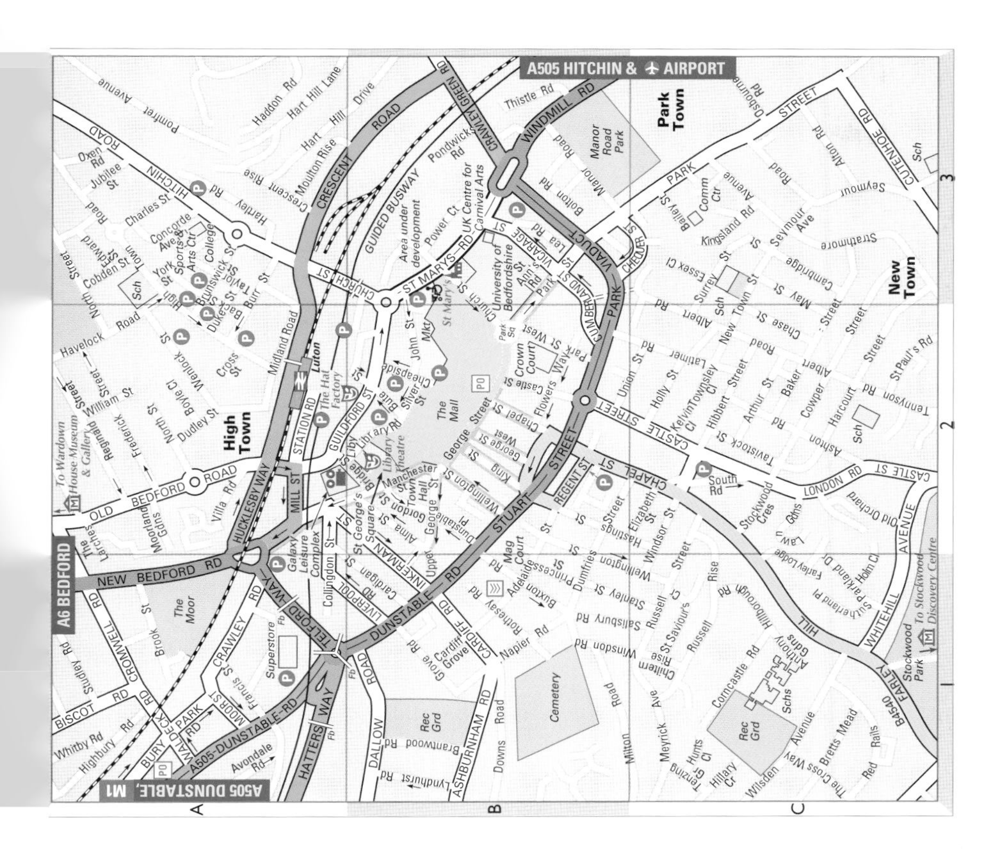
A505 HITCHIN & AIRPORT
A505 DUNSTABLE M1
A6 BEDFORD
High Town
New Town
Park Town

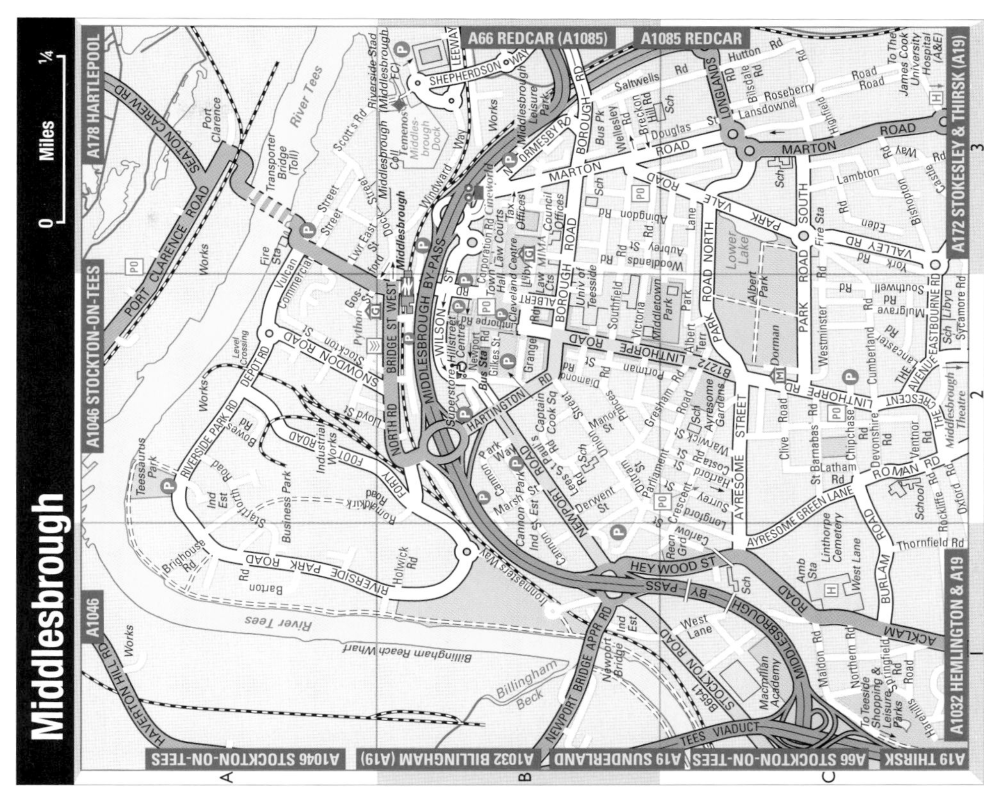
Middlesbrough
A66 REDCAR (A1085)
A1085 REDCAR
A178 HARTLEPOOL
A1046 STOCKTON-ON-TEES
A172 STOKESLEY & THIRSK (A19)
A1032 HEMLINGTON & A19
River Tees

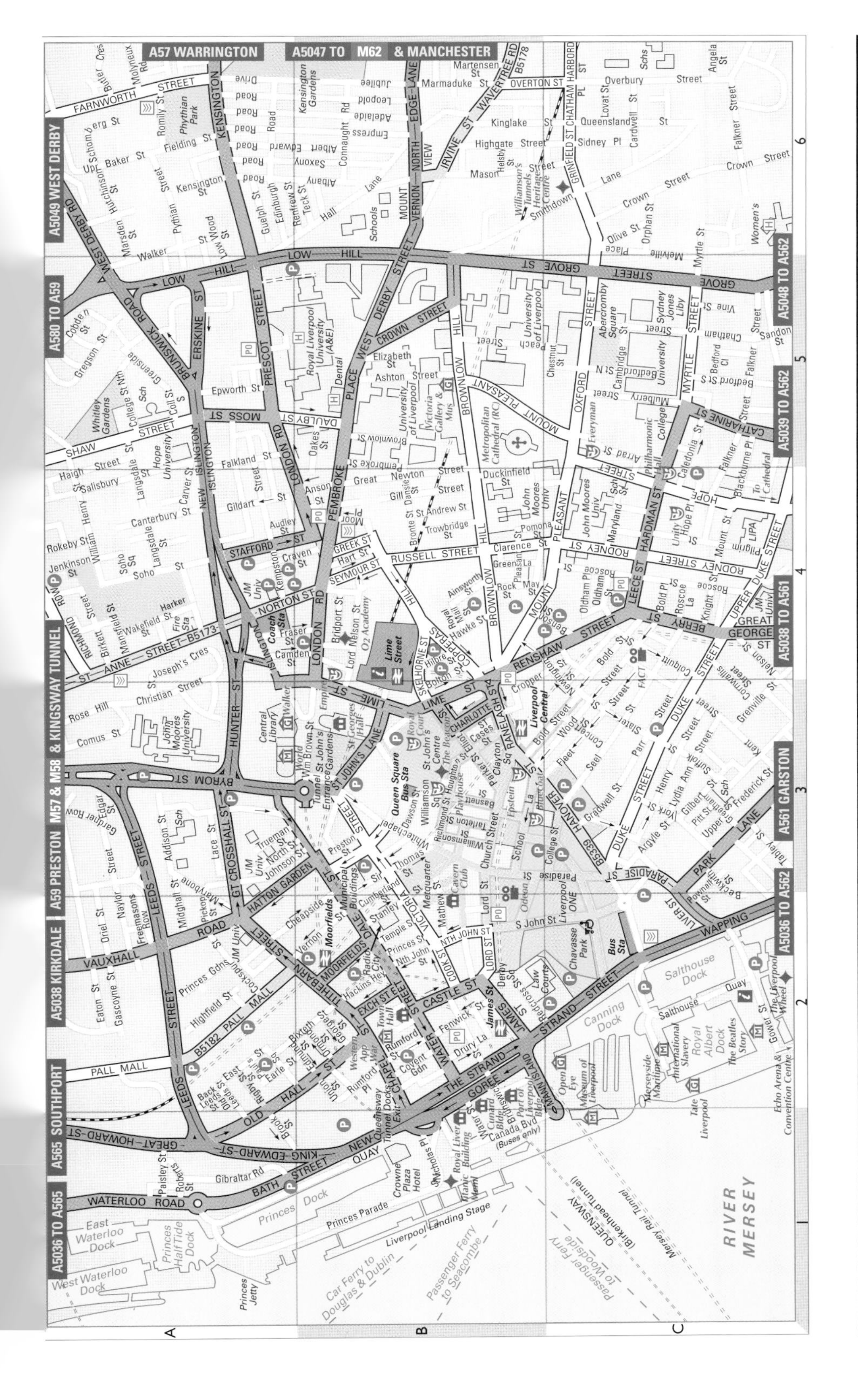
A57 WARRINGTON
A5047 TO M62 & MANCHESTER
A5049 WEST DERBY
A580 TO A59
A5038 KIRKDALE
A59 PRESTON
M57 & M58 & KINGSWAY TUNNEL
A565 SOUTHPORT
A5036 TO A565
A5048 TO A562
A5039 TO A562
A5038 TO A561
A561 GARSTON
A5036 TO A562
RIVER MERSEY

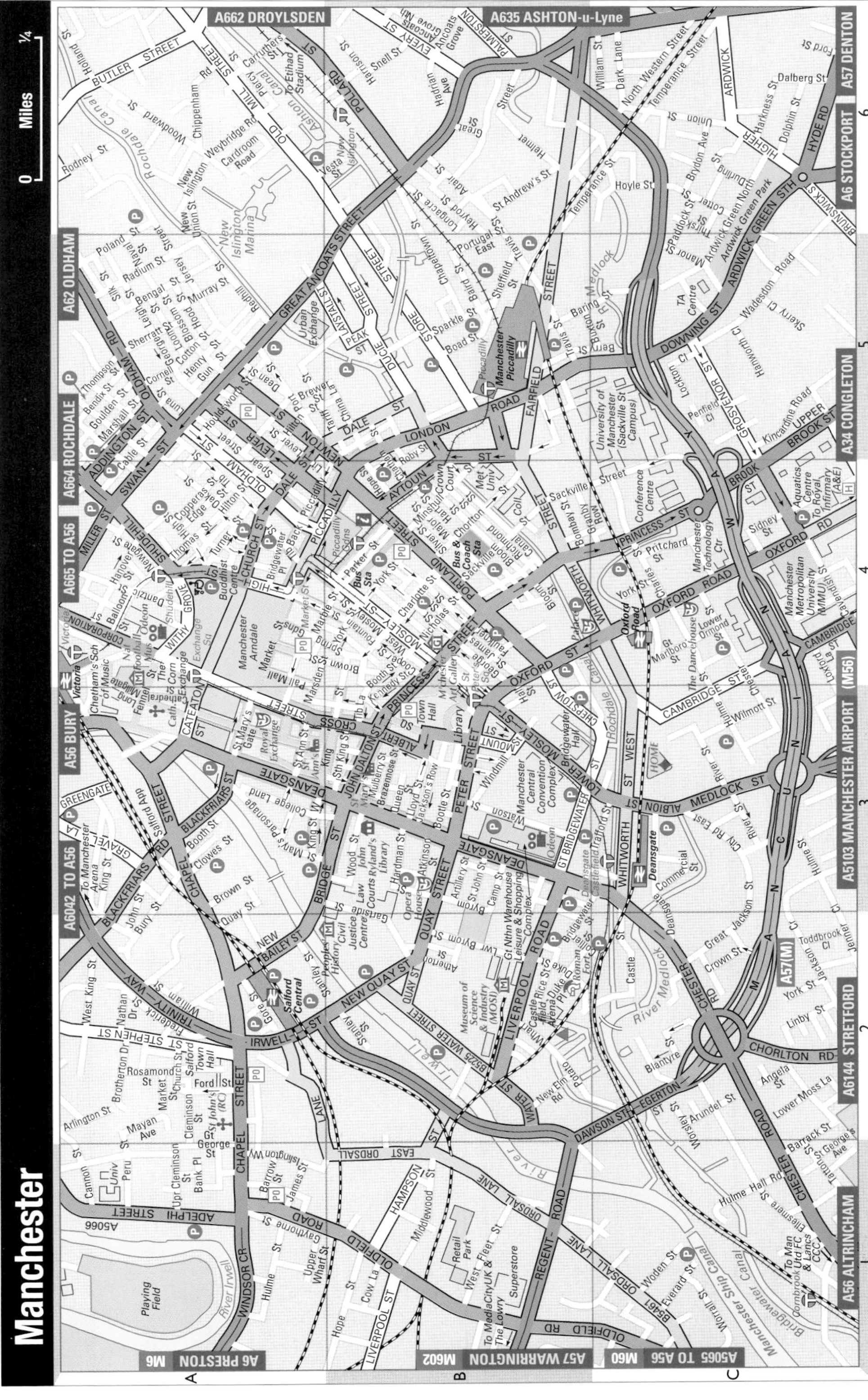
Manchester
A662 DROYLSDEN
A635 ASHTON-u-Lyne
A62 OLDHAM
A664 ROCHDALE
A665 TO A56
A56 BURY
A6042 TO A56
A57 DENTON
A6 STOCKPORT
A34 CONGLETON
A5103 MANCHESTER AIRPORT (M56)
A5144 STRETFORD
A56 ALTRINCHAM
A6 PRESTON M6
A57 WARRINGTON M602
A5065 TO A56 M60

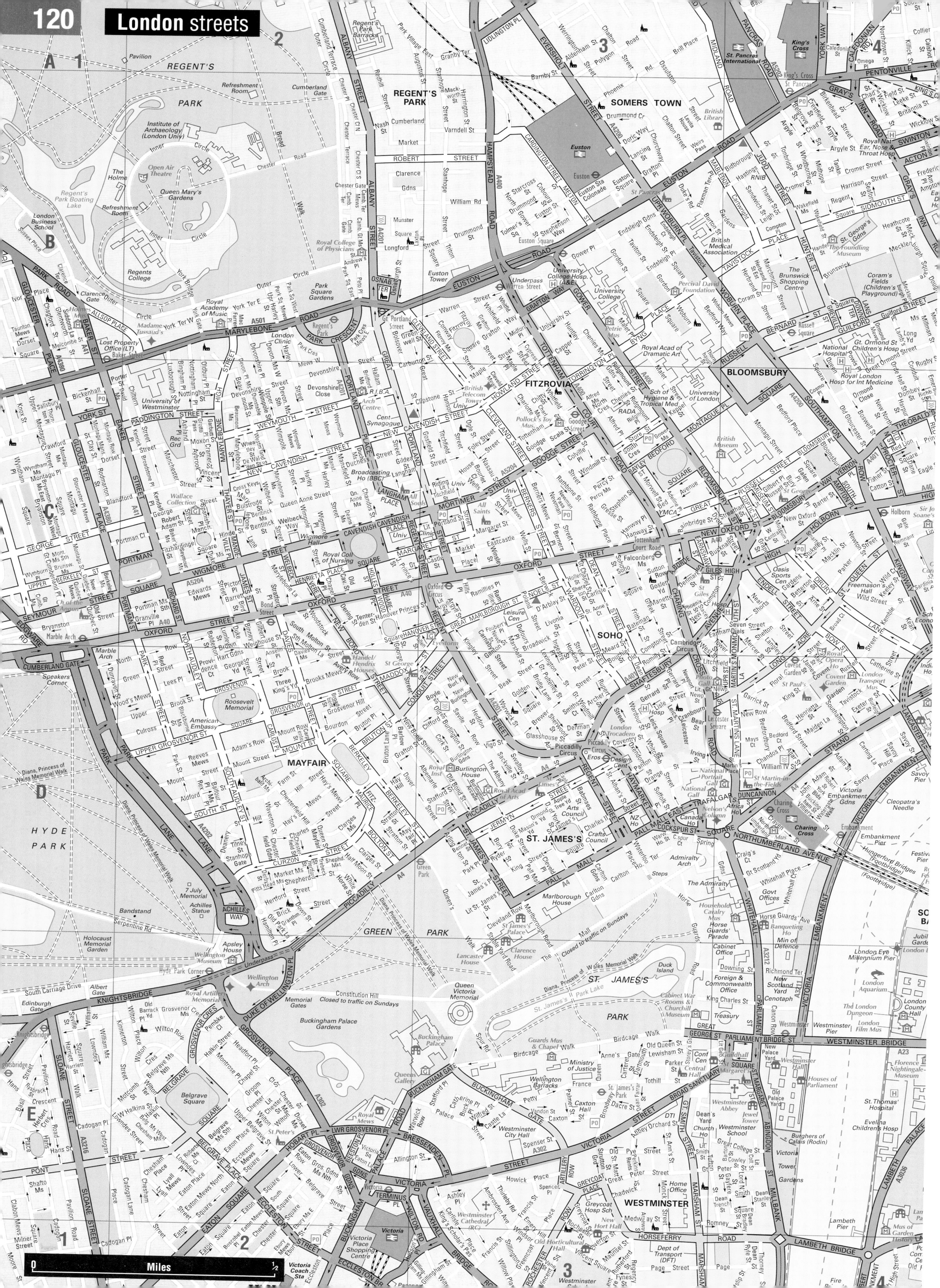

REGENT'S PARK
REGENT'S PARK
SOMERS TOWN
FITZROVIA
BLOOMSBURY
SOHO
MAYFAIR
ST. JAMES'S
WESTMINSTER
HYDE PARK
GREEN PARK
ST. JAMES'S PARK
MARYLEBONE ROAD
EUSTON ROAD
OXFORD STREET
PICCADILLY
KNIGHTSBRIDGE
VICTORIA STREET
PARK LANE
REGENT STREET
TOTTENHAM COURT ROAD
SHAFTESBURY AVENUE
CHARING CROSS ROAD
STRAND
VICTORIA EMBANKMENT
WHITEHALL
PARLIAMENT SQUARE
BUCKINGHAM PALACE ROAD
GROSVENOR PLACE
PALL MALL
PENTONVILLE ROAD
KINGSWAY
Euston
St. Pancras International
King's Cross
Victoria
Charing Cross
Buckingham Palace
Houses of Parliament
Westminster Abbey
British Museum
Miles

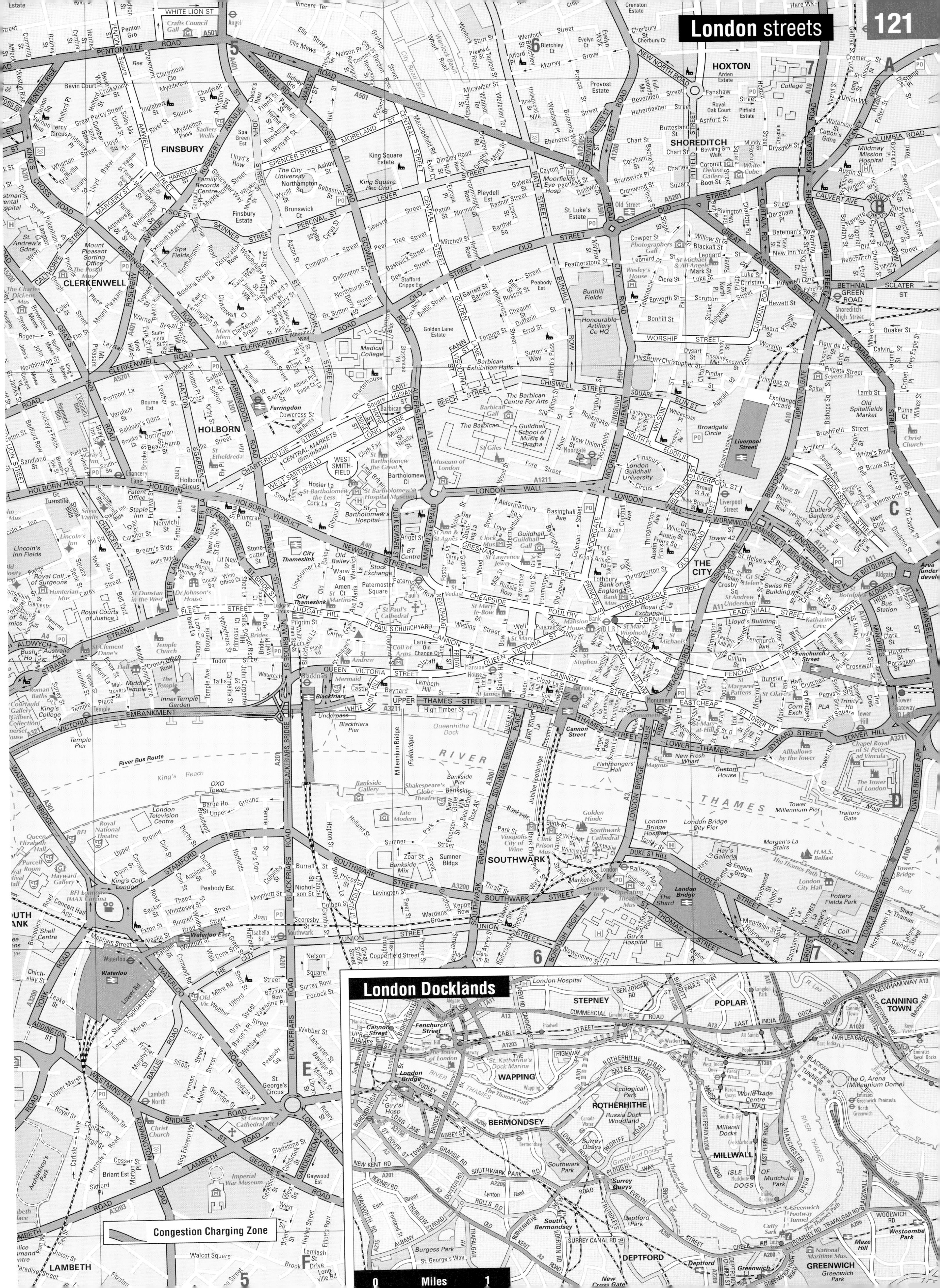

London Docklands

Congestion Charging Zone

0 Miles 1

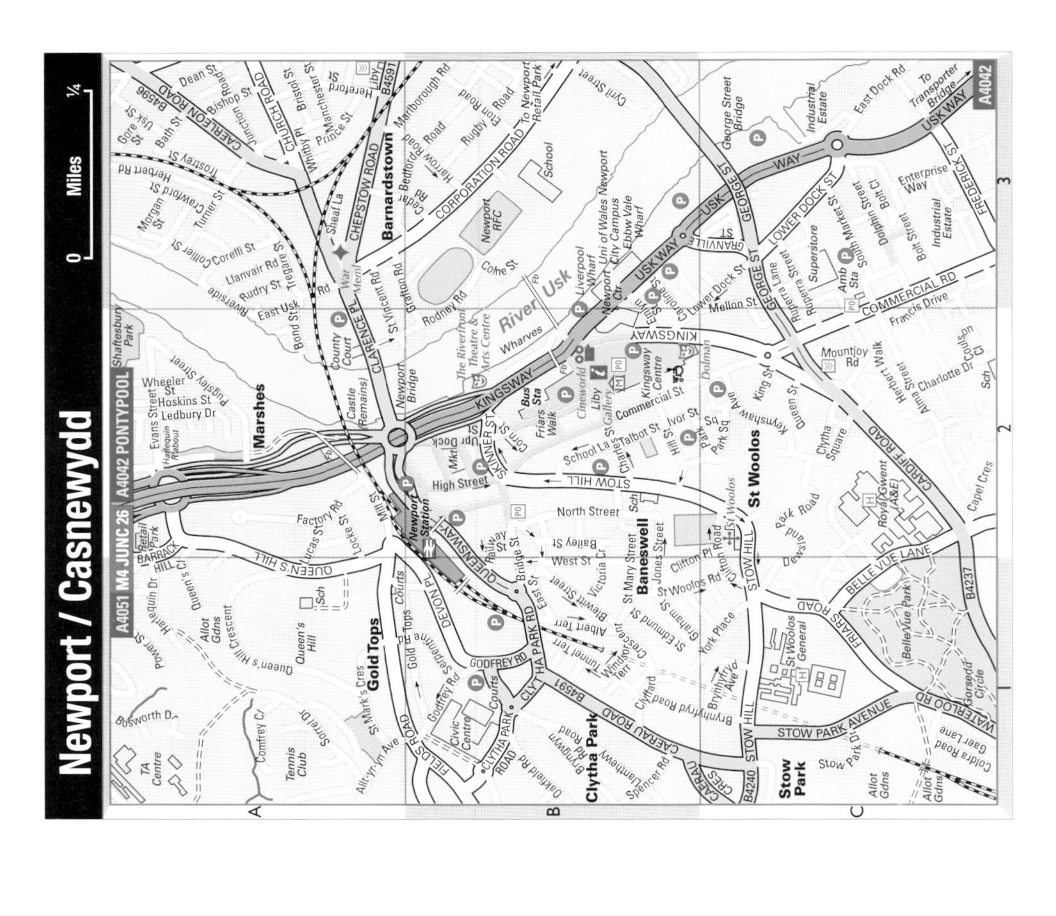

Newport / Casnewydd

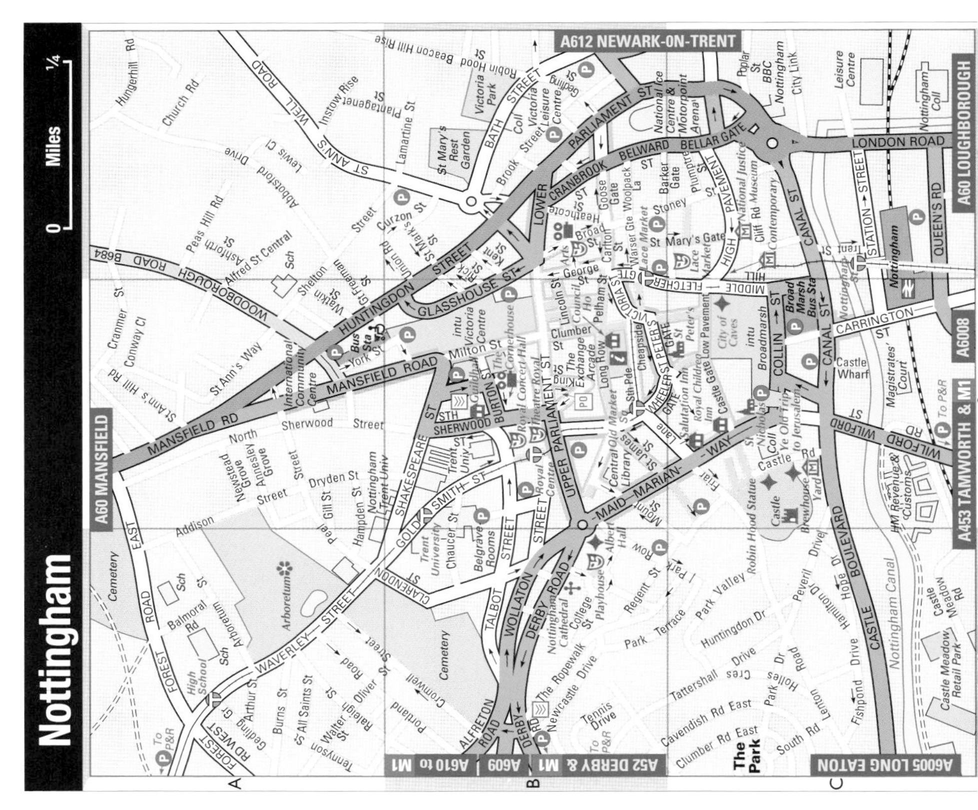

Nottingham

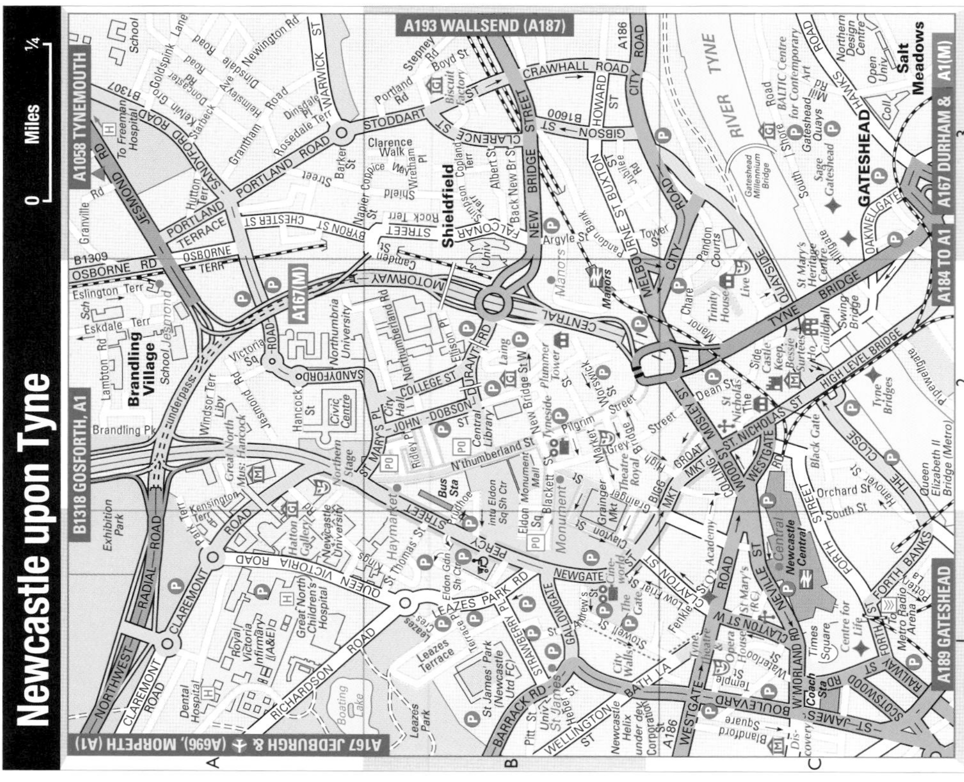

Newcastle upon Tyne

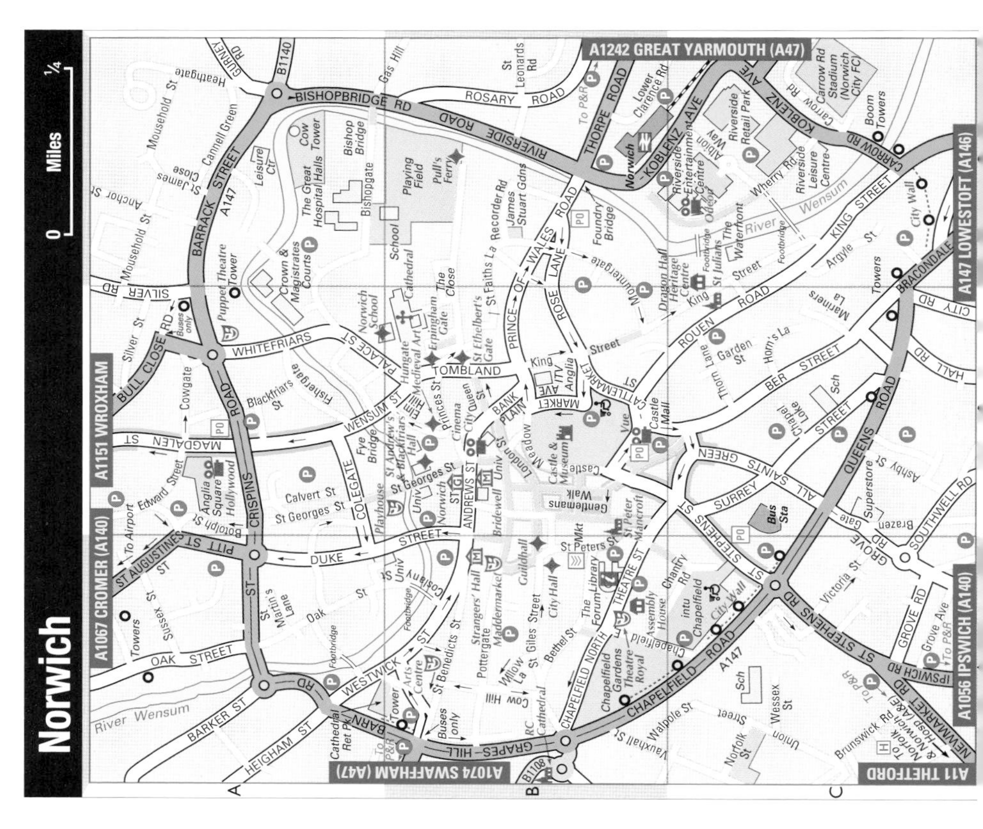

Norwich

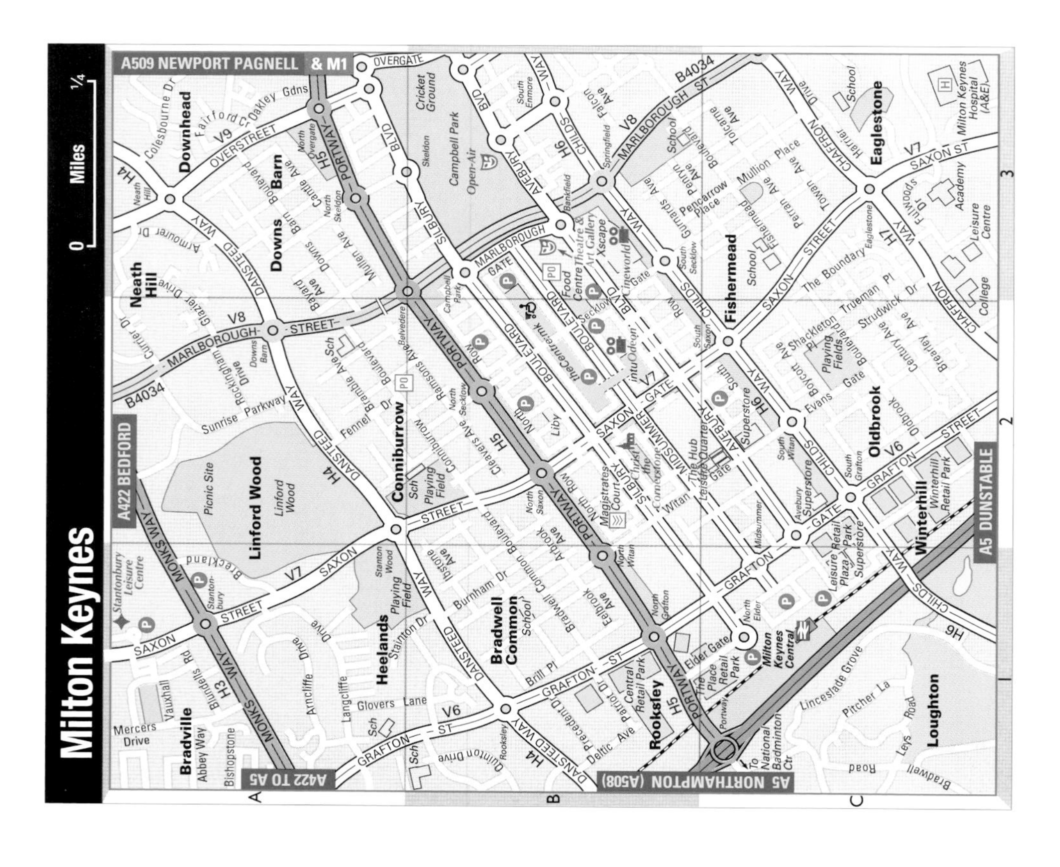

Milton Keynes

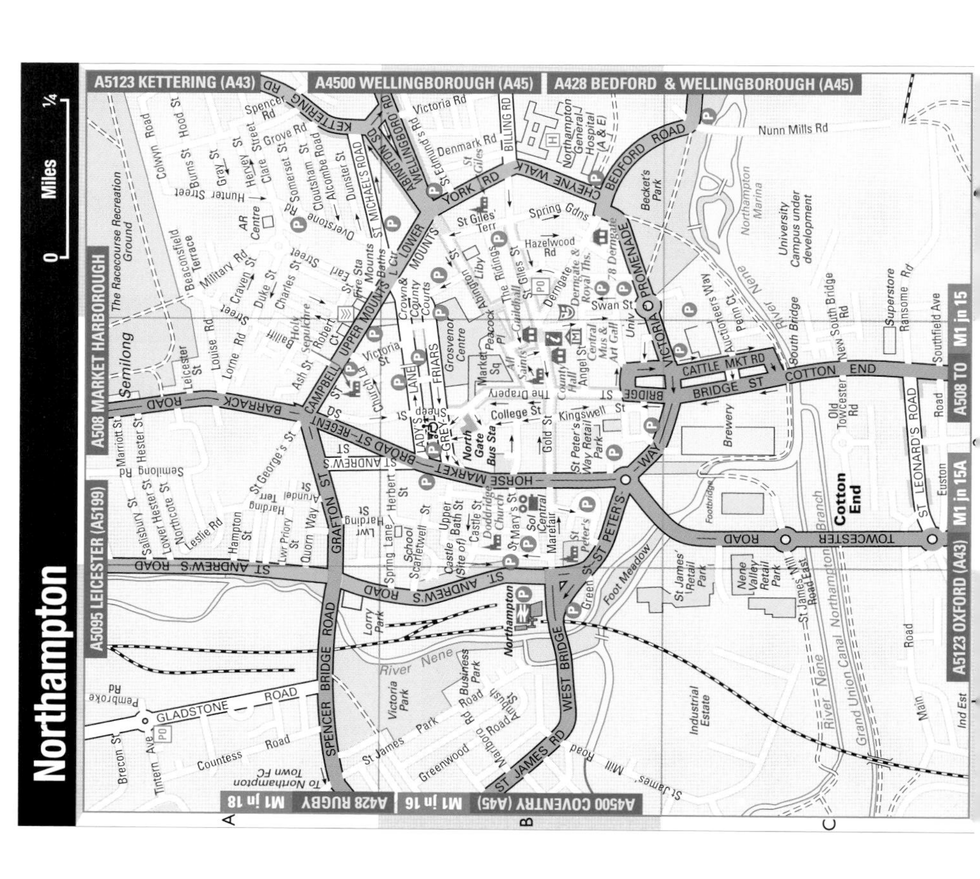

Northampton

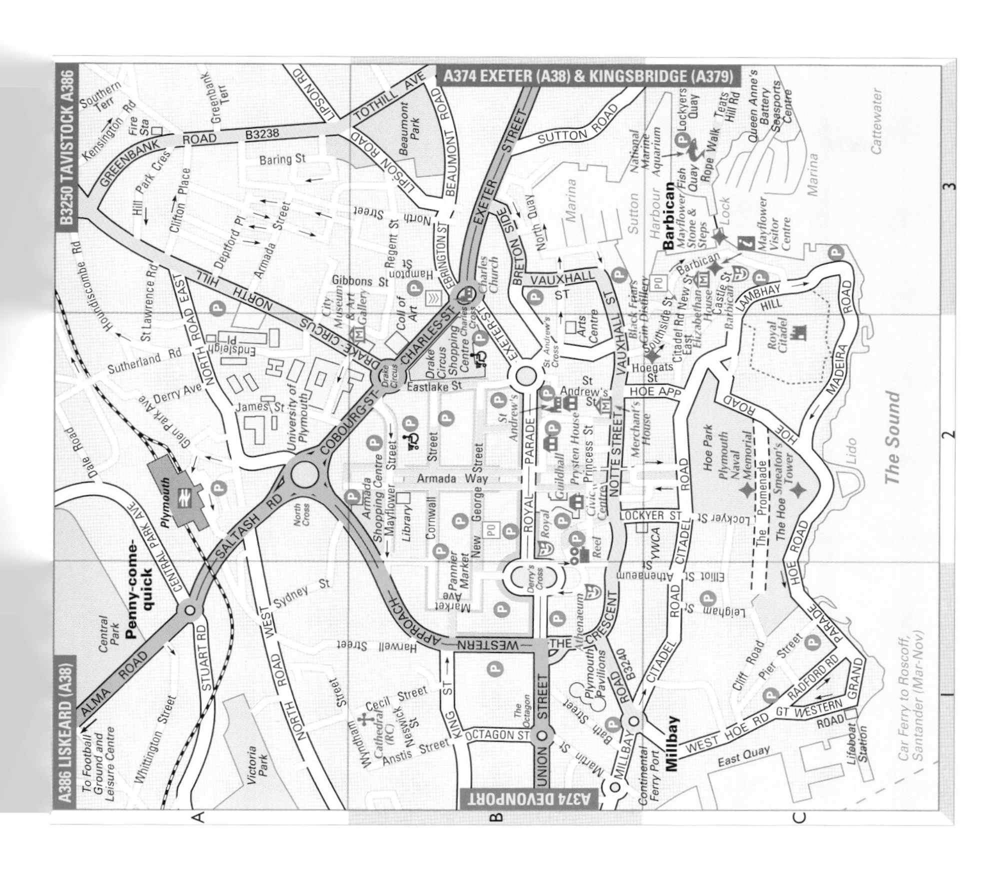
A374 EXETER (A38) & KINGSBRIDGE (A379)
B3250 TAVISTOCK A386
A386 LISKEARD (A38)
A374 DEVONPORT
Penny-come-quick
Plymouth
Barbican
Millbay
The Sound
Royal Citadel

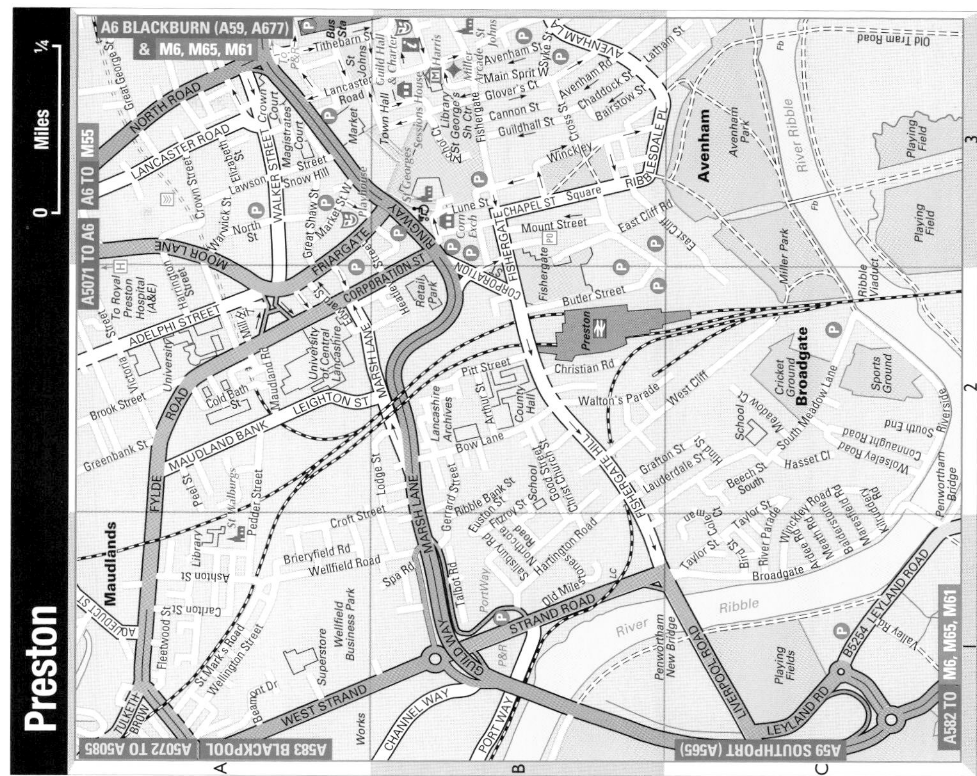
Preston
A6 BLACKBURN (A59, A677) & M6, M65, M61
A6 TO M55
A5071 TO A6
A583 BLACKPOOL
A5072 TO A5085
A59 SOUTHPORT (A565)
A582 TO M6, M65, M61
Maudlands
Avenham
Broadgate
River Ribble

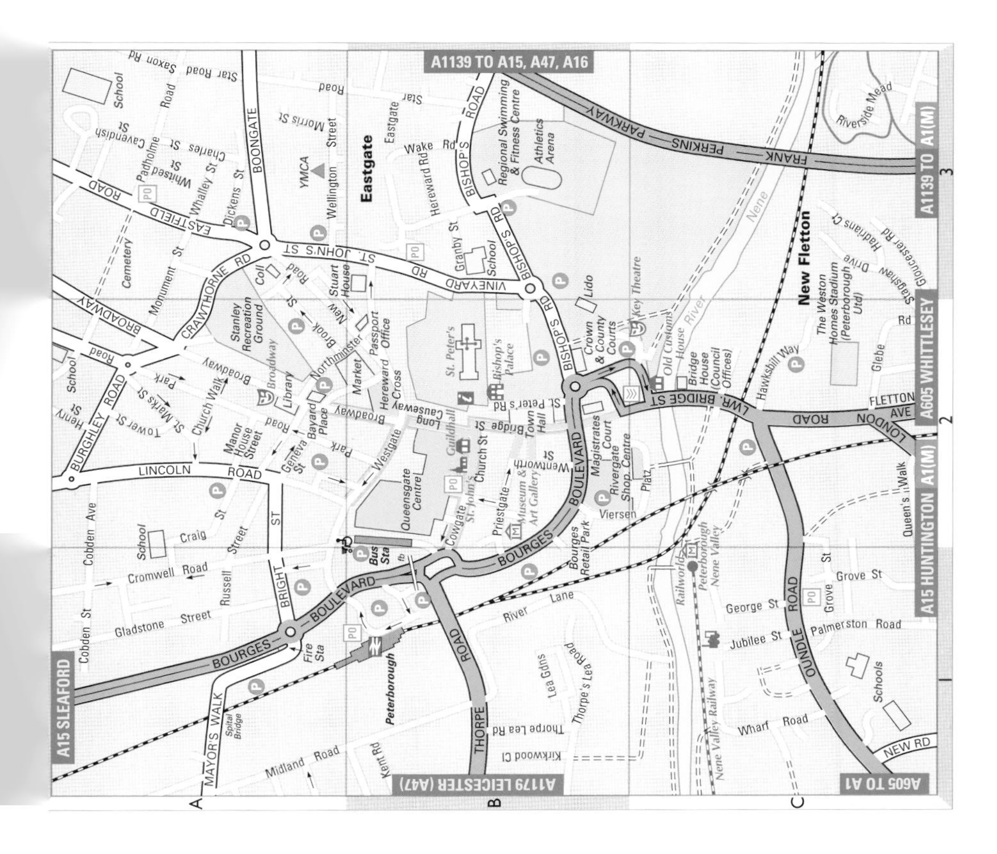
A1139 TO A15, A47, A16
A15 SLEAFORD
A1179 LEICESTER (A47)
A605 TO A1
A15 HUNTINGTON A1(M)
A605 WHITTLESEY
A1139 TO A1(M)
Eastgate
New Fletton
Peterborough

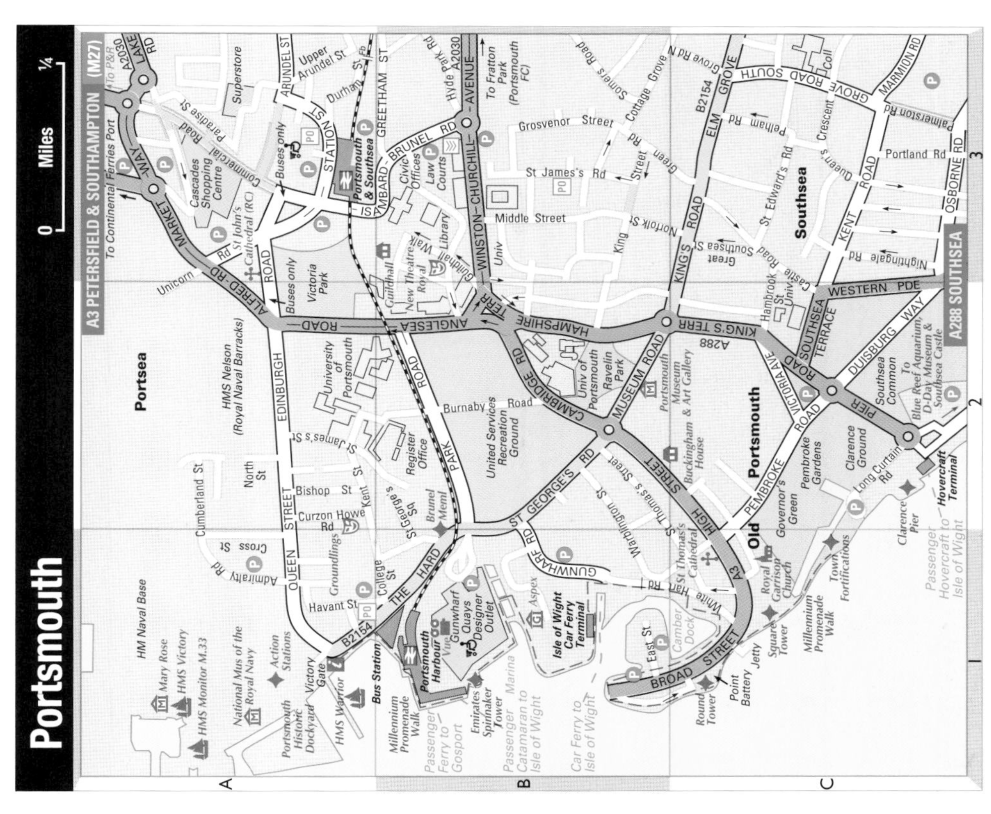
Portsmouth
A3 PETERSFIELD & SOUTHAMPTON (M27)
A288 SOUTHSEA
Portsea
Southsea
Old Portsmouth
Isle of Wight Car Ferry Terminal

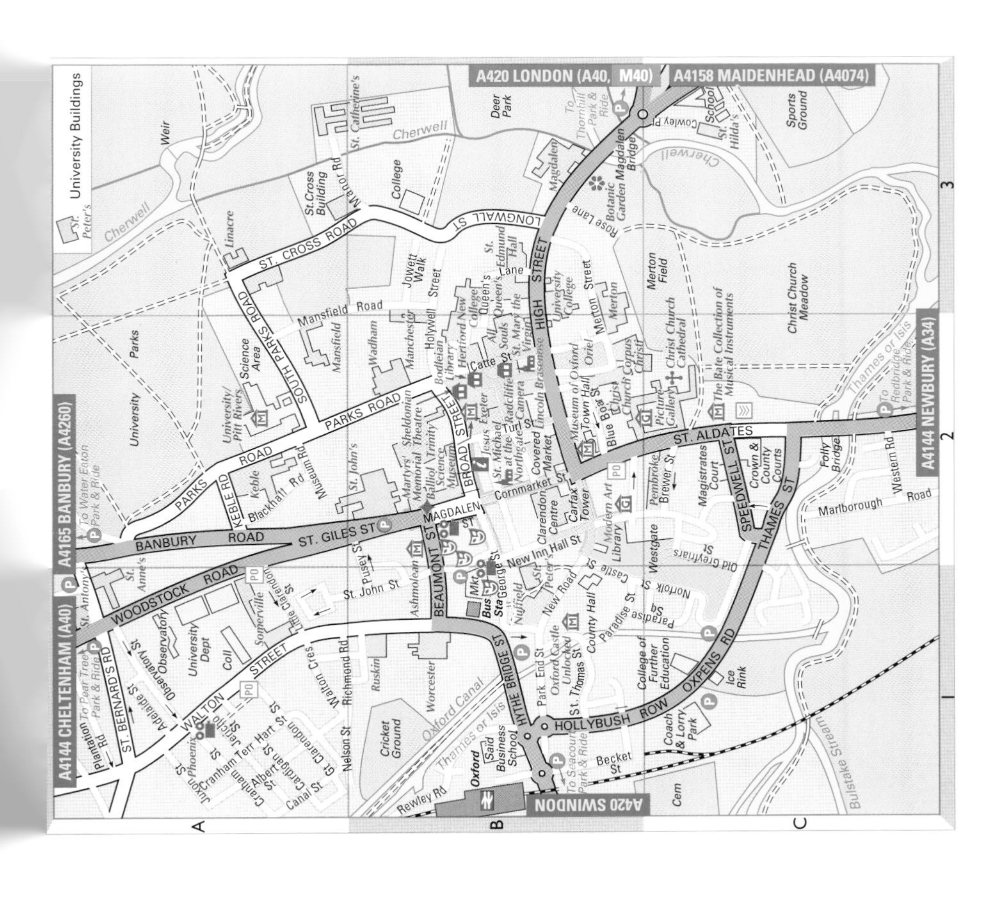
A420 LONDON (A40, M40)
A4158 MAIDENHEAD (A4074)
A4165 BANBURY (A4260)
A4144 CHELTENHAM (A40)
A420 SWINDON
A4144 NEWBURY (A34)
University Parks
Christ Church Meadow
Oxford

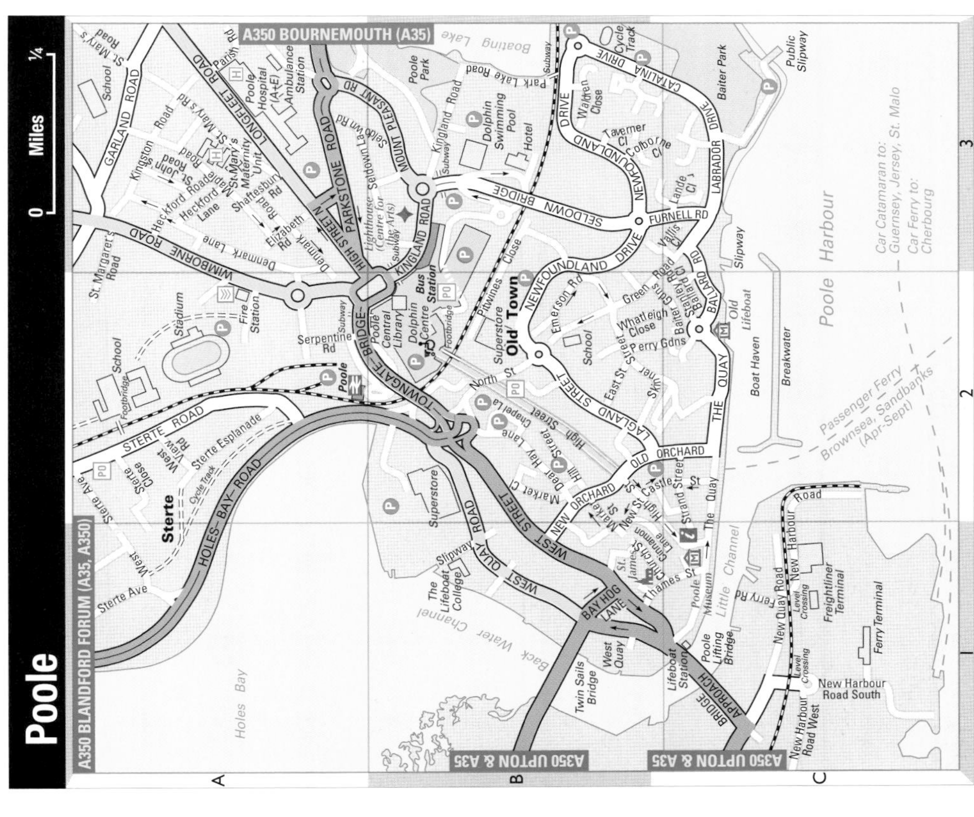
Poole
A350 BOURNEMOUTH (A35)
A350 BLANDFORD FORUM (A35, A350)
A350 UPTON & A35
Sterte
Old Town
Holes Bay
Poole Harbour

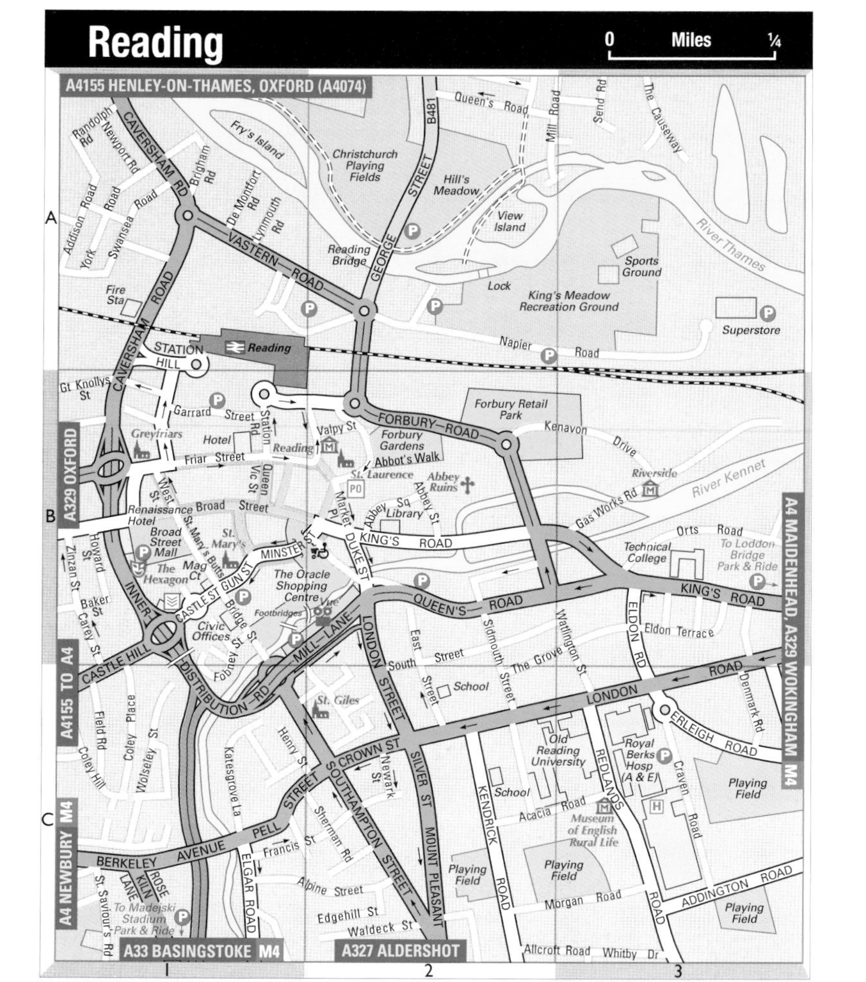
Reading
0 Miles ¼
A4155 HENLEY-ON-THAMES, OXFORD (A4074)
A329 OXFORD
A4155 TO A4
A4 NEWBURY M4
A33 BASINGSTOKE M4
A327 ALDERSHOT
A4 MAIDENHEAD, A329 WOKINGHAM M4

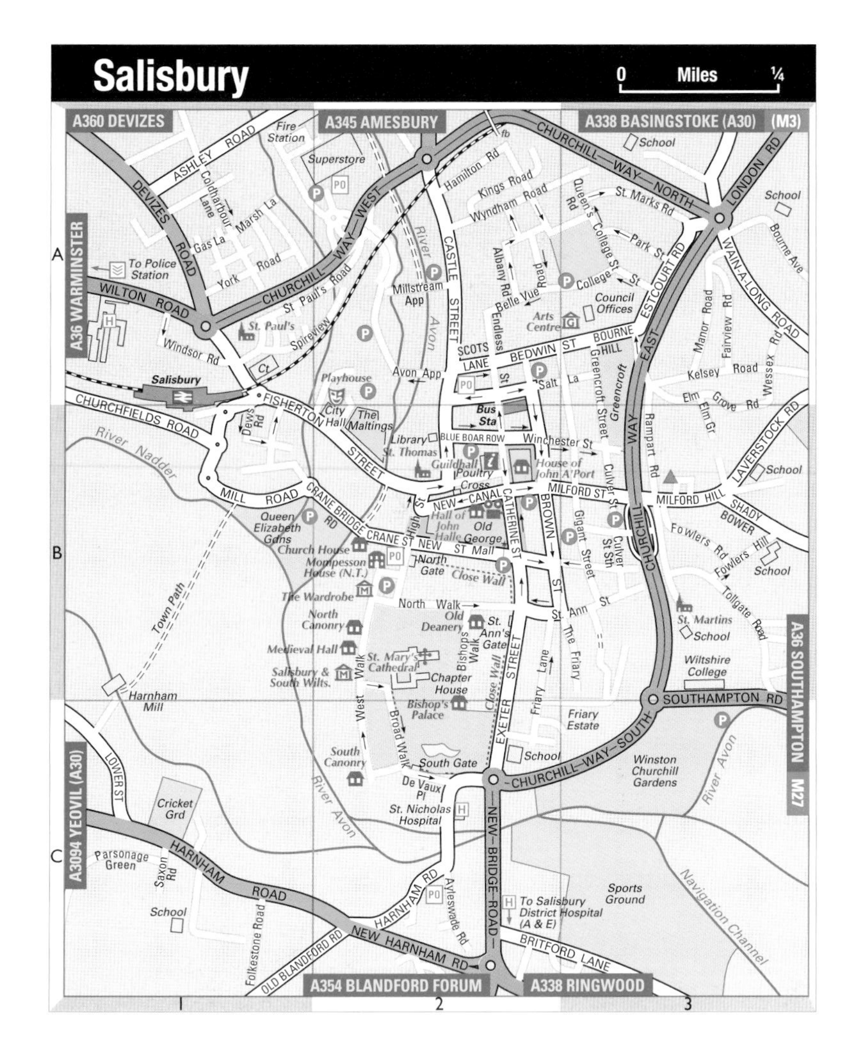
Salisbury
0 Miles ¼
A360 DEVIZES
A345 AMESBURY
A338 BASINGSTOKE (A30) (M3)
A36 WARMINSTER
A3094 YEOVIL (A30)
A354 BLANDFORD FORUM
A338 RINGWOOD
A36 SOUTHAMPTON M27

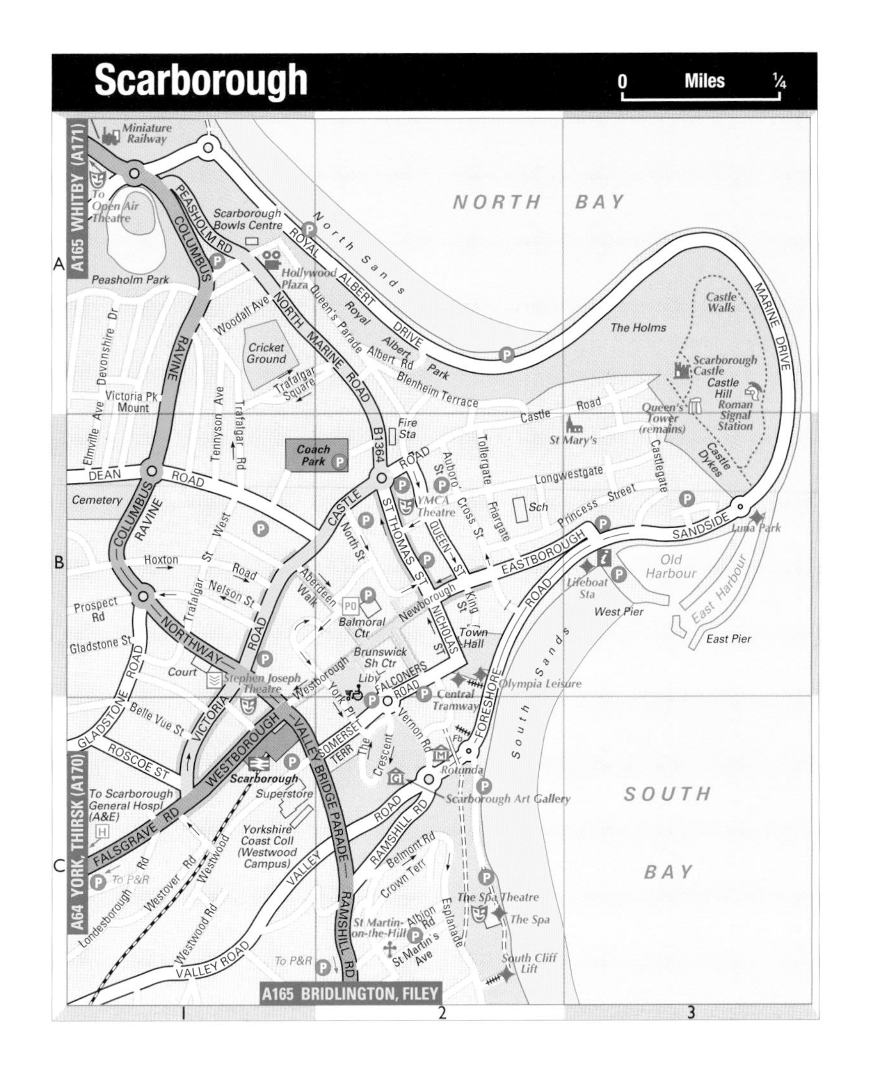
Scarborough
0 Miles ¼
NORTH BAY
SOUTH BAY
A165 WHITBY (A171)
A64 YORK, THIRSK (A170)
A165 BRIDLINGTON, FILEY

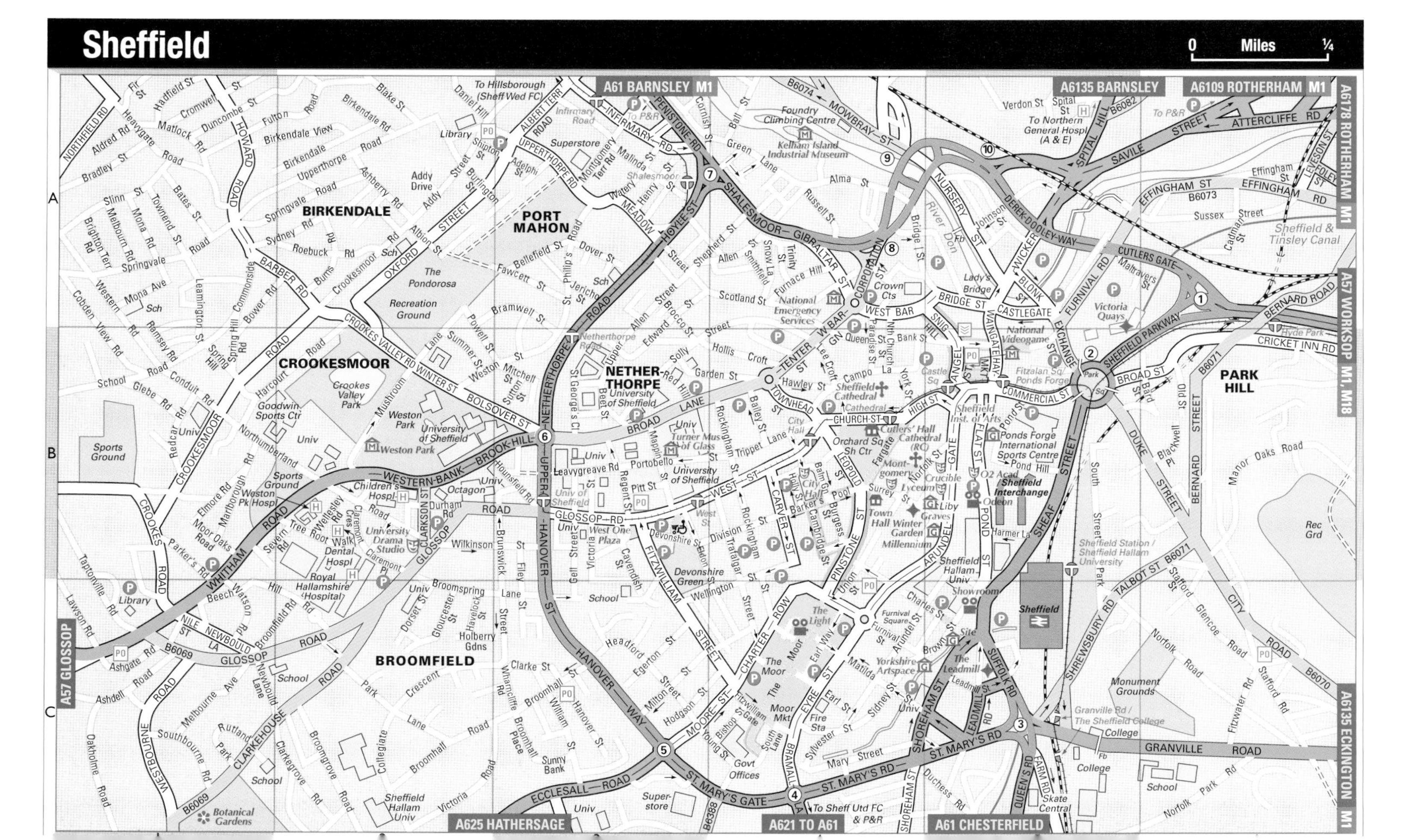
Sheffield
0 Miles ¼
A61 BARNSLEY M1
A6135 BARNSLEY
A6109 ROTHERHAM M1
A6178 ROTHERHAM M1
A57 WORKSOP M1, M18
A6135 ECKINGTON M1
A57 GLOSSOP
A625 HATHERSAGE
A621 TO A61
A61 CHESTERFIELD
BIRKENDALE
PORT MAHON
CROOKESMOOR
NETHER-THORPE
PARK HILL
BROOMFIELD

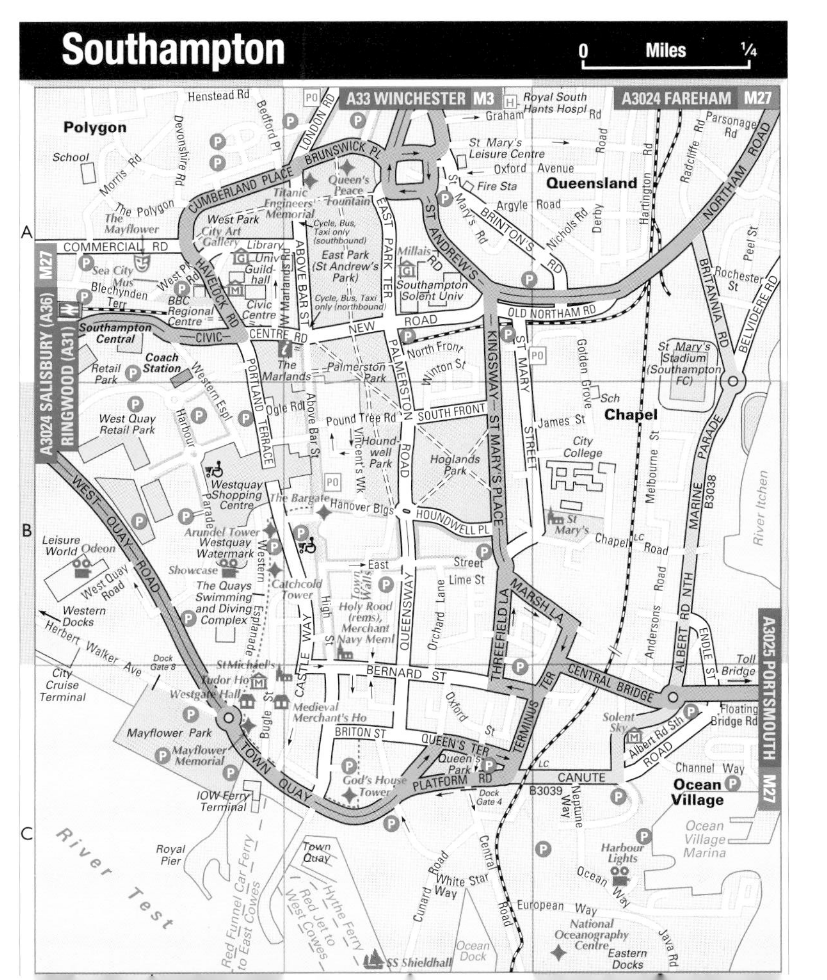
Southampton
0 Miles ¼
A33 WINCHESTER M3
A3024 FAREHAM M27
A3024 SALISBURY (A36) RINGWOOD (A31) M27
A3025 PORTSMOUTH M27
Polygon
Queensland
Chapel
Ocean Village
River Test

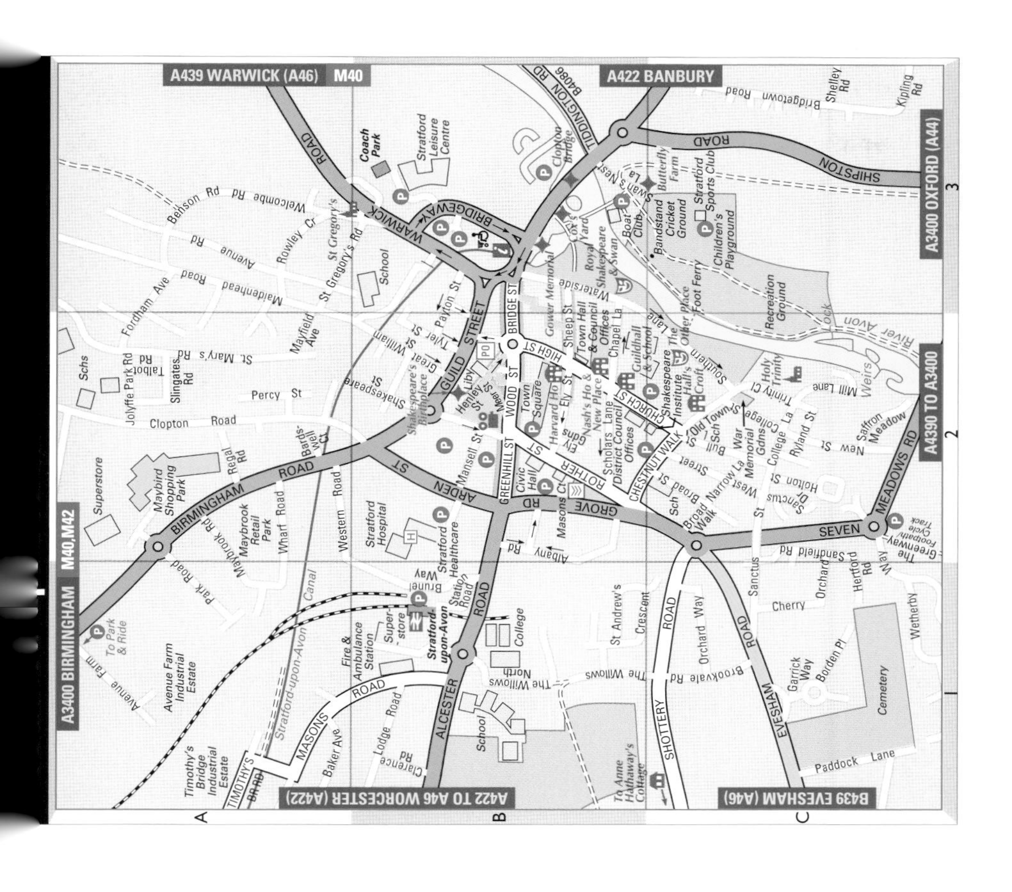
Stratford-upon-Avon

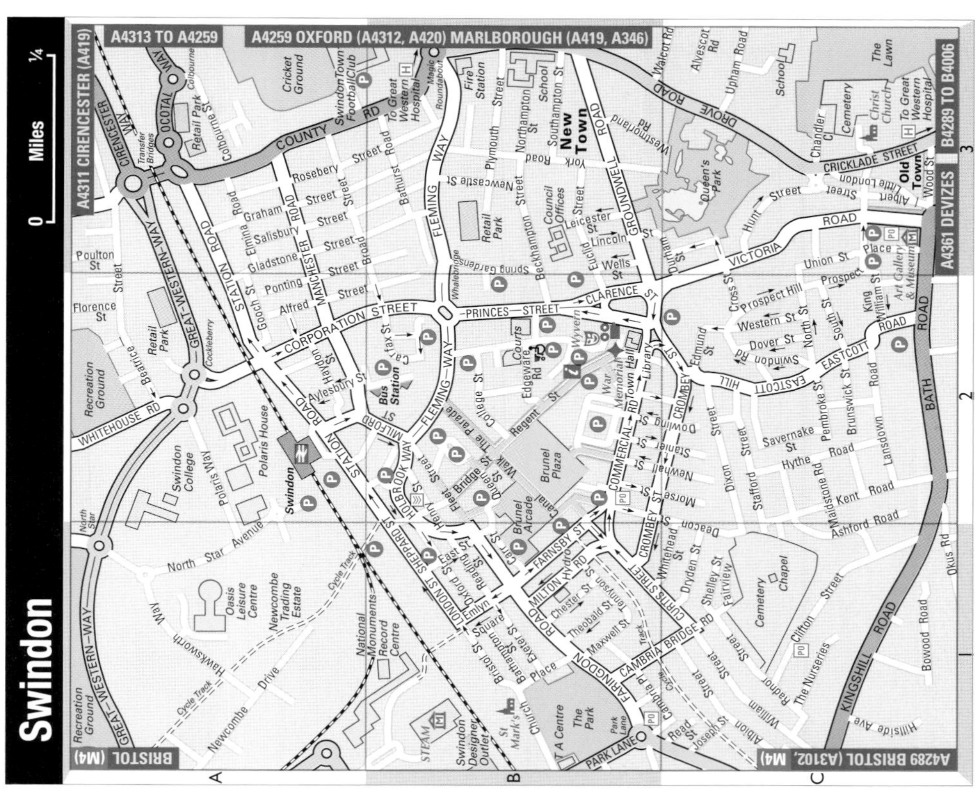
Swindon

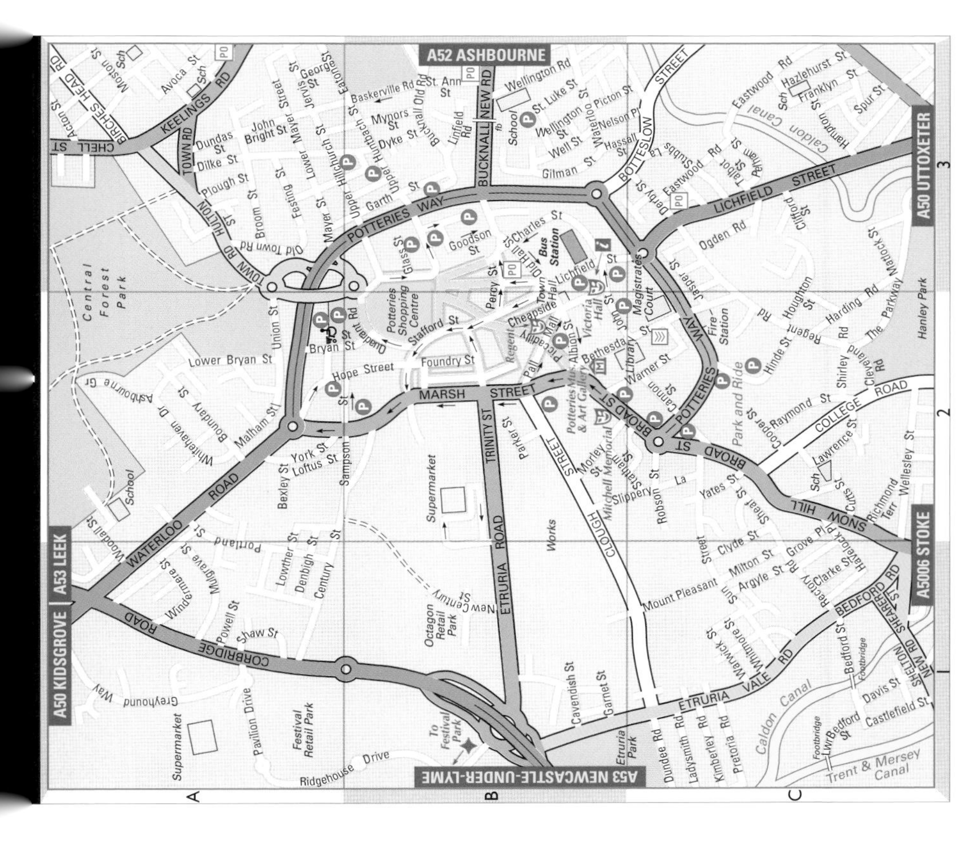
Stoke-on-Trent (Hanley)

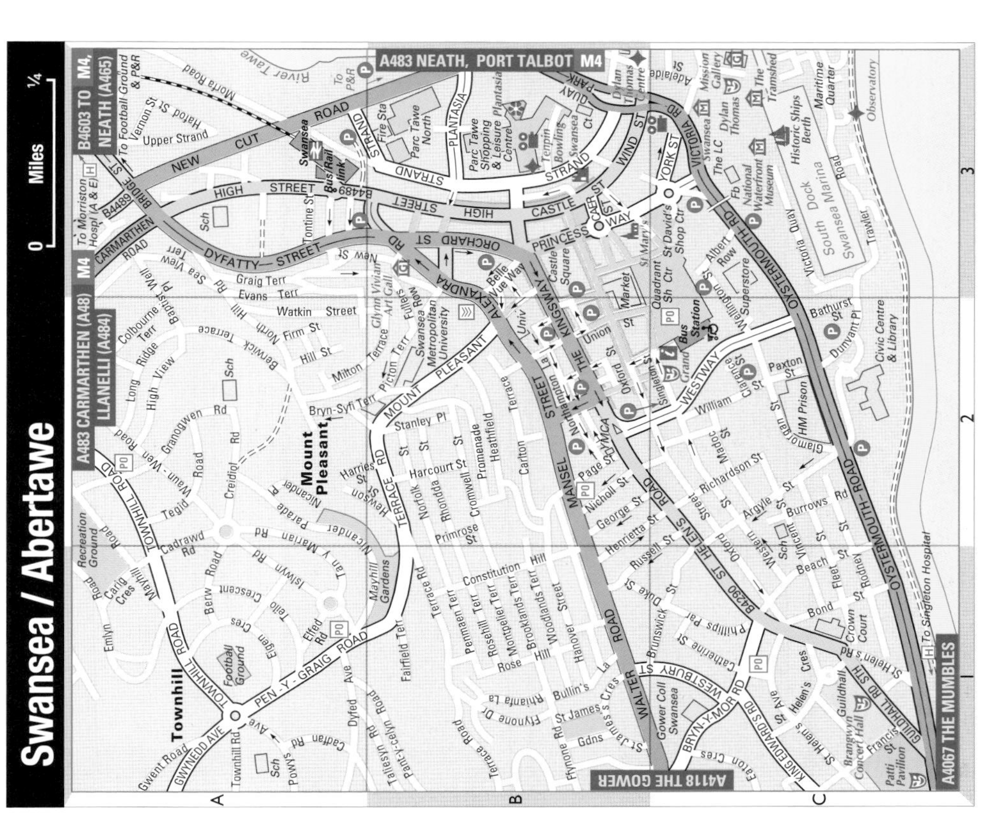
Swansea / Abertawe

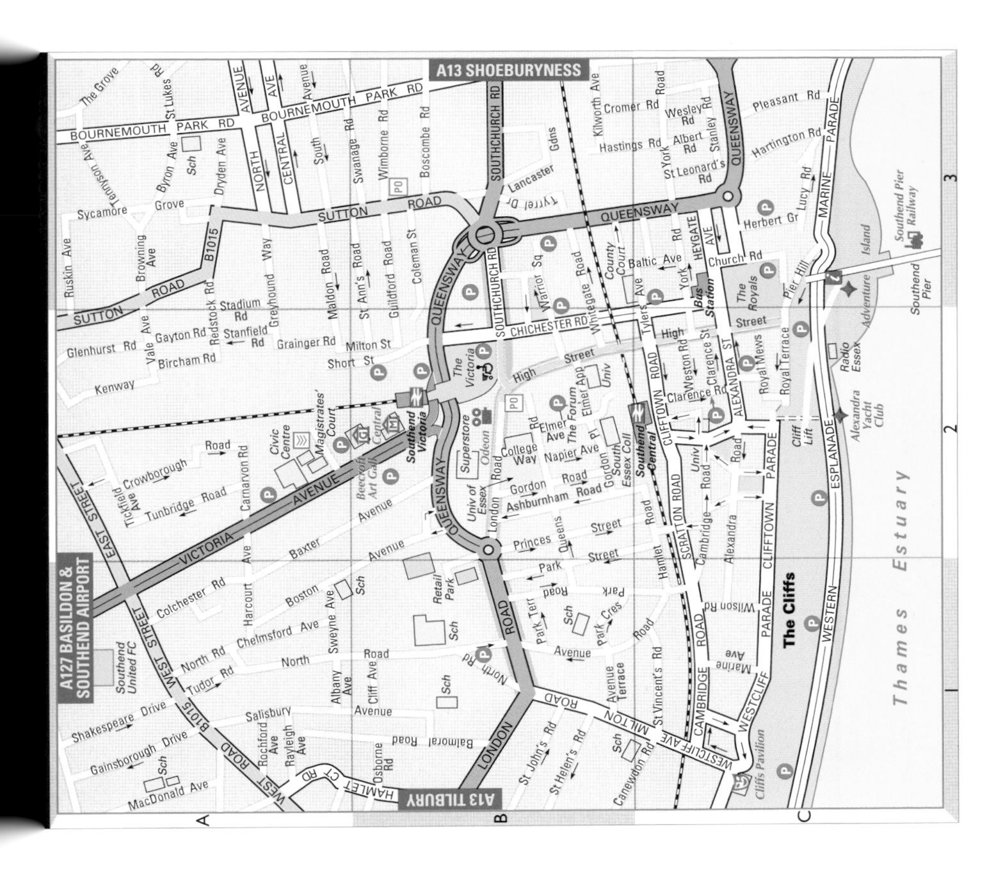
Southend-on-Sea

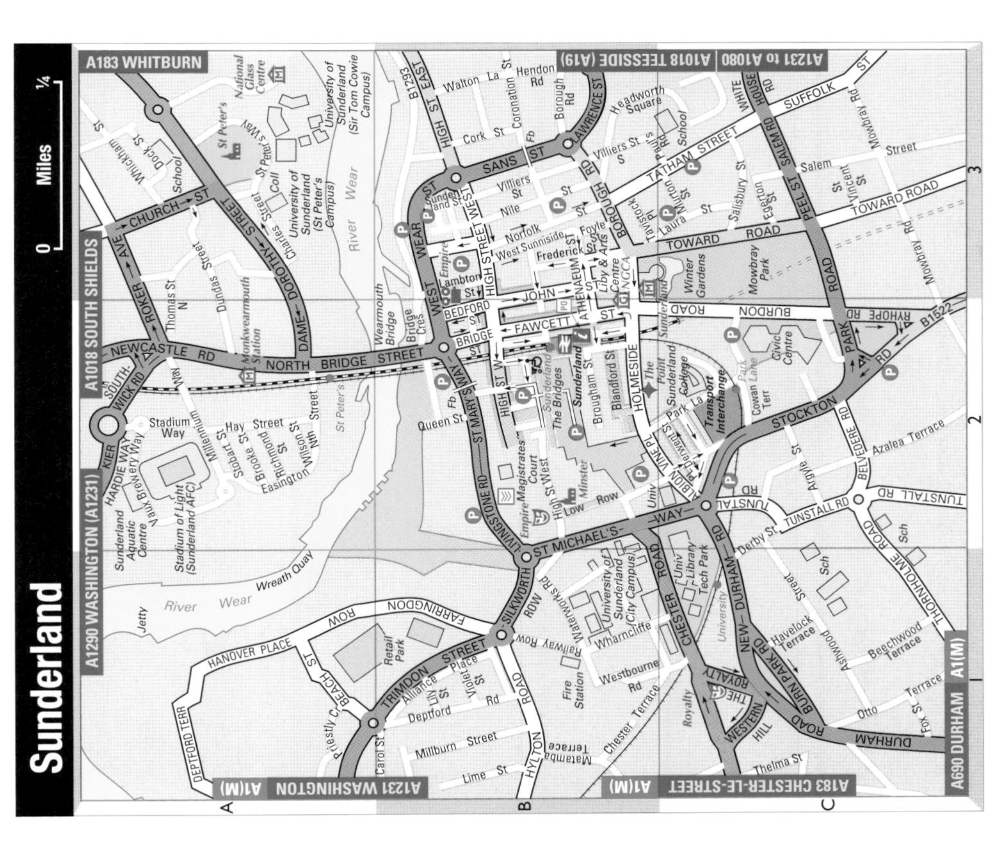
Sunderland

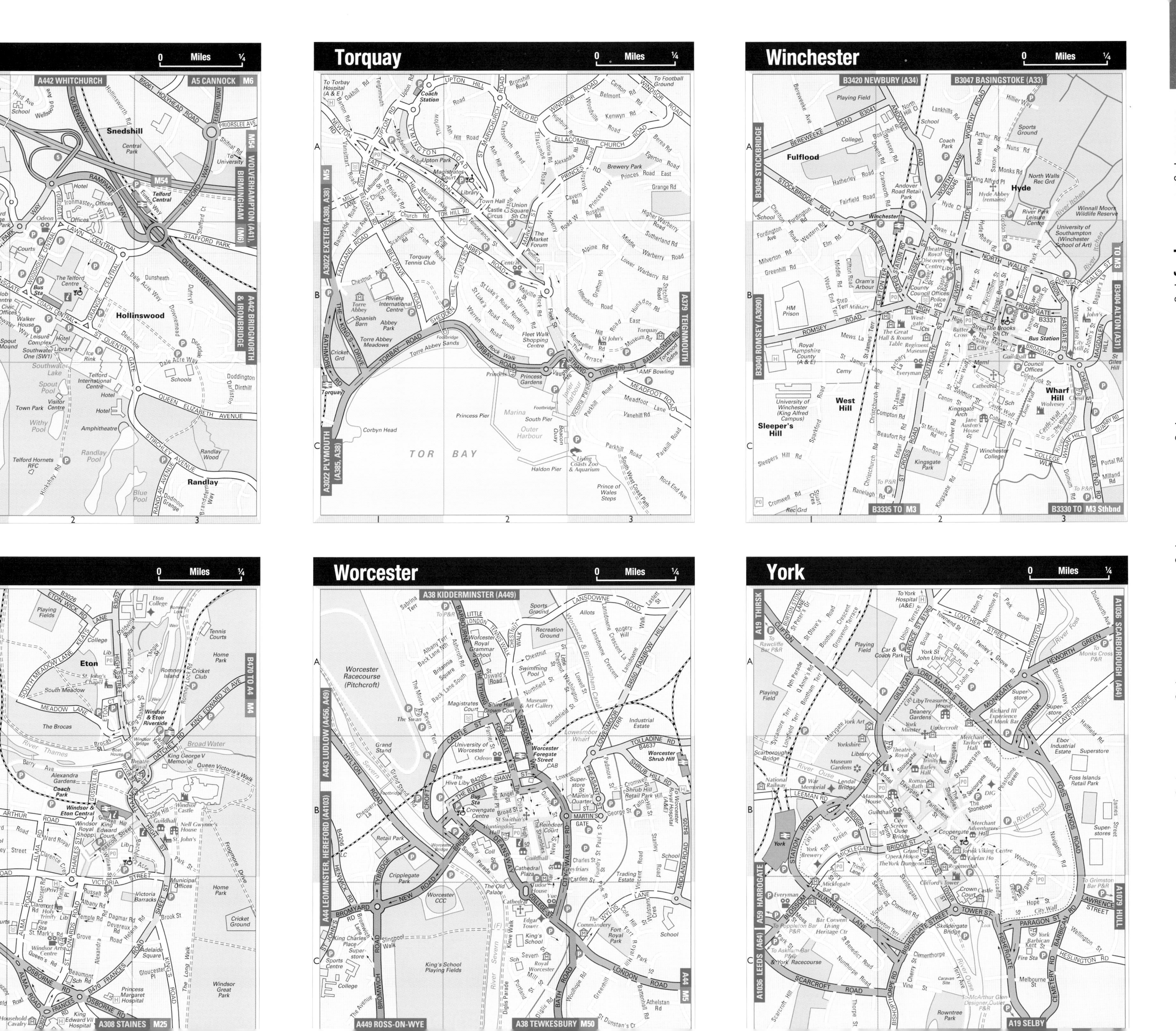
Telford
Torquay
Winchester
Windsor
Worcester
York

Town plan indexes

Chester • Chichester • Colchester • Coventry • Derby • Dundee • Durham • Edinburgh 129

Margarets Rd A2
Mary's B2
Matthew's B2
Paul's La A2
Paul's Rd A2
Paul's St A2
Stephen's Rd C1
andford Parks
Lido C3
andford Mill Road C3
andford Park C3
andford Rd C2
elkirk St A3
herborne Pl B3
herborne St B3
hopmobility B2
uffolk Parade C2
uffolk Rd C1
uffolk Sq C1
un St A1
windon Rd B1
ydenham Villas Rd C3
ewkesbury Rd A1
he Courtyard B1
hirlstaine Rd C1
voli Rd C1
voli St C1
own Hall &
Theatre B2
ownsend St A1
rafalgar St C2
nion St B3
niv of
Gloucestershire
(Francis Close
Hall) A2
niversity of
Gloucestershire
(Hardwick) A1
ctoria Pl B3
ctoria St A2
ttoria Walk C2
el Pl B2
ellesley Rd A2
ellington Rd A3
ellington Sq A3
ellington St B2
est Drive A3
estern Rd B1
inchcombe St B3
inston Churchill
Meml Gardens A1

hester 115

bbey Gateway A2
ppleyards La C3
ars,The B2
edward Row B1
eeston View C3
shop Lloyd's
Palace B2
ack Diamond St A2
ottoms La C3
oughton B3
ouverie St A1
us Interchange A2
ridge St B2
ridgegate C2
rook St A3
rown's La C2
ambrian Rd A1
anal St A2
arrick Rd C1
astle C2
astle Dr C2
athedral A2
atherine St A1
hester ≥ A3
heyney Rd A1
hichester St A1
ty Rd A3
ty Walls B1/B2
ty Walls Rd B1
ornwall St A2
ross Hey C3
ross,The B2
rown Ct C2
uppin St B2
urzon Park North C1
urzon Park South C1
ee Basin A1
ee La B3
elamere St A2
ewa Roman
Experience B2
uke St B2
astgate B2
astgate St B2
aton Rd C2
dinburgh Way C3
lizabeth Cres B3
re Station A2
oregate St B2
orum,The B2
rodsham St B2
amul House B2
arden La A1
eorge St A2
ladstone Ave A1
od's Providence
House B2
orse Stacks A2
reenway St C2
rosvenor Bridge C1
rosvenor Mus B2
rosvenor Park B3
rosvenor Pk Terr C1
rosvenor
Shopping Centre B2
rosvenor St B2
roves Rd B3
roves,The B3
uildhall Mus B1
andbridge C2
artington St C3
oole Way A2
unter St B2
nformation Ctr B2
ing Charles'
Tower A2
ing St A2
eisure Centre A2
ibrary B2
ightfoot St A3
Little Roodee C2
Liverpool Rd A2
Love St B3
Lower Bridge St B2
Lower Park Rd B3
Lyon St A2
Magistrates Court B2
Meadows La C3
Meadows,The B3
Military Mus C2
Milton St A3
New Crane St B1
Nicholas St B2
Northgate A2
Northgate St A2
Nun's Rd B1
Old Dee Bridge C2
Overleigh Rd C2
Park St B2
Police Station B2
Post Office
A2/A3/B2
Princess St B2
Queen St B2
Queen's Park Rd C3
Queen's Rd A3
Race Course B1
Raymond St A1
River La C2
Roman Amphitheatre
& Gardens B2
Roodee (Chester
Racecourse),The B1
Russell St A3
St Anne St A2
St George's Cres C3
St Martin's Gate A1
St Martin's Way B1
St Mary's Priory B2
St Oswalds Way A2
Saughall Rd A1
Sealand Rd A1
South View Rd A1
Stanley Palace B1
Station Rd A3
Steven St A3
Storyhouse B2
Superstore B2
Tower Rd B1
Town Hall B2
Union St B3
Univ of Chester C2
Vicar's La B2
Victoria Cres C3
Victoria Rd A2
Walpole St A1
Water Tower St A1
Water Tower,The B1
Watergate B1
Watergate St B2
Whipcord La A1
White Friars B2
York St B3

Chichester 115

Adelaide Rd A3
Alexandra Rd A3
Arts Centre B2
Ave de Chartres B1/B2
Barlow Rd A1
Basin Rd C2
Beech Ave B1
Bishops Palace
Gardens B2
Bishopsgate Walk A3
Bramber Rd C3
Broyle Rd A2
Bus Station B2
Caledonian Rd B3
Cambrai Ave B3
Canal Place C1
Canal Wharf C2
Canon La B2
Cathedral B2
Cavendish St A1
Cawley Rd B2
Cedar Dr A1
Chapel St A2
Cherry Orchard Rd C3
Chichester ≥ B2
Chichester
By-Pass C2/C3
Chichester Coll B1
Chichester
Cinema B3
Chichester
Festival B2
Chichester Gate
Leisure Pk C1
Churchside A2
Cineworld C1
City Walls B2
Cleveland Rd B3
College La A2
Cory Cl C2
Council Offices B2
County Hall B2
District B2
Duncan Rd A1
Durnford Cl A1
East Pallant B2
East Row B2
East St B2
East Walls B3
Eastland Rd C3
Ettrick Cl B3
Ettrick Rd B3
Exton Rd C3
Fire Station A2
Football Ground A2
Franklin Pl A2
Friary (Rems of) A2
Garland Close C3
Green La A3
Grove Rd C3
Guilden Rd B3
Guildhall A2
Hawthorn Close A1
Hay Rd C3
Henty Gdns B1
Herald Dr C3
Hornet,The B3
Information Ctr B2
John's St B2
Joys Croft A3
Jubilee Pk A3
Jubilee Rd A3
Juxon Cl B2
Kent Rd A3
King George Gdns A2
King's Ave C2
Kingsham Ave C3
Kingsham Rd C2
Laburnum Grove B2
Leigh Rd C1
Lennox Rd A3
Lewis Rd A3
Library B2
Lion St B2
Litten Terr A3
Litten,The A3
Little London B2
Lyndhurst Rd B3
Market B3
Market Ave B2
Market Cross B2
Market Rd B3
Melbourne Rd A3
Minerva B2
Mount La B1
New Park Rd A3
Newlands La A1
North Pallant B2
North St A2
North Walls A2
Northgate A2
Novium,The B2
Oak Ave A1
Oak Cl A1
Oaklands Park A2
Oaklands Way A2
Orchard Ave A1
Orchard St A1
Ormonde Ave B3
Pallant House B2
Parchment St A1
Parklands Rd A1/B1
Peter Weston Pl B3
Police Station C2
Post Office
A1/B2/C3
Priory La A2
Priory Park A2
Priory Rd A2
Queen's Ave C1
Riverside A3
Roman
Amphitheatre B3
St Cyriacs A2
St Martins' St B2
St Pancras A3
St Paul's Rd A2
St Richard's Hospital
(A&E) A3
Shamrock Cl A3
Sherbourne Rd A1
Somerstown A2
South Bank C2
South Downs
Planetarium C2
South Pallant B2
South St B2
Southgate B2
Spitalfield La A3
Stirling Rd B3
Stockbridge Rd C1/C2
Swanfield Dr A3
Terminus Ind Est C1
Tower St A2
Tozer Way A3
Turnbull Rd A3
Upton Rd C1
Velyn Ave B3
Via Ravenna B1
Walnut Ave A1
West St B2
Westgate B1
Westgate Fields B1
Westgate Leisure
Centre B1
Weston Ave C1
Whyke Cl C3
Whyke La B3
Whyke Rd C3
Winden Ave B3

Colchester 115

Abbey Gateway C2
Albert St A1
Albion Grove C2
Alexandra Rd C1
Artillery St C3
Arts Centre B1
Balkerne Hill B1
Barrack St C3
Beaconsfield Rd C1
Beche Rd C3
Bergholt Rd A1
Bourne Rd C3
Brick Kiln Rd A1
Brigade Grove C2
Bristol Rd B2
Broadlands Way A3
Brook St B3
Bury Cl B2
Bus Sta B2
Butt Rd C1
Campion Rd C2
Cannon St C3
Canterbury Rd C2
Captain Gardens C2
Castle B2
Castle Park B2
Castle Rd B2
Catchpool Rd A1
Causton Rd B1
Chandlers Row C3
Circular Rd East C2
Circular Rd North C1
Circular Rd West C1
Clarendon Way A1
Claudius Rd C2
Colchester ≥ A1
Colchester Camp
Abbey Field C1
Colchester
Retail Park B1
Colchester Town ≥ C2
Colne Bank Ave A1
Colne View
Retail Park A2
Compton Rd A3
Cowdray Ave A1/A2
Cowdray Ctr,The A2
Crouch St B1
Crowhurst Rd B1
Culver Square
Shopping Centre B1
Culver St East B2
Culver St West B1
Dilbridge Rd A3
East Hill B2
East St B3
East Stockwell St B1
Eld La B1
Essex Hall Rd A1
Exeter Dr B2
Fairfax Rd C2
Fire Station A2
Firstsite B2
Flagstaff Rd C1
Garrison Parade C2
George St B2
Gladstone Rd C2
Golden Noble Hill C2
Goring Rd A3
Granville Rd C3
Greenstead Rd B3
Guildford Rd B2
Harsnett Rd C3
Harwich Rd B3
Head St B1
High St B1/B2
High Woods Country
Park A2
Hollytrees B2
Hyderabad Cl C2
Hythe Hill C3
Information Ctr B2
Jarmin Rd A2
Kendall Rd C2
Kimberley Rd C3
King Stephen Rd C3
Leisure World A2
Library B1
Lincoln Way B2
Lion Walk Shopping
Centre B1
Lisle Rd C2
Lucas Rd C2
Magdalen Green C3
Magdalen St C2
Maidenburgh St B2
Maldon Rd C1
Manor Rd B1
Margaret Rd A1
Mason Rd A2
Mercers Way A1
Mercury B1
Mersea Rd C2
Meyrick Cres C2
Mile End Rd A1
Military Rd C2
Mill St C2
Minories B2
Moorside B3
Morant Rd C3
Napier Rd C2
Natural History B2
New Town Rd C2
Norfolk Cres A3
North Hill B1
North Station Rd A1
Northgate St B1
Nunns Rd B1
Odeon B1
Old Coach Rd B3
Old Heath Rd C3
Osborne St B2
Petrolea Cl A1
Police Station C1
Popes La B1
Port La C3
Post Office B2/C1
Priory St B2
Queen St B2
Rawstorn Rd B1
Rebon St C3
Recreation Rd C3
Ripple Way A3
Roberts Rd C2
Roman Rd B2
Roman Wall B2
Romford Cl A3
Rosebery Ave B2
St Andrews Ave B3
St Andrews Gdns B3
St Botolph St B2
St Botolphs B2
St John's Abbey
(site of) C2
St John's St B1
St Johns Walk
Shopping Centre B1
St Leonards Rd C3
St Marys Fields B1
St Peter's St B1
St Peters B1
Salisbury Ave C1
Saw Mill Rd C3
Sergeant St C2
Serpentine Walk A1
Sheepen Pl B1
Sheepen Rd B1
Sir Isaac's Walk B1
Smythies Ave B2
South St C1
South Way C1
Sports Way A2
Suffolk Close A3
Superstore A1
Town Hall B1
Valentine Dr A3
Victor Rd C3
Wakefield Close B2
Wellesley Rd C1
Wells Rd B2/B3
West St C1
West Stockwell St B1
Weston Rd C3
Westway A1
Wickham Rd C1
Wimpole Rd C3
Winchester Rd C2
Winnock Rd C2
Worcester Rd B2

Coventry 116

Abbots La A1
Albany B1
Albany Rd B1
Alma St B3
Ambulance Sta A2
Art Faculty B3
Asthill Grove C2
Bablake School A1
Barras La A1/B1
Barr's Hill School A1
Belgrade B2
Bishop St A2
Bond's Hospital B1
Broad Gate B2
Broadway C1
Burges,The B2
Bus Station A3
Butts Radial B1
Byron St A3
Canal Basin A2
Canterbury St A3
Cathedral B3
Central Six
Retail Park C1
Chester St A1
Cheylesmore Manor
House B2
Christ Church
Spire B2
City Coll A3
City Walls &
Gates A2
Corporation St B2
Council House B2
Coundon Rd A1
Coventry Station ≥ C2
Coventry Transport
Museum A2
Coventry University
Technology Park C3
Cox St A3
Croft Rd B1
Dalton Rd C1
Deasy Rd C3
Earl St B2
Eaton Rd C2
Fairfax St B2
Foleshill Rd A2
Ford's Hospital B2
Fowler Rd A1
Friars Rd C2
Gordon St C1
Gosford St B3
Greyfriars Green B2
Greyfriars Rd B2
Gulson Rd B3
Hales St A2
Harnall Lane East A3
Harnall Lane West A2
Herbert Art Gallery &
Museum B3
Hertford St B2
Hewitt Ave A1
High St B2
Hill St B1
Holy Trinity B2
Holyhead Rd A1
Howard St A3
Huntingdon Rd C1
Information Ctr B2
Jordan Well B3
King Henry VIII
School C1
Lady Godiva
Statue B2
Lamb St A2
Leicester Row A2
Library B2
Lincoln St A2
Little Park St B2
London Rd C3
Lower Ford St B3
Lower Precinct
Shopping Centre B2
Magistrates &
Crown Courts B2
Manor House Drive B2
Manor Rd C2
Market B2
Martyrs Meml C2
Meadow St B1
Meriden St A1
Michaelmas Rd C2
Middleborough Rd A1
Mile La C3
Millennium Pl A2
Much Park St B3
Naul's Mill Park A1
New Union B2
Odeon B1
Park Rd C2
Parkside C3
Planet Ice Arena B1
Post Office B2
Primrose Hill St A3
Priory Gardens &
Visitor Centre B2
Priory St B3
Puma Way C3
Quarryfield La C3
Queen's Rd B1
Quinton Rd C2
Radford Rd A2
Raglan St B3
Ringway
(Hill Cross) A1
Ringway (Queens) B1
Ringway (Rudge) B1
Ringway
(St Johns) B3
Ringway
(St Nicholas) A2
Ringway
(St Patricks) C2
Ringway
(Swanswell) A2
Ringway
(Whitefriars) B3
St John St B2
St John the
Baptist B2
St Nicholas St A2
Sidney Stringer
Academy A3
Skydome B1
Spencer Ave C1
Spencer Rec Gnd C1
Spencer Rd C1
Spon St B1
Sports Centre B3
Stoney Rd C2
Stoney Stanton Rd A3
Superstore B2
Swanswell Pool A3
Technocentre C3
Thomas Landsdail
St C2
Tomson Ave A1
Top Green C1
Trinity St B2
University B3
Univ Sports Ctr B3
Upper Hill St A1
Upper Well St A2
Victoria St A3
Vine St A3
Warwick Rd C2
Waveley Rd B1
West Orchards
Shopping Ctr B2
Westminster Rd C1
White St A3
Windsor St B1

Derby 116

Abbey St C1
Agard St B1
Albert St B2
Albion St B2
Ambulance Station B1
Arthur St A1
Ashlyn Rd B3
Assembly Rooms B2
Babington La C2
Becket St B1
Belper Rd A1
Bold La B1
Bradshaw Way C2
Bradshaw Way
Retail Park C2
Bridge St B1
Brook St B1
Burton Rd C1
Bus Station B2
Business Park A3
Caesar St A2
Canal St C3
Carrington St C3
Cathedral B2
Cathedral Rd B1
Charnwood St C2
Chester Green Rd A2
City Rd A2
Clarke St A3
Cock Pitt B3
Council House B2
Courts B1
Cranmer Rd B3
Crompton St C1
Crown & County
Courts B2
Curzon St B1
Darley Grove A1
Derby ≥ C3
Derby C2
Derwent Bsns Ctr A2
Derwent St B2
Drewry La C1
Duffield Rd A1
Duke St A2
Dunton Cl B3
Eagle Market C2
East St B2
Eastgate B3
Exeter St B2
Farm St C1
Ford St B1
Forester St C1
Fox St A2
Friar Gate B1
Friary St B1
Full St B2
Gerard St C1
Gower St C2
Green La C2
Grey St C1
Guildhall B2
Harcourt St C1
Highfield Rd A1
Hill La C2
Information Ctr B2
intu Derby C2
Iron Gate B2
John St C3
Joseph Wright Ctr B1
Kedleston Rd A1
Key St B2
King Alfred St C1
King St A1
Kingston St A1
Lara Croft Way C2
Leopold St C2
Library B1
Liversage St C3
Lodge La B1
London Rd C2
London Rd Com
Hosp C2
Macklin St C1
Mansfield Rd A2
Market B2
Market Pl B2
May St C1
Meadow La B3
Melbourne St C2
Mercian Way C1
Midland Rd C3
Monk St C1
Morledge B2
Mount St C1
Museum &
Art Gallery B1
Noble St C3
North Parade A1
North St A1
Nottingham Rd B3
Osmaston Rd C2
Otter St A1
Park St C3
Parker St A1
Pickfords House B1
Police HQ A2
Police Station B2
Post Office
A1/A2/B1/C2/C3
Pride Parkway C3
Prime Enterprise
Park A2
Prime Parkway A2
QUAD B2
Queens Leisure Ctr B1
Racecourse Park A3
Railway Terr C3
Register Office B2
Sadler Gate B1
St Alkmund's
Way B1/B2
St Helens House A1
St Mary's A1
St Mary's Bridge A2
St Mary's Bridge
Chapel A2
St Mary's Gate B1
St Paul's Rd A2
St Peter's C2
St Peter's St C2
Showcase
De Lux C2
Siddals Rd C3
Sir Frank Whittle
Rd A3
Spa La C1
Spring St C1
Stafford St B1
Station Approach C3
Stockbrook St C1
Stores Rd A3
The Pattonair
County Ground
(Derbyshire CCC) B3
Traffic St C2
Wardwick B1
Werburgh St C1
West Ave A1
West Meadows
Industrial Estate B3
Wharf Rd A2
Wilmot St C2
Wilson St C1
Wood's La C1

Dundee 116

Abertay University B2
Adelaide Pl A1
Airlie Pl C1
Albany Terr A1
Albert St A3
Alexander St A2
Ann St A2
Arthurstone Terr A3
Bank St B2
Barrack Rd A1
Barrack St B2
Bell St B2
Blinshall St B1
Broughty Ferry Rd A3
Brown St B1
Bus Station B3
Caird Hall B2
Camperdown St B3
Candle La B3
Carmichael St A1
City Churches B2
City Quay B3
City Sq B2
Commercial St B2
Constable St A3
Constitution Cres A1
Constitution Ct A1
Constitution St A1/B2
Cotton Rd A3
Courthouse Sq B1
Cowgate A3
Crescent St A3
Crichton St B2
Dens Brae A3
Dens Rd A3
Discovery Point C2
Douglas St B1
Drummond St A1
Dudhope Castle A1
Dudhope St A2
Dudhope Terr A1
Dundee ≥ C2
Dundee
Contemporary Arts
C2
Dundee High
School B2
Dundee Law A1
Dundee
Repertory C2
Dunhope Park A1
Dura St A3
East Dock St B3
East Marketgait B3
East Whale La B3
Erskine St A3
Euclid Cres B2
Forebank Rd A2
Foundry La A3
Gallagher Retail Pk B3
Gellatly St B3
Government
Offices C2
Guthrie St B1
Hawkhill B1
Hilltown A2
HMS Unicorn B3
Howff Cemetery,
The B2
Information Ctr B2
Keiller Shopping
Centre B2
Keiller Ctr,The B2
King St A3
Kinghorne Rd A1
Ladywell Ave A3
Laurel Bank A2
Law Rd A1
Law St A1
Library A2/A3
Library and Steps
Theatre A2
Little Theatre,
The A2
Lochee Rd B1
Lower Princes St A3
Lyon St A3
McManus Art Gallery
& Museum,The B2
Meadow Side B2
Meadowside
St Pauls B2
Mercat Cross B2
Murraygate B2
Nelson St A2
Nethergate B2/C1
North Lindsay St B2
North Marketgait B2
Old Hawkhill B1
Olympia Leisure Ctr B3
Overgate Shopping
Centre B2
Park Place B1
Perth Rd C1
Police Station B1
Post Office B2
Princes St A3
Prospect Pl A2
Reform St B2
Riverside Dr C2
Riverside
Esplanade C2
Roseangle C1
Rosebank St A2
RRS Discovery C2
St Andrew's C2
St Pauls
Episcopal B3
Science Centre C2
Seagate B2
Sheriffs Court B1
Shopmobility B2
South George St A2
South Marketgait B3
South Tay St B2
South Victoria Dock
Road B3
South Ward Rd B2
Tay Road Bridge C3
Thomson Ave B2
Trades La B3
Union St B2
Union Terr A1
University Library B2
Univ of Dundee B1
Upper Constitution
St A1
Verdant Works B1
V&A Museum of
Design C2
Victoria Dock B3
Victoria Rd A2
Victoria St A3
Ward Rd B1
Wellgate B2
West Bell St B1
West
Marketgait B1/B2
Westfield Pl C1
William St A3
Wishart Arch A3

Durham 116

Alexander Cres B2
Allergate B2
Archery Rise C1
Avenue,The B1
Back Western Hill A1
Bakehouse La A3
Baths B3
Baths Bridge B3
Boat House B3
Bowling A2
Boyd St C3
Bus Station B2
Castle B2
Castle Chare B2
Cathedral B2
Church St C3
Clay La C1
Claypath B3
College of St Hild &
St Bede B3
County Hall A1
County Hospital B1
Crescent,The A1
Crook Hall &
Gardens A3
Crossgate B2
Crossgate Peth C1
Crown Court B3
Darlington Rd C1
Durham ≥ A2
Durham School C2
Durham University
Science Site C3
Ellam Ave C1
Elvet Bridge B3
Elvet Court B3
Farnley Hey B1
Ferens Cl A3
Fieldhouse La A1
Flass St B1
Framwelgate
Bridge B2
Framwelgate A2
Framwelgate Peth A2
Framwelgate
Waterside A2
Frankland La A3
Freeman's Pl A3
Freeman's Quay
Leisure Centre A3
Gala Theatre &
Cinema B3
Geoffrey Ave C1
Gilesgate B3
Grey College C3
Grove,The A1
Hallgarth St C3
Hatfield College B3
Hawthorn Terr B1
Heritage Centre B3
HM Prison B3
Information Ctr B3
John St B1
Kingsgate Bridge B3
Laburnum Terr B1
Lawson Terr B1
Leazes Rd B2/B3
Library B2
Library C3
Margery La B2
Market B2
Mavin St C3
Millburngate B2
Millburngate
Bridge B2
Millennium Bridge
(foot/cycle) A2
Mountjoy Research
Centre C3
Museum of
Archaeology B2
Nevilledale Terr B1
New Elvet B3
New Elvet Bridge B3
North Bailey B3
North End A1
North Rd A1/B2
Observatory C1
Old Elvet B3
Open Treasure B2
Oriental Mus C2
Oswald Court C3
Parkside B2
Passport Office A2
Percy Terr B1
Pimlico C2
Police Station B3
Post Office A1/B2
Potters Bank C1/C2
Prebends Bridge C2
Prebends Walk C2
Prince Bishops
Shopping Centre B3
Princes St A1
Providence Row A3
Quarryheads La C2
Redhills La B1
Redhills Terr B1
Riverwalk,The B2
Saddler St B3
St Chad's College C3
St Cuthbert's
Society C2
St John's College C2
St Margaret's B2
St Mary the Less C2
St Mary's College C2
St Monica Grove B1
St Nicholas' B3
St Oswald's C3
Sands,The A3
Shopmobility B3
Sidegate A2
Silver St B2
Sixth Form College A3
South Bailey C2
South Rd C3
South St B2
Springwell Ave A1
Stockton Rd C3
Student Union B3
Sutton St B2
Town Hall B2
Univ Arts Block B3
University Coll B2
Walkergate Centre A3
Wearside Dr A3
Western Hill A1
Wharton Park A2
Whinney Hill C3
Whitehouse Ave C1
YHA C3

Edinburgh 116

Abbey Strand B6
Abbeyhill A6
Abbeyhill Cres B6
Abbeymount A6
Abercromby Pl A3
Adam St C5
Albany La A4
Albany St A4
Albert Memorial B2
Albyn Pl A2
Alva Pl A6
Alva St B1
Ann St A1
Appleton Tower C4
Archibald Pl C3
Assembly Rooms &
Musical Hall A3
Atholl Cres B1
Atholl Crescent La C1
Bank St B4
Barony St A4
Beaumont Pl C5
Belford Rd B1
Belgrave Cres A1
Belgrave Cres La A1
Bell's Brae B1
Blackfriars St B4
Blair St B4
Bread St C2
Bristo Pl C4
Bristo St C4
Brougham St C2
Broughton St A4
Brown St C5
Brunton Terr A6
Buckingham Terr A1
Burial Ground A6
Bus Station A4
Caledonian Cres C1
Caledonian Rd C1
Calton Hill A4
Calton Hill A5
Calton Rd B4
Camera Obscura &
Outlook Tower B3
Candlemaker Row C4
Canning St B2
Canongate B5
Canongate B5
Carlton St A1
Carlton Terr A6
Carlton Terrace La A6
Castle St B2
Castle Terr B2
Castlehill B3
Central Library B4
Chalmers Hosp C3
Chalmers St C3
Chambers St C4
Chapel St C4
Charles St C4
Charlotte Sq B2
Chester St B1
Circus La A2
Circus Pl A2
City Art Centre B4
City Chambers B4
City Observatory A5
Clarendon Cres A1
Clerk St C5
Coates Cres B1
Cockburn St B4
College of Art C3
Comely Bank Ave A1
Comely Bank Row A1
Cornwall St C2
Cowans Cl C5
Cowgate B4
Cranston St B5
Crichton St C4
Croft-An-Righ A6
Cumberland St A2
Dalry Pl C1
Dalry Rd C1
Danube St A1
Darnawy St A2
David Hume Tower C4
Davie St C5
Dean Bridge A1
Dean Gdns A1
Dean Park Cres A1
Dean Park Mews A1
Dean Park St A1
Dean Path B1
Dean St A1
Dean Terr A1
Dewar Pl C1
Dewar Place La C1
Doune Terr A2
Drummond Pl A3
Drummond St C5
Drumsheugh Gdns B1
Dublin Mews A3
Dublin St A4
Dublin St La South A4
Dumbiedykes Rd B5
Dundas St A3
Dynamic Earth B6
Earl Grey St C2
East
Crosscauseway C5
East Market St B4
East Norton Pl A6
East Princes St
Gdns B3
Easter Rd A6
Edinburgh
(Waverley) ≥ B4
Edinburgh
Castle B3
Edinburgh
Dungeon B4
Edinburgh Int
Conference Ctr C2
Elder St A4
Esplanade B3
Eton Terr A1
Eye Pavilion C3
Festival Office B3
Festival Theatre
Edinburgh C4
Filmhouse C2
Fire Station C2
Floral Clock B3
Forres St A2
Forth St A4
Fountainbridge C2
Frederick St A3
Freemasons' Hall B3
Fruitmarket B4
Gardner's Cres C2
George Heriot's
School C3
George IV Bridge B4
George Sq C4
George Sq La C4
George St B3
Georgian House B2
Gladstone's Land
B3
Glen St C3
Gloucester La A2
Gloucester Pl A2
Gloucester St A2
Graham St C3
Grassmarket C3
Great King St A3
Great Stuart B1
Greenside La A5
Greenside Row A5
Greyfriars Kirk C4
Grindlay St C2
Grosvenor St C1
Grove St C1
Gullan's Close B5
Guthrie St B4
Hanover St A3
Hart St A4
Haymarket C1
Haymarket Sta ≥ C1
Heriot Pl C3
Heriot Row A2
High School Yard B5
High St B4
Hill Pl C5
Hill St A2
Hillside Cres A5
Holyrood Abbey,
remains of
(AD 1128) A6
Holyrood Gait B6

Holyrood Park C6
Holyrood Rd B5
Home St C2
Hope St B2
Horse Wynd B6
Howden St C5
Howe St A2
Hub,The ✦ B3
India Pl A2
India St A2
Infirmary St B4
Information Ctr B4
Jeffrey St B4
John Knox Ho B4
Johnston Terr C3
Keir St C3
Kerr St A2
King's Stables Rd B2
Lady Lawson St C3
Lauriston Gdns C3
Lauriston Park C3
Lauriston Pl C3
Lauriston St C3
Lawnmarket B3
Learmonth Gdns A1
Learmonth Terr A1
Leith St A4
Lennox St A1
Lennox St La A1
Leslie Pl A2
London Rd A5
Lothian Rd B2
Lothian St C4
Lower Menz Pl A6
Lynedoch Pl B1
Manor Pl B1
Market St B4
Marshall St C4
Maryfield A6
McEwan Hall C4
Medical School C4
Melville St B1
Meuse La B4
Middle Mdw Walk C4
Milton St A6
Montrose Terr A6
Moray Place A2
Morrison Link C1
Morrison St C1
Mound Pl B3
Mound,The B3
Multrees Walk A4
Mus Collections Ctr A4
Museum of Childhood B5
Museum of Edinburgh B5
Museum of Fire C3
Museum on the Mound B4
National Archives of Scotland A4
National Museum of Scotland C4
National Gallery B3
National Library of Scotland B4
National Monument ✦ A5
National Portrait Gallery B4
National War Museum B3
Nelson Monument ✦ A5
Nelson St A3
New St B5
Nicolson Sq C4
Nicolson St C4
Niddry St B4
North Bank St B3
North Bridge B4
North Castle St A2
North Charlotte St A2
North Mdw Walk C3
North St Andrew St A4
North St David St A3
North West Cir Pl A2
Northumberland St A3
Odeon C2
Old Royal High School A5
Old Tolbooth Wynd B5
OMNi Centre ✦ A4
Oxford Terr A1
Palace of Holyroodhouse B6
Palmerston Pl B1
Panmure Pl C3
Parliament Sq B4
People's Story, The B5
Playhouse Theatre A4
Pleasance C5
Police Station A4
Ponton St C2
Post Office A3/B4/B5/C1/C2/C4
Potterrow C4
Princes Mall B4
Princes St B3
Princes St B3
Prisoners of War B3
Queen's Gallery B6
Queen St A2
Queen Street Gdns A3
Queen's Dr B6/C6
Queensferry Rd A1
Queensferry St B1
Queensferry St La B2
Radical Rd C6
Randolph Cres B1
Regent Gdns A5
Regent Rd B5
Regent Rd Park A6
Regent Terr A5
Richmond La C5
Richmond Pl C5
Rose St B2
Ross Open Air Theatre B3
Rothesay Pl B1
Rothesay Terr B1
Roxburgh Pl C5
Roxburgh St C5
Royal Bank of Scotland A4
Royal Circus A2
Royal Lyceum C2
Royal Mile,The B5
Royal Scottish Academy B3
Royal Terr A5
Royal Terrace Gdns A5
Rutland Sq B2
Rutland St B2
St Andrew Sq A4
St Andrew Sq A4
St Andrew's House A4
St Bernard's Cres A1
St Bernard's Well ✦ A1
St Cecilia's Hall B4
St Colme St A2
St Cuthbert's B2
St Giles' B4
St John St B5
St John's B2
St John's Hill B5
St Leonard's Hill C5
St Leonard's La C5
St Leonard's St C5
St Mary's A4
St Mary's Scottish Episcopal B1
St Mary's St B5
St Michael & All Saints C3
St Stephen St A2
Salisbury Crags C6
Saunders St A2
Scotch Whisky Experience ✦ B3
Scott Monument ✦ B4
Scottish Parliament B6
Scottish Storytelling Centre ✦ B5
Semple St C2
Shandwick Pl B2
South Bridge B4
South Charlotte St B2
South College St C4
South Learmonth Gdns A1
South St Andrew St A4
South St David St A3
Spittal St C2
Stafford St B1
Student Centre C4
Surgeons' Hall C5
Supreme Courts B4
Teviot Pl C4
Thistle St A3
Torphichen Pl C1
Torphichen St C1
Traverse Theatre B2
Tron Sq B4
Tron,The ✦ B4
Union St A4
University C4
University Library C4
Univ of Edinburgh B5
Upper Grove Pl C1
Usher Hall C2
Vennel C3
Victoria St B3
Viewcraig Gdns B5
Viewcraig St B5
Vue A4
Walker St B1
Waterloo Pl A4
Waverley Bridge B4
Wemyss Pl A2
West Approach Rd C1
West Crosscauseway C5
West End Princess St B1
West Maitland St C1
West of Nicholson St C4
West Port C3
West Princes Street Gardens B3
West Richmond St C5
West Tollcross C2
White Horse Cl ✦ B6
William St B1
Windsor St A5
Writer's Museum, The B4
York La A4
York Pl A4
York Pl A4
Young St B2

Exeter 117

Alphington St C1
Athelstan Rd B3
Bampfylde St B2
Barnardo Rd C3
Barnfield Hill B3
Barnfield Rd B2/B3
Barnfield Theatre B2
Bartholomew St East B1
Bartholomew St West B1
Bear St B2
Beaufort Rd C1
Bedford St B2
Belgrave Rd A3
Belmont Rd A3
Blackall Rd A2
Blackboy Rd A3
Bonhay Rd B1
Bull Meadow Rd C2
Bus & Coach Sta B3
Castle St B2
Cecil Rd C1
Cheeke St A3
Church Rd C1
Chute St A3
City Wall B1/B2
Civic Centre B2
Clifton Rd B3
Clifton St B3
Clock Tower A1
College Rd B3
Colleton Cres C2
Commercial Rd C1
Coombe St B2
Cowick St C1
Crown Courts B2
Custom House C2
Cygnet New Theatre C2
Danes' Rd A2
Denmark Rd B3
Devon County Hall C3
Devonshire Pl A3
Dinham Cres B1
East Grove Rd C3
Edmund St C1
Elmgrove Rd A1
Exe St B1
Exeter Cathedral B2
Exeter Central Station A1
Exeter City Football Ground A3
Exeter College A1
Exeter Picture House B1
Fire Station A1
Fore St B1
Friars Walk C2
Guildhall B2
Guildhall Shopping Centre B2
Harlequins Shopping Centre B1
Haven Rd C2
Heavitree Rd B3
Hele Rd A1
High St B2
HM Prison A2
Holloway St C2
Hoopern St A2
Horseguards A2
Howell Rd A1
Information Ctr B3
Iron Bridge B1
Isca Rd C1
Jesmond Rd A3
King St B1
King William St A2
Larkbeare Rd C2
Leisure Centre C1
Library B2
Longbrook St A2
Longbrook Terr A2
Lower North St B1
Lucky La C2
Lyndhurst Rd C3
Magdalen Rd B3
Magdalen St B2
Market B2
Market St B2
Marlborough Rd C3
Mary Arches St B1
Matford Ave C3
Matford La C3
Matford Rd C3
May St A3
Mol's Coffee House B2
New Bridge St B1
New North Rd A1/A2
North St B1
Northernhay St B1
Norwood Ave C3
Odeon A3
Okehampton St C1
Old Mill Cl C2
Old Tiverton Rd A3
Oxford Rd A3
Paris St B2
Parr St A3
Paul St B1
Pennsylvania Rd A2
Police HQ B3
Portland Street A3
Post Office A3/B2/B3/C1
Powderham Cres A3
Preston St B1
Princesshay Shopping Centre B2
Pyramids Leisure Centre B3
Quay,The C2
Queen St A1
Queen's Terr A1
Queens Rd C1
Radford Rd C2
Richmond Rd A1
Roberts Rd C2
Rougemont Castle A2
Rougemont Ho ✦ B2
Royal Albert Memorial Mus B2
St David's Hill A1
St James' Pk Sta A3
St James' Rd A3
St Leonard's Rd C3
St Mary Steps C1
St Nicholas Priory B1
St Thomas Sta C1
Sandford Walk B3
School for the Deaf C2
School Rd C1
Sidwell St A2
Smythen St B1
South St B2
Southernhay East B2
Southernhay West B2
Spacex Gallery B1
Spicer Rd B3
Sports Centre A3
Summerland St A3
Sydney Rd C1
Tan La C2
Thornton Hill A2
Topsham Rd C3
Tucker's Hall B1
Tudor St B1
Underground Passages ✦ B2
Univ of Exeter (St Luke's Campus) B3
Velwell Rd A1
Verney St A3
Water La C1/C2
Weirfield Rd C2
Well St A3
West Ave A2
West Grove Rd C3
Western Way A3/B1/B2
Willeys Ave C1
Wonford Rd B3/C3
York Rd A2

Glasgow 117

Admiral St C2
Albert Bridge C5
Albion St B5
Anderston B3
Anderston Quay B3
Argyle Arcade B5
Argyle St A1/A2/B3/B4/B5
Argyle Street B5
Arlington St A3
Arts Centre B3
Ashley St A3
Bain St C6
Baird St A6
Baliol St A3
Ballater St C5
Barras (Mkt),The C6
Bath St A3
BBC Scotland B1
Bell St C6
Bell's Bridge B1
Bentinck St A2
Berkeley St A3
Bishop La B3
Black St A6
Blackburn St C2
Blackfriars St B6
Blantyre St A1
Blythswood Sq A4
Blythswood St B4
Bothwell St B4
Brand St C1
Breadalbane St A2
Bridge St C4
Bridge St C4
Bridgegate C5
Briggait C5
Broomielaw B4
Broomielaw Quay Gardens B3
Brown St B4
Brunswick St B5
Buccleuch St A3
Buchanan Bus Sta A5
Buchanan Galleries A5
Buchanan St B5
Buchanan St B5
Cadogan St B4
Caledonian Univ A5
Calgary St A5
Cambridge St A4
Canal St A5
Candleriggs B5
Carlton Pl C4
Carnarvon St A3
Carrick St B4
Castle St B6
Cathedral Sq B6
Cathedral St B5
Central Mosque C5
Ctr for Contemporary Arts A4
Centre St C4
Cessnock C1
Cessnock St C1
Charing Cross A3
Charlotte St C6
Cheapside St B3
Cineworld A5
Citizens' Theatre C5
City Chambers Complex B5
City Halls B5
City of Glasgow Coll (City Campus) B5
City of Glasgow Coll (Riverside Campus) C5
Clairmont Gdns A2
Claremont St A2
Claremont Terr A2
Claythorne St C6
Cleveland St A3
Clifford La C1
Clifford St C1
Clifton Pl A2
Clifton St A2
Clutha St C1
Clyde Arc B2
Clyde Pl C4
Clyde Place Quay C4
Clyde St C5
Clyde Walkway C3
Clydeside Expressway B2
Coburg St C4
Cochrane St B5
College St B6
Collins St B6
Commerce St C4
Cook St C4
Cornwall St C2
Couper St A5
Cowcaddens A4
Cowcaddens Rd A4
Crimea St B3
Custom House Quay Gdns C4
Dalhousie St A4
Dental Hospital A4
Derby St A2
Dobbie's Loan A4/A5
Dobbie's Loan Pl A5
Dorset St A3
Douglas St B4
Doulton Fountain ✦ C6
Dover St A2
Drury St B4
Drygate B6
Duke St B6
Dunaskin St A1
Dunblane St A4
Dundas St B5
Dunlop St C5
East Campbell St C6
Eastvale Pl A1
Eglinton St C4
Elderslie St A3
Elliot St B2
Elmbank St A3
Esmond St A1
Exhibition Ctr B2
Festival Park C1
Film Theatre A4
Finnieston Quay B2
Finnieston St B2
Fire Station C6
Florence St C5
Fox St C5
Gallowgate C6
Garnet St A3
Garnethill St A4
Garscube Rd A4
George Sq B5
George St B5
George V Bridge C4
Gilbert St A1
Glasgow Bridge C4
Glasgow Cath B6
Glasgow Central B4
Glasgow City Free Church B4
Glasgow Green C6
Glasgow Necropolis ✦ B6
Glasgow Royal Concert Hall A5
Glasgow Science Centre ✦ B1
Glasgow Tower ✦ B1
Glassford St B5
Glebe St A6
Gorbals Cross C5
Gorbals St C5
Gordon St B4
Govan Rd B1/C1/C2
Grace St B3
Grafton Pl A5
Grand Ole Opry ✦ C2
Grant St A3
Granville St A3
Gray St A2
Greendyke St C6
Grey Eagle St B7
Harley St C1
Harvie St C1
Haugh Rd A1
Havanah St B6
Heliport B1
Henry Wood Hall A2
High Court C5
High St B6
High Street B6
Hill St A3
Holland St A3
Holm St B4
Hope St A5
Houldsworth St B2
Houston Pl C3
Houston St C3
Howard St C5
Hunter St C6
Hutcheson St B5
Hydepark St B3
Imax Cinema B1
India St A3
Information Ctr B5
Ingram St B5
Jamaica St B4
James Watt St B4
John Knox St B6
John St B5
Kelvin Hall ✦ A1
Kelvin Statue ✦ A2
Kelvin Way A2
Kelvingrove Art Gallery & Mus A1
Kelvingrove Park A2
Kelvingrove St A2
Kelvinhaugh St A1
Kennedy St A6
Kent Rd A2
Killermont St A5
King St B5
King's,The A3
Kingston Bridge C3
Kingston St C4
Kinning Park C2
Kyle St A5
Lancefield Quay B2
Lancefield St B3
Langshot St C1
Lendel Pl C1
Lighthouse,The ✦ B4
Lister St A6
Little St B3
London Rd C6
Lorne St C1
Lower Harbour B1
Lumsden St A1
Lymburn St A1
Lyndoch Cres A3
Lynedoch Pl A3
Lynedoch St A3
Maclellan St C1
Mair St C2
Maitland St A4
Mansell St C7
Mavisbank Gdns C2
Mcalpine St B3
Mcaslin St A6
McLean Sq C2
McLellan Gallery A4
McPhater St A4
Merchants' Ho B5
Middlesex St C2
Middleton St C1
Midland St B4
Miller St B5
Millennium Bridge B1
Millroad St C6
Milnpark St C2
Milton St A4
Minerva St B2
Mitchell St West B4
Mitchell Library, The ✦ A3
Modern Art Gallery B5
Moir St C6
Molendinar St C6
Moncur St C6
Montieth Row C6
Montrose St B5
Morrison St C3
Nairn St A1
National Piping Centre,The ✦ A5
Nelson Mandela Sq B5
Nelson St C4
Nelson's Monument C6
Newton Pl A3
Newton St A3
Nicholson St C4
Nile St B5
Norfolk Court C4
Norfolk St C4
North Frederick St B5
North Hanover St B5
North Portland St B6
North St A3
North Wallace St A5
O2 ABC A4
O2 Academy ✦ C4
Odeon C3
Old Dumbarton Rd A1
Osborne St B5/C5
Oswald St B4
Overnewton St A1
Oxford St C4
Pacific Dr B1
Paisley Rd C3
Paisley Rd West C1
Park Circus A2
Park Gdns A2
Park St South A2
Park Terr A2
Parkgrove Terr A2
Parnie St C5
Parson St A6
Partick Bridge A1
Passport Office A5
Pavilion Theatre A4
Pembroke St A3
People's Palace C6
Pinkston Rd A6
Pitt St A4/B4
Plantation Park C1
Plantation Quay B1
Police Mus B5
Police Station A4/A6
Port Dundas Rd A5
Port St B2
Portman St C2
Prince's Dock B1
Princes Sq B5
Provand's Lordship B6
Queen St B5
Queen Street B5
Ramshorn B5
Renfrew St A3/A4
Renton St A5
Richmond St B5
Robertson St B4
Rose St A4
Rottenrow B5
Royal Concert Hall A5
Royal Conservatoire of Scotland A4
Royal Cres A2
Royal Exchange Sq B5
Royal Highland Fusiliers Mus A3
West Glasgow Ambulatory Care A1
Royal Infirmary B6
Royal Terr A2
Rutland Cres C2
St Andrew's in the Square C6
St Andrew's (RC) ⊕ C5
St Andrew's St C5
St Enoch B5
St Enoch Shopping Centre B5
St Enoch Sq B4
St George's Rd A3
St James Rd B6
St Kent St C6
St Mungo Ave A5/A6
St Mungo Museum of Religious Life & Art B6
St Mungo Pl A6
St Vincent Cres A2
St Vincent Pl B5
St Vincent St B3/B4
St Vincent Terr B3
Saltmarket C5
Sandyford Pl A3
Sauchiehall St A2/A4
SEC Armadillo B2
School of Art A4
Sclater St B7
Scotland St C2
Scott St A4
Scottish Exhibition & Conference Ctr B1
Seaward St C2
Shaftesbury St B3
Sheriff Court C5
Shields Rd C3
Shopmobility A5
Shuttle St B6
Somerset Pl A2
South Portland St C4
Springburn Rd A6
Springfield Quay C3
SSE Hydro The B2
Stanley St C2
Stevenson St C6
Stewart St A4
Stirling Rd B6
Stobcross Quay B1
Stobcross Rd B1
Stock Exchange B5
Stockwell Pl C5
Stockwell St B5
Stow College A4
Sussex St C2
Synagogue A3
Taylor Pl A6
Tenement Ho A3
Teviot St A1
Theatre Royal A4
Tolbooth Steeple & Mercat Cross ✦ C6
Tower St C2
Trades House B5
Tradeston St C4
Transport Mus A1
Tron C5
Trongate B5
Tunnel St B2
Turnbull St C5
Union St B4
Univ of Strathclyde B6
Victoria Bridge C5
Virginia St B5
Wallace St C3
Walls St B6
Walmer Cres C1
Warrock St B3
Washington St B3
Waterloo St B4
Watson St B6
Watt St C3
Wellington St B4
West Campbell St B4
West George St B4
West Graham St A4
West Greenhill Pl B2
West Regent St A4
West Regent St B4
West St C4
West St C4
Whitehall St B3
Wilkes St C7
Wilson St B5
Woodlands Gate A3
Woodlands Rd A3
Woodlands Terr A2
Woodside Pl A3
Woodside Terr A3
York St B4
Yorkhill Parade A1
Yorkhill St A1

Gloucester 117

Albion St C1
Alexandra Rd B3
Alfred St C3
All Saints Rd C2
Alvin St B2
Arthur St C2
Barrack Square B1
Blackfriars ⊕ B1
Blenheim Rd C2
Bristol Rd C1
Brunswick Rd C2
Bruton Way B2
Bus Station B2
Cineworld C1
City Council Offices B1
City Mus, Art Gall & Library B2
Clarence St B2
Commercial Rd B1
Council Offices B1
Courts B1
Cromwell St C2
Deans Way A2
Denmark Rd A3
Derby Rd C3
Docks ✦ C1
Eastgate St B2
Eastgate,The B1
Edwy Pde A2
Estcourt Cl A3
Estcourt Rd A3
Falkner St C2
GL1 Leisure Centre C2
Gloucester Cath ⊕ B1
Gloucester Life B1
Gloucester Quays Outlet C1
Gloucester Sta B2
Gloucester Waterways C1
Gloucestershire Archive B2
Gloucestershire Royal Hospital (A&E) B3
Goodyere St C2
Gouda Way A1
Great Western Rd B3
Guildhall B2
Heathville Rd A3
Henry Rd B3
Henry St B2
Hinton Rd A2
India Rd C3
Information Ctr B1
Jersey Rd C3
King's C2
King's Walk Shopping Centre B2
Kingsholm (Gloucester Rugby) A2
Kingsholm Rd A2
Lansdown Rd A3
Library C2
Llanthony Rd C1
London Rd B3
Longhorn Ave A1
Longsmith St B1
Malvern Rd A3
Market B2
Market Pde B2
Mercia Rd A1
Metz Way C3
Midland Rd C2
Millbrook St C3
Montpellier C1
Napier St C3
Nettleton Rd C2
New Inn B2
New Olympus C3
North Rd A3
Northgate St B2
Oxford Rd A2
Oxford St B2
Park & Ride Gloucester A1
Park Rd C2
Park St B2
Park,The C2
Parliament St C1
Peel Centre,The C1
Pitt St B1
Police Station B1
Post Office B2
Quay St B1
Quay,The B1
Recreation Gd A1/A2
Regent St C2
Robert Raikes Ho B1
Royal Oak Rd B1
Russell St B2
Ryecroft St C2
St Aldate St B2
St Ann Way C1
St Catherine St A2
St Mark St A2
St Mary de Crypt B1
St Mary de Lode B1
St Nicholas's B1
St Oswald's Rd A1
St Oswald's Retail Park A1
St Peter's B2
Seabroke Rd A3
Sebert St A2
Severn Rd C1
Sherborne St B2
Shire Hall B1
Sidney St C3
Soldiers of Gloucestershire B1
Southgate St B1/C1
Spa Field C1
Spa Rd C1
Sports Ground A2/B2
Station Rd B2
Stratton Rd C3
Stroud Rd C1
Superstore A1
Swan Rd A2
Trier Way C1/C2
Union St A2
Vauxhall Rd C3
Victoria St C2
Walham Lane A1
Wellington St C2
Westgate Retail Pk B1
Westgate St B1
Widden St C2
Worcester St B2

Harrogate 117

Albert St C2
Alexandra Rd B2
Arthington Ave B2
Ashfield Rd A2
Back Cheltenham Mount B2
Beech Grove C1
Belmont Rd C1
Bilton Dr A2
BMI The Duchy Hospital C1
Bower Rd B2
Bower St B2
Bus Station B2
Cambridge Rd B2
Cambridge St B2
Cemetery A2
Chatsworth Grove A2
Chatsworth Pl A2
Chatsworth Rd A2
Chelmsford Rd B3
Cheltenham Cres B2
Cheltenham Mt B2
Cheltenham Pde B2
Christ Church B3
Christ Church Oval B3
Chudleigh Rd B3
Clarence Dr B1
Claro Rd A3
Claro Way A3
Coach Park B2
Coach Rd B3
Cold Bath Rd C1
Commercial St B2
Coppice Ave A1
Coppice Dr A1
Coppice Gate A1
Cornwall Rd B1
Council Offices B1
Crescent Gdns B1
Crescent Rd B1
Dawson Terr A2
Devonshire Pl B3
Dixon Rd A2
Dixon Terr A2
Dragon Ave B3
Dragon Parade B2
Dragon Rd B2
Duchy Rd B1
East Parade B2
East Park Rd C3
Esplanade B1
Everyman B2
Fire Station A2
Franklin Mount A2
Franklin Rd B2
Franklin Square A2
Glebe Rd C1
Grove Park Ct A3
Grove Park Terr A3
Grove Rd A2
Hampsthwaite Rd A1
Harcourt Dr B3
Harcourt Rd B3
Harrogate B2
Harrogate Convention Centre B1
Harrogate Justice Ctr (Magistrates' and County Courts) C2
Harrogate Ladies College B1
Harrogate Theatre B2
Heywood Rd C1
Hollins Cres A1
Hollins Mews A1
Hollins Rd A1
Hydro Leisure Centre,The A1
Information Ctr B1
James St B2
Jenny Field Dr A1
John St B2
Kent Dr A1
Kent Rd A1
Kings Rd A2
Kingsway B3
Kingsway Dr B3
Lancaster Rd C1
Leeds Rd C2
Lime Grove B3
Lime St A3
Mayfield Grove B2
Mercer B1
Montpellier Hill B1
Mornington Cres A3
Mornington Terr B3
Mowbray Sq B3
North Park Rd B3
Oakdale Ave A1
Oatlands Dr C3
Odeon B2
Osborne Rd A2
Otley Rd C2
Oxford St B2
Parade,The B2
Park Chase B3
Park Parade B3
Park View B2
Parliament St B1
Police Station C3
Post Office B2/C1
Providence Terr A2
Queen Parade C3
Queen's Rd C1
Raglan St C2
Regent Ave A3
Regent Grove A3
Regent Parade A3
Regent St A3
Regent Terr A3
Ripon Rd A1
Robert St C2
Royal Baths & Turkish Baths B1
Royal Pump Room B1
St Luke's Mount A2
St Mary's Ave C1
St Mary's Walk C1
Scargill Rd A1
Skipton Rd A3
Skipton St A2
Slingsby Walk C3
South Park Rd C2
Spring Grove A1
Springfield Ave B1
Station Ave B2
Station Parade B2
Stray Rein C3
Stray,The C2/C3
Studley Rd A2
Superstore B2/C1
Swan Rd B1
Tower St C2
Trinity Rd C2
Union St B2
Valley Dr C1
Valley Gardens C1
Valley Mount C1
Victoria Ave C2
Victoria Rd C1
Victoria Shopping Centre B2
Waterloo St A2
West Park C2
West Park St C2
Wood View A1
Woodfield Ave A3
Woodfield Dr A3
Woodfield Grove A3
Woodfield Rd A3
Woodfield Square A3
Woodside B3
York Pl C3
York Rd B1

Hull 117

Adelaide St C1
Albert Dock C1
Albion St B2
Alfred Gelder St B2
Anlaby Rd B1
Arctic Corsair ✦ B3
Beverley Rd A1
Blanket Row C2
Bond St B2
Bonus Arena B2
Bridlington Ave A2
Brook St B1
Brunswick Ave A1
Bus Station B1
Camilla Cl C3
Cannon St A2
Caroline St A2
Carr La B2
Castle St C2
Central Library B1
Charles St A2
Citadel Way B3
City Hall B2
City Hall Theatre B2
Clarence St B3
Cleveland St A3
Clifton St A1
Colonial St B1
Court B2
Deep,The C3
Dinostar C2
Dock Office Row B3
Dock St
Drypool Bridge
Egton St
English St
Ferens Gallery
Ferensway
Fire Sta
Francis St
Francis St West
Freehold St
Freetown Way
Früit Theatre
Garrison Rd
George St
Gibson St
Great Thornton St
Great Union St
Green La
Grey St
Grimston St
Grosvenor St
Guildhall
Guildhall Rd
Hands-on History
Harley St
Hessle Rd
High St
Hull Minster
Hull Paragon Interchange Station
Hull & East Riding Museum
Hull Ice Arena
Hull College
Hull History Centre
Hull New Theatre
Hull Truck Theatre
Humber Dock Marina
Humber Dock St
Humber St
Hyperion St
Information Ctr
Jameson St
Jarratt St
Jenning St
King Billy Statue ✦
King Edward St
King St
Kingston Retail Pk
Kingston St
Liddell St
Lime St
Lister St
Lockwood St
Maister House
Maritime Mus
Market
Market Place
Minerva Pier
Mulgrave St
Myton Swing Bridge
Myton St
NAPA (Northern Academy of Performing Arts)
Nelson St
New Cleveland St
New George St
Norfolk St
North Bridge
North St
Odeon
Old Harbour
Osborne St
Paragon St
Park St
Percy St
Pier St
Police Station
Porter St
Portland St
Post Office B1/
Posterngate
Prince's Quay
Prospect Centre
Prospect St
Queen's Gdns
Railway Dock Marina
Railway St
Real
Red Gallery
Reform St
Retail Park
Riverside Quay
Roper St
St James St
St Luke's St
St Mark St
St Mary the Virgin
St Stephens Shopping Centre
Scale Lane Footbridge
Scott St
South Bridge Rd
Sport's Centre
Spring Bank
Spring St
Spurn Lightship
Spyvee St
Stage @ the Dock
Streetlife Transport Museum
Sykes St
Tidal Surge Barrier ✦
Tower St
Trinity House
Vane St
Victoria Pier ✦
Waterhouse La
Waterloo St
Waverley St
Wellington St
Wellington St West
West St
Whitefriargate

Wilberforce Dr.... B2
Wilberforce Ho 🅿... B3
Wilberforce
  Monument ◆... B3
William St.... C1
Wincolmlee.... A3
Witham.... A3
Wright St.... A1

Ipswich 118
Alderman Rd.... A3
All Saints' Rd.... A1
...ll St.... B2
Ancaster Rd.... C1
Ancient House 🏛.. B3
Anglesea Rd.... B2
...nn St.... B2
Arboretum.... A2
Austin St.... C2
Avenue,The.... A3
Belstead Rd.... A2
Berners St.... B1
Bibb Way.... B1
Birkfield Rd.... C1
Parkfield Rd.... C1
Bolton La.... A2
Bond St.... C3
Bowthorpe Cl.... B2
Bramford La.... A1
Bramford Rd.... A1
Bridge St.... B2
Brookfield Rd.... A1
Brooks Hall Rd.... A1
Broomhill Park.... A1
Broomhill Rd.... A1
Broughton Rd.... A2
Bulwer Rd.... B1
Burrell Rd.... B2
Bus Station.... B3
Buttermarket
  Shopping Ctr,The.. B3
Cardinal Park
  Leisure Park.... C2
Carr St.... B3
Cecil Rd.... B2
Cecilia St.... C2
Chancery Rd.... C2
Charles St.... B2
Chevallier St.... A1
Christchurch Mansion
  & Wolsey Art Gallery
  🏛.... B3
Christchurch Park.. A3
Christchurch St.... B3
Civic Centre.... B2
Civic Dr.... B2
Clarkson St.... B1
Cobbold St.... B2
Commercial Rd.... C2
Constable Rd.... A3
Constantine Rd.... C1
Constitution Hill.. A3
Corder Rd.... A2
Corn Exchange 🏛.. B2
Cotswold Ave.... A2
Council Offices.... A2
County Hall.... B3
Crown Court.... B2
Crown St.... B2
Cullingham Rd.... B1
Cumberland St.... B1
Curriers La.... A2
Dale Hall La.... A2
Dales View Rd.... A1
Dalton Rd.... B2
Dillwyn St.... B1
Eliot St.... B2
Elm St.... B2
...smere Rd.... A2
Falcon St.... C2
Fire Station.... C2
Flint Wharf.... C2
Fonnereau Rd.... B2
Fore St.... C3
Foundation St.... C3
Franciscan Way.... C2
Friars St.... C2
Gainsborough Rd... A3
Gatacre Rd.... B1
Geneva Rd.... B1
Gippeswyk Ave.... C1
Gippeswyk Park.... C1
Grafton Way.... C2
Graham Rd.... A1
Great Whip St.... C3
Grimwade St.... B3
Handford Cut.... B1
Handford Rd.... B1
Henley Rd.... A2
Hervey St.... A2
High St.... B2
Holly Rd.... A2
Information Ctr ℹ.. B3
Ipswich Haven
  Marina ◆.... C3
Ipswich Museum &
  Art Gallery 🏛.. B2
Ipswich School.... A2
Ipswich Station ≥.. C2
Ipswich Town FC
  (Portman Road).. C2
Ivry St.... A2
Kensington Rd.... A1
Kesteven Rd.... C1
Kingsfield Ave.... A1
Little's Cres.... C2
Lisle Rd.... C2
London Rd.... B1
Low Brook St.... B3
Lower Orwell St.... C3
Luther Rd.... C2
Magistrates Court.. B2
Manor Rd.... A3
Mornington Ave.... A1
Museum St.... B2
Neale St.... B2
New Cardinal St.... C2
New Cut East.... C3
New Cut West.... C3
New Wolsey 🎭.. B2

Newson St.... B2
Norwich Rd.... A1/B1
Oban St.... B2
Old Custom Ho 🏛.. C3
Old Foundry Rd.... B3
Old Merchant's
  House 🏛.... C3
Orford St.... B2
Paget Rd.... A2
Park Rd.... A2
Park View Rd.... A2
Peter's St.... C2
Philip Rd.... C2
Pine Ave.... A2
Pine View Rd.... A2
Police Station 🏛.. C2
Portman Rd.... C2
Portman Walk.... C2
Post Office 🅿
  Rd.... A2
Princes St.... B1
Prospect St.... B1
Queen St.... C2
Ranelagh Rd.... C1
Recreation Ground B1
Rectory Rd.... C2
Regent Theatre 🎭.. B3
Retail Park.... C1
Retail Park.... C3
Richmond Rd.... A1
Rope Walk.... C3
Rose La.... C2
Russell Rd.... C2
St Edmund's Rd.... A2
St George's St.... B2
St Helen's St.... B3
Sherrington Rd.... A1
Shopmobility.... B3
Silent St.... C2
Sir Alf Ramsey Way C1
Sirdar Rd.... A1
Soane St.... B3
Springfield La.... A1
Star La.... C2
Stevenson Rd.... A1
Suffolk College.... C3
Suffolk Retail Park B1
Superstore.... B3
Surrey Rd.... A1
Tacket St.... C3
Tavern St.... B3
Tower Ramparts
  Shopping Centre.. B3
Tower Ramparts.... B3
Tower St.... B3
Town Hall.... B2
Tuddenham Rd.... A3
University.... C3
Upper Brook St.... B3
Upper Orwell St.... B3
Valley Rd.... A2
Vermont Cres.... A3
Vermont Rd.... A3
Vernon St.... C2
Warrington Rd.... A2
Waterloo Rd.... A1
Waterworks St.... C3
Wellington St.... B1
West End Rd.... B1
Westerfield Rd.... A3
Westgate St.... B2
Westholme Rd.... A1
Westwood Ave.... A1
Willoughby Rd.... C2
Withipoll St.... B3
Woodbridge Rd.... B3
Woodstone Ave.... B1
Yarmouth Rd.... B1

Lancaster 118
Aberdeen Rd.... C3
Adult College,The.. A3
Aldcliffe Rd.... C2
Alfred St.... B3
Ambleside Rd.... A3
Ambulance Sta.... A2
Ashfield Ave.... B1
Ashton Rd.... C2
Assembly Rooms
  Emporium ◆.... A2
Balmoral Rd.... B3
Bath House 🏛.... B3
Bath Mill La.... B3
Bath St.... B3
Blades St.... B2
Borrowdale Rd.... C3
Bowerham Rd.... C3
Brewery La.... A2
Bridge La.... B2
Brook St.... C1
Bulk Rd.... B3
Bulk St.... B2
Bus Station.... B2
Cable St.... B2
Canal Cruises &
  Waterbus ◆.... C2
Carlisle Bridge.... A1
Carr House La.... C3
Castle 🏛.... B2
Castle Park.... B2
Caton Rd.... A3
China St.... B2
Church St.... B2
City Museum 🏛.. B2
Clarence St.... B1
Common Gdn St.... B2
Coniston Rd.... A3
Cott Museum 🏛 B2
Council Offices.... C1
County Court &
  Family Court.... C1
Cromwell Rd.... C1
Crown Court.... B1
Dale St.... C2
Dallas Rd.... B1/C1
Dalton Rd.... B3
Dalton Sq.... B2
Damside St.... B2
De Vitre St.... B3
Dee Rd.... A1
Denny Ave.... A2
Derby Rd.... A3
Dukes,The 🎭... B2
Earl St.... B3
East Rd.... B3

Eastham St.... C3
Edward St.... B3
Fairfield Rd.... B1
Fenton St.... B2
Firbank Rd.... B2
Fire Station.... B2
Friend's Meeting
  House 🏛.... B3
Garnet St.... C3
George St.... B2
Giant Axe Field.... B1
Grand 🎭.... B2
Grasmere Rd.... B3
Greaves Rd.... C2
Green St.... A3
Gregson Ctr,The.... C3
Gregson Rd.... C3
Greyhound Bridge.. A2
Greyhound Bridge
  Rd.... A2
High St.... B2
Hill Side.... B1
Hope St.... C2
Hubert Pl.... B1
Information Ctr ℹ.. B2
Kelsy St.... B3
Kentmere Rd.... B3
King St.... B2
Kingsway.... A3
Kirkes Rd.... C3
Lancaster &
  Lakeland Ⓗ.... C2
Lancaster City
  Football Club.... B1
Lancaster Sta ≥.... B1
Langdale Rd.... B3
Ley Ct.... B1
Library.... B2
Lincoln Rd.... C1
Lindow St.... C2
Lodge St.... A3
Long Marsh La.... B1
Lune Rd.... A1
Lune St.... A2
Lune Valley Ramble A3
Mainway.... A2
Maritime Mus 🏛 A1
Marketgate
  Shopping Centre.. B2
Market St.... B2
Meadowside.... C2
Meeting House La.. B3
Millennium Bridge.. A2
Moor La.... B2
Moorgate.... B3
Morecambe Rd.... A1/A2
Nelson St.... B2
North Rd.... B2
Orchard La.... C1
Owen Rd.... A3
Park Rd.... B3
Parliament St.... A2
Patterdale Rd.... A3
Penny St.... B2
Police Station 🏛 B2
Portland St.... C2
Post Office 🅿.... C2
Primrose St.... C3
Priory 🏛.... B2
Prospect St.... C3
Quarry Rd.... B3
Queen St.... C2
Regent St.... C2
Ridge La.... A3
Ridge St.... A3
Royal Lancaster
  Infirmary (A&E) Ⓗ C2
Rydal Rd.... B3
Ryelands Park.... A1
St Georges Quay.... A2
St John's 🏛.... B2
St Leonard's Gate.. B3
St Martin's Rd.... C2
St Nicholas Arcades
  Shopping Centre.. B2
St Oswald St.... C3
St Peter's 🏛... B3
St Peter's Rd.... B3
Salisbury Rd.... B1
Scotch Quarry Urban
  Park.... C3
Sibsey St.... B1
Skerton Bridge.... A2
South Rd.... C2
Station Rd.... B1
Stirling Rd.... C3
Storey Ave.... B1
Sunnyside La.... C1
Sylvester St.... C1
Tarnsyke Rd.... A1
Thurnham St.... C2
Town Hall.... B2
Troutbeck Rd.... C3
Ulleswater Rd.... B3
Univ of Cumbria.... B1
Vicarage Field.... B1
Vue 🎬.... B2
West Rd.... B1
Westbourne Dr.... A1
Westbourne Rd.... B1
Westham St.... C2
Wheatfield St.... B1
White Cross Business
  Park.... C2
Williamson Rd.... B3
Willow La.... B1
Windermere Rd.... A3
Wingate-Saul Rd.... B1
Wolseley St.... B3
Woodville St.... B3
Wyresdale Rd.... C3

Leeds 118
Aire St.... B3
Albion Pl.... B4
Albion St.... B4
Albion Way.... B1
Alma St.... A6
Ambulance Sta.... B5
Arcades 🏛.... B4
Armley Rd.... A1
Armories Dr.... C5
Back Burley Lodge
  Rd.... A1

Back Hyde Terr.... A2
Back Row.... C3
Bath Rd.... C3
Beckett St.... A6
Bedford St.... B3
Belgrave St.... A4
Belle Vue Rd.... A2
Benson St.... A5
Black Bull St.... C5
Blenheim Walk.... A3
Boar La.... B4
Bond St.... B4
Bow St.... B5
Bowman La.... B4
Brewery ◆.... C4
Brewery Wharf.... C5
Bridge St.... A5/B5
Briggate.... B4
Bruce Gdns.... C1
Burley Rd.... A1
Burley St.... B2
Burmantofts St.... B6
Bus & Coach Sta.... B5
Butterly St.... C4
Butts Cres.... B4
Byron St.... A5
Call La.... B4
Calls,The.... B5
Calverley St.... A3/B3
Canal St.... B1
Canal Wharf.... C3
Carlisle Rd.... C5
Cavendish Rd.... A1
Cavendish St.... A2
Chadwick St.... C5
Cherry Pl.... A6
Cherry Row.... A5
City Museum 🏛 A4
City Varieties
  Music Hall 🎭.. B4
City Sq.... B3
Civic Hall 🏛.... A3
Clarence Road.... C5
Clarendon Rd.... A2
Clarendon Way.... A3
Clark La.... C6
Clay Pit La.... A4
Cloberry St.... A2
Close,The.... B6
Clyde Approach.... C1
Clyde Gdns.... C1
Coleman St.... B2
Commercial St.... B4
Concord St.... A5
Cookridge St.... A4
Copley Hill.... C1
Core,The.... B4
Corn Exchange 🏛 B4
Cromer Terr.... A2
Cromwell St.... A5
Cross Catherine St.. B6
Cross Green La.... C6
Cross Stamford St.. A5
Crown & County
  Courts.... B5
Crown Point
  Bridge.... C5
Crown Point Rd.... C4
Crown Point
  Retail Park.... C4
David St.... C3
Dent St.... C6
Derwent Pl.... C3
Dial St.... C6
Dock St.... C4
Dolly La.... A6
Domestic St.... C2
Drive,The.... B6
Duke St.... B5
Duncan St.... B4
Dyer St.... B5
East Field St.... B6
East Parade.... B3
East St.... C5
Eastgate.... B5
Easy Rd.... C6
Edward St.... B4
Ellerby La.... C6
Ellerby Rd.... C6
Fenton St.... A3
Fire Station.... B6
First Direct Arena.. A4
Fish St.... B4
Flax Pl.... B5
Garth,The.... B5
Gelderd Rd.... C1
George St.... B4
Globe Rd.... C2
Gower St.... A5
Grafton St.... A4
Grand Theatre 🎭 B4
Granville Rd.... A5
Great George St.... A3
Great Wilson St.... C4
Greek St.... B3
Green La.... C1
Hanover Ave.... A2
Hanover La.... A2
Hanover Sq.... A2
Hanover Way.... A2
Harewood St.... B4
Harrison St.... B4
Haslewood Close.... B6
Haslewood Drive.... B6
Headrow,The.... B3/B4
High Court.... B5
Holbeck La.... C2
Holdforth Close.... B1
Holdforth Gdns.... B1
Holdforth Grove.... B1
Holdforth Place.... B1
Holy Trinity 🏛.. B4
Hope Rd.... A5
Hunslet La.... C4
Hunslet Rd.... C4
Hyde Terr.... A2
Infirmary St.... B3
Information Ctr ℹ.. B3
Ingram Row.... C3
ITV Yorkshire.... A1
Junction St.... C4
Kelso Gdns.... A2
Kelso Rd.... A2
Kelso St.... A2
Kendal La.... A2

Kendell St.... C4
Kidacre St.... C4
King Edward St.... B4
King St.... B3
Kippax Place.... C6
Kirkgate.... B4
Kirkgate Market.... B4
Kirkstall Rd.... A1
Kitson St.... C6
Knight's Way
  Bridge.... C5
Lady La.... A4
Lands La.... B4
Lane,The.... B5
Lavender Walk.... B6
Leeds
  Art Gallery 🏛.. B3
Leeds Beckett Univ A4
Leeds Bridge.... C4
Leeds Coll of Music B5
Leeds Discovery
  Centre.... C5
Leeds General
  Infirmary (A&E) Ⓗ A3
Leeds Minster 🏛 B5
Leeds Station ≥.... B3
Library.... B3/B4
Light,The.... B4
Lincoln Green Rd.... A6
Lincoln Rd.... A6
Lindsey Gdns.... A6
Lindsey Rd.... A6
Lisbon St.... B3
Little Queen St.... B3
Long Close La.... C6
Lord St.... C2
Lovell Park.... A4
Lovell Park Hill.... A4
Lower Brunswick
  St.... A5
Mabgate.... A5
Macauly St.... A4
Magistrates Court.. A4
Manor Rd.... C3
Mark La.... B4
Marlborough St.... B2
Marsh La.... B5
Marshall St.... C3
Meadow La.... C4
Meadow Rd.... C3
Melbourne St.... A5
Merrion Centre.... A4
Merrion St.... A4
Merrion Way.... A4
Mill St.... B5
Millennium Sq.... A3
Monk Bridge.... A2
Mount Preston St.. A2
Mushroom St.... A5
Neville St.... C4
New Briggate.... A4/B4
New Market St.... B4
New York Rd.... A5
New York St.... B5
Nile St.... A5
Nippet La.... A6
North St.... A4
Northern Ballet 🎭 B5
Northern St.... B3
Oak Rd.... B1
Oxford Pl.... B3
Oxford Row.... A3
Parade,The.... A6
Park Cross St.... B3
Park La.... A2
Park Pl.... B3
Park Row.... B4
Park Sq.... B3
Park Sq East.... B3
Park Sq West.... B3
Park St.... B3
Police Station.... C6
Pontefract La.... B6
Portland Cres.... A3
Portland Way.... A3
Post Office 🅿.... B4/B5
Quarry Ho
  (NHS/DSS HQ).... B5
Quebec St.... B3
Queen St.... B3
Radio Aire.... A1
Railway St.... B5
Rectory St.... A6
Regent St.... A5
Richmond St.... C5
Rigton Approach.... B6
Rigton Dr.... B6
Rillbank La.... A1
Rosebank Rd.... A1
Rose Bowl
  Conference Ctr.... A3
Royal Armouries 🏛 C5
Russell St.... B3
St Anne's
  Cathedral (RC) ✝.. A4
St Anne's St.... B4
St James' Hosp Ⓗ.. A6
St John's Rd.... A2
St Johns Centre.... B4
St Mary's St.... B5
St Pauls St.... B3
Saxton La.... B5
Sayner La.... C5
Shakespeare Ave.... A6
Shannon St.... B6
Sheepscar St South A5
Siddall St.... C3
Skinner La.... A5
South Pde.... B3
Sovereign St.... C4
Spence La.... C1
Springfield Mount.. A2
Springwell Ct.... C2
Springwell Rd.... C2
Springwell St.... C2
Stoney Rock La.... A6
Studio Rd.... A1
Sutton St.... C2
Sweet St.... C3
Sweet St West.... C3
Swinegate.... B4
Templar St.... B5
Thoresby Pl.... A3

Torre Rd.... A6
Town Hall 🏛.... A3
Trinity Leeds.... B4
Union Pl.... B4
Union St.... B5
University of Leeds A4
Upper Accomodation
  Rd.... C6
Upper Basinghall St B4
Vicar La.... B4
Victoria Bridge.... C4
Victoria Gate.... B4
Victoria Quarter.... B4
Vue 🎬.... B4
Wade La.... A4
Washington St.... A1
Water La.... C3
Waterloo Rd.... C4
Wellington Rd.... B2/C1
Wellington St.... B3
West St.... B2
West Yorkshire
  Playhouse 🎭.. B5
Westfield Rd.... A1
Westgate.... A3
Whitehall Rd.... B3/C2
Whitelock St.... A5
Willis St.... C6
Willow Approach.... A1
Willow Ave.... A1
Willow Terrace Rd.. A3
Wintoun St.... A5
Woodhouse La.... A3/A4
Woodsley Rd.... A2
York Pl.... B3
York Rd.... B6

Leicester 118
Abbey St.... A2
All Saints' 🏛.... A2
Aylestone Rd.... C2
Bath La.... B1
Bede Park.... C1
Bedford St.... A3
Bedford St South.. A3
Belgrave Gate.... A2
Belvoir St.... B2
Braunstone Gate.. B1
Burleys Way.... A2
Burnmoor St.... C2
Bus & Coach Sta.... A2
Canning St.... A2
Carlton St.... C2
Castle 🏛.... B1
Castle Gardens.... B1
Cathedral ✝.... B2
Causeway La.... A2
Charles St.... B2
Chatham St.... B2
Christow St.... A3
Church Gate.... A2
City Gallery 🏛.. A2
City Hall.... A2
Clank St.... B2
Clock Tower ◆.... B2
Clyde St.... A3
Colton St.... B2
Conduit St.... B3
Crafton St.... A3
Craven St.... A1
Crown Courts.... B1
Curve 🎭.... B3
De Lux 🎬.... B2
De Montfort Hall 🎭 C3
De Montfort St.... C3
De Montfort Univ.. C1
Deacon St.... C2
Dover St.... B3
Duns La.... B1
Dunton St.... A1
East St.... B3
Eastern Boulevard.. C1
Edmonton Rd.... A3
Erskine St.... A3
Filbert St.... C1
Filbert St East.... C2
Fire Station.... A3
Fleet St.... A3
Friar La.... B2
Friday St.... A2
Gateway St.... C2
Gateway,The.... C2
Glebe St.... B3
Granby St.... B2
Grange La.... C2
Grasmere St.... C1
Great Central St.... A1
Guildhall 🏛.... B2
Guru Nanak Sikh
  Museum 🏛.... A1
Halford St.... B2
Havelock St.... C2
Haymarket Shopping
  Centre.... A2
High St.... B2
Highcross
  Shopping Centre.. A2
Highcross St.... A1
HM Prison.... B1
Horsefair St.... B2
Humberstone Gate.. A2
Humberstone Rd.... A3
Infirmary St.... C2
Information Ctr ℹ.. B2
Jarrom St.... C1
Jewry Wall 🏛.. B1
Kamloops Cres.... A3
King St.... B2
Lancaster Rd.... C2
LCB Depot.... A3
Lee St.... A2
Leicester Royal
  Infirmary (A&E) Ⓗ C2
Leicester Station ≥ B3
Library.... B2
London Rd.... B3
Lower Brown St.... B2
Magistrates' Court.. B2
Manitoba Rd.... A3
Mansfield St.... A2
Market 🏛.... B2
Market St.... B2
Mill La.... C2

Montreal Rd.... A3
Narborough Rd
  North.... C1
Nelson Mandela Pk C2
New Park St.... B1
New St.... B2
New Walk.... C3
New Walk Museum
  & Art Gallery 🏛 C3
Newarke Houses 🏛 B2
Newarke,The.... B1
Northgate St.... A1
Orchard St.... A2
Ottawa Rd.... A3
Oxford St.... C2
Phoenix Arts Ctr 🎭 B3
Police Station 🏛 B2
Post Office 🅿
  .... A1/B2/C3
Prebend St.... C3
Princes Rd East.... C3
Princes Rd West.... C3
Queen St.... B3
Rally Com Pk,The.. C1
Regent College.... C3
Regent Rd.... C2/C3
Repton St.... A1
Rutland St.... B3
St Augustine Rd.... B1
St Georges
  Retail Park.... B3
St George St.... A3
St Georges Way.... B3
St John St.... A2
St Margaret's 🏛 A2
St Margaret's Way.. A2
St Martins.... B2
St Mary de
  Castro 🏛.... B1
St Matthew's Way.. A3
St Nicholas 🏛.. B1
St Nicholas Circle.. B1
Sanvey Gate.... A1
Silver St.... B2
Slater St.... A1
Soar La.... A1
South Albion St.... B3
Southampton St.... B3
Sue Townsend
  Theatre 🎭.... B2
Swain St.... B3
Swan St.... A1
Tigers Way.... C3
Tower St.... C2
Town Hall.... B2
Tudor Rd.... B1
Univ of Leicester.. C3
University Rd.... C3
Upper Brown St 🎭 B2
Upperton Rd.... C1
Vaughan Way.... A1
Walnut St.... C1
Watling St.... A2
Welford Rd.... B2
Welford Rd Leicester
  Tigers RC.... C2
Wellington St.... B2
West St.... C2
West Walk.... C3
Western Boulevard C1
Western Rd.... C1
Wharf St North.... A3
Wharf St South.... A3
Y Theatre,The 🎭 B3
Yeoman St.... B3
York Rd.... B2

Lincoln 118
Alexandra Terr.... B1
Anchor St.... C2
Arboretum.... B3
Arboretum Ave,The B3
Avenue,The.... B1
Baggholme Rd.... B3
Bailgate.... A2
Beaumont Fee.... B1
BMI The Lincoln
  Hospital Ⓗ.... A1
Brayford Way.... C1
Brayford Wharf
  East.... C1
Brayford Wharf
  North.... B1
Bruce Rd.... A2
Burton Rd.... A1
Bus Station (City).. C2
Canwick Rd.... C2
Cardinal's Hat ◆.... B2
Carline Rd.... A1
Castle 🏛.... B1
Castle St.... B1
Cathedral ✝.... B2
Cathedral St.... B2
Cecil St.... A2
Chapel La.... A2
Cheviot St.... B3
Church La.... A2
City Hall.... B1
Clasketgate.... B2
Clayton Sports Gd.. A3
Coach Park.... B2
Collection,The 🏛 B2
County Hospital
  (A&E) Ⓗ.... A3
County Office.... C1
Courts.... B2
Cross St.... C2
Crown Courts.... B2
Curle Ave.... A3
Danesgate.... B2
Drill Hall 🎭.... B2
Drury La.... B1
East Bight.... A2
East Gate.... A2
Eastcliff Rd.... B3
Eastgate.... B2
Egerton Rd.... A3
Ellis Windmill ◆.... A1
Engine Shed,
  The 🎭.... C1
Environment
  Agency.... C1
Exchequer Gate ◆.. B2

Firth Rd.... C1
Flaxengate.... B2
Florence St.... B3
George St.... C1
Good La.... A2
Gray St.... A1
Great Northern
  Terrace.... C3
Great Northern
  Terrace Ind Est.... C3
Greetwell Rd.... B3
Greetwellgate.... B3
Grove,The.... A3
Haffenden Rd.... A2
High St.... B2/C1
HM Prison.... A1
Hungate.... B2
James St.... A2
Jews House & Ct 🏛 B2
Kesteven St.... C2
Langworthgate.... A2
Lawn,The.... B1
Lee Rd.... A3
Library.... B2
Lincoln Central
  Station ≥.... C2
Lincoln College.... B2
Lincolnshire Life/
  Royal Lincolnshire
  Regiment Mus 🏛 A1
Lincoln Univ Technical
  Coll (UTC).... B2
Lindum Rd.... B2
Lindum Sports Gd.. A3
Lindum Terr.... B3
Mainwaring Rd.... A3
Manor Rd.... A1
Market.... B2
Massey Rd.... A3
Medieval Bishop's
  Palace 🏛.... B2
Mildmay St.... A1
Mill Rd.... A1
Millman Rd.... A3
Minster Yard.... B2
Monks Rd.... B3
Montague St.... B2
Mount St.... A1
Nettleham Rd.... A2
Newland.... B1
Newport.... A2
Newport Arch 🏛 A2
Newport Cemetery A2
Northgate.... A2
Odeon 🎬.... C1
Orchard St.... B1
Oxford St.... C2
Park St.... C1
Pelham Bridge.... C2
Pelham St.... C2
Police Station 🏛 C2
Portland St.... C2
Post Office 🅿
  .... A1/B3/C2
Potter Gate.... A2
Priory Gate.... B2
Queensway.... A3
Rasen La.... A1
Ropewalk.... C1
Rosemary La.... B2
St Anne's Rd.... B3
St Benedict's 🏛 B1
St Giles Ave.... A3
St Mark's Shopping
  Centre.... C1
St Marks St.... C1
St Mary-le-
  Wigford 🏛.... C1
St Mary's St.... C2
St Nicholas St.... A2
St Rumbold's St.... B2
St Swithin's 🏛 B2
Saltergate.... B2
Saxon St.... A1
Sewell Rd.... B3
Silver St.... B2
Sincil St.... C2
Spital St.... A2
Spring Hill.... B1
Stamp End.... C3
Steep Hill.... B2
Stonebow &
  Guildhall 🏛.... C2
Stonefield Ave.... A2
Tentercroft St.... C1
Theatre Royal 🎭 B2
Tritton Rd.... C1
Tritton Retail Park.. C1
Union Rd.... B1
Univ of Lincoln.... C1
Upper Lindum St... B3
Upper Long Leys Rd A1
Usher 🏛.... B2
Vere St.... A3
Victoria St.... B1
Victoria Terr.... B1
Vine St.... B3
Wake St.... A1
Waldeck St.... A1
Waterside North.... B2
Waterside Shopping
  Centre.... B2
Waterside South.... C2
West Pde.... B1
Westgate.... A2
Wigford Way.... C1
Williamson St.... A2
Winn St.... B3
Wragby Rd.... A3
Yarborough Rd.... A1

Liverpool 119
Abercromby Sq.... C5
Addison St.... A4
Adelaide Rd.... B6
Ainsworth St.... B4
Albany Rd.... B6
Albert Edward Rd.. B6
Angela St.... C6
Anson St.... B4
Argyle St.... C3
Arrad St.... C5
Ashton St.... B5

Audley St.... A4
Back Leeds St.... A2
Basnett St.... B3
Bath St.... A1
Beacon,The ◆.... B2
Beatles Story,
  The ◆.... C2
Beckwith St.... C3
Bedford Close.... C5
Bedford St North.. C5
Bedford St South.. C5
Benson St.... C4
Berry St.... C4
Birkett St.... A4
Bixteth St.... B2
Blackburne Place.. C4
Bluecoat 🏛.... B3
Bold Place.... C4
Bold St.... C4
Bolton St.... B3
Bridport St.... B4
Bronte St.... B4
Brook St.... A1
Brownlow Hill.... B4/B5
Brownlow St.... B5
Brunswick Rd.... A5
Brunswick St.... B1
Bus Station.... C2
Butler Cres.... A6
Byrom St.... A3
Caledonia St.... C4
Cambridge St.... C5
Camden St.... A4
Canada Blvd.... B1
Canning Dock.... C2
Canterbury St.... A4
Cardwell St.... C6
Carver St.... A4
Cases St.... B3
Castle St.... B2
Catherine St.... C5
Cavern Club 🏛 B3
Central Library.... B3
Chapel St.... B2
Charlotte St.... B3
Chatham Place.... C6
Chatham St.... C5
Cheapside.... B2
Chavasse Park.... C2
Chestnut St.... C5
Christian St.... A3
Church St.... B3
Clarence St.... B4
Clayton Square
  Shopping Centre.. B3
Coach Station.... B4
Cobden St.... A5
Cockspur St.... A2
College La.... B3
College St North.. A5
College St South.. A5
Colquitt St.... C4
Comus St.... A3
Concert St.... C4
Connaught Rd.... B6
Cook St.... B2
Copperas Hill.... B3
Cornwallis St.... C3
Covent Garden.... B2
Craven St.... A4
Cropper St.... B3
Crown St.... B5/C6
Cumberland St.... B2
Cunard Building 🏛 B1
Dale St.... B2
Dansie St.... B4
Daulby St.... B5
Dawson St.... B3
Dental Hospital.... B5
Derby Sq.... B2
Drury La.... B2
Duckinfield St.... B4
Duke St.... C3
Earle St.... A2
East St.... A2
Eaton St.... A2
Echo Arena ◆.... C2
Edgar St.... A3
Edge La.... B6
Edinburgh Rd.... A6
Edmund St.... B2
Elizabeth St.... B5
Elliot St.... B3
Empire Theatre 🎭 B4
Empress Rd.... B6
Epstein Theatre 🎭 B3
Erskine St.... A5
Everyman
  Theatre 🎭.... C5
Exchange St East.. B2
FACT 🎬.... C4
Falkland St.... A5
Falkner St.... C5/C6
Farnworth St.... A6
Fenwick St.... B2
Fielding St.... A6
Fire Sta.... B4
Fleet St.... C3
Fraser St.... B4
Freemasons Row.. A2
Gardner Row.... A3
Gascoyne St.... A2
George St.... B2
Gibralter Road.... A1
Gilbert St.... C3
Gildart St.... B4
Gill St.... B5
Goree.... B2
Gower St.... C2
Gradwell St.... C3
Great Crosshall St.. A3
Great George St.... C4
Great Howard St.. A1
Great Newton St.. B5
Greek St.... B4
Greenland St.... C3
Greenside.... A5
Greetham St.... C3
Grenville St.... C3
Grinfield St.... C6
Grove St.... C5
Guelph St.... A6

Haigh St.... A4
Hall La.... B6
Hanover St.... B3
Harbord St.... C6
Hardman St.... C4
Harker St.... A4
Hart St.... B4
Hatton Garden.... A2
Hawke St.... B4
Helsby St.... B6
Henry St.... C3
Highfield St.... A2
Highgate St.... B6
Hilbre St.... B4
Hope Place.... C4
Hope St.... C4
Hope University.... A5
Houghton St.... B3
Hunter St.... A4
Hutchinson St.... A6
Information Ctr ℹ
  .... B4/C2
Institute for the
  Performing Arts.. C4
International
  Slavery Mus 🏛 C1
Irvine St.... B6
Irwell St.... B2
Islington.... A4
James St.... B2
James St Sta ≥.... B2
Jenkinson St.... A4
John Moores
  University
  .... A2/A3/A4/B4/C4
Johnson St.... A3
Jubilee Drive.... B6
Kempston St.... A4
Kensington.... A6
Kensington Gdns.. B6
Kensington St.... A6
Kent St.... C3
King Edward St.... A1
Kinglake St.... B6
Knight St.... C4
Lace St.... A3
Langsdale St.... A4
Law Courts.... C2
Leece St.... C4
Leeds St.... A2
Leopold Rd.... B6
Lime St.... B3
Lime St Station ≥ B4
Liver St.... C2
Liverpool Central
  Station ≥.... B3
Liverpool Landing
  Stage.... B1
Liverpool Institute for
  Performing
  Arts (LIPA).... C4
Liverpool ONE.... C2
Liverpool Wheel,
  The ◆.... C2
London Rd.... A4/B4
Lord Nelson St.... B4
Lord St.... B2
Lovat St.... C6
Low Hill.... A6
Low Wood St.... A6
Lydia Ann St.... C3
Mansfield St.... A4
Marmaduke St.... B6
Marsden St.... A5
Martensen St.... B6
Marybone.... A3
Maryland St.... C4
Mason St.... B6
Mathew St.... B3
May St.... B4
Melville Place.... C6
Merseyside Maritime
  Museum ◆.... C1
Metquarter.... B3
Metropolitan
  Cathedral (RC) ✝.. B5
Midghall St.... A2
Molyneux Rd.... A6
Moor Place.... B4
Moorfields.... B2
Moorfields Sta ≥.. A5
Moss St.... A5
Mount Pleasant.... B4/B5
Mount St.... C4
MountVernon.... B6
Mulberry St.... C5
Mus of Liverpool 🏛 C1
Myrtle St.... C5
Naylor St.... A3
Nelson St.... C4
New Islington.... A4
New Quay.... B1
Newington St.... B3
North John St.... B2
North St.... A3
North View.... A6
Norton St.... A4
O2 Academy.... B4
Oakes St.... B5
Odeon 🎬.... B4
Old Hall St.... A1
Old Leeds St.... A2
Oldham Place.... C4
Oldham St.... C4
Olive St.... C6
Open Eye
  Gallery 🏛.... C2
Oriel St.... A2
Ormond St.... B2
Orphan St.... C6
Overbury St.... C6
Overton St.... C6
Oxford St.... C5
Paisley St.... A1
Pall Mall.... A2
Paradise St.... C3
Park La.... C3
Parker St.... B3
Parr St.... C3
Peach St.... C5
Pembroke Place.... B4
Pembroke St.... C5
Philharmonic
  Hall 🎭.... C5

Phythian Park . . . A6
Pickop St . . . A2
Pilgrim St . . . C4
Pitt St . . . C3
Playhouse Theatre . . . B3
Pleasant St . . . B4
Police HQ . . . C2
Police Station . . . A4/A6/B4
Pomona St . . . B4
Port of Liverpool Building . . . B2
Post Office . . . A2/A4/A5/B2/B3/B4/C4
Pownall St . . . C2
Prescot St . . . A5
Preston St . . . B3
Princes Dock . . . A1
Princes Gdns . . . A2
Princes Jetty . . . A1
Princes Parade . . . B1
Princes St . . . B2
Pythian St . . . A6
Queen Sq Bus Sta . . . B3
Queensland St . . . C6
Queensway Tunnel (Docks exit) . . . B1
Queensway Tunnel (Entrance) . . . B3
Radio City . . . B2
Ranelagh St . . . B3
Redcross St . . . B2
Renfrew St . . . B6
Renshaw St . . . B4
Richmond Row . . . A4
Richmond St . . . B3
Rigby St . . . A2
Roberts St . . . A1
Rock St . . . B4
Rodney St . . . C4
Rokeby St . . . A4
Romily St . . . A6
Roscoe La . . . C4
Roscoe St . . . C4
Rose Hill . . . A3
Royal Albert Dock . . . C2
Royal Court Theatre . . . B3
Royal Liver Building . . . B1
Royal Liverpool Hospital (A&E) . . . B5
Royal Mail St . . . B4
Rumford Place . . . B2
Rumford St . . . B2
Russell St . . . B4
St Andrew St . . . B4
St Anne St . . . A4
St Georges Hall . . . B3
St John's Centre . . . B3
St John's Gdns . . . B3
St John's La . . . B3
St Joseph's Cres . . . A4
St Minishull St . . . B5
St Nicholas Place . . . B1
St Paul's Sq . . . A2
Salisbury St . . . A4
Salthouse Dock . . . C2
Salthouse Quay . . . C2
Sandon St . . . C5
Saxony Rd . . . B6
Schomberg St . . . A6
School La . . . B2
Seel St . . . C3
Seymour St . . . B4
Shaw St . . . A5
Shopmobility . . . C2
Sidney Place . . . C6
Sir Thomas St . . . B3
Skelhorne St . . . B4
Slater St . . . C3
Smithdown La . . . B6
Soho Sq . . . A4
Soho St . . . A4
South John St . . . B2
Springfield . . . A4
Stafford St . . . A4
Standish St . . . A3
Stanley St . . . B2
Strand St . . . C2
Strand, The . . . B2
Suffolk St . . . C3
Sydney Jones Liby . . . C5
Tabley St . . . C3
Tarleton St . . . B3
Tate Liverpool Gallery . . . C2
Teck St . . . B6
Temple St . . . B2
Titanic Memorial . . . B1
Tithebarn St . . . B2
Town Hall . . . B2
Trowbridge St . . . B4
Trueman St . . . A3
Union St . . . B2
Unity Theatre . . . C4
University . . . C5
Univ of Liverpool . . . B5
Upper Baker St . . . A6
Upper Duke St . . . C4
Upper Frederick St . . . C3
Vauxhall Rd . . . A2
Vernon St . . . B2
Victoria Gallery & Museum . . . B5
Victoria St . . . B2
Vine St . . . C5
Wakefield St . . . A4
Walker Art Gallery . . . A3
Walker St . . . A6
Wapping . . . C2
Water St . . . B1/B2
Waterloo Rd . . . A1
Wavertree Rd . . . B6
West Derby Rd . . . A6
West Derby St . . . B5
Western Approaches War Museum . . . B2
Whitechapel . . . B3
Whitley Gdns . . . A5
William Brown St . . . B3
William Henry St . . . A4
Williamson Sq . . . B3
Williamson St . . . B3
Williamson's Tunnels Heritage Ctr . . . C6
Women's Hosp . . . C6
Wood St . . . B3
World Museum, Liverpool . . . A3
York St . . . C3

London 120

Abbey Orchard St . . . E3
Abchurch La . . . D6
Abingdon St . . . E4
Achilles Way . . . D2
Acton St . . . B4
Addington St . . . E4
Air St . . . D3
Albany St . . . B2
Albemarle St . . . D3
Albert Emb . . . F4
Aldenham St . . . A3
Aldersgate St . . . C6
Aldford St . . . D2
Aldgate . . . C7
Aldgate High St . . . C7
Aldwych . . . C4
Allsop Pl . . . B1
Amwell St . . . B5
Andrew Borde St . . . C3
Angel . . . A5
Appold St . . . C7
Argyle Sq . . . B4
Argyle St . . . B4
Argyll St . . . C3
Arnold Circus . . . B7
Artillery La . . . C7
Artillery Row . . . E3
Association of Photographers Gallery . . . B6
Baker St . . . B1
Baker St . . . B1
Baldwin's Gdns . . . C5
Baltic St . . . B6
Bank . . . C6
Bank Museum . . . C6
Bank of England . . . C6
Bankside . . . D6
Bankside Gallery . . . D5
Banner St . . . B6
Barbican . . . C6
Barbican Centre for Arts, The . . . C6
Barbican Gallery . . . C6
Basil St . . . E1
Bastwick St . . . B6
Bateman's Row . . . B7
Bath St . . . B6
Bayley St . . . C3
Baylis Rd . . . E5
Beak St . . . D3
Bedford Row . . . C4
Bedford Sq . . . C3
Bedford St . . . D4
Bedford Way . . . B3
Beech St . . . C6
Belgrave Pl . . . E2
Belgrave Sq . . . E2
Bell La . . . C7
Belvedere Rd . . . E4
Berkeley Sq . . . D2
Berkeley St . . . D2
Bernard St . . . B4
Berners Pl . . . C3
Berners St . . . C3
Berwick St . . . C3
Bethnal Green Rd . . . B7
Bevenden St . . . B6
Bevis Marks . . . C7
BFI (British Film Institute) . . . D4
BFI London IMAX Cinema . . . D5
Bidborough St . . . B4
Binney St . . . C2
Birdcage Walk . . . E3
Bishopsgate . . . C7
Blackfriars . . . D5
Blackfriars Bridge . . . D5
Blackfriars Rd . . . E5
Blandford St . . . C1
Blomfield St . . . C6
Bloomsbury St . . . C3
Bloomsbury Way . . . C4
Bolton St . . . D2
Bond St . . . C2
Borough High St . . . E6
Boswell St . . . C4
Bow St . . . C4
Bowling Green La . . . B5
Brad St . . . D5
Bressenden Pl . . . E3
Brewer St . . . D3
Brick St . . . D2
Bridge St . . . E4
Britannia Walk . . . B6
British Film Institute (BFI) . . . D4
British Library . . . B3
British Museum . . . C4
Britton St . . . B5
Broad Sanctuary . . . E3
Broadway . . . E3
Brook Dr . . . F5
Brook St . . . D2
Brunswick Pl . . . B6
Brunswick Shopping Centre, The . . . B4
Brunswick Sq . . . B4
Brushfield St . . . C7
Bruton St . . . D2
Bryanston St . . . C1
BT Centre . . . C6
Buckingham Gate . . . E3
Buckingham Palace . . . E3
Buckingham Palace Rd . . . F2
Bunhill Row . . . B6
Byward St . . . D7
Cabinet War Rooms & Churchill Mus . . . E3
Cadogan La . . . E2
Cadogan Pl . . . E1
Cadogan Sq . . . F1
Caledonian Rd . . . A4
Calshot St . . . A4
Calthorpe St . . . B4
Calvert Ave . . . B7
Cambridge Circus . . . C3
Camomile St . . . C7
Cannon St . . . D6
Cannon St . . . D6
Carey St . . . C4
Carlisle La . . . E4
Carlisle Pl . . . E3
Carlton House Terr . . . D3
Carmelite St . . . D5
Carnaby St . . . C3
Carter La . . . C5
Carthusian St . . . C6
Cartwright Gdns . . . B4
Castle Baynard St . . . D5
Cavendish Pl . . . C2
Cavendish Sq . . . C2
Caxton Hall . . . E3
Caxton St . . . E3
Central St . . . B6
Chalton St . . . B3
Chancery Lane . . . C5
Chapel St . . . E2
Charing Cross . . . D4
Charing Cross Rd . . . C3
Charles II St . . . D3
Charles Dickens Museum . . . B4
Charles Sq . . . B6
Charles St . . . D2
Charlotte Rd . . . B7
Charlotte St . . . C3
Chart St . . . B6
Charterhouse Sq . . . C5
Charterhouse St . . . C5
Cheapside . . . C6
Chenies St . . . C3
Chesham St . . . F2
Chester Sq . . . F2
Chesterfield Hill . . . D2
Chiltern St . . . C2
Chiswell St . . . C6
City Garden Row . . . A5
City Rd . . . B6
City Thameslink . . . C5
City University, The . . . B5
Claremont Sq . . . A5
Clarges St . . . D2
Clerkenwell Cl . . . B5
Clerkenwell Green . . . B5
Clerkenwell Rd . . . B5
Cleveland St . . . C3
Clifford St . . . D3
Clink Prison Museum . . . D6
Clock Museum . . . C6
Club Row . . . B7
Cockspur St . . . D3
Coleman St . . . C6
Columbia Rd . . . B7
Commercial St . . . C7
Compton St . . . B5
Conduit St . . . D2
Constitution Hill . . . E2
Copperfield St . . . E5
Coptic St . . . C4
Cornhill . . . C6
Cornwall Rd . . . D5
Coronet St . . . B7
Courtauld Gallery . . . D4
Covent Garden . . . D4
Covent Garden . . . D4
Cowcross St . . . C5
Cowper St . . . B6
Cranbourn St . . . D3
Craven St . . . D4
Crawford St . . . C1
Creechurch La . . . C7
Cremer St . . . A7
Cromer St . . . B4
Cumberland Gate . . . D1
Cumberland Terr . . . A2
Curtain Rd . . . B7
Curzon St . . . D2
Cut, The . . . E5
D'arblay St . . . C3
Davies St . . . C2
Dean St . . . C3
Deluxe Gallery . . . B7
Denmark St . . . C3
Dering St . . . C2
Devonshire St . . . C2
Diana, Princess of Wales Meml Walk . . . E3
Dingley Rd . . . B6
Dorset St . . . C1
Doughty St . . . B4
Dover St . . . D2
Downing St . . . E4
Druid St . . . E7
Drummond St . . . B3
Drury La . . . C4
Drysdale St . . . B7
Duchess St . . . C2
Dufferin St . . . B6
Duke of Wellington Place . . . E2
Duke St . . . C2
Duke St . . . D3
Duke St Hill . . . D6
Duke's Pl . . . C7
Duncannon St . . . D4
East Rd . . . B6
Eastcastle St . . . C3
Eastcheap . . . D7
Eastman Dental Hospital . . . B4
Eaton Pl . . . E2
Eaton Sq . . . E2
Eccleston St . . . E2
Edgware Rd . . . C1
Eldon St . . . C6
Embankment . . . D4
Endell St . . . C4
Endsleigh Pl . . . B3
Euston . . . B3
Euston Rd . . . B3
Euston Square . . . B3
Evelina Children's Hospital . . . E4
Eversholt St . . . A3
Exmouth Market . . . B5
Fann St . . . B6
Farringdon . . . C5
Farringdon Rd . . . C5
Farringdon St . . . C5
Featherstone St . . . B6
Fenchurch St . . . D7
Fenchurch St . . . D7
Fetter La . . . C5
Finsbury Circus . . . C6
Finsbury Pavement . . . C6
Finsbury Sq . . . B6
Fitzalan St . . . F5
Fitzmaurice Pl . . . D2
Fleet St . . . C5
Floral St . . . D4
Florence Nightingale Museum . . . E4
Folgate St . . . C7
Foot Hospital . . . B3
Fore St . . . C6
Foster La . . . C6
Francis St . . . F3
Frazier St . . . E5
Freemason's Hall . . . C4
Friday St . . . C6
Gainsford St . . . E7
Garden Row . . . E5
Gee St . . . B6
George St . . . C1
Gerrard St . . . D3
Giltspur St . . . C5
Glasshouse St . . . D3
Gloucester Pl . . . C1
Golden Hinde . . . D6
Golden La . . . B6
Golden Sq . . . D3
Goodge St . . . C3
Goodge St . . . C3
Gordon Sq . . . B3
Goswell Rd . . . B5
Gough St . . . B4
Goulston St . . . C7
Gower St . . . B3
Gracechurch St . . . D6
Grafton Way . . . B3
Gray's Inn Rd . . . B4
Great College St . . . E4
Great Cumberland Place . . . C1
Great Eastern St . . . B7
Great Guildford St . . . D6
Great Marlborough St . . . C3
Great Ormond St . . . B4
Great Ormond St Children's Hosp . . . B4
Great Percy St . . . B4
Great Peter St . . . E3
Great Portland St . . . B2
Great Portland St . . . C2
Great Queen St . . . C4
Great Russell St . . . C3
Great Scotland Yd . . . D4
Great Smith St . . . E3
Great Suffolk St . . . D5
Great Titchfield St . . . C3
Great Tower St . . . D7
Great Windmill St . . . D3
Greek St . . . C3
Green Park . . . D3
Green St . . . D2
Greencoat Pl . . . F3
Gresham St . . . C6
Greville St . . . B4/C5
Greycoat Hosp Sch . . . E3
Greycoat Pl . . . E3
Grosvenor Cres . . . E2
Grosvenor Gdns . . . E2
Grosvenor Pl . . . E2
Grosvenor Sq . . . D2
Grosvenor St . . . D2
Guards Museum and Chapel . . . E3
Guildhall Art Gallery . . . C6
Guilford St . . . B4
Guy's Hospital . . . D6
Haberdasher St . . . B6
Hackney Rd . . . B7
Half Moon St . . . D2
Halkin St . . . E2
Hall St . . . B5
Hallam St . . . C2
Hampstead Rd . . . B3
Hanover Sq . . . C2
Hans Cres . . . E1
Hanway St . . . C3
Hardwick St . . . B5
Harley St . . . C2
Harrison St . . . B4
Hastings St . . . B4
Hatfields . . . D5
Hay's Galleria . . . D7
Hay's Mews . . . D2
Hayles St . . . F5
Haymarket . . . D3
Hayne St . . . C5
Hayward Gallery . . . D4
Helmet Row . . . B6
Herbrand St . . . B4
Hercules Rd . . . E4
Hertford St . . . D2
High Holborn . . . C4
Hill St . . . D2
HMS Belfast . . . D7
Hobart Pl . . . E2
Holborn . . . C4
Holborn . . . C5
Holborn Viaduct . . . C5
Holland St . . . D5
Holmes Mus . . . B1
Holywell La . . . B7
Horse Guards' Rd . . . D3
Houndsditch . . . C7
Houses of Parliament . . . E4
Howland St . . . C3
Hoxton Sq . . . B7
Hoxton St . . . B7
Hunter St . . . B4
Hunterian Mus . . . C4
Hyde Park . . . D1
Hyde Park Corner . . . E2
Imperial War Museum . . . E5
Inner Circle . . . B2
Inst of Archaeology (London Univ) . . . B2
Ironmonger Row . . . B6
James St . . . C2
James St . . . D4
Jermyn St . . . D3
Jockey's Fields . . . C4
John Carpenter St . . . D5
John St . . . B4
Judd St . . . B4
Kennington Rd . . . E5
King Charles St . . . E4
King St . . . D3
King St . . . D4
King William St . . . C6
King's Coll London . . . D5
King's Cross . . . A4
King's Cross Rd . . . B4
King's Cross St Pancras . . . A4
King's Rd . . . E2
Kingley St . . . C3
Kingsland Rd . . . B7
Kingsway . . . C4
Kinnerton St . . . E2
Knightsbridge . . . E1
Lamb St . . . C7
Lamb's Conduit St . . . C4
Lambeth Bridge . . . F4
Lambeth High St . . . F4
Lambeth North . . . E5
Lambeth Palace . . . E4
Lambeth Palace Rd . . . E4
Lambeth Rd . . . E5
Lambeth Walk . . . F4
Lancaster Pl . . . D4
Langham Pl . . . C2
Leadenhall St . . . C7
Leake St . . . E4
Leather La . . . C5
Leicester Sq . . . D3
Leicester St . . . D3
Leonard St . . . B6
Lever St . . . B6
Lexington St . . . D3
Lidlington Pl . . . A3
Lime St . . . D7
Lincoln's Inn Fields . . . C4
Lindsey St . . . C5
Lisle St . . . D3
Liverpool St . . . C7
Liverpool St . . . C7
Lloyd Baker St . . . B5
Lloyd Sq . . . B5
Lombard St . . . C6
London Aquarium . . . E4
London Bridge . . . D6
London Bridge Hospital . . . D6
London City Hall . . . D7
London Dungeon, The . . . E4
London Film Museum . . . E4
London Guildhall University . . . C6
London Rd . . . E5
London Transport Museum . . . D4
London Wall . . . C6
London Eye . . . E4
Long Acre . . . D4
Long La . . . C5
Longford St . . . B2
Lower Belgrave St . . . E2
Lower Grosvenor Pl . . . E2
Lower Marsh . . . E5
Lower Thames St . . . D6
Lowndes St . . . E2
Ludgate Circus . . . C5
Ludgate Hill . . . C5
Luxborough St . . . C2
Lyall St . . . E2
Macclesfield Rd . . . B6
Madame Tussaud's . . . B2
Maddox St . . . D2
Malet St . . . C3
Mall, The . . . E3
Manchester Sq . . . C2
Manchester St . . . C2
Mandeville Pl . . . C2
Mansell St . . . D7
Mansion House . . . C6
Mansion House . . . D6
Maple St . . . C3
Marble Arch . . . C1
Marble Arch . . . D1
Marchmont St . . . B4
Margaret St . . . C3
Margery St . . . B5
Mark La . . . D7
Marlborough Rd . . . D3
Marshall St . . . C3
Marsham St . . . E3
Marylebone High St . . . C2
Marylebone La . . . C2
Marylebone Rd . . . B2
Marylebone St . . . C2
Mecklenburgh Sq . . . B4
Middle Temple La . . . C5
Middlesex St (Petticoat La) . . . C7
Midland Rd . . . A3
Migration Mus . . . F5
Minories . . . C7
Monck St . . . E3
Monmouth St . . . C4
Montagu Pl . . . C1
Montagu Sq . . . C1
Montagu St . . . C4
Montague Pl . . . C3
Monument . . . D6
Monument St . . . D6
Monument, The . . . D6
Moor La . . . C6
Moorfields . . . C6
Moorfields Eye Hospital . . . B6
Moorgate . . . C6
Moorgate . . . C6
Moreland St . . . B5
Morley St . . . E5
Mortimer St . . . C3
Mount Pleasant . . . B5
Mount St . . . D2
Murray Grove . . . A6
Museum of Garden History . . . E4
Mus of London . . . C6
Museum St . . . C4
Myddelton Sq . . . B5
Myddelton St . . . B5
National Gallery . . . D3
National Hosp . . . B4
National Portrait Gallery . . . D3
Neal St . . . C4
Nelson's Column . . . D4
New Bond St . . . C2/D2
New Bridge St . . . C5
New Cavendish St . . . C2
New Change . . . C6
New Fetter La . . . C5
New Inn Yard . . . B7
New North Rd . . . A6
New Oxford St . . . C3
New Scotland Yard . . . E3
New Sq . . . C4
Newgate St . . . C5
Newton St . . . C4
Nile St . . . B6
Noble St . . . C6
Noel St . . . C3
North Audley St . . . D2
North Cres . . . C3
North Row . . . D2
Northampton Sq . . . B5
Northington St . . . B4
Northumberland Ave . . . D4
Norton Folgate . . . C7
Nottingham Pl . . . C2
Obstetric Hosp . . . B3
Old Bailey . . . C5
Old Broad St . . . C6
Old Compton St . . . C3
Old County Hall . . . E4
Old Gloucester St . . . C4
Old King Edward St . . . C6
Old Nichol St . . . B7
Old Paradise St . . . F4
Old Spitalfields Mkt . . . C7
Old St . . . B6
Old St . . . B6
Old Vic . . . E5
Open Air Theatre . . . B2
Operating Theatre Museum . . . D6
Orange St . . . D3
Orchard St . . . C2
Ossulston St . . . A3
Outer Circle . . . B1
Oxford Circus . . . C3
Oxford St . . . C2/C3
Paddington St . . . C2
Palace St . . . E3
Pall Mall . . . D3
Pall Mall East . . . D3
Pancras Rd . . . A4
Panton St . . . D3
Paris Gdn . . . D5
Park Cres . . . B2
Park La . . . D2
Park Rd . . . B1
Park St . . . D2
Park St . . . D6
Parker St . . . C4
Parliament Sq . . . E4
Parliament St . . . E4
Paternoster Sq . . . C5
Paul St . . . B6
Pear Tree St . . . B5
Penton Rise . . . B4
Penton St . . . A5
Pentonville Rd . . . A4/A5
Percival St . . . B5
Petticoat La (Middlesex St) . . . C7
Petty France . . . E3
Phoenix Pl . . . B4
Phoenix Rd . . . A3
Photo Gallery . . . D3
Piccadilly . . . D2
Piccadilly Cir . . . D3
Pitfield St . . . B7
Pollock's Toy Museum . . . C3
Polygon Rd . . . A3
Pont St . . . E1
Portland Pl . . . C2
Portman Mews . . . C2
Portman Sq . . . C2
Portman St . . . C1
Portugal St . . . C4
Postal Museum, The . . . B4
Poultry . . . C6
Primrose St . . . C7
Princes St . . . C6
Procter St . . . C4
Provost St . . . B6
Quaker St . . . B7
Queen Anne St . . . C2
Queen Elizabeth Hall . . . D4
Queen Sq . . . B4
Queen St . . . D6
Queen Street Pl . . . D6
Queen Victoria St . . . D5
Queens Gallery . . . E3
Radnor St . . . B6
Rathbone Pl . . . C3
Rawstorne St . . . B5
Red Lion Sq . . . C4
Red Lion St . . . C4
Redchurch St . . . B7
Redcross Way . . . D6
Regency St . . . F3
Regent Sq . . . B4
Regent St . . . C3
Regent's Park . . . B2
Richmond Terr . . . E4
Ridgmount St . . . C3
Rivington St . . . B7
Robert St . . . B2
Rochester Row . . . F3
Ropemaker St . . . C6
Rosebery Ave . . . B5
Roupell St . . . D5
Royal Academy of Arts . . . D3
Royal Academy of Dramatic Art . . . B3
Royal Academy of Music . . . B2
Royal Artillery Memorial . . . E2
Royal College of Nursing . . . C2
Royal College of Surgeons . . . C4
Royal Festival Hall . . . D4
Royal London Hosp for Integrated Medicine . . . C4
Royal National Theatre . . . D5
Royal National Throat, Nose and Ear Hospital . . . B4
Royal Opera Ho . . . D4
Russell Sq . . . B3
Russell Square . . . B4
Sackville St . . . D3
Sadlers Wells . . . B5
Saffron Hill . . . C5
St Alban's St . . . D3
St Andrew St . . . C5
St Bartholomew's Hospital . . . C5
St Botolph St . . . C7
St Bride St . . . C5
St George's Circus . . . E5
St George's Rd . . . E5
St Giles High St . . . C3
St James's Pal . . . D3
St James's Park . . . E3
St James's St . . . D3
St John St . . . B5
St Margaret St . . . E4
St Mark's Hosp . . . B5
St Martin's La . . . D4
St Martin's Le Grand . . . C6
St Mary Axe . . . C7
St Pancras Int . . . A4
St Paul's . . . C6
St Paul's Cath . . . C6
St Paul's Churchyard . . . C5
St Peter's Hosp . . . D4
St Thomas St . . . D6
St Thomas' Hosp . . . E4
Savile Row . . . D3
Savoy Pl . . . D4
Savoy St . . . D4
School of Hygiene & Tropical Medicine . . . C3
Scrutton St . . . B7
Sekforde St . . . B5
Serpentine Rd . . . D1
Seven Dials . . . C4
Seward St . . . B5
Seymour St . . . C1
Shad Thames . . . D7
Shaftesbury Ave . . . D3
Shakespeare's Globe Theatre . . . D6
Shepherd Market . . . D2
Sherwood St . . . D3
Shoe La . . . C5
Shoreditch High St . . . B7
Shoreditch High St . . . B7
Shorts Gdns . . . C4
Sidmouth St . . . B4
Silk St . . . C6
Sir John Soane's Museum . . . C4
Skinner St . . . B5
Sloane St . . . E1
Snow Hill . . . C5
Soho Sq . . . C3
Somerset Ho . . . D4
South Audley St . . . D2
South Carriage Dr . . . E1
South Molton St . . . C2
South Pl . . . C6
South St . . . D2
Southampton Row . . . C4
Southampton St . . . D4
Southwark . . . D5
Southwark Bridge . . . D6
Southwark Bridge Rd . . . D6
Southwark Cath . . . D6
Southwark St . . . D6
Speakers' Corner . . . D1
Spencer St . . . B5
Spital Sq . . . C7
Stamford St . . . D5
Stanhope St . . . B3
Stephenson Way . . . B3
Stock Exchange . . . C5
Stoney St . . . D6
Strand . . . C5
Stratton St . . . D2
Sumner St . . . D5
Sutton's Way . . . B6
Swanfield St . . . B7
Swinton St . . . B4
Tabernacle St . . . B6
Tate Modern . . . D6
Tavistock Pl . . . B4
Tavistock Sq . . . B3
Tea & Coffee Museum . . . D6
Temple . . . D5
Temple Ave . . . D5
Temple Pl . . . D4
Terminus Pl . . . E2
Thayer St . . . C2
Theobald's Rd . . . C4
Thorney St . . . F4
Threadneedle St . . . C6
Throgmorton St . . . C6
Tonbridge St . . . B4
Tooley St . . . D7
Torrington Pl . . . B3
Tothill St . . . E3
Tottenham Ct Rd . . . B3
Tottenham Ct Rd . . . C3
Tottenham St . . . C3
Tower Bridge . . . D7
Tower Bridge App . . . D7
Tower Bridge Rd . . . E7
Tower Hill . . . D7
Tower Hill . . . D7
Tower of London, The . . . D7
Toynbee St . . . C7
Trafalgar Square . . . D3
Trinity Sq . . . D7
Trocadero Centre . . . D3
Tudor St . . . D5
Turnmill St . . . C5
Ufford St . . . E5
Union St . . . D5
Univ Coll Hosp . . . B3
Univ of London . . . C3
University of Westminster . . . C2
University St . . . B3
Upper Belgrave St . . . E2
Upper Berkeley St . . . C1
Upper Brook St . . . D2
Upper Grosvenor St . . . D2
Upper Ground . . . D5
Upper Montague St . . . C1
Upper St Martin's La . . . D4
Upper Thames St . . . D6
Upper Wimpole St . . . C2
Upper Woburn Pl . . . B3
Vere St . . . C2
Vernon Pl . . . C4
Vestry St . . . B6
Victoria . . . E2
Victoria Emb . . . D4
Victoria Place Shopping Centre . . . F2
Victoria St . . . E3
Villiers St . . . D4
Vincent Sq . . . F3
Vinopolis City of Wine . . . D6
Virginia Rd . . . B7
Wakley St . . . B5
Walbrook . . . C6
Wallace Collection . . . C2
Wardour St . . . C3/D3
Warner St . . . B5
Warren St . . . B3
Warren St . . . B3
Waterloo . . . E5
Waterloo Bridge . . . D4
Waterloo East . . . D5
Waterloo Rd . . . E5
Watling St . . . C6
Webber St . . . E5
Welbeck St . . . C2
Wellington Arch . . . E2
Wellington Mus . . . E2
Wells St . . . C3
Wenlock St . . . A6
Wentworth St . . . C7
West Smithfield . . . C5
West Sq . . . E5
Westminster . . . E4
Westminster Abbey . . . E4
Westminster Bridge . . . E4
Westminster Bridge Rd . . . E5
Westminster Cathedral (RC) . . . E3
Westminster City Hall . . . E3
Westminster Hall . . . E4
Weymouth St . . . C2
Wharf Rd . . . A6
Wharton St . . . B4
Whitcomb St . . . D3
White Cube . . . B7
White Lion Hill . . . D5
White Lion St . . . A5
Whitecross St . . . B6
Whitefriars St . . . C5
Whitehall . . . D4
Whitehall Pl . . . D4
Wigmore Hall . . . C2
Wigmore St . . . C2
William IV St . . . D4
Wilmington Sq . . . B5
Wilson St . . . C6
Wilton Cres . . . E2
Wimpole St . . . C2
Windmill Walk . . . D5
Woburn Pl . . . B4
Woburn Sq . . . B3
Women's Hosp . . . C3
Wood St . . . C6
Woodbridge St . . . B5
Wootton St . . . D5
Wormwood St . . . C7
Worship St . . . B6
Wren St . . . B4
Wynyatt St . . . B5
York Rd . . . E4
York St . . . C1
York Terrace East . . . B2
York Terrace West . . . B2
York Way . . . A4

Luton 119

Adelaide St . . . B1
Albert Rd . . . C2
Alma St . . . B2
Alton Rd . . . C3
Anthony Gdns . . . C1
Arthur St . . . C2
Ashburnham Rd . . . B1
Ashton Rd . . . C2
Avondale Rd . . . A1
Back St . . . A2
Bailey St . . . C3
Baker St . . . C2
Biscot Rd . . . A1
Bolton Rd . . . B3
Boyle Close . . . A2
Brantwood Rd . . . B1
Bretts Mead . . . C1
Bridge St . . . B2
Brook St . . . A1
Brunswick St . . . A3
Burr St . . . A3
Bury Park Rd . . . A1
Bute St . . . B2
Buxton Rd . . . B2
Cambridge St . . . C3
Cardiff Grove . . . B1
Cardiff Rd . . . B1
Cardigan St . . . A2
Castle St . . . B2/C2
Chapel St . . . C2
Charles St . . . A3
Chase St . . . C2
Cheapside . . . B2
Chequer St . . . C3
Chiltern Rise . . . C1
Church St . . . B2/B3
Cinema . . . A2
Cobden St . . . A3
College . . . A3
Collingdon St . . . A1
Community Centre . . . C3
Concorde Ave . . . A3
Corncastle Rd . . . C1
Cowper St . . . C2
Crawley Green Rd . . . B3
Crawley Rd . . . A1
Crescent Rd . . . A3
Crescent Rise . . . A3
Cromwell Rd . . . A1
Cross St . . . A2
Cross Way, The . . . C1
Crown Court . . . B2
Cumberland St . . . B2
Cutenhoe Rd . . . C3
Dallow Rd . . . B1
Downs Rd . . . B1
Dudley St . . . A2
Duke St . . . A2
Dumfries St . . . B1
Dunstable Place . . . B2
Dunstable Rd . . . A1/B1
Edward St . . . A3
Elizabeth St . . . C2
Essex Cl . . . C3
Farley Hill . . . C1
Farley Lodge . . . C1
Flowers Way . . . B2
Francis St . . . A1
Frederick St . . . A2
Galaxy Leisure Complex . . . A2
George St . . . B2
George St West . . . B2
Gordon St . . . B2
Grove Rd . . . B1
Guildford St . . . A2
Haddon Rd . . . A3
Harcourt St . . . C2
Hart Hill Drive . . . A3
Hart Hill Lane . . . A3
Hartley Rd . . . A3
Hastings St . . . B2
Hat Factory, The . . . B2
Hatters Way . . . A1
Havelock Rd . . . A2
Hibbert St . . . C2
High Town Rd . . . A3
Highbury Rd . . . A1
Hightown Community Sports & Arts Ctr . . . A3
Hillary Cres . . . C1
Hillborough Rd . . . C1
Hitchin Rd . . . A3
Holly St . . . C2
Holm . . . C1
Hucklesby Way . . . A2
Hunts Cl . . . C1
Inkerman St . . . A2
John St . . . B2
Jubilee St . . . A3
Kelvin Cl . . . C2
King St . . . B2
Kingsland Rd . . . C3
Larches, The . . . A2
Latimer Rd . . . C2
Lawn Gdns . . . C2
Lea Rd . . . B3
Library . . . B2
Library Rd . . . B2
Library Theatre . . . B2
Liverpool Rd . . . B1
London Rd . . . C2
Luton Station . . . A2
Lyndhurst Rd . . . B1
Magistrates Court . . . B2
Mall, The . . . B2
Manchester St . . . B2
Manor Rd . . . B3
Manor Road Park . . . B3
May St . . . C3
Meyrick Ave . . . C1
Midland Rd . . . A2
Mill St . . . A2
Milton Rd . . . B1
Moor St . . . A1
Moor, The . . . A1
Moorland Gdns . . . A2
Moulton Rise . . . A3
Napier Rd . . . B1
New Bedford Rd . . . A1
New Town St . . . C2
North St . . . A3
Old Bedford Rd . . . A2
Old Orchard . . . C2
Osbourne Rd . . . C3
Oxen Rd . . . A3
Park Sq . . . B2
Park St . . . B3/C3
Park St West . . . B2
Park Viaduct . . . B3
Parkland Drive . . . C1
Police Station . . . B1
Pomfret Ave . . . A3
Pondwicks Rd . . . B3
Post Office . . . A1/
Power Court . . .
Princess St . . .
Red Rails . . .
Regent St . . .
Reginald St . . .
Rothesay Rd . . .
Russell Rise . . .
Russell St . . .
St Ann's Rd . . .
St George's Square
St Mary's . . .
St Marys Rd . . .
St Paul's Rd . . .
St Saviour's Cres . . .
Salisbury Rd . . .
Seymour Ave . . .
Seymour Rd . . .
Silver St . . .
South Rd . . .
Stanley St . . .
Station Rd . . .
Stockwood Cres . . . C
Stockwood Park . . . C
Strathmore Ave . . . C
Stuart St . . .
Studley Rd . . .
Surrey St . . .
Sutherland Place . . . C
Tavistock St . . . C
Taylor St . . . A
Telford Way . . . A
Tennyson Rd . . . C
Tenzing Grove . . . C
Thistle Rd . . . B
Town Hall . . . B
Townsley Cl . . . C
UK Centre for Carnival Arts . . . B
Union St . . . B
University of Bedfordshire . . . B
Upper George St . . . B
Vicarage St . . . B
Villa Rd . . . A
Waldeck Rd . . . A
Wardown House Mus & Gallery . . . A
Wellington St . . . B1/B
Wenlock St . . . A
Whitby Rd . . . A
Whitehill Ave . . . C
William St . . . A
Wilsden Ave . . . C
Windmill Rd . . . B
Windsor St . . . C
Winsdon Rd . . . B
York St . . . A

Manchester 119

Adair St . . . B
Addington St . . . A
Adelphi St . . . A
Albert Sq . . . B
Albion St . . . C
Ancoats Grove . . . B
Ancoats Grove North . . . B
Angela St . . . C
Aquatics Centre . . . C
Ardwick Green North . . . C
Ardwick Green Park . . . C
Ardwick Green South . . . C
Arlington St . . . A2
Artillery St . . . B3
Arundel St . . . C2
Atherton St . . . B2
Atkinson St . . . B3
Aytoun St . . . B4
Back Piccadilly . . . A4
Baird St . . . B5
Balloon St . . . A4
Bank Pl . . . A1
Baring St . . . B5
Barrack St . . . C1
Barrow St . . . A1
Bendix St . . . A5
Bengal St . . . A5
Berry St . . . C5
Blackfriars Rd . . . A3
Blackfriars St . . . A3
Blantyre St . . . C2
Bloom St . . . B4
Blossom St . . . A5
Boad St . . . B5
Bombay St . . . B4
Booth St . . . A3
Booth St . . . B4
Bootle St . . . B3
Brazennose St . . . B3
Brewer St . . . A5
Bridge St . . . A3
Bridgewater Hall . . . B3
Bridgewater Pl . . . A4
Bridgewater St . . . B2
Brook St . . . C4
Brotherton Dr . . . A2
Brown St . . . A3
Brown St . . . B4
Brunswick St . . . C6
Brydon Ave . . . C6
Buddhist Centre . . . A4
Bury St . . . A2
Bus & Coach Sta . . . B4
Bus Station . . . B4
Butler St . . . A6
Buxton St . . . C5
Byrom St . . . B3
Cable St . . . A5
Cambridge St . . . C3/C4
Camp St . . . B3
Canal St . . . B4
Cannon St . . . A1
Cardroom Rd . . . A6
Carruthers St . . . A6
Castle St . . . C2
Castlefield Arena . . . B2
Cateaton St . . . A3
Cathedral . . . A3
Cathedral St . . . A3
Cavendish St . . . C4

hapel St A1/A3
hapeltown St B5
harles St C4
harlotte St B4
hatham St B4
hepstow St B3
hester Rd C1/C2
hester St C4
hetham's School of Music A3
hina La B5
hippenham Rd A6
horlton Rd C2
horlton St B4
hurch St A2
hurch St A4
ty Park A4
ty Rd East C3
vil Justice Ctr B2
eminson St A2
owes St A3
ollege Land A3
ollier St B2
ommercial St C3
onference Centre C4
ooper St B4
opperas St A4
orn Exchange,The A4
ornbrook C1
ornell St A5
orporation St A4
otter St C6
otton St A5
ow La B1
oss St B3
own Court B4
own St C2
alberg St C6
ale St A4/B5
ancehouse,The C4
antzic St A4
ark La C6
awson St C2
ean St A5
eansgate A3/B3/C2
eansgate Castlefield C3
eansgate Sta C3
olphin St C6
owning St C5
ucie St B5
uke Pl B2
uke St B2
urling St C6
ast Ordsall La A2/B1
dge St A4
erton St C2
llesmere St C1
verard St C1
ery St B6
xchange Sq A4
airfield St B5
aulkner St B4
ennel St A3
ord St A2
ord St C6
ountain St B4
rederick St A2
artside St B2
aythorne St A1
eorge Leigh St A5
eorge St B4
ore St A2
oulden St A5
ranby Row B4
ravel La A3
reat St B6
reat Ancoats St A5
reat Bridgewater St B3
reat George St A1
reat Jackson St C2
reat Marlborough St C4
reat Northern Warehouse Leisure & Shopping Complex B3
reengate A3
rosvenor St C5
un St A5
adrian Ave B6
all St B3
ampson St B1
anover St A4
anworth Cl C5
ardman St B3
arkness St C6
arrison St B6
art St B4
elmet St B6
enry St A5
eyrod St B6
igh St A4
igher Ardwick C6
ilton St A4/A5
olland St A6
OME ✦ C2
ood St A5
ope St B1
ope St B4
ouldsworth St A5
oyle St C6
ulme Hall Rd C1
ulme St A1
ulme St C3
yde Rd C6
ington Way A2
nformation Ctr B4
well St A2
ackson Cres C2
ackson's Row B3
ames St A1
enner Cl C2
ersey St A5
ohn Dalton St B3
ohn Ryland's Library B3
ohn St A4
ennedy St B3
incardine Rd C5
ing St A3
ing St West A3
aw Courts B3
aystall St B5
Lever St A5
Library B3
Linby St C2
Little Lever St A4
Liverpool Rd B2
Liverpool St B1
Lloyd St B3
Lockton Cl C5
London Rd B5
Long Millgate A3
Longacre St B6
Loom St A5
Lower Byrom St B2
Lower Mosley St B3
Lower Moss La C2
Lower Ormond St C4
Loxford La C4
Luna St A5
Major St B4
Manchester Arndale A4
Manchester Art Gallery B4
Manchester Central Convention Complex B3
Manchester Metropolitan Univ (MMU) B4/C4
Manchester Piccadilly Station B5
Manchester Technology Ctr C4
Mancunian Way C3
Manor St C5
Marble St A4
Market St A2
Market St A4
Market St A4
Marsden St A3
Marshall St A5
Mayan Ave A2
Medlock St C3
Middlewood St B1
Miller St A4
Minshull St B4
Mosley St A4
Mount St B3
Mulberry St B3
Murray St A5
Museum of Science & Industry (MOSI) B2
Nathan Dr A2
National Football Museum A4
Naval St A5
New Bailey St A2
New Elm Rd B2
New Islington A6
New Islington Station B6
New Quay St B2
New Union St A6
Newgate St A4
Newton St A5
Nicholas St B4
North Western St C6
Oak St A4
Odeon A4/B3
Old Mill St A6
Oldfield Rd A1/C1
Oldham Rd A5
Oldham St A4
Opera House B3
Ordsall La C1
Oxford Rd C4
Oxford Rd C4
Oxford St B4
Paddock St C6
Palace Theatre B4
Pall Mall A3
Palmerston St B6
Parker St B4
Peak St B5
Penfield Cl C5
Peoples' History Museum B2
Peru St A1
Peter St B3
Piccadilly A4
Piccadilly B5
Piccadilly Gdns B4
Piercy St A6
Poland St A5
Police Sta B3/B5
Pollard St B6
Port St A5
Portland St B4
Portugal St East B5
Post Office A1/A2/A4/A5/B3/B4
Potato Wharf B2
Princess St B3/C4
Pritchard St C4
Quay St A2
Quay St B2
Queen St B3
Radium St A5
Redhill St A5
Regent Rd B1
Retail Park A5
Rice St B2
Richmond St B4
River St C3
Roby St B5
Rodney St A6
Roman Fort B2
Rosamond St A2
Royal Exchange A3
Sackville St B4
St Andrew's St B6
St Ann St A3
St Ann's A3
St George's Ave C1
St James St B4
St John St B3
St John's Cathedral (RC) A2
St Mary's B3
St Mary's Gate A3
St Mary's Parsonage A3
St Peter's Sq B3
St Stephen St A2
Salford Approach A3
Salford Central A2
Sheffield St B5
Sherratt St A5
Shopmobility A4
Shudehill A4
Shudehill A4
Sidney St C4
Silk St A5
Silver St B4
Skerry Cl C5
Snell St B6
South King St B3
Sparkle St B5
Spear St A4
Spring Gdns A4
Stanley St A2/B2
Store St B5
Superstore B1
Swan St A4
Tariff St B5
Tatton St C1
Temperance St B6/C6
Thirsk St C6
Thomas St A4
Thompson St A5
Tib La B3
Tib St A4
Town Hall (Manchester) B3
Town Hall (Salford) A2
Trafford St C3
Travis St B5
Trinity Way A2
Turner St A4
Union St C6
Univ of Manchester (Sackville Street Campus) C5
Univ of Salford A1
Upper Brook St C5
Upper Cleminson St A1
Upper Wharf St A1
Urban Exchange A5
Vesta St B6
Victoria A4
Victoria Station A4
Wadesdon Rd C5
Water St B2
Watson St B3
West Fleet St B1
West King St A2
West Mosley St B4
Weybridge Rd A6
Whitworth St B4
Whitworth St West C3
William St A2
William St C6
Wilmott St C3
Windmill St B3
Windsor Cres A1
Withy Grove A4
Woden St C1
Wood St B3
Woodward St A6
Worrall St C1
Worsley St C2
York St B4
York St C2
York St C4

Middlesbrough 119

Abingdon Rd C3
Acklam Rd C1
Albert Park C3
Albert Rd B2
Albert Terr C2
Ambulance Station C1
Aubrey St C3
Avenue,The C2
Ayresome Gdns C2
Ayresome Green La C1
Ayresome St C2
Barton Rd A1
Bilsdale Rd C3
Bishopton Rd C3
Borough Rd B2/B3
Bowes Rd A2
Breckon Hill Rd B3
Bridge St West B2
Brighouse Rd A1
Burlam Rd C1
Bus Station B2
Cannon Park B1
Cannon Park Way B2
Cannon St B1
Captain Cook Sq B2
Carlow St C1
Castle Way C3
Chipchase Rd C2
Cineworld B3
Cleveland Centre B2
Clive Rd C2
Commercial St A2
Corporation Rd B2
Costa St C2
Council Offices B3
Crescent Rd C2
Crescent,The C2
Cumberland Rd C2
Depot Rd A2
Derwent St B2
Devonshire Rd C2
Diamond Rd B2
Dock St B3
Dorman Mus C2
Douglas St B3
Eastbourne Rd C2
Eden Rd C3
Fire Sta A3
Forty Foot Rd A2
Gilkes St B2
Gosford St A2
Grange Rd B2
Gresham Rd B2
Harehills Rd C1
Harford St C2
Hartington Rd B2
Haverton Hill Rd A1
Hey Wood St B1
Highfield Rd C3
Hillstreet Centre B2
Holwick Rd B1
Hutton Rd C3
Ironmasters Way B1
Lambton Rd C3
Lancaster Rd C2
Lansdowne Rd C3
Latham Rd C2
Law Courts B2/B3
Lees Rd B2
Leeway B3
Library B2/C2
Linthorpe Cemetery C1
Linthorpe Rd B2
Lloyd St B2
Longford St C2
Longlands Rd C3
Lower East St A3
Lower Lake C3
Macmillan Acad C1
Maldon Rd C1
Manor St B2
Marsh St B2
Marton Rd B3
Middlesbrough By-Pass B2/C1
Middlesbrough College B3
Middlesbrough Dock B3
Middlesbrough Leisure Park B3
Middlesbrough Station B2
Middletown Park C2
MIMA B3
Mulgrave Rd C2
Newport Bridge B1
Newport Bridge Approach Rd B1
Newport Rd B2
North Ormesby Rd B3
North Rd B2
Northern Rd C1
Outram St B2
Oxford Rd C2
Park La C2
Park Rd North C2
Park Rd South C2
Park Vale Rd C3
Parliament Rd B1
Police Station A2
Port Clarence Rd A3
Portman St B2
Post Office B3/C1/C2
Princes Rd B2
Python A2
Riverside Park Rd A1
Riverside Stadium (Middlesbrough FC) B3
Rockliffe Rd C2
Romaldkirk Rd B1
Roman Rd C2
Roseberry Rd C3
St Barnabas' Rd C2
St Paul's Rd B2
Saltwells Rd B3
Scott's Rd A3
Seaton Carew Rd A3
Shepherdson Way B3
Shopmobility B2
Snowdon Rd A2
South West Ironmasters Park B1
Southfield Rd B2
Southwell Rd C2
Springfield Rd C1
Startforth Rd A2
Stockton Rd C1
Stockton St A2
Superstore B2
Surrey St C2
Sycamore Rd C2
Tax Offices B3
Tees Viaduct C1
Teessaurus Park A2
Teesside Tertiary College C3
Temenos ✦ B3
Thornfield Rd C1
Town Hall B2
Transporter Bridge (Toll) A3
Union St B2
Univ of Teesside B2
Upper Lake C2
Valley Rd C3
Ventnor Rd C2
Victoria Rd B2
Vulcan St A2
Warwick St C2
Wellesley Rd B3
West La B1
West Lane Hosp C1
Westminster Rd C2
Wilson St B2
Windward Way B3
Woodlands Rd B2
York Rd C3

Milton Keynes 122

Abbey Way A1
Arbrook Ave B1
Armourer Dr A3
Arncliffe Dr A1
Avebury C2
Avebury Blvd C2
Bankfield B3
Bayard Ave A2
Belvedere A2
Bishopstone A1
Blundells Rd A1
Boundary,The C3
Boycott Ave C2
Bradwell Common Boulevard B1
Bradwell Rd C1
Bramble Ave A2
Brearley Ave C2
Breckland A1
Brill Place B1
Burnham Dr B1
Campbell Park B3
Cantle Ave A3
Central Retail Park C1
Century Ave C2
Chaffron Way C3
Childs Way C1
Christ the Cornerstone B2
Cineworld B2
Civic Offices B2
Cleavers Ave B2
Colesbourne Dr A3
Conniburrow Blvd B2
Currier Dr A2
Dansteed Way A2/A3/B1
Deltic Ave B1
Downs Barn A2
Downs Barn Blvd A3
Eaglestone C3
Eelbrook Ave B1
Elder Gate B1
Evans Gate C2
Fairford Cres A3
Falcon Ave B3
Fennel Dr A2
Fishermead Blvd C3
Food Centre B3
Fulwoods Dr C3
Glazier Dr A2
Glovers La A1
Grafton Gate C1
Grafton St A1/C2
Gurnards Ave B3
Harrier Dr C3
The Hub Leisure Quarter B2/C2
Ibstone Ave B1
intu Milton Keynes B2
Langcliffe Dr A1
Leisure Centre C3
Leisure Plaza C1
Leys Rd C1
Library B2
Linceslade Grove C1
Linford Wood A2
Magistrates Court B2
Marlborough Gate B3
Marlborough St A2/B3
Mercers Dr A1
Midsummer C2
Midsummer Blvd B2
Milton Keynes Central C1
Milton Keynes Hospital (A&E) C3
Monks Way A1
Mullen Ave A3
Mullion Pl C3
Neath Hill A3
North Elder C1
North Grafton B1
North Overgate A3
North Row B2
North Saxon B2
North Secklow B2
North Skeldon A3
North Witan B1
Oakley Gdns A3
Odeon B2
Oldbrook Blvd C2
Open-Air Theatre B3
Overgate A3
Overstreet A3
Patriot Dr B1
Pencarrow Pl B3
Penryn Ave B3
Perran Ave C3
Pitcher La C1
Place Retail Pk,The C1
Police Station B2
Portway B2
Post Office A2/B2/B3
Precedent Dr B1
Quinton Dr B1
Ramsons Ave B2
Retail Park C2
Rockingham Dr A2
Rooksley B1
Saxon Gate B2
Saxon St A1/C3
Secklow Gate B2
Shackleton Pl C2
Shopmobility B2
Silbury Blvd B2
Skeldon A3
South Enmore B3
South Grafton C2
South Row C2
South Saxon C2
South Secklow B3
South Witan C2
Springfield B3
Stainton Dr A1/B1
Stanton Wood A1
Stantonbury A1
Stantonbury Leisure Centre ✦ A1
Strudwick Dr C2
Sunrise Parkway A2
Superstore C1/C2
Theatre & Art Gallery B3
theCentre:mk B2
Tolcarne Ave C3
Towan Ave C3
Trueman Pl C2
Vauxhall A1
Winterhill Retail Pk C2
Witan Gate B2
Xscape B3

Newcastle upon Tyne 122

Albert St B3
Argyle St B3
Back New Bridge St B3
BALTIC Centre for Contemporary Art C3
Barker St A3
Barrack Rd B1
Bath La B1
Bessie Surtees House ✦ C2
Bigg Market C2
Biscuit Factory B3
Black Gate C2
Blackett St B2
Blandford Sq C1
Boating Lake A1
Boyd St B3
Brandling Park A2
Bus Station B2
Buxton St B3
Byron St A3
Camden St B2
Castle Keep C2
Central C1
Central Library B2
Central Motorway B2
Chester St A3
Cineworld B1
City Hall B2
City Rd B3/C3
City Walls ✦ C1
Civic Centre A2
Claremont Rd A1
Clarence St B3
Clarence Walk B3
Clayton St C1/B1
Clayton St West C1
Close,The C2
Coach Station C1
College St B2
Collingwood St C2
Copland Terr B3
Coppice Way B3
Corporation St B1
Courts C3
Crawhall Rd B3
Dean St C2
Dental Hospital A1
Dinsdale Pl A3
Dinsdale Rd A3
Discovery C1
Doncaster Rd A3
Durant Rd B2
Eldon Sq B1
Ellison Pl B2
Eskdale Terr A2
Eslington Terr A2
Exhibition Park A1
Falconar St B3
Fenkle St C1
Forth Banks C1
Forth St C1
Gallowgate B1
Gate,The ✦ B1
Gateshead Millennium Bridge C3
Gateshead Quays C3
Gibson St B3
Goldspink La A3
Grainger Market B2
Grainger St B2
Grantham Rd A3
Granville Rd A3
Great North Children's Hosp A1
Great North Mus:Hancock A2
Grey St B2
Groat Market C2
Guildhall C2
Hancock St A2
Hanover St C2
Hatton Gallery A1
Hawks Rd C3
Haymarket B2
Heber St B1
Helmsley Rd A3
High Bridge B2
High Level Bridge C2
Hillgate C3
Howard St B3
Hutton Terr A3
intu Eldon Sq Shopping Centre B2
Jesmond A2
Jesmond Rd A2/A3
John Dobson St B2
Jubilee Rd B3
Kelvin Grove A3
Kensington Terr A2
Laing Gallery B2
Lambton Rd A2
Leazes Cres B1
Leazes La B1
Leazes Park B1
Leazes Park Rd B1
Leazes Terr B1
Library A2
Live C2
Low Friar St C1
Manor Chare C2
Manors B2
Manors Station B2
Market St B2
Melbourne St B2
Mill Rd C3
Monument B2
Monument Mall Shopping Centre B2
Morpeth St A2
Mosley St C2
Napier St A3
New Bridge St West B2/B3
Newcastle Central Station C1
Newcastle Univ A1
Newgate St B1
Newington Rd A3
Northern Design Centre C3
Northern Stage Theatre A2
Northumberland Rd B2
Northumberland St B2
Northumbria Univ A2
Northwest Radial Rd A1
O2 Academy ✦ C1
Oakwellgate C3
Open Univ C3
Orchard St C2
Osborne Rd A2
Osborne Terr A3
Pandon C3
Pandon Bank B3
Park Terr A1
Percy St B1
Pilgrim St B2
Pipewellgate C2
Pitt St B1
Plummer Tower A2
Police Station C1
Portland Rd A3/B3
Portland Terr A3
Post Office B1/B2
Pottery La C1
Prudhoe Pl B1
Prudhoe St B1
Quayside C2
Queen Elizabeth II Bridge C2
Queen Victoria Rd A1
Richardson Rd A1
Ridley Pl B2
Rock Terr B3
Rosedale Terr A3
Royal Victoria Infirmary A1
Sage Gateshead ✦ C3
St Andrew's St B1
St James B1
St James' Blvd C1
St James' Park (Newcastle Utd FC) B1
St Mary's Heritage Centre ✦ C3
St Mary's (RC) C1
St Mary's Place B2
St Nicholas C2
St Nicholas St C2
St Thomas' St B1
Sandyford Rd A2/A3
Shield St B3
Shieldfield B3
Shopmobility B1
Side,The C2
Simpson Terr B3
South Shore Rd C3
South St C1
Starbeck Ave A3
Stepney Rd B3
Stoddart St B3
Stowell St B1
Strawberry Pl B1
Swing Bridge C2
Temple St C1
Terrace Pl B1
Theatre Royal B2
Times Sq C1
Tower St B3
Trinity House C2
Tyne Bridge C2
Tyne Bridges ✦ C2
Tyne Theatre & Opera House C1
Tyneside B2
Victoria Sq A2
Warwick St A3
Waterloo St C1
Wellington St B1
Westgate Rd C1/C2
Windsor Terr A2
Worswick St B2
Wretham Pl B3

Newport Casnewydd 122

Albert Terr B1
Allt-yr-Yn Ave A1
Alma St C2
Ambulance Station C3
Bailey St B2
Barrack Hill A2
Bath St A3
Bedford Rd B3
Belle Vue La C1
Belle Vue Park C1
Bishop St A3
Blewitt St B1
Bolt Cl C3
Bolt St C3
Bond St A2
Bosworth Dr A1
Bridge St B1
Bristol St A3
Bryngwyn Rd B1
Brynhyfryd Ave C1
Brynhyfryd Rd C1
Bus Station B2
Caerau Cres C1
Caerau Rd B1
Caerleon Rd A3
Capel Cres C2
Cardiff Rd C2
Caroline St B3
Castle (Remains) A2
Cedar Rd B3
Charles St B2
Charlotte Dr C2
Chepstow Rd A3
Church Rd A3
Cineworld B2
Civic Centre B1
Clarence Pl A2
Clifton Pl B1
Clifton Rd C1
Clyffard Cres B1
Clytha Park Rd B1
Clytha Sq C2
Coldra Rd C1
Collier St A3
Colne St B3
Comfrey Cl A1
Commercial Rd C3
Commercial St B2
Corelli St A3
Corn St B2
Corporation Rd B3
Coulson Cl C2
County Court A2
Courts A1
Courts B1
Crawford St A3
Cyril St B3
Dean St A3
Devon Pl B1
Dewsland Park Rd C2
Dolman B2
Dolphin St C3
East Dock Rd C3
East St B1
East Usk Rd A3
Ebbw Vale Wharf B3
Emlyn St B2
Enterprise Way C3
Eton Rd B3
Evans St A2
Factory Rd A2
Fields Rd B1
Francis Dr C2
Frederick St C3
Friars Rd C1
Friars Walk B2
Gaer La C1
George St C3
George St Bridge C3
Godfrey Rd B1
Gold Tops B1
Gore St A3
Gorsedd Circle C1
Grafton Rd A3
Graham St B1
Granville St C3
Harlequin Dr A1
Harrow Rd B3
Herbert Rd A3
Herbert Walk C2
Hereford St A3
High St B2
Hill St B2
Hoskins St A2
Information Ctr B2
Ivor St B2
Jones St B1
Junction Rd A3
Keynshaw Ave C2
King St C2
Kingsway B2
Kingsway Centre B2
Ledbury Dr A2
Library A3
Library, Museum & Art Gallery B2
Liverpool Wharf B3
Llanthewy Rd B1
Llanvair Rd A3
Locke St A2
Lower Dock St C3
Lucas St A2
Manchester St A3
Market B2
Marlborough Rd B3
Mellon St C3
Mill St A2
Morgan St A3
Mountjoy Rd C2
Newport Bridge A2
Newport Ctr B2
Newport RFC B3
Newport Station B2
North St B2
Oakfield Rd B1
Park Sq C2
Police Sta A3/C2
Post Office B2/C3
Power St A1
Prince St A3
Pugsley St A2
Queen St C2
Queen's Cl A1
Queen's Hill A1
Queen's Hill Cres A1
Queensway B2
Railway St B2
Riverfront Theatre & Arts Ctr,The B2
Riverside A3
Rodney Rd B2
Royal Gwent (A&E) C2
Rudry St A3
Rugby Rd B3
Ruperra La C3
Ruperra St C3
St Edmund St B1
St Mark's Cres A1
St Mary St B1
St Vincent Rd A3
St Woolos C2
St Woolos General (no A&E) C1
St Woolos Rd B1
School La B2
Serpentine Rd B1
Shaftesbury Park A2
Sheaf La A3
Skinner St B2
Sorrel Dr A1
South Market St C3
Spencer Rd B1
Stow Hill B2/C1/C2
Stow Park Ave C1
Stow Park Dr C1
TA Centre A1
Talbot St B2
Tennis Club A1
Tregare St A3
Trostrey St A3
Tunnel Terr B1
Turner St A3
Univ of Wales Newport City Campus B3
Upper Dock St B2
Usk St A3
Usk Way B3/C3
Victoria Cres B1
War Memorial A3
Waterloo Rd C1
West St B1
Wharves B2
Wheeler St A2
Whitby Pl A3
Windsor Terr B1
York Pl C1

Northampton 122

78 Derngate B3
Abington Sq B3
Abington St B3
Alcombe St A3
All Saints' B2
Ambush St B1
Angel St B2
AR Centre A3
Arundel St A2
Ash St A2
Auctioneers Way C2
Bailiff St A2
Barrack Rd A2
Beaconsfield Terr A3
Becket's Park C3
Bedford Rd B3
Billing Rd B3
Brecon St A1
Brewery C2
Bridge St C2
Broad St B2
Burns St A3
Bus Station B2
Campbell St A2
Castle (Site of) B2
Castle St B2
Cattle Market Rd C2
Central Museum & Art Gallery B2
Charles St A3
Cheyne Walk B3
Church La A2
Clare St A3
Cloutsham St A3
College St B2
Colwyn Rd A3
Cotton End C2
Countess Rd A1
County Hall B2
Court A2
Craven St A3
Crown & County Courts B3
Denmark Rd B3
Derngate B3
Derngate & Royal Theatres B3
Doddridge Church B2
Drapery,The B2
Duke St A3
Dunster St A3
Earl St A3
Euston Rd C2
Fire Station A3
Foot Meadow B2
Gladstone Rd A1
Gold St B2
Grafton St A2
Gray St A3
Green St B1
Greenwood Rd B1
Greyfriars B2
Grosvenor Centre B2
Grove Rd A3
Guildhall B2
Hampton St A2
Harding Terr A2
Hazelwood Rd B3
Herbert St B2
Hervey St A3
Hester St A2
Holy Sepulchre A2
Hood St A3
Horse Market B2
Hunter St A3
Information Ctr B1
Kettering Rd A3
Kingswell St B2
Lady's La B2
Leicester St A2
Leslie Rd A2
Library B3
Lorne Rd A2
Lorry Park A1
Louise Rd A2
Lower Harding St A2
Lower Hester St A2
Lower Mounts B3
Lower Priory St A2
Main Rd C1
Marefair B2
Market Sq B2
Marlboro Rd B1
Marriott St A2
Military Rd A3
Mounts Baths Leisure Centre A3
Nene Valley Retail Park C1
New South Bridge Rd C2
Northampton General Hospital (A&E) B3
Northampton Marina C3
Northampton Station B1
Northcote St A2
Nunn Mills Rd C3
Old Towcester Rd C2
Overstone Rd A3
Peacock Pl B2
Pembroke Rd A1
Penn Court C2
Police Station B3
Post Office A1/B3
Quorn Way A2
Ransome Rd C3
Regent Sq A2
Ridings,The B3
Robert St A2
St Andrew's Rd B1
St Andrew's St A2
St Edmund's Rd B3
St George's St A2
St Giles B3
St Giles St B3
St Giles' Terr B3
St James Park Rd B1
St James Rd B1
St James Retail Pk C1
St James' Mill Rd B1
St James' Mill Rd East C1
St Leonard's Rd C2
St Mary's St B2
St Michael's Rd A3
St Peter's B2
St Peter's Way Shopping Prec B2
St Peter's Way B2
Salisbury St A2
Scarletwell St B2
Semilong Rd A2
Sheep St B2
Sol Central (Leisure Centre) B2
Somerset St A3
South Bridge C2
Southfield Ave C2
Spencer Bridge Rd A1
Spencer Rd A3
Spring Gdns B3
Spring La B2
Superstore C2
Swan St B3
Tintern Ave A1
Towcester Rd C2
Upper Bath St B2
Upper Mounts A2
Victoria Park A1
Victoria Prom B2
Victoria Rd B3
Victoria St A2
Wellingborough Rd B3
West Bridge B1
York Rd B3

Norwich 122

Albion Way C3
All Saints Green C2
Anchor St A3
Anglia Sq A2
Argyle St C3
Arts Centre B1
Ashby St C2
Assembly House B1
Bank Plain B2
Barker St A1
Barn Rd A1
Barrack St A3
Ber St C2
Bethel St B1
Bishop Bridge A3
Bishopbridge Rd A3
Bishopgate A3
Blackfriars St A2
Botolph St A2
Bracondale C3
Brazen Gate C2
Bridewell B2
Brunswick Rd C1
Bull Close Rd A2
Bus Station C2
Calvert St A2
Cannell Green A3
Carrow Rd C3
Castle & Mus B2
Castle Mall B2
Castle Meadow B2
Cathedral B2
Cath Retail Park A1
Cattlemarket St B2
Chantry Rd C1
Chapel Loke C2
Chapelfield East B1
Chapelfield Gdns B1
Chapelfield North B1
Chapelfield Rd B1
Cinema City B2
City Hall ✦ B1
City Rd C2
City Wall C1/C3
Close,The B2/B3
Colegate A2
Coslany St B1
Cow Hill B1
Cow Tower A3
Cowgate A2
Crown & Magistrates' Courts A2
Dragon Hall Heritage Ctr C3
Duke St A1
Edward St A2
Elm Hill B2
Erpingham Gate ✦ B2
Fishergate A2
Forum,The B1
Foundry Bridge B3
Fye Bridge A2
Garden St C2
Gas Hill B3
Gentlemans Walk B2
Grapes Hill B1
Great Hospital Halls,The A3
Grove Ave C1
Grove Rd C1
Guildhall ✦ B1
Gurney Rd A3
Hall Rd C2
Heathgate A3
Heigham St A1
Hollywood A2
Horn's La C2
Hungate Medieval Art ✦ B2
Information Ctr B1
intu Chapelfield C1
Ipswich Rd C1
ITV Anglia C3
James Stuart Gdns B3
King St B2
King St C3
Koblenz Ave C3
Leisure Centre A3
Library B1
London St B2
Lower Clarence Rd B3
Maddermarket B1
Magdalen St A2
Mariners La C2
Market B2
Market Ave B2
Mountergate B3

Mousehold St.....A3
Newmarket Rd....C1
Norfolk St.......C1
Norwich City FC..C3
Norwich Gallery...B2
Norwich School...B2
Norwich Station...B2
Oak St..........A1
Odeon..........A2
Palace St.......A2
Pitt St.........A1
Playhouse.......B2
Police Station...B1
Post Office
  ....A2/B2/B3/C1
Pottergate......B2
Prince of Wales Rd..B2
Princes St.......B2
Pull's Ferry.....B3
Puppet Theatre...A2
Queen St........B2
Queens Rd.......C2
RC Cathedral....B2
Recorder Rd.....B3
Riverside
  Entertainment Ctr C3
Riverside Leisure
  Centre........C3
Riverside Rd.....C3
Riverside Retail Pk..C3
Rosary Rd.......C2
Rose La.........C2
Rouen Rd.......C2
St Andrews St....B2
St Augustines St...A1
St Benedicts St...B1
St Ethelbert's
  Gate..........B2
St Faiths La.....B3
St Georges St....A2
St Giles St......B1
St James Cl......A3
St Julians St.....B3
St Leonards Rd...B3
St Martin's La....A1
St Peter
  Mancroft......B2
St Peters St.....C1
St Stephens Rd...C1
St Stephens St...B2
Shopmobility....C1
Silver Rd.......A2
Silver St.......A2
Southwell Rd....C2
St. Andrew's &
  Blackfriars' Hall
  ....B2
Strangers' Hall...B1
Superstore......C2
Surrey St.......C2
Sussex St.......A1
Theatre Royal....B1
Theatre St......B1
Thorn La........C1
Thorpe Rd......B3
Tombland.......B2
Union St........B1
Vauxhall St.....B1
Victoria St......B1
Vue............B2
Walpole St......B1
Waterfront, The...C2
Wensum St......A2
Wessex St......A2
Westwick St.....A1
Wherry Rd......C2
Whitefriars......B2
Willow La.......B1

Nottingham 122
Abbotsford Dr....A3
Addison St......A1
Albert Hall......B1
Alfred St Central...A1
Alfreton Rd.....A1
All Saints St.....A1
Annesley Grove...A1
Arboretum......A1
Arboretum St....A1
Arthur St.......A1
Arts Theatre.....B3
Ashforth St.....A1
Balmoral Rd.....A1
Barker Gate.....B3
Bath St.........B3
BBC Nottingham..C1
Beacon Hill Rise...B3
Belgrave Rooms...B1
Bellar Gate.....B3
Belward St......B3
Brewhouse Yard...C2
Broad Marsh Bus
  Station........C2
Broad St........B2
Brook St........B3
Burns St........A1
Burton St.......B2
Bus Station......A2
Canal St........C2
Carlton St......B3
Carrington St....C2
Castle..........C2
Castle Blvd......C1
Castle Gate......C2
Castle Meadow Rd..C1
Castle Meadow
  Retail Park.....C1
Castle Rd.......C2
Castle Wharf.....C2
Cavendish Rd East..C1
Cemetery.......A1/B1
Chaucer St......B2
Cheapside.......B2
Church Rd.......A3
City Link.......C3
City of Caves....C2
Clarendon St....B1
Cliff Rd........C3
Clumber Rd East..C1
Clumber St......B3
College St.......B1
Collin St........C2
Contemporary....C3
Conway Cl.......A2

Cornerhouse, The
  ....B2
Council House....B2
Cranbrook St....B3
Cranmer St......A2
Cromwell St.....B1
Curzon St.......B3
Derby Rd.......B1
Dryden St......A2
Exchange Ctr, The..B2
Fishpond Dr.....C2
Fletcher Gate....B3
Forest Rd East...A1
Forest Rd West...A1
Friar La........B2
Gedling Grove...A1
Gedling St......B3
George St.......B3
Gill St.........A2
Glasshouse St....B2
Goldsmith St....B2
Goose Gate.....B3
Great Freeman St..B2
Guildhall.......B2
Hamilton Dr.....C1
Hampden St.....A1
Heathcote St....B2
High Pavement...C3
High School.....A1
HM Revenue &
  Customs......C2
Holles Cres......C1
Hope Dr........C1
Hungerhill Rd....A3
Huntingdon Dr...C1
Huntingdon St...A2
Information Ctr...B2
Instow Rise......A3
Int Com Ctr.....A2
intu Broadmarsh..C2
intu Victoria Centre..B2
Kent St.........A3
King St.........B2
Lace Market.....B3
Lace Market
  Theatre.......C3
Lamartine St....C3
Leisure Ctr......C2
Lenton St.......C1
Lewis Cl........A3
Lincoln St.......B3
London Rd......C3
Long Row.......B2
Low Pavement....C2
Lower
  Parliament St....B3
Magistrates' Court..C2
Maid Marian Way...B2
Mansfield Rd....A2/B2
Middle Hill......C3
Milton St.......B2
Mount St.......C1
National Ice Centre &
  Motorpoint Arena..C3
National Justice
  Museum.......C3
Newcastle Dr....C1
Newstead Grove..A2
North Sherwood St..A1
Nottingham Arena..C3
Nottingham Cath...B1
Nottingham Coll...C3
Nottingham
  Station.......C3
Nottingham Trent
  University.....A2/B2
Old Mkt Square...B2
Oliver St........A1
Park Dr........C1
Park Row.......B1
Park Terr.......B1
Park Valley......C1
Park, The.......C1
Peas Hill Rd.....A3
Peel St.........A2
Pelham St......B2
Peveril Dr......C1
Plantagenet St...A3
Playhouse
  Theatre.......B1
Plumptre St.....C3
Police Sta......B1/B2
Poplar St.......C3
Portland Rd.....C1
Post Office......B2
Queen's Rd......C3
Raleigh St......A1
Regent St......B1
Rick St.........B3
Robin Hood St...A3
Robin Hood
  Statue........B3
Ropewalk, The...B1
Royal Centre....B2
Royal Children
  Inn...........B2
Royal Concert
  Hall..........B2
St Ann's Hill Rd...A3
St Ann's Way....A3
St Ann's Well Rd...A3
St James' St.....B2
St Mark's St.....A3
St Mary's Rest Gdn..B3
St Mary's Gate...B3
St Nicholas......B2
St Peter's.......B2
St Peter's Gate...B2
Salutation Inn...C2
Shakespeare St...B2
Shelton St.......A2
Shopmobility....B2
South Pde.......B2
South Rd.......C1
South Sherwood St..B2
Station Street....C3
Stoney St.......B3
Talbot St.......B1
Tattershall Dr....C1
Tennis Dr......C1
Tennyson St....A1
Theatre Royal....B1
Trent St........C3
Trent University...B2
Union Rd.......B3

Upper
  Parliament St....B2
Victoria Leisure Ctr..B3
Victoria Park....B3
Victoria St......A1
Walter St.......A1
Warser Gate....B3
Watkin St......A2
Waverley St.....A1
Wheeler Gate....B2
Wilford Rd......C2
Wilford St.......C2
Wollaton St.....B1
Woodborough Rd..A3
Woolpack La....B3
Ye Old Trip to
  Jerusalem.....C2
York St.........A2

Oxford 123
Adelaide St.....A1
Albert St.......A1
All Souls (Coll)...B2
Ashmolean Mus...B1
Balliol (Coll)....B2
Banbury Rd.....A2
Bate Collection
  of Musical
  Instruments....B2
Beaumont St....B1
Becket St.......B1
Blackhall Rd.....A2
Blue Boar St.....B2
Bodleian Library...B2
Botanic Garden...B3
Brasenose (Coll)..B2
Brewer St.......C2
Broad St.......B2
Burton-Taylor
  Theatre.......B1
Bus Station.....B1
Canal St........A1
Cardigan St.....A1
Carfax Tower....B2
Castle..........B1
Castle St.......B1
Catte St........B2
Cemetery......C1
Christ Church
  (Coll).........B2
Christ Church
  Cathedral.....B2
Christ Church
  Meadow.......C2
Clarendon Centre..B2
Coach & Lorry Park..C1
College.........A3
Coll of Further Ed..C1
Cornmarket St...B2
Corpus Christi
  (Coll).........B2
County Hall.....B1
Covered Market...B2
Cowley Pl.......C3
Cranham St.....A1
Cranham Terr....A1
Cricket Ground...B1
Crown & County
  Courts........C2
Deer Park......B2
Exeter (Coll)....B2
Folly Bridge.....C2
George St.......B1
Great Clarendon St..A1
Hart St.........A1
Hertford (Coll)...B2
High St........B2
Hollybush Row...B1
Holywell St.....B2
Hythe Bridge St...B1
Ice Rink........C1
Information Ctr...B2
Jericho St.......A1
Jesus (Coll).....B2
Jowett Walk.....B2
Juxon St........A1
Keble (Coll).....A3
Keble Rd.......A2
Library.........B2
Linacre (Coll)....A3
Lincoln (Coll)....B2
Little Clarendon St..A1
Longwall St.....B2
Magdalen (Coll)..B3
Magdalen Bridge..B3
Magdalen St.....B2
Magistrate's Court..B2
Manchester (Coll)..B2
Manor Rd.......A2
Mansfield (Coll)...A2
Mansfield Rd....A2
Market.........B1
Marlborough Rd...C2
Martyrs' Meml...B2
Merton (Coll)....B2
Merton Field....C2
Merton St......B2
Museum of
  Modern Art...B2
Mus of Oxford...B2
Museum Rd.....A2
New College (Coll)..B3
New Inn Hall St...B1
New Rd........B1
New Theatre....B2
Norfolk St.......C1
Nuffield (Coll)....B1
Observatory.....A1
Observatory St...A1
Odeon.........B1/B2
Old Fire Station...B1
Old Greyfriars St..B1
Oriel (Coll).....B2
Oxford Station...B1
Oxford University
  Research Centres..A1
Oxpens Rd......C1
Paradise Sq.....C1
Paradise St......B1
Park End St.....B1
Parks Rd.......A2/B2
Pembroke (Coll)..B2
Phoenix........A1
Picture Gallery...C2

Plantation Rd....A1
Playhouse......B2
Police Station....B1
Post Office
  ....A3/B1/B2/B3/C1
Pusey St.......A1
Queen's (Coll)...B2
Queen's La.....B2
Radcliffe
  Camera.......B2
Rewley Rd......B1
Richmond Rd....B1
Rose La........B3
Ruskin (Coll)....A1
Said Bsns School..B1
St Aldates......B2
St Antony's (Coll)..A1
St Bernard's Rd...A1
St Catherine's
  (Coll).........B3
St Cross Building..A3
St Cross Rd.....A3
St Edmund Hall
  (Coll).........B2
St Giles St......B1
St Hilda's (Coll)..C3
St John St......B2
St John's (Coll)..B2
St Mary the
  Virgin........B2
St Michael at the
  Northgate.....B1
St Peter's (Coll)..B1
St Thomas St....B1
Science Area.....A2
Science Mus.....B2
Sheldonian
  Theatre.......B2
Somerville (Coll)..A1
South Parks Rd...A2
Speedwell St....C2
Sports Ground...C3
Thames St......C1
Town Hall.......B2
Trinity (Coll)....B2
Turl St.........B2
Univ Coll (Coll)..B2
Univ Mus & Pitt
  Rivers Mus.....A2
University Parks...A2
Wadham (Coll)...B2
Walton Cres.....A1
Walton St......A1
Western Rd......C2
Westgate.......C1
Woodstock Rd...A1
Worcester (Coll)..B1

Peterborough 123
Athletics Arena...B3
Bishop's Palace...B2
Bishop's Rd.....B2/B3
Boongate.......A3
Bourges Boulevard..A2
Bourges Retail
  Park..........B1/B2
Bridge House
  (Council Offices)..C2
Bridge St.......B2
Bright St.......A1
Broadway......A2
Broadway......B2
Brook St.......A2
Burghley Rd.....A3
Bus Station.....B2
Cavendish St....A3
Charles St......A1
Church St......B2
Church Walk....A2
Cobden Ave.....A1
Cobden St......A1
Cowgate.......A2
Craig St........A1
Crawthorne Rd...A2
Cromwell Rd....A1
Dickens St......A3
Eastfield Rd.....A3
Eastgate.......B3
Fire Station.....C2
Fletton Ave.....C2
Frank Perkins
  Parkway......C3
Geneva St......A1
George St......A1
Gladstone St....A1
Glebe Rd.......C1
Gloucester Rd...C1
Granby St.......A3
Grove St........C1
Guildhall........B2
Hadrians Ct.....C1
Hawksbill Way...C1
Henry St.......A1
Hereward Cross
  (shopping)....B2
Hereward Rd....B3
Information Ctr...B2
Jubilee St......C1
Kent Rd.......A2
Key Theatre.....B2
Kirkwood Cl.....C1
Lea Gdns......A1
Library.........B2
Lincoln Rd......A2
London Rd......C2
Long Causeway...B2
Lower Bridge St..C2
Magistrates Court..B2
Manor House St...A1
Mayor's Walk....A1
Midland Rd.....B1
Monument St....A3
Morris St.......A3
Museum &
  Art Gallery....B2
Nene Valley
  Railway.......C1
New Rd........A2
New Rd........B2
Northminster....B2
Old Customs Ho..B2
Oundle Rd......C1
Padholme Rd....A3
Palmerston Rd...C1

Park Rd.......A2
Passport Office...B2
Peterborough Nene
  Valley........C2
Peterborough
  Station.......B1
Police Station....B2
Post Office
  ......A3/B1/B2/B3/C1
Priestgate......B2
Queen's Walk...C3
Queensgate Centre..B2
Railworld......C1
Regional Swimming &
  Fitness Centre...B3
River La........B2
Rivergate Shopping
  Centre........B2
Riverside Mead...B2
Russell St.......A1
St John's.......B2
St John's St.....A3
St Marks St.....A2
St Peter's.......B2
St Peter's Rd....B2
Saxon Rd......A3
Spital Bridge....A1
Stagshaw Dr....C3
Star Rd........B3
The Weston
  Homes Stadium
  (Peterborough
  United).......C2
Thorpe Lea Rd...B1
Thorpe Rd......B1
Thorpe's Lea Rd..B1
Tower St.......A2
Town Hall.......B2
Viersen Platz....B2
Vineyard Rd.....B3
Wake Rd.......B3
Wellington St....A3
Wentworth St...B2
Westgate.......A2
Whalley St.....A3
Wharf Rd......C1
Whitsed St.....A3
YMCA.........B2

Plymouth 123
Alma Rd.......A1
Anstis St.......A1
Armada Shopping
  Centre........A2
Armada St......A2
Armada Way....B2
Arts Centre.....B2
Athenaeum.....B2
Athenaeum St...B2
Barbican.......C3
Baring St.......A3
Bath St........A1
Beaumont Park...B3
Beaumont Rd...B3
Black Friars
  Gin Distillery...C2
Breton Side.....B3
Castle St.......C3
Cathedral (RC)...B1
Cecil St........B1
Central Park....A1
Central Park Ave..A1
Charles Church...B3
Charles Cross....B3
Charles St......B2
Citadel Rd......C2
Citadel Rd East...C2
City Museum &
  Art Gallery....B2
Civic Centre.....B2
Cliff Rd........C1
Clifton Pl.......A3
Cobourg St.....B2
College of Art....B2
Continental
  Ferry Port.....A3
Cornwall St.....B2
Crescent, The....C1
Dale Rd.......A2
Deptford Pl......A3
Derry Ave......A2
Derry's Cross....B2
Drake Circus.....B3
Drake Circus
  Shopping Centre..B2
Eastlake St......B2
Ebrington St....B3
Elliot St........C2
Endsleigh Pl.....A2
Exeter St.......B3
Fire Station.....B2
Fish Quay......C3
Gibbons St......A3
Glen Park Ave....A2
Grand Parade....C1
Great Western Rd..A1
Greenbank Rd...A3
Greenbank Terr...A3
Guildhall........B2
Hampton St.....B3
Harwell St......B1
Hill Park Cres....A3
Hoe Approach...C2
Hoe Rd.......C2
Hoe, The......C2
Hoegate St.....C2
Houndiscombe Rd..A2
Information Ctr...C2
James St.......A2
Kensington Rd...A3
King St........B1
Lambhay Hill....C3
Leigham St.....C1
Library.........B2
Lipson Rd......A3/B3
Lockyer St......C2
Lockyers Quay...C3
Madeira Rd.....C3
Marina.........C3
Market Ave.....B1
Martin St.......B1
Mayflower St....B2

Mayflower Stone &
  Steps.........C3
Mayflower Visitor
  Centre........C3
Mayflower St....B2
Merchant's Ho...B1
Millbay Rd.....B1
National Marine
  Aquarium.....C3
Neswick St.....B1
New George St...B2
New St........C3
North Cross.....A2
North Hill......A3
North Quay.....C3
North Rd East...A3
North Rd West...A2
North St.......A3
Notte St.......C2
Octagon, The....B1
Octagon St.....B1
Pannier Market...B2
Pennycomequick
  ....A1
Pier St........C1
Plymouth Naval
  Memorial.....C2
Plymouth Pavilions..B1
Plymouth Sta....A2
Police Station....B3
Post Office......B2
Princess St......B2
Promenade, The...C2
Prysten House....B3
Queen Anne's Battery
  Seaports Centre..C3
Radford Rd......C1
Reel...........B3
Regent St......B3
Rope Walk......C3
Royal Citadel....C3
Royal Pde......B2
Royal Theatre....B2
St Andrew's
  Cross........B2
St Andrew's St...B2
St Lawrence Rd..A2
Saltash Rd......A2
Shopmobility....B2
Smeaton's Tower..C2
Southern Terr....A3
Southside St....C3
Stuart Rd.......A1
Sutherland Rd...A3
Sutton Rd......B3
Sydney St......A1
Teats Hill Rd....C3
Tothill Ave.....A3
Union St.......B1
Univ of Plymouth..A2
Vauxhall St.....B2/3
Victoria Park....A1
West Hoe Rd....C1
Western Approach..B1
Whittington St...A1
Wyndham St....A1
YMCA.........B2
YWCA.........B2

Poole 123
Ambulance Station..A3
Baiater Gdns.....C2
Baiter Park......C3
Ballard Cl.......C2
Ballard Rd......C2
Bay Hog La.....B1
Bridge Approach..C1
Bus Station.....B2
Castle St.......B2
Catalina Dr.....C3
Chapel La......B1
Church St......B1
Cinnamon La...B1
Colborne Cl.....B3
Dear Hay La....B2
Denmark La....A2
Denmark Rd....A2
Dolphin Ctr.....B2
East St........B2
Elizabeth Rd....A3
Emerson Rd....B2
Ferry Rd.......C1
Ferry Terminal...C1
Fire Station.....C1
Freightliner
  Terminal......A1
Furnell Rd......B3
Garland Rd.....A3
Green Rd......B2
Heckford La....A3
Heckford Rd....A3
High St........B2
High St North....A2
Hill St.........A2
Holes Bay Rd...A1
Hospital (A&E)...A3
Information Ctr...C2
Kingland Rd....B2
Kingston Rd....A3
Labrador Dr.....C1
Lagland St......B2
Lander Cl......C3
Lifeboat Coll, The..C1
Lighthouse, Poole Ctr
  for the Arts....B2
Longfleet Rd....A3
Maple Rd......A3
Market Cl......B2
Market St......B2
Mount Pleasant Rd..B3
New Harbour Rd..C1
New Harbour Rd
  South........C1
New Harbour Rd
  West.........C1
New Orchard....B1
New Quay Rd...C1
New St........B2
Newfoundland Dr..B2
North St.......B2
Old Lifeboat....C1
Old Orchard....B2
Parish Rd......A2
Park Lake Rd...B2

Parkstone Rd....A3
Perry Gdns......B2
Pitwines Cl......B2
Police Station....B2
Poole Central Liby..B2
Poole Lifting
  Bridge........C1
Poole Park......C3
Poole Station....A2
Poole Museum...C1
Post Office......A2/B2
Quay, The......C1
St John's Rd.....A3
St Margaret's Rd..A2
St Mary's
  Maternity Unit...A3
St Mary's Rd....A3
Seldown Bridge..B3
Seldown La.....B3
Serpentine Rd...B2
Shaftesbury Rd...A3
Skinner St......B2
Slipway........C1
Stanley Rd......C2
Sterte Ave......A2
Sterte Ave West..A2
Sterte Cl.......A2
Sterte Esplanade..A1
Sterte Rd......A2
Strand St......C1
Swimming Pool...B3
Taverner Cl.....B2
Thames St.....C1
Towngate Bridge..B3
Twin Sails Bridge..B1
Vallis Cl........C3
Walden Cl......A3
West Quay......C1
West Quay Rd...B1
West St........B1
West View Rd...A3
Whatleigh Cl....B2
Wimborne Rd...A3

Portsmouth 123
Action Stations...C1
Admiralty Rd....A1
Alfred Rd......A2
Anglesea Rd....B2
Arundel St.....B3
Aspex.........C1
Bishop St......A2
Broad St.......C1
Buckingham Ho...B2
Burnaby Rd.....B2
Bus Station.....B3
Camber Dock....C1
Cambridge Rd...B2
Car Ferry to Isle of
  Wight........B1
Cascades Shopping
  Centre........A3
Castle Rd.......C2
Civic Offices....B3
Clarence Pier....C2
College St......B1
Commercial Rd...A3
Cottage Grove...C3
Cross St.......A1
Cumberland St...A1
Duisburg Way....C2
Durham St......A3
East St........B1
Edinburgh Rd...B2
Elm Grove.....C3
Emirates Spinnaker
  Tower........B1
Governor's Grn...C1
Great Southsea St..C3
Green Rd......C3
Greetham St....B3
Grosvenor St....C3
Groundlings
  Theatre.......A2
Grove Rd North..C3
Grove Rd South..C3
Guildhall........B3
Guildhall Walk...B2
Gunwharf Quays
  Designer Outlet..B1
Gunwharf Rd....B1
Hambrook St....C2
Hampshire Terr...B2
Hanover St.....A1
Hard, The......B1
High St........C1
HM Naval Base...B1
HMS Nelson (Royal
  Naval Barracks)..A2
HMS Monitor
  M.33.........A1
HMS Victory....A1
HMS Warrior....B1
Hovercraft
  Terminal......C2
Hyde Park Rd...B3
Information
  Centre........A1/B3
Isambard Brunel Rd B3
Isle of Wight Car
  Ferry Terminal...B1
Kent Rd.......C2
Kent St........A1
King St........B2
King's Rd......C2
King's Terr......C2
Lake Rd.......A3
Law Courts.....B2
Library.........B3
Long Curtain Rd..C2
Marina.........B1
Market Way.....A3
Marmion Rd....C3
Mary Rose......A1
Middle St......B2
Millennium Prom
  Walk.........B1
Museum Rd....B2
National Museum of
  the Royal Navy..A1
Naval Rec Gd....C2
Nightingale Rd...C2
Norfolk St......B2
North St.......A2

Osborne Rd......C3
Paradise St......A3
Park Rd.......B2
Passenger Catamaran
  to Isle of Wight...B1
Passenger Ferry to
  Gosport.......B1
Pelham Rd......B3
Pembroke Gdns...C2
Pier Rd........C1
Point Battery....C1
Police Station....B2
Portsmouth &
  Southsea Sta....A3
Portsmouth Harbour
  Station.......B1
Portsmouth Historic
  Dockyard......A1
Portsmouth Museum
  & Art Gallery...B2
Post Office
  ....A1/A3/B2
Queen St......A1
Queen's Cres....C3
Ravelin Park.....B2
Register Office....B3
Round Tower....C1
Royal Garrison
  Church.......C1
St Edward's Rd...C3
St George's Rd...B2
St George's Sq...B1
St George's Way..C3
St James's Rd...B3
St James's St....B2
St John's Cathedral
  (RC)..........B2
St Thomas's Cath..C1
Shopmobility....A3/B1
Somers Rd......C3
Southsea Common..C2
Southsea Terr....C2
Square Tower....C1
Station St......A3
Unicorn Rd.....A2
United Services
  Recreation Gd...B2
University of
  Portsmouth....A2/B2
Univ of Portsmouth..B2
Upper Arundel St..A3
Victoria Ave.....C2
Victoria Park....B2
Victory Gate....A1
Vue..........B1
Warblington St...B1
Western Pde....C2
White Hart Rd...C1
Winston Churchill
  Ave...........B3

Preston 123
Adelphi St......A2
Anchor Ct......B3
Aqueduct St....A1
Ardee Rd......A3
Arthur St......A1
Ashton St......A2
Avenham La....B3
Avenham Park...C3
Avenham Rd....B3
Avenham St....B3
Bairstow St.....B2
Balderstone Rd...C2
Beamont Dr....A1
Beech St South..C2
Bird St........C1
Bow La.......C2
Brieryfield Rd....B1
Broadgate......C1
Brook St.......A2
Bus Station.....A2
Butler St......B2
Cannon St.....B2
Carlton St......A1
Chaddock St....B3
Channel Way....B1
Chapel St......B2
Christ Church St..B2
Christian Rd....A2
Cold Bath St....A2
Coleman Ct....A2
Connaught Rd...C1
Corn Exchange...B3
Corporation St...A2/B2
County Hall.....B3
Cricket Ground...A1
Croft St.......A1
Cross St.......B2
Crown Court....A3
Crown St.......A3
East Cliff.......C2
East Cliff Rd....C2
Edward St......A2
Elizabeth St....A3
Euston St......A2
Fishergate......B2
Fishergate Hill...C2
Fishergate Shopping
  Centre........B2
Fitzroy St......A3
Fleetwood St....A2
Friargate.......A2
Fylde Rd......A1/A2
Gerrard St......B3
Glover's Ct.....B3
Good St.......A2
Grafton St......A2
Great George St..A3
Great Shaw St...A2
Greenbank St....A3
Guild Way.....C1
Guild Hall &
  Charter........B2
Harrington St....A2
Harris Museum...B3
Hartington Rd...B3
Hasset Cl......A2
Heatley St.....B2
Hind St.......C2

Information Ctr...B3
Kilruddery Rd...C1
Lancashire
  Archives......B2
Lancaster Rd....A3/B3
Latham St......B1
Lauderdale St....A2
Lawson St......B2
Leighton St.....A2
Leyland Rd.....A3
Library.........A1
Library.........B2
Liverpool Rd....C1
Lodge St......A2
Lune St.......B2
Magistrate's Court..A3
Main Sprit West..B3
Maresfield Rd...C1
Market St West...A2
Marsh La.......B1/B2
Maudland Bank..A2
Maudland Rd...A2
Meadow Ct....C2
Meath Rd.....A3
Mill Hill.......B3
Miller Arcade....B3
Miller Park.....C3
Moor La.......A3
Mount St......A2
North Rd......A3
North St.......A3
Northcote Rd...A2
Old Milestones...B1
Old Tram Rd....C3
Pedder St......A1/A2
Peel St........A3
Penwortham
  Bridge........C2
Penwortham
  New Bridge....C2
Pitt St.........B2
Playhouse......A3
Police Station....A2
Port Way......B1
Post Office......A3
Preston Station...B2
Retail Park......B2
Ribble Bank St...B1
Ribble Viaduct...C2
Ribblesdale Pl...B3
Ringway.......A3
River Parade....B1
Riverside......C2
St George's
  Shopping Centre..B3
St Georges......B2
St Johns
  Shopping Centre..B3
St Mark's Rd...A1
St Walburges....A1
Salisbury Rd....B1
Sessions House...B3
Snow Hill......B3
South End......C2
South Meadow La..C2
Spa Rd.......A3
Sports Ground...C1
Strand Rd......B1
Syke St.......B3
Talbot Rd......A1
Taylor St.......C1
Tithebarn St....B2
Town Hall......B3
Tulketh Brow....A1
University of Central
  Lancashire.....A2
Valley Rd......C1
Victoria St......B3
Walker St......A3
Walton's Parade..B3
Warwick St.....A3
Wellfield Bsns Park..A1
Wellfield Rd....A1
Wellington St....A1
West Cliff......C2
West Strand....A1
Winckley St.....B2
Winckley Square..B2
Wolseley Rd.....C1

Reading 124
Abbey Ruins....B3
Abbey Sq......B2
Abbey St......B2
Abbot's Walk....B2
Acacia Rd.....C3
Addington Rd...C2
Addison Rd....A1
Allcroft Rd.....C3
Alpine St......C3
Baker St......B1
Berkeley Ave....C1
Bridge St.......B2
Brigham Rd....A1
Broad St.......B2
Broad Street Mall..B2
Carey St.......B1
Castle Hill.....C1
Castle St.......B1
Causeway, The...A3
Caversham Rd...A1
Christchurch
  Playing Fields..A3
Civic Offices....B1
Coley Hill......C1
Coley Pl.......C1
Craven Rd.....C3
Crown St......C2
De Montfort Rd..A1
Denmark Rd....C3
Duke St.......B2
East St........B2
Edgehill St.....C2
Eldon Rd......B3
Eldon Terr......C3
Elgar Rd......C1
Erleigh Rd.....C3
Field Rd.......C1
Fire Station.....B3
Fobney St......C2
Forbury Gdns...B2
Forbury Rd.....B2
Forbury Retail Park..B2

Francis St.......C1
Friar St........B2
Garrard St......B2
Gas Works Rd...B3
Great Knollys St..B1
Greyfriars......B1
Grove, The......A3
Gun St........B2
Henry St.......C2
Hexagon Theatre,
  The..........B2
Hill's Meadow....A2
Howard St......B1
Inner Distribution
  Rd...........B1
Katesgrove La...C2
Kenavon Dr....A3
Kendrick Rd....C3
King's Meadow
  Recreation Gd...A2
King's Rd......B3
Library........B2
London Rd.....C3
London St......C2
Lynmouth Rd...A2
Magistrate's Court..B1
Market Pl......B2
Mill La........B1
Mill Rd........A3
Minster St......B2
Morgan Rd....C3
Mount Pleasant..C3
Museum of English
  Rural Life.....C3
Napier Rd......A2
Newark St......C3
Newport Rd....A3
Old Reading Univ..C2
Oracle Shopping
  Centre, The....B2
Orts Rd.......B3
Pell St........C2
Police Station....B1
Police Station....B2
Post Office......B2
Queen Victoria St..B2
Queen's Rd.....B3
Queen's Rd.....C1
Randolph Rd....A1
Reading Bridge..A2
Reading Station...B2
Redlands Rd....C3
Renaissance Hotel..B2
Riverside Mus...A2
Rose Kiln La....C1
Royal Berks Hospital
  (A&E)........C3
St Giles.......C2
St Laurence....B2
St Mary's......B1
St Mary's Butts..B1
St Saviour's Rd..C1
Send Rd......A3
Sherman Rd....C2
Sidmouth St....C3
Silver St.......C2
South St......B2
Southampton St..C2
Station Hill.....B2
Station Rd......B2
Superstore.....B1
Swansea Rd....A1
Technical College..B1
Valpy St.......B2
Vastern Rd.....A1
Vue..........B2
Waldeck St.....C2
Watlington St....B3
West St.......B1
Whitby Dr.....A1
Wolseley St.....C1
York Rd.......A1
Zinzan St......B1

Salisbury 1
Albany Rd
Arts Centre
Ashley Rd
Avon Approach
Ayleswade Rd
Bedwin St
Belle Vue
Bishop's Palace
Bishops Walk
Blue Boar Row
Bourne Ave
Bourne Hill
Britford La
Broad Walk
Brown St
Bus Station
Castle St
Catherine St
Chapter House
Church Rd
Churchfields Rd
Churchill Way East
Churchill Way
  North
Churchill Way
  South
Churchill Way West
City Hall
Close Wall
Coldharbour La
College St
Council Offices
Court
Crane Bridge Rd
Crane St
Cricket Ground
Culver St South
De Vaux Pl
Devizes Rd
Dews Rd
Elm Grove
Elm Grove Rd
Endless St
Estcourt Rd
Exeter St
Fairview Rd
Fire Station
Fisherton St
Folkestone Rd